W9-CNQ-767

DOS Programmer's Reference

Terry R. Dettmann

Que® Corporation
Carmel, Indiana

DOS Programmer's Reference.
Copyright © 1988 by Que® Corporation.

All rights reserved. Printed in the United States of America. No part of this book may be reproduced in any form or by any means, or stored in a database or retrieval system, without prior written permission of the publisher except in the case of brief quotations embodied in critical articles or reviews. Making copies of any part of this book for any purpose other than your own personal use is a violation of United States copyright laws. For information, address Que Corporation, 11711 N. College Ave., Carmel, IN 46032.

Library of Congress Catalog No.: 87-60811
ISBN 0-88022-327-8

This book is sold *as is*, without warranty of any kind, either express or implied, respecting the contents of this book, including but not limited to implied warranties of the book's quality, performance, merchantability, or fitness for any particular purpose. Neither Que Corporation nor its dealers or distributors shall be liable to the purchaser or any other person or entity with respect to any liability, loss, or damage caused or alleged to be caused directly or indirectly by this book.

92 91 90 89 88   7 6 5 4 3 2

Interpretation of the printing code: the rightmost double-digit number is the year of the book's printing; the rightmost single-digit number, the number of the book's printing. For example, a printing code of 89-3 shows that the third printing of the book occurred in 1989.

This book was written for DOS V3.3. The examples in this book should work with the following versions of MASM, Microsoft C, Turbo C, QuickBASIC, Turbo BASIC, and Turbo Pascal:

MASM versions through 5.1
Microsoft C versions through 5.1
QuickBASIC versions through 4.0
Turbo BASIC versions through 1.1
Turbo C versions through 1.5
Turbo Pascal versions through 4.0

Dedication

This book is dedicated to friends who were hackers before "hacker" became a dirty word, for without them much of the information in this book would not be as freely available as it is.

Publishing Manager

Allen L. Wyatt, Sr.

Product Development Specialist

Bill Nolan

Editors

Gail S. Burlakoff

Gregory Croy

Rebecca Whitney

Technical Editors

V. Mitra Gopaul

Gregory L. Guntle

Acquisitions Editor

Pegg Kennedy

Illustrators

Barabara Bennett

Susan Moore

Index

Brown Editorial Service

Production and Design

Dan Armstrong

Cheryl English

Joe Ramon

Peter Tocco

About the Author

Terry Dettmann

Terry Dettmann's love affair with computers began in the 1960s and has continued sporadically ever since. He has written numerous articles about computers, taught computer courses, and has been a consultant, programmer, and editor. Mr. Dettmann has done doctoral work in electrical engineering and computer science. Currently, he is the Chief Scientist for Digital Systems International in Redmond, Washington, where he designs computer-based solutions to productivity problems in the telecommunications and banking industries.

Table of Contents

I   Introduction to DOS

III   Disks, Directories, and Files

IV Memory Management and Miscellaneous Topics

V Reference

Acknowledgments

There is no way to acknowledge the many people who contributed to this book.

I am grateful to those who spent hours studying DOS and the BIOS and then shared what they learned, and to my friends and coworkers for their encouragement on this project.

Special thanks to Pegg Kennedy and Allen Wyatt of Que Corporation, who worked closely with me from the original concept (a 300-page reference work) to the final product. Thanks also to others at Que.

Last—and most important—thanks (and love) go to my wife Pauline and son TJ, who tolerate my love affair with writing and computers.

Trademark Acknowledgments

Que Corporation has made every attempt to supply trademark information about company names, products, and services mentioned in this book. Trademarks indicated below were derived from various sources. Que Corporation cannot attest to the accuracy of this information.

1-2-3, Lotus, and VisiCalc are registered trademarks of Lotus Development Corporation.

3Com is a registered trademark of 3Com Corporation.

86-DOS is a registered trademark of Seattle Computer Products, Inc.

ANSI is a registered trademark of American National Standards Institute.

Apple DOS is a registered trademark of Apple Computer, Inc. Macintosh is a trademark of Apple Computer, Inc.

Ashton-Tate is a registered trademark of Ashton-Tate Corporation.

COMPAQ Deskpro 286 and COMPAQ Portable Computer are registered trademarks of COMPAQ Computer Corporation.

CompuServe is a registered trademark of CompuServe Incorporated.

CP/M and CP/M-86 are registered trademarks of Digital Research Inc.

DESQview is a trademark of Quarterdeck Office Systems.

EPSON and Epson RX-80 are trademarks of Epson America, Inc.

Guide is a registered trademark of Owl International, Inc.

IBM and IBM Personal System/2 are registered trademarks of International Business Machines Corporation. IBM PC*jr*, OS/2, and PS/2 are trademarks of International Business Machines Corporation.

Intel is a registered trademark of Intel Corporation.

MCI Mail is a registered servicemark of MCI Communications Corporation.

Microsoft, Microsoft C, Microsoft C Compiler, Microsoft QuickBASIC, Microsoft Windows, Microsoft Word, MS-DOS, and XENIX are registered trademarks of Microsoft Corporation.

Norton Utilities is a trademark of Peter Norton Computing.

PostScript is a registered trademark of Adobe Systems Incorporated.

Quadram is a registered trademark of Quadram Corporation.

SideKick, Turbo BASIC, Turbo C, and Turbo Pascal are registered trademarks of Borland International, Inc.

TRS-80 and TRSDOS are registered trademarks of Radio Shack.

UNIX is a trademark of AT&T.

Introduction

Welcome to *DOS Programmer's Reference*. I wrote this book for two reasons. First, I wanted to show people beginning to program at the DOS-level how using DOS (and BIOS) functions can help their programming. Second, I wanted to encourage high-level language programmers to use DOS functions in order to extend their control of the PC system.

Most books about DOS or BIOS programming seem to focus on assembly language. A few discuss using DOS functions from high-level languages, but most are spotty in their coverage and virtually useless as references. *DOS Programmer's Reference* provides you with a range of techniques that serve as starting points for greater use of the DOS functions in your programs. You will want to keep it next to your computer—not on a dusty bookshelf.

To make this book as useful as possible, I have balanced breadth of coverage with enough depth to give you a start into any one programming topic. Entire books could be written about many programming topics and techniques. I do not provide exhaustive coverage of any particular techniques—I give you a starting point.

DOS Programmer's Reference covers each major area in which BIOS and DOS functions can be applied. The discussion and examples in this book should help novices learn how to use these functions and give more advanced programmers a way to organize what they have learned. I emphasize the *why* wherever possible.

A book like this is truly useful only if it provides programmers with pertinent reference information. The last part of this book is devoted to a detailed function-by-function listing of all DOS and BIOS functions (including many that are undocumented). For each function, I have summarized the available information and provided details of the register requirements before the function is called and on return. The function listings alone should make this a useful reference for any DOS programmer, whether you work in assembly language, BASIC, C, or Pascal.

What You Should Know
To Use this Book

This book is written for C, BASIC, or Pascal programmers. It includes little or no explanatory information about assembly language or bits and bytes. If you want to learn more about these topics, I suggest that you read *Using Assembly Language,* also published by Que Corporation, or some of the other books listed in Appendix C.

The examples in *DOS Programmer's Reference* are drawn from assembly language, BASIC, C, and Pascal, with a definite tendency toward C. I have tried to make the examples clear, no matter what your programming background may be. The listings help demonstrate the actual use of the DOS and BIOS functions used throughout the book.

Purpose of This Book

A principal aim of this book is to show you how to work at appropriate levels to program the DOS system. I discuss available functions but emphasize that you do not *always* have to resort to assembly language to use them. Some programming tasks can be done efficiently only in assembly language. (Some things, in fact, can be done only by going "right down to the bare metal"—even BIOS and DOS services sometimes get in your way.) But working at the highest possible level has definite benefits. This book provides the information you need in order to decide which level to use in your own programming.

The examples I use are oriented toward high-level interfaces to the DOS and BIOS routines. Although I minimize the use of assembly language, I do not neglect it. By emphasizing that you can access and effectively use the routines from C, BASIC, or Pascal, I hope to make these techniques more widely usable.

Who Should Use This Book?

If you are a programmer interested in working with DOS to make the most effective programs possible, *DOS Programmer's Reference* is for you. It deals with DOS at many levels, from high-level programming-language services down to the BIOS interrupts.

This book is intended for intermediate to advanced programmers who have some experience in C, BASIC, or Pascal and are comfortable with assembly language. I assume that you are familiar with at least one programming language and curious about others, and that you are familiar also with MS-DOS® or its IBM® cousin, PC DOS.

A fundamental assumption is that you want to speed up your programs or to access facilities that are unavailable in your language. We will go after these facilities through DOS and BIOS functions. This book deals with advanced program design and freely uses elements from high-level languages as well as assembly language.

Although a certain technique may be illustrated in a particular programming language, the *technique*—not the *language*—is of primary interest. Once you learn how to use a technique, it is equally applicable whether you use it in C, Pascal, BASIC, or assembly language. It will apply, in fact, in any language that provides access to DOS and BIOS interrupts.

How To Use This Book

DOS Programmer's Reference is divided into five parts. Readers interested in learning the fundamentals of DOS programming will want to start with Part I. Those who want specific information about various aspects of programming at the system level can find useful information in Parts II, III, and IV. More advanced programmers who simply want a quick reference should concentrate on Part V.

The four chapters in **Part I, "An Introduction to DOS,"** lay the groundwork. You first look at some of the history of the system and at how DOS works, both statically and dynamically. Then you are introduced to the general principles of programming at the DOS level and to the language resources available for this type of work. Finally, we explore the "nitty-gritty" of programming at the DOS level.

In **Part II, "Character Devices and Serial Devices,"** Chapters 5 and 6 cover output devices (the video display and printer) and input devices (the keyboard and mouse). Chapter 7 deals with serial input and output devices; the 8250 UART is discussed also.

Part III, "Disks, Directories, and Files," contains two chapters. Chapter 8 describes the partition table, boot record, and file allocation table (the FAT) and discusses disk functions. Chapter 9 covers the root directory, directory entries, subdirectories, and volume labels. You also learn in this chapter about how files are handled through DOS—about file control blocks (FCBs) and handle functions and when to use them.

Part IV, "Memory Management and Miscellaneous Topics," covers program and memory management (Chapter 10); interrupt handlers (Chapter 11), and device drivers (Chapter 12). Chapter 13, "Miscellaneous Functions," provides information on such topics as equipment information and extended error processing.

Each chapter in Parts II, III, and IV introduces you to the subject and illustrates it with practical examples that you can use as the basis for your own library of functions.

All of the sample programs illustrate basic techniques only. If you learn a basic technique from one of these simple programs, you can then extend it into your own programming.

Part V is a reference section. Typography, icons, and other design elements were carefully planned to make this section easy to use. The BIOS and DOS services are presented in numerical order. Each function is listed in a standard reference format, with cautions or restrictions for the various functions included in the comments. In addition to the BIOS and standard DOS functions, Part V includes sections on the mouse functions (DOS Int 33h) and expanded memory functions (DOS Int 67h).

Appendix A contains the ASCII character set; **Appendix B**, a table of selected memory locations; and **Appendix C** is a resource list of other titles.

DOS Programmer's Reference was designed and developed as a tutorial and a reference manual on programming DOS. It is *not* a reference manual devoted to assembly language, BASIC, C, or any other programming language.

Talk to Us

Any errors and omissions from the book are solely my responsibility. I have done my best to make the information as accurate and useful as possible, but errors may have crept in. Let us know of any errors or omissions you may find. And please take a moment to fill in and mail the registration card at the back of this book. Que Corporation is interested in your reaction to *DOS Programmer's Reference*.

Part I

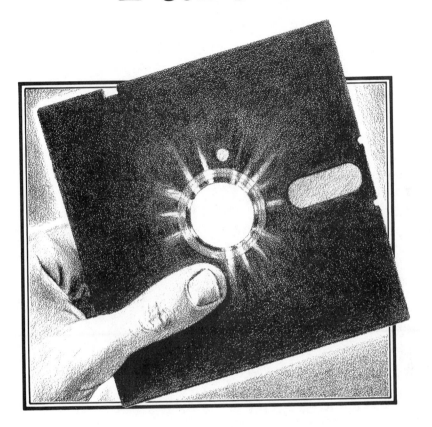

Introduction
to DOS

An Introduction to DOS

It will be helpful for you to have a clear idea about what DOS is before you read further. This chapter is designed to provide a quick overview of DOS, as well as a short history of the operating system. In addition, it touches quickly on DOS structure and interfacing. Because this is a cursory examination, do not be concerned if some terms seem unclear. Each will be explained in detail in the coming chapters.

What is DOS?

DOS consists of four basic modules:

❏ *The boot record:* This record begins on track 0, sector 1, side 1 on every disk formatted by the DOS FORMAT command. On fixed disks, the boot record is on the first sector of the DOS partition. This record, which requires one sector of space, identifies the disk and contains the initial boot program for the disk.

❏ *The BIOS:* The Basic Input/Output System usually is split between a portion located in ROM and an interface module loaded from disk. This low-level interface to the physical machine is responsible for hiding the vagaries of the hardware from the DOS software.

❑ *The DOS program:* The computer's operating system is the high-level interface for programs that will be run on the computer. It contains file-management, data-blocking and unblocking routines, and other high-level services necessary for program implementation. It is accessed through a series of interrupt calls that invoke services provided by DOS.

❑ *The command processor:* Most people think of this module as DOS. The command processor, the normal interface to DOS services for people working with the system, generates the command prompt (C>), accepts commands, and executes programs requested by users of the system.

Each of these modules is covered in detail in Chapters 2 and 3. Some basic explanations may be in order at this point.

The BIOS provides a series of functions that programmers can use to perform operations without having to concern themselves with the details of the underlying hardware. Throughout this book BIOS functions are used to perform necessary operations in programming examples. Part V of this book contains a function-by-function reference to the capabilities of the BIOS.

Even though it is powerful, BIOS is far from comprehensive. DOS, built on the platform provided by the BIOS, provides many services that are essential to programming. In the early days of computers, before general-purpose operating systems (such as DOS) became available, programmers wrote programs that included the functional equivalent of DOS. This made the process of debugging applications terribly complex.

With the DOS functions left to Microsoft® and other vendors, much of the burden for system operation is shifted to them; they become our partners in program development. Although you should not assume that *everything* in DOS works without error, you can assume that (unless proven otherwise) DOS is solid. Part V of this book contains a function-by-function breakdown of the DOS functions.

History of DOS

Over the years, DOS has emerged as the primary operating system for microcomputers. DOS, without a doubt, has more users today than any other operating system. It has become a sophisticated environment with tools and applications to meet a wide spectrum of needs.

DOS's foreseeable growth involves expansion to handle more sophisticated microprocessors such as the 80386. Future releases of DOS may even handle multitasking and multiuser operations (some may question this statement, in light of the emergence of OS/2™).

DOS was first marketed by Seattle Computer Products as 86-DOS® with that company's proprietary line of computers. The original DOS, which was extremely limited in its application, was written by Tim Paterson in 1980. At that time, Digital Research's CP/M® was the most widely used microcomputer operating system. 86-DOS was designed to make porting applications from CP/M easy: it kept the same basic structure for file control blocks and functions so that a mechanical translator could convert a program directly to 86-DOS.

Because 86-DOS worked only on Seattle Computer Products' line of S-100 based microcomputers, no other hardware vendors bothered to use it. Few people even knew that it existed. Then IBM started looking for an operating system.

The story of how IBM approached Microsoft is almost apocryphal now. With no operating system of its own, Microsoft licensed 86-DOS in October, 1980. Then, in July, 1981, Microsoft bought all rights to 86-DOS. When IBM released the PC in late 1981, Microsoft was ready with MS-DOS 1.0 (PC DOS, for IBM machines).

Had you looked for a PC after its original release, you would have noticed that PC DOS was not prominently displayed in some stores. IBM had selected Digital Research's CP/M-86® and Softech's P-system as alternative PC operating systems. But vendors were slow to deliver both products, and few programming languages were available for development of applications under those operating systems. Microsoft already had earned a reputation for programming languages. IBM released its own software using PC DOS, and developers rapidly picked up the ball, which has never stopped rolling. CP/M-86 and the P-system never "got off the ground" as serious contenders in the PC marketplace.

DOS has been changed officially many times (and several versions exist that were not available for general use). Although improvements and bug fixes have both figured in this evolution, each release usually has involved a response to some hardware change—particularly, a change in disk-drive format or capability.

Table 1.1 lists each official DOS release (to date) and the primary change involved.

Table 1.1. *DOS Versions*

Version	Date	Hardware Change
86-DOS	1980	Seattle Computer Products' version
1.0	August, 1981	Original PC, single-sided disk
1.1	May, 1982	Double-sided disk
2.0	March, 1983	PC XT system, including hard disk
2.1	October, 1983	IBM PC*jr* and Portable PC
3.0	August, 1984	PC AT system, including high-capacity disk
3.1	March, 1985	Networking
3.2	1986	Enhanced support for new media
3.3	April, 1987	Support for PS/2

As you look at this list, notice the trade-off between memory and features that each new version of DOS has required. DOS V1 was capable of existing in 16K of memory, and the original IBM PC was available with only 64K (try to put 1-2-3 ® into *that*!). Version 2 needed at least 24K of memory (more, if device drivers were installed). Any useful programming required a minimum of 128K of memory. As of V3, DOS needs 36K of memory (and can require much more for file-sharing and installed device drivers). Machines with less than 512K are almost impractical. The move to expanded and extended memory (see Chapter 2) is gaining momentum. As DOS continues to expand, machines will need megabytes of memory to do practical work. Let's look at each version of DOS to see what is involved in each change.

Version 1.0

DOS V1.0 was the original support for the PC system. It supported the basic single-sided, eight-sector disk format and provided all the basic disk services. Changes (from CP/M) included a much improved disk-directory structure that managed file attributes, exact file size, and last modification date. Version 1.0 also added improved disk allocation and management, better operating-system services, and an AUTOEXEC batch file for start-up initialization. IBM was the only vendor to ship this version.

Version 1.1

This was the first version to be widely distributed by original equipment manufacturers other than IBM. (As MS-DOS, it was referred to as Version 1.25). The kernel's hardware independence was improved in this version, and support for double-sided disk drives was added, as were some bug fixes.

Version 2.0

In DOS V2.0, support was added for double- and single-sided nine-sector diskettes, for fixed disks, and for cartridges that would be used on the PC*jr*™. DOS services were enhanced significantly. This version also added hierarchical file systems similar to those in UNIX™. Here are some of the significant changes incorporated into DOS V2.0:

❏ File handles
❏ I/O redirection
❏ Pipes
❏ Filters
❏ Print spooling
❏ Volume labels
❏ Expanded file attributes
❏ System-configuration file
❏ Program-environment block maintenance
❏ ANSI® display driver
❏ Dynamic control of memory by programs
❏ Support of user-customized command processors
❏ International support

Version 2.1

In this version, only timing changes were made to allow better handling of IBM's PC*jr* and Portable PC.

Version 3.0

DOS V3.0 added support for high-capacity (1.2M) diskettes and additional hard disk formats, as well as the foundation for support of networked disks. Some major new features include the following:

❑ Control of the print spooler by applications
❑ Extended error reporting
❑ Suggested error-recovery codes
❑ Support for file and record locking

Version 3.1

DOS V3.1 has been standard for some time with many vendors. This version added networked disks, including support for file sharing, as well as some bug fixes.

Version 3.2

This version added support for 3 1/2-inch floppy disks. It also integrated formatting control into the peripheral device drivers.

Version 3.3

In DOS V3.3, two new user commands (NLSFUNC and FASTOPEN) and two new functions have been added, many other services have been upgraded, and device support has been expanded to cover IBM's new PS/2™ line.

And the Future

As DOS continues to evolve, new services and options become available to programmers. The advent of windowed environments such as Microsoft® Windows and DESQView™ has made sophisticated new services available for DOS-level programmers. Each new service hides more of the machine from our programs and allows us to do more without having to reinvent the proverbial wheel. The cost of any high-level service, however, tends to be a compromise in the maximum amount of speed and responsiveness that we can achieve. But as processors get faster, the need for lower-level tricks will diminish. Applications programs will use the services of DOS and its cousins. Only systems-level programmers working inside DOS, Windows, or DESQView will have to worry about direct access to the machine or its services. Such is progress.

The Structure of DOS

As this book examines DOS and the PC system, you will notice a definite layering of functions. Figure 1.1 should help you visualize this layering.

Fig. 1.1. *System layering.*

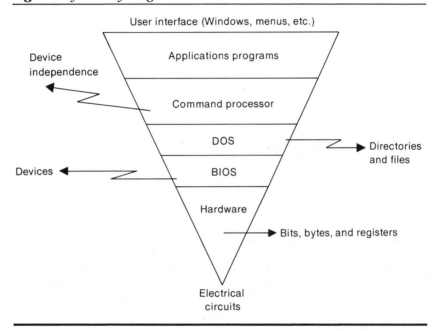

Fundamental to the design of the whole DOS/PC system is a kind of "system within a system" approach to design. Starting with the electrical circuits at the bottom of the system, for example, you will notice that the circuits implement a device (called a computer) with definite capabilities and features.

The BIOS integrates this circuitry level into a new "computer system" with well-defined features and functions. The BIOS level is characterized by the presence of devices that have standard features. No matter which kind of display you use or whose keyboard you bought, the BIOS makes them all respond similarly. Taken together, all of BIOS's features make it capable of supporting a programming environment. Within this environment, Microsoft developed DOS.

The DOS environment defines yet another computer system—but at a much higher level. A computer language that can manage files and file systems is introduced at this level, as are the devices on which the language is based. And at this level DOS integrates the features we need in order to operate in a standardized environment. Whether you use a Toshiba or Maxtor disk drive, the operating system treats them the same way. To programs working with DOS, the lower-level details are unimportant.

On the next level (that of the command processor) is yet another computer: an interactive one characterized by device independence. At this level, you can deal with devices and files as though they were the same. Although DOS has to keep things straight, at the command-processor level you can direct output (that was *supposed* to go to the screen) to a file. (You do not have to worry about the implications of speed or handling differences between the devices.)

Up one more level is a computer system defined by your applications programs. The system is even simpler when it interfaces with users rather than with programmers. Now the "computer language" consists of menu selections and windows. This layer, like all the others, is built on what precedes it.

As you read this book, working your way down through these levels (or layers), keep in mind what you gain (and lose) by skipping parts of the systems hierarchy. Because DOS is built on the BIOS routines, programs that skip around DOS to the BIOS *can* affect the way DOS works. You *could* use the disk read and write functions, for example, to write your own file handling at the BIOS level. But you probably would need to work for years to make it work as well as DOS does. Conversely, you can stay at the highest level—but all of the lower levels will eat away at your program speed. There are trade-offs all up and down the hierarchy.

For many programs, the trade-off is easy: users don't need submillisecond responses when they write characters to a printer. But a spreadsheet program, which has to maintain thousands of individual details, can use all the tightening it can get. The choice is yours.

The Programmer's Interface to DOS

Programmers who work in high-level languages are accustomed to working with predefined functions. In BASIC, all the functions (like PRINT and INPUT) are defined in the language. Pascal also defines the standard functions that you can access. C compilers come with a standard set of library functions. For many people, these functions represent the limits of the language.

In fact, the functions provided with BASIC, C, and Pascal are based on a much lower level of interaction with DOS and the BIOS functions. The language functions are written to handle requests for services in standard ways. In some cases, language functions are defined to be compatible with national or international standards for the way in which these functions are supposed to work. But in order to be implemented, the functions must refer directly to DOS, the BIOS, or the hardware.

Ordinarily, you are protected from the world of functionality beneath the level of language functions. Because they are written for general use by many people who could not "program their way out of a paper bag," language functions must provide error checking and control for generalized cases. Generalizing slows things down—but you do not have have to give up on speed. DOS and BIOS services are directly available from any language, if you take the time to learn how to work with that language.

The software interrupt is the mechanism for using DOS and BIOS services. (Chapter 11 is devoted to interrupts.) In the present context, think of a software interrupt as a high-level language's subroutine call. You have to set entry parameters and you get a result. But you can run into trouble if you don't have the language functions to smooth the way.

By accessing DOS and BIOS functions, you strip a layer of programming from your work. You can build in your own error checking and control based on what *you* need, not on what a Microsoft or Borland programmer thought would be suitable for the mass market. But by doing so, you take your life and your program into your own hands.

By going beyond the language functions, you give up not only their error-checking, control capabilities, and the reliability of standard libraries; you also give up a considerable amount of portability. C programs written in standard Microsoft or Turbo C® functions often can be taken, with few changes, directly to a UNIX system. DOS and BIOS functions cannot.

By slipping down to the DOS and BIOS level, you regain control and speed up your programs. The cost (some extra programming effort) is minimal. For the highest speed possible, you need to access the hardware directly. Doing so makes sense for screen displays and serial ports, both of which are too slow for what they need to do. This direct approach makes little or no sense for other devices such as disks.

Disk systems are controlled at a high level in DOS. If you try to go below this level (even just to the BIOS level), you do not make your programs faster— you make them completely incompatible with DOS. Although some game programs intentionally are written this way, most programs need DOS compatibility.

Throughout this book, I lay out the pros and cons of working at the various programming levels. *You* decide what is appropriate for your application. As a general rule, however, you should always work at the highest possible level. When software works for you, errors are easier to find. The lower you go, the more subtle the errors—and the harder they are to locate.

Ordinarily, a slow program that works correctly can be made faster by recoding critical modules at a lower level or by changing the programming algorithm. But if you spend your time making a tight, fast program that doesn't do the job, you may be stuck with a tight, fast plate of "spaghetti." Remember that it is easier to make a slow program fast than it is to make a fast program correct.

Summary

The IBM-compatible line of computers has been built on a firm foundation of BIOS and DOS. BIOS provides the low-level interface to the outside world, whereas DOS provide the functionality of higher level services that augment the development of computer programs. As the most popular operating system in the world, each successive version of DOS has provided a solid footing upon which to build.

How you develop your programs—which language you use, whether you use BIOS or DOS services, etc.—depends largely on your programming needs. There are trade-offs to any programming decision you may make. As you think through options and formulate strategies, you will begin to find ways to make your computer system work for you (not against you). *DOS Programmer's Reference* is designed with that end in mind—to make your programming experience the best it can be by making full use of your computer environment.

In the next chapter, which covers the structure of DOS, we will look more closely at the conceptual foundation upon which DOS is built and how it relates to your programs. We also will examine the tools, resources, and building blocks available to you as a programmer in a DOS environment.

2

Structure of a DOS System

The structure of the disk operating system (DOS) involves the whole machine—not just the operating system itself, but the whole computer from the hardware on up. You must understand the structure of DOS if you are to make the best decisions about which functions to use and how to use them.

The "Virtual Machine" Concept

A useful way to think about a DOS system is to view it as a hierarchical structure in which functions are distributed among subsystems. Each level in the hierarchy provides a well-defined set of services upon which the next higher level can build. Thus, each level becomes a virtual machine—it is the computer to the next higher level. Figure 2.1 illustrates this concept in relation to a DOS system.

The physical machine, or hardware, is the lowest level of the hierarchy. At this level there are many differences between systems. The common threads among the various machines include:

❏ A processor from the Intel® 8086 family: the 8086, the 8088, the 80186, the 80286, or the 80386

❏ A similar mapping of physical equipment within the system (in other words, similarly assigned interrupts and addresses)

17

Fig. 2.1. *The virtual machine hierarchy.*

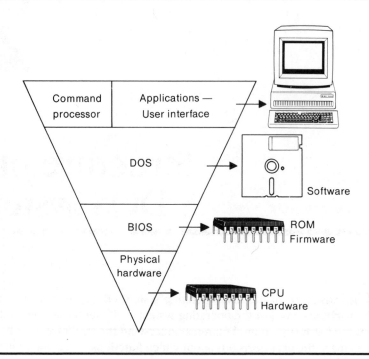

☐ One of a limited number of bus designs, the IBM PC bus being
   the basic type

One of the major purposes of DOS is to hide physical differences between
machines so that there is a standard method of accessing the computer's
capabilities at both the programming and user levels. DOS quite successfully
provides a uniformity that has made it the operating system of choice on a
wide variety of IBM-compatible computers.

But this design philosophy (of a general-purpose DOS that can be used on a
wide variety of computers) has limitations. Perhaps the most apparent
limitation is DOS's amazing lack of speed. For many applications, DOS is
simply not fast enough to serve the needs of programmers. The extra
overhead built into DOS (the extra code needed to make a general-purpose
DOS) takes time to execute and slows down DOS's overall performance.

To get around this bottleneck, many programmers have resorted to working at lower levels of the virtual machine. For instance, some computing tasks can be completed more rapidly by working with BIOS instead of DOS; other tasks require that you work directly with the hardware to achieve the maximum speed.

The Physical Machine

One of the difficulties inherent in bypassing DOS or BIOS to gain speed is that this method frequently can make your software incompatible with certain computers. The greatest differences between machines occur at the hardware level, the level at which you generally discover whether "compatibles" are truly compatible. Programs that operate at this level will not work on machines with any major hardware differences.

The physical computer system (see fig. 2.2) can be broken down into several major components:

1. The central processing unit (CPU), which performs the operations of the computer system

2. ROM and RAM memory, which hold programs and data

3. The input channel(s), which feed information to the computer

4. The output channel(s), which feed information to the user

5. The storage devices (floppy disks and hard disks) used to hold information temporarily or permanently

An understanding of each of these elements of the computer system is integral to the successful development of quality software—particularly when you use DOS and BIOS functions. Let's look at each of these elements.

The Processor

The *central processing unit* (CPU) used in a PC or compatible is a member of Intel Corporation's 8086 series of processor chips—you are likely to see an 8088, 80186, 80286, or 80386 chip in the computers you program. Each of these chips not only implements unique qualities that set it apart from its predecessors but also retains compatibility with its earlier versions. Thus, an 80186 can do all that an 8086 or 8088 can, as well as its own unique

Fig. 2.2. Block diagram of the basic computer.

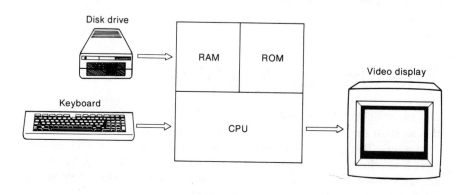

operations. Further, an 80286 can do all that the 80186 can (plus some), and an 80386 (the latest member of the 8086 family) can do all that the earlier chips can do—and quite a bit more.

This book does not explore specific differences between the chips, but you should be aware that DOS is based on the capabilities of the 8086 or 8088 chips. And because the 80186, 80286, and 80386 are compatible with these earlier processors, DOS also works well on the more recent chips. In this book's discussions of DOS, BIOS, and programming, I use examples that run on the 8086 or 8088 (without taking advantage of the unique capabilities of the newer chips). This is not a fault, but a recognition of the fact that you do not need to use these unique capabilities to program successfully with DOS. Throughout this book, all references to the 8086 imply the entire family of processors: the 8086, 8088, 80186, 80286, and 80386.

CPUs are basic processing engines that perform only the simplest of operations. Because you need to know something about this basic processor engine, this section provides an overview of microprocessors in the 8086 series. Far from trying to give an exhaustive overview of the CPU that DOS is built around, this section provides a quick introduction to the things you'll need to know in order to access system resources from your programs. If you are already familiar with the subject, you can skip this section. If you want information about programming the 8086 family, see the bibliography at the end of this book.

Later in this section, I discuss the CPU registers that are accessible to you as a programmer. But first, because memory addressing is fundamental to many of the programming operations you perform at a DOS level, it is important that you understand how the 8086 addresses memory. Let's take a look at this area.

8086 Memory Addressing

Some programmers criticize the 8086's segmented memory-addressing scheme. Memory segmentation not only places limits on the sizes of data items but also complicates pointer arithmetic. For DOS programmers, however, segmented memory is here to stay—it represents a reasonable solution to a problem inherent in the 8086's design: finding the best way to represent 20-bit address values, using the 16-bit registers of the 8086. The 8086 has 20 address pins, which allows the addressing of 2^{20} (1,048,576, or 1M) unique memory locations, yet its registers are only 16 bits wide (register usage is discussed shortly).

The solution is to divide an absolute memory address into "pieces" that can be stored individually in the 16-bit registers. Thus, two registers are used to represent a single address; one of these registers stores a base (or segment) address, and the other stores an offset from that base. Theoretically, such a method can generate 2^{32} (more than four billion) unique addresses. Even though such an address range would require 32 address lines for the microprocessor and therefore is beyond the capabilities of the 8086, an example that uses this address range is helpful.

Figure 2.3 shows the four corners of a memory space containing 100000000h (4,294,967,296, or 2^{32}) locations. Each row is a portion, or *segment*, containing 10000h (65,536, or 2^{16}) locations. The address of each location in a segment can be expressed as an offset from where the segment begins, with the first location at offset 0. The convention for writing addresses in this segment-offset form is *segment:offset*, and is always expressed in hexadecimal notation.

Fig. 2.3. Memory segments with 10000h-byte intervals.

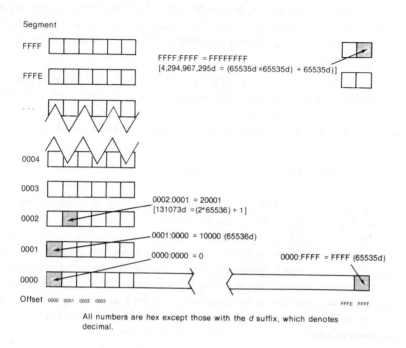

All numbers are hex except those with the *d* suffix, which denotes decimal.

The last byte of the first segment (at 0000:FFFFh) is followed immediately by the first byte of the next segment (at 0001:0000h). Therefore, the absolute address of each memory location—its ordinal position, counted from the very first memory location—can be calculated from the following formula:

actual_address = (segment_number × segment_interval) + offset

Figure 2.3 shows that when the segment interval is 10000h, the segment number forms, in effect, the four most-significant digits of the 8-digit absolute address. Similarly, the offset address can be regarded as the four least-significant digits of the absolute address.

In practice, the relationship between the base address and the absolute address does not have to be as simple as that shown in figure 2.3. Sophisticated hardware can rapidly perform address translations equivalent to those we humans use to calculate absolute addresses from segments and offsets.

Even though an understanding of this example is helpful, it still leaves us with a quandary—the 8086 uses 20 (not 32) bits for addresses. Thus, this example must be adapted to the reality of the situation. The addressing scheme developed by Intel regards the contents of the segment register (the segment portion of the absolute address) as the 16 most-significant bits of the absolute address; the 4 least-significant bits are assumed to be zero. In other words, the segment register contains the four most-significant hex digits of the address, and the least-significant (rightmost) digit are zero. Adding the contents of the offset register to this calculated address results in the desired absolute address. Figure 2.4 shows how an absolute address is determined from a segment-offset pair under the Intel addressing scheme.

Fig. 2.4. Calculating an absolute-memory address.

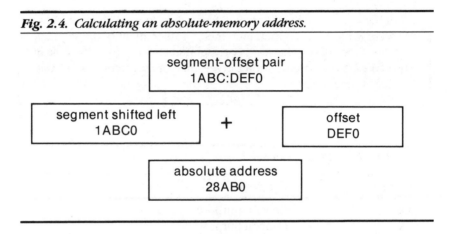

Now that you have a conceptual basis of how the 8086 addresses memory, let's take a look at the register set of the 8086.

The 8086 Register Set

The 8086 family uses 14 separate 16-bit registers which can be grouped, by purpose, into the following four categories:

- ❏ General-purpose registers
- ❏ Segment registers
- ❏ Offset registers
- ❏ The flags register

The actual registers and their categorization are shown in table 2.1.

8086 Memory Addressing

The 8086's use of segment-offset pairs for addressing memory results in an interesting anomaly: virtually every absolute memory address can be addressed in a multitude of ways. For instance, all of the following valid segment-offset pairs reference the same absolute memory address:

```
Ø1Ø1:FFFØ        1ØØØ:1ØØØ
Ø3F1:DØFØ        1ØØ1:ØFFØ
Ø9ØØ:8ØØØ        1ØØ2:ØFEØ
ØCB7:449Ø        1ØØ3:ØFDØ
ØFFF:1Ø1Ø        11ØØ:ØØØØ
```

All of these segmented addresses refer to the same absolute address: Ø11ØØØh. Notice that for each increment or decrement of the segment portion of the address there is a corresponding increase or decrease of 10h in the offset portion. As you can see, memory segments can overlap in many different ways.

Table 2.1. The 8086 Register Set

Register	Category	Use
AX	General purpose	
BX	General purpose	
CX	General purpose	
DX	General purpose	
CS	Segment	Code Segment
DS	Segment	Data Segment
ES	Segment	Extra Segment
SS	Segment	Stack Segment
SP	Offset	Stack Pointer
BP	Offset	Base Pointer
SI	Offset	Source Index
DI	Offset	Destination Index
IP	Offset	Instruction Pointer
Flags	Flags	Status Flags

Clearly, when you deal with individual registers you work directly with the CPU at a hardware level. Note that although this usually is accomplished through assembly language, high-level languages such as BASIC, C, and Pascal all have convenient ways to access the 8086 registers. (Some of the techniques used to do this are covered in Chapter 4.)

As I mentioned earlier, the 8086 register set can be divided, according to purpose, into four different categories. Let's examine each category and its registers.

General-Purpose Registers

As their name implies, the general-purpose registers are used for such general purposes as the storage of immediate results or other temporary needs. When you use DOS or BIOS functions, you load these registers with values needed for the completion of the function. You will always include a value that represents the specific function, as well as other parameters that may be needed. The function number and parameters vary from function to function, and are the subject of many sections of this book. Similarly, upon return from a DOS or BIOS function, values that can be used by your program may be returned in the registers.

The general-purpose registers are AX, BX, CX, and DX. To facilitate use of 8- and 16-bit values, each of these 16-bit registers can be addressed also as a pair of 8-bit registers. The register names AL, AH, BL, BH, etc. are used to address the lower or higher 8 bits (*L* and *H* signify *low* and *high*, respectively). Figure 2.5 shows this relationship.

Fig. 2.5. *The 16-bit registers can be addressed as a pair of 8-bit registers.*

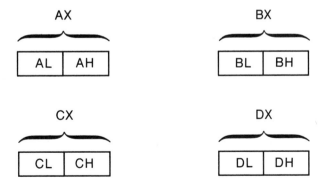

These registers are used extensively in programming, whether you are working in assembly language or using high-level language calls to access the DOS or BIOS routines.

Segment Registers

The segment registers play an important role in the 8086's memory-addressing scheme. They store 16-bit values representing the base addresses of 64K memory segments. As you may recall, these values represent the upper 16 bits of a 20-bit base address; the lower four bits are assumed to be zero. The 8086's memory-addressing hardware combines these base addresses with offset values stored in one of the CPU's offset registers, which are discussed in the following section.

The segment registers are

- ❏ The CS (*code segment*) register
- ❏ The DS (*data segment*) register
- ❏ The ES (*extra segment*) register
- ❏ The SS (*stack segment*) register

Each segment register specifies a distinct segment. As a programmer, you basically are free to use these segment registers in any way you choose, within certain limits (described shortly). In Chapter 3, you will see how programs are developed and how these segment registers are put to use. These segment registers are designed to be used in the following manner:

- ❏ CS holds the base address of the segment containing the code that is currently executing

- ❏ DS holds the base address of the segment containing the program's data

- ❏ ES supplements the DS register, holding the base address of an "extra" segment often used for data

- ❏ SS holds the base address of the program's stack, which is used for temporary storage of data

The previously mentioned limits on the use of segment registers include restrictions on the use of the CS and SS registers. In order to operate properly, the 8086 expects that the CS register will *always* point to the segment of the program that currently is executing and that the SS register will *always* point to the current stack (which is necessary for 8086 operations). (Because most programmers are comfortable with the concept of a stack by the time they begin programming with DOS and BIOS functions, I won't describe the stack or its use in detail.)

The Stack

Processors in the 8086 family use a structure called a *stack* to keep track of information during function calls and other operations. The processor puts registers on the stack whenever a subroutine is called (a PUSH operation) and takes them off again (a POP operation) on return from the subroutine.

Programmers use the stack to store intermediate values in calculations or to pass values to subroutines. Programming languages make extensive use of the stack for the same purpose.

The stack works like a stack of dishes in a cafeteria: as items are added (PUSHed on) to the stack, the stack gets larger. When something is removed (POPped off), the first item to come off is the last item added to the stack. This type of structure is called a *last-in-first-out* (LIFO) structure.

Offset Registers

As the name implies, the offset registers generally are used as the offset portion of memory addresses. The segment portions of the addresses usually are stored in the segment registers.

The five offset registers are

- The SP (*stack pointer*) register
- The BP (*base pointer*) register
- The SI (*source index*) register
- The DI (*destination index*) register
- The IP (*instruction pointer*) register

Because the registers in this group differ in their common uses, they frequently are subdivided into two separate classes: pointer registers and index registers.

Pointer Registers

The pointer registers (SP and BP) provide a convenient way to access values in the current stack segment. SP always points to the current top of the stack and is updated automatically by various assembly language instructions. The other pointer register, BP, typically is used as a base (or reference) pointer for indexed operations. For instance, some programmers use BP to point to a fixed position within the stack. This position then is used as a reference point for retrieving variables that were placed on the stack before the subroutine was called. With high-level language compilers, this use of the BP register is a standard means of accessing parameters.

The instruction pointer (IP) holds the offset address of the next instruction to be executed by the CPU. When the IP and code segment (CS) registers combine, they point to the absolute address of the instruction. (The CS:IP register pair is always used in this manner.) The value of IP is incremented automatically by the CPU after each instruction is fetched from the current code segment.

Index Registers

The index registers, SI and DI, are specialized offset registers. Typically, SI and DI are used in conjunction with the DS and ES segment registers. In string operations, for example, you would use DS:SI to point to the address of the source string and ES:DI to point to the destination string. In non-string operations, programmers generally use SI and DI for what their name implies—an index (offset) to the source or destination data.

The Flags Register

The flags register uses nine of its 16 bits as flags that reflect the processor's status or control its operations. These flags are divided into two categories: status flags and control flags.

The status flags are

- ❑ The CF (*carry flag*)
- ❑ The PF (*parity flag*)
- ❑ The AF (*auxiliary carry flag*)
- ❑ The ZF (*zero flag*)
- ❑ The OF (*overflow flag*)
- ❑ The SF (*sign flag*)

These flags report on the status of the last instruction executed. If the last instruction generated a value of zero, for example, the zero flag is set. The status flags are set and cleared automatically, but programs also can set and clear the flags. Many DOS and BIOS routines use the carry flag to signal errors.

The control flags are

- ❑ The DF (*direction flag*)
- ❑ The TF (*trap flag*)
- ❑ The IF (*interrupt flag*)

The direction flag controls certain aspects of the 8086's instructions for copying ranges of memory, the trap flag puts the CPU in "single-step" mode, and the interrupt flag enables or disables interrupts.

Memory

PCs and compatible computers have four classes of memory:

1. *ROM (read only memory)* is permanent memory installed in the computer. Usually it holds a portion of BIOS specific to the physical machine. On the original IBM PC, the ROM also holds cassette BASIC.

2. *RAM (random access memory)* holds nonpermanent program code and data.

3. *Extended memory* (memory above one megabyte) can be accessed by an 80286 processor running in protected mode (on the IBM Personal Computer AT, for example).

4. *Expanded memory*, which is added to the system and is not part of the memory mapped directly by the processor. This memory is accessed through a special expanded memory driver system.

You may hear also about PROM (programmable read only memory) and other variations but, for practical purposes, I have lumped all such memory under the ROM heading. Although purists may object to this move, from the standpoint of those programming the DOS system, PROM and other such variations represent permanent memory.

The memory map in figure 2.6 shows how the basic system memory is allocated.

In Chapter 10, which discusses in greater detail the allocation and uses of memory, you will learn how to control memory and how to use it for your programs.

I/O Channels

The standard input/output (I/O) devices on the PC and compatibles are the keyboard, the video monitor, and the printer (see Chapters 5 and 6). In addition to these standard devices, you frequently will see a mouse and one or more serial ports (see Chapters 6 and 7).

Fig. 2.6. *Memory map for a machine with one megabyte of memory.*

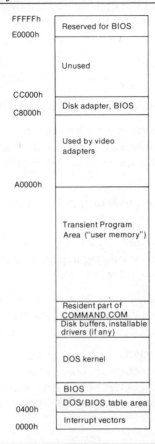

FFFFFh	Reserved for BIOS
E0000h	
	Unused
CC000h	
	Disk adapter, BIOS
C8000h	
	Used by video adapters
A0000h	
	Transient Program Area ("user memory")
	Resident part of COMMAND.COM
	Disk buffers, installable drivers (if any)
	DOS kernel
	BIOS
	DOS/BIOS table area
0400h	
	Interrupt vectors
0000h	

You also can add custom devices, such as touch-sensitive screens and sensors of all types, to a PC system. Although such specialized devices are beyond the scope of this book, Chapter 12 shows you how to write your own drivers for specialized devices.

The Keyboard

The PC keyboard knows nothing about *what* you type. The keyboard doesn't interpret your keystrokes—it simply tells the computer that a given key has been pressed or released. The keyboard assigns no meaning to the keys.

However, it does assign a unique number (a *scan code*) to each key. This scan code is passed to the PC for interpretation by BIOS. Figure 2.7 shows the keyboard scan codes.

Fig. 2.7. The keyboard scan codes.

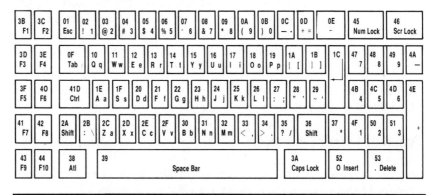

As you type, the keyboard notifies the computer (via Int 09h) that a key has been pressed or released. When the processor executes Int 09h, the BIOS takes momentary control of the computer and reads the key's scan code, checking first for toggle keys such as Shift and Num Lock. If a toggle key has been pressed or released, the BIOS updates the keyboard status bits kept in memory addresses 0417h–0418h. Next, the BIOS checks for special key combinations (such as Ctrl-Alt-Del) and, if necessary, executes their special handlers.

If the scan code still has not been "weeded out" as a special-purpose character (such as Num-Lock, Ctrl-Alt-Del, the Shift or Ctrl keys, etc.), BIOS translates it into its ASCII equivalent. If no corresponding ASCII character is available for the key, it is given an ASCII value of zero. Then the ASCII character, along with its original scan code, is stored in the keyboard buffer. This buffer is large enough to hold 15 characters and their scan codes. If the buffer is full, BIOS issues a "beep" (signalling that the keyboard buffer is full) and then discards the character.

Once the character is in the keyboard buffer, it is available for use by any program (including DOS) that is currently running. Because the computer usually responds within a fraction of a second, the chances of filling the keyboard buffer are slim—*unless the computer is busy performing another task*. In this case, the keyboard buffer is likely to fill, and you will hear the familiar beep when BIOS cannot handle any more keyboard input.

This quick overview of the keyboard should suffice for the time being. (Programming the keyboard is discussed in greater detail in Chapter 6.)

The Display Screen

The PC supports several different types of video adapters, and most adapters work in more than one mode—text or graphics. Writing programs to accommodate the various kinds of adapters is not as difficult as you might think, however, because DOS provides facilities for determining what kind of adapter is present and what the current mode is.

Chapter 6 discusses these matters in detail. The following sections are an introduction to kinds of adapters you are likely to encounter.

Types of Display Adapters

For most PC programming, you should be familiar with six types of display adapters. (Others exist but are used for special applications.)

The original "standard" display was the Monochrome Display Adapter (MDA). This system, with its crisp, clear characters and a nice professional appearance, was expected to be the standard for business use of the computer. Other video adapters (the CGA, EGA, MCGA, and VGA) became available as users began to demand color, higher resolution, and other display enhancements. Table 2.2 lists these display adapters and the year each became available.

Table 2.2. Display Adapters and Year Each Became Available

Adapter	Year Introduced
MDA	1981
CGA	1982
EGA	1984
MCGA	1987
VGA	1987

In addition to the monochrome adapter, the Color Graphics Adapter (CGA) was available for those to whom color was important. The CGA display shows color and graphics, but the characters are not as sharp as those displayed by the MDA. This difference in sharpness is due to the number of dots, or pixels, used to create each character. The MDA uses a 9 × 14 character box to create characters, whereas the CGA uses an 8 × 8 box. Because of this difference in resolution, the characters on the CGA tend to look "fuzzy" when compared to the MDA. Many users find the CGA display impossible to use for any extended length of time in text-oriented work such as word-processing or spreadsheet applications.

The Hercules Graphics Adapter (HGA) display, which combines the monochrome screen's clear characters with the graphics capabilities of the color graphics display, produces high-resolution monochrome displays that rapidly became the standard of comparison for text and graphics. Although HGAs are not capable of producing color, the lack of color was not a big drawback.

With the introduction of the Enhanced Graphics Adapter (EGA) color graphics system, people (and businesses) began to discover that color added a rich new dimension to their work. Highlighting alone is never adequate for showing a wide range of things on-screen; you can use color to call attention to many more things than you could with a monochrome screen. Business packages that produce graphic output in color are rapidly becoming the standard against which new packages are judged.

The standards for displays have again been revised, albeit only slightly, by the introduction of the Multi-Color Graphics Array (MCGA) for IBM Personal System/2™ Models 25 and 30 and the Video Graphics Array (VGA) for IBM PS/2 Models 50, 60, and 80. The MCGA is similar to the CGA but has higher resolution. (The MCGA's resolution is 320 × 400; the CGA's is 320 × 400). The VGA's resolution (640 × 480) is a modest extension of the EGA (640 × 350). The big improvement in both displays is that they now use analog instead of digital monitors. By working with analog signals, these new video systems can display palettes of 256 colors (of the possible 262,144 colors available).

Memory Mapping and Display Adapters

The video displays of the IBM family all use *memory mapping*. In other words, what you see on the screen is a direct reflection of what resides within the memory area controlled by the display adapter you are using. The memory areas used by the different display adapters vary according to the type of display. Table 2.3 details the starting memory locations and length of video buffers for each display adapter.

Let's take a closer look at the concept of memory mapping. To put it simply: first, characters are written to the display memory; then the display adapter reads the characters from the display memory and shows them on the video screen. In graphics modes, the display adapter treats the data in the video memory as an array of individual bits that control the dots on the screen.

Table 2.3. Memory Configurations for Display Adapters

Display Type	Mode	Buffer Segment Address	Buffer Length	Display Pages
MDA	Text	B000h	4K	1
CGA	Text	B800h	16K	4/8
	Graphics	B800h	16K	1
EGA	Mono	B000h	-- varies --	
	Text	B800h	-- varies --	
	CGA Graphics	B800h	-- varies --	
	Graphics	A000h	-- varies --	
MCGA	Text	B800h	64K	8
	CGA Graphics	B800h	64K	1
	Graphics	A000h	64K	1
VGA	Mono	B000h	256K	8
	Text	B800h	256K	8
	CGA Graphics	B800h	256K	1
	Graphics	A000h	256K	1/2/4/8

Although this section provides a brief overview of the way display adapters function, you should refer to Chapter 5 for more detailed information. That chapter provides specifics on how the display adapters interpret the video memory and how to use the BIOS and DOS functions to display information.

The Printer

Fortunately, you can rely on the printer to work in the simplest way possible. Generally, all you need to know about a printer is that if you send it characters, it will print them (provided that the cable between the computer and the printer is connected properly and that the power is turned on).

In this book, the term *printer* generally refers to a printer attached to the parallel printer port—not to the serial port. (Serial ports are touched upon in the next section; Chapter 7 discusses them in greater detail.) With a parallel printer interface, you can send the printer an initialization message that tells it to get ready and you can read the printer's status to find out, for example, whether it is out of paper. This is typically what you will do with a printer at the DOS level.

Printer gymnastics are beyond the scope of this book. However, if you have a good printer with high-resolution graphics capability, or color, or one that can respond to sophisticated page layout commands (such as PostScript®), you can do wonderful things.

In Chapter 5 you will learn how to write programs that access the printer directly, using the BIOS and DOS functions. You can access several printers (LPT1:, LPT2:, etc.) and interpret the return codes to determine the printer's status.

The Serial Port

With a parallel printer connection, you have limited control of the parallel printer port. The hardware has been designed to handle almost every task. You can buy a printer off the shelf and be confident that it will run correctly as soon as you plug it in. But serial ports are different.

Most of today's computers are equipped with at least one serial port. Used predominantly to drive serial printers or modems, serial ports pose special problems. Their parameters must be set identically on both sides of the connection; if the parameters are not set correctly, nothing gets through. These parameters include baud rate, parity, stop and start bits, and data length. Although standards govern the way that wires are physically connected for most (but not all) devices, the parameters have not been completely standardized. Even if you make the correct physical connections, you still have to make the correct *logical* connections.

There is no quick-and-easy way to make these connections. Serial port parameters specify the number of bits-per-second at which information is transferred; the number of bits that make up a character; whether there is parity checking and, if there is, the type of parity; and the number of stop bits used to indicate the end of a character. You may have to specify flow control over the line with software, such as XON/XOFF or ETX/ACK; or you may have to use a special line protocol, such as Xmodem or Kermit. It is no wonder that neophytes rarely succeed in getting their computers connected to the telephone line the first time they try.

In Chapter 7, which is devoted to the intricacies of serial channels and how to program them, you will find the meaning of all the serial port parameters and determine how best to incorporate this information into the programs you write. You will learn also that you cannot use DOS or BIOS to do certain things on serial channels. For example, you will have to bypass DOS and BIOS and go directly to the hardware level to write practical programs that deal in real-time communications between computers, either to emulate terminals or to transfer files.

The Mouse

When the original PC was designed, the mouse was not considered an important device. Routines inside the BIOS allowed programmers to access the more popular joysticks and light pens. But times (and users) change—today, the mouse has a sizeable following.

Generally, a mouse is connected to a PC either through a custom hardware board that plugs into the PC's internal system bus or through one of the installed serial ports. The mouse driver software determines the location of the mouse and handles the interface to the board.

The Mouse

In its simplest form, a mouse is a device with a small ball fitted on the bottom. When you roll the mouse across a flat surface, sensors measure the device's movement in both X and Y directions. The mouse sends signals indicating changes in position to the computer system. An *optical mouse* does not use a ball; rather, it tracks the movement of the device across a reflective grid. No matter which type of mouse you use, the computer responds to the changes in position by moving a visible pointer on the screen as the mouse moves. All of this activity is handled at the driver level. Whenever the program is ready for input, it can simply check the mouse.

In addition to sensors that track its movement, the mouse usually is fitted with one, two, or three switches (called *buttons*) that you can press to initiate or terminate the system's actions.

You use DOS Int 33h to access the mouse by using the standard mouse driver software. The interrupt allows access to information about the mouse and its movement.

To some users, a program that doesn't use the mouse has one strike against it; others won't even consider a program that does use the mouse. You, the programmer, will have to decide whether to use it. (Even though the mouse is an add-on to the DOS system, you can learn more about it and how to manipulate its information in Chapter 6.)

Storage Devices

As DOS has evolved, so have its capabilities for greater disk storage capacity. Table 2.4 shows the increases in disk capacity and in the number of drive formats supported.

Table 2.4. Disk Capacities

DOS Version	Disk	Capacity
1.0	5 1/4" SSDD	160K
	5 1/4" DSDD	320K
2.0	5 1/4" SSDD	180K
	5 1/4" DSDD	360K
2.1	5 1/4" High capacity	1.2M
3.2	3 1/2" DSDD	720K
3.3	3 1/2" High capacity	1.44M

Physical Disk Structure

The recording surface of a disk is divided into concentric tracks, and each track is divided into sectors. The numbers of tracks and sectors vary according to the type of disk (floppy disk or hard disk; single, double, or high density; 3 1/2-inch or 5 1/4-inch). Figure 2.8 shows the arrangement of tracks and sectors on the disk.

Because hard disk drives contain more than one platter, hard-disk space is divided into cylinders. Each cylinder includes one track on each side of each platter present in the drive. Figure 2.9 shows how tracks combine to make cylinders.

Fig. 2.8. Disk track formatting.

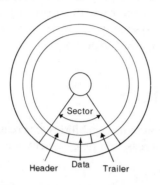

Fig. 2.9. A fixed disk.

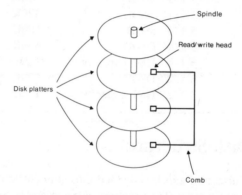

In Chapter 8, which deals with disk structure, you will find a more detailed discussion of the disk's physical format. Chapter 8 also shows how to access the internal formatting routines that control the lowest level of the track-formatting operation.

Logical Disk Structure

The FORMAT program establishes not only the disk's sector structure but also a logical structure, unique to DOS, that controls how data is stored on the disk. Figure 2.10 shows this logical structure.

Fig. 2.10. *The disk's logical structure.*

Boot sector	FAT 1	FAT 2	Root directory	Data ⟶

FORMAT's largest, most time-consuming task is that of formatting the disk—dividing the physical disk into logical tracks and sectors and filling them with an initial value.

Then the FORMAT program creates three areas on the disk: the *boot record*, the *file allocation table* (FAT), and the *root directory*. The rest of the disk (the portion not included in any of these areas) is the file-storage area.

The Boot Record

The boot record is the first sector on every logical disk. Beginning with DOS V2, the boot record contains the disk boot program and a table of the disk characteristics. After the boot program, which is only a few hundred bytes long, is loaded into memory when the system is started, it loads the operating system files from the disk. If those files are not found, the boot program gives you an error message. The booting process is covered in greater detail in Chapter 3.

The File Allocation Table (FAT)

The FAT is a map of the disk. It shows you which portions of the disk are assigned, which are unassigned, and which are not assignable (because of formatting errors, for example). Areas of the disk are assigned to files in clusters, with each cluster represented by an entry in the FAT. Depending on the disk's size, clusters can vary in size from one to eight or more sectors. To accommodate the increased storage capacity of hard disks, FAT entries (originally 12 bits per entry) are now 16 bits per entry.

I want to stress that the FAT is essential to the proper functioning of DOS in relation to a disk. A detailed description and discussion of the FAT would be premature at this point; for more detailed information on the FAT, see Chapter 8.

The Root Directory

The last part of the system information on the disk, the root directory, is located immediately after the FAT. It contains the following information about the files accessible through the root directory:

- ❏ An eight-byte file name
- ❏ A three-byte file extension
- ❏ The file size (in bytes)
- ❏ A date and time stamp for the file
- ❏ The starting cluster number for the file
- ❏ The file attribute codes

Each entry is 32 bytes long, with extra space reserved for future expansion. The root directory for a given disk is a fixed size. On 160K, single-sided disks, the root directory can accommodate 64 entries; on a 20-megabyte hard disk, it can hold 512 entries. Directory size is limited so that DOS can tell where the disk's data area begins. In DOS V2 and later versions, this limitation is not a problem; you can bypass the limit on the number of files by creating subdirectories, which have no size limit.

For a more detailed discussion of the structure of disks and directories, see Chapters 8 and 9.

The Software

Above the physical machine, the software provided with a PC or compatible system builds another layer on the virtual machine. This software starts with the BIOS, which builds a standard view of the machine that attempts to hide the specifics of the installed hardware. Above the BIOS, DOS builds the machine we are familiar with (in terms of files and directories).

The BIOS

The first software level in the virtual machine is the BIOS (Basic Input/Output System). This software forms the lowest-level machine with which you normally will deal. In certain cases, the BIOS is neither powerful enough nor fast enough to accomplish what you want to do—you have to go directly to the hardware.

The BIOS software consists of two parts: a ROM portion containing the most basic machine functions, and a portion loaded from disk, which extends these functions so that they can handle all of the system's input and output requests. The purpose of the BIOS is to insulate higher levels of software from possible hardware changes in the computer. The BIOS provides a defined set of services as a base for higher software levels.

Each computer manufacturer (including IBM) provides the BIOS for its machines. Microsoft provides a module called SYSINIT (see Chapter 3), which manages system initialization and the loading of DOS. The BIOS has to meet certain specifications to allow the higher-level software to function properly. For example, Microsoft's DOS kernel uses the BIOS services to implement many of its own operations.

PC-compatible computers often come with versions of the BIOS ROM provided by the manufacturer. Clearly, none of them can duplicate the exact code in an IBM BIOS ROM; they *can*, however, provide BIOS services by handling the same interrupt structure and using the same data table areas used by the IBM BIOS. Although the code is different, they provide the BIOS services needed to run DOS.

If third-party BIOS ROMs are accessed through the defined BIOS interrupts, you can expect them to work the way the IBM PC services work. If you write a program that uses an internal knowledge of the BIOS ROM to get something done, all bets are off.

From its position between the hardware and DOS, the BIOS enables Microsoft to provide a standard operating system kernel regardless of the hardware. Whether a computer is from IBM or from some other manufacturer, programs that use the standard DOS or BIOS interface for all of their system functions are portable between DOS machines. In other words, such a program can be taken unchanged (at least in source-code form) from one machine and made to work on another.

The BIOS Reference Section at the back of this book describes the BIOS interrupt functions in detail. All of these functions work with the BIOS ROMs provided by all manufacturers of IBM-compatible computers.

The DOS Kernel

Microsoft provides the DOS kernel as a proprietary program based on the standard BIOS services. The DOS kernel provides hardware-independent services that can be used by application programs on a variety of systems. You will spend a great deal of time working with these DOS services. *Note:* "DOS" refers to PC DOS *or* MS-DOS unless specifically mentioned otherwise. DOS services can be divided arbitrarily into the following categories:

❑ Character I/O
❑ Directory operations
❑ Disk control
❑ Dynamic Memory Allocation (DMA)
❑ Error handling
❑ File operations
❑ Miscellaneous system functions
❑ Network functions
❑ Program execution/termination

You can access the DOS services in two ways. Some services are accessed directly through software interrupts. Most DOS services, however, are accessed through DOS function calls by placing a function number in register AH and then executing Int 21h.

The DOS Reference Section at the back of this book describes the DOS interrupt functions in detail. These interrupts are available on all PCs and compatibles. Known differences between systems are pointed out in this section.

The Command Processor

To most people who work with a PC, the command processor (or *shell*) *is* the operating system. These people are used to thinking of the **A**> prompt as coming from the operating system and not from a program. Only a few years ago, interactive operating systems *were* built this way.

Today, however, shell interfaces are the standard. The shell makes the process of changing and adding new features easy, because only one part of the operating system has to be changed. Although the shell interface was not invented by the designers of UNIX™, this type of program (COMMAND.COM, for example) was popularized by the UNIX operating system. UNIX systems have several standard shells (csh, ksh, sh, to name a few).

The structure of COMMAND.COM is important to its operation. The program has three parts: an initialization section, a resident section, and a transient section.

When COMMAND.COM starts, the initialization and resident sections are loaded from disk. The initialization section sets up the system, runs the AUTOEXEC.BAT file, and then loads and turns control over to the transient section. As its name implies, the transient section comes and goes (according to the demands of memory); the resident section, which "is always there," is responsible for reloading the transient section, among other things.

If all of COMMAND.COM's capabilities were coded in a single program, the program would take up a substantial amount of memory (more than 20K). This amount of memory is a drop in the bucket compared to that required by most applications but, if you were trying to get the last few paragraphs into a document or the last few cells into a spreadsheet, it could be considerable. To minimize the program's memory consumption, the COMMAND.COM code for normal operations and the code for the program's built-in commands are kept in the transient section. Because this section is sometimes overwritten by another program, COMMAND.COM's resident section checks to see whether the transient section needs to be reloaded and, if it does, reloads it.

COMMAND.COM executes programs from three categories of commands:

1. *Internal commands* (built into COMMAND.COM)

2. *External commands* (programs stored on the disk)

3. *Batch files* (also stored on the disk)

The transient section of COMMAND.COM includes the code for the internal commands. When the user types a command name, COMMAND.COM first searches to see whether the command is an internal command. If COMMAND.COM does not find the named command among the internal commands, the program searches for it first in the current directory and then along the search path. COMMAND.COM searches for an external command with the .COM extension, and then for one with the .EXE extension. If it finds neither of these in a given directory, COMMAND.COM looks for a batch file (extension .BAT) with the appropriate name.

Batch files are scripts of commands to execute. These commands may be internal, external, or other batch files. The transient portion of COMMAND.COM reads in each line of the batch file and then executes it.

Batch files are a special type of "program" allowed by a command processor. These files consist of scripts of commands to execute in a given sequence, with a small control language that allows for parameter substitution, decisions, and branching within the batch file.

Batch files are executed by COMMAND.COM on a line-by-line basis. Each line consists of a command to be executed: either an executable command or an internal control command allowed in batch files only. Actual operation is simple. COMMAND.COM takes one line of the batch file, performs any parameter replacements, and then uses the DOS EXEC function to execute the command.

As each line is finished, COMMAND.COM gets the next line and executes it. The batch command language is a mini programming language. Some internal commands allow branching within the batch file (GOTO), decision making (IF), or looping (FOR). Although batch files can call other batch files directly, doing so terminates the operation of the first batch file. COMMAND.COM will never return to the first batch file when it starts a second.

Device Drivers

Most advances in the art of software have involved ways to make the underlying hardware disappear. High-level languages, for example, definitely are an advance because they don't require the programmer to know about registers, bits, and bytes. (Not everyone will agree with that statement.) Similarly, operating systems are a big improvement over the days when we all had to write our own drivers for each device we wanted to use.

CP/M used standard devices for handling the console and printer. DOS has gone a step further by making the devices more interchangeable and making it possible to install your own devices without having to recompile the entire operating system. Think about it! Previously, if you wanted to add new devices to a system you had to get down to the internals of the operating system to make your devices work. Today, DOS includes a more flexible driver model that allows you to write a driver for a device and to choose whether to add it when the system starts. To understand how this works, you need to understand a little about device drivers.

The operating system software includes a set of device drivers (the resident drivers) that run the hardware. Each driver meets certain specifications for its calling interface so that DOS can operate the hardware *without having to know how it works*. It makes no difference to DOS what kind of keyboard or screen display a system has, if the driver works as it should.

When you boot the computer, DOS initializes all of the drivers through standard initialization entry points, as you will learn in Chapter 3. For the time being, all you need to know is that you operate a device through a series of functions that are defined by standard entry points. The type of device you are trying to control determines which entry points are meaningful. In Chapter 12, you will learn a great deal about device drivers—in fact, you will create a simple one.

DOS divides devices into *character devices* and *block devices*. Character devices operate on a character-by-character basis (the keyboard and video display, for example); block devices (disks and RAM disks) operate on a block-transfer basis. Each type of driver has entry points appropriate for handling specific functions.

Basically, DOS is a collection of standard device drivers. This provides a degree of independence from the underlying hardware and allows Microsoft to deliver the basic operating system kernel (MSDOS.SYS) as a standard file, compatible with all standard hardware.

You can write your own device drivers and then add them to your CONFIG.SYS file. These device drivers will be added to the system the next time you boot the system. (You will learn how to do this in Chapter 12.) Your drivers will operate on an equal footing with the resident drivers. You can even replace an existing character driver with completely new code, as ANSI.SYS and other drivers do for the video display.

Installable drivers let you add to the system new equipment that was not envisioned in the original design of the system. (MOUSE.SYS does this for the mouse; EMM.SYS, for expanded memory). In short, DOS has created an environment that you can expand to meet your needs as new equipment becomes available.

All device handling in OS/2 is done through device drivers. OS/2's only BIOS functions are those for DOS compatibility and booting. Whenever input or output is needed, OS/2 gets it done by referring directly to a driver device.

Now that you understand something of the statics of DOS, let's move on to DOS in a dynamic environment and learn how it all works.

Summary

In this chapter, you have learned that DOS systems exist as a hierarchy of "virtual computers." Starting with the hardware at the lowest level and continuing up through the BIOS and DOS systems, each level provides a consistent logical computer with special functions needed to implement the next level of the computer system.

The lowest level, hardware (the combination of components that comprise a system) can vary widely between systems. Then, the BIOS provides a "computer" with defined services that we can depend on to work in the same way from one system to another. These Basic Input/Output Services allow raw access to the devices on the system. DOS provides a higher level of services (and therefore a higher level of abstraction) than the BIOS. The DOS services create what we commonly think of as "the system"—files, directories, and so on. At the highest level, COMMAND.COM provides a user interface that gives control of the different services.

The Dynamics of DOS

Chapter 2 described the layout of DOS, its hardware support, and its basic software modules. This chapter shows you what happens when these elements operate in a dynamic environment. We will see what happens as the system starts up, how it processes commands, and how programs are executed.

Then, having gained an overview of system and program operation, we will take a more detailed look at interrupts and memory management under DOS. This chapter lays the groundwork for the practical programming in Chapters 5 through 13.

The DOS Boot Sequence

When you power up or reset a system based on the 8086 family of micro-processors, the microprocessor automatically starts program execution at address FFFF:0000h. This happens because of the processor design and has nothing to do with DOS. The ROM BIOS at FFFF:0000h provides a jump instruction to the beginning of the hardware test routines and the ROM bootstrap code. (In the following discussion, *ROM BIOS* applies to PCs and compatibles.)

When a system is turned on (a cold start), a series of hardware tests called the *Power-On Self Test* (POST) check the amount of installed memory and test which peripheral devices are available and operable. At this point during startup, most machines show rapidly changing memory-size figures and report on serial ports, parallel ports, and so forth. When these steps are complete, control is transferred to the ROM bootstrap initialization procedure.

The bootstrap initialization routine sets up important parts of the interrupt vector table in low memory (especially vectors for hardware located by the POST). The routine also initializes the ROM BIOS tables at memory location 0400:0000h, and may do some hardware setup, such as starting dynamic memory refresh. The routine then searches the memory area from A000:0000 through F000:0000 to locate other ROM extensions; these extensions are marked with a unique byte sequence that identifies them as ROM. (Typical ROM extensions are the EGA graphics ROM and the PC XT fixed disk controller ROM.) The bootstrap routine initializes any ROM extensions it finds. After initialization is complete, the ROM bootstrap code starts the system itself.

The ROM bootstrap routines now read the disk bootstrap code from the first sector (the *boot sector*) of the boot disk. The bootstrap code is a minimal-services routine responsible for getting the system up and running. The ROM bootstrap routines check all bootable disk drives for the presence of a boot sector on the disk. On a hard disk system with a single floppy disk, the ROM routines first check drive C and then drive A. If no boot sector is found, an IBM PC transfers control to ROM BASIC and starts up as a diskless system; PC compatibles prompt you to insert a system disk and then wait for you to press a key.

When a bootstrap record is located, the ROM bootstrap loads it into high memory, away from where DOS itself will be loaded. Control is then transferred to the disk bootstrap routine.

After the disk bootstrap code has been loaded and has control, it looks back to the disk to locate the files IO.SYS and MSDOS.SYS.

Note: On an IBM PC and many compatibles, these files are named IBMBIO.COM and IBMDOS.COM. In this discussion, *MSDOS.SYS* refers to two modules (MSDOS.SYS and IBMDOS.COM) and *IO.SYS* refers to two others (IO.SYS and IBMBIO.COM). Unless a specific difference is pointed out, all operations are performed alike in either set of modules.

The disk bootstrap doesn't know about file systems or disk structures—indeed, it can't. All of the information about a disk's file layout is held in the file MSDOS.SYS and, because that file has not yet been loaded and initialized, that data is not available. Therefore, the following requirements are imposed on a boot disk:

1. IO.SYS must be the *first* entry in the root directory.

2. MSDOS.SYS must be the *second* entry in the root directory.

3. The files themselves *must* be the first files on the disk and they must be stored in contiguous clusters in the correct order.

Now you know why the SYS.COM program "complains" when it tries to make bootable a disk that already has something stored on it. A bootable disk must be built when the disk is empty. Otherwise, SYS.COM won't work.

If the disk bootstrap doesn't know about the file system, how does it know about the directory entries and where the files are located? It learns this information from the *BIOS parameter block* (BPB)—the area of the boot sector from byte 0Bh through 17h (see fig. 3.1).

Fig. 3.1. *The boot sector.*

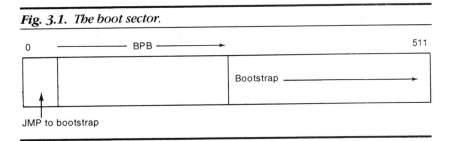

The BPB tells the boot program enough about the disk layout that the boot program can locate the beginning of the directory and the file space. After locating the files, the boot program copies IO.SYS (IBMBIO.COM) into low memory above the BIOS tables. Then, depending on which system you are using, either the boot program or the IO.SYS initialization routine will also copy MSDOS.SYS to memory in an area above IO.SYS.

When you load IO.SYS, it has two parts. The system manufacturer supplies the first part—the BIOS. The BIOS contains the resident device drivers as well as hardware-specific initialization code that is run only when the BIOS is loaded. Microsoft and IBM supply the second part: a module called SYSINIT.

When IO.SYS takes control of the computer, it runs any hardware-specific initialization the system may need. During initialization, IO.SYS checks the interrupt vector table (set up earlier by the ROM BIOS initialization) to see what hardware is being used. (Unneeded drivers are deleted automatically at this point.) Then control is transferred to the SYSINIT module.

SYSINIT checks the available memory and relocates itself into high memory. Permanent memory space does not have to be allocated for SYSINIT, a temporary module whose services will be needed for a short time only. The relocation of SYSINIT to high memory allows the module to continue long enough to serve its purpose, but gets it out of the way so that memory is available for use by DOS.

This high-memory copy of SYSINIT copies MSDOS.SYS over the IO.SYS initialization code (including the original copy of SYSINIT). This operation recovers and makes available to DOS all of the memory used for initialization (memory that is used once—during system startup). SYSINIT then calls the MS-DOS (or PC DOS) initialization code.

The MSDOS.SYS initialization code sets up its internal tables and the interrupt vectors. Then it starts initializing drivers. MSDOS.SYS calls the initialization function for each resident device driver. This function checks the driver's status, initializes the hardware, and sets up any interrupts serviced by that driver.

MSDOS.SYS also examines the BIOS parameter block to determine how many disk drives are attached to the system and determines the largest disk-sector size for all these disk drives. MSDOS.SYS uses this value to set up a disk-sector buffer for use by the system. Finally, MSDOS.SYS displays the DOS copyright and returns control to SYSINIT.

Next, using the DOS Int 21h file services, SYSINIT opens the CONFIG.SYS file. The entire file is loaded into memory, all characters are converted to uppercase, and CONFIG.SYS is interpreted for system configuration information. Memory is allocated for disk buffers and file control blocks, and default values are assigned if CONFIG.SYS does not exist or doesn't specify explicit values through the buffers and FCB directives. Additionally, any drivers referenced in CONFIG.SYS are loaded, initialized, and added to the list of drivers maintained by the system. If new character drivers and resident drivers have the same name, the new drivers are listed in such a way that they always are found first when access to a driver is needed, thereby effectively replacing the existing driver.

After completing the initialization process, SYSINIT closes all file handles and opens the console device (CON) as standard input, standard output, and standard error; the printer device (PRN) as standard list; and the auxiliary device (AUX) as standard auxiliary. Finally, SYSINIT calls the DOS EXEC function to load and execute COMMAND.COM or the shell specified in CONFIG.SYS. (The EXEC function is described in this chapter's "Command Processing" section.) SYSINIT is no longer necessary by design. Because its functions are limited to support of system startup, its memory now can be reused for other purposes. SYSINIT will be overwritten as its space is needed.

When COMMAND.COM is loaded, it immediately relocates part of itself into high memory. The low-memory section of COMMAND.COM (the resident section of the code) contains code essential for restarting COMMAND.COM when it regains control, as well as handlers for three interrupts: Int 22h (Terminate Address), Int 23h (Ctrl-C), and Int 24h (Critical Error). The high-memory section of COMMAND.COM (the transient portion) holds the code necessary for the internal commands and for batch-file processing. By splitting itself in two, COMMAND.COM tries to use the smallest possible amount of memory for functions that *must* remain in memory at all times.

When first loaded by SYSINIT, COMMAND.COM sets up the vectors for interrupts 22h through 24h. Then COMMAND.COM executes the AUTOEXEC.BAT file. When that step is complete, control is transferred to the transient portion of COMMAND.COM, the DOS prompt is displayed, and the system is ready to go.

Now that all the software necessary for running the computer has been loaded and initialized, let's see how COMMAND.COM processes commands.

Command Processing

COMMAND.COM is a shell program that controls access to system resources and provides a working environment for users. This working environment consists of defined ways in which users can locate and execute functions on the system. When you ask COMMAND.COM to execute a command, the program tries to locate the command in the following manner:

1. By searching for the requested operation in the list of internal commands (such as DIR, COPY, DEL, etc.)

2. By searching for an executable file (with the extension .COM, .EXE, or .BAT) in the current directory, as external commands

3. By searching for a program in the directories listed in the PATH environment variable

When COMMAND.COM searches a directory, it looks first for the command file with a .COM extension, then with a .EXE extension, and then with a .BAT extension, thereby setting up a precedence of program types for execution. If two programs in the same directory have the same root name but different extensions (FORMAT.COM and FORMAT.EXE, for example), DOS will always execute the .COM file. The extension is disregarded. Even if you enter FORMAT.EXE, DOS will execute the .COM file. (A common misconception, repeated in some other books, is that by entering the extension you can "force" DOS to run the executable file of your choice. You cannot!)

When a program is identified as either a .COM or .EXE file, COMMAND.COM calls the DOS EXEC function to execute that program. The EXEC function:

1. Checks whether enough memory is available to load the program. If sufficient memory is available, the required memory is allocated. If the memory is not available, EXEC issues an error message and does not execute the program.

2. Builds a program segment prefix (PSP) at the bottom of the allocated memory area (see fig. 3.2). (For a more detailed discussion of the PSP, see Chapter 10.)

Fig. 3.2. Program segment prefix (PSP).

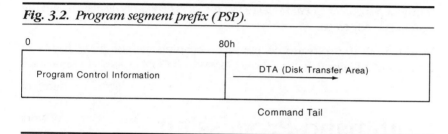

3. Loads the program into the memory space above the PSP. COM programs simply are copied as a memory image; EXE programs are loaded according to the loading information in the header.

4. Transfers control to the program's entry point. .COM files *always* have an entry point at 100h (just after the PSP), whereas the entry points for an .EXE file are specified in the EXE program header.

5. Returns control, when the program terminates, to the resident portion of COMMAND.COM. The resident portion of COMMAND.COM does a checksum of the area occupied by the transient portion. If the checksum is OK, control of the computer is transferred back to the transient portion, and the system prompt reappears; otherwise, the transient portion is reloaded from disk and regains control.

A shell program intended to replace COMMAND.COM *must* provide handlers for interrupts 22h through 24h; the shell can provide other features as needed. On Hewlett-Packard systems, COMMAND.COM has been replaced by a simplified shell that is friendlier to novice users.

You may want to play with ideas for a shell to front-end a system you put together, considering some of the following advantages:

❑ By controlling users' access to disk files, you can prevent unauthorized tampering.

❑ By guiding users to certain choices, you can eliminate frustrating, costly mistakes.

❑ You can provide users with context-sensitive help (help appropriate to specific parts of a program).

Writing a shell can be challenging. But writing a shell that makes a large, complex system less complicated to use can be well worth your effort. No matter what else a shell may do, its primary purpose is to run programs in the DOS environment. Let's look at the way programs work, so that you can see what happens when you run them.

Programs under DOS

Applications programs under DOS take two basic and significantly different forms: .COM files (COM programs) and .EXE files (EXE programs). You must have a thorough understanding of the differences if you are to do useful work on the system.

COM Programs

COM programs are the smallest and simplest of programs. On disk, they exist as memory images; in memory, they are loaded into a single 64K memory segment. Even though COM programs are supposed to exist totally within a single segment, they frequently stray outside. COM programs that access video memory directly, for example, *must* access memory outside their assigned 64K memory area.

Early programs for the PC and compatibles often did much more than simply access video memory. Frequently, because the rest of memory was assumed to be available for its use, a program would set up tables, load program overlays, or control the extra memory in any way needed for its function. Some fairly nice programs acted this way. If DOS assumed that a COM program used only its assigned segment of memory, another program executed by DOS could easily mess up a program that was already there. To eliminate the problem, DOS gives all of free memory to a COM program that is being executed. Later in this chapter (and again in Chapter 10) you will learn in greater detail about the way this memory is assigned.

A COM program easily can exceed the assumed bounds of the data area. It simply modifies the processor's segment registers to point to memory areas that the program needs to access. For example, by modifying the data segment (DS) register, a COM program can manipulate data in any portion of memory. This capability is absolutely necessary if the program is going to modify the screen memory directly instead of using DOS services for video output, because the screen memory cannot be in the program's data segment.

Although you may consider access to all of the system's memory a great capability, it leaves DOS with the possibility that a program can modify anything—thus, nothing is "safe." To obviate this problem, DOS takes the safe way out by assigning all available memory to the program. (Technically, this statement is only partly correct; for a more detailed explanation, check the section on memory allocation, at the end of this chapter).

If you write a COM program that uses DOS's EXEC function (the program and overlay loader) to execute another program, your COM program should release any memory it is not using. DOS provides memory-management functions that can be used to allocate, deallocate, and change the size of memory blocks used by your programs. These functions are detailed in the last part of this chapter and in the "DOS Reference Section" at the end of this book (see DOS functions 48h through 4Ah). Because high-level languages handle memory-management automatically, you will not need to worry about memory management unless you are programming in assembly language.

Listing 3.1, a sample COM program written in assembly language, is the simplest of programs. It uses a standard DOS function (09h) to write a string to the screen.

Listing 3.1

```
;                       Sample COM Program

        name        dosbook
;
; Democm.asm - .COM file version of simple print
; Prints 'DOS Programmer's Reference
;
;------ Beginning of the CODE Segment ------
cseg    segment     para public 'CODE'
        org         100h            ; Program origin
;
; All of the segment registers are set to point
;to the same segment (required for a
; COM program)
        assume      cs:cseg,ds:cseg,es:cseg,ss:cseg
```

Listing 3.1 continues

Listing 3.1 continued

```
;
;------ Procedure Book ------
; PURPOSE:        To illustrate programming for
;                 a .COM file. Displays a defined
;                 string on the screen
; USES:           DX, AX
; RETURNS:        Nothing
;
book   proc       near
       mov        dx,offset msg  ; Get message location
       mov        ah,9           ; Output character string
       int        21h
       mov        al,Ø           ; Exit code zero
       mov        ah,4ch         ; Terminate
       int        21h
book   endp
;------ End of Procedure Book ------
msg    db             'DOS Programmer',Ø27h,'s Reference',Ødh,Øah,'$'
cseg   ends
;------ End of the CODE Segment ------
       end        book
```

Let's go through the program, line-by-line, to see what it does.

After the initial three-line comment section, a *segment* instruction declares the start of the program's code segment, and the program's origin is established at location 100h. Starting at 100h allows space in the segment for the program's PSP. (See Chapter 10 for a discussion of the PSP's layout and use.)

Another three-line comment section precedes the next step, the *assume* statement, which tells the assembler that all of the segment registers will point to the code segment. Because all of the segment registers point to the same location and a segment can refer to only 64K of memory, the program effectively is limited to 64K of space.

With the program established, the next step is that of creating the program's only procedure (book) and declaring it a NEAR procedure (all references will be within the single segment). The body of the program is simplicity itself. To create it, you follow these steps:

1. Put the offset address of the message into the DX register.

2. Set the AH register to 9 (the code for the DOS function that writes a string to the screen).

3. Execute Int 21h to invoke the DOS interrupt processor.

4. Set the AL register to zero (the exit code for the program) in preparation for program termination.

5. Set AH to 4Ch (the function number for a DOS program-termination call).

6. Make a final call to Int 21h to process program termination.

At the end of the procedure, the data string for printing is defined in memory with special ASCII characters 27h (the apostrophe, '), 0Dh (carriage return), and 0Ah (line feed). The DOS function requires that the string be terminated with a dollar sign ($).

When you assemble the program, the macro assembler creates an object file from the source code. This object file is a direct translation of the source file into assembly language. But before the program can be executed, it must be linked to any library routines specified in the source code; the linker creates an .EXE file, which is an executable version of the original program. To turn this .EXE file into a .COM file, you use the EXE2BIN program.

As you can see from figure 3.3, which shows a COM program dump as it exists on disk, only the program code is kept in the file. The program uses minimal disk space.

EXE Programs

EXE programs are much more complex and versatile than COM programs. Instead of being limited to a single memory segment, EXE programs frequently occupy several segments and may include more than one segment of code and data. EXE program files have a special header area, which is used by the DOS EXEC function to load the program. This header block contains information that DOS uses to relocate the file and determine memory requirements. The program header is essential if the program is to operate because, unlike a COM program, which is stored as an absolute memory image, an EXE program is stored as a relocatable memory image. The system can adjust such an image to conform to overall space and memory-usage needs as determined by DOS. Each program contains a checksum.

EXE programs are more flexible than COM programs, and sometimes much larger (reaching the limits of memory). They also coexist better in memory because they can be broken into discrete segments and assigned to available free space. This coexistence is of little use on PC systems in a single-user, single-task environment. Coexistence will become more and more of a problem, however, as we move either into multitasking (using systems such

Fig.3.3. Disk sector containing the sample COM program.

```
ØØØØ  BA ØD Ø1 B4 Ø9 CD 21 BØ-ØØ B4 4C CD 21 44 4F 53   ......!...L.!DOS
ØØ1Ø  2Ø 5Ø 72 6F 67 72 61 6D-6D 65 72 27 73 2Ø 52 65   Programmer's Re
ØØ2Ø  66 65 72 65 6E 63 65 ØD-ØA 24 ØØ ØØ ØØ ØØ ØØ ØØ   ference..$......
ØØ3Ø  ØØ ØØ ØØ ØØ ØØ ØØ ØØ ØØ-ØØ ØØ ØØ ØØ ØØ ØØ ØØ ØØ   ................
ØØ4Ø  ØØ ØØ ØØ ØØ ØØ ØØ ØØ ØØ-ØØ ØØ ØØ ØØ ØØ ØØ ØØ ØØ   ................
ØØ5Ø  ØØ ØØ ØØ ØØ ØØ ØØ ØØ ØØ-ØØ ØØ ØØ ØØ ØØ ØØ ØØ ØØ   ................
ØØ6Ø  ØØ ØØ ØØ ØØ ØØ ØØ ØØ ØØ-ØØ ØØ ØØ ØØ ØØ ØØ ØØ ØØ   ................
ØØ7Ø  ØØ ØØ ØØ ØØ ØØ ØØ ØØ ØØ-ØØ ØØ ØØ ØØ ØØ ØØ ØØ ØØ   ................
ØØ8Ø  ØØ ØØ ØØ ØØ ØØ ØØ ØØ ØØ-ØØ ØØ ØØ ØØ ØØ ØØ ØØ ØØ   ................
ØØ9Ø  ØØ ØØ ØØ ØØ ØØ ØØ ØØ ØØ-ØØ ØØ ØØ ØØ ØØ ØØ ØØ ØØ   ................
ØØAØ  ØØ ØØ ØØ ØØ ØØ ØØ ØØ ØØ-ØØ ØØ ØØ ØØ ØØ ØØ ØØ ØØ   ................
ØØBØ  ØØ ØØ ØØ ØØ ØØ ØØ ØØ ØØ-ØØ ØØ ØØ ØØ ØØ ØØ ØØ ØØ   ................
ØØCØ  ØØ ØØ ØØ ØØ ØØ ØØ ØØ ØØ-ØØ ØØ ØØ ØØ ØØ ØØ ØØ ØØ   ................
ØØDØ  ØØ ØØ ØØ ØØ ØØ ØØ ØØ ØØ-ØØ ØØ ØØ ØØ ØØ ØØ ØØ ØØ   ................
ØØEØ  ØØ ØØ ØØ ØØ ØØ ØØ ØØ ØØ-ØØ ØØ ØØ ØØ ØØ ØØ ØØ ØØ   ................
ØØFØ  ØØ ØØ ØØ ØØ ØØ ØØ ØØ ØØ-ØØ ØØ ØØ ØØ ØØ ØØ ØØ ØØ   ................
Ø1ØØ  ØØ ØØ ØØ ØØ ØØ ØØ ØØ ØØ-ØØ ØØ ØØ ØØ ØØ ØØ ØØ ØØ   ................
Ø11Ø  ØØ ØØ ØØ ØØ ØØ ØØ ØØ ØØ-ØØ ØØ ØØ ØØ ØØ ØØ ØØ ØØ   ................
Ø12Ø  ØØ ØØ ØØ ØØ ØØ ØØ ØØ ØØ-ØØ ØØ ØØ ØØ ØØ ØØ ØØ ØØ   ................
Ø13Ø  ØØ ØØ ØØ ØØ ØØ ØØ ØØ ØØ-ØØ ØØ ØØ ØØ ØØ ØØ ØØ ØØ   ................
Ø14Ø  ØØ ØØ ØØ ØØ ØØ ØØ ØØ ØØ-ØØ ØØ ØØ ØØ ØØ ØØ ØØ ØØ   ................
Ø15Ø  ØØ ØØ ØØ ØØ ØØ ØØ ØØ ØØ-ØØ ØØ ØØ ØØ ØØ ØØ ØØ ØØ   ................
Ø16Ø  ØØ ØØ ØØ ØØ ØØ ØØ ØØ ØØ-ØØ ØØ ØØ ØØ ØØ ØØ ØØ ØØ   ................
Ø17Ø  ØØ ØØ ØØ ØØ ØØ ØØ ØØ ØØ-ØØ ØØ ØØ ØØ ØØ ØØ ØØ ØØ   ................
Ø18Ø  ØØ ØØ ØØ ØØ ØØ ØØ ØØ ØØ-ØØ ØØ ØØ ØØ ØØ ØØ ØØ ØØ   ................
Ø19Ø  ØØ ØØ ØØ ØØ ØØ ØØ ØØ ØØ-ØØ ØØ ØØ ØØ ØØ ØØ ØØ ØØ   ................
Ø1AØ  ØØ ØØ ØØ ØØ ØØ ØØ ØØ ØØ-ØØ ØØ ØØ ØØ ØØ ØØ ØØ ØØ   ................
Ø1BØ  ØØ ØØ ØØ ØØ ØØ ØØ ØØ ØØ-ØØ ØØ ØØ ØØ ØØ ØØ ØØ ØØ   ................
Ø1CØ  ØØ ØØ ØØ ØØ ØØ ØØ ØØ ØØ-ØØ ØØ ØØ ØØ ØØ ØØ ØØ ØØ   ................
Ø1DØ  ØØ ØØ ØØ ØØ ØØ ØØ ØØ ØØ-ØØ ØØ ØØ ØØ ØØ ØØ ØØ ØØ   ................
Ø1EØ  ØØ ØØ ØØ ØØ ØØ ØØ ØØ ØØ-ØØ ØØ ØØ ØØ ØØ ØØ ØØ ØØ   ................
Ø1FØ  ØØ ØØ ØØ ØØ ØØ ØØ ØØ ØØ-ØØ ØØ ØØ ØØ ØØ ØØ ØØ ØØ   ................
```

as Microsoft Windows or DESQview) or to OS/2. Programs that ignore the possibility of coexistence may not run.

The sample COM program in listing 3.1 can be rewritten as an EXE program (see listing 3.2). Because this program does not restrict all its parts to one segment of memory, you cannot run EXE2BIN on it. It simply will fail.

Listing 3.2

```
;                         Sample EXE Program

      name          dosbook
;
; Demoex.asm - EXE version of simple print
; Prints 'DOS Programmer's Reference
;
;------ Beginning of the CODE Segment ------
cseg  segment       para public 'CODE'
      assume        cs:cseg,ds:dseg,ss:stack
;
;------ Procedure Book ------
; PURPOSE:          Demonstrates programming for
;                   an .EXE file
; USES:             AX, DX
; RETURNS:          Nothing
;
book  proc          far
      mov           ax,dseg         ; Set data segment register
      mov           ds,ax
      mov           dx,offset msg   ; Get message location
      mov           ah,9            ; Output character string
      int           21h
      mov           al,Ø            ; Exit code zero
      mov           ah,4ch          ; Terminate
      int           21h
book  endp
;------ End of Procedure Book ------
;
cseg  ends
;------ End of the Code Segment ------
;
;------ Beginning of the Data Segment ------
dseg  segment       para 'DATA'
msg   db            'DOS Programmer',Ø27h,'s Reference',Ødh,Øah,'$'
dseg  ends
;------ End of the Data Segment ------
;
;------ Beginning of the Stack Segment
stack segment       para stack 'STACK'
      db            20 dup ('stack   ')
stack ends
;------ End of the Stack Segment ------
;
      end           book
```

You can see immediately that the EXE version of the program in listing 3.2 is longer and more complex than the COM version in listing 3.1. The program code does the same job in both versions but, in the EXE version, more program lines are needed to do that job. If you compare the COM and EXE versions, you will find that many portions are identical but that significant differences also are apparent.

In both versions, the CODE segment is declared in the same way. But the *assume* statements are different. In the EXE version, this statement assigns different values to every segment register. Each register points to a different section of the program. (Notice that SS now points to a defined stack segment.)

In listing 3.2, the procedure book starts with a FAR label, which indicates that book can be called from other segments.

Because the EXE program has a data segment, you must explicitly set the data segment register to the beginning of the data segment. The first step in this procedure puts the address into the AX register; the second step moves the address into the DS register.

Then you create the body of the EXE program by following the six steps used for the COM version:

1. Load the offset address of the message into the DX register.

2. Set the AH register to 9 (the code for the DOS function that writes a string).

3. Execute Int 21h to invoke the DOS processor.

4. Set the AL register to zero (the exit code for the program) in preparation for program termination.

5. Set AH to 4Ch (the function number for program termination).

6. Make a final call to Int 21h to process program termination.

But the EXE program does not end here. Now you must declare the data segment as a separate part of the program. (In this program, the data segment contains one string—the same constant string that is used in the COM version.) And you have to declare and initialize the stack segment. This stack was created with the repeating string 'stack' in it, to make memory dumps more readable. (Stacks are discussed briefly in a sidebar in Chapter 2.)

Figure 3.4 shows a complete dump of the disk image of the EXE program. Because it includes the EXE header and the relocation table, this program is much larger than the COM version. The EXE version needs considerably more disk space and is slower to load than its COM counterpart.

Fig. 3.4. Disk sector containing the sample EXE program.

```
0000   4D 5A E0 00 02 00 01 00-20 00 00 00 FF FF 04 00   MZ...... ........
0010   A0 00 9A CF 00 00 00 00-1E 00 00 00 01 00 01 00   ................
0020   00 00 00 00 00 00 00 00-00 00 00 00 00 00 00 00   ................
0030   00 00 00 00 00 00 00 00-00 00 00 00 00 00 00 00   ................
0040   00 00 00 00 00 00 00 00-00 00 00 00 00 00 00 00   ................
0050   00 00 00 00 00 00 00 00-00 00 00 00 00 00 00 00   ................
0060   00 00 00 00 00 00 00 00-00 00 00 00 00 00 00 00   ................
0070   00 00 00 00 00 00 00 00-00 00 00 00 00 00 00 00   ................
0080   00 00 00 00 00 00 00 00-00 00 00 00 00 00 00 00   ................
0090   00 00 00 00 00 00 00 00-00 00 00 00 00 00 00 00   ................
00A0   00 00 00 00 00 00 00 00-00 00 00 00 00 00 00 00   ................
00B0   00 00 00 00 00 00 00 00-00 00 00 00 00 00 00 00   ................
00C0   00 00 00 00 00 00 00 00-00 00 00 00 00 00 00 00   ................
00D0   00 00 00 00 00 00 00 00-00 00 00 00 00 00 00 00   ................
00E0   00 00 00 00 00 00 00 00-00 00 00 00 00 00 00 00   ................
00F0   00 00 00 00 00 00 00 00-00 00 00 00 00 00 00 00   ................
0100   00 00 00 00 00 00 00 00-00 00 00 00 00 00 00 00   ................
0110   00 00 00 00 00 00 00 00-00 00 00 00 00 00 00 00   ................
0120   00 00 00 00 00 00 00 00-00 00 00 00 00 00 00 00   ................
0130   00 00 00 00 00 00 00 00-00 00 00 00 00 00 00 00   ................
0140   00 00 00 00 00 00 00 00-00 00 00 00 00 00 00 00   ................
0150   00 00 00 00 00 00 00 00-00 00 00 00 00 00 00 00   ................
0160   00 00 00 00 00 00 00 00-00 00 00 00 00 00 00 00   ................
0170   00 00 00 00 00 00 00 00-00 00 00 00 00 00 00 00   ................
0180   00 00 00 00 00 00 00 00-00 00 00 00 00 00 00 00   ................
0190   00 00 00 00 00 00 00 00-00 00 00 00 00 00 00 00   ................
01A0   00 00 00 00 00 00 00 00-20 00 00 00 00 00 00 00   ................
01B0   00 00 00 00 00 00 00 00-00 00 00 00 00 00 00 00   ................
01C0   00 00 00 00 00 00 00 00-00 00 00 00 00 00 00 00   ................
01D0   00 00 00 00 00 00 00 00-00 00 00 00 00 00 00 00   ................
01E0   00 00 00 00 00 00 00 00-00 00 00 00 00 00 00 00   ................
01F0   00 00 00 00 00 00 00 00-00 00 00 00 00 00 00 00   ................
0200   B8 02 00 8E D8 BA 00 00-B4 09 CD 21 B0 00 B4 4C   ...........!...L
0210   CD 21 00 00 00 00 00 00-00 00 00 00 00 00 00 00   .!..............
0220   44 4F 53 20 50 72 6F 67-72 61 6D 6D 65 72 27 73   DOS Programmer's
0230   20 52 65 66 65 72 65 6E-63 65 0D 0A 24 00 00 00   Reference..$...
0240   73 74 61 63 6B 20 20 20-73 74 61 63 6B 20 20 20   stack   stack
0250   73 74 61 63 6B 20 20 20-73 74 61 63 6B 20 20 20   stack   stack
0260   73 74 61 63 6B 20 20 20-73 74 61 63 6B 20 20 20   stack   stack
0270   73 74 61 63 6B 20 20 20-73 74 61 63 6B 20 20 20   stack   stack
0280   73 74 61 63 6B 20 20 20-73 74 61 63 6B 20 20 20   stack   stack
0290   73 74 61 63 6B 20 20 20-73 74 61 63 6B 20 20 20   stack   stack
02A0   73 74 61 63 6B 20 20 20-73 74 61 63 6B 20 20 20   stack   stack
02B0   73 74 61 63 6B 20 20 20-73 74 61 63 6B 20 20 20   stack   stack
02C0   73 74 61 63 6B 20 20 20-73 74 61 63 6B 20 20 20   stack   stack
02D0   73 74 61 63 6B 20 20 20-73 74 61 63 6B 20 20 20   stack   stack
02E0   00 00 00 00 00 00 00 00-00 00 00 00 00 00 00 00   ................
```

Fig. 3.4 continues

Fig. 3.4 *continued*

```
02F0  00 00 00 00 00 00 00 00-00 00 00 00 00 00 00 00   ................
0300  00 00 00 00 00 00 00 00-00 00 00 00 00 00 00 00   ................
0310  00 00 00 00 00 00 00 00-00 00 00 00 00 00 00 00   ................
0320  00 00 00 00 00 00 00 00-00 00 00 00 00 00 00 00   ................
0330  00 00 00 00 00 00 00 00-00 00 00 00 00 00 00 00   ................
0340  00 00 00 00 00 00 00 00-00 00 00 00 00 00 00 00   ................
0350  00 00 00 00 00 00 00 00-00 00 00 00 00 00 00 00   ................
0360  00 00 00 00 00 00 00 00-00 00 00 00 00 00 00 00   ................
0370  00 00 00 00 00 00 00 00-00 00 00 00 00 00 00 00   ................
0380  00 00 00 00 00 00 00 00-00 00 00 00 00 00 00 00   ................
0390  00 00 00 00 00 00 00 00-00 00 00 00 00 00 00 00   ................
03A0  00 00 00 00 00 00 00 00-00 00 00 00 00 00 00 00   ................
03B0  00 00 00 00 00 00 00 00-00 00 00 00 00 00 00 00   ................
03C0  00 00 00 00 00 00 00 00-00 00 00 00 00 00 00 00   ................
03D0  00 00 00 00 00 00 00 00-00 00 00 00 00 00 00 00   ................
03E0  00 00 00 00 00 00 00 00-00 00 00 00 00 00 00 00   ................
03F0  00 00 00 00 00 00 00 00-00 00 00 00 00 00 00 00   ................
```

You can see from the dump that the stack initialization is stored as an image of the stack memory area. Table 3.1 decodes the EXE header shown in this dump. (All entries in the table are 2-byte words.)

The EXE program header provides the information that the EXEC module needs to control the loading of the program and to assign its segments correctly. Each entry consists of a 2-byte data word stored low-order-byte first. Let's look at the meaning of each entry in table 3.1.

1. At offset 00h, a unique word (5A4Dh—ASCII code ZM) identifies the file as an EXE file. Whenever the DOS EXEC function sees a file that starts with this word, the function automatically handles it as an EXE file.

2. At offset 02h, the length of the file (modulo 512) is stored. This value, along with the values at offsets 04h and 08h, is used to determine the size of the program.

3. At offset 04h, the length of the file (including the header) in 512-byte pages is stored.

4. Offset 06h has the number of items in the relocation table (the location of the relocation table is stored at offset 18h).

5. Offset 08h is the size, in paragraphs (16 bytes per paragraph), of the EXE program header.

Table 3.1. *Decoding of an EXE Program Header*

Offset	Typical Values	Meaning
00h	4Dh 5Ah	Link program .EXE file signature
02h	E0h 00h	Length of image
04h	02h 00h	Size of file in 512-byte pages (2)
06h	01h 00h	Number of relocation-table items (1)
08h	20h 00h	Size of header in paragraphs (32)
0Ah	00h 00h	Minimum number of paragraphs above (MINALLOC)
0Ch	FFh FFh	Maximum number of paragraphs above (65,535) (MAXALLOC)
0Eh	04h 00h	Displacement of stack segment in paragraphs
10h	A0h 00h	Offset in SP register
12h	9Ah CFh	Word checksum
14h	00h 00h	IP register offset
16h	00h 00h	Code segment displacement
18h	1Eh 00h	Displacement of first relocation item
1Ah	00h 00h	Overlay number (Resident code = 0)

6. Offset 0Ah is the minimum number of paragraphs needed to run the program (MINALLOC). If this much memory is not available, the program will not run.

7. Offset 0Ch is the maximum number of paragraphs the program would like to get. The linker sets this to FFFFh (1 Mb) unless overridden by a LINK command-line switch.

8. Offset 0Eh is the offset of the stack segment, in paragraphs, from the beginning of the program.

9. Offset 10h is the initial value of the SP register when the program is started.

10. Offset 12h is a checksum of the program for use by the EXEC function at runtime.

11. Offset 14h is the initial value of the IP register when the program starts (the program's entry point).

12. Offset 16h is the segment displacement of the program's code segment.

13. Offset 18h is the offset (in the .EXE file) of the relocation table's first entry.

14. Offset 1Ah is the overlay number. For a program, this value is zero.

Immediately after the header, a small amount of reserved space is followed by the program's relocation table. Items in the relocation table are read, one at a time, into a work area. Each item's segment value is added to the program's start segment value, which the EXE loader calculates from the values at offsets 04h, 08h, and 02h in the EXE header. The resulting segment value and the item's offset value point to a word in the program; the calculated segment value is written to that location.

The relocation table is followed by another small amount of reserved space. (Either of the reserved spaces can vary in size.) Then comes the program itself, followed by the stack segment.

Figure 3.5 pulls together for comparison the dumps of the EXE and COM programs. The EXE program dump includes the stack area, initialized according to the instructions in the program source. Because the COM program does not have a defined stack area, no initialization is provided for one.

Although the two programs are nearly identical, the need for addressing modes that reach beyond a single segment creates slightly different instructions when you look at the files this way.

Fig. 3.5. COM vs. EXE program.

```
0000  BA 0D 01 B4 09 CD 21 B0-00 B4 4C CD 21 44 4F 53    ......!...L.!DOS  ⎤
0010  20 50 72 6F 67 72 61 6D-6D 65 72 27 73 20 52 65    Programmer's Re   ⎬ COM
0020  66 65 72 65 6E 63 65 0D-0A 24                       ference..$        ⎦


0000  B8 02 00 8E D8 BA 00 00-B4 09 CD 21 B0 00 B4 4C    ...........!...L  ⎤
0010  CD 21 00 00 00 00 00 00-00 00 00 00 00 00 00 00    .!..............  │
0020  44 4F 53 20 50 72 6F 67-72 61 6D 6D 65 72 27 73    DOS Programmer's  │
0030  20 52 65 66 65 72 65 6E-63 65 0D 0A 24 00 00 00    Reference..$...   │
0040  73 74 61 63 6B 20 20 20-73 74 61 63 6B 20 20 20    stack   stack     │
0050  73 74 61 63 6B 20 20 20-73 74 61 63 6B 20 20 20    stack   stack     │
0060  73 74 61 63 6B 20 20 20-73 74 61 63 6B 20 20 20    stack   stack     │
0070  73 74 61 63 6B 20 20 20-73 74 61 63 6B 20 20 20    stack   stack     ⎬ EXE
0080  73 74 61 63 6B 20 20 20-73 74 61 63 6B 20 20 20    stack   stack     │
0090  73 74 61 63 6B 20 20 20-73 74 61 63 6B 20 20 20    stack   stack     │
00A0  73 74 61 63 6B 20 20 20-73 74 61 63 6B 20 20 20    stack   stack     │
00B0  73 74 61 63 6B 20 20 20-73 74 61 63 6B 20 20 20    stack   stack     │
00C0  73 74 61 63 6B 20 20 20-73 74 61 63 6B 20 20 20    stack   stack     │
00D0  73 74 61 63 6B 20 20 20-73 74 61 63 6B 20 20 20    stack    stack    ⎦
```

Some High-level Language Examples

Having looked at assembly language programs as examples of COM and EXE programs, let's look at some examples that use high-level languages to do the same simple function. In a high level language, the program source is *much* simpler to write. This is a significant advantage. As programs grow in complexity, program maintenance is easier if the source code is less complex.

Frequently, the high-level language version of the executable program is longer than the assembly language version for the same program. This happens because high level languages must provide for many variations of use. For example, printf in C is loaded with special features not used in my simple example.

To provide a basis for comparison, I used several available language compilers (in various high-level languages) to compile programs with the same function as the assembly language examples in the preceding section. As you will see, the high-level language versions have much larger executable files loaded and stored on disk.

Although it is difficult to detect differences in execution speed in programs this small, you can easily set up experiments to test their speed. I am interested in focusing on the simplicity of the programs, not on their speed or size.

A Compiled BASIC Program

With a single PRINT statement, you can build a BASIC program that prints a line to the screen. Listing 3.3 is an example of a three-line BASIC program that includes comments.

Listing 3.3

```
REM  A simple BASIC print program
REM  Prints 'DOS Programmer's Reference'
print "DOS Programmer's Reference"
```

This program compiles in either Turbo BASIC® or QuickBASIC®. Although not all BASIC programs are 100 percent compatible with both compilers, most programs compile without problems.

Because of its simplicity and ease of use, BASIC has a large following. The sample program shows this ease of use: only the print line is essential to the compiler. The remark lines are essential only to the programmer.

If you add line numbers, this program will run using Microsoft's BASIC interpreter. The capability of prototyping a program with an interpreter can be a decided advantage to the BASIC programmer. Interpreters for Pascal and C are not widely available.

As you will learn from Chapters 5 through 13, BASIC can make effective use of DOS and BIOS functions. But BASIC does not provide enough flexibility to use these functions effectively in certain applications, such as program execution and memory management (see Chapter 10). BASIC is able to provide its simplicity of programming by controlling the computer to such a degree that programmers cannot deal effectively with the more sophisticated DOS and BIOS control functions.

A Turbo Pascal Program

Many people prefer working in BASIC to working in Turbo Pascal®. To print just one line in Turbo Pascal, for example, you must deal with overhead on a program-language level. You must identify your program code as a program module and use a Begin-End pair to set off the program's executable code (see listing 3.4). Although this organizational detail may seem ridiculous at such a trivial level, you will find that as the program expands, your work also expands. The overhead then becomes more of a device for guarding against mistakes.

Listing 3.4

```
Program Demo;

{
     demotp.pas - Turbo Pascal version of simple print
     Prints 'DOS Programmer's Reference'
}
Begin
     writeln('DOS Programmer''s Reference');
End.
```

Although Pascal is much better suited than BASIC to programming on the DOS and BIOS level, existing Pascal compilers control the computer's memory to a large extent. Because determinations about memory usage are made at compile time, the use of functions such as program execution and memory management requires a considerable amount of forethought.

A Compiled C Program

The C programming language was designed with systems-level programming in mind. Because access to system resources is much easier in C than in Pascal or BASIC, C generally is the language chosen for programs that have to make extensive use of DOS or BIOS functions.

As in the Pascal version of the program, the overhead is greater in the C version (see listing 3.5) than it is in the BASIC version. As with Pascal, this overhead is minor in large, complex programs and is a major help in keeping the program understandable.

C compilers produce code that gives the programmer the most direct control of the underlying machine. This is intentional: the C programming language was designed to be used for writing operating systems.

Listing 3.5

```
#include <stdio.h>

main()

/*
        demo.c - A C version of the simple print program
        Prints "Dos Programmer's Reference"
*/

{
        printf("DOS Programmer's Reference\n");
}
```

The capability of providing tight control of a machine while still providing high-level language functions and control structures similar to those provided in Pascal make C the language of choice for most serious applications.

All of the applications in this book are written in C. The examples in BASIC and Pascal are included to illustrate how you can use the same techniques in other languages. (Limited space precludes duplication of all examples in all languages.)

Comparing Different Versions of a Program

The results of a comparison of the compiled modules from each version of the program are shown in table 3.2. This table reflects neither an exhaustive test of one compiler versus another nor a performance test—it simply shows the comparative sizes (in bytes) of the compiled modules.

Clearly, the tightest code is in the assembly language programs. Microsoft C and Turbo C® turn out files of comparable size, followed by Turbo Pascal. Overhead is greatest in the two BASIC programs.

This is neither the time nor the place for further comparisons. Even if I were to write an entire book about which language and compiler is best—people *still* would object. (And for good reasons.)

Any comparison of compilers depends on your perspective and your needs. Speed, the most frequently cited yardstick, is important in some programs but not in others. For example, if a program that transfers characters to a printer is

Table 3.2. Size (in Bytes) of Compiled Modules

Language	Source File	Object File	Executable
Assembly (COM)	1145	108	43
Assembly (COM)	512	107	811 (before EXE2BIN)
Assembly (EXE)	1293	183	736
Microsoft C	184	339	6378
Turbo C	182	235	5416
Turbo Pascal 3.0	181	x	10667 (COM file)
Turbo BASIC	132	x	29040
QuickBASIC	132	842	27644

Note: I included Turbo Pascal 3.0 in the comparison because it generates .COM files on output. For other examples in this book, I used Turbo Pascal 4.0.

already faster than the printer and has to wait, what difference does speed make? If speed is important to your programming, you can find the most recent speed comparisons in *BYTE*, *PC Tech Journal*, and other magazines devoted to bringing the most recent compiler information to your attention. Anything I do here will be out-of-date before you see it.

This exercise *is* useful if you understand that your choice of a language influences the size and operation of your program and makes your conceptual work easier or more difficult. And remember—no matter what the benefits of a high-level language may be, nothing beats assembly language and hand coding if you need to squeeze the most from the available memory space and processor speed.

COM versus EXE Programs

Should you or shouldn't you? Is it worthwhile to write a program that you can convert to COM format, or should you leave it in EXE format? To decide, you should consider the following factors:

❏ A COM program is faster to load and start because it is a direct memory image.

❏ A COM program is limited to a maximum of 64K, including data and program code. (You can increase these limits by manipulating the segment registers, however.)

❏ A COM program hogs all memory and has to release memory in order to EXEC other programs. (This item is important only if you are using concurrent programs. It is unimportant if the program will run on a single-user, single-task system.)

❏ A COM program uses less space on disk because it does not include the EXE program header or relocation table. In some cases, the difference is considerable, because the relocation table may be the largest part of the program.

❏ COM programs run faster because they cannot use FAR calls, which are a bit slower than NEAR calls. In most programs, the difference is imperceptible unless many such calls are executed per second.

COM programs are most useful when you need to squeeze as many programs as possible into a limited space. For example, if you wanted to take with you a floppy disk filled with simple utilities, .COM files would be the answer. But for most programming, building a COM program makes no sense. An EXE program does as good a job and is likely to remain compatible with extensions to the DOS system well into the future. A well-designed EXE program can limit FAR calls to those needed for crossing segment boundaries. And, by using NEAR calls for most of the repetitive work, an EXE program can eliminate much of the overall speed advantage of a COM program.

If you work with a high-level language, you may not have a choice. Most compilers produce either COM or EXE programs; others produce both. Basically, the decision to convert an EXE program to a COM program will be determined in large part by your particular circumstances.

Now, having laid the groundwork, let's look at interrupts. Interrupts affect the way DOS, the BIOS—the whole system—work.

Interrupts

Old-style computer systems, which ran one program at a time to completion, were simple in theory, simple in design, and simple to operate. An early system that I worked on had punch-card input and a line printer for output. Large data sets were stored on one of five magnetic-tape drives (disks did not exist) and memory was 32K of magnetic core. When you programmed that system, you *knew* you had total control of your computer. When your program needed some data from a tape drive, the program simply waited. When it needed some input from the console (not even a keyboard—just switches!), it waited again. Working with that computer was extremely uncomplicated—but you waited much of the time.

Interrupts are a way to eliminate the waiting. When a computer requests a hardware service, such as a disk read, it waits for the results in one of three ways:

- ❏ It waits until the operation is completed.

- ❏ It continues with other tasks and checks periodically to see whether the operation is completed.

- ❏ It continues with other tasks and is notified by the operating system when the operation is completed.

Each method has its advantages and disadvantages. Consider serial communications, for example.

When your computer communicates with another computer over the telephone line, characters arrive at your serial port at random intervals. If all you had to do was read the characters from the line and dump them in a buffer, you could simply wait for a character to arrive, read it and write it to the buffer, and then wait again. This type of tightly looping process is frequently called a *busy wait*. Everything will work as it should, provided that the characters arrive slowly enough to give you time to read one, write it, and get back in time to read the next one.

This method would be acceptable if your computer were handling only communications between computers—nothing else. But you want your computer to pay attention to *you*. If you want the computer to pay attention to you *and* the serial line, you have to use a different method.

For example, you could write a program that checks repeatedly for something to do and, if it finds something to do, does it. You might write a simple program that performs the following steps:

1. If a character is at the keyboard, write it to the serial port.

2. If a character is at the serial port, write it to the screen.

3. Go to Step 1.

(In Chapter 7, you will build a program just like this one to demonstrate basic serial communications.)

However, with communications at 1200 baud (1,200 bits per second), about 120 characters arrive each second. A new character reaches the serial port every 8.33 milliseconds; if you are not ready to receive an incoming character, you lose it. How much can *you* do in 8.33 milliseconds? In computer terms, 8.33 milliseconds is a relatively long time, but not if you want to:

❏ Place a character on-screen

❏ Scroll the screen up and blank the bottom line if the character was at the end of your screen

❏ Carry out a sequence if the character is part of a screen-control sequence

❏ Decide how to handle a nonprintable character

In addition to all this activity, you want to be ready to handle each character the moment it is typed on the keyboard. As you will discover, even if you work through the DOS and BIOS functions or read directly from the serial port, there is simply not enough time for you to do everything.

Your only option is to use the interrupt system. Some people are afraid of interrupts, which have a reputation as an arcane technique known only to gurus and hackers. Nothing could be farther from the truth. As soon as you understand basic interrupt operation, you can write an interrupt handler yourself. (You will write several in Chapter 11.)

Think of an interrupt as a doorbell. If you didn't have a doorbell on your home, you would have to check periodically to see whether someone was at your door. This repeated checking, or *polling*, tends to be inefficient and wastes your time—as it would the computer's time in a computer environment. Going to the door only when the doorbell rings is much more efficient. An interrupt works like a doorbell for your computer.

When a program is running, events such as a character's arrival on the serial line cause an interrupt to occur. When an interrupt occurs, the system stops your program, saves the program's *state* (the CS, IP, and FLAGS registers) on the stack, and branches to a handler for that interrupt. Basically, an interrupt handler is just another program although (as you will discover in Chapter 11) interrupt handlers are somewhat restricted in what they can do.

Whether you realize it or not, the system you work with interrupts your work regularly. For example, the timer interrupt (an internal metronome that updates the system time and date) occurs about 18.2 times per second. Some programs tie in to this interrupt in order to display an on-screen clock.

Another important interrupt is generated whenever you press a key. This keyboard interrupt handles the keystroke. All you see is the characters appearing on-screen. But interrupt control makes everything happen.

A PC has 256 interrupt routines. It accesses them through an interrupt vector table located at 0000:0000h through 0000:03FFh. Every four-byte entry in this table corresponds to an interrupt routine. To understand the interrupts, you need to know how they are classified.

The 8086 processor family has four basic types of interrupts:

- Internal interrupts
- The non-maskable interrupt
- Hardware interrupts (also called *maskable* interrupts)
- Software interrupts

Let's look briefly at each type.

Internal Interrupts

The 8086 microprocessor family generates many interrupts that are sensed directly by the CPU. In the divide-by-zero interrupt, for example, the processor automatically issues the appropriate interrupt request when it detects a divide-by-zero error.

The Non-Maskable Interrupt

This interrupt is tied directly to a special non-maskable interrupt (NMI) pin on the processor chip. The non-maskable interrupt forces the processor to deal immediately with some kind of catastrophic system failure. (You can think of the NMI as the "Now Move Immediately" interrupt.)

On the PC and compatibles, this interrupt is activated by a memory-parity error—an error indicating a major problem in the system's memory. The standard handler for this interrupt writes the message Memory Parity Error to the screen and then shuts down the computer.

You could divert the interrupt (Int 02h) to a special handler, but then you wouldn't know whether the memory was any good. You wouldn't know where to find the error, which might be in data you want to save. It might even be in the program that will save the data. Either way, you severely compromise the integrity of your data. Because there is no safe way to recover on a PC when a memory parity error occurs, the system simply shuts down.

Hardware (Maskable) Interrupts

Interrupts generated by external devices are called *maskable* interrupts. They come through a pin on the CPU that you can tell the processor to ignore temporarily. On a PC, interrupts come through the 8259 Programmable Interrupt Controller chip and can be masked individually. (You will learn more about the 8259 in Chapter 11.) The state of the interrupt flag in the flags register determines whether the processor pays attention to a maskable interrupt. To mask an interrupt, you use the clear interrupt instruction (CLI) to clear the flag. (See Chapter 2 for a detailed discussion of flags and the flags register.)

Maskable interrupts tend to be frequent and unpredictable. Because they come from external hardware, a program cannot predict when such interrupts will occur. Maskable interrupts need to be handled quickly so that the program can continue. Interrupt handlers should be optimized to perform only necessary operations.

Software Interrupts

Software interrupts are generated by programs, not by hardware. All DOS and BIOS functions are accessed through software interrupts. These interrupts don't have to "know" anything about the system in order to create a flexible method for programs to access system resources.

Ordinarily, software interrupts are synchronized to your program's operations. Handlers for these interrupts frequently provide special functions, such as mouse control and file handling. Although software interrupts are not as critical as hardware interrupts, they are called frequently and must be efficient.

As you will discover from the discussion of TSRs (Terminate and Stay Resident programs) in Chapter 11, some software interrupts are used to trigger special programs that may take complete control of the computer. (Borland's Sidekick is a good example of this type of program.) Efficiency becomes more a matter of packing features into as little space as possible than of operating speed, although speed remains important. To keep the entire system from bogging down, other services (such as a handler for keyboard characters or a clock handler that updates a screen display) must be extremely speed efficient.

In order to understand how Int 24h affects the stack, you need to examine how DOS uses the stack. When an Int 21h function is invoked, the Int 21h handler pushes all CPU registers on the stack. DOS then uses an internal stack for its own purposes. If a critical error occurs, the user stack is selected again but the register values pushed by Int 21h are left on the user stack. Then Int 24h is invoked and the resulting stack appears (see fig. 3.6).

Fig. 3.6. *A stack on entry to Int 24h (the critical-error handler).*

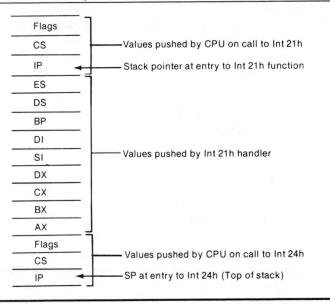

With all of these registers available, you can easily determine where you were before the error occurred. The critical-error handler is extremely important. We all are familiar with its characteristic message:

```
<Error Message>
Abort, Retry, Ignore?
```

The error message usually tells you that a floppy disk drive is not ready. The default handler handles the situation in a straightforward, simple way. If you press *I* to ignore the error, control returns to the program and processing continues. If you press *R* (for Retry), the handler tries the function again to see whether the problem has been fixed. When you press *A* (for Abort), the handler aborts the process, returning to DOS.

You must be wary of DOS critical errors. If a critical error occurs during execution of a program that creates its own general interrupt handlers (such as a terminal program that creates an interrupt handler for the serial port), the program will be terminated and its interrupt handlers will *not* be restored to their previous state. Chaos can result. If a program-generated interrupt occurs after the program has been terminated by a critical error, the system probably will lock up. Because you have no way of knowing where program-generated interrupts are sending data, a program-generated interrupt will transfer control to a location where no interrupt handler is available to deal with the data.

If you want to write foolproof programs that are safe from such errors, you can write your own critical-error handlers. After you begin dealing with interrupts, you will find that their "domino effect" pulls you ever deeper into the system. You must be alert to all possible ramifications and add appropriate safeguards to your programs in order to do one thing well.

When you understand interrupts well enough to be able to add interrupt handlers for various conditions, you probably will want to write some of your own.

Interrupt handlers are not limited to dealing with an external event or processing a hardware function; they can do straight software work such as sorting and searching. There are several advantages to building a software package with standard utilities needed by a system. For example, you might be writing a system that needs standard menu displays, command input controls, or search procedures. If the system involves several independent programs, you might include all of the standard functions in a package accessed through a system interrupt. All of the programs then have access to the same routines.

This approach has specific advantages. First, because the common routines are tied to an interrupt and not compiled into each program, the programs themselves are smaller. Second, because the functions are accessed through a common interrupt, you do not have to relink the individual programs when you change functions in the library.

The DOS function interrupt (Int 21h) is a collection of standard functions which are available to all programs that need them. Mouse functions (Int 33h) and expanded memory functions (Int 67h) are other examples of such collections. With the functions provided in this form, people do not have to change their programs when newer versions of the functions become available—they can continue using the same programs.

With a standard run-time package loaded in memory, you can share its resources with all your programs. When you change the package, all programs receive the change without your having to relink them. You can include interrupt handlers in a resident package without having to worry about critical errors crashing the program. A handler always will be in the correct place. And because memory-resident run-time routines do not have to be added to a compiled module, your compiled programs will be smaller and simpler to work with. One drawback to such a package is that, because bugs in an interrupt library are hard to find, your library must be bug-free.

Most programs do not use this technique. Rather, they build programs with overlays; the common routines are in the master overlay, which is always resident (even for programs that do not use it). If you have a mouse, you already have some experience with this. You cannot UNLOAD the mouse driver after it has been loaded—the memory has already been used.

The problems with this approach can be carried to extremes. On a Personal Computer AT system with 512K of memory, I recently loaded the mouse and expanded memory drivers as well as those needed by the TOPS networking system. With all of this loaded, I went into DESQview, checked memory available, and found only 88K available in which to run programs. By adding other libraries of functions, I would have used even more of the available space. 88K is enough space for small programs—but try to find a word processor or spreadsheet that can run in 88K!

All of these techniques are options. You can use them when appropriate, but you have to be aware of the trade-offs.

Finally, let's look at another important topic: memory management.

Memory Allocation and Management

After the operating system is loaded and you are running programs, memory allocation becomes extremely important. Unless enough memory is available, you cannot even load your program. You must understand how memory is managed before you can understand how memory management affects your programs.

DOS organizes available memory as a pool of blocks that are chained together from bottom to top. This chain, or *memory arena*, includes all available memory. Every *memory block* (or *arena entry*) is made up of a 16-byte (one paragraph) *memory control block* and the memory controlled by that block. Table 3.3 shows how the control block is organized.

Memory blocks are organized as a chain (or *linked list*) in which each memory control block represents a contiguous area of memory directly above the control block. Each control block points to the next control block in the chain (bytes 3–4 serve as this pointer). Figure 3.7 shows a conceptual picture of this memory-allocation chain. Starting from a DOS pointer to the

Table 3.3. *The Memory Control Block*

Byte	Meaning
0	ASCII 90h if last block
	ASCII 77h otherwise
1–2	0 if the block has been allocated
3–4	Size of the block in paragraphs

first memory control block, each block gives the offset to the next block when it records the size of its own block. If two free blocks come together, DOS combines them into a single memory block. When they are separated by a block in use for some other reason (see fig. 3.7), no attempt is made to relocate the information and reassign the block locations.

A block can be as small as a single paragraph (16 bytes) or as large as all available memory. DOS uses the blocks to assign memory to programs, as necessary.

When DOS receives a request for memory, it looks through the chain of memory blocks to find a block large enough to fill the request. If DOS finds a break in the chain or some other anomaly, it returns an error. For example, if the calling program is COMMAND.COM trying to execute a program, DOS displays *Memory allocation error* and then halts the system. You must reboot to recover.

When a request for memory can be filled, DOS uses one of the following memory-allocation strategies to return a block:

❑ First Fit: DOS allocates the first memory block on the chain big enough to fill the request.

❑ Best Fit: DOS allocates the smallest memory block big enough to fill the request.

❑ Last Fit: DOS allocates the highest memory block big enough to fill the request.

The first-fit strategy, which minimizes the time spent searching for a block of memory, is the fastest—but it may fragment memory. When a block is assigned, it is divided into two blocks: one that exactly matches the request, and the remainder (which is returned to the chain for later use).

No matter which allocation strategy is used, if more than one block is in use at any given time, memory will be fragmented into smaller and smaller blocks. A

Fig. 3.7. A chain of memory blocks.

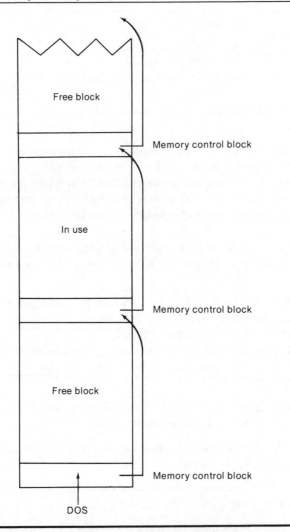

program that alternately grabs and frees blocks of memory can create free blocks surrounded by blocks in use. Requests for memory may fail when a program has created a large number of small blocks that can't be recombined into a single block large enough to handle the request.

Suppose, for example, that a program grabs all of available memory in 16K blocks and then releases to the operating system 10 of those blocks, none of which is next to another. Even though 160K of memory is available, a request for 32K of memory will fail because no single block is large enough to handle the request.

Memory fragmentation like this can be a serious problem in some systems. DOS does not do any special cleanup (often called *garbage collection*) to move allocated blocks around in order to recover space. If this sort of problem is important for one of your programs, look in any good book on algorithms or data structures for information on garbage collection techniques.

DOS provides access to the following three basic memory-allocation functions:

❏ *Allocate a memory block*: a function that requests assignment of a memory block to meet program requirements

❏ *Free memory block*: a function that returns a previously allocated memory block to the pool after the program has finished using it

❏ *Resize memory block:* a function that lets you make a previously allocated memory block larger or smaller, as needed. This function normally is called to shrink a program's memory block needed for a program to the smallest size possible.

Beginning with DOS V3.3, you can use an additional function to determine the memory-allocation strategy. DOS defaults to the First Fit strategy, but the new function lets you override the default.

The most obvious use of the allocation functions is during program execution. When a program starts up, it receives memory for its operation. As you may recall from the discussion earlier in this chapter, a COM program gets all of memory and an EXE program gets the amount requested. Let's see how that arrangement works in terms of the memory-allocation scheme.

When a COM program is executed, it is allocated all of the available memory in the first block large enough to hold the program, the PSP, and the stack (at least two bytes). Although all of memory is not allocated directly to the COM program, it might as well be. Ordinarily only one block is in the chain at program execution time, and that block holds all of memory.

EXE programs, on the other hand, are allocated the amount of memory requested in the MAXALLOC field of the EXE program header, if that amount of memory is available. (If MINALLOC is not available, the program will not be executed.) When a program is linked, MAXALLOC is set to FFFFh (1 Mb); therefore, an EXE program (like a COM program) is allocated all of memory on entry. However, you can override this allocation and use command-line switches to request less than 1Mb of memory—you can't do that with a COM program. Although most programmers don't bother with it, they should.

EXE programs, on the other hand, are allocated the amount of memory requested in the EXE program header's MAXALLOC field (maximum memory to allocate to the program), if that amount of memory is available. If the amount of memory specified in the MINALLOC field (minimum memory needed for the program to run) is not available, the program will not be executed.

When a program is linked, the linker automatically sets the MAXALLOC field to FFFFh (1 Mb) unless it is overridden by command-line switches to request a smaller amount of memory. Thus, EXE programs, just like COM programs, are given all of available memory. Most programmers simply ignore the fact that this can be overridden when the linker is executed.

When you program in C, the program's start-up code (supplied with the compiler) ordinarily releases unused memory without your having to worry about it. Pascal and BASIC use all available memory for their data structures.

When you work in Pascal, a portion of memory set aside by the compiler is used for an area called the *heap*. This area of memory is used by the compiler for allocation of dynamic variables (those created within specific program blocks) and for memory allocated with the standard Pascal routines. If you want memory available for running other programs when you are using Pascal or BASIC, you have to tell the compiler to leave the space available.

This overall management scheme works well. Because programs usually occupy the highest available memory (parents usually are at a lower memory address, although TSRs do not have to be), the allocation scheme ordinarily results in all of the available memory being held in a single block—the largest (and usually the only) block. But inherent in this scheme is the capability of allocating memory to multiple tasks that run concurrently.

Summary

This chapter has introduced the dynamics of DOS, showing how the hardware and software elements of the system interact dynamically in operations such as the boot sequence, command processing, and program execution. You have learned that the ROM bootstrap code is executed automatically when the PC's CPU is powered up. That code, in turn, loads and transfers control to the bootstrap record, which then loads IO.SYS and MSDOS.SYS (or their PC DOS analogues, IBMBIO.COM and IBMDOS.COM). Those programs perform other work needed to get the system up and running.

Command processing is a function of COMMAND.COM, the DOS shell. COMMAND.COM interprets user commands by searching its internal table for a command matching the user's command; if no match is found, COMMAND.COM then searches for an executable file with a name matching that of the user's command.

The differences between COM and EXE programs were also discussed in this chapter. Each has its advantages and disadvantages: COM programs are easier to code and faster to load, but are limited in the code and data they can contain. EXE programs, on the other hand, are more complex and somewhat slower in loading but offer the programmer greater control over memory allocation and other parameters.

Interrupts, an important feature of the DOS landscape, were another topic covered here. Interrupt-driven control of the computer was compared with other methods, and its advantages were made clear. Interrupts are of four major types:

- ❑ Internal interrupts
- ❑ The non-maskable interrupt
- ❑ Hardware (or *maskable* interrupts)
- ❑ Software interrupts

Software interrupts are the principle programming interface to DOS.

And finally, you learned about DOS's memory-management functions. DOS manages memory as a series of blocks. Each memory block includes a memory-control block, which tells whether the memory block is allocated to a program and tells the location of the next block. DOS makes available three memory-allocation strategies. DOS provides services for allocating, deallocating, and resizing memory blocks, as well as (in version 3.0) a function for determining the memory-allocation strategy.

Now you have learned the fundamentals of DOS as a system of dynamically interacting parts. In the next chapter, you'll learn about exploiting DOS's capabilities in your own programs.

The DOS and BIOS Interface

This chapter shows how your programs can access the services available from the DOS kernel and the BIOS. To access these services, you can invoke software interrupts from any language covered in this book. You won't learn everything about accessing system resources, but you will learn enough to get started.

This book focuses on four languages: assembly language, C, Pascal, and BASIC. The implementations described are Microsoft Macro Assembler, Microsoft® C, Turbo C, Turbo Pascal version 4.0 (with a few notes about version 3.0), Turbo BASIC®, and Microsoft® QuickBASIC. All four languages have features that let you access directly the DOS and BIOS functions. But because not every necessary operation is provided by a built-in language feature, you have to code some operations yourself. In this chapter you will learn what is ready-made in the language you use, as well as what you need to do for yourself and how to do it.

Accessing DOS and BIOS from Your Programs

To access DOS and BIOS resources, you follow these simple steps:

1. Load the CPU's registers with appropriate values.

2. Generate a software interrupt to invoke the desired system resource.

3. Interpret the results (if any) returned in the CPU's registers.

Ordinarily, the values loaded into the registers are either 8- or 16-bit numeric parameters or the addresses of larger data structures. All the languages discussed in this book provide a convenient means for loading the CPU's registers, generating interrupts, and reading the returned results. If you need a quick overview of the CPU's registers and their uses, refer to Chapter 2.

Figure 4.1 is a diagram of the contents of the CPU's registers immediately before and after a system call.

Fig. 4.1. The contents of registers before and after a system call.

Before call

xx =Not used in this system call

After call

BIOS
Printer Status Request

Invoked with Int 17h (BIOS Printer services interrupt)

AH =2 for Printer Status Request

DX =0 for LPT1

Result returned in AH

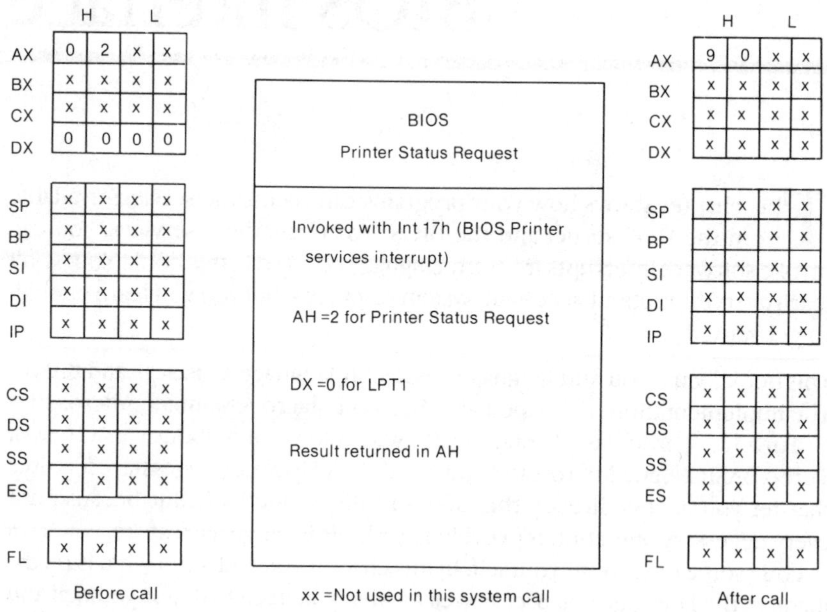

Depending on which resource you want to invoke, you may need to do some additional work before you load the registers and generate the interrupt. Many file-oriented services, for example, require your program to load registers with the segment:offset address of a string or other data structure before the interrupt is generated. (If you are not familiar with the segment:offset form of address representation, refer to the "Memory Segmentation and the 8086" section in Chapter 2.)

First, your program must get the data item's address. Getting an item's address is a fairly simple procedure; any complexity is to some degree a function of the language you use. For each language covered in this book, a section later in this chapter demonstrates techniques for taking addresses of data items.

The string or other item must be in the appropriate form. Many DOS functions that take string arguments require strings in *ASCIIZ* (ASCII plus Zero) format: the characters are represented in their ASCII format and the final character in the string is ASCII character zero ('\Ø' in C, CHR$(Ø) in BASIC, or Chr(Ø) in Pascal). Figure 4.2 shows the structure of an ASCIIZ string.

Fig. 4.2. The structure of an ASCIIZ string.

Null character

Character:	M	Y	F	I	L	E	.	D	A	T	
ASCII code:	4 D	59	46	49	4 C	45	2 E	44	41	54	0 0

If you program in C, you probably know that ASCIIZ is precisely the format in which the C language stores strings internally. In BASIC or Pascal you have a little more work to do because neither language stores strings in the ASCIIZ format. The work is not complicated, however, and the examples later in this chapter show how it is done.

Because assembly language provides the most direct access to the CPU and to DOS and BIOS resources, the introductory examples in the following sections are in assembly language. For an introduction to the general principles of accessing DOS and BIOS resources, be sure to read the following subsections; the examples are clear, even if you are not fluent in assembly language.

Higher-level language resources for talking to the operating system are described later in this chapter. But we will look first at some simple assembly language examples that explore the DOS and BIOS interface.

A Simple Call to DOS

Each of the programming languages in this book has several services that provide access to the basic DOS and BIOS interrupts. The simplest of these languages is assembly language, which allows you to access the INT (interrupt) instruction directly in order to generate calls to BIOS or DOS functions.

The following code fragment, which uses Int 21h, Function 02h to output the character *X* to the console, is a typical call to DOS.

```
mov       ah,2       ; Character output function
mov       dl,'X'     ; Character 'X'
int       21h        ; Execute DOS function interrupt
```

Int 21h, Function 02h is easy to use:

1. *Load registers with the appropriate values:* The value 2 is loaded immediately into AH to select DOS Function 2 (Console Character Output). The character *X* is loaded immediately into DL.

2. *Generate the interrupt:* The assembly language mnemonic INT is followed by the value 21h, the "generic" DOS interrupt number. (Because Microsoft's Macro Assembler [MASM] is almost everyone's standard, the INT instruction should be available with any assembler you choose.)

Because Function 2 of Int 21h returns nothing, the third part of this DOS-call prototype is missing. The following example demonstrates the third step and illustrates basic techniques for obtaining and passing to DOS the addresses of data items "wider" than 16 bits.

Passing String Addresses to DOS

As was mentioned earlier, the CPU's registers often must be loaded with the segment and offset of data items "wider" than 16 bits. The following code fragment demonstrates one method for passing the address of a character string:

```
; PATH_NAME contains name of file to be opened
MOV       AX,SEG PATH_NAME          ; Segment address of path
MOV       DS,AX                     ;    in DS
MOV       DX,OFFSET PATH_NAME       ; Offset address of path
MOV       AL,C2h                    ; Mode for opening file
MOV       AH,3Dh                    ; Open the file
INT       21h                       ; DOS interrupt
JC        ERROR                     ; Carry set signals error
MOV       FILE_HANDLE,AX            ; Save file handle
```

This code fragment uses Int 21h, Function 3Dh to open a file. This function requires that DS and DX contain the segment and offset, respectively, of the file's path name. The first three lines of the code fragment load the registers accordingly. The next line puts C2h into AL; the value in AL specifies the mode in which the file is to be opened. (The encoding of modes in this value is explained in the DOS Reference section of this book.) With registers properly loaded, the DOS interrupt is then generated.

Like many DOS services, this one sets the carry flag if the service fails (if, that is, the file could not be opened); the code therefore jumps to an error-handling routine if the carry flag is set (JC ERROR). But if the carry flag is clear, indicating success (that the file was opened), the file handle, returned in AX, is stored to a data byte allocated for that purpose.

High-Level Language Resources

High-level languages offer many different ways to call DOS and BIOS routines. Each language has a unique method that does not resemble that of any other language. Even within the same language, different implementations have different resources.

Compare Microsoft QuickBASIC version 4.0 and its chief competitor, Turbo BASIC version 1.0. QuickBASIC provides the function

```
CALL INTERRUPT (interrupt_number,
                registers_in,registers_out)
```

The equivalent function in Turbo BASIC is

```
CALL INTERRUPT interrupt_number
```

In Turbo BASIC, register values are global to the program and don't need to be passed explicitly in the CALL INTERRUPT statement. (Clearly, before using either of these instructions, you must load registers with the appropriate values.)

Variations between releases are common also. Turbo Pascal 3.0 provided no ready means for accessing all files matching a wild-card file specification (such as C:\QTRLY\QTR?1988.DAT). To access such a group of files, you had to write two procedures: one that called DOS Int 21h, Function 4Eh to find the first file matching the specification, and another that called Function 4Fh to find any remaining matching files. Turbo Pascal 4.0 provides the procedures FindFirst and FindNext for those purposes.

Each of the following subsections presents two sample programs. For each language, the first sample program (a simple one that illustrates the basic operations required for accessing operating-system resources) uses BIOS Int

17h, Function 2 to check the printer's status. The second example is a slightly more complex program that illustrates the interpretation of results returned from a system call.

The more complex example differs according to the language. In accordance with my philosophy that you should not do unnecessary work, I have chosen programming examples that provide services you can't get from the language. The BASIC examples show how to use DOS Int 21h, Functions 4Eh and 4Fh to retrieve file names matching a wild-card file specification. Because analogous functions are built into Turbo Pascal 4.0 (but not 3.0) and C, the sample programs in those languages perform different actions. The Pascal example uses DOS Int 21h, Function 57h to get the date and time of a specified file. The C example uses DOS Int 21h, Function 43h to get and set file attributes (archive, hidden, system, and read-only). The examples use other functions as needed to perform necessary setup and cleanup work. Those ancillary function calls are described in the text and documented in the code.

Avoiding Unnecessary Work

Many high-level languages have predefined functions, procedures, or variables that provide "ready-made" access to system resources. In most cases, these language elements access the same DOS and BIOS functions you would work with directly if you had to implement the system call yourself; the people who implemented the languages already have built the code for you. If you are considering the use of system resources in a language that's new to you—or in a new implementation of a familiar language—make sure that you are not reinventing the wheel. A principle I repeatedly return to in this book is that you should go to the system only when necessary. You should, therefore, use the built-in language resources unless your program has special needs that the language resources don't answer.

Always read your manual carefully. This basic advice is worth repeating: *Read your manual!* Many programmers, particularly those who are new to a language or operating system, have spent hours or days on unnecessary work. Had they read their language manuals more carefully, they would not have wasted time in reinventing the wheel.

The C Programming Language

For talking to an operating system, C is a programmer's delight. If you read the sections about other languages, you see that the high-level character of Pascal and BASIC often gets in your way. The languages obscure or limit your access to system-level data structures and other information you have to get your hands on when you access DOS and BIOS resources.

The C programming language, with its handy blend of high-level and low-level resources, has been described as "high-level assembly language." C lets you "think like a microprocessor" while sparing you the drudgery of a detailed setup for operations in which you don't care about what happens at the level of bits and bytes.

C has a similar relationship to the operating system: many C functions are "DOS in C clothing." Those functions often take the same arguments as their DOS equivalents, and the same results are returned; indeed, the data structures accepted as input and returned as output often are identical to those used by their DOS equivalents.

Consequently, the more complex sample program in this section is presented in two versions: one (chmd.c) that calls DOS directly and one (chmc.c) that uses the equivalent C function. Only one version of the simpler example (pronok.c) is presented (see listing 4.1); the program provides a capability not directly available from the Turbo C library.

The C programs in this section were developed with the Turbo C compiler, version 1.5. For information concerning the differences between Turbo C and Microsoft C, be sure to read the comments in the listings (including code fragments).

Accessing Registers and Generating Interrupts

The principal data structures for the interface between C and DOS are defined by the REGS union and the SREGS and REGPACK structures. These objects are declared in the header file DOS.H. Their declarations are shown in the following code fragment:

```
struct WORDREGS {
    unsigned int  ax, bx, cx, dx, si, di, cflag, flags;
};

/*Microsoft C lacks flags element */

struct BYTEREGS {
    unsigned char al, ah, bl, bh, cl, ch, dl, dh;
};
```

Fragment continues

Fragment *continued*

```
union REGS {
    struct WORDREGS x;
    struct BYTEREGS h;
};

struct SREGS {
    unsigned int es;
    unsigned int cs;
    unsigned int ss;
    unsigned int ds;
};

struct REGPACK {        /* Not defined in Microsoft C */
    unsigned r_ax, r_bx, r_cx, r_dx;
    unsigned r_bp, r_si, r_di, r_ds, r_es, r_flags;
};
```

In addition, the contents of the CPU registers are available in Turbo C through the pseudovariables _AX, _AL, _AH, and so on. Each of the 8086's general-purpose, offset, and segment registers (except IP) has a corresponding pseudovariable. Variables corresponding to the 16-bit and 8-bit registers are used (but not declared) as though they were of the type unsigned int and unsigned char, respectively:

```
unsigned int _AX;
unsigned char _AL;
```

These declarations should *not* be included in your programs.

The pseudovariables described in the preceding paragraph are not available in Microsoft C. Their absence necessitates small changes in the programs at some points, so be sure to read the comments in the listings if you want to adapt the code for Microsoft's C compiler.

The header file DOS.H contains the following prototypes of the C functions for generating software interrupts:

```
int int86 (int intno, union REGS *inregs,
                    union REGS *outregs);

int int86x (int intno, union REGS *inregs,
                     union REGS *outregs,
                        struct SREGS *segregs);
```

```
int intdos (union REGS *inregs,
            union REGS *outregs);
int intdosx (union REGS *inregs,
             union REGS *outregs,
             struct SREGS *segregs);

void intr (int int_type, struct REGPACK *preg);
```

The function intdos() generates Int 21h, the principal DOS interrupt; int86() and intr() each generate the interrupt specified by the function's first argument (intno or int_type). Each intdos and int86 has an "x" version that uses the segment registers as well as the general-purpose and offset registers. The intr() function is not available in Microsoft C.

The program in listing 4.1 demonstrates the use of the int86() function to verify that LPT1 is on-line.

Listing 4.1

```
/* prnok.c */
#include <conio.h>
#include <dos.h>

#define PRN_INT 0x17    /* Printer-services interrupt */
#define STAT_RQ 0x02    /* Status-request service number */

int prnok(void)
{
    union REGS regs;

    regs.h.ah = STAT_RQ;   /* AH = 02 for printer status */
    regs.x.dx = 0;         /* DX = 00 for LPT1 */

    int86(PRN_INT, &regs, &regs);

    return( ((regs.h.ah & 0x80) == 0x80 ) ? 1 : 0 );

}

main()
{
    if (prnok())
        cputs("Ready to print!\n");
    else
        cputs("Please check the printer!\n");
}
```

A Note about the BIOS Printer-Status Request

The first sample program for each language uses BIOS Int 17h, Function 2 to verify that LPT1 is on-line. For this function, put 2 in AH and the printer number (0 for LPT1, 1 for LPT2, and so on) in DX. The function returns the printer's status, encoded in the bits of AH as follows:

Bit	Meaning (if set)
0	Time-out
1	Unused
2	Unused
3	I/O error
4	Printer is selected
5	Out of paper
6	Acknowledge
7	Printer not busy

The meaning of bits 0 and 3 through 7 is well-defined, but the two hardware configurations I tested do not return the same result for the same condition. In every test case, the high bit of AH was set when the printer was powered up and on-line. Note, however, that on a Toshiba P351 printer connected to an IBM Personal System/2 Model 50, the program reports Ready to print when the printer is connected but not powered up. On an Epson RX-80™ printer connected to a COMPAQ Portable Computer®, the program responds Please check the printer! if the printer is connected but powered down. This is just a "demo" routine; a program with truly powerful status-checking capabilities needs more sophisticated logic.

Getting and Setting File Attributes

This section presents two sample C programs for changing the attributes of a specified file. These programs resemble the useful FA (File Attribute) program included in the Norton Utilities™; they differ from FA in that they accept only a literal file name, not a file specification containing wild-card characters. To keep the code as simple as possible, I have not included options for simply inquiring about the file's attributes or for changing more than one attribute at a time. The programs, which "expect" a command-line argument specifying an attribute to be set or cleared, terminate with an error message if an invalid argument is given.

If you are proficient in C programming, you should have no difficulty adding further options (such as "inquire") to the capabilities of this program. The information provided throughout this book makes it easy to add a capability for processing files specified by a wild card.

The two sample programs differ in that one calls the DOS interrupt directly, whereas the other uses a corresponding C library function to call the interrupt. The first example, shown in listing 4.2, makes a direct call to DOS Int 21h, Function 43h.

Listing 4.2

```
/* chmd.c */
/* Note: For Turbo C version 1.Ø
        or Microsoft C, replace \n with \r\n*/

#include <conio.h>
#include <stdio.h>
#include <ctype.h>
#include <process.h>
#include <dos.h>

#include <attrmask.h>

#define GS_FATTR    Øx43
#define GET_FATTR   ØxØØ
#define SET_FATTR   ØxØ1

typedef enum { clr, set } clrorset;

void showattr(int attr);
int parsearg(char *thearg, clrorset *action, char *selection);

main( int argc, char *argv[] )
{
    extern char *sys_errlist[];    /* Provided by Turbo C */
    extern int errno;              /*  Ditto             */

    union REGS regs;
    struct SREGS sregs;

    clrorset action;
    char selection;

    unsigned attrib, setting;
    int goahead;

    if (argc == 3) goahead = parsearg(argv[2], &action, &selection);
     else goahead = Ø;
```

Listing 4.2 continues

Listing 4.2 *continued*

```
    if (!goahead) {
        cputs("Can't parse "); cputs(argv[2]);
        exit(1);
    }

    switch(selection) {
        case 'A': setting = ARCHIVE_BIT; break;
        case 'H': setting = HIDDEN_BIT;  break;
        case 'R': setting = RDONLY_BIT;  break;
        case 'S': setting = SYSTEM_BIT;  break;
        default:
            cputs("Bad input: "); cputs(argv[2]); cputs("\n");
            exit(1);
    }

    regs.h.ah = GS_FATTR;    regs.h.al = GET_FATTR;
    regs.x.dx = (unsigned) argv[1];    /* Offset of first argument */
    sregs.ds  = _DS;

/* ----------------------
   For Microsoft C, use the following in place of the
   preceding line:

   segread(&sregs);
*/

    intdosx(&regs,&regs,&sregs);  /* Get the current attribute word */

    if (!regs.x.cflag) {          /* If carry is clear, success */
        attrib = regs.x.cx;
        cputs("------------ Initial ------------\n");
        showattr(attrib);

        if (action == clr) {
            setting = ( (~setting)&attrib );
        } else {
            setting = (setting | attrib);
        }

        regs.h.ah = GS_FATTR;
        regs.h.al = SET_FATTR;
        regs.x.cx = setting;
        regs.x.dx = (unsigned) argv[1];
        sregs.ds  = _DS;

        intdosx(&regs,&regs,&sregs);  /* Set the attribute */

        attrib = regs.x.cx;
```

Listing 4.2 *continues*

Listing 4.2 *continued*

```
        cputs("------------- Final -------------\n");
        showattr(attrib);

   } else {          /* i.e., if carry is not set */
      char *msg;
      cputs("function Øx43 failed: ");
      switch (regs.x.ax) {
         case 1:  msg = "Bad function code\n"; break;
         case 2:  msg = "Bad file name\n"; break;
         case 3:  msg = "Bad path\n"; break;
         case 5:  msg = "Can't change attribute\n"; break;
         default: msg = "Unknown cause\n";
      }
      cputs(msg);
   }
} /* End main */
```

Int 21h, Function 43h takes the following input:

Register	*Value*
AH	43h
AL	0 to get file attribute,
	1 to set file attribute
DS:DX	Segment:offset address of the file pathname

The program uses #define preprocessor directives to "name" the DOS function and the desired action (get or set). The file pathname is provided as a command-line argument.

For a program compiled under the small memory model in Turbo C, you use the following statements to put the pathname's segment and offset into DS and DX:

```
regs.x.dx = (unsigned) argv[1];
sregs.ds  = _DS;
```

Other methods of assignment may be necessary in other memory models. Because Microsoft C lacks the register pseudovariables, the statement

```
segread(&sregs);
```

should be used instead.

If the operation is successful, the carry flag is clear and CX contains the file's attribute word. Bits of the attribute word and their corresponding attributes are

Bit	Meaning (if set)
0	Read Only
1	Hidden
2	System
5	Archive

If the bit is set, the file has the corresponding attribute. (A set archive bit means that the file has not been backed up since the file was created or last modified.)

For convenience and legibility, #define directives are used also to create bit masks for the meaningful bits of the attribute word. (These definitions are contained in the file ATTRMASK.H; see the following code fragment). The bit masks are used for changing the file attribute word as well as for reading it.

```
/* attrmask.h */

#define ARCHIVE_BIT  Øx2Ø   /* Bit 5 of CX is archive bit */
#define SYSTEM_BIT   Øx04   /* Bit 2 of CX is system bit */
#define HIDDEN_BIT   ØxØ2   /* Bit 1 of CX is hidden bit */
#define RDONLY_BIT   ØxØ1   /* Bit Ø of CX is read-only bit */
```

Listings 4.3 and 4.4 show miscellaneous functions used by the two versions of the second sample program.

Listing 4.3

```
/* parsarg.c */
/* Note: For Turbo C version 1.Ø, replace \n with \xØD\xØA */

#include  <conio.h>
#include  <ctype.h>

typedef enum { clr, set } clrorset;

int parsearg(char *thearg, clrorset *action, char *selection)
{

    if (*(thearg) == '/') {
        switch( *(thearg+2) ) {
            case '+':
                *action = set; break;
            case'-':
                *action = clr; break;
            default:
                cputs("Use '+' to set or '-' to clear\n");
                return(Ø);
```

Listing 4.3 continues

Listing 4.3 continued

```
        }
        *selection = toupper(*(thearg+1));
        return(1);
    } else {
        cputs("Usage: chmc filename /xy\n"
                "where x = A (archive) or H (hidden) or\n"
                "            R (read-only) or S (system),\n\
                "  and y = + (set) or - (clear)\n");
        return(Ø);
    }
}
```

Listing 4.4

```
/* showatr1.c */
/* Note: For Turbo C version 1.Ø, replace \n with \xØD\xØA */

#include  <conio.h>

#include  <attrmask.h>

#define CLEAR Ø
#define isclear(x,y) ((x&y)==CLEAR)        /* Parens around x, y ? */
#define putstat(x,y) cputs( isclear(x,y) ? "clear   " : "set     " )

void showattr(int attr)
{
    cputs("Archive System  Hidden  Read-only\n");

    putstat(attr,ARCHIVE_BIT);
    putstat(attr,SYSTEM_BIT);
    putstat(attr,HIDDEN_BIT);
    putstat(attr,RDONLY_BIT);
    cputs("\n");
}
```

If you compare listing 4.2 (the first version of this program) to listing 4.5 (the second version), you can see that error-checking is slightly more sophisticated in a program that uses the interrupt instead of the C library function. Because of differences in the libraries, this program compiles under Turbo C only. Modifications are needed for Microsoft C, which lacks the _chmod function.

Listing 4.5

```
/* chmc02.c */
/* Note: For Turbo C version 1.0, replace \n with \x0D\x0A */

#include <conio.h>
#include <stdio.h>
#include <io.h>
#include <ctype.h>
#include <process.h>

#include <attrmask.h>

#define GET_FATTR    0x00
#define SET_FATTR    0x01

typedef enum { clr, set } clrorset;

void showattr(int attr);          /* Show file attribute */
int parsearg(char *thearg,        /* Parse cmd.-line arg */
            clrorset *action,     /* Clear or set attrib. */
            char *selection);     /* Selected attrib      */

main( int argc, char *argv[] )
{
    extern char *sys_errlist[];   /* Provided by Turbo C */
    extern int errno;             /* Ditto               */

    clrorset action;
    char selection;

    unsigned attrib, setting;
    int goahead;

    if (argc == 3) goahead = parsearg(argv[2], &action, &selection);

    if (!goahead) {
        cputs("Can't parse "); cputs(argv[2]);
        exit(1);
    }

    switch(selection) {
        case 'A': setting = ARCHIVE_BIT; break;
        case 'H': setting = HIDDEN_BIT;  break;
        case 'R': setting = RDONLY_BIT;  break;
        case 'S': setting = SYSTEM_BIT;  break;
        default:
            cputs("Bad input: "); cputs(argv[2]); cputs("\n");
            exit(1);
    }
```

Listing 4.5 continues

Listing 4.5 *continued*

```
    attrib = _chmod(argv[1], GET_FATTR );

    if (attrib != -1) {
        cputs("------------ Initial ------------\n");
        showattr(attrib);
        if (action == clr) {
            setting = ( (~setting)&attrib );
        } else {
            setting = (setting | attrib);
        }
        attrib = _chmod(argv[1], SET_FATTR, setting );
        cputs("------------ Final -------------\n");
        showattr(attrib);
    } else {
        cputs("function _chmod failed:\n");
        cputs(sys_errlist[errno]); cputs("\n");
    }
} /* end main */
```

Notice also that the C library function _chmod( ) returns the file-attribute word as a functional return value (with –1 signaling an error), whereas Int 21h, Function 43h returns the attribute word in register CX and signals an error (as do most DOS functions) by setting the carry flag. Because the results returned by the C library function are the same as those returned in CX by the DOS function, you can use the function showattr( ) to decode the attribute word for both programs.

Turbo Pascal

Version 4.0 of Turbo Pascal improves on version 3.0, which provided excellent support for calling DOS and BIOS functions. Moreover, the language has an extensive set of built-in facilities that provide access to system resources and minimize the need for programmers to write their own system-level code. The language's file and console input/output functions meet almost any programming need; most common file and directory operations (get file size, get current directory, change directory, make directory, and so on) are fully supported. As I mentioned earlier in this chapter, version 4.0 simplifies the writing of programs that process a group of files selected by a wild-card file specification.

Turbo Pascal 4.0 provides a complete set of procedures, functions, and data items that support access to system-level resources. So complete is this collection of resources that you would have difficulty finding a DOS or BIOS service you would want to call directly from your program. Why call DOS or the BIOS for console input and output when Turbo has a full complement of functions and procedures for those operations?

Turbo's Dos unit contains ready-made functions and procedures for almost anything you may want to do to a file or directory (rename or erase file, get or set file date and time, get or set file attributes, make directory, etc.). But the time may come—if it hasn't already—when your program needs something that the language does not provide. This section, therefore, presents two sample programs that make direct calls to DOS and the BIOS. For tutorial purposes, the programs duplicate operations available on a higher level, within Turbo itself.

The first of these programs uses BIOS Int 17h, Function 2 to verify that the printer is on-line. (Similar results—with equally sophisticated error checking—are available through the language's built-in procedures and functions.) The second sample program, which also duplicates a function built into Turbo Pascal 4.0, gets a file's date and time of creation or most recent modification.

Accessing Registers and Generating Interrupts

Turbo Pascal's main data structure for accessing registers is the Registers record. The structure of this record, which is defined in the Dos unit of Turbo Pascal 4.0, is shown in the following lines of code. In version 3.0, the record must be user-defined.

```
Type
    Registers = Record
        Case Integer of
            Ø: (AX,BX,CX,DX,BP,SI,DI,DS,ES,FLAGS : Word);
            1: (AL,AH,BL,BH,CL,CH,DL,DH : Byte)
        End;
```

Turbo Pascal has the following two procedures for generating interrupts:

```
MsDos(Regs : Registers)
```

```
MLIntr(InterruptNum : Word; Regs : Registers)
```

MsDos generates Int 21h, the "generic" DOS interrupt. Intr can generate *any* software interrupt, including 21h. (In version 3.0, the first argument of Intr is an integer.)

The first sample program (see listing 4.6) demonstrates a simple call to the BIOS. The function PrinterOnline invokes BIOS Int 17h, Function 2 (Printer Status Request) to verify that the printer is on-line. Function 2 returns in AH a byte that indicates whether the printer is busy, selected, out of paper, and so on. (Be sure to see the note about this BIOS interrupt in the "High-Level Language Resources" section, earlier in this chapter.) This program, however, checks only bit 7 of AH; if the bit is set, the printer is selected.

Listing 4.6

```
Program PrinterDemo;
Uses Dos;

    Function PrinterOnline : Boolean;
        Const
            PrnStatusInt : Byte = $17;
            StatusRequest : Byte = $02;
            PrinterNum : Word = 0; { 0 for LPT1, 1 for LPT2, etc. }
        Var
            Regs : Registers;          { Type is defined in Dos unit. }
        Begin
        Regs.AH := StatusRequest;
        Regs.DX := PrinterNum;
        Intr(PrnStatusInt, Regs);
        PrinterOnline := (Regs.AH and $80) = $80
        End;

Begin                { Program }
If PrinterOnline Then
    WriteLn('Ready to print!')
Else
    WriteLn('Please check the printer!')
End.
```

Reading a File's Date and Time Stamp

The date and time that you created or last modified a file is available through DOS Int 21h, Function 57h. The Pascal procedure GetDateAndTime demonstrates that DOS function's use (see listing 4.7).

The principal input item for Function 57h is a file handle. Turbo Pascal has a full complement of file-oriented procedures and functions, but the system-level details of Turbo's file management are concealed from the programmer. To use Function 57h, the procedure GetDateAndTime must "go around" Turbo's normal file-management routines. Thus, instead of using Pascal's procedures for opening a file (Assign and either Reset or Rewrite), the

Listing 4.7

```
{ ================================================ }
Procedure GetDateAndTime(PathName : PathNameType;
                         Var DateWord, TimeWord : Word);
    Const
        GetDateAndTime : Byte = $57;
        CloseFile : Byte = $3E;
    Var
        Regs : Registers;
        Handle : Word;

    Function CarryClear(Regs : Registers) : Boolean;
    Begin CarryClear := ((Regs.Flags and 1) = Ø) End;

    { =============================================== }
    Function GetFileHandle(PathName : PathNameType) : Word;
        Const GetHandle : Byte = $3D; ReadAccess : Byte = Ø;
        Var PathSeg, PathOfs : Word;
    Begin
    PathName := PathName + Chr(Ø);
    PathSeg := Seg(PathName[1]);  PathOfs := Ofs(PathName[1]);

    Regs.AH := GetHandle; Regs.AL := ReadAccess;
    Regs.DS := PathSeg;    Regs.DX := PathOfs;
    MsDos(Regs);
    If CarryClear(Regs) Then
        GetFileHandle := Regs.AX   { (no semicolon before Else!) }
    Else
        Begin
        WriteLn('Handle function failed!');
        Exit
        End; { If carry is clear }
    End;                     { Function GetFileHandle }

{ ===================================================== }
Begin                       { Procedure GetDateAndTime }

Handle := GetFileHandle(PathName);

Regs.AH := GetDateAndTime; Regs.AL := Ø;  Regs.BX := Handle;
MsDos(Regs);
If CarryClear(Regs) Then
    Begin  DateWord := Regs.DX;  TimeWord := Regs.CX  End
Else
    Begin
    DateWord := Ø; TimeWord := Ø; { Error flag for caller }
    End;
```

Listing 4.7 continues

Listing 4.7 *continued*

```
Regs.AH := CloseFile;    Regs.BX := Handle;
MsDos(Regs);
If NOT CarryClear(Regs) Then
    WriteLn(
        'Warning: Procedure GetDateAndTime didn"t close ',
        pathname)
End;              { Procedure GetDateAndTime }
```

---

function calls DOS Int 21h, Function 3Dh. This system call is performed by the function GetFileHandle, which is nested within the procedure GetDateAndTime.

Function 3Dh requires the address of an ASCIIZ string whose contents are the file's pathname. Because Turbo Pascal strings are not terminated by a zero byte, the function appends Chr(Ø) to the string PathName. And because the length byte at the first position in the Turbo Pascal string must not be included in the string argument passed to Function 3Dh, the address of PathName[1] is passed to the function. The functions Seg and Ofs give straightforward access to the components of the string's address.

Having obtained the file handle, the procedure GetDateAndTime passes it to DOS Function 57h. The AL register is set to 0, signaling that the DOS function is to get (not set) the file's date and time. If Function 57h succeeds (as indicated by a clear carry flag), it returns the file's encoded time and date in CX and DX, respectively.

The program FileDateAndTime, shown in listing 4.8, demonstrates the use of the Turbo Pascal function GetDateAndTime.

Listing 4.8

```
{ TPEXØ2Ø3.PAS }

Program FileDateAndTime;

    Uses Dos;
    Type
        PathNameType = String[64];
        String5 = String[5];
        { Max DOS path is 63; add 1 for the null. }
```

Listing 4.8 *continues*

Listing 4.8 *continued*

```
    Var
         PathName : PathNameType;
         DateWord, TimeWord : Word;    { Use Integer in 3.0 }
         Hours, Mins, Secs, Year, Month, Day : Integer;
         Ch : Char;

{$i GETDTTM.PAS}

{ ========================================================== }
Begin                       { Program }

Write('Pathname? >');  ReadLn(PathName);
GetDateAndTime(PathName, DateWord, TimeWord);
If (DateWord <> 0) Then
    Begin
    { Decode date }
    Year  := ((DateWord AND $FE00) SHR  9) + 1980;
    Month := (DateWord AND $01E0) SHR  5;
    Day   := (DateWord AND $001F);

    { Decode time }
    Hours := (TimeWord AND $F800) SHR 11;
    Mins  := (TimeWord AND $07E0) SHR  5;
    Secs  := (TimeWord AND $001F) SHL  1; { Shift left to double }

    WriteLn('File Time: ', Hours:2,':', Mins:02,  ':', Secs:2);
    WriteLn('File Date: ', Year:4, '/', Month:02, '/', Day:2);

    End                 { (No semicolon before Else) }
Else
    WriteLn('GetDateAndTime has failed!');

End.
```

QuickBASIC

QuickBASIC and Turbo BASIC share the familiar file-oriented statements of their forerunners, BASICA and GW—BASIC. The gratuitously violent KILL FileName$ statement deletes files, CHDIR changes the current directory, and so on. Input and output routines are flexible.

But BASIC's file-handling capabilities are lacking in some respects. For instance, the procedure for processing file names that match a wild-card file specification (with * or ?) is convoluted. You have to monkey around with passing a DOS command to the SHELL, directing the command's output to a file, and reading the output file into your program one line at a time, parsing file names (and skipping superfluous lines) as you go. Empty disk drives, write-protect tabs, and full disks can bring your program to an abrupt halt. And how do you *know* that the name you are using for SHELL's output isn't the same as that of an existing file?

By programming at the DOS level, you can avoid all that hassle. The second sample program in this section shows how to call DOS Int 21h, Functions 4Eh and 4Fh to find the names of all files that match a file specification, which may contain one or more wild-card characters. (Some of the best uses of programming at the DOS level not only make programming convenient but also make running your programs more convenient for the user.)

First, let's look at a simpler program that introduces the fundamentals of calling DOS from BASIC. This first QuickBASIC example (like those in the other languages) uses BIOS Int 17h, Function 2 to verify that the printer is on-line. If you want to use Int 17h, Function 2 in your own program, be sure to read "A Note about the BIOS Printer-Status Request" in this chapter's section on C.

Accessing Registers and Generating Interrupts

QuickBASIC's principal data structure for the DOS and BIOS interface is the Registers record:

```
TYPE Registers
      AX AS INTEGER
      BX AS INTEGER
      CX AS INTEGER
      DX AS INTEGER
      BP AS INTEGER
      SI AS INTEGER
      DI AS INTEGER
      SI AS INTEGER
      FLAGS AS INTEGER
      DS AS INTEGER
      ES AS INTEGER
END TYPE
```

Register-type variables are declared by means of the DIM statement:

```
DIM InRegs AS Registers, OutRegs AS Registers
```

Because these variables obey the normal scoping rules, they can be declared as local to procedures.

QuickBASIC has two built-in procedures for generating interrupts:

```
CALL INTERRUPT(IntNumber, InRegs, OutRegs)
```

and

```
CALL INTERRUPTX(IntNumber, InRegs, OutRegs)
```

CALL INTERRUPT ignores the DS and ES registers (or the DS and ES fields of the Registers arguments), whereas CALL INTERRUPTX uses these registers or fields. If you want to leave DS and ES unchanged in a call to INTERRUPTX, assign the value –1 to the record's DS and ES fields.

Listing 4.9 demonstrates the use of the BIOS Printer Status Request function. Because the results of this function are not entirely consistent across hardware configurations, be sure to read "A Note about the BIOS Printer-Status Request" (in this chapter's section on C) if you want to use the function in a program.

Listing 4.9

```
'PRNOKQB.BAS
CONST PRN.Status.rq% = &H200          '2 in AH
CONST BIOS.PRN.INT% = &H17

TYPE Registers
     AX AS INTEGER
     BX AS INTEGER
     CX AS INTEGER
     DX AS INTEGER
     BP AS INTEGER
     SI AS INTEGER
     DI AS INTEGER
     FLAGS AS INTEGER
     DS AS INTEGER
     ES AS INTEGER
END TYPE

DIM InRegs AS Registers, OutRegs AS Registers

InRegs.AX = PRN.Status.rq%

CALL INTERRUPT(BIOS.PRN.INT%, InRegs, OutRegs)

IF ((OutRegs.AX AND &H8000) = &H8000) THEN
    PRINT "Printer OK"
ELSE
    PRINT "Please check the printer"
END IF

END        'PROGRAM
```

Finding Files that Match a File Specification

Frequently, sophisticated programs must process groups of files described by wild-card file specifications. QuickBASIC does not provide a built-in facility for finding the file names that match a user-supplied file specification; by building such a facility, you can make the language much more useful.

The DOS resources for using file specifications are Functions 4Eh (Find First) and 4Fh (Find Next) of Int 21h. These functions find, respectively, the first matching file name and any remaining matching names. Both place their output—the file names and other information—in the Disk Transfer Area (DTA). By default, the DTA is a 128-byte buffer at offset 80h in the Program Segment Prefix. But the sample program presented in this section uses DOS Function 1Ah to set a different DTA address, to avoid any possibility of interference with other DOS functions.

Most BASIC implementations, QuickBASIC included, do not store strings at a fixed location. A four-byte string descriptor keeps track of each string's location. The descriptor contains a 16-bit pointer to the string; this pointer contains the string's offset into the default data area. You do not have to bother with locating this descriptor and retrieving the address because the QuickBASIC function

    SADD(TheString$)

returns the offset of the string supplied as an argument. (If you need to access the string descriptor, you can retrieve its segment and offset with the VARSEG and VARPTR functions.) SADD should be called immediately before your program accesses the string because a string can be "moved around" in memory during program execution, especially if your program changes its length.

The program in listing 4.10 demonstrates the use of Functions 4Eh and 4Fh to retrieve file names that match a file specification.

The procedure

    SetDTA(TheDTA$)

sets the Disk Transfer Area address to the address of its string argument.

The procedures

    FindFirst(FileSpec$, FileName$)

and

    FindNext(FileName$)

Listing 4.10

```
' QBEXØ2Ø1.BAS
' listing 4.1Ø, QuickBASIC
' Demonstrates QuickBASIC techniques for
' taking addresses of string variables and
' passing them to DOS.
'    Uses QB.QLB
DECLARE SUB SetDTA (TheDTA$)
DECLARE SUB FindFirst (FileSpec$, FileName$)
DECLARE SUB FindNext (FileName$)
DECLARE SUB BuildName (TheName$)

TYPE Registers
      AX AS INTEGER
      BX AS INTEGER
      CX AS INTEGER
      DX AS INTEGER
      BP AS INTEGER
      SI AS INTEGER
      DI AS INTEGER
      FLAGS AS INTEGER
      DS AS INTEGER
      ES AS INTEGER
END TYPE

DTA$ = SPACE$(43)

INPUT "Filespec? >", FileSpec$

CALL SetDTA(DTA$)
' Get the first matching filename
CALL FindFirst((FileSpec$), FileName$)

IF FileName$ <> "" THEN
    PRINT "First match: "; FileName$
    DO
        CALL FindNext(FileName$)
        IF FileName$ <> "" THEN
            PRINT " Next match: "; FileName$
        END IF
    LOOP UNTIL FileName$ = ""
ELSE
    PRINT "No files match "; FileSpec$
END IF
```

Listing 4.10 continues

Listing 4.10 continued

```
END             ' PROGRAM
SUB BuildName (TheName$)
SHARED DTA$
    EndOfStr% = INSTR(31, DTA$, CHR$(Ø))
    TheName$ = MID$(DTA$, 31, EndOfStr% - 31)
END SUB


SUB FindFirst (FileSpec$, FileName$)
FileSpec$ = FileSpec$ + CHR$(Ø)   'make ASCIIZ
DIM InRegs AS Registers, OutRegs AS Registers
InRegs.AX = &H4EØØ                  'find first matching file
InRegs.DX = SADD(FileSpec$)        'offset of FileSpec$
InRegs.DS = VARSEG(FileSpec$)      'seg of FileSpec$
InRegs.CX = Ø                      'normal files only--no dirs, etc.
CALL INTERRUPT(&H21, InRegs, OutRegs)
' Got a match? Yes, if CARRY FLAG (bit Ø of FLAGS) is clear.
IF (OutRegs.FLAGS AND 1) = Ø THEN
    CALL BuildName(FileName$):
ELSE
    FileName$ = ""
END IF
END SUB


SUB FindNext (FileName$)
   DIM InRegs AS Registers, OutRegs AS Registers
   InRegs.AX = &H4FØØ                    'find next matching file
   CALL INTERRUPT(&H21, InRegs, OutRegs)
   IF (OutRegs.FLAGS AND 1) = Ø THEN
       CALL BuildName(FileName$):
   ELSE
       FileName$ = ""
   END IF
END SUB


SUB SetDTA (DTA$)
DIM InRegs AS Registers, OutRegs AS Registers
' Set the Disk Transfer Area address
InRegs.DX = SADD(DTA$)          'offset of DTA
InRegs.DS = VARSEG(DTA$)        'segment of DTA
InRegs.AX = &H1AØØ              'DOS function for setting DTA addr
CALL INTERRUPT(&H21, InRegs, OutRegs)
' no return value for function &H1A
END SUB
```

locate the matching file names. If matching file names are found, both procedures assign the matching name to `FileName$`; if matching names are not found, they assign the empty string (`""`). Although the sample program simply displays the file names, you can have your program do whatever you want with the returned values. A simple loop can easily assign file names to array elements and then repeat

```
WHILE FileName$  < ""
```

and increment an array index on each repetition.

Turbo BASIC

The difficulties imposed by BASIC's limited file and directory support hinder Turbo BASIC as well as QuickBASIC. (See the introductory text in the QuickBASIC section for a discussion of these difficulties.) Like QuickBASIC, Turbo BASIC lacks a built-in facility for retrieving the names of files that match a wild-card file specification. Although the interface to system resources in Turbo BASIC is not quite as supple as it is in QuickBASIC, DOS resources can be used to compensate for Turbo BASIC's shortcomings.

The sample programs in this section demonstrate a simple call to the BIOS Printer Status Request function and a more complicated call to DOS Int 21h, Functions 4Eh and 4Fh. (Again, see the QuickBASIC section for a discussion of these DOS functions.) Because the process of passing string arguments to DOS is slightly more complex in Turbo BASIC than in QuickBASIC, the text in this section is devoted to Turbo BASIC details rather than to DOS.

Accessing Registers and Generating Interrupts

Turbo BASIC's primary data structure for the DOS and BIOS interface is a register buffer (best thought of as an array of integers). The following code fragment illustrates both the layout of the register buffer and a convenient means for referencing locations within it:

```
%FLAGS = 0
%AX = 1: %BX = 2: %CX = 3: %DX = 4
%SI = 5: %DI = 6: %BP = 7
%DS = 8: %ES = 9
```

(Note that, in Turbo BASIC, a data-type flag character—such as %—that precedes the identifier indicates a constant.) Because the register-buffer components that correspond to the 8-bit general-purpose registers cannot be accessed separately, you cannot write or read AL without writing or reading AH at the same time unless you perform a few mathematical operations that, fortunately, are not needed here.

The register buffer is accessed through the REG statement and the REG function. These constructs write input and read results, respectively, to a register buffer. With the preceding constant declarations in effect, the statement

```
REG %AX, $H2100
```

loads AX with the value 21h. The statement

```
Result% = REG(%AX)
```

uses the REG function to assign the result in the AX portion of the register buffer to Result%.

The Turbo BASIC procedure for generating interrupts is called as follows:

```
CALL INTERRUPT InterruptNumber%
```

The register buffer is accessed as a global variable. You have to do extra work because you cannot store input register values and return values in separate data structures. To repeatedly call a function that changes the registers used for input, you must rewrite the register-buffer values before each call.

The program in listing 4.11 demonstrates the use of BIOS Int 17h, Function 2 to verify that the printer is on-line. Before you use this code in a program, be sure to read "A Note about the BIOS Printer-Status Request" (in this chapter's section on C).

Listing 4.11

```
'PRNOKTB.BAS
%PRN.Status.rq = &H0200          '2 in AH
%BIOS.PRN.INT = &H17

%FLAGS = 0
%AX = 1: %BX = 2: %CX = 3: %DX = 4
%SI = 5: %DI = 6: %BP = 7
%DS = 8: %ES = 9

REG %AX, %PRN.Status.rq

CALL INTERRUPT %BIOS.PRN.INT
```

Listing 4.11 continues

Listing 4.11 continued

```
IF ( (REG(%AX) AND &H8000) = &H8000 ) THEN
    PRINT "Printer OK"
ELSE
    PRINT "Please check the printer"
END IF

END        'PROGRAM
```

Finding Files that Match a File Specification

Like QuickBASIC, Turbo BASIC manages strings by means of a string descriptor. Turbo BASIC, however, has no analogue to QuickBASIC's convenient SADD function. The sample program presented in this section includes code for the procedure StrAddr, which retrieves the same information as SADD and works around peculiarities in Turbo BASIC's VARPTR and VARSEG functions.

In Turbo BASIC, the VARPTR function returns the offset of a string descriptor instead of the address of a string argument; the VARSEG function returns the segment of the string descriptor instead of the segment of the string itself. Bytes 2 and 3 (counting from 0) of the four-byte string descriptor contain the low and high bytes, respectively, of the string's offset from the default string segment. The string segment, in turn, is contained in the first two bytes of the default data segment. These complicated (and potentially confusing) relationships between data items and addresses are diagrammed in figure 4.3.

Fig.4.3. Data items used in getting a Turbo BASIC string address.

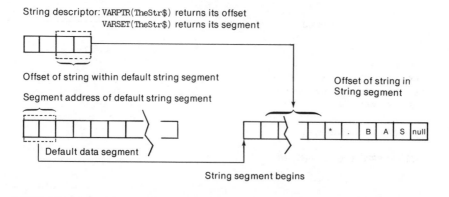

The function

```
StrAddr (TheStr$, StrSeg%, StrOfs%)
```

is shown in listing 4.12. Notice that the low and high bytes of the addresses manipulated in this procedure are converted to long integers for calculation of the segment and offset addresses. Unsigned integers are not available in Turbo BASIC; all integers are stored as signed integers, with negative values in two's-complement form. The range for signed integers is –8000h to 7FFFh (–32,768 to 32,767). But DOS regards segment and offset addresses as unsigned integers with a range of 0 to FFFFh (65,536). To avoid value-out-of-range errors, the StrAddr procedure calculates these address components as long integers, normalizes them to the range of unsigned integers, and then assigns their values to StrSeg% and StrOfs%.

Listing 4.12

```
'STRADDR.BAS
' Procedure to return segment and offset of a string
SUB StrAddr (TheStr$, StrSeg%, StrOfs%)
LOCAL StrSegLong&, StrOfsLong&, LO%, HI%
'Get string segment from word at data_segment:0000

DEF SEG : LO% = PEEK(0): HI% = PEEK(1)

StrSegLong& = (CLNG(HI%) * 256) + CLNG(LO%)

IF StrSegLong& > 32767 THEN
    StrSeg% = CINT(StrSegLong& - 65536)
ELSE
    StrSeg% = CINT(StrSegLong&)
END IF

'Get address of string descriptor
StrDescAdr% = VARPTR(TheStr$)
DEF SEG = VARSEG(TheStr$)

'Get offset of string from bytes
' at offset 2 of string descriptor
LO% = PEEK(StrDescAdr% + 2): HI% = PEEK(StrDescAdr% + 3)
StrOfsLong& = (CLNG(HI%) * 256) + CLNG(LO%)

IF StrOfsLong& > 32767 THEN
    StrOfs% = CINT(StrOfsLong& - 65536)
ELSE
    StrOfs% = CINT(StrOfsLong&)
END IF

END SUB
```

After all the gyrations of StrAddr, the procedures in listing 4.13 seem simple. Listing 4.13 has procedures for setting the address of the Disk Transfer Area and extracting a file name from the DTA. For specifics about the use of DOS Int 21h, Function 1Ah, see the description of listing 4.10. The procedure SetDTA uses StrAddr to get the address of the string that is passed to it as an argument. This string's space is used as the Disk Transfer Area.

Listing 4.13

```
' USEDTA.BAS
' Routines for setting the DTA
' and for extracting file names from it

SUB SetDTA(DTA$)
CALL StrAddr (DTA$, StrSeg%, StrOfs%)
REG %DX, StrOfs%              'Offset of DTA
REG %DS, StrSeg%              'Segment of DTA
REG %AX, &H1A00               'DOS function for setting DTA addr
CALL INTERRUPT &H21
' No return value for function &H1A
END SUB 'SetDTA

SUB BuildName (TheName$)
SHARED DTA$
    EndOfStr% = INSTR(31, DTA$, CHR$(0))
    TheName$ = MID$(DTA$, 31, EndOfStr% - 31)
END SUB
```

The FindFirst and FindNext procedures in listing 4.14 work just like their equivalents in QuickBASIC. (See the QuickBASIC discussion for details about DOS Int 21h, Functions 4Eh and 4Fh.) Like SetDTA, these Turbo BASIC procedures call StrAddr to get the segment and offset addresses of their string arguments.

Listing 4.14

```
'FFFN.BAS
SUB FindFirst (FileSpec$,FileName$)
LOCAL Carry%
FileSpec$ = FileSpec$ + CHR$(0)
CALL StrAddr (FileSpec$, StrSeg%, StrOfs%)
REG %AX, &H4E00              'find first matching file
REG %DX, StrOfs%            'offset of FileSpec$
REG %DS, StrSeg%            'seg of FileSpec$
REG %CX, 0                  'normal files only--no dirs, etc.
CALL INTERRUPT &H21
```

Listing 4.14 continues

Listing 4.14 *continued*

```
' Got a match? Yes, if CARRY FLAG (bit Ø of FLAGS) is clear.
Carry% = (REG(%FLAGS) AND 1%)
IF (Carry% = Ø) THEN
    CALL BuildName (FileName$)
ELSE
    FileName$ = ""
END IF

END SUB 'FindFirst

SUB FindNext(FileName$)
'Now find the next. No problem if this executes following
' error in call to FindFirst (interrupt &H4E)
    REG %AX, &H4FØØ                    'Find next matching file
    CALL INTERRUPT &H21
    Carry% = (REG(%FLAGS) AND 1%)   'Carry is clear
    IF (Carry% = Ø) THEN             'if we have a match
        CALL BuildName (FileName$)
    ELSE
        FileName$ = ""
    END IF
END SUB         'FindNext
```

Listing 4.15 uses the procedures shown in the preceding listings to display all names matching a file specification. This program also works just like its QuickBASIC equivalent; the only differences are dictated by differences in the DOS and BIOS interface of the two language implementations.

Listing 4.15

```
' TBEXØ2Ø3.BAS
' Listing 4.15

' Demonstrates Turbo BASIC techniques for
' taking addresses of string variables and
' passing them to DOS.
' Also see listing for STRADDR.BAS procedure

$INCLUDE "STRADDR.BAS" 'Procedure for getting string address
                       ' (not necessary in QB: use SADD function)
$INCLUDE "USEDTA.BAS" 'Procedures for setting DTA address
                       '  and getting file name from DTA
$INCLUDE "FFFN.BAS"    'FindFirst FindNext procedures
```

Listing 4.15 *continues*

Listing 4.15 *continued*

```
%FLAGS = Ø                    'constants for register names
%AX = 1: %BX = 2: %CX = 3: %DX = 4
%SI = 5: %DI = 6: %BP = 7
%DS = 8: %ES = 9

DTA$ = SPACE$(43)

CALL SetDTA (DTA$)

INPUT "Filespec? >", FileSpec$

CALL FindFirst (FileSpec$,FileName$)

IF FileName$ <> "" THEN
    PRINT "First match: "; FileName$
    DO
        CALL FindNext(FileName$)
        IF FileName$ <> "" THEN
            PRINT " Next match: "; FileName$
        END IF
    LOOP UNTIL FileName$ = ""
ELSE
    PRINT "No files match "; FileSpec$
END IF

END        'PROGRAM
```

Summary

This chapter introduced the fundamentals of system-level programming in assembly language, C, Pascal, and BASIC. The procedure for accessing DOS and BIOS resources has three major components:

- ❑ Loading registers with appropriate values
- ❑ Generating a software interrupt
- ❑ Interpreting the results returned in registers

Sometimes additional work is needed, as when your program must pass to the system the address of a string or other data item. Each language offers resources for getting the addresses of items; the simplicity of using addresses varies according to the language.

If you have read the sections about each language (not just about your language of choice) you probably have noticed that the languages differ greatly in the convenience and the amount of support they provide for accessing DOS and BIOS resources. You may want to consider these differences when you choose a language for your next programming project.

Part II

Character Devices
and
Serial Devices

Output Devices

This chapter discusses the video display and the printer, the two fundamental output devices. They are perhaps the most important devices in computer programming because they serve as the interaction points between the program and the programmer. In DOS, programmers can access the video display and the printer easily.

Most computer books treat the auxiliary devices (the RS-232 ports) as character-output devices and describe them in chapters similar to this one. Because of the unique nature and diverse capabilities of the RS-232 ports, they are treated separately in Chapter 7, "Serial Devices."

Like other chapters, this one emphasizes the utility of working with the highest available coding level to complete a task. Generally, you should use a service available directly from a high-level language. But in many situations you must go lower, to either the DOS or BIOS level, to perform specific tasks. This chapter describes the DOS and BIOS services that control the video display and printer.

Basic Character Devices

Programming the video display and the printer can be a simple procedure or an extremely sophisticated one. Beyond the level of simple character I/O, programming can quickly become a complex process, particularly when you work with graphics.

119

This book is not a comprehensive manual about graphics, but it does provide the basic principles for working with graphics. In this chapter, useful routines for system programming are developed and, most important, useful tools for working with output are constructed.

When you program in C, you find that the services already available for working with the display and printer are adequate for typical programming chores. When you build a program, these services generally are the best ones to use for two reasons:

❑ By using standard library functions, you increase your program's insensitivity to changes in DOS design.

❑ If standard calls are used properly, they can make your program compatible with UNIX or XENIX systems.

If you need to move beyond the level of standard library functions, you must balance carefully what might be lost against what might be gained. By moving from standard library functions to DOS services, you gain great control over output operations while preserving a fair amount of insensitivity to system design. You lose the convenience of the standard library functions, and you lose compatibility with UNIX or XENIX. Whenever you work directly with DOS or BIOS functions, you lose compatibility with other systems not built on the DOS or BIOS platforms.

When are insensitivity and compatibility important considerations for programmers? Obviously, if you work with both DOS and UNIX or XENIX, having program code that successfully compiles without modification under the various operating systems can simplify program development and maintenance. These programs typically are simple utilities or simple interactive programs.

This dual-world approach does not work well with real-time interactive programs. Programs such as 1-2-3, Microsoft Word, and others would suffer from this approach. These types of programs are not acceptable unless they are written to utilize the fastest possible routines. In many instances, the hardware then would be programmed directly, thus eliminating compatibility.

How the Display System Works

The PC display system has evolved from simple beginnings to encompass the following variety of standards in use today:

- ☐ Monochrome Display Adapter (MDA)
- ☐ Color Graphics Adapter (CGA)
- ☐ Hercules Graphics Adapter (HGA)
- ☐ Enhanced Graphics Adapter (EGA)
- ☐ MultiColor Graphics Array (MCGA)
- ☐ Virtual Graphics Array (VGA)

All of the standards except the Hercules Graphics Adapter are endorsed and supported by IBM through standard BIOS and DOS services. The MDA, CGA, and EGA are used in the PC line of computers, and the MCGA and VGA are used in the Personal System/2 line. The HGA's popularity makes it the de facto standard for high-resolution monochrome graphics on the PC line, but it requires a special driver to take advantage of its graphics capabilities. Neither BIOS nor DOS has built-in services to take full advantage of the HGA. The HGA's unique nature and lack of support directly through BIOS or DOS services make an explanation of its programming beyond the scope of this book.

The video display can be accessed in one of three ways:

1. *Through DOS function calls.* This method is the most compatible, but slowest, form of access. With DOS V2.0 and greater, the ANSI.SYS driver lets programs using this method of access have control of the screen through control-code sequences.

2. *Through BIOS function calls.* This fairly compatible method of accessing the display is faster than DOS. Most systems, but not all of them, are compatible with this screen-access method. Through BIOS function calls, graphics and other screen effects not available from the DOS level can be used.

3. *Directly at the hardware level.* This method is incompatible because wide hardware differences may exist among systems. Programs that use this method are not generally compatible with all systems considered PC-compatible. This method is not compatible in multiuser or multitasking systems. Both its advantage and the reason for its frequent use stem from the snappy displays and fast operations that occur at this level.

Programmers who decide to build sophisticated displays do not need to start at the hardware level (which, in fact, should be the "level of last resort"). Most good programs begin at the other end of the spectrum, with a high-level language. BASIC prototypes of major commercial programs frequently are a starting point for development. (VisiCalc®, the original spreadsheet pro-

Types of Display Monitors

A multitude of display monitors are available on the market, and more of them are becoming available all the time. Not all of the available types of display monitors can be mentioned in this chapter, but some of them are described in the following list:

Direct monochrome monitors: These monitors display high-resolution text and character-level graphics. They can be driven by a monochrome adapter (MDA), the Hercules adapter (HGA), or an EGA card set to emulate a monochrome adapter.

Composite monochrome monitors: These inexpensive monochrome monitors (often amber or green) can be driven from a CGA output. They can display CGA graphics but not color. Some of these monitors implement shading to indicate color differences.

Composite color monitors: These monitors produce color and graphics output, but their resolution typically is poor on 80-column text displays. Television sets are at the low end of this range, but their poor resolution produces unsatisfactory results in text-display modes, except when you use 40-column lines.

RGB monitors: These monitors produce clear, crisp color output in both text and graphics modes by using separate electrical lines for each primary color (red, green, and blue).

Enhanced RGB monitors: These monitors provide color text and graphics that are superior to those provided by normal RGB monitors. They use the same technology (separate RGB lines) but use advanced display circuitry to provide a higher-quality image.

Multisync monitors: These monitors currently provide the highest-quality text and graphics plus added flexibility. Using RGB connections, multisync monitors go beyond the capabilities of normal or enhanced RGB monitors. Multisync monitors can imitate any other type of monitor and provide enhanced display capabilities.

gram, was first coded in BASIC; the author's popular Minicalc program for the TRS-80® Model 100 was always an interpreted BASIC program.) Once a program is working correctly, you can increase its speed and sophistication to make it as fast and tight as possible. Making a correct program fast is easier than making a fast program correct.

You *can* write sophisticated, useful programs using DOS and BIOS screen access. Programs that do sophisticated processing can work without direct access to the screen display. As you begin to work with multitasking environments such as Windows or DESQview, you start to appreciate this access level.

Let's look quickly at the basics of display adapters. For a solid understanding of how a computer operates, understanding display devices "from the ground up" is helpful.

Storing and Displaying Video Data

The PC display system is based on the Motorola 6845 Cathode Ray Tube Controller (CRTC) chip. The EGA and VGA systems use custom chips based on this design. These chips manage many important display tasks so that programmers don't have to manage them:

❏ detect light pen signals
❏ increment video buffer address counter
❏ synchronize display and timing
❏ select the video buffer
❏ determine the size and location of the hardware cursor

The system's design is conceptually simple. A PC display is a *memory-mapped* device, in which everything that appears on-screen reflects what is in the computer's memory (see fig. 5.1). A memory buffer stores information that appears on the display. The memory buffer's starting address and length vary, depending on the type of video display in use, the current display mode, and the amount of memory allocated to the display.

Display adapters generally contain from 4K to 256K of memory. Because the data needed to define a display screen may occupy significantly less space than this amount, some display adapters can control more than one display screen. Notice that I said display *screen* and not display *monitor*. Display screens, or *pages*, are the memory representation of what appears on your screen. Table 5.1 shows the beginning memory-buffer locations, the buffer lengths, and the number of display pages for the different display types.

Fig. 5.1. *A display system that shows memory mapping.*

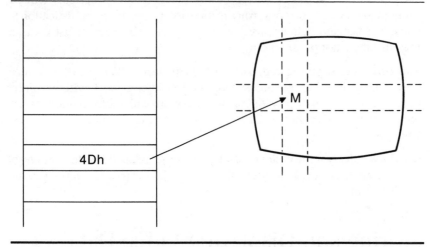

Table 5.1 *Memory Configurations for Display Adapters*

Display Type	Mode	Buffer Segment Address	Buffer Length	Display Pages
MDA	Text	B000h	4K	1
CGA	Text	B800h	16K	4/8
	Graphics	B800h	16K	1
EGA	Mono	B000h	Varies	Varies
	Text	B800h	Varies	Varies
	Graphics	A000h	Varies	Varies
	CGA Graphics	B800h	Varies	Varies
MCGA	Text	B800h	64K	8
	Graphics	A000h	64K	1
	CGA Graphics	B800h	64K	1
VGA	Mono	B000h	256K	8
	Text	B800h	256K	8
	Graphics	A000h	256K	1/2/4/8
	CGA Graphics	B800h	256K	1

For all display adapters, the number of display pages available for text modes is the result of two bytes per screen position. With 80 text characters per line, the result of 2*80*25 is 4,000 bytes, or approximately 4K. If you use the adapter for 40 text characters per line (2*40*25), each screen occupies 2,000 bytes, or about 2K of space. Using these calculations, you can easily see why the CGA can get eight display pages from 16K of buffer space.

The EGA card's buffer size varies because the EGA can have 64K, 128K, or 256K of memory. This RAM is a video buffer for the screen images and also holds patterns (fonts) for as many as 1,024 display characters. The calculations from the preceding paragraph can help you determine the number of display pages available.

Table 5.1 shows that the EGA, MCGA, and VGA have two different graphics-buffer beginning addresses. These adapters can emulate the CGA (segment address B800h) as well as their native beginning segment address of A000h.

The CRTC chip, independent of a computer system's operation, scans the display memory area and, based on the information stored there, updates the video display. The actual screen display is produced by an electron beam that turns small screen dots (called picture elements or *pixels*) on or off as each line of the screen is scanned. The beam traces a path from left to right and top to bottom over the entire screen.

To provide a steady image, the screen is refreshed (the electron beam makes one complete cycle of the entire screen) at a rate of 60 times per second. At the end of each line, the beam has to move from the right side of the screen back to the left side. This time period is called the *horizontal retrace interval* (HRI). Similarly, after the beam completes one cycle it must move from the lower right to the upper left corner of the screen to begin a new cycle. This movement is called the *vertical retrace interval* (VRI). During both the HRI and the VRI, the beam is turned off and nothing is written to the screen.

Programmers whose programs write directly to the display memory should be aware of the HRI or VRI for some types of display adapters, because of the way that the adapter uses the display memory. The memory assigned to the display is actually a special *dual-ported* memory, in which a computer can write values to memory at the same time that the CRTC reads them. If your computer happens to be changing a value at one memory location while the CRTC is reading the value, you may see a display-screen distortion called *snow*. To avoid snow, you should change the screen memory only during either the HRI or VRI.

Paying attention to the HRI or VRI is particularly important when you work with a CGA adapter. You can tell whether an HRI or VRI condition exists by polling the CRTC status register at I/O port 3DAh. Bit 0 indicates whether an

HRI exists; bit 3 reflects the same information about the VRI. The respective bit is on when the retrace interval begins and off when it is complete. Because HRIs happen much more often than VRIs and are easier to detect when you are programming, most direct screen-memory routines test only for the HRI condition. When the bit goes on, you can put as many characters as possible in the display memory without screen interference.

This guideline about screen interference applies primarily to the CGA, which has the most interference problems, and only when you *write* to the screen memory. Because reading from the screen memory causes no interference, you do not need to wait for either the HRI or VRI when you read.

Video Display Formats

The display adapter's interpretation of video data depends on the display *mode*, which controls the way data appears on-screen. Table 5.2 details the display modes available with the different display adapters.

Table 5.2 *Video Modes*

Mode	Type	Colors	Resolution	MDA	CGA	EGA	MCGA	VGA	PCjr
00h	Text	16	40×25		X	X	X	X	
01h	Text	16	40×25		X	X	X	X	
02h	Text	16	80×25		X	X	X	X	
03h	Text	16	80×25		X	X	X	X	
04h	Graphics	4	320×200		X	X	X	X	X
05h	Graphics	4	320×200		X	X	X	X	X
06h	Graphics	2	640×200		X	X	X	X	X
07h	Text	Mono	80×25	X		X		X	X
08h	Graphics	16	160×200						X
09h	Graphics	16	320×200						X
0Ah	Graphics	4	640×200						X
0Bh	----- RESERVED -------								
0Ch	----- RESERVED -------								
0Dh	Graphics	16	320×200			X		X	
0Eh	Graphics	16	640×200			X		X	
0Fh	Graphics	Mono	640×350			X		X	
10h	Graphics	16	640×350			X		X	
11h	Graphics	2	640×480				X	X	
12h	Graphics	16	640×480					X	
13h	Graphics	256	320×200				X	X	

The numbers in the resolution column represent rows and columns for text modes, and pixels for graphics modes.

The monochrome adapter supports only one screen-display mode (mode 7), the CGA supports seven, and the EGA supports 12. The most sophisticated adapter is the VGA system, which supports 15 display modes. The VGA also supports graphics on a monochrome display, a display of 43 lines per screen, and a color palette of up to 256 colors.

BIOS keeps track of the current display mode and stores the number at memory address 0040:0049. The number of columns per line is stored at 0040:004A. Although you can change these values directly, doing so is not wise because the BIOS not only changes the numbers at these memory locations but also performs other operations necessary for setting a video mode correctly.

Now let's look at the two major display-mode categories: text and graphics.

Text-Mode Display

Text mode is also called alphanumeric mode, as most IBM documentation refers to it. In text modes, two bytes of memory are assigned to each character position displayed on the screen: one byte to hold the character, one to hold its *attribute*. Character attributes indicate to the display adapter how the character should be displayed. Table 5.3 shows the meaning of the character-attribute bits for monochrome text mode; table 5.4 shows the bit meanings for color text mode.

Table 5.3 *Monochrome Character Attributes*

Bits 76543210	*Meaning*
0.	Normal character
1.	Blinking character
.000. . . .	Black background (normal)
.111. . . .	White background (inverse)
. . . .0. . .	Normal intensity
. . . .1. . .	High intensity
. 000	White foreground (normal)
. 001	Underlined white foreground
. 111	Black foreground (inverse)

Table 5.4. *Color Character Attributes*

Bits 76543210	Meaning
0	Normal character
1	Blinking character
. xxx	Background (see table 5.5)
. . . . xxxx	Foreground (see table 5.5)

Notice in table 5.4 that only three bits are allowed for the background color and that four bits are allowed for the foreground. Table 5.5 lists the possible bit settings for each color. Be aware, however, that because the background is determined by three bits, only values up to 7 can be stored in the background.

Table 5.5. *Possible Bit Settings for Color Text Mode*

| | Bit Value | |
Binary	Decimal	Color
0000	0	Black
0001	1	Blue
0010	2	Green
0011	3	Cyan
0100	4	Red
0101	5	Magenta
0110	6	Brown
0111	7	White
1000	8	Gray
1001	9	Light blue
1010	10	Light green
1011	11	Light cyan
1100	12	Light red
1101	13	Light magenta
1110	14	Yellow
1111	15	High-intensity white

After the character's ASCII value is stored in the character's memory location and the attribute is set in the attribute byte, the adapter card's display circuitry creates the physical display of the character. Each character is converted on-screen to a dot pattern that corresponds to the character generated by the display adapter. The characters are converted from data contained within a ROM character generator on the adapter. The EGA and VGA cards also allow programmers to specify alternate user-defined character sets for character display.

In addition to monochrome and color text displays, two other types of text displays exist. The distinction between these displays lies in the number of characters displayed per line.

Some display adapters can display either 40 or 80 characters per line. The basic video-display format is the 80-by-25 display screen. Because the 40-column format generally is useful only when your video display is a television set, in which 40 characters per line is about right for readability, the major emphasis in this book is given to the 80-column format, which closely matches the standard 80-by-24 computer-terminal display.

Graphics-Mode Display

IBM refers to the graphics display modes as the APA, or *all-points addressable* modes. In graphics modes, each screen pixel is specified by a set number of memory bits. Each bit indicates whether the pixel is on or off and what color it is. The number of bits used for each pixel depends on the type of display adapter and the graphics mode being used. For example, the EGA system can display 16 colors from a palette of 64 available colors. To indicate which of the 16 colors a specific pixel should be, you need four bits. The number of bits required for each pixel can be represented by the following equation:

$$\text{BITS} = \frac{\log(\text{COLORS})}{\log(2)}$$

COLORS is the number of colors to be represented, and BITS is the number of bits required. With 16 colors available at any time for each EGA-screen pixel, the equation would look like the following:

$$\frac{\log(16)}{\log(2)} = \frac{1.20412}{0.30103} = 4 \text{ bits}$$

If only four colors were available, you could determine from this equation that each pixel would require two bits. Similarly, if only two colors were used, each pixel could be represented by a single bit.

The resolution of a graphics display screen (refer to table 5.2) is expressed by pixels, with a horizontal and vertical resolution. For example, table 5.2 lists the resolution for mode 0Eh as 640-by-200, or 640 pixels wide by 200 scan lines (pixels) deep. This number represents a total of 128,000 pixels for the display screen. Using the figures developed earlier, if each pixel can be one of 16 colors, then it takes four bits per pixel, or one byte for every two pixels to code each of the 16 colors. Therefore, 128,000 pixels (a full screen for mode 0Eh) can be represented in 64,000 bytes (approximately 64K of memory). When you work with graphics, keep in mind the relationship between resolution, available colors, and memory requirements.

Video Functions

Now that you know how screen displays work, you can try out some simple functions to see how they work. Like most of the topics discussed in this book, the video functions are available in two categories: DOS and BIOS. Unlike other programming areas, however, the preponderance of video functions are relegated to BIOS. No DOS services are available for controlling the screen; only a few DOS services are available for displaying information on the screen.

The DOS services are simplest to use. Each DOS service provides a simple output mechanism that is redirectable and compatible with all system operations.

The BIOS services generally are the functions of choice for serious programming in which you do not directly access video memory. These services not only provide extensive control of a video system but also are faster and much more flexible than the DOS services. The BIOS services provide access to the cursor, to attributes for display, and to other controls.

Remember that DOS and BIOS simply provide the building blocks for creating screens. A programmer's imagination and skill provide much of the "glitz" that makes a program perform well or look snappy. If your abilities in creating displays are not on a par with your programming techniques, your displays may look shoddy.

Programming with DOS and BIOS Video Functions

In this section we will build some simple window functions to see how easy using the BIOS and DOS functions can be. The purpose of this chapter is not to build a complete windowing system—such an endeavor is beyond the scope of this book. We're going to investigate screen operations in terms of some simple window display functions that illustrate the use of the BIOS and DOS functions.

The first program, testscn.c, is a simple test that fills the screen with data and then clears a window in the middle of it. You will write more data to the screen and then put the original window data back into place and scroll it. Listing 5.1 shows the testscn.c program.

Listing 5.1

Testscn.c:

```
#include <stdio.h>

/*
    Test Screen Display ... simple window functions
*/
main()
{
    int i;

    /*
        Display a screen full of lines
    */
    cls();
    for (i=Ø; i <5Ø; i++)
        printf("DOS Programmer's Reference            ");

    /*
        Save the data in the rectangle (5,5) to (12,4Ø),
        then clear that area and put a border around it
    */
    savewin(5,5,12,4Ø);
    clearwin(5,5,12,4Ø);
    border(5,5,12,4Ø);

    /*
        Wait 5 seconds and then scroll the screen again.
        (NOTE: Everything scrolls, including the window.)
    */
    sleep(5);
    gotoxy(24,Ø);
    for (i=Ø; i <5Ø; i++)
        printf("This is the Second Screen of the Demo   ");
```

Listing 5.1 continues

Listing 5.1 continued

```
/*
    Wait 5 seconds, then clear the window and fill it
*/
sleep(5);
clearwin(5,5,12,40);
putwin(5,5,12,40);

/*
    Scroll the inside of the window up one line every
    2 seconds for 10 steps
*/
for (i=0; i <10; i++) {
    sleep(2);
    upwin(1,6,6,11,39);
}

/*
    Finally, clear the screen again and then end the
    program.
*/
cls();
}
```

Testscn.c is built on three simple function collections contained in the files window.c, screen.c, and chario.c. Window.c (see listing 5.2) handles the window functions called for by testscn.c. With the functions in window.c, you can do the following:

savewin( )	Save the current data in the window
clearwin( )	Clear the window
putwin( )	Put data into a window
border( )	Put a border around a window
upwin( )	Scroll the window up

This small collection of functions makes no attempt to be super sophisticated. It simply handles single, nonoverlapping windows such as those you might use to display help information and so forth. Because it uses nothing lower than the BIOS functions, it is compatible with other environments such as DESQview.

Listing 5.2

Window.c:

```
/*
     Name:     Window.c
     Purpose:  Basic window control functions
     Note:     Throughout, the following special variables
               are defined as follows:

                    lr = left row (upper left corner)
                    lc = left column (upper left corner)
                    rr = right row (lower right corner)
                    rc = right column (lower right corner)
*/


#include <stdio.h>
#include <dos.h>

#define VIDEO 0x10

/*   Basic screen size definitions */

#define      LINES    24
#define      COLS     80

/*
     Structure for each character position...Character and
     attribute.
*/
struct  charpos {
     char ch;
     char att;
};

/*   Screen is made up of LINES*COLS of character positions */
struct charpos screen[LINES][COLS];

/*
     Function: savewin()
     Purpose:  Saves a rectangular area of the screen into the
               master screen buffer by reading the character and
               attribute at each position
*/
savewin(lr,lc,rr,rc)

int  lr,  lc,  rr,  rc;
```

Listing 5.2 continues

Listing 5.2 continued

```
{
    int i, j;

    for (i=lr; i <=rr; i++)
        for (j=lc; j <=rc; j++) {
            gotoxy(i,j);
            rch(&screen[i][j].ch,&screen[i][j].att);
        }
}

/*
    Function: Clearwin()
    Purpose:  Clears the designated area on the screen
              using the BIOS scroll-window function
*/
clearwin(lr,lc,rr,rc)

int  lr,  lc,  rr,  rc;

{
    union REGS regs;

    regs.h.ah = 0x06;
    regs.h.al = 0;
    regs.h.bh = 7;
    regs.h.ch = lr;
    regs.h.cl = lc;
    regs.h.dh = rr;
    regs.h.dl = rc;
    int86(VIDEO,&regs,&regs);
}

/*
    Function: Putwin()
    Purpose:  Writes to the designated area on the screen,
              from the data in the screen buffer
*/
putwin(lr,lc,rr,rc)

int lr, lc, rr, rc;

{
    int  i,   j;
```

Listing 5.2 continues

Listing 5.2 continued

```
    for (i=lr; i <=rr; i++)
        for (j=lc; j <=rc; j++) {
            gotoxy(i,j);
            wch(screen[i][j].ch,screen[i][j].att);
        }
    border(lr,lc,rr,rc);
}

#define VERTLINE    186
#define UPPERRIGHT  187
#define LOWERRIGHT  188
#define LOWERLEFT   200
#define UPPERLEFT   201
#define HORIZLINE   205

/*
    Function: Border()
    Purpose:  Puts a 2-line border around the designated
              screen area
*/
border(lr,lc,rr,rc)

int lr, lc, rr, rc;

{
    int  i, j;

    for (i=lr; i <=rr; i++) {
        gotoxy(i,lc); wch(VERTLINE,7);
        gotoxy(i,rc); wch(VERTLINE,7);
        if (i==lr || i==rr) {
            for (j=lc; j <=rc; j++) {
                gotoxy(i,j);
                wch(HORIZLINE,7);
            }
            if (i==lr) {
                gotoxy(lr,lc); wch(UPPERLEFT,7);
                gotoxy(lr,rc); wch(UPPERRIGHT,7);
            }
            if (i==rr) {
                gotoxy(rr,lc); wch(LOWERLEFT,7);
                gotoxy(rr,rc); wch(LOWERRIGHT,7);
```

Listing 5.2 continues

Listing 5.2 continued

```
            }
        }
    }
}

/*
    Function: Upwin()
    Purpose:  Scrolls the designated area on the screen
              up n lines, using the BIOS scroll window
*/
upwin(n,lr,lc,rr,rc)

int n;
int lr, lc, rr, rc;

{
    union REGS regs;

    regs.h.ah = 0x06;
    regs.h.al = n;
    regs.h.bh = 7;
    regs.h.ch = lr;
    regs.h.cl = lc;
    regs.h.dh = rr;
    regs.h.dl = rc;
    int86(VIDEO,&regs,&regs);
}
```

The functions in the file screen.c handle screen-related functions such as positioning the cursor and clearing the screen (functions gotoxy() and cls(), respectively). Note that cls() is just clearwin() with set values of the upper left and lower right corners corresponding to the whole screen.

The screen.c functions (see listing 5.3) are intended to be global to the whole screen display. They act on a screen-wide basis. Window.c functions are intended to work within a single window. Additional functions could be added to a handle working within a window.

Listing 5.3

Screen.c:

```
#include <stdio.h>
#include <dos.h>

#define     VIDEO  0x10

/*
     Function: Gotoxy()
     Purpose:  Moves the cursor to the designated screen
               location, using the BIOS cursor-position function
*/
gotoxy(r,c)

int r, c;

{
    union REGS regs;

    regs.h.ah = 0x02;
    regs.h.bh = 0;
    regs.h.dh = r;
    regs.h.dl = c;
    int86(VIDEO,&regs,&regs);
}

/*
     Function: Cls()
     Purpose:  Clears the screen using the BIOS scroll window function
*/
cls()
{
    union REGS regs;

    regs.h.ah = 0x06;
    regs.h.al = 0;
    regs.h.bh = 7;
    regs.h.ch = 0;
    regs.h.cl = 0;
    regs.h.dh = 25;
    regs.h.dl = 80;
    int86(VIDEO,&regs,&regs);
}
```

At the lowest level of the program, screen-character functions allow us to
look at a single screen position or to change it by using the BIOS screen-
display functions (see listing 5.4).

Listing 5.4

Chario.c:

```
#include <stdio.h>
#include <dos.h>

#define VIDEO Øx1Ø

union REGS regs;

/*
    Function: Wch()
    Purpose:  Write a character and attribute to the screen,
              using the BIOS write-character function
*/
wch(ch, attr)

char ch,  attr;

{
    regs.h.ah = ØxØ9;
    regs.h.bh = Ø;
    regs.h.bl = attr;
    regs.h.al = ch;
    regs.x.cx = 1;
    int86(VIDEO,&regs,&regs);
}

rch(ch, attr)
/*
    Function: Rch()
    Purpose:  Read a character and its attribute from the screen
*/

char *ch, *attr;

{
    regs.h.ah = ØxØ8;
    regs.h.bh = Ø;
    int86(VIDEO,&regs,&regs);
    *ch = regs.h.al;
    *attr = regs.h.ah;
}
```

If you are using Microsoft C, then you do not have a sleep() function as of version 4.0. The following function will wait until a specified number of seconds have passed:

```
#include  <stdio.h>

sleep(n)

/*
    Function: Sleep()
    Purpose:  Needed w/Microsoft C compiler to provide
              sleep function... sleep for n seconds
*/

int  n;

{
    long timeval,  time();

    timeval = time(NULL);
    while(time(NULL)  < timeval + n);
}
```

Using Multiple Display Pages

All of the display functions used for this simple windowing system deal specifically with only one screen page (page zero), so they are independent of the type of monitor system you are using. You could add screen-page control, but not all functions allow it. For example, the scrolling functions have no page assignment among their arguments. Thus, you cannot use these facilities for paging the display. (If you write your own window functions to access display memory directly, you are not bound by this limitation.) Also, Function 0Eh does not work with all pages on all BIOS ROMs. In all of the non-IBM ROMs that I was able to test, this function worked only on the currently displayed page and not on a nondisplayed page.

One way to add screen page control is to change the routines to include a current screen page number and a way to set it. For example, you could change screen.c to include a setpage command (see listing 5.5).

In the preceding listing, the function pgprint() has also been added to allow you to print strings to the current page. By adding page control to your screen functions, you can build programs in which you use the window and page functions together to preserve displays that can be recovered rapidly simply by shifting display page. The sample program testpage.c (see listing 5.6) lets you try the new functions setpage() and pgprint().

Listing 5.5

Screenpg.c:

```c
#include <stdio.h>
#include <dos.h>

#define    BOOL  int
#define    VIDEO 0x10

static int cpage = 0;         /* Current display page */

/*
    Function: Gotoxy()
    Purpose:  Moves the cursor to the designated screen
              location, using the BIOS cursor-position function
*/
gotoxy(r,c)

int  r,   c;

{
    union REGS regs;

    regs.h.ah = 0x02;
    regs.h.bh = cpage;
    regs.h.dh = r;
    regs.h.dl = c;
    int86(VIDEO,&regs,&regs);
}

/*
    Function: Cls()
    Purpose:  Clears the screen, using the BIOS scroll-window
              function
*/
cls()

{
    union REGS regs;

    regs.h.ah = 0x06;
    regs.h.al = 0;
    regs.h.bh = 7;
    regs.h.ch = 0;
    regs.h.cl = 0;
    regs.h.dh = 25;
    regs.h.dl = 80;
    int86(VIDEO,&regs,&regs);
```

Listing 5.5 continues

Listing 5.5 *continued*

```
}

/*
    Function: Setpage()
    Purpose:  Sets the current video display page
*/
setpage(n,clrflg)

int  n;
BOOL clrflg;

{
    union REGS regs;

    cpage = n;
    regs.h.ah = ØxØ5;
    regs.h.al = n;
    int86(VIDEO,&regs,&regs);
    if(clrflg)
        cls();
}

/*
    Function: Pgprint()
    Purpose:  Prints the string to the current display page
*/
pgprint(str)

char *str;

{
    union REGS regs;

    regs.h.ah = ØxØe;
    regs.h.bh = cpage;
    while (*str) {
        regs.h.al = *str;
        int86(VIDEO,&regs,&regs);
        str++;
    }
}
```

Listing 5.6

```
Testpage.c:

#include <stdio.h>

/*
    Test Screen Paging
*/

#define FALSE Ø
#define TRUE  !FALSE

main()

{
    int     i;

    /*
        Display a screen full of lines
    */
    setpage(1,TRUE);
    for (i=Ø; i <5Ø; i++)
        pgprint("DOS Programmer's Reference            ");
    sleep(5);
    setpage(Ø,FALSE);
}
```

If you have a monochrome monitor system, you will not be able to see anything. In fact, when the setpage() function is executed, your screen will not change and you simply will see everything remain static for a few seconds and then return. But if you have a CGA or EGA monitor or better, you will see the screen change, display the test line, and then return to the same display you had on the screen when you executed the program.

Using a current display page for all functions is not as impressive as working with undisplayed pages. By including the display page in the function arguments, you can apply a function like gotoxy() to pages that are not yet displayed. You then can build a complete display before the user sees it and, by making it the current display, the user will see it generate instantaneously.

Printer Functions

The only other major output device over which we have direct control in the system is the printer. Printer functions are much simpler than screen functions because they deal only with character output and minimally with input from the printer.

The simplest way to write to the printer is to use the DOS-level printer-output function (Int 21h, Function 05h) as shown in listing 5.7. This function allows you to send characters to the printer device. DOS will handle error conditions by invoking the critical-error handler if there is a problem using the function.

Listing 5.7

```
Print.c:

#include  <stdio.h>
#include  <dos.h>

/*
    Output a line to the printer
*/
main()

{
    outprt("This is a line to the printer\012\015");
}

/*
    Output the string to the printer, using the
    printer function in Int 21h
*/
outprt(str)

char    *str;

{
    union REGS regs;

    regs.h.ah = 0x05;
    while (*str) {
        regs.h.dl = *str;
        intdos(&regs,&regs);
        str++;
    }
}
```

At a lower level, you can invoke the BIOS print functions (Int 17h) to get greater control over the print function. At this level, you can check the printer's status directly and respond to printer errors within your program as needed. Listing 5.8 shows an example of how you might use the BIOS functions to handle printer interfacing.

Listing 5.8

Print2.c

```c
#include  <stdio.h>
#include  <dos.h>

/*
    Output a line to the printer
*/
main()

{
    int     i;

    for (i=0; i <10; i++) {
        if(!prtrdy())
            exit(1);
        outprt("This is a line to the printer\012\015");
    }
}

#define PRINTER 0x17

/*
    Output the string to the printer, using the
    printer function in Int 21h
*/
outprt(str)

char    *str;

{
    union REGS regs;

    regs.x.dx = 0;
    while (*str) {
        regs.h.ah = 0x00;
        regs.h.al = *str;
        int86(PRINTER,&regs,&regs);
        putchar(*str);
        str++;
    }
}

/*
    Check the printer ready for printing
*/
prtrdy()
```

Listing 5.8 continues

Listing 5.8 continued

```
{
    union REGS regs;

    regs.h.ah = 2;
    regs.x.dx = Ø;
    int86(PRINTER,&regs,&regs);
    printf("Printer Status: %x\n",regs.h.ah);
    if (regs.h.ah & Øx2Ø)
        printf("Printer out of paper\n");
    if (regs.h.ah & ØxØ8)
        printf("Printer I/O error\n");
    return((regs.h.ah&Øx2Ø)==Ø && (regs.h.ah&ØxØ8)==Ø);
}
```

As these examples show, you can perform printer output directly from your programs and recognize what is happening with the printer at the same time.

Sophisticated printer-control functions such as graphics, font control, and other specialized printer functions are specific to the printer you are using. Neither BIOS or DOS has any built-in functions for handling printers beyond simply sending characters to them. Specialized printer-control functions are beyond the scope of this book.

Summary

This chapter has covered a wide range of functions for output, primarily related to the video display. You have learned about the various screen modes available and the various screen displays you can use.

Within DOS, screen control is limited to a few simple functions that allow basic output to the screen and little else. More sophisticated control requires access to the BIOS functions to allow cursor positioning, character-attribute control, and so forth. At the BIOS level, you can do graphical displays, screen positioning, and even window functions. Programs intended to do sophisticated screens will almost always have to work at the BIOS level or below, using direct access to the screen-display memory.

Printer functions are even more limited than screen functions. There are no primitive functions for anything other than outputing characters to the printer and checking the printer's status. We cannot call BIOS or DOS functions to do printer graphics or special printer functions such as font changing and so forth. Any special control must be performed by your programs.

In the next chapter, we'll move on to input functions. These will serve as a complement to the output functions we've just covered.

CHAPTER 6

Input Devices

Input and output are so tied together in most people's minds that we normally think in terms of "I/O" or "Input/Output" and rarely deal only with one or the other. In this chapter, which complements Chapter 5's discussion of output devices, you will learn about input devices.

This chapter focuses on the two most popular input devices: the keyboard and the mouse. The keyboard is handled by DOS and BIOS functions included in the system, whereas a driver must be added to the system to make the mouse's functions available.

Keyboards are much more sophisticated than most people realize. The keyboard itself is a sophisticated piece of engineering. It works with low-level functions in the BIOS and, by buffering character input and providing interrupts to allow the BIOS to handle keyboard characters as they are typed, makes keyboard operations almost invisible to programs.

Because interrupts are not covered until Chapter 11, this chapter deals with the mouse in a simplistic manner. But even that makes for an interesting program. By using the mouse functions (when they are present), you can build mouse-control functions into a variety of programs.

Both keyboard and mouse functions can be made much more interesting by combining them with interrupt-handling functions. Terminate and Stay Resident programs that use hot keys to start or mouse-driven programs that interrupt on mouse input provide for immediate response to the user's needs. Chapter 11 discusses interrupts in greater detail. At this point, however, you need to learn the basic input functions.

147

Keyboards

You can always count on the PC to have a keyboard as an input device—every PC has one, and most programs use them. Although alternative input devices such as the mouse have gained popularity for some types of programs, few programs can operate without *some* keyboard input.

In this section we look at the use of BIOS and DOS functions for keyboard input. These functions, when used instead of the normal input functions of a high-level language, result in the following advantages:

- ❏ Maximum control over your input. (You can add user-oriented editing features, special help functions, and so forth.)

- ❏ Smaller programs than those possible when using the keyboard input routines provided with high-level languages. (These routines, which are written to provide for virtually every possible input situation and condition, carry a great deal of "overhead code."

- ❏ Snappier, more responsive input because you can make the program react however you choose.

Before I discuss programming, let's look at how the keyboard works.

How the Keyboard Works

To programmers, the keyboard probably is the most familiar but least understood device on a computer. Most of us understand file systems and disk operations because we have read books about them. But the lowly keyboard is discussed minimally and is well known to only a few specialists.

Instead of trying to describe the hardware that makes keyboards work, this book concentrates on the sequence of events you must understand if you want to use the keyboard-related DOS and BIOS services.

First, imagine that you are looking from your computer through the cable which connects your computer and the keyboard. As you press keys, you can see numbers (the keyboard "scan codes") coming from the keyboard through the cable to the computer.

Each keystroke generates a unique 8-bit number, with even the left and right Shift keys represented by different numbers. These scan codes indicate exactly which keys were pressed. Figures 6.1, 6.2, and 6.3 show the scan codes (hexadecimal) on the PC, Personal Computer AT, and enhanced keyboards.

Fig. 6.1. *Hexadecimal scan codes for a PC keyboard.*

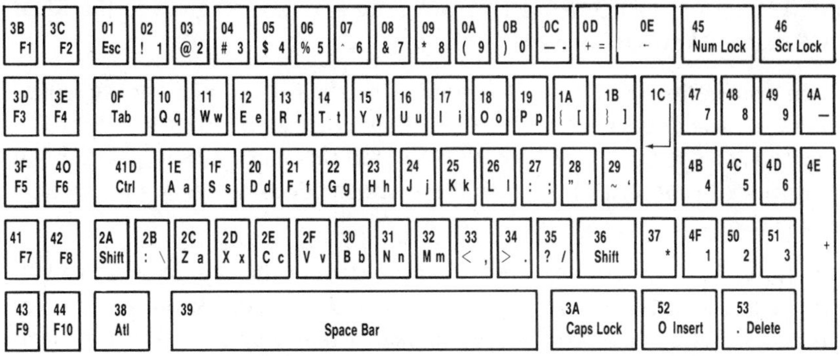

Fig. 6.2. *Hexadecimal scan codes for an AT keyboard.*

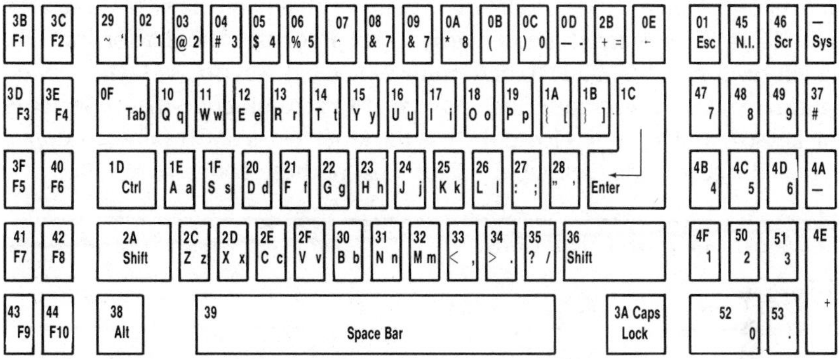

FIg. 6.3. *Hexadecimal scan codes for an enhanced keyboard.*

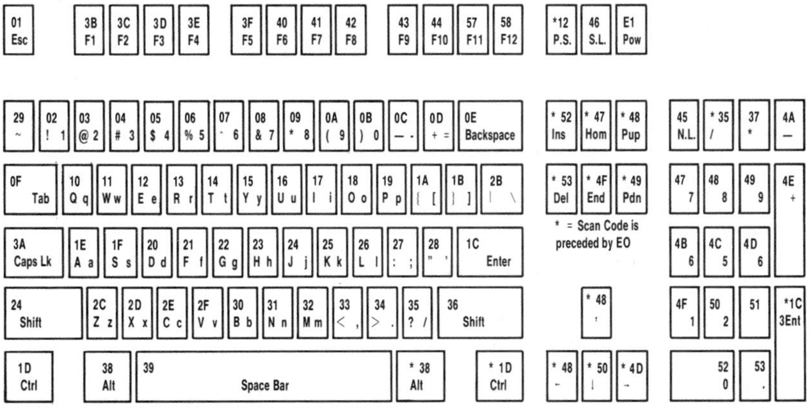

Whenever a key is released, another scan code is generated. This code is the same as that for the keystroke, except that the high-order bit is set (which adds 128 to the scan code). In this way, the scan code signals to the ROM BIOS that the key has been released.

When you hold down a key for more than half a second, the keyboard generates a sequence of scan codes that correspond to the keystroke, repeated at a specified rate. The BIOS can tell that a key is being held down (not pressed repeatedly) because the keyboard does not generate any key-release codes in this sequence.

Clearly, the keyboard recognizes only the *keys* (not the characters) that you press. The keyboard supplies only the scan code that corresponds to the key you press. (The scan code simply indicates that a specific key has been pressed.) The BIOS interprets the scan codes to determine which ASCII character corresponds to the keystroke.

Whenever you press a key, the keyboard generates not only the scan code but also Int 09h, which tells the ROM BIOS that a key has been pressed. Control of the system is transferred momentarily to the interrupt handler for Int 09h, which reads port 96 (60h) to determine which key was pressed. The service routine reads the scan code and converts it to a 16-bit code that represents the keystroke. The code's lower byte is the keystroke's ASCII value; its upper byte is the scan code (see table 6.1 for a list of these codes.)

Table 6.1. *ASCII and Scan Codes*

Scan Code	Key
01	Esc
02	! 1
03	@ 2
04	# 3
05	$ 4
06	% 5
07	^ 6
08	& 7
09	* 8
0A	(9
0B	) 0
0C	_ -
0D	+ =
0E	Backspace
0F	Tab

Table 6.1 continues

Table 6.1 *continued*

Scan Code	Key
10	Q q
11	W w
12	E e
13	R r
14	T t
15	Y y
16	U u
17	I i
18	O o
19	P p
1A	{ [
1B	}]
1C	Enter
1D	Ctrl
1E	A a
1F	S s
20	D d
21	F f
22	G g
23	H h
24	J j
25	K k
26	L l
27	: ;
28	″ ′
29	~ `
2A	Left Shift
2B	| \
2C	Z z
2D	X x
2E	C c
2F	V v
30	B b
31	N n
32	M m
33	< ,
34	> .

Table 6.1 continues

Table 6.1 *continued*

Scan Code	Key
35	? /
36	Right Shift
37	PrtSc *
38	Alt
39	Space bar
3A	Caps Lock
3B	F1
3C	F2
3D	F3
3E	F4
3F	F5
40	F6
41	F7
42	F8
43	F9
44	F10
45	Num Lock
46	Scroll Lock
47	7 Home
48	8 Cursor Up
49	9 PgUp
4A	Gray –
4B	4 Cursor Left
4C	5
4D	6 Cursor Right
4E	Gray +
4F	1 End
50	2 Cursor Down
51	3 PgDn
52	0 Ins
53	. Del
54	SysRq

Special keys, such as the function keys and numeric keypad keys, have a zero in their lower byte to indicate that the keystroke is not a standard ASCII character and must be specially processed.

When the BIOS keyboard interrupt handler finishes processing a keystroke, it places the code in the keyboard buffer, where it is stored until a program requests it.

We will not write any programs that access the keyboard data at this level. Instead, we will rely on the BIOS or DOS to preprocess all keyboard input data so that we have to deal only with the ASCII codes for normal keys and the scan codes for special keys.

Reading the Keyboard from BASIC

Before you start using DOS and BIOS calls to read the keyboard, let's look at a BASIC program that uses standard BASIC functions for keyboard input. The program KEYBD.BAS (see listing 6.1) uses functions available in the BASIC interpreter.

Listing 6.1

```
10 REM --- KEYBD.BAS    Basic keyboard demonstration
20 C$=INKEY$:IF C$="" THEN 20
30 GOSUB 100:GOTO 20
100 REM --- Display keyboard input
110 IF LEN(C$)>1 THEN GOSUB 200 ELSE GOSUB 300
120 PRINT USING "Character: ! ### ###";CH$;C;SC
130 RETURN
200 REM --- Keystroke has scan code included
210 CH$=".":C=ASC(MID$(C$,1,1)):SC=ASC(MID$(C$,2,1))
220 RETURN
300 REM --- Keystroke is character only
310 CH$=C$:C=ASC(C$):SC=0
320 RETURN
```

For compatibility with the BASIC interpreter, this program is written with line numbers. The simple structure of this program follows:

1. Wait for a keystroke.

2. Print the keystroke character, ASCII code, and scan code.

3. Repeat from Line 1.

INKEY$ (which is put into a tight loop in line 20 of listing 6.1) gives you a way to read the keyboard without having to wait for a keystroke. Subroutine 100 translates the return from INKEY$ according to whether the string is more than one character long. In BASIC, if the string returned by INKEY$ is more than one character long, the first character is the character's ASCII value and the second one is the scan code. (The subroutine beginning at line 200 deals with such a case.) Usually, the string is one character long. The subroutine at line 300 is used to decode the string.

If you run the program in listing 6.1, you will notice that the scan codes correspond only to a limited extent to individual keys (refer to figs. 6.1 and 6.2). Program KEYBD.BAS has the following limitations:

❑ INKEY$ returns only "meaningful" characters (in this case, only characters that are "meaningful" to the BASIC interpreter).

❑ Scan codes are returned only for completed keystrokes that are *not* ASCII characters. (You do not see the Shift keys, the Ctrl key, or the Alt key.)

From now on, instead of continuing with an interpreter-compatible BASIC program, we will work with a BASIC compiler: either QuickBASIC or Turbo BASIC. Listing 6.2 shows the program modified for QuickBASIC in order to take advantage of the features of the compiler.

Listing 6.2

```
' KEYBD2.BAS

'QuickBASIC Keyboard Demonstration

Start:
    C$ = INKEY$: IF C$ = "" THEN GOTO Start
    GOSUB Display: GOTO Start

Display:
    'Display Keyboard Input
    IF LEN(C$) > 1 THEN GOSUB Scan ELSE GOSUB Char
    PRINT USING "Character: ! ### ###"; CH$; C; SC
    RETURN

Scan:
    'Keystroke includes scan code
    CH$ = ".": C = ASC(MID$(C$, 1, 1)): SC = ASC(MID$(C$, 2, 1))
    RETURN

Char:
    'Keystroke is character only
    CH$ = C$: C = ASC(C$): SC = Ø
    RETURN
```

Starting from the sample program in listing 6.2, we will substitute BIOS function calls to perform input. As we do, we will be able to see more of the keystrokes on the keyboard.

Accessing the Keyboard Using Int 16h

When you get ready to use the BIOS functions, the first thing you notice is that Int 16h, Function 0 (the BIOS keyboard input function) waits for a keystroke. In this way, the BIOS function is unlike BASIC's INKEY$ function. The result of rewriting the program to use this BIOS function is the program KEYBD3.BAS (see listing 6.3).

Listing 6.3

```
'Turbo Basic Keyboard Demonstration
' NOTE: Enable "keyboard break" (Ctrl-Break) option
' before running

' Constants for register names
%FLAGS = 0
%AX = 1: %BX = 2: %CX = 3: %DX = 4
%SI = 5: %DI = 6: %BP = 7
%DS = 8: %ES = 9

Start:
    GOSUB Getchar
    GOSUB Display
    GOTO Start
    END

Display:
'Display Keyboard Input
    CH$ = CHR$(ch)
    PRINT USING "Character: ! ### ###";CH$;CharCode;ScanCode
    RETURN

Getchar:
    REG %ax, &H0000
    call interrupt &H16
    ScanCode = (REG(%AX) AND &HFF00)/256%
    CharCode = (REG(%AX) AND &HFF)
    RETURN
```

To emphasize the use of the BIOS function, the program has been slightly restructured so that the getchar subroutine waits until it gets a character; then the subroutine returns. The result is similar to that of a loop with INKEY$ except that, if no key was pressed, the program cannot do another task while it waits for a keystroke.

QuickBASIC and Turbo Basic give you direct access to the 16-bit general-purpose registers only: you can address the registers as AX, BX, CX, and DX, but not as AH, AL, and so on. In order to examine individual 8-bit registers, you must use masking and division.

As you learned from Chapter 2, the 16-bit AX register can be regarded as two 8-bit registers: AH and AL. In other words, you can think of AH and AL as the high and low bytes, respectively, of the 16-bit AX value. If you know the values in AH and AL, you can use the following equation to calculate the value of the AX register:

$$AX = (256 \times AH) + AL$$

If you know the value of AX, you can derive the value of either the high or low byte (AH or AL). To derive the value in AL, use the following equation:

$$AL = AX \text{ AND } \&HFF$$

The bitwise AND operation, with FFh (255, or binary 11111111) as the other argument, forces all the bits in AH to zero.

The value in AH is

$$AH = (AX \text{ AND } \&HFF00)/256$$

To get the value into the proper range, you clear all the bits in the low byte and then divide the result by 256.

Instead of waiting for a keystroke, you can read a keystroke only when one is available. Int 16h, Function 1 indicates whether a keystroke is waiting. If no key is waiting, the zero flag is set in the processor's flag register. You can test that register as shown in listing 6.4.

Listing 6.4

```
' KEYBD4.BAS
' Turbo Basic Keyboard Demonstration

' NOTE: Enable "keyboard break" (Ctrl-Break) option
' before running

%FLAGS = Ø
%AX = 1: %BX = 2: %CX = 3: %DX = 4
%SI = 5: %DI = 6: %BP = 7
%DS = 8: %ES = 9

cls
print"Input Test"
start:
```

Listing 6.4 continues

Listing 6.4 *continued*

```
    GOSUB getchar
    GOSUB display
    GOTO start
    END

display:
'Display Keyboard Input
    ch$ = chr$(ch)
    PRINT USING "Character: ! ### ###";CH$;CH;SC
    RETURN

getchar:
    do
        gosub stuff
        reg %ax,&h0100
        call interrupt &h16
        zf = reg(%flags) AND &H40
    loop while zf <> 0
    reg %ax, &h0000
    call interrupt &h16
    sc = (reg(%ax) AND &hff00)/256
    ch = (reg(%ax) AND &hff)
    return

stuff:
    print ".";
    return
```

Before getting the key from the keyboard, the program first looks to see whether a key is ready. If no key is ready, the stuff subroutine is called. (It simply prints a dot on the screen.) Whenever a key is pressed, the dots stop momentarily and the program displays information that tells you which key was pressed. Then the program resumes printing dots.

Instead of "idling" while they wait for a keystroke, programs that have a way to check for keyboard input can do other tasks. For example, you might use such a routine to move data on the screen and terminate the operation when a key is pressed.

Int 16h, Function 2 lets you determine the state of keys that even BASIC's INKEY$ function cannot "see": the Ins, Caps Lock, Num Lock, Scroll Lock, Alt, Ctrl, and left and right Shift keys. The next version of the keyboard input program lets you check the status of these keys (see listing 6.5).

Listing 6.5

```
'KBD.BAS
'Turbo BASIC Demonstration using Int 16h, Function 2
' NOTE: Enable "keyboard break" (Ctrl-Break) option
' before running

%FLAGS = Ø
%AX = 1: %BX = 2: %CX = 3: %DX = 4
%SI = 5: %DI = 6: %BP = 7
%DS = 8: %ES = 9

CLS
PRINT "Input Test"
Start:
    GOSUB Getchar
    GOSUB Display
    GOTO Start
    END

Display:
'Display Keyboard Input
    ch$ = chr$(ch)
    PRINT
    PRINT USING "Character: ! ### ###";CH$;CH;SC
    RETURN

Getchar:
    DO
        GOSUB Getspec
        REG %AX,&hØ1ØØ
        CALL INTERRUPT &h16
        zf = reg(%flags) AND &H4Ø
    LOOP WHILE zf <> Ø
    REG %ax, &hØØØØ
    CALL INTERRUPT &h16
    sc = (reg(%ax) AND &hffØØ)/256
    ch = (reg(%ax) AND &hff)
    RETURN

Getspec:
'Gets the special keyboard flags

    REG %ax, &hØ2ØØ
    CALL INTERRUPT &h16
    keyflg = (reg(%ax) AND &hff)
    ins = keyflg AND &h8Ø
    caps = keyflg AND &h4Ø
    num = keyflg AND &h2Ø
```

Listing 6.5 continues

Listing 6.5 continued

```
scroll = keyflg AND &h10
alt = keyflg AND &h08
ctrl = keyflg AND &h04
left = keyflg AND &h02
right = keyflg AND &h01

locate 12,10
print       " INS CAPS  NUM SCRL  ALT CTRL LEFT RIGHT"
locate 13,10
print using "#### #### #### #### #### #### ####  ####"; _
            ins; caps;num;scroll;alt;ctrl;left;right
RETURN
```

In the program in listing 6.5, the stuff routine has been replaced by a routine that checks the status of the special keys and prints their status in the center of the screen. This status information gives you a complete picture of what is happening on the keyboard. If you want your program to check for a trigger event such as both the left and right Shift keys being pressed, Int 16h, Function 2 can tell when that event occurs.

The program in listing 6.5 shows the value returned when the appropriate bit of the keyboard status byte is turned on. Int 16h, Function 2 returns a single byte in the AL register. (Remember that AL = AX AND &h00FF.) Every bit corresponds to a specific keystroke. Table 6.2 shows the bit assignments for this function.

BIOS functions for keyboard input represent the most primitive level of access short of going to the machine. The BIOS level is the lowest level you can use and still be guaranteed that a program is portable to compatible PCs.

When you do not need maximum flexibility and you can allow the operating system kernel to do some of the work, you can use the DOS Int 21h functions for input.

Accessing the Keyboard Using Int 21h

When you go to the DOS level to get keyboard input, you lose immediate access to every possible keystroke. DOS input functions indicate whether special keys have been pressed (if the first byte returned is a zero, the next byte is the scan code). But DOS functions do not give you the scan code for

Table 6.2. *Keyboard Flag Byte*

Bit 76543210	Meaning
.......0	Right Shift key not pressed
.......1	Right Shift key pressed
......0.	Left Shift key not pressed
......1.	Left Shift key pressed
.....0..	Ctrl key not pressed
.....1..	Ctrl key pressed
....0...	Alt key not pressed
....1...	Alt key pressed
...0....	Scroll Lock off
...1....	Scroll Lock on
..0.....	Num Lock off
..1.....	Num Lock on
.0......	Caps Lock off
.1......	Caps Lock on
0.......	Insert off
1.......	Insert on

any key that has an ASCII code, nor does DOS report on the status of Alt, Shift, and so on.

Int 21h, Function 1 (Character Input with Echo) is the most basic DOS character input function you might want to use (see listing 6.6).

Listing 6.6

```
/*   Keyin.c - Test Int 21h keyboard input functions
*/

#include <stdio.h>
#include <dos.h>

#define CTRL_D    0x04
#define LF        0x0a
#define ENTER     0x0d
```

Listing 6.6 continues

Listing 6.6 *continued*

```
main( )

{
    int c;

    printf("Testing Int 21h Input Functions\n");
    while ((c = keyin( ))!=CTRL_D)
        if (c >= 256)
            printf("SPECIAL: %d\n",c - 256);
        else if (c==ENTER)
            putchar(LF);
}

keyin( )
/* Inputs a single character from the keyboard.
 * The interrupt automatically echoes the character to
 * the display ... special characters (those with no
 * ASCII code) are returned as integers with an
 * offset of 256.
 */

{
    union REGS regs;
    int offset;

    offset = Ø;
    regs.h.ah = ØxØ1;
    intdos(&regs,&regs);
    if (regs.h.al == Ø) {
        offset = 256;
        regs.h.ah = ØxØ1;
        intdos(&regs,&regs);
    }
    return(regs.h.al + offset);
}
```

Program KEYIN.C takes the following approach:

1. Wait for a character from the keyboard.

2. If that character is a special character (a function key or a cursor key, for example), print *SPECIAL* and the key's scan code.

3. If the character is the Enter key, the character input function will output a Return without a line feed; you will have to output a line feed to the screen.

4. Repeat from Step 1.

If you try to run the program without the special portion that prints the line-feed character to the screen, you will see the characters echoed by the DOS function as you type them; but when you press Enter, the cursor will not move to the next line. Remember that the function echoes the *characters you type* and that the Enter key represents only the carriage return—not the line-feed character.

One of the program's interesting features is its special coding that distinguishes function keys from regular keys. Because ASCII characters are always less than or equal to 255, this feature creates an extended character set by adding 256 to the scan value of a key that returns a zero ASCII code. In practice, this method often simplifies the process of decoding the keystrokes and causes no problems. Many programmers do not use this method because they associate the keystrokes with character variables. By associating the returned characters with integers, you have a larger range of special codes to represent special keystrokes.

A problem with this approach to reading in characters when you expect special keys (function keys and arrows, for example) is that when you make the second call to get the special key's scan code, the DOS function prints the scan code's ASCII equivalent as though you were retrieving the ASCII code rather than the scan code. To prevent this situation from occurring, you can use Int 21h, Function 8, and echo the characters yourself (see listing 6.7).

Listing 6.7

```
/* Keyin2.c - Test Int 21h keyboard input functions */

#include  <stdio.h>
#include  <dos.h>

#define CTRL_D   0x04
#define LF       0x0a
#define ENTER    0x0d

main()
{
    int c;
```

Listing 6.7 continues

Listing 6.7 *continued*

```
    printf("Testing Int 21h Input Functions\n");
    while ((c = keyin())!=CTRL_D)
        if (c >= 256) {
            printf("SPECIAL: %d\n",c - 256);
        } else {
            putchar(c);
            if (c == ENTER)
                putchar(LF);
        }
}

keyin()

/* Inputs a single character from the keyboard.
 * The interrupt automatically echoes the character to
 * the display ... special characters (those with no
 * ASCII code) are returned as integers with an
 * offset of 256.
 */

{
    union REGS regs;
    int offset;

    offset = 0;
    regs.h.ah = 0x08;
    intdos(&regs,&regs);
    if (regs.h.al == 0) {
        offset = 256;
        regs.h.ah = 0x08;
        intdos(&regs,&regs);
    }
    return(regs.h.al + offset);
}
```

The differences between this program and the one in listing 6.6 are so subtle that you can miss them if you don't look closely. First, in the keyin() function, you set up to call Int 21h, Function 8 instead of Function 1. Your main routine must echo every character to the screen as it is typed (because the DOS kernel isn't echoing characters for you). Because the special keys are handled separately, you are not plagued by the echo of bogus function-key codes—only the keys you type are echoed.

Every DOS function used so far in this chapter waits for a keystroke but, as with the BIOS functions, you can check periodically to see whether a character is waiting (this process is called *polling*). Interrupt 21h, Function

0Bh indicates whether a character is waiting to be read. Listing 6.8 shows how to use this function to perform a task while you wait for a keystroke.

Listing 6.8

```
/*  Keyin3.c - Test Int 21h keyboard input functions
 */

#include <stdio.h>
#include <dos.h>

#define CTRL_D 0x04
#define LF      0x0a
#define ENTER   0x0d

main()

{
    int c;

    printf("Testing Int 21h Input Functions\n");
    while ((c = keyin())!=CTRL_D)
        if (c >= 256) {
            printf("SPECIAL: %d\n",c - 256);
        } else {
            putchar(c);
            if (c == ENTER)
                putchar(LF);
        }
}

keyin()
/* Inputs a single character from the keyboard.
 * The interrupt automatically echoes the character to
 * the display ... special characters (those with no
 * ASCII code) are returned as integers with an
 * offset of 256.
 */

{
    union REGS regs;
    int offset;

    while (!charwait())
        putchar('.');
    offset = 0;
    regs.h.ah = 0x08;
```

Listing 6.8 continues

Listing 6.8 continued

```
    intdos(&regs,&regs);
    if (regs.h.al == Ø) {
        offset = 256;
        regs.h.ah = Øx08;
        intdos(&regs,&regs);
    }
    return(regs.h.al + offset);
}

charwait()
/* Watches for a character at the keyboard: if there
 * is one, returns TRUE; otherwise, returns FALSE.
 */

{
    union REGS regs;

    regs.h.ah = ØxØb;
    intdos(&regs,&regs);
    return(regs.h.al);
}
```

This program introduces a new function charwait(), which watches for a character at the keyboard. If a character is waiting, charwait() returns TRUE; otherwise, it returns FALSE.

Function charwait() is based on Int 21h, Function 0Bh, which sets the AL register to FFh (255) if a character is waiting and to 0 otherwise. By returning the value of the AL register, function charwait() indicates whether a character is waiting (FALSE is a zero value and TRUE is a nonzero value).

To gauge how quickly the program checks for characters, run it and watch the periods march across the screen while the program waits for you to type a character. This program is fairly responsive to input. You can make it extremely sluggish by substituting a long, complicated operation for the simple putchar('.').

If you are willing to relinquish control over the input until Enter is pressed, you can call the buffered input function (Int 21h, Function 0Ah) and let it get your input, echo it, and allow line editing. Some books on DOS programming indicate that the function will return function keys, arrows, and other special keys by returning a 2-byte sequence (including a zero byte and the scan code). The program KEYIN4.C (see listing 6.9) was written to show these special keys if they are returned—but they aren't. The *IBM Technical Reference* manual states that the 2-byte key codes are not included.

Listing 6.9

```
/* Keyin4.c - Test Int 21h keyboard input functions
*/

#include <stdio.h>
#include <dos.h>

#define CTRL_D   0x04
#define LF        0x0a
#define ENTER    0x0d

main()

{
    char buffer[11];

    printf("Testing Int 21h Input Functions\n");
    while ( getline(buffer,10) > 0 ) {
        printf(" <<%>>\n",buffer);
    }
}


getline(buffer,n)
/* Gets a line from the keyboard using the buffer
 * input DOS function
 */

char *buffer;
int n;

{
    union REGS regs;
    char locbuf[514];
    int i, j;

    locbuf[0] = n;
    locbuf[1] = 0;
    regs.h.ah = 0x0a;
    regs.x.dx = (int)&locbuf;
    intdos(&regs,&regs);
    for(i=0, j=0; i <locbuf[1]; i++, j++)
        if (locbuf[i+2]==0) {
            i++;
            buffer[j] = 'X';
        } else {
            buffer[j] = locbuf[i+2];
        }
    buffer[j] = NULL;
    return(locbuf[1]);
}
```

The requirements of the buffered input function make it special. Because of its layout, the buffer does not fit naturally with the way strings are handled in BASIC, C, or Pascal. When the function is invoked, you must pass it a buffer large enough to handle the input characters plus two extra characters. The first character in the buffer is the *maximum* number of characters to input; the second, which is filled in by DOS, represents the number of characters read.

Other input functions, including functions based on file access, can be used for keyboard input. The topic of using file handles to access files is discussed in Chapter 9. You can look up other input functions in the "DOS Reference Section" at the end of this book.

Mouse

As you look at computer systems, you will find increasing use of a mouse (or some equivalent device, such as a roller ball) as part of the computer systems. Furthermore, you will find that more and more software depends on a mouse for its effective use. Microsoft Windows can be used with the keyboard, but the graphics interface is much easier to use with a mouse. And although programs such as Microsoft's Paint (which runs under Windows) *can* be used with a keyboard, doing so is almost impossible. Guide ® (Owl International's Hypertext system) simply cannot be used without a mouse.

DOS does not include a mouse driver. Although Microsoft chose to include a light pen driver (not used in many software packages) and a game paddle driver (not used in many business packages), they did not include a mouse driver. Nevertheless, a discussion of the mouse is appropriate to this book.

For protection in case of a wrong guess, Microsoft allowed new drivers to be added easily to the system. One of these drivers, Microsoft's MOUSE.SYS, is added to the operating system when you boot the system. (MOUSE.SYS is provided by Microsoft if you purchase one of their mice.) In this section, we see how the mouse software works.

How the Mouse Works

The mouse is one of the truly simple pieces of equipment that can be attached to a computer. It consists of virtually nothing more than a little ball inside a "mouse" that rolls on a flat surface. As the ball rotates, circuitry in the mouse reports the movement to the computer, which interprets and translates that movement into movement of the mouse cursor on the screen.

Initializing the Mouse Driver

Depending on which software you have, you may have one of several ways to set up the mouse driver. Some packages create a TSR to handle the mouse; others have a driver. If you have a driver, you install it on the system by including in your CONFIG.SYS file a line that tells the system to load the driver when it boots. Use the following line:

DEVICE =C:\MOUSE.SYS

if you have Microsoft's mouse driver stored in the root directory on drive C:.

Where Is the Mouse?

First, your program must determine whether a mouse is installed. Int 33h, Function 0 tells you that a mouse is available if AX is nonzero on return. If you know that a mouse is available, you can use it by periodically polling it for changes in position and key clicks.

Because the mouse driver takes care of the mouse cursor's on-screen position, your program doesn't have to do so. You simply need to know that the mouse is positioned where users want something done. The sample program MOUSE.C, which is based on KEYIN3.C, shows how you can the check the mouse while you wait for other input (see listing 6.10).

Listing 6.10

```
/* Mouse.c--Demonstrates the mouse integrated with
 * keyboard operation
 */

#include <stdio.h>
#include <dos.h>

#define CTRL_D   0x04
#define LF       0x0a
#define ENTER    0x0d

main()
{
    int c;
```

Listing 6.10 continues

Listing 6.10 continued

```
        printf("Testing Mouse Input\n");
        chk_mouse();
        while ((c = keyin())!=CTRL_D)
            if (c >= 256) {
                printf("SPECIAL: %d\n",c - 256);
            } else {
                putchar(c);
                if (c == ENTER)
                    putchar(LF);
            }
}

keyin()
/* Inputs a single character from the keyboard.
 * The interrupt automatically echoes the character to
 * the display ... special characters (those with no
 * ASCII code) are returned as integers with an
 * offset of 256.
 */

{
    union REGS regs;
    int offset;

    while (!charwait())
        mousepos();
    offset = 0;
    regs.h.ah = 0x08;
    intdos(&regs,&regs);
    if (regs.h.al == 0) {
        offset = 256;
        regs.h.ah = 0x08;
        intdos(&regs,&regs);
    }
    return(regs.h.al + offset);
}

charwait()
/* Watches for a character at the keyboard: returns TRUE
 * if there is one; otherwise, returns FALSE.
 */
{
    union REGS regs;
```

Listing 6.10 continues

Listing 6.10 *continued*

```
    regs.h.ah = ØxØb;
    intdos(&regs,&regs);
    return(regs.h.al);
}

#define MOUSE Øx33

static int mouse = Ø;

chk_mouse()


/* Checks for the presence of a mouse, sets the
 * static variable mouse to the number of buttons.
 * If mouse is zero, then chk_mouse didn't find
 * a mouse installed. If it finds a mouse, it
 * turns it on for use.
 */

{
    union REGS regs;

    regs.x.ax = Ø;
    int86(MOUSE,&regs,&regs);
    if (regs.x.ax != Ø) {
        mouse = regs.x.bx;
        regs.x.ax = ØxØ1;
        int86(MOUSE,&regs,&regs);
    }
}

/* Checks the current position of the mouse and
 * prints position and button status to the screen.
 * If no mouse is installed, prints NO MOUSE.
 */
mousepos()
  {
    union REGS regs;
    char buttons[6];

    gotoxy(12,1Ø);
    if (mouse) {
        regs.x.ax = ØxØ3;
        int86(MOUSE,&regs,&regs);
        switch(regs.x.bx & ØxØ3) {
            case Ø:    /* no buttons */
```

Listing 6.10 *continues*

Listing 6.10 *continued*

```
                    strcpy(buttons,"NONE ");
                    break;
            case 1:     /* left button */
                    strcpy(buttons,"LEFT ");
                    break;
            case 2:     /* right button */
                    strcpy(buttons,"RIGHT");
                    break;
            case 3:     /* both buttons */
                    strcpy(buttons,"BOTH ");
                    break;
        }
        printf("X = %4.4d Y = %4.4d %s",
            regs.x.cx,regs.x.dx,buttons);
    } else {
        printf("NO MOUSE");
    }
}

#define VIDEO 0x10

/* Positions the cursor to the designated row
 * column position.
 */
gotoxy(row,col)

int row, col;

{
    union REGS regs;

    if (row < 0 || row > 24) return;
    if (col < 0 || col > 79) return;

    regs.h.ah = 2;
    regs.h.bh = 0;
    regs.h.dh = row;
    regs.h.dl = col;
    int86(VIDEO,&regs,&regs);
}
```

MOUSE.C includes function chk_mouse( ), which checks for the existence of a mouse. Instead of printing periods as it waits for input, the program moves the cursor to the center of the screen and displays information about the mouse's position and buttons.

If you have a mouse installed, move it around and watch the mouse status change to reflect the mouse's movement. Within these basic functions is a minimum level of operability for mouse functions. The function gotoxy( ), which uses the BIOS screen-addressing routines to position the cursor on-screen, also has been added to program MOUSE.C. (Chapter 5 explains how this function operates.)

The sample program includes only three basic mouse functions. The first, which determines whether a mouse is installed and how many buttons it has, sets the number of buttons into a global variable. When other mouse functions are called, they can check this variable to determine whether they have anything to do.

If a mouse *is* installed, you call the second function (Int 33h, Function 1) to display the mouse cursor on-screen. With the mouse available, you call Int 33h, Function 3 to check for the mouse status (position and button status) whenever you check for (but don't find) a character. This function returns the status of the buttons coded into the bottom two bits of the BX register. If bit 0 is set, the left button has been pressed; if bit 1 is set, the right button has been pressed.

The mouse's position on-screen is always given in the range 0 to 639 across the screen (x coordinate) and 0 to 199 down the screen (y coordinate). Depending on the current display mode, you can determine from table 6.3 the mouse's position in terms of columns or coordinates.

Table 6.3. Mouse Coordinates

Screen Mode	Coordinates
0 to 1	row = DX/8, col = CX/16
2 to 3	row = DX/8, col = DX/8
4 to 5	x = CX/2, y = DX
6	x = CX, y = DX
7	row = DX/8, col = CX/8
14 to 16	x = CX, y = DX

Additional mouse functions (described in the "Mouse Reference Section" at the end of this book) help you control the size, shape, and on-screen boundaries of the mouse cursor, as well as the speed of on-screen movement in response to that of the mouse. You also can set a function to be called whenever a mouse event (such as a key press or release) occurs. You will learn about this type of routine, called an interrupt handler, in Chapter 11.

Summary

In this chapter we have looked at keyboard and mouse functions and learned some basic operations that can be used to implement input functions. By using the keyboard functions available through the BIOS, you can tell which keys are pressed on the keyboard and keep track of operations. You can see not only the ASCII codes for character input (like those returned from high-level language input functions) but also the scan codes, which are returned only for some keys. And you can monitor the position of the Shift, Alt, Ctrl, Scroll Lock, Num Lock, and Caps Lock keys.

Using the mouse functions on DOS Int 33h, you can monitor the position of the keys on the mouse as well as the position of the mouse on the screen. You can even set interrupts for mouse functions that execute special handlers whenever mouse events (such as a key click) occur.

7

Serial Devices

The modern computing world's serial devices are fascinating. Thanks to serial devices we can communicate effectively with many different people around the world through such services as CompuServe® or MCI Mail. Why serial devices work the way they do and how you can exploit their properties is the subject of this chapter.

Throughout this chapter, we will be working with serial devices in terms of communications with other computers—the most visible use of such communications today. Serial communications can be used also with printers, sensors, and many other devices, and the communications need not be two-way. Communications with printers, for example, are predominantly one-way—from computer to printer. Or you might build a program to read the Associated Press news wire (a 1,200 bps [bits per second] one-way data feed) or the NOAA weather wire (50 bps, one-way).

This chapter concentrates on two-way terminal communication, which embodies all aspects of serial communication. Before you write a terminal program, however, you should understand how the serial interface works.

After defining some basic terminology, I provide specifics about the way the IBM PC's serial interface chip (the 8250) works. Then the discussion focuses on how to control the chip directly.

With the groundwork laid, we will write two terminal programs. The first one uses the BIOS functions to access the serial port. You will find that such a program, however practical, is too slow for serious communications except at speeds under 1200 baud. You can gain some speed and control by working directly with the 8250 chip. The second terminal program illustrates this technique, but even this program is too slow for practical communications at 1200 baud. For a truly practical communications program, however, you will have to wait for Chapter 11, which introduces interrupt processing.

Serial Interfaces

Fundamentally, a serial interface transforms the computer's internal, parallel format of data (an 8-bit byte) into a serial format (one bit) that can be transmitted over a single data line. This transformation can be done by software; in a PC, however, it is done more effectively by hardware.

Figure 7.1 illustrates the basic purpose of a serial interface: to convert information from parallel to serial format or from serial to parallel format. Data enters one side of the interface and emerges, translated, from the other side. The interface converts data to a serial format by converting each character into a "packet" of information that can be transmitted in a way agreed upon by both the sender and the receiver. (Serial format will be discussed shortly in greater detail.) Computers can communicate successfully with one another only if each end of the *serial link* (the serial connection between two computers or between a computer and another device) uses the same format for the data and the same transmission speed.

Fig. 7.1. *A serial interface converts the format of data from parallel (in) to serial (out).*

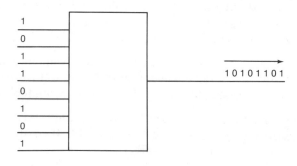

Two methods of transmitting serial information are generally accepted. Both are named for the timing method that *paces* the information transmitted and received over the serial link. The first method, called *synchronous communications*, maintains rigid control of transmission and reception of data through the link. In this process, data is transmitted at precisely timed intervals. The clocking information is transmitted with the data so that the receiving computer can be synchronized with the information received. This type of communications link, which generally is used in mini- or mainframe computer applications, is beyond the scope of this book.

In the second method, called *asynchronous communication*, individual information packets are placed on the communications line with no precisely defined timing between them. These data packets can be transmitted quickly, one after another, or with varying time delays between each transmission. The asynchronous communication method is native to most microcomputers, including the IBM family.

Although you can buy hardware interfaces that allow other types of serial communication (such as the previously mentioned synchronous method), asynchronous communications should suffice for most general-purpose needs.

Figure 7.2 is a graphic representation of a serial information packet (as a function of time for asynchronous communications) on a communications line. The line usually is kept in a *mark* state (high voltage). The start of a character (the start bit) is signaled by a drop to the *space* state (low voltage). To determine whether the next bit is high or low, the line is sampled at precisely timed intervals based on the bit rate. The data bits are followed by one or more stop bits, in *mark state*, which allow sufficent time for the character to be processed and for the system to get ready for the next character.

Fig. 7.2. Serial transmission.

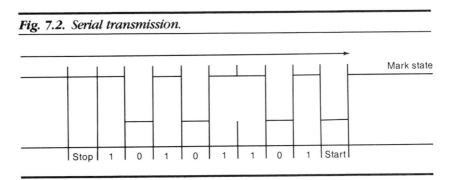

In preparation for a more detailed discussion of asynchronous communications, I want to be sure that you understand the basic communications terminology. As you will recall, a serial interface converts parallel data into packets of information that can be transmitted easily through a serial communications link. These packets are made up of a specific number of bits of information, each with a specific purpose: start bits, data bits, stop bits, and parity. Definitions of these and a few other critical terms follow:

❑ *Start bit:* A bit sent before the actual character data to alert the receiving computer that a character is coming. Start bits are sent automatically by the serial device.

❑ *Data bits:* The bits representing the individual character being transmitted. (The number of data bits is often referred to as the *word length*.) Normal communications to serial devices use a word length of either seven bits if parity is computed (see the following definition) or eight bits if no parity is computed. The serial communications chip on an IBM PC can handle from five to eight data bits.

❑ *Parity:* A simple character-level "goodness" check in which the receiver tests to see whether the character was received correctly. Parity is computed by counting the number of bits set to 1 in the data portion of the information packet being transmitted and then appending a parity bit representative of the type of parity you want. For EVEN parity, the total number of data bits set to 1 plus the parity bit must result in an even number. Conversely, for ODD parity, the number of data bits set to 1 plus the parity bit must result in an odd number. Other possible settings for the parity bit include MARK (always set to 1), SPACE (always set to 0), or NONE (always ignored).

❑ *Stop bits:* The bits sent at the end of the information packet to give the receiver time to process a character before the next one arrives. One stop bit is normal for all communications you are likely to handle. (Two stop bits are needed only when communications occur at extremely slow speeds, such as 110 bps).

❑ *Baud rate:* An electrical term that represents the signaling (or transfer) rate of a communications line. This term frequently is used interchangeably (albeit incorrectly) with the bit rate.

❑ *Bit rate:* The transmission speed, expressed as bits per second (bps), and frequently referred to as the baud rate. Bit rate, the more accurate term, is used in this book.

❑ *Full duplex:* A means of communication in which the information displayed on your screen is an echo of the character you have transmitted to a remote computer

❑ *Half duplex:* A means of communication in which the information sent to a remote computer is not echoed back to your computer

When one computer communicates with another, both machines must operate by a set of predefined parameters that define the format in which information is transferred. If both computers are not set to the same values, communication between them will not be reliable. One reason that communications between computers are less widespread than they might be is that those of us who work with computers have been unable to agree on a standard for communications between computers (without involving users in specialized, frustrating terminology).

Several configurations, however, are fairly standard. Generally, either eight data bits, no parity, and one stop bit or seven data bits, EVEN or ODD parity, and one stop bit will work. The bit rate for most on-line computer systems is fairly well established at 300, 1,200, or 2,400 bps.

If you try one of these configurations, you almost always can match one of the on-line computer systems. But some systems are not always what they seem to be. For example, a computer system advertising seven bits, EVEN parity was best accessed with seven bits, ODD parity. In this case, the results of determining the cause of the problem were not worth the cost of the equipment needed to determine it. If a configuration works, use it.

After an information packet has been transmitted, timing is critical. The communication line is idle until the start bit is received. After the start bit arrives, the line has to be sampled at precise intervals in order to receive the individual bits that make up the character. The parity bit, which is used to calculate the correctness of the transmitted character, follows the data. Finally, the stop bits are received and discarded, and the receiver again waits for a start bit.

If this background information has confused you—relax. IBM microcomputers are equipped with hardware that manages the low-level details of serial communication. After you have determined which communications parameters to use and have entered that information, the serial-conversion hardware ensures that you get what you want.

PC Serial Conversion: The 8250 UART

IBM microcomputers (and most compatibles) use a hardware chip that is based on the Intel 8250 Asynchronous Communications Controller, also known as UART (Universal Asynchronous Receiver Transmitter). Compared to some systems that rely on software to manage their communications properly, the UART is a wonder. By attending to the details of receiving and transmitting bits of information, the UART frees the programmer for other tasks.

Suppose that you want to send data across a series of wires while the voltage level on the line changes. If you were to write a program to manage the line, you could control the line directly and signal anything you wanted. Sound difficult? In concept, it isn't. But the process is tedious and subject to subtle errors. Some systems (the original TRS-80 Color Computer, for example) can handle serial communications only in this way.

With the 8250 UART, you don't have to go to the trouble of programming a software controller to get data on to and off of a communications line. For much less effort than you would spend writing and testing a software UART, the UART chip gives you an enormous amount of control and allows rapid, standard communications with other devices.

Each 8250 has 10 programmable 1-byte registers that control and monitor the serial port. Most of these registers are for initialization, and only a few are used regularly. All of the registers are accessed through seven I/O port addresses. These addresses are calculated as an offset from a base address that varies according to which communications port is used. The base addresses for COM1: through COM4: are shown in table 7.1; the offsets from these addresses, which control each UART register, are listed in table 7.2.

Table 7.1. Base Addresses for the IBM Communications Ports

Communications Port	Base Address
COM1:	03F8h
COM2:	02F8h
COM3:	03E8h
COM4:	02E8h

Table 7.2. 8250 Registers: Offset from Base Address

Offset	LSR Bit 7	Meaning
0	0	Transmitter holding register (THR) and receiver data register (RDR)
0	1	Baud rate divisor, low byte (BRDL)
1	1	Baud rate divisor, high byte (BRDH)
1	0	Interrupt enable register (IER)
2	?	Interrupt identification register (IIR)
3	?	Line control register (LCR)
4	?	Modem control register (MCR)
5	?	Line status register (LSR)
6	?	Modem status register (MSR)

Although the 8250 UART has 10 registers to control its operation, there are only seven port addresses for these 10 registers. Three of the seven addresses serve more than one register. At offset 0, the THR is accessed whenever you *write* to the port, and the RDR is accessed whenever you *read* from the port. Because neither register requires both *read* and *write* access, this combination makes sense.

Register offsets 0 and 1 are made to serve another function when bit 7 of the LSR is set to 1. When this happens, these two ports access the BRD registers. (Because the BRD registers are accessed only during initialization of the chip, they can be kept safely out of the way during normal operations.)

Let's look at what each 8250 register does.

The Transmitter Holding Register (THR)

The THR holds the byte of data that is about to be sent. You write data to this register when bit 5 of the line status register (LSR) indicates that the register is empty.

The Receiver Data Register (RDR)

The RDR holds the byte of data most recently received from the communications line. You read this register when LSR bit 0 indicates that a byte has been received.

The Baud Rate Divisor (BRD)

This 16-bit number, which specifies the bit transfer rate used by the UART, is divided between two 8-bit ports (BRDL and BRDH). To determine the bit transfer rate, you divide the UART's internal clock rate (1.8432 MHz) by the BRD, as in the following formula:

$$BRD = \frac{\text{clock speed}}{16 \times \text{desired bps}}$$

If you use this formula, determining the settings for different bit speeds is easy. For example, you can calculate the BRD for 1,200 bps as follows:

$$BRD = \frac{1843200}{16 \times 1200} = \frac{1843200}{19200} = 96 = 0060h$$

Thus, BRDH must be set to 0, and BRDL to 60h.

You can use the equation to construct the BRD for the typical bit rates listed in table 7.3.

Table 7.3. Baud Rate Divisors

Bit Rate	BRDH	BRDL
50	09h	00h
110	04h	17h
300	01h	80h
1200	00h	60h
2400	00h	30h
4800	00h	18h
9600	00h	0Ch
19200	00h	06h

Note: IBM cautions users of its early versions of BIOS not to set the baud rate (*bit rate*) above 9,600 bps. But you can safely drive the 8250 UART at rates of 19,200 bps (or even higher).

To set the BRD, you first must set bit 7 of the line control register (LCR) to 1. Then you can safely output the required divisors to their I/O locations (refer to table 7.2). After you have set the BRD, good practice dictates that you immediately clear bit 7 of the LCR.

The Interrupt Enable Register (IER)

The IER controls the type of interrupts generated by the UART. You can enable one or more interrupts at a time, depending on how you have written your interrupt handler. Note that whenever an interrupt is enabled, a specific action must be taken to clear it. Table 7.4 shows the assignments of interrupts to bits in the register and the appropriate action needed to clear each interrupt.

Table 7.4. *Interrupt Enable Register*

Bit	Activates	Action
0	Data received	Read RDR
1	THR empty	Output to THR
2	Data error or break	Read LSR
3	MSR change	Read MSR
4–7	Unused, always set to zero	

Interrupts are generated when one of the activating conditions shown in table 7.4 occurs and the corresponding IER bit is set to 1.

The Interrupt Identification Register (IIR)

When an interrupt occurs, a communications program can identify it from the interrupt identification register's bit settings. Table 7.5 lists the meanings of these bits.

Table 7.5. *Interrupt Identification Register*

Bit	Meaning
0	More than one interrupt has occurred
1–2	Interrupt ID
	00 = Change in modem status register (MSR)
	01 = Transmitter holding register (THR) empty
	10 = Data received
	11 = Data reception error or break

If your software is interrupt driven, you first must specify the type of interrupts you want to generate (refer to table 7.4). Then, after an interrupt request is received, you must examine the IIR to see what type of interrupt actually occurred. Again, this process is described in greater detail in Chapter 11.

The Line Control Register (LCR)

The line control register is the primary control register for the serial line. Table 7.6 details the bit assignments for this register.

Table 7.6. *Line Control Register*

Bit	Meaning	Settings	Notes
0–1	Character length		
	5 bits	00	
	6 bits	01	
	7 bits	10	
	8 bits	11	
2	Stop Bits		
	1 bit	0	
	1.5 bits	1	If using 5-bit characters
	2 bits	1	If using 6-, 7-, or 8-bit characters
3–5	Parity		
	IGNORE	000	
	ODD	100	
	EVEN	110	
	MARK	101	
	SPACE	111	
6	Break Condition		
	Disabled	0	
	Enabled	1	
7	Port Toggle		
	Normal	0	Use THR/RDR and IER registers
	Alternate	1	Use BRDL and BRDH registers

The Modem Control Register (MCR)

The MCR sets control lines to the modem and, through these lines, tells the modem that the computer is ready to send and/or receive characters. Table 7.7 gives the bit assignments for this register.

Table 7.7. *Modem Control Register*

Bit	Meaning
0	Set DTR line active
1	Set RTS line active
2	User output #1
3	User output #2
4	UART loopback
5–7	Unused, set to zero

The data terminal ready (DTR) line tells the modem that the computer is powered on and ready to receive information from the modem. The request to send (RTS) line tells the modem that the computer is ready to send something to the line. Ordinarily, you can safely set both DTR and RTS to 1 to turn on these lines. Some modems ignore (or can be set to ignore) these signals, but older modems cannot be set to ignore them. Bit 2 (user output #1), which is tied to the interrupt servicing for the 8250, can block interrupt handling. Bit 3 is used only by specialized hardware (such as the Hayes Smartmodem internal board, which uses bit 3 to reset the modem). Bit 4 allows testing of a communications program without any over-the-line communications. In this *loopback* state, data that you send out the port reappears as input.

The Line Status Register (LSR)

The LSR gives you the status of the communication line (see table 7.8). From this register, you can determine information about the status (the condition) of the individual characters being sent or received over the communications line. Then, from this information, you can diagnose common line problems.

Table 7.8. *Line Status Register*

Bit	Meaning
0	Data received, byte in RDR
1	Overrun error occurred because the previous byte was not read before the next byte arrived
2	Parity error
3	Framing error occurred because the transmission was not in sync (no stop bit was found after the character had been read).
4	Break detect
5	THR is empty, OK to output a character to the line
6	Transmitter shift register (TSR) empty. (The TSR takes the character from the THR and places it on the line, one bit at a time.)
7	Time out

The Modem Status Register (MSR)

The modem's status depends on whether a certain status line is high or low and whether the status on a specified line has changed since the last register read. Table 7.9 shows how the bits are assigned.

Table 7.9. *Modem Status Register*

Bit	Meaning
0	Change in clear to send (CTS)
1	Change in data set ready (DSR)
2	Change in ring indicator (RI)
3	Change in data carrier detect (DCD)
4	Clear to send (CTS) set high
5	Data set ready (DSR) set high
6	Ring indicator (RI) set high
7	Data carrier detect (DCD) set high

The modem signals correspond to changes in the status of an electrical signal line connecting the computer and the serial device. Depending on the device, these hardware signals may or may not be used. Some modems make no use of them and rely solely on the Hayes command set to handle communications. Because your modem (or other serial device) may use modem signals, their meaning is described in table 7.10.

Table 7.10. *Modem Signals*

Signal	Meaning
CTS	Clear to send: The modem is ready to receive characters from the computer.
DSR	Data set ready: The modem is powered on and ready to operate.
RI	Ring indicator: The telephone line is ringing. As the line rings, RI is held high (electrically) so that your computer can detect the rings.
DCD	Data carrier detect: The modem is connected to another modem.

Initializing the Communications Port

Working directly with the 8250 serial controller is not as easy as it may seem. Even initialization can become a complex operation that depends on sequencing registers in the correct order to produce a specific effect. However, direct control of the chip offers more options than any other method of controlling the serial line. Direct programming of the 8250 UART is beyond the scope of this book—an entire book could be dedicated to the subject.

For many programs (even those that intend to access the 8250 directly), you do not have to initialize the UART directly. You can control initialization through a BIOS function designed to simplify the task. In this area of programming (as elsewhere), never make more work for yourself than you have to.

To access the BIOS function that initializes a communications port, you load the AH register with 0 and you load DX with a zero-based number that represents the communications port to be initialized (thus, 0 =COM1:, 1 =COM2:, 2 =COM3:, and 3 =COM4:). Because some versions of the IBM BIOS do not intrinsically support four communications ports, you may be limited to a DX setting of either 0 or 1. All of the PS/2 series of computers support four communications ports.

Finally, you load AL with the initialization parameters you want; each bit has a significant purpose. Table 7.11 lists the possible AL settings.

Table 7.11. BIOS Communications Port Initialization Settings for AL

Bit	Meaning	Settings
0–1	Word length	
	Not used	00
	Not used	01
	7 bits	10
	8 bits	11
2	Stop bits	
	1 bit	0
	2 bits	1
3–4	Parity	
	NONE	00
	ODD	01
	NONE	10
	EVEN	11
5–7	Bit rate	
	110 bps	000
	150 bps	001
	300 bps	010
	600 bps	011
	1200bps	100
	2400bps	101
	4800 bps	110
	9600 bps	111

After you have loaded AH, AL, and DX with the necessary values, issue an Int 14h; the communications port will be set according to your specifications. (For a summary of the register settings necessary for this BIOS function, see table 7.14. Further information on this function is available in the BIOS Reference Section at the end of this book.)

As you can see from table 7.11, you cannot set a data length of 5 or 6 bits, nor can you set a bit rate below 110 bps or above 9,600 bps. Your initialization options are quite limited for certain applications. For example, when you try to tie in to a specialized application such as the NOAA weather wire, which is 50 bps with a 5-bit word length, your only option is to initialize the communications port through direct manipulation of the UART registers.

The IBM PS/2 series computers have another BIOS function that provides an additional degree of control over your communications interface. You access this function by loading the AH register with 4 and, as in the normal BIOS function, loading DX with a zero-based number that represents the communications port to be initialized. Next, AL is set to either 0 or 1, depending on whether you want a break condition on the line. Ordinarily, AL is set to 0 (0 =no break). BH must be set to the desired parity, as outlined in table 7.12.

Table 7.12. *Parity Settings for BH (Function 14/4)*

Setting	Parity Meaning
0	NONE
1	ODD
2	EVEN
3	MARK
4	SPACE

BL must be set to the number of stop bits you want: 0 represents 1 stop bit, and 1 represents either 1.5 (for a 5-bit data length) or 2 (for 6-, 7-, or 8-bit data lengths) stop bits.

The data length is specified in CH, with the value in CH equaling five less than the number of data bits required. Thus, a value of 0 represents five data bits, and a value of 3 equals eight data bits.

Finally, CL is loaded with the bit rate you want. This value is determined by the settings detailed in table 7.13.

Table 7.13. *Bit Rate Settings for CL (Function 14/4)*

Setting	Bit Rate
0	110 bps
1	150 bps
2	300 bps
3	600 bps
4	1200 bps
5	2400 bps
6	4800 bps
7	9600 bps
8	19200 bps

After you have loaded all of the registers (AH, AL, BH, BL, CH, CL, and DX), issue an Int 14h to set the communications port as specified. Table 7.14 summarizes the register settings needed for the two BIOS functions presented in this section. Further information about these functions is available in the BIOS Reference Section at the end of this book.

Table 7.14. *Summary of BIOS Communications Port Initialization Functions*

Function	Parameter	Notes and Possible Settings
AH =0	AL	Set according to information in table 7.11.
	DX	Communications port desired: 0 (COM1:) through 3 (COM4:)
AH =4		**(Works only on PS/2 series)**
	AL	Break condition setting
	BH	Parity
	BL	Stop bits
	CH	Word length
	CL	Bit rate
	DX	Communications port desired: 0 (COM1:) through 3 (COM4:)

Note: To access all of these functions, load a function value into AH before you call interrupt 14h.

Despite the BIOS's capabilities for initializing communication ports, you may have to access the UART directly if you cannot set a certain register (through the BIOS function) to a value you need. Before you make the assumption that "BIOS can't do it," try to work with the BIOS initialization functions—you may find them more than adequate.

Modems

Modem is a contraction of the term *modulator-demodulator*. Although detailed instructions about using a specific modem are beyond the scope of this book, some general observations should be made.

First, most modems are advertised as Hayes compatible, which means that all modem control is in the command sequences (character strings) sent to the modem rather than in the modem control lines. Many sophisticated terminal programs use these Hayes command sequences to communicate with the modem; these programs can program the modem's many functions directly. All you have to do is tell the program what you want.

If your modem uses the modem control lines instead of a string command set, you will be able to control the modem only by manipulating the modem control lines directly at the BIOS or hardware level. The BIOS and DOS functions generally do a good job of hiding these control lines from your program, which means that you have to go directly to the 8250 UART to control them.

You don't need a modem for all serial communications. In most offices with serial connections to a central computer, for example, the connections can be wired directly to a PC if the central computer and the PC are fairly close to each other. Technically, they should be no more than 150 feet apart, although runs of up to 400 feet can work if no outside interference exists. And you also can run printers and serial devices without a modem if they meet the cable-length requirements.

To communicate through a telephone line you *must* use a modem. The bandwidth of most telephone systems is relatively limited (300 to 3000 Hz). The output from the 8250 UART is a series of square waves that will be distorted beyond recognition if you try to send them, unaltered, through a telephone line. The result would be no communication at all. A modem translates the square wave output from an 8250 UART into a series of tones that fall within the telephone line's bandwidth.

Older, slower modems translated the output simply: one tone corresponded to 0, another to 1. The newer, faster modems use not only tones but also multiplexing, phasing, and other electrical-signal components to pass a greater volume of information through a line.

Writing a Terminal Program

Now that you have seen how the 8250 UART functions and how modems work, you are almost ready to design a simple terminal program. But before you begin, you should be aware of several other considerations.

A communications program can be implemented in two ways. The first uses a polling method: your program periodically checks the serial port to determine whether an incoming character is available. If a character is available, you can process it and continue. The second method, which is more efficient in terms of computer time, is based on interrupts: you and the computer work until interrupted by the UART when an incoming character is available. You process the character and then return to the task you were working on before the interruption.

Only the polling method of serial interfacing is described in this chapter. The interrupt method is discussed in greater detail in Chapter 11.

Duplex Considerations

Before you can use the polling method of serial control, you must decide whether you want your communications to be full duplex or half duplex. You may recall from the terms introduced earlier in this chapter that in full-duplex communications, every character sent over the communications link is echoed back from the remote computer. A character that you see on-screen is the character received by the other computer, echoed back (or retransmitted) by the other computer. These characters travel in both directions simultaneously—you can send characters to the remote computer while it sends others back. Therefore, the outline for a full-duplex implementation of a simple terminal program is as follows:

1. If a character is at the keyboard, send it.

2. If a character is at the serial port, display it.

3. Go to Step 1.

Although most computers use full-duplex communications, some use half duplex (characters travel in only one direction at a time). Because the remote computer does not echo back (retransmit) the characters it receives, the concept of a half-duplex terminal program differs from that of the full-duplex version in only one minor point:

1. If a character is at the keyboard, send *and* display it.

2. If a character is at the serial port, display it.

3. Go to Step 1.

The differences in implementation rest in the coding section that handles getting a character from the keyboard. In the next section, you will see how your coding is affected.

The Controlling Program: Term.c

Implementation of the communications program at the highest conceptual level is quite simple. The following program, written in C, implements the basic concepts discussed so far in this chapter.

Listing 7.1

```
/* Term.c */

/*******************************************************

PROGRAM:  term.c
PURPOSE:  Demonstrates simple serial communications
*******************************************************/
#include <stdio.h>

#define FALSE Ø
#define TRUE !FALSE

main()
{
    cls();
    printf("Simple Terminal Program\n\n\n");
    setup();
    while(TRUE){
        if(!keybd())
            exit(Ø);
        serial();
    }
}
```

Except for clearing the terminal screen (accomplished by the cls() function) and setting up the port (through the setup() function), this is a simple application of the terminal procedure. It repeats forever, alternately retrieving characters from the keyboard (with the keybd() function) or from the serial port (with the serial() function).

Notice that, as all reasonable programs should, this program provides a way to end the program—if the keyboard-handling routine ever returns FALSE, the program ends. (As you will see in listing 7.4, the keyboard function has been programmed to return FALSE whenever the Shift-F1 key combination is pressed.)

Supporting Functions

Let's look at each of the supporting functions. Two versions of the keybd( ) function are provided: one handles full-duplex operation and the other handles half-duplex. Use whichever fits your needs.

Initialization: Setup( )

Setup( ), the first user-developed function, initializes the serial port. As presented here, the function uses a simplified, hard-coded setup for 1200 baud, 8 bits, no parity, and 1 stop bit. Listing 7.2 shows how this setup is implemented.

Listing 7.2

```
/* Setup.c */

#include  <stdio.h>
#include  <dos.h>

#define    COM1      Ø
#define    RS232     Øx14
#define    SETUP     Øx83

setup()

/********************************************************
    Sets up the COM1 port with a standard setup string
    12ØØ baud, 8 bits, no parity, 1 stop bit
********************************************************/

{
    union REGS regs;
    printf("Setup the serial port\n");
    regs.h.ah = Ø;
    regs.x.dx = COM1;
    regs.h.al = SETUP;
    int86(RS232, &regs, &regs);
}
```

As the program comments state, setup( ) initializes COM1: to 1,200 bps, an 8-bit word length, no parity, and 1 stop bit. Setup( ) uses the basic BIOS communications-port initialization function presented earlier in this chapter.

An Initialization Alternative

The setup( ) function in listing 7.2 is not flexible—it can be used only to set the serial port to one specific bit rate and data format. As an alternative, you can create a more flexible setup( ) function to handle multiple initialization parameters (see listing 7.3).

Listing **7.3**

```
/* Setup.c */

#include  <stdio.h>
#include  <dos.h>

#define    RS232          Øx14

#define    B3ØØ           Øx4Ø
#define    B12ØØ          Øx8Ø
#define    B24ØØ          ØxaØ

#define    NOPARITY       ØxØØ
#define    EVEN           Øx18
#define    ODD            ØxØ8

#define    WORD7          ØxØ2
#define    WORD8          ØxØ3

#define    STOP1          ØxØØ
#define    STOP2          Øx4Ø

setup(port,baud,word,parity,stop)

/***********************************************************
     Sets up the port with the specified parameters.
     Performs error-checking on the input, and returns:
          Ø    Setup complete
          -1   Invalid COM port
          -2   Invalid baud rate
          -3   Invalid word length
          -4   Invalid parity
          -5   Invalid stop bits
***********************************************************/

int  port,          /* COM port, Ø=COM1, 1=COM2, etc.*/
     baud,          /* baud rate */
     word,          /* word length */
```

Listing **7.3** *continues*

Listing 7.3 *continued*

```
parity,          /* Ø = off, 1 = EVEN, 2 = ODD */
stop;            /* number of stop bits */

{
    union REGS regs;
    unsigned char setup;

    setup = Ø;
    printf("Setup the serial port\n");

    /*   Error check for allowable COM port */
    if(port!=Ø && port!=1)
        return(-1);

    /*   Allowed speeds are 3ØØ/12ØØ/24ØØ baud */
    switch(baud){
        case 3ØØ:
            setup |= B3ØØ;
            break;
        case 12ØØ:
            setup |= B12ØØ;
            break;
        case 24ØØ:
            setup |= B24ØØ;
            break;
        default:
            return(-2);
            break;
    }

    /*   Allowed word lengths are 7 or 8 bits */
    if(word==7)
        setup |= WORD7;
    else if(word==8)
        setup |= WORD8;
    else
        return(-3);

    /*   Allowed to have NO, EVEN, or ODD parity */
    if(parity==Ø)
        setup |= NOPARITY
    else if(parity==1)
        setup |= EVEN;
    else if(parity==2)
        setup |= ODD;
    else
        return(-4);
```

Listing 7.3 continues

Listing 7.3 *continued*

```
/*    Allowed to have 1 or 2 stop bits */
if(stop==1)
      setup  |= STOP1;
else if(stop==2)
      setup  |= STOP2;
else
      return(-5);

/*    Set up the port */
regs.h.ah = Ø;
regs.x.dx = port;
regs.h.al = setup;
int86(RS232, &regs, &regs);
return(Ø);
}
```

This longer version of setup( ) allows you to error-check each parameter and gives you greater flexibility in setting parameters. The version of term.c in listing 7.1 cannot use this alternate setup( ) function. It is written on the assumption that the setup values are built into the program. You can add it if you want to, but then you also must provide a means of setting the proper initialization parameters, either from the command line or as inputs to the program.

If you initialize a port other than COM1:, you must change also the other supporting functions—xmit( ), chrdy( ), rch( ), and loopback( )—to support other communications ports. For testing purposes, and until you feel comfortable with basic serial-port programming, you may want to use the limited version of setup( ) shown in listing 7.2 and then experiment later with the version in listing 7.3.

Keyboard Control: Keybd( )

Through the keybd( ) function, which manages the keyboard, you can determine whether a character has been entered at the keyboard and then, if it has, transmit the character (see listing 7.4).

Listing 7.4

```
/* Keybd.c */

#include  <stdio.h>
#include  <dos.h>
```

Listing 7.4 continues

Listing 7.4 continued

```
#define    FALSE      Ø
#define    TRUE       !FALSE
#define    SF1        84

keybd()

/***********************************************************
     Examines the keyboard for a keystroke. If there is one,
     reads it. Automatically handles multiple-character
     keystrokes ... Shift-F1 returns FALSE.
 ***********************************************************/

{
     char c;

     if((c=get_ch())>=Ø){
          /* There has been a keystroke */
          if(c == Ø){
          /* The first character was zero */
               if((c = get_ch())==SF1)
                    return(FALSE);
               return(TRUE);
          }
          /* Send the character */
          xmit(c);
     }
     return(TRUE);
}
```

Operation of the get_ch() function, which is integral to keybd() operation, is discussed in the following section. What you need to understand now is that if get_ch() returns a 0, a special character or key combination has been entered from the keyboard. In this case, get_ch() must be called again in order to retrieve the keyboard scan code of the key pressed.

Keybd() specifically looks for this special character value (a zero) and, if it finds the value, keybd() looks for a second character. If the second character is a Shift-F1, that character returns FALSE to the calling routine; if it is not a Shift-F1 (for example, if you pressed another special key combination or non-ASCII character), the value TRUE is returned and the character entry is ignored.

If you enter a normal ASCII value from the keyboard, the get_ch() function does not return a 0; the character is transmitted (as entered, without alteration) through the xmit() function.

Keybd( ) for Half-Duplex Communications

Only one additional line is necessary to make the keybd( ) function compatible with half-duplex operations. Insert the following line immediately after the line containing the xmit( ) function:

```
putscrn(c);
```

Basically, this function displays a character to the screen. (You will learn about the exact development and usage of putscrn(c) later in this chapter.)

I/O Control: Get_ch( ) and Xmit( )

Two functions support the basic keybd( ) function: get_ch( ), shown in listing 7.5, retrieves a character from the keyboard (if a character is available), and xmit( ) transmits a character through the serial port.

Listing 7.5

```
/* Get_ch.c */

#include  <stdio.h>
#include  <dos.h>

#define   MASK       Øx7f
#define   ZFLAG      Øx4Ø

get_ch()

/**********************************************************
      Reads a character from the keyboard
**********************************************************/

{
    union REGS regs;
    /*
          Int 21h Function 6 - Direct Console I/O

          AH = Function number
          DL = Function requested (FFH)

          Returns AL = Character
          Zero flag will indicate whether character was ready
    */
```

Listing 7.5 continues

Listing 7.5 continued

```
        regs.h.ah = 6;
        regs.h.dl = Øxff;
        intdos(&regs,&regs);
        if(regs.x.flags & ZFLAG)
                return(-1);
        return(regs.h.al & MASK);
}
```

Get_ch( ) uses the DOS direct console I/O function (see Chapter 6) to input characters. You may recall that this DOS function sets the zero flag (ZFLAG) to indicate whether a character is available. Get_ch( ) tests the ZFLAG to see whether a character is available. If a character is available, it is in AL; the function returns it to the calling routine with the high-order bit set to 0. (The high-order bit is stripped by ANDing it with the MASK value.) This masking process eliminates any possible problems with transmitting 8-bit characters.

Xmit.c( ), the other routine needed for the successful completion of keybd( ), is shown in listing 7.6.

Listing 7.6

```
/* Xmit.c */

#include <stdio.h>
#include <dos.h>

#define    RS232     Øx14
#define    WRITECH   1
#define    COM1      Ø

xmit(ch)

/***********************************************************
     Sends a character out the RS232 port
***********************************************************/

char ch;

{
     union REGS regs;
```

Listing 7.6 continues

Listing 7.6 *continued*

```
/*
        Int 14h Function 1 - Write character to communications port

        AH = Function number
        AL = Character to write
        DX = Comm port number (Ø = COM1)
*/
    regs.h.ah = WRITECH;
    regs.x.dx = COM1;
    regs.h.al = ch;
    int86(RS232, &regs, &regs);
}
```

The xmit( ) function simply writes the character to the serial port handler in the BIOS. As you can see from listing 7.6, this BIOS function requires the use of only three registers: AH contains the desired function number (1), AL is the character value to transmit (passed to xmit( ) by the calling routine, and DX is the communications port to use for the transmission (0, designating COM1:). For additional information about this BIOS function, see the BIOS Reference Section at the back of this book.

Receiving Characters: Serial( )

Now that you understand keybd( ), get_ch( ), and xmit( ), you are ready to examine the other major part of your terminal program—the part that receives and displays any incoming characters. Listing 7.7 shows this function, called serial( ).

Listing 7.7

```
/* Serial.c */

#include  <stdio.h>
#include  <dos.h>

serial()

/*********************************************************
    Checks for a character from the serial port. If one is
    available, gets it and displays it.
*********************************************************/
```

Listing 7.7 *continues*

Listing 7.7 continued

```
{
    char c;

    if(chrdy()){
        c = rch();
        putscrn(c);
    }
}
```

Let's examine each of the three functions necessary for the successful completion of serial(): chrdy(), rch(), and putscrn().

Serial Port Status: Chrdy()

Chrdy() checks whether an incoming character is available at the serial port. It uses BIOS Int 14h, Function 03h, which returns the communications port status. (For details about this BIOS function, see the BIOS Reference Section at the back of this book.) Listing 7.8 shows how chrdy() is implemented.

Listing 7.8

```
/* Chrdy.c */

#include <stdio.h>
#include <dos.h>

#define   RS232    Øx14
#define   STATUS   3
#define   COM1     Ø
#define   DTARDY   Øx1ØØ

chrdy()

/*********************************************************
    Checks to see whether a character is ready at COM1:.
    Returns TRUE if one is available, FALSE otherwise.
    This is accomplished by checking the Data Ready Bit
    returned by the BIOS function in register AH
*********************************************************/

{
    union REGS regs;
```

Listing 7.8 continues

Listing 7.8 continued

```
/*
        Int 14h Function 3 - Communications Port Status Request

        AH = Function number
        DX = Comm port number

        returns:
            AH = Port status
            AL = Modem status

        If bit Ø of AH = 1, then data is ready
*/
regs.h.ah = STATUS;
regs.x.dx = COM1;
int86(RS232, &regs, &regs);
return(regs.x.ax & DTARDY);
}
```

Accessing Received Characters: Rch( )

When chrdy( ) returns TRUE, informing you that a character is waiting, the
rch( ) function is used to retrieve the character (see listing 7.9).

Listing 7.9

```
/* Rch.c */

#include  <stdio.h>
#include  <dos.h>

#define    COM1     Ø
#define    RS232    Øx14
#define    READCH   2
#define    MASK     Øx7f

rch()

/********************************************************
    Reads character from the communications port
********************************************************/

{
    union REGS regs;

    /*
        Int 14h Function 2 - Read character from communications port
```

Listing 7.9 continues

Listing 7.9 *continued*

```
        AH = Function number
        DX = Comm port number (Ø = COM1)

        returns:
              AH bit 7 = Ø (successful)
              AL = Character

              AH bit 7 = 1 (error)
              AH bits Ø-6 = port status
    */
    regs.h.ah = READCH;
    regs.x.dx = COM1;
    int86(RS232, &regs, &regs);
    return(regs.h.al & MASK);
}
```

The high-order bit of the incoming character is stripped here, as it was in get_ch( ), by ANDing the value in AL with the MASK value.

Screen Display: Putscrn( ) and Put_ch( )

The final portion of serial( ) is the routine for displaying a character on-screen. Because only printable characters can be displayed, putscrn( ), shown in listing 7.10, is designed to ignore all control characters except carriage-return and line-feed.

Listing 7.10

```
/* Putscrn.c */

#include  <stdio.h>
#include  <dos.h>

#define   CR    ØxØd
#define   LF    ØxØa

putscrn(c)

/**********************************************************
    Displays printable characters on the screen.
    Control codes are ignored.
**********************************************************/
```

Listing 7.10 *continues*

***Listing 7.10** continued*

```
char c;

{
    if(c>=' ' || c==CR || c==LF)
        put_ch(c);
}
```

Putscrn( ) calls put_ch( ) to write the character to the display, using the basic character-out DOS function. (For a detailed description of this function, see the DOS Reference Section at the back of this book.) Listing 7.11 shows how put_ch( ) works.

Listing 7.11

```
/* Put_ch.c */

#include  <stdio.h>
#include  <dos.h>

#define   CHAROUT   2

put_ch(c)

/**********************************************************
    Puts a character to the screen
**********************************************************/

char c;

{
    union REGS regs;

    /*
        Int 21h Function 2 - Character output

        AH = Function number
        DL = Character
    */
    regs.h.ah = CHAROUT;
    regs.h.dl = c;
    intdos(&regs,&regs);
}
```

Using Term.c

Now that you have learned about each of the functions neeeded for term.c, enter them and try using term.c. You will discover that, although your computer can communicate with other computers, you may lose some of the incoming characters if more than a few arrive in quick succession. A short message of only one or two lines probably will overload the program. What's wrong?

Several problems exist:

❑ Because the terminal program has not been programmed for efficiency, it includes many subroutine calls—each of which eats time. You could speed it up by coding it with fewer individual functions.

❑ DOS function calls were used to handle the keyboard and screen. Although you are not likely to type faster than the characters can be read, the time spent on DOS function calls is time taken away from the needs of the serial channel.

❑ The BIOS function calls used are not spectacularly efficient.

Despite these problems, you will not change the program's basic design—its primary purpose is to show *how* to use the BIOS and DOS functions within the program. But you *can* speed up the program by changing it so that it can work directly with the 8250 chip.

Directly Accessing the 8250 UART

Direct UART access is one way to make the program tighter and faster, but you need to know when direct access is suitable and justifiable. You should be aware of some important trade-offs when you go directly to the UART.

Working directly at the hardware level:

❑ Results in the greatest speed increases you can get from the computer

❑ Provides the greatest programming flexibility

❏ Is the most machine-dependent type of programming and is most susceptible to compatibility problems when you transfer the program to another type of computer

IBM's promise to maintain serial-interface compatibility with the 8250 UART may be a great comfort if you work with computers produced by IBM. However, this promise is not a guarantee. Nor is it a safe bet when you work with other computers that use DOS. Although most of these computers currently use the 8250, be on the lookout for subtle differences in some models that use different UARTs.

As I mentioned in the preceding section, the version of term.c in listing 7.1 causes loss of incoming characters because that version cannot keep up with a steady stream of characters. Because they cannot get the required performance from the DOS or BIOS serial-interface functions, many programmers have solved this dilemma by always working directly with the 8250.

DOS designers seem to be trying to create an operating system that shields us from the machine in much the same way that large system operating systems do. Although this attempt is essential and understandable for a multiuser or multitasking system, most people currently use IBM microcomputers as individual workstations where responsiveness still is the most important factor.

To work directly with the 8250 chip, you must access it through I/O ports. Although some languages do not provide ways to access the I/O ports, every language used in this book does.

Assembly

In assembly language, you access the ports with the IN and OUT instructions: IN reads a word or byte into the AL or AX register; OUT writes a word or byte from the AL or AX register to the port. Variations in the OUT instruction include OUTS (BL or CX registers), OUTSB (byte from DS:[SI]), and OUTSW (word from DS:[SI]).

C

In Microsoft and Turbo C, the inport and outport functions input or output words to a port. Inportb and Outportb do the same for bytes.

BASIC

Basic functions INP and OUT read bytes from or write bytes to a port.

Pascal

Unlike the other languages, Pascal has no function for accessing the ports. Instead, Turbo Pascal treats the ports as an array (Port for bytes, Portw for words). Input and output to the port is accomplished by reading and writing to the array.

Modifying Term.c

To modify the terminal program, you simply change the three serial-port routines: chrdy(), xmit(), and rch(). You can (and will) safely leave control of the setup to the BIOS function.

When you access the 8250 directly, chrdy() is simplified considerably (see listing 7.12).

Listing 7.12

```
/* Chrdy.c */

#include  <stdio.h>

#define    COM1       Øx3f8
#define    LSR        5
#define    DTARDY     Øx01

chrdy()

/**********************************************************
    Checks to see whether a character is ready at COM1:.
    Returns TRUE if one is available, FALSE otherwise.
**********************************************************/

{
    return(inportb(COM1+LSR) & DTARDY);
}
```

The rch( ) function for reading a character also is simplified considerably (see listing 7.13).

Listing 7.13

```
/* Rch.c */

#include  <stdio.h>

#define   COM1        Øx3f8
#define   RDR         Ø
#define   MASK        Øx7f

rch( )

/*********************************************************
     Reads character from the communications port
*********************************************************/


{
     return(inportb(COM1+RDR) & MASK);
}
```

The modified xmit( ) function takes the form shown in listing 7.14.

Listing 7.14

```
/* Xmit.c */

#include  <stdio.h>

#define   COM1        Øx3f8
#define   LSR         5
#define   THR         Ø
#define   THRRDY      Øx2Ø

xmit(ch)

/*********************************************************
     Sends a character out the RS232 port
*********************************************************/

char ch;

{
     register int cnt;
```

Listing 7.14 continues

Listing 7.14 continued

```
    cnt = 0;
    while(!(inportb(COM1+LSR) & THRRDY) && cnt  < 10000) cnt++;
    if(cnt>=10000)
        return(-1);
    outportb(COM1+THR,ch);
    return(0);
}
```

The modified version of xmit( ) is slightly more complicated than the earlier version because you need to be sure that the transmitter holding register (THR) is ready for a character before you write one to that port. A maximum-retry counter is set to prevent the system from locking into an infinite loop.

The other term.c functions do not need to be modified to make the program work. My comments about the BIOS version of term.c and why it is slow still apply here. Even when you access the 8250 UART directly, you will not have enough speed to handle 1,200 bps without some problems.

In this instance, the problems are caused by the method used for handling the incoming serial characters. As you may recall, a polling method is used in the examples in this chapter. In other words, the program sequentially checks the keyboard and then the serial interface, ad infinitum. If a couple of characters arrive at the serial port while the program's attention is focused on the keyboard, those incoming characters may be lost before the program has a chance to record them.

Loopback Testing

When you use the modified version of term.c, you can add also a function that allows loopback testing. In other words, the UART will "think" that it is talking to a remote computer; what really happens is a local echo (within the UART) of what is being sent to the serial interface. The process is implemented as follows:

```
#include  <stdio.h>

#define   MCR        0x3fc
```

```
#define   LOOPBACK  Øx1Ø

loopback()

int  mcr_value;

/*      Toggles the status of the loopback bit in the modem
        control register.
*/
{
     printf("Toggling Loopback\n");
     inportb(MCR,mcr_value);
     mcr_value = mcr_value ^ LOOPBACK;
     outportb(MCR,mcr_value);
     mcr_value = mcr_value & LOOPBACK;
     printf("Loopback ");
     if(mcr_value == Ø)
          printf("cleared");
     else
          printf("set");
     printf(" ... continuing\n");
}
```

Invoking loopback() from term.c (immediately after the setup() function is called) causes all characters you type to be echoed back instead of being transmitted over the serial communications link. Why use loopback()? Because it is helpful for testing to make sure that communications software functions properly before you test the software on-line with another computer.

Note also that this routine accesses directly the modem control register (MCR) for COM1:. After your computer has been set in loopback mode with this function, the only way to turn off loopback is to turn off your computer and then turn it on again or to invoke loopback() a second time. (The best place to add this second loopback() to the term.c program is immediately preceding the final closing brace).

Evaluation of the Serial I/O Services

The basic serial I/O services are wholly inadequate for the job of high-performance communications applications. In high-speed (greater than 1200 baud), error-free file transfers or multihost, real-time terminal operations, speed is essential and should not be sacrificed to the god of compatibility (not lightly, at any rate). In order to achieve throughput and responsiveness, direct access to hardware is often more justifiable in communications than in other applications.

The basic term.c terminal program is adequate but cannot handle high speeds. Before you can improve its capability, you need to learn about interrupts and interrupt handlers.

I don't mean that a noninterrupt-driven program is useless. If you can put together a program in which the PC's undivided attention is devoted to the communication link, you can manage safely without interrupts. A package created on exactly this basis is used nationwide as a master control system; it provides control of a PC from a UNIX-based system. All communications to the PC are in packets and are either file transfers or commands to be executed. This program, which was built in a few hours by programmers using only the simplest techniques, has been in use for several years. It runs at speeds as high as 19,200 bps. Simple, direct programming can sometimes be the best solution to problems.

Summary

This chapter has focused on the use and control of the IBM microcomputer family's serial interface. This interface, which is based on the 8250 UART, offers programmers a good deal of hands-off control over a serial communications link.

Despite the capabilities and freedom presented by the 8250, the task of programming serial-communications software can be tedious and frustrating. Although BIOS and DOS services can be used to simplify the task somewhat, their value is diminished because they offer only limited access to the 8250's power. Furthermore, they introduce overhead that can seriously degrade the performance of time-critical software.

Part III

Disks, Directories, and Files

8

Disks

When you learn a programming language, you usually start by learning about basic input and output (as you did by reading Chapters 5, 6, and 7). You learn how to get data into and out of a computer, and you play with it.

Before you can begin to write serious programs, you need to learn about files (and you will, in Chapter 9) because most programs work with different types of files. Some programs work directly with the disk and directory structure. To lay the groundwork for Chapter 9, let's examine disks.

First you will learn how basic magnetic-disk technology works. Floppy disks and hard disks differ in capacity but are alike in the way they can be accessed through the DOS functions. The function calls used to open or close files, read or write files, or access directories are the same on any disk. As you work through this chapter, you will learn about tracks, sectors, and clusters and the role they play when you build a program.

Then, by applying your newfound knowledge about how disks work, you will produce a basic track-formatting function with which to reformat disks. Using this function requires special caution, however; you can easily make a mistake that may destroy critical disks.

Disk Internals

Anyone who uses a PC works with disks. No matter what kind of system you have, you most likely store information on disks. Given the importance of

215

disks in the operation of personal computers, you would expect people to know how disks work—but they don't. If you plan to work on the disks themselves (even if only to examine their structure or the data stored on them), you should understand how they work.

You can think of a disk as a collection of files—not unlike a drawer in a file cabinet. Each disk holds many files, and you can access any file "folder" directly. In a file drawer, you locate a certain folder by looking for the tab that identifies its contents. On a disk, the file structure is the operating system's interpretation of data stored on the disk. Files do not exist at levels below DOS.

During the formatting process, the operating system imposes the familiar file structure on your disks. DOS creates an index to the files (the directory) as well as a way to determine the files' location on the disk (the file allocation table, or FAT). DOS records information about the disk's layout (the boot record) which, even on disks without the system files, includes a start-up program.

Each side of a disk is a magnetically coated surface. This surface is magnetized by a "read/write" head that passes over the rotating disk. Double-sided disks have two recording surfaces; single-sided disks have only one (although both sides are coated, only one side is certified to meet quality standards). Hard disks typically have two to four platters, or disks, with recording surfaces on both sides.

On any disk drive, the read/write head (or heads) are moved across the disk surface by a special *stepper motor*. This motor has precisely defined stops (called *steps*) at which the head comes to rest. Each of these resting points defines a *track* on which data can be recorded. Most hard disks have a multiple-platter system in which the heads move together on all platters. The tracks (on all platters) corresponding to one step of the stepper motor are referred to as a *cylinder*.

The FORMAT program divides the tracks into 512-byte sectors in order to create more manageable disk segments: eight or nine sectors per track on a floppy disk; 17 sectors per track on a hard disk.

DOS allocates space to a file in units called *clusters*. Each cluster is made up of from two to eight sectors, depending on the type of disk. When a file needs additional disk space, the operating system allocates one or more additional clusters to that file. Figure 8.1 shows a typical disk platter layout.

Fig. 8.1. *A disk platter (showing a track, sector, and cluster).*

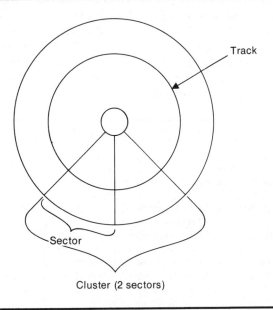

The disk is divided into the five important areas:

- ❏ The partition table
- ❏ The boot record
- ❏ The file allocation table (FAT)
- ❏ The directory
- ❏ The data space

discussed in the following sections.

The Partition Table

Every hard disk has a master boot record that resides at cylinder (track) 0, head (side) 0, sector 1. This boot record is responsible for reading and deciphering the disk partition table contained at the end of the master boot record. Based upon the contents of the partition table, the master boot record is then responsible for passing control to the boot record of the currently bootable hard disk partition.

The partition table describes how the hard disk is divided. To be recognizable by programs like FDISK, this partition table must conform to a standard layout. There can be as many as four partitions on a hard disk, each with a corresponding entry in the partition table. Figure 8.2 shows a memory dump of the master boot record from a COMPAQ Deskpro 286®. Notice the partition table information that is stored at the end of the sector. Entries begin at offset 01BEh for partition 1, 01CEh for partition 2, 01DEh for partition 3, and 01EEh for partition 4. The last two bytes of the sector (those immediately following the partition table at offset 01FEh) are a signature word for the sector, in this case AA55h.

Fig. 8.2.   Hard disk master boot record, disk partition table.

```
0000   33 C0 8E D8 8E C0 FA 8E-D0 BC 00 7C FB 8B F4 BF   3..........|....
0010   00 06 B9 00 01 FC F3 A5-50 B8 1E 06 50 CB B9 04   ........P...P...
0020   00 BE BE 07 80 3C 80 74-2C 83 C6 10 E2 F6 B4 0F   .....<.t,.......
0030   CD 10 B3 07 BE 97 06 B9-78 00 AC B4 0E CD 10 E2   ........x.......
0040   F9 C7 06 72 04 34 12 B8-FF FF 50 1E B4 0F CD 10   ...r.4....P.....
0050   32 E4 CD 16 CB B2 80 8B-DC 8A 74 01 BD 05 00 8B   2.........t.....
0060   4C 02 B8 01 02 CD 13 73-1E 80 FC 11 75 10 1E B8   L......s....u...
0070   00 F0 8E D8 33 FF 81 7D-EA 43 4F 1F 74 09 32 E4   ....3..}.CO.t.2.
0080   CD 13 4D 75 DD EB A7 81-BF FE 01 55 AA 75 9F 8B   ..Mu.......U.u..
0090   EE 1E 53 CB 43 52 4A 0D-0A 45 72 72 6F 72 20 6C   ..S.CRJ..Error l
00A0   6F 61 64 69 6E 67 20 6F-70 65 72 61 74 69 6E 67   oading operating
00B0   20 73 79 73 74 65 6D 20-66 72 6F 6D 20 66 69 78    system from fix
00C0   65 64 20 64 69 73 6B 2E-0D 0A 0D 0A 49 6E 73 65   ed disk.....Inse
00D0   72 74 20 43 4F 4D 50 41-51 20 44 4F 53 20 64 69   rt COMPAQ DOS di
00E0   73 6B 65 74 74 65 20 69-6E 20 64 72 69 76 65 20   skette in drive
00F0   41 2E 0D 0A 50 72 65 73-73 20 61 6E 79 20 6B 65   A...Press any ke
0100   79 20 77 68 65 6E 20 72-65 61 64 79 3A 20 07 00   y when ready: ..
0110   00 00 00 00 00 00 00 00-00 00 00 00 00 00 00 00   ................
0120   00 00 00 00 00 00 00 00-00 00 00 00 00 00 00 00   ................
0130   00 00 00 00 00 00 00 00-00 00 00 00 00 00 00 00   ................
0140   00 00 00 00 00 00 00 00-00 00 00 00 00 00 00 00   ................
0150   00 00 00 00 00 00 00 00-00 00 00 00 00 00 00 00   ................
0160   00 00 00 00 00 00 00 00-00 00 00 00 00 00 00 00   ................
0170   00 00 00 00 00 00 00 00-00 00 00 00 00 00 00 00   ................
0180   00 00 00 00 00 00 00 00-00 00 00 00 00 00 00 00   ................
0190   00 00 00 00 00 00 00 00-00 00 00 00 00 00 00 00   ................
01A0   00 00 00 00 00 00 00 00-00 00 00 00 00 00 00 00   ................
01B0   00 00 00 00 00 00 00 00-00 00 00 00 00 00 80 01   ................
01C0   01 00 04 04 51 E9 11 00-00 00 A1 A2 00 00 00 00   ....Q...........
01D0   41 EA 05 04 D1 D2 B2 A2-00 00 5D A2 00 00 00 00   A.........].....
01E0   00 00 00 00 00 00 00 00-00 00 00 00 00 00 00 00   ................
01F0   00 00 00 00 00 00 00 00-00 00 00 00 00 00 55 AA   ..............U.
                           Partition table
```

Notice that the partition table information shown in figure 8.2 has only two entries filled in—there are only two partitions on this hard disk. Each entry in the partition table is 16 bytes long. Table 8.1 details the layout for each partition table entry, using sample values taken from the partition table shown in figure 8.2.

Table 8.1. *Hard Disk Partition Table Entry Layout*

Byte Offset	Field Length	Sample Value	Meaning
00h	Byte	80h	Boot indicator
			00h = Nonbootable
			80h = Bootable
01h	Byte	01h	Starting head
02h	Byte	01h	Starting sector
03h	Byte	00h	Starting cylinder
04h	Byte	04h	System ID
			00h = Unknown
			01h = DOS, 12-bit FAT
			04h = DOS, 16-bit FAT
			05h = DOS, extended disk, 16-bit FAT
05h	Byte	04h	Ending head
06h	Byte	51h	Ending sector
07h	Byte	E9h	Ending cylinder
08h	Double word	0000:0011	First partition sector
0Ch	Double word	0000:A2A1	Sectors in partition

Notice the information stored in the partition table. Most of this information describes boundaries for each partition, but two fields, the boot indicator and the system ID, are of particular interest. The boot indicator signals whether the partition is bootable. Only one of the four possible partitions can be labeled as bootable. The system ID is used to designate the partition type. Table 8.1 indicates several possible system ID values, but various other operating systems (XENIX, UNIX, Pick, etc.), will necessarily expand the possbile system ID list.

During system boot, the BIOS consults the first sector on the disk to continue with the booting process. With a floppy disk, this is the boot sector (see the following section). With a hard disk, this fist sector is the master boot record described earlier. Within this master boot record, the partition table is located and BIOS determines (by the settings of the boot-indicator fields) which partition is bootable. After the bootable partition has been located, control is passed to the boot sector of that partition and booting continues as it would for a floppy disk.

The disk partitioning establishes a set of logical disks on the hard disk. Each logical disk acts like a smaller disk drive (and is assigned a drive letter by the disk driver). A single hard disk can use the logical drives for one operating system, or each can hold a different one. Systems often have MS-DOS in one partition and XENIX in another—not unlike having two computers for the price of one.

Partitioning is often necessary when you use hard disks with a capacity greater than 32M. Some versions of DOS are limited to 32M or less in a single partition. By using multiple partitions, you can make use of disks as large as 128M. Commercial utilities are available to eliminate the 32M limit with special disk drivers. But because the disks frequently cannot be used without the drivers, this can lead to problems if you are trying to run other operating systems or booting from floppy disks.

The Boot Record

When the system has determined where to locate the boot record for the bootable disk partition, the BIOS loads the boot record into memory. A typical boot sector for a floppy disk is shown in figure 8.3.

The boot sector begins with a jump to the start of the bootstrap loader routine, which "bootstraps" the system into operation. The small bootstrap program is loaded and, in turn, loads the larger operating system. (See Chapter 3 for a more detailed discussion of the DOS loading procedures.)

The 3-byte jump instruction is followed by an 8-byte system-name field that can be filled in to indicate the manufacturer whose system formatted the disk (some manufacturers do not put a name here). This is followed by the BIOS Parameter Block (BPB), which provides the information listed in table 8.2. The sample values shown in table 8.2 are taken from the boot sector in figure 8.3. (These values are from a 360K DSDD floppy disk.)

This BPB is critical to the operation of the bootstrap program because it must know these parameters to be able to find IO.SYS and MSDOS.SYS (the operating system BIOS and kernel). It is also the basis for what DOS knows about whether a disk is bootable.

The File Allocation Table (FAT)

The file allocation table (or FAT) is the area used by DOS to manage access to the disk's data area. DOS uses the FAT to indicate which portions of the disk belong to each file. Older operating systems have not used a dynamic concept of file management as embodied in the FAT; rather, they allocated a specific

Fig. 8.3.   *The boot sector layout.*

Jump instruction   System name   BPB

```
0000  E9 8D 00 00 00 00 00 00-00 00 00 00 02 02 01 00  ...............
0010  02 70 00 D0 02 FD 02 00-09 00 02 00 00 00 00 00  .p..............
0020  00 DF 02 25 02 0F 2A FF-50 F6 00 02 0D 0A 4E 6F  ...%..*.P.....No
0030  6E 2D 53 79 73 74 65 6D-20 64 69 73 6B 20 6F 72  n-System disk or
0040  20 64 69 73 6B 20 65 72-72 6F 72 2E 0D 0A 52 65   disk error...Re
0050  70 6C 61 63 65 20 61 6E-64 20 70 72 65 73 73 20  place and press
0060  61 6E 79 20 6B 65 79 20-77 68 65 6E 20 72 65 61  any key when rea
0070  64 79 0D 0A 07 00 49 4F-20 20 20 20 20 20 53 59  dy....IO      SY
0080  53 4D 53 44 4F 53 20 20-20 53 59 53 00 00 00 00  SMSDOS   SYS....
0090  FC 33 C0 8E D8 8E C0 FA-8E D0 BC 00 7C FB A1 78  .3..........|..x
00A0  00 A3 8C 7C A1 7A 00 A3-8E 7C 8D 06 21 7C A3 78  ...|.z...|..!|.x
00B0  00 8C 1E 7A 00 E8 38 00-A1 8E 7C A3 7A 00 A1 8C  ...z..8...|.z...
00C0  7C A3 78 00 8A 16 20 7C-EA 00 00 70 00 A1 8E 7C  |.x... |...p...|
00D0  A3 7A 00 A1 8C 7C A3 78-00 BE 2C 7C AC 0A C0 74  .z...|.x..,|...t
00E0  09 B4 0E BB 07 00 CD 10-EB F2 B4 00 CD 16 CD 19  ................
00F0  33 C0 CD 13 72 D7 8B 36-0E 7C A0 10 7C B4 00 F7  3...r..6.|..|...
0100  26 16 7C 03 F0 8B EE BB-20 00 A1 11 7C F7 E3 B1  &.|..... ...|...
0110  09 05 FF 01 D3 E8 03 E8-8D 1E 00 05 B8 01 00 E8  ................
0120  3B 00 BE 76 7C BF 00 05-B9 0B 00 F3 A6 74 02 EB  ;..v|........t..
0130  9C BF 20 05 B9 0B 00 F3-A6 74 02 EB 90 BB 00 07  .. .....t.....
0140  8B F5 A1 1C 05 B1 09 05-FF 01 D3 E8 E8 0E 00 8B  ................
0150  1E 1C 7C 03 DD 8B 0E 1E-7C 83 D1 00 C3 96 03 06  ..|.....|.......
0160  1C 7C 8B 16 1E 7C 83 D2-00 F7 36 18 7C 8B CA 41  .|...|....6.|..A
0170  BA 00 00 F7 36 1A 7C 8A-E8 B0 00 D1 E8 D1 E8 8A  ....6.|.........
0180  E1 0A C8 8A F2 8A 16 20-7C A0 18 7C 2A C4 FE C0  ....... |..|*...
0190  B4 00 3B F0 73 02 8B C6-BF 03 00 50 B4 02 CD 13  ..;.s......P....
01A0  58 73 06 4F 75 F5 E9 24-FF 2B F0 74 26 8A E0 B0  Xs.Ou..$.+.t&...
01B0  00 D1 E0 03 D8 80 E1 C0-80 C9 01 80 C6 01 3A 36  ..............:6
01C0  1A 7C 75 0A B6 00 80 C5-01 73 03 80 C1 40 A1 18  .|u......s...@..
01D0  7C EB BF C3 00 00 00 00-00 00 00 00 00 00 00 00  |...............
01E0  00 00 00 00 00 00 00 00-00 00 00 00 00 00 00 00  ................
01F0  00 00 00 00 00 00 00 00-00 00 00 00 00 00 55 AA  ..............U.
```

Loader routine

fixed-size disk area to each file. Because files can be virtually any size, the drawback to this method is that a fixed-size file tends to waste file space.

The FAT follows the boot record on the disk. Because the boot record is only one sector long (sector 0), the FAT starts with sector 1. The length of the FAT (in sectors) can be determined from the boot record itself, as well as from the number of FAT copies. Because of the FAT's critical nature, DOS usually maintains two copies which reside, one after the other, on the disk. As changes are made to the original FAT, DOS religiously updates the second

Table 8.2. *BIOS Parameter Block (BPB) Layout*

Byte Offset	Field Length	Sample Value	Meaning
00h	Word	0200	Number of bytes per sector
02h	Byte	02	Number of sectors per cluster
03h	Word	0001	Number of reserved sectors starting at sector 0
05h	Byte	02	Number of FATs
06h	Word	0070	Maximum number of root directory entries
08h	Word	02D0	Total number of sectors
0Ah	Byte	FD	Media descriptor
0Bh	Word	0002	Number of sectors per FAT
0Dh	Word	0009	Number of sectors per track
0Fh	Word	0002	Number of heads
11h	Double word	0000:0000	Number of hidden sectors
15h	11 bytes	----	Reserved

copy. It is interesting to note that no native DOS commands make use of the second FAT copy. If the original FAT is somehow damaged, a separate utility program can use be used with the second FAT copy to recover disk files.

The FAT is composed of a series of bytes used to record the status of each cluster on the disk drive. There are codes to indicate whether the cluster is available, in use, reserved, or damaged. The exact coding scheme used for the FAT depends on the capacity of the disk drive. Because each FAT entry must be able to represent a disk cluster number, the length of each FAT entry must be equal to the number of bits necessary to represent the disk's highest possible cluster number. DOS versions prior to V2 were limited to 12-bit FAT entries; the largest disk that could be represented was comprised of 2^{12} (or 4,096) clusters. Because some FAT entry values are used to represent the status of a cluster, the number of actual clusters representable in a 12-bit FAT is reduced by 16, to 4,080 clusters. If each cluster represents four 512-byte sectors, the 12-bit FAT limits the size of the disk to 8,355,840 bytes—just under 8M. Although 8M of storage space seemed huge when the PC was introduced, it is not much by today's standards. Even if the number of sectors per cluster is increased to 8, the disk limit is increased only to just under 16M—a severe limitation of DOS.

This barrier was circumvented by allowing DOS to understand a FAT that is encoded differently. Beginning with DOS V2, if the disk drive was large enough, DOS would use a 16-bit FAT entry. This 16-bit FAT allows tracking of 65,536 clusters (actually 65,520 clusters, when accounting for possible status values), or 268,369,920 bytes (just under 256M), using eight 512-byte sectors per cluster.

When a disk is formatted, the FORMAT program determines which coding scheme to use. If the size of the disk indicates that it can be represented adequately with a 12-bit FAT, that scheme is used; otherwise, a 16-bit FAT is used. Let's take a look at each type of FAT.

The 12-Bit FAT

The 12-bit FAT allows for a FAT that is 25 percent smaller than the 16-bit FAT. This fact was probably responsible for the adoption of the 12-bit FAT. Two 12-bit numbers can be be held in three bytes. Figure 8.4 shows a sample sector from a 12-bit FAT.

Notice the composition of the file allocation table. In this example, the first two FAT entries (the first three bytes) are used to represent system information. Thus, clusters 0 and 1 of the data area are inaccessible by the FAT. The following one and one half bytes (12 bits) (an FAT entry for cluster 2) are followed by the entry for cluster 3, and so on. Notice the three bytes at offset 0103h, which are the FAT entries for clusters 2 and 3. You can divide Ø3 4Ø ØØ into two separate FAT entries by using the following formulas (all values are hexadecimal):

> Entry 1 = (Byte2 AND 0F) * 10000 + Byte1
> Entry 2 = Byte3 * 10 + (Byte2 AND F0) / 10

Thus, the FAT entry for cluster 2 is

> FAT Cluster 2 = (40 AND 0F) * 10000 + 03
>   = (0) * 10000 + 03
>   = 03

and the FAT entry for cluster 3 is

> FAT Cluster 3 = 00 * 10 + ((40 AND F0) / 10)
>   = 0 + (40 / 10)
>   = 04

Each FAT entry points to the next cluster occupied by the file. Thus, the FAT entries form a chain; when all of the "links" in this chain are put together, the chain signifies the clusters occupied by a specific file.

Fig. 8.4. *A sample 12-bit FAT.*

```
2D14:0100  FD FF FF 03 40 00 05 60-00 07 80 00 09 A0 00 0B   ....@..`........
2D14:0110  C0 00 0D E0 00 0F 00 01-11 20 01 13 40 01 15 60   ......... ..@..`
2D14:0120  01 17 F0 FF 19 A0 01 1B-C0 01 1D E0 01 1F 00 02   ................
2D14:0130  21 20 02 23 40 02 25 60-02 27 80 02 29 A0 02 2B   ! .#@.%.`.')..+
2D14:0140  C0 02 2D E0 02 2F 00 03-31 20 03 33 40 03 35 F0   ..-../..1 .3@.5.
2D14:0150  FF 37 80 03 39 A0 03 3B-C0 03 3D E0 03 3F 00 04   .7..9..;..=..?..
2D14:0160  41 20 04 43 40 04 45 60-04 47 80 04 49 A0 04 4B   A .C@.E`.G..I..K
2D14:0170  C0 04 4D E0 04 FF 0F 00-00 00 00 00 00 00 00 00   ..M.............
2D14:0180  00 00 00 00 00 00 00 00-00 00 00 00 00 00 00 00   ................
2D14:0190  00 00 00 00 00 00 00 00-00 00 00 00 00 00 00 00   ................
2D14:01A0  00 00 00 00 00 00 00 00-00 00 00 00 00 00 00 00   ................
2D14:01B0  00 00 00 00 00 00 00 00-00 00 00 00 00 00 00 00   ................
2D14:01C0  00 00 00 00 00 00 00 00-00 00 00 00 00 00 00 00   ................
2D14:01D0  00 00 00 00 00 00 00 00-00 00 00 00 00 00 00 00   ................
2D14:01E0  00 00 00 00 00 00 00 00-00 00 00 00 00 00 00 00   ................
2D14:01F0  00 00 00 00 00 00 00 00-00 00 00 00 00 00 00 00   ................
2D14:0200  00 00 00 00 00 00 00 00-00 00 00 00 00 00 00 00   ................
2D14:0210  00 00 00 00 00 00 00 00-00 00 00 00 00 00 00 00   ................
2D14:0220  00 00 00 00 00 00 00 00-00 00 00 00 00 00 00 00   ................
2D14:0230  00 00 00 00 00 00 00 00-00 00 00 00 00 00 00 00   ................
2D14:0240  00 00 00 00 00 00 00 00-00 00 00 00 00 00 00 00   ................
2D14:0250  00 00 00 00 00 00 00 00-00 00 00 00 00 00 00 00   ................
2D14:0260  00 00 00 00 00 00 00 00-00 00 00 00 00 00 00 00   ................
2D14:0270  00 00 00 00 00 00 00 00-00 00 00 00 00 00 00 00   ................
2D14:0280  00 00 00 00 00 00 00 00-00 00 00 00 00 00 00 00   ................
2D14:0290  00 00 00 00 00 00 00 00-00 00 00 00 00 00 00 00   ................
2D14:02A0  00 00 00 00 00 00 00 00-00 00 00 00 00 00 00 00   ................
2D14:02B0  00 00 00 00 00 00 00 00-00 00 00 00 00 00 00 00   ................
2D14:02C0  00 00 00 00 00 00 00 00-00 00 00 00 00 00 00 00   ................
2D14:02D0  00 00 00 00 00 00 00 00-00 00 00 00 00 00 00 00   ................
2D14:02E0  00 00 00 00 00 00 00 00-00 00 00 00 00 00 00 00   ................
2D14:02F0  00 00 00 00 00 00 00 00-00 00 00 00 00 00 00 00   ................
```

Other values for FAT entries, however, do not represent a subsequent cluster number; rather, these values represent a status of the cluster. Table 8.3 summarizes the possible codes for a FAT entry.

Table 8.3. *12-Bit FAT Assignment Bytes*

Category	Code
Free for assignment	0
Part of a file (pointers to next clusters)	2–FEF
Reserved	FF0–FF6
Bad cluster	FF7
End of cluster chain	FF8–FFF

Using the 12-bit FAT shown in figure 8.3, let's follow a cluster chain. A file's directory entry points to the first cluster occupied by a file (directory entries are discussed in Chapter 9). In this illustration, the directory entry for IBMBIO.COM (22,100 bytes in length) points to a beginning cluster number of 2. If you look at the entry for cluster 2, you will see a pointer to cluster 3—and cluster 3 points to cluster 4 (remember, we just worked out the math for this). Cluster 4 then points to 5, which points to 6, and so on until cluster 18h is reached. Here the FAT entry is FFFh, which indicates that the end of the cluster chain has been reached.

The 16-Bit FAT

The release of DOS V2 brought support for larger hard disks and a FAT that uses 16 bits (2 bytes) per entry. Figure 8.5 shows a sample sector from a 16-bit FAT.

Translation of this file allocation table is much more straightforward than with the 12-bit FAT. The first two entries are used for system information; each subsequent entry occupies two bytes. Notice the two bytes at offset 0104h (the FAT entry for cluster 2). The value here (0003h) points to the entry for cluster 3.

Each FAT entry points to the next cluster occupied by the file. Thus, the FAT entries form a chain that, when all its "links" are put together, signifies the clusters occupied by a specific file. As with the 12-bit FAT, other values for FAT entries do not represent a subsequent cluster number; rather, these values represent the status of the cluster. Table 8.4 summarizes the possible codes for a FAT entry.

Table 8.4. *16-Bit FAT Assignment Bytes*

Category	Code
Free for assignment	0
Part of a file (pointers to next clusters)	2–FFEF
Reserved	FFF0–FFF6
Bad cluster	FFF7
End of cluster chain	FFF8–FFFF

Let's follow a cluster chain, using the 16-bit FAT shown in figure 8.5. A file's directory entry points to the first cluster occupied by a file (directory entries are discussed in Chapter 9). In this illustration, the directory entry for IBMBIO.COM (22,100 bytes in length) points to a beginning cluster number of 2. The entry for cluster 2 points to cluster 3. Cluster 3 points to cluster 4, which points to 5, which points to 6, and so on until cluster 0Ch is reached. The FAT entry at cluster 0Ch is FFFFh, which indicates that the end of the cluster chain has been reached.

Fig. 8.5. *A sample 16-bit FAT.*

```
2D14:Ø1ØØ   F8 FF FF FF Ø3 ØØ Ø4 ØØ-Ø5 ØØ Ø6 ØØ Ø7 ØØ Ø8 ØØ   ................
2D14:Ø11Ø   Ø9 ØØ ØA ØØ ØB ØØ ØC ØØ-FF FF ØE ØØ ØF ØØ 1Ø ØØ   ................
2D14:Ø12Ø   11 ØØ 12 ØØ 13 ØØ 14 ØØ-15 ØØ 16 ØØ 17 ØØ 18 ØØ   ................
2D14:Ø13Ø   19 ØØ 1A ØØ 1B ØØ FF FF-78 ØA FF FF 2Ø ØØ FF FF   ........x... ...
2D14:Ø14Ø   FF FF FF FF FF FF 6D Ø4-26 ØØ FF FF 27 ØØ 28 ØØ   ......m.&...'.(.
2D14:Ø15Ø   29 ØØ 2A ØØ 2B ØØ 2C ØØ-2D ØØ 2F ØØ FF FF 32 ØØ   ).*.+.,.-./...2.
2D14:Ø16Ø   FF FF ØØ ØØ 33 ØØ 51 ØØ-42 ØØ 36 ØØ 37 ØØ 38 ØØ   ....3.Q.B.6.7.8.
2D14:Ø17Ø   FF FF 3A ØØ 3B ØØ 3C ØØ-3D ØØ 3E ØØ 3F ØØ 41 ØØ   ..:.;. <.=.>.?.A.
2D14:Ø18Ø   FF FF FF FF 43 ØØ 44 ØØ-45 ØØ 48 ØØ FF FF FF FF   ....C.D.E.H.....
2D14:Ø19Ø   49 ØØ 4A ØØ 4B ØØ 4C ØØ-4F ØØ FF FF FF FF 5Ø ØØ   I.J.K.L.O.....P.
2D14:Ø1AØ   FF FF 52 ØØ 53 ØØ 54 ØØ-55 ØØ 57 ØØ FF FF 81 ØØ   ..R.S.T.U.W.....
2D14:Ø1BØ   59 ØØ 5A ØØ 5B ØØ 5C ØØ-61 ØØ 72 ØØ FF FF 6Ø ØØ   Y.Z.[.\.a.r...`.
2D14:Ø1CØ   FF FF 62 ØØ 6B ØØ FF FF-FF FF 66 ØØ FF FF FF FF   ..b.k.....f.....
2D14:Ø1DØ   FF FF 6A ØØ FF FF 6C ØØ-6D ØØ 78 ØØ 6F ØØ FF FF   ..j...l.m.x.o...
2D14:Ø1EØ   71 ØØ FF FF 83 ØØ FF FF-FF FF 76 ØØ 77 ØØ FF FF   q.........v.w...
2D14:Ø1FØ   7B ØØ FF FF FF FF 7C ØØ-7D ØØ 7E ØØ 7F ØØ 8Ø ØØ   {.....|.}.¯.....
2D14:Ø2ØØ   FF FF 82 ØØ DØ ØØ 84 ØØ-85 ØØ 86 ØØ 87 ØØ 88 ØØ   ................
2D14:Ø21Ø   8C ØØ 8A ØØ 8B ØØ FF FF-8D ØØ 8E ØØ FF FF ØØ ØØ   ................
2D14:Ø22Ø   ØØ ØØ ØØ ØØ 93 ØØ 94 ØØ-95 ØØ 96 ØØ 97 ØØ 98 ØØ   ................
2D14:Ø23Ø   99 ØØ 9A ØØ 9B ØØ 9C ØØ-9D ØØ C3 ØØ FF FF AØ ØØ   ................
2D14:Ø24Ø   A1 ØØ A2 ØØ A3 ØØ A4 ØØ-A5 ØØ A6 ØØ A7 ØØ A8 ØØ   ................
2D14:Ø25Ø   A9 ØØ AA ØØ AB ØØ AC ØØ-AD ØØ AE ØØ AF ØØ BØ ØØ   ................
2D14:Ø26Ø   B1 ØØ B2 ØØ B3 ØØ B4 ØØ-C2 ØØ B6 ØØ B7 ØØ B8 ØØ   ................
2D14:Ø27Ø   B9 ØØ BA ØØ BB ØØ BC ØØ-BD ØØ BE ØØ BF ØØ CØ ØØ   ................
2D14:Ø28Ø   C1 ØØ FF FF FF FF C4 ØØ-C5 ØØ C7 ØØ FF FF C8 ØØ   ................
2D14:Ø29Ø   CF ØØ CA ØØ CB ØØ CC ØØ-CD ØØ CE ØØ FF FF FC Ø1   ................
2D14:Ø2AØ   D1 ØØ D2 ØØ D3 ØØ D9 ØØ-D5 ØØ D6 ØØ D7 ØØ D8 ØØ   ................
2D14:Ø2BØ   FF FF DA ØØ DB ØØ DC ØØ-DD ØØ DE ØØ DF ØØ EØ ØØ   ................
2D14:Ø2CØ   E1 ØØ E2 ØØ E3 ØØ E4 ØØ-E5 ØØ E6 ØØ E7 ØØ E8 ØØ   ................
2D14:Ø2DØ   E9 ØØ EA ØØ EB ØØ EC ØØ-ED ØØ EE ØØ EF ØØ FØ ØØ   ................
2D14:Ø2EØ   F1 ØØ F2 ØØ F3 ØØ F4 ØØ-F5 ØØ F6 ØØ F7 ØØ F8 ØØ   ................
2D14:Ø2FØ   F9 ØØ FA ØØ FB ØØ FC ØØ-FD ØØ FE ØØ FF ØØ ØØ Ø1   ................
```

More FAT Information

When DOS requests space for a file, that space is assigned to the file in units of one or more clusters. As you have seen from the discussions of the 12- and 16-bit FATs, the clusters in a file are chained together, with each FAT entry giving the cluster number of the next entry (see fig. 8.6).

Fig. 8.6. FAT cluster chaining.

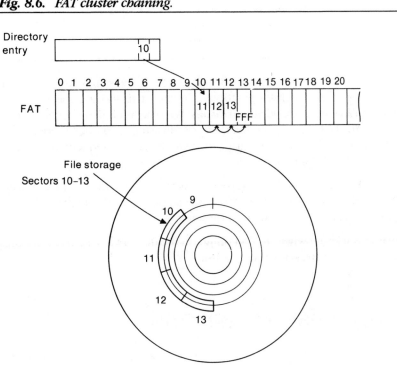

The FAT reserves, but does not use, the space for entries 0 and 1. The first byte of the FAT is used for a disk identification (ID) byte that helps identify the disk format (see table 8.5). Because clusters 0 and 1 are reserved for the system, cluster 2 is the first cluster that can be assigned.

Note that DOS allocates the space needed by files according to the number of complete clusters. Thus, regardless of the size of the file, the minimum disk usage for a file is one cluster. A 1-byte file may occupy 512, 1024, 2048, or 4096 bytes of disk space, depending on the number of sectors per cluster.

Table 8.5. Some Possible FAT ID Byte Values

Value	Disk characteristics
F0	Not identifiable
F8	Fixed disk
F9	Double sided, 15 sectors/track
F9	Double sided, 9 sectors/track (720K)
FC	Single sided, 9 sectors/track
FD	Double sided, 9 sectors/track (360K)
FE	Single sided, 8 sectors/track
FF	Double sided, 8 sectors/track

As you learned from decoding the floppy disk BPB, the sample disk had two FAT tables. Whenever disk operations allocate or deallocate space on the disk, both FATs are updated automatically. When a disk is first accessed, DOS compares the FATs to see whether they are consistent. Although there can be more than two FATs, in which case they will be stored sequentially on the disk, most disks have two.

After the FATs comes the root directory, with 32 bytes for each entry. The BPB gives the size of the directory so you can determine where the file area begins (immediately after the root directory).

Now that you know where to find things on the disk, let's see what functions DOS provides for manipulating the disk.

Using Disk Functions

There are no BIOS functions for dealing with a DOS file system, because the file system (including all of the tables just discussed) is a construction of DOS. To the BIOS, the disk is just a series of sectors starting at sector number 0 and proceeding sequentially to the highest numbered sector. The BIOS knows about tracks, sectors, and disk heads, but not about files, FATs, or directories. All of the functions you will use are DOS-oriented functions.

Drive Information

You can use DOS function calls to get information about the disk drive. The program drvinfo.c illustrates how you can get and display this information (see listing 8.1).

To get information about the drive, drvinfo.c calls three subroutines:

1. get—drive( ), to get the current drive number

2. get—drvinfo( ), to get general information about the drive

3. get—drvspace( ), to get other information

All of this information is entered into the drvinfo structure (in file drvinfo.h) as follows:

```
struct drvinfo {
      int  spc;              /* Sectors per cluster */
      int  avail;            /* Available clusters */
      int  fatseg;           /* FAT segment of ID byte */
      int  fatoff;           /* FAT offset of ID byte */
      int  secsize;          /* Physical sector size */
      int  clusters;         /* Number of clusters */
      char fatid;            /* FAT ID byte */
} info;
```

By defining a structure to hold related information about the disk, you can keep the information organized logically as you work with it.

Notice that program drvinfo.c (see listing 8.1) includes two subroutine calls which illustrate that the same information can be obtained in more than one way.

Listing 8.1

```
#include <stdio.h>
#include "drvinfo.h"

main(argc,argv)

int  argc;
char *argv[];

{
     int  drive;

     /* Gets the current drive information and displays it */
     drive = get_drive();
     printf("Current Drive Code = %d\n",drive);
     printf("Drive is %c:\n",'A'+drive);
```

Listing 8.1 continues

Listing 8.1 *continued*

```
/*
        Gets the following basic drive information:

                Sectors per cluster on the drive
                Physical sector size
                Number of clusters on the disk

        The capacity of the disk is computed from this information
*/

get_drvinfo(*argv[1],&info);
printf("Drive Information for drive %c:\n",*argv[1]);
printf("    Number of Sectors per cluster = %d\n",info.spc);
printf("    Size of Physical Sector = %d\n",info.secsize);
printf("    Number of Clusters = %d\n",info.clusters);
printf("\n");
printf("    Drive size is = %dK\n",
        info.clusters * ((info.spc * info.secsize)/1024));
printf("\n\n");

/*
        Gets the following basic drive information:

                Sectors per cluster on the drive
                Physical sector size
                Number of clusters on the disk

        This call also adds the number of available clusters.
        We can now compute both capacity and available space.

*/
get_drvspace(*argv[1],&info);
printf("Drive Information for drive %c:\n",*argv[1]);
printf("    Number of Sectors per cluster = %d\n",info.spc);
printf("    Size of Physical Sector = %d\n",info.secsize);
printf("    Number of Clusters = %d\n",info.clusters);
printf("    Number of Available Clusters = %d\n",info.avail);
printf("\n");
printf("    Drive size is = %dK\n",
        info.clusters * ((info.spc * info.secsize)/1024));
printf("    Available Space is = %dK\n",
        info.avail * ((info.spc * info.secsize)/1024));
}
```

Getting the drive information is a simple procedure—you call the DOS services interrupt (Int 21h). This call is performed in C by function intdos; in Pascal, by the Msdos function. The DOS service returns the drive code in register AL.

The function get—drive() does not interpret the drive code; it simply returns the code to drvinfo.c in the following manner:

```
#include <stdio.h>
#include <dos.h>

get—drive()

{
    union REGS regs;

    regs.h.ah = Øx19;
    intdos(&regs,&regs);

    return(regs.h.al);
}
```

But the process of requesting drive information is more complex than a simple request for the drive number. Information is returned in segment registers as well as in the general-purpose registers. To access the segment registers, you must use the function intdosx (see listing 8.2).

The functions get_drvinfo() and get_drvspace() are examples of a good programming practice—that of hiding implementation details inside the functions. In this case, the functions determine the correct drive code from the standard user-oriented designation for the drives (A:, B:, C:, and so forth). Allowing the drive name to be passed as a letter is a way to hide the fact that the drive designations in DOS and BIOS routines are not always consistent. Some routines use *0* to designate drive A:, whereas some use *0* to designate the default drive.

Functions (such as get_drvinfo() and get_drvspace) that will be included in a library for many programmers to use should hide as many implementation details as they can. This type of "programmer friendly" library routine helps programmers build programs without having to worry about the details of the machine.

The get_drvinfo() function in listing 8.2 is ready for use. It is written for inclusion in a library of functions and can be compiled alone as an object module.

Listing 8.2

```
#include <stdio.h>
#include <dos.h>
#include "drvinfo.h"

get_drvinfo(drv,info)

char drv;
struct drvinfo *info;

{
    union REGS regs;
    struct SREGS segs;
    int dn;

    /* Converts drive letter to internal representation */
    drv = toupper(drv);
    dn = drv - 'A' + 1;

    /* set up and call DOS */
    regs.h.ah = 0x1c;
    regs.h.dl = dn;
    intdosx(&regs,&regs,&segs);
    info->spc = regs.h.al;
    info->fatseg = segs.ds;
    info->fatoff = regs.x.bx;
    info->secsize = regs.x.cx;
    info->clusters = regs.x.dx;
}
```

After the function calls DOS (the intdosx function call), it saves the returned information from the registers in the info structure that was passed by the function call. Putting the information in this structure allows someone with no knowledge of registers and DOS calls to access it from the program that calls the function. The function can be included in a library for programmers who do not know how to deal with DOS.

DOS function 36h provides another, more complete way of getting disk information. The function get_drvspace(), shown in listing 8.3, not only loads disk information into the info structure but also returns the available space on the disk. Clearly, this function is useful for programs that work with large disk files or with many files.

Listing 8.3

```c
#include <stdio.h>
#include <dos.h>
#include "drvinfo.h"

get_drvspace(drv,info)

char drv;
struct drvinfo *info;

{
    union REGS regs;
    struct SREGS segs;
    int  dn;

    /* Converts drive letter to internal representation */

    drv = toupper(drv);
    dn = drv - 'A' + 1;

    /* Set up and make the DOS call */
    regs.h.ah = 0x36;
    regs.h.dl = dn;
    intdosx(&regs,&regs,&segs);
    info->spc = regs.x.ax;
    info->avail = regs.x.bx;
    info->secsize = regs.x.cx;
    info->clusters = regs.x.dx;
}
```

To determine how much free space is available on the disk, you use the following information (returned by DOS function 36h):

Register	Contains
AX	Number of sectors per cluster
BX	Number of available sectors
CX	Bytes per sector
DX	Clusters per drive

To calculate the free space on the drive, use the following formula:

BX * AX * CX

The total drive capacity is calculated by the following formula:

DX * AX * CX

If you want to find out only how much free space is on the disk, you can write a function (get_free()) to return only this information. The program free.c gets this information by calling get_free() with the drive name and pointers to integers for both the available and total disk space:

Program: Free.c

```
#include <stdio.h>

main(argc,argv)

int   argc;
char *argv[];

{
     int  avail, total;

     get_free(*argv[1],&avail,&total);
     if(*argv[1])
          printf("Disk Free Space on drive %c: is %dK of %dK\n",
               *argv[1],avail,total);
     else
          printf("Disk Free Space on default drive is %dK of %dK\n",
               avail,total);
}
```

The program is written to check the first command-line argument for the drive name. If *no* first argument is supplied, the program assumes that it should find the information for the default drive.

The function get_free() determines which drive it should check and then sets up and makes the call to DOS (see listing 8.4). Function 36h is used again to determine the free space, but most of the disk information is thrown away because it is not needed for the limited purpose of the function.

Listing 8.4

```
#include <stdio.h>
#include <dos.h>

get_free(drv,avail,total)

char drv;
int  *avail,
     *total;
```

Listing 8.4 continues

Listing 8.4 continued

```
{
    union REGS regs;
    struct SREGS segs;
    int  dn;

    /* Determines the drive and sets the drive number */
    if(drv){
        drv = toupper(drv);
        dn = drv - 'A' + 1;
    } else {
        dn = Ø;
    }

    /* Sets up and makes the DOS function call */
    regs.h.ah = Øx36;
    regs.h.dl = dn;
    intdosx(&regs,&regs,&segs);
    *avail = ((regs.x.ax * regs.x.cx)/1Ø24) * regs.x.bx;
    *total = ((regs.x.ax * regs.x.cx)/1Ø24) * regs.x.dx;
}
```

The same operations can be performed in BASIC, as you can see from the program free.bas in listing 8.5.

Listing 8.5

```
$include "REGNAMES.INC"

def fnchkspc(drv)
'determine the Free Space from Int 21h, Function 36
    reg %ax, &h36ØØ
    reg %dx, drv
    call interrupt &h21

    fnchkspc = reg(%bx) * (reg(%ax) * reg(%cx)/1Ø24)
end def

def fnsize(drv)
'determine the Space from Int 21h, Function 36h
    reg %ax, &h36ØØ
    reg %dx, drv
    call interrupt &h21
```

Listing 8.5 continues

Listing 8.5 continued

```
    fnsize = reg(%dx) * (reg(%ax) * reg(%cx)/1024)
end def

'MAIN PROGRAM
'
    input "Drive: ",dv$
    dv$ = left$(dv$,1)
    drive = int((instr("AaBbCcDdEeFfGg",dv$)+1)/2)
    print "Free Space on Drive ";dv$;" Is " ;fnchkspc(drive);"K"
    print "Drive Capacity Is ";fnsize(drive);"K"
end
```

If you want to build a truly useful utility for yourself, why not build one that copies a group of files to a floppy disk or to a series of floppies. Such a utility checks the size of the next file that you want to copy. If sufficient space is available on the disk, the utility copies the file; if not, the utility prompts for another floppy. Such a program might look like this:

```
FOR i=1 TO number_of_arguments
    TOP:
    size = size of file i
    space = get space on target drive
    IF size>space THEN
        ask for another floppy disk
        wait for user to press a key
        GOTO TOP:
    ELSE
        copy file i to floppy
    ENDIF
NEXT i
```

Although you do not yet know how to do everything needed to make this program a practical reality, you will learn about file sizes and executing other programs in Chapters 9 and 10. Then you will be able to build the program directly.

If you write commercial applications, your program is responsible for preventing all foreseeable errors. *Whenever* you build applications in which you add information to files, you risk running out of disk space. To prevent disk crashes, be sure to include checks for available space.

Formatting Disks

Disk formatting is a simple yet dangerous task most people do not need to do for themselves. The basic FORMAT program distributed with DOS is one of several adequate disk-formatting programs available. Special formatters are available (often as part of utility packages such as PCTOOLS) for those who want faster or more sophisticated formatting.

Beginners should plan carefully before they try to write disk-formatting programs because these programs, if handled incorrectly, can wipe out critical disk systems and destroy months of work. In this section, I describe some basic formatting techniques and show a few examples of ways to access the formatting routines present in the system. But remember: *You put your system at risk if you make a mistake here!* When you test a formatting program, follow these simple precautions:

❑ Whenever possible, test a formatting program on a "floppy disk only" system (no fixed disk). Use system disks that you can afford to lose if something goes wrong.

❑ If you must make test runs on a system that includes a hard disk, disable the hard disk if you can (by pulling the hard disk controller, for example).

❑ Be sure to have a current backup of your system. (*You should always have a current backup!*)

Good programming practice dictates that you recognize the inevitability of mistakes and that your testing provides for possible errors. If you are careful, nothing is likely to happen to your system when you test your programs.

DOS provides a BIOS function (Int 13h, Function 05h) for formatting disk tracks. The concept is simple and the function is easy to use. Let's take a look at how you use this function to format a disk.

If you start with an unformatted disk (or if you want to clear an old one), you must use Int 13h Function 05h to format the disk, track-by-track, as follows:

For each track from 0 to the last track
Set up the call for the track
Call the track-formatting routine

The disk will be formatted correctly and BIOS routines will be able to read it—but it is *not* a DOS disk. As you may recall from the discussion earlier in this chapter, DOS requires that a disk have certain structures (such as the boot sector, FAT, and root directory). The format procedure provides none of these.

To produce a disk acceptable to DOS, you must not only give a disk its basic format but also initialize the disk structure as follows:

> *For each track from 0 to the last track*
> > *Set up the call for the track*
> > *Call the track formatting routine*
> *Write boot sector to the disk*
> *Write FAT information to the disk*
> *Write root directory information to the disk*

You can handle the last two steps by simply writing zeros into the FAT and disk-directory areas. Zero entries in the FAT table indicate that the clusters are free and ready for reassignment. Zeros in the disk directory indicate that the directory entries have never been used. Except for the boot sector, then, the formatting process can be fairly simple: format the tracks, write the boot sector, and then zero the FAT and root-directory areas.

Let's write a routine for formatting a disk track. After you know how to format one track, you can format a disk simply by "stepping through" all the tracks.

You call BIOS Int 13h, Function 05h with the register settings shown in table 8.6.

***Table 8.6.** Register Settings for BIOS Int 13h, Function 05h*

Register	Meaning
AH	05h (the function code)
ES:BX	Pointer to track-address field table
CH	Track number
DH	Head number
DL	Drive number

The track-address table is the heart of the formatting operation. It specifies the order of logical disk sectors on the physical disk track. Each disk sector is represented in the table by a 4-byte entry that gives the label for each sector on the track. You can use the table to assign logical sector numbers in a different order than the physical sectors on the disk (a process known as *interleaving*).

The number of tracks varies according to the type of disk you use: 5 1/4-inch disks (360K, double-sided, double density) have 40 tracks per side; 3 1/2-inch disks (720K, double-sided, double density) have 80 tracks per side. The head number (for floppy disks) should be 0 or 1.

The drive number (DL) indicates which physical drive you want to work on. (Physical drives are specified by counting from zero: drive A: is number 0, drive B: is 1, and so on.)

On an unformatted disk, a track is an unstructured blank section of the magnetic surface. The formatting procedure imposes a structure on the disk by magnetically creating "storage bins" on the track (see fig. 8.7). Information can be stored in these bins, which are called *sectors*.

Fig. 8.7. *Disk track.*

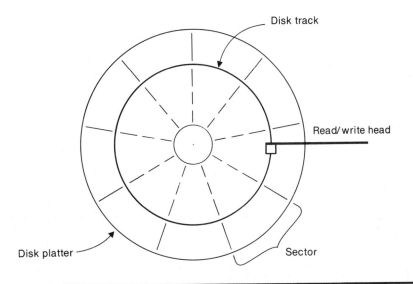

You can place the bins around the track in the physical order in which they occur, but this method can have drawbacks.

Think about reading from a set of disk sectors. Suppose that you copy a disk sector into memory, work with it briefly, and then come back to read the next sector. It's no problem: simply tell the disk controller which sector you want, and the controller gets the right one. But what if the two sectors are one after another on the disk? Your request for the second sector will occur after the beginning of that sector has passed the read/write head. To get the sector, you must wait while the disk makes a full revolution (about a fifth of a second for a floppy at 300 rpm). That amount of time adds up.

If you try to read an entire disk, one sector after another, those fifths of a second add up to the more than two minutes that the program spends waiting for a specific sector to rotate into position under the read/write head! In applications that do a great deal of disk I/O, the time overhead doesn't add up as quickly. By doing something to eliminate the problem, you can significantly improve such applications.

One way to avoid the wait for disk sectors is to interleave them so that one physical sector separates consecutive logical sectors. In other words, you alternate the sector numbers around the track. Figure 8.8 shows how nine sector-sized pieces of a file can be interleaved on a nine-sector track.

Fig. 8.8. *Storing file sectors.*

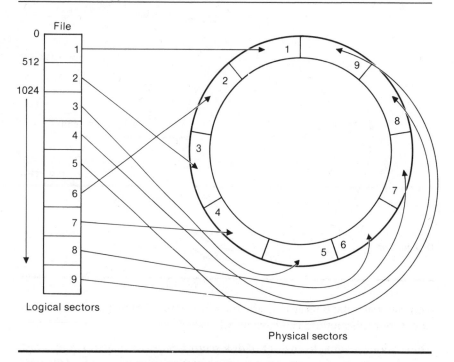

The track-address table lets you specify (to the BIOS function) what the logical sector numbers will be for each physical sector on the track. By specifying the size of each sector, you can change the sector size around the track. The information from the track address table is stored on the disk so that the disk controller can find a specific sector without having to consult special tables and figure out the disk's layout. When you use the track-address table to establish the layout, you create the interleaving for the track as a permanent part of the disk's logical structure.

The track-address table is a series of 4-byte entries (one for each sector on the track) that represent the track, the head, the logical sector number, and the code size. Table 8.7 lists the allowable code sizes.

Table 8.7. *Size Codes*

Code	Sector Size (in Bytes)
0	128
1	256
2	512
3	1024

The entries in the track-address table are always arranged on the disk by physical sector number. Each physical sector can have a logical sector number (in any order you want) so that interleaving can be implemented. The track-address table sets the access order of the sectors on a track; PCs read the disk by accessing the sector header in order to determine which sector has been requested.

The track-address table for track 3 of a 360K, double-sided, double-density disk with nine sectors per track might look like the one in figure 8.8. The logical sector numbers in figure 8.8 correspond to the following physical sectors:

Physical Sector   1 2 3 4 5 6 7 8 9
Logical Sector   1 6 2 7 3 8 4 9 5

To indicate a formatting error, the carry flag is set on return from the function. If the flag is set, AH will contain an error code. The meanings of the individual bits of this error code are shown in table 8.8. If an error occurs, your program should immediately call BIOS Int 13h, Function 00h (which resets the disk) and then handle the error appropriately.

Function fmt_trk( ) is an example of the track-formatting procedure implemented in C (see listing 8.6). This function assumes that you are formatting a 360K, DSDD disk in a standard PC drive. The function provides only for simple error recovery; it also assumes that the calling routine handles all interaction with the user.

Table 8.8. *Disk-Error Status Bits*

---Error Code---		Meaning
Hex Value	Binary Value	
	76543210	
01	1	Bad command
02	......1.	Bad sector address mark
03	11	Write-protect error
04	.....1..	Bad sector/sector not found
08	....1...	DMA overrun
09	....1..1	DMA error
10	...1....	Bad CRC on disk read
20	..1.....	Controller malfunction
40	.1......	Seek failure
80	1.......	Time out

Listing 8.6

```
/*
    Formats the specified disk track with a standard
    36ØK, DSDD track format. Returns Ø if the format
    is successful; otherwise, returns an error code
    that can be used by the calling routine to determine
    the next step.

*/

#include  <stdio.h>
#include  <dos.h>

#define DISK    Øx13

fmt_trk(dsk,trk,head)

int   dsk;
int   trk;
int   head;

{
```

Listing 8.6 continues

Listing 8.6 *continued*

```
    union REGS regs;
    char trktbl[36];
    int  i;

    for(i=0; i< 9; i++){
        trktbl[ i*4]   = trk;
        trktbl[ i*4+1] = head;
        trktbl[ i*4+2] = i;
        trktbl[ i*4+3] = 2;
    }
    regs.h.ah = 0x05;
    regs.h.ch = trk;
    regs.h.dh = head;
    regs.h.dl = dsk;
    regs.x.bx = trktbl;
    int86(DISK,&regs,&regs);
    if(regs.x.cflag)
        return(fmt_error(regs.h.ah));
    return(0);
}

fmt_error(code)

/*

    Processes a disk-formatting error by resetting the drive and
    returning an error code. The code passed to this routine is
    a bit code interpreted as shown in table 8.6. This routine
    returns an error code of 1 to indicate that a write-protect
    error (which can be recoverable) occurred. The routine
    assumes that all other errors can be treated as
    nonrecoverable and thus are lumped together.

*/

char code;

{
    union REGS regs;

    regs.h.ah = 0;
    int86(DISK,&regs,&regs);
    return((code==3)?1:2);
}

/* ========================================================= */
```

Summary

In this chapter, you have learned about the basic structure of disks and how they are formatted. And you have learned that the BIOS knows only about tracks, sectors, and disk heads, not about files and directories. The BIOS knows how to locate the disk's partition table as well as the boot record for the disk, but its knowledge stops there. Other than these special structures, the rest of the disk is just a set of data sectors.

All file-related disk operations are DOS-level functions. DOS maintains the disk's directories, files, and File Allocation Tables (FATs). The structure and location of these tables are given in the BIOS Parameter Block (BPB) stored in the boot record (the first sector of the bootable partition).

Once you have the basic information about the disk, you can access information about the disk (free space, disk capacity, and so forth) from standard DOS calls. Armed with what you have learned from this chapter, you are ready to tackle Chapter 9.

CHAPTER 9

Directories and Files

Nothing is more basic to programming than disk files. As programmers, we have to deal with disk files no matter which audience (business, development, entertainment, or scientific) we program for. Most programming languages, therefore, provide a wealth of easy ways to create, open, read, write, close, and delete files.

Dealing with files from within a high-level language is so easy that we generally do not have to think about file operations on a DOS level. With the file-handling functions provided by C, BASIC, and Pascal, you can do your job safely without much fuss. But if you work in assembly language, you need to become familiar with DOS's file-manipulation functions.

Even if you do not program in assembly language, some functions are not readily available from C, BASIC, or Pascal libraries; you cannot do certain types of operations effectively unless you use the DOS functions.

You may be wondering why I refer only to DOS file functions—not to the BIOS. The answer is that files and directories are beyond the realm of BIOS. The BIOS "knows" nothing about files. It assigns no structure (other than tracks and sectors) to disks. Disk file structure is under the direct control of DOS, which contains all the functions necessary for accessing disk files and directories.

This chapter begins with a look at the structure of directories and proceeds by discussing disk files and file functions. Finally, I show you how you can use your newly acquired knowledge of directories and files to build a program that allows you to locate a specific file anywhere in the directory system.

245

Disk Directories

Directories represent a major advance in the way disk operating systems handle disk files. The early operating systems (CP/M, TRSDOS®, Apple DOS®, and a myriad of others) all treated files in much the same way. In these *flat file systems*, *all* of the disk files were available through a single directory. DOS treated files this way until the advent of DOS V2.

Beginning with DOS V2, a file-ordering concept was borrowed from UNIX and XENIX. This *hierarchical directory scheme* allows easy ordering and manipulation of a large number of disk files (usually stored on a hard disk). In a system with hierarchical directories, every disk starts with a predefined, fixed-size *root directory* that is stored at a known location on the disk. Like the flat-file concept described in the preceding paragraph, the root directory can contain a specific number of equally accessible files. If we were to stay within the confines of a single directory, we would be no better off than before. But thanks to DOS's hierarchical directory system, you can create special entries in the root directory. These entries (called *subdirectories*) are similar to files except that their file space contains additional directory entries. Like the root directory, subdirectories are directories in their own right.

Unlike the root directory, subdirectories are not limited by arbitrary size restrictions. They can grow to accommodate additional files. Furthermore, you can create subdirectory entries within subdirectories, with each entry containing references to individual groups of files. Let's look at the way DOS keeps track of the individual files and directories on a disk.

The Root Directory

The root directory is located in a fixed position on the disk and has a fixed size, which is determined by the FORMAT program when it formats the disk. The root directory's size and disk location are held in the BIOS parameter block of the disk's boot sector (refer to Chapter 8).

In DOS V1, the root directory was the only directory on a disk. Support for subdirectories began with DOS V2. As you now know, a subdirectory is simply a file that contains other directory entries.

The first two entries in a root directory are reserved for the BIOS and DOS-kernel system file entries. The disk bootstrap program uses these entries during system start-up (refer to Chapter 3). Figure 9.1 shows the first sector of a typical root directory which includes the operating system.

Fig. 9.1. *A root-directory dump (first sector only).*

Nonbootable disk

```
00   53 52 43 20 20 20 20 20-20 20 20 10 00 00 00 00    SRC        .....
10   00 00 00 00 00 00 6E 00-9B 10 02 00 00 00 00 00    ......n.........
20   44 45 4D 4F 43 4D 20 20-41 53 4D 20 00 00 00 00    DEMOCM ASM ....
30   00 00 00 00 00 00 D7 83-4F 0F 09 00 79 04 00 00    ........O...y...
40   44 45 4D 4F 43 4D 20 20-4F 42 4A 20 00 00 00 00    DEMOCM OBJ ....
50   00 00 00 00 00 00 7B BD-9B 10 0B 00 6C 00 00 00    ......{.....l...
60   44 45 4D 4F 43 4D 20 20-45 58 45 20 00 00 00 00    DEMOCM EXE ....
70   00 00 00 00 00 00 81 BD-9B 10 0C 00 2B 03 00 00    ............+...
80   44 45 4D 4F 43 4D 20 20-43 4F 4D 20 00 00 00 00    DEMOCM COM ....
90   00 00 00 00 00 00 84 BD-9B 10 0D 00 2B 00 00 00    ............+...
A0   44 45 4D 4F 43 4D 20 20-44 4D 50 20 00 00 00 00    DEMOCM DMP ....
B0   00 00 00 00 00 00 2A BE-9B 10 0E 00 29 05 00 00    ......*.....)...
C0   00 00 00 00 00 00 00 00-00 00 00 00 00 00 00 00    ...............
D0   00 00 00 00 00 00 00 00-00 00 00 00 00 00 00 00    ...............
E0   00 00 00 00 00 00 00 00-00 00 00 00 00 00 00 00    ...............
F0   00 00 00 00 00 00 00 00-00 00 00 00 00 00 00 00    ...............
```

Bootable disk (system files included, first sector only)

```
00   49 4F 20 20 20 20 20 20-53 59 53 07 00 00 00 00    IO      SYS.....
10   00 00 00 00 00 00 00 00-66 EA 0C 02 00 3C 1F 00 00    ......f....<...
20   4D 53 44 4F 53 20 20 20-53 59 53 07 00 00 00 00    MSDOS   SYS.....
30   00 00 00 00 00 00 75 6B-06 0B 0A 00 E0 6C 00 00    ......uk.....l..
40   43 4F 4D 4D 41 4E 44 20-43 4F 4D 00 00 00 00 00    COMMAND COM.....
50   00 00 00 00 00 00 1A 00-AF 0A 26 00 95 58 00 00    ..........&..X..
60   53 52 43 20 20 20 20 20-20 20 20 10 00 00 00 00    SRC        .....
70   00 00 00 00 00 00 80 01-9B 10 3D 00 00 00 00 00    ..........=.....
80   44 45 4D 4F 43 4D 20 20-41 53 4D 20 00 00 00 00    DEMOCM ASM ....
90   00 00 00 00 00 00 D7 83-4F 0F 44 00 79 04 00 00    .......O.D.y...
A0   44 45 4D 4F 43 4D 20 20-4F 42 4A 20 00 00 00 00    DEMOCM OBJ ....
B0   00 00 00 00 00 00 7B BD-9B 10 46 00 6C 00 00 00    ......{...F.l...
C0   44 45 4D 4F 43 4D 20 20-45 58 45 20 00 00 00 00    DEMOCM EXE ....
D0   00 00 00 00 00 00 81 BD-9B 10 47 00 2B 03 00 00    ..........G.+...
E0   44 45 4D 4F 43 4D 20 20-43 4F 4D 20 00 00 00 00    DEMOCM COM ....
F0   00 00 00 00 00 00 84 BD-9B 10 48 00 2B 00 00 00    ..........H.+...
```

The root directory must start at a clearly defined point so that it can be found by a program that does not understand the file system. The kernel and BIOS programs must be the very first files stored on disk so that they can be located quickly during the process of booting to the disk. The bootstrap program assumes that both programs are the first ones in the root directory and that they are stored contiguously on the disk.

Directory Entries

Understanding the structure of directory entries is imperative if you are to understand how DOS keeps track of files and directories. After you learn the structure of directory entries, interpreting the entries is easy.

Each directory entry (32 bytes of data) contains identifying information about the file: the file's name, extension, attribute, size, and starting location on the disk, as well as the date and time of the directory entry's most recent update. Table 9.1 shows the basic structure of a 32-byte directory entry.

Table 9.1. Structure of the Directory Entry

Offset	Size	Meaning
00h	8 bytes	File name
08h	3 bytes	File extension
0Bh	Byte	File attribute
0Ch	10 bytes	Reserved (not used)
16h	Word	Time of last update
18h	Word	Date of last update
1Ah	Word	Beginning disk cluster
1Ch	Double word	File size

Every directory entry is formatted in this way; each piece of information about the file is stored at a fixed offset within the 32-byte entry. Each field in the directory entry tells you something unique about the file. With the exception of the 10 bytes reserved by DOS (offset 0Ch), we will take a fairly detailed look at each field in the directory entry.

File Name (Offset 00h)

The first eight bytes of the entry are the file's root name (stored as ASCII text). Now you can see why file names in DOS are limited to eight characters—only that amount of space is available in the directory entry.

In many DOS programs, you can use file names longer than eight characters, but DOS will truncate them to fit within its eight-character limit. If the root file name is less than eight characters long, it is left-justified within the field and padded with spaces. DOS stores all file names as uppercase ASCII characters.

The first byte of the file-name field has several special meanings (see table 9.2).

Table 9.2. *Special Meanings of File Name's First Byte*

Value of First Byte	Meaning
00h	Entry has never been used; no further entries follow this one.
05h	First character of the file name is actually E5h.
2Eh	Entry is an alias for the current or parent subdirectory. If the next byte is 2Eh, the directory entry's beginning disk cluster field contains the cluster number of the parent of the current directory.
E5h	File erased

Ordinarily, the 00h code is used only in the root directory. This code saves DOS from fruitless searches of unused directory entries.

The E5h character (displayed on an IBM as the Greek *sigma* character) can be used as the first character of a file name but is stored in the directory entry as 05h.

Because coding E5h marks files that have been erased, DOS may ignore or reuse this coding. Only the first byte changes to mark the entry (as deleted); the rest of the directory entry remains unaltered. Theoretically, you can resurrect an erased file by changing the first character to a valid ASCII character. But if another file is using the disk space previously occupied by the erased file, you cannot unerase the file.

The entry 2Eh is a period (.) Found only in subdirectories, it marks a directory entry for the current directory. If the next byte also is a period, it points to the parent of the current directory. You see these dot (.) and dot-dot (..) entries at the beginning of every subdirectory whenever you use the DOS DIR command.

File Extension (Offset 08h)

The three characters that begin at offset 08h are the file extension (also stored as ASCII characters). If the file has no extension, or if the extension is shorter than three characters, then the extension is left-justified within the field and the name is padded with spaces. Notice that the period, which generally is used as a delimiter between the root file name and the extension, is not stored with the file name in the directory entry. DOS assumes the presence of a period between the eighth and ninth bytes of the directory entry.

File Attribute (Offset 0Bh)

The file's attribute (the byte at offset 0Bh) indicates both the type of file represented by the directory entry and its accessibility. Each bit of the attribute marks one of the file's characteristics or features (see table 9.3).

Table 9.3. *An Attribute Byte*

Bit	Meaning
76543210	
. . . . x	Read only
. . . . . . x .	Hidden
. . . . . x . .	System
. . . . x . . .	Volume label
. . . x	Subdirectory
. . x	Archive
x x	Reserved (unused)

The read-only characteristic means exactly what it says—that the file can only be read—not written to. If this bit is set, the file cannot be deleted. Although this precaution provides some security to the file, the file can be renamed and then modified.

What about the other attributes? Hidden files are not available to DIR or most other DOS commands. The term *system* refers specifically to the DOS kernel and BIOS files but could be used also for other files. The volume label is a label (or name) for a given disk. Each disk should have a label but, during most disk functions, DOS does not check for it. Volume labels are discussed more fully later in this chapter.

The subdirectory bit marks the file as a special file containing other directory entries. A subdirectory is another directory subordinate to the current one. (We'll come back to directories and subdirectories later in this chapter.)

The archive bit (a status bit for the file) is set whenever the file is updated. Typically, hard-disk backup programs use the archive bit to indicate which files need to be backed up.

Time of Last Update (Offset 16h)

The word (two bytes) beginning at offset 16h is the time of the file's last update. Sometimes called the file's *time stamp*, it is stored least-significant byte first.

The file's time field is set when you create the file and updated thereafter whenever you close the file, but only *after* information has been written to the file. This field is not updated if the file is read from, copied (with the DOS COPY command), or renamed (with the DOS REN command). When the time field is updated, the new time is retrieved from the system clock.

Table 9.4 shows the meaning of each bit in the time field. The hour is contained in five bits (24-hour clock) and the minutes, in six bits; the seconds are divided by 2 and stored in five bits.

Table 9.4. *Encoding of the Time Field*

Bits	Meaning
FEDCBA98 76543210	
xxxxx...	Hours
.....xxx xxx.....	Minutes
....xxxxx	Two-second increments

Note that because the seconds are divided by 2, the time stamp is accurate only to an even number of seconds. (This limitation is not significant in most applications.)

Date of Last Update (Offset 18h)

The word (two bytes) beginning at offset 18h is the date of the file's last update. Sometimes referred to as a file's *date stamp*, it is stored least-significant byte first.

The date field is similar to the time field—it is set when you create the file and updated thereafter whenever you close the file, but only *after* information has been written to the file. The date field is not updated if the file is read from, copied (with the DOS COPY command), or renamed (with the DOS REN command). When the date field is updated, it encodes (from the system clock) the date of the file's most recent modification.

Table 9.5 shows the layout of the date field. Each bit has meaning: the year is stored in seven bits, the month in four, and the day in five.

Table 9.5. *Encoding of the Date Field*

Bits	Meaning
FEDCBA98 76543210	
xxxxxxx.	Year count (relative to 1980)
.......x xxx.....	Month
....xxxxx	Day

Notice that the year entry is relative to 1980. In other words, it is an offset from 1980, not an absolute value (such as 1988). The year 1988, for example, is stored as 8. To identify the absolute year, you simply add the offset to 1980. Seven bits are allocated for the year; because 127 is the largest value that can be represented in 7 bits, the year can range from 1980 (offset 0) to 2107 (offset 127).

Beginning Disk Cluster (Offset 1Ah)

The word (two bytes) beginning at offset 1Ah is the file's beginning disk cluster. This word is stored with its least significant byte first.

This works for files that occupy only one cluster of disk space, but many files exceed one cluster. In these cases, the value of the beginning disk cluster field is used to calculate the offset into the *file allocation table* (FAT). From the FAT, additional clusters used by the file can be located. (See Chapter 8 for a detailed discussion of how to use the FAT effectively.)

File Size (Offset 1Ch)

Some high-level languages (early versions of BASIC, in particular) were notorious for setting this value equal to the total number of bytes in the sectors occupied by the file. If the file contained 520 bytes and occupied two 512-byte sectors, the file size would be set to a clearly misleading 1024. Normally, however, this entry will reflect accurately the file's size in bytes.

Subdirectories

I have already mentioned that each directory entry contains an attribute byte for the file. Bit 4 of this attribute byte marks a directory entry as a pointer to a subdirectory.

A subdirectory is a file, like all the others on the system. The subdirectory entry points to the number of the directory file's beginning cluster; you "step through" subsequent file clusters to find subsequent entries. Figure 9.2 shows a dump of a typical subdirectory.

Fig. 9.2. A subdirectory dump.

```
00   2E 20 20 20 20 20 20 20-20 20 20 10 00 00 00 00   .           ....
10   00 00 00 00 00 00 6E 00-9B 10 02 00 00 00 00 00   ......n........
20   2E 2E 20 20 20 20 20 20-20 20 20 10 00 00 00 00   ..          ....
30   00 00 00 00 00 00 6E 00-9B 10 00 00 00 00 00 00   ......n........
40   44 45 4D 4F 45 58 20 20-41 53 4D 20 00 00 00 00   DEMOEX  ASM ....
50   00 00 00 00 00 00 DC 8B-4F 0F 03 00 0D 05 00 00   ........O.......
60   44 45 4D 4F 45 58 20 20-4F 42 4A 20 00 00 00 00   DEMOEX  OBJ ....
70   00 00 00 00 00 00 91 BD-9B 10 05 00 B7 00 00 00   ...............
80   44 45 4D 4F 45 58 20 20-45 58 45 20 00 00 00 00   DEMOEX  EXE ....
90   00 00 00 00 00 00 94 BD-9B 10 06 00 E0 02 00 00   ...............
A0   44 45 4D 4F 45 58 20 20-44 4D 50 20 00 00 00 00   DEMOEX  DMP ....
B0   00 00 00 00 00 00 5A BE-9B 10 07 00 2A 05 00 00   ......Z.....*...
C0   00 00 00 00 00 00 00 00-00 00 00 00 00 00 00 00   ...............
D0   00 00 00 00 00 00 00 00-00 00 00 00 00 00 00 00   ...............
E0   00 00 00 00 00 00 00 00-00 00 00 00 00 00 00 00   ...............
F0   00 00 00 00 00 00 00 00-00 00 00 00 00 00 00 00   ...............
```

The structure of a subdirectory is just like that of the root directory. At the beginning of each 32-byte subdirectory entry are two special entries: the files (.) and (..). The first of these files (.) refers to the location of the current directory; the beginning cluster field in this directory entry points to the first cluster of the current subdirectory. The (..) entry refers to the parent directory; the beginning cluster field in this file entry points to the parent directory's first cluster. If this cluster number is 0, the parent directory is the root directory. Neither of these two special directory entries can be deleted.

You cannot handle subdirectories as you would normal files. DOS Function 43h cannot set a subdirectory's attribute bit. The subdirectory's system and hidden bits can be set to exclude the directory from normal directory listings, but its accessibility can't be changed. CHDIR still can reach it.

Volume Labels

A volume label is a directory entry in which bit 3 of the file attribute byte is set. To interpret the entry, all you need to do is locate it—the file name is the volume label.

Although generally not used by most software, volume labels can be extremely useful for software written to take advantage of them. A program can use unique volume labels as disk identifiers. By remembering which disks are in use, a program can prompt for a specific disk by name rather than by a general title. The Macintosh, for example, does this when you use more than one disk on a single drive system. On the Macintosh desktop, the names of disks that have been identified to the system are shown and, if one of these disks is needed, it is requested by name. The system, which can tell whether you have inserted the wrong disk, will continue to ask for the proper disk by name.

Although most PC programs do not handle disks this way, they could—thanks to the volume label. The only way to create a disk label is through the extended FCB functions, which are described in this chapter's "Extended File Control Blocks" section. (For a list of DOS functions for all FCB operations, see the DOS Reference Section at the end of this book.)

What Is a File?

We use files for all sorts of things. Simply speaking, a file is an organized place in which to store information. The term *files* is used also to refer to devices. Following the lead of UNIX, DOS V2 introduced the concept of the *file handle*. The file handle can assign unique numbers, called *handles*, to devices such as the printer, the RS-232 port, the keyboard, and the video screen. Many of us were accustomed to treating these devices as special objects, but file handles have changed that.

The concept of using file handles is more powerful than many people realize. With a file handle, you can use the same techniques to access either files or devices. For example, in a program written to deal with the keyboard and the video screen (using STDIN and STDOUT), you not only can redirect the input so that it comes from a file but you also can redirect the output to a file. The *same program* works in each case—you change only the handle used for input or output.

How Files Are Handled through DOS

DOS provides two basic ways to deal with files: the FCB method or the handle-function method.

Before DOS V2 was introduced, the *file control block* (FCB) method (an outgrowth of the old CP/M system) was the only way to access files. FCB functions are built around the presence of a file control block that the programmer controls directly. In this powerful method of accessing file information, the FCB is kept in the programmer's data space and the programmer explicitly carries out all related operations. But such a degree of control often is not necessary.

You do not need to have all the details of the file at your fingertips for most operations—such as opening, closing, reading, writing, or maintaining a file (renaming or deleting it). For these types of file operations, you use the other method—the handle functions.

Handle functions give programmers only limited access to file information; DOS controls the files internally. Programmers request file operations either by a specific file name (to open or create files) or by using a file handle (to read or write files). DOS uses the handle to look up information about the file.

Handle functions have several advantages over FCB functions:

❏ Because handle functions are simpler to use, it is easier to prevent or correct mistakes.

❏ Handle functions are likely to remain compatible with changes in DOS and, later, in OS/2.

❏ Handle functions can take advantage of DOS's hierarchical directory structure.

❏ Handle functions relieve programmers of a great deal of bookkeeping. (The bookkeeping—file location and everything that is stored in an FCB—is done inside the DOS kernel.)

I recommend that, whenever you can, you use the handle functions for accessing files. You have to use FCB functions to create disk volume labels but, for any other file operation, handles are a better way to work with files.

Regardless of whether you use FCB or handle functions, DOS is quite adept at informing you of any errors it may detect. For a comprehensive list of DOS error codes, see the DOS Reference Section at the end of this book (see particularly Int 21h, Function 59).

Standard File Control Blocks

The standard FCB used by all FCB functions comes almost directly from the original CP/M environment. Its 36 bytes make up 11 fields, as you can see from the layout of the standard FCB shown in table 9.6.

Table 9.6. *The Standard File Control Block*

Offset	Length	Meaning	Notes
00h	1	Drive specification	0 =default, 1 =A:, 2 =B:, and so on
01h	8	File name	Left-justified ASCII; padded with blanks
09h	3	Extension	Left-justified ASCII; padded with blanks
0Ch	2	Current block number	
0Eh	2	Record size	Default of 80h bytes with DOS *open* or *create* functions
10h	4	File size	
14h	2	Date created/updated	Same format as directory entry
16h	2	Time created/updated	Same format as directory entry
18h	8	Reserved	
20h	1	Current record number	
21h	4	Random record number	Only three bytes used if record size is less than 64 bytes

The file control block is made up of information supplied by DOS, some of which comes directly from the values in a file's directory entry. Notice that no allowance is made for using path names with FCBs. All FCB functions operate within the confines of the current directory.

The file name, extension, file size, and date and time of last update are all reflections of the file's directory entry. The other fields are either initialized by the individual FCB functions or modified by the programmer to indicate to DOS what he or she wants.

Extended File Control Blocks

Extended FCBs allow additional file information to be included in the FCB. The extended portion of the FCB is composed of seven bytes (three fields) added to the beginning of the traditional FCB.

By examining the FCB's first byte, DOS can tell which type of FCB you are using. If the first byte is FFh, DOS assumes that you are using an extended FCB. (The first byte in a standard FCB represents the disk drive designator. FFh is an illegal value as a disk drive number.)

All DOS FCB functions can use extended FCBs. If you decide to use FCB functions, use extended FCBs so that you will have to keep track of only one structured FCB area.

Most of the information in an extended FCB is identical to that in a standard FCB. If you compare table 9.6 with table 9.7, which details the layout of an extended FCB, you can see that (beginning with byte offset 07h) the two layouts are identical.

Basic FCB File Handling

In order to work successfully with FCBs, follow these basic steps:

1. Set all the bytes of the FCB to 0.

2. Get the file-name information. To do so, you may need to use the DOS parse function (29h).

3. OPEN (Function 0Fh) or CREATE (Function 16h) the file.

4. If the record-size field should not be 80h, change it.

5. Set the record-number field if you are doing random-access operations.

Table 9.7. *An Extended File Control Block*

Offset	Length	Meaning	Notes
00h	1	FFh	Signals DOS that this is an extended FCB
01h	5	Reserved	Used by DOS; normally zeroes
06h	1	Attribute byte	Same meaning as directory entry
07h	1	Drive specification	0 =default, 1 =A:, 2 =B:, and so on
08h	8	File name	Left-justified ASCII; padded with blanks
10h	3	Extension	Left-justified ASCII; padded with blanks
13h	2	Current block number	
15h	2	Record size	Default of 80h bytes with DOS *open* or *create* functions
17h	4	File size	
1Bh	2	Date created/updated	Same format as directory entry
1Dh	2	Time created/updated	Same format as directory entry
1Fh	8	Reserved	
27h	1	Current record number	
28h	4	Random record number	Only three bytes used if record size is less than 64 bytes

6. Set the DTA address (if it has not been set).

7. Execute the appropriate function.

8. After you have finished, close the file.

When To Use FCB Functions

Even in DOS V3, the use of FCB functions is justified for the following reasons:

❏ When you use FCBs, you can have an unlimited number of open files.

❏ FCBs provide the only way to create a volume label for a disk.

❏ FCBs ensure that methods of accessing files are compatible with DOS V1.

The first point is true because you have total control of the "housekeeping" associated with file I/O. (In the most recent versions of DOS, users can specify in the CONFIG.SYS file how many files can be open simultaneously.)

The second point is important, no matter which version of the operating system you use. If your program creates a volume label for a disk, you *must* use FCBs.

The third reason may be the most important: FCBs are the only way to verify compatibility with systems that use DOS V1. If you are sure that the software will be used on a system with DOS V2 or later, or if you can sacrifice the compatibility of earlier systems, you always should choose handle functions.

Handle Functions

As I mentioned earlier in this chapter, the handle functions are an advance in programming technique. Their introduction to DOS provides file control similar to that found in UNIX. In fact, you can port UNIX applications (written in C) to DOS. These applications will run just like their UNIX counterparts.

You should recognize the two basic features of handle functions:

❏ Under the handle functions, no distinction is made between sequential and random-access files. All files are seen as a string of bytes, much like an array. This view of a file is standard for UNIX files.

❏ Handles are kept internally by DOS. The only information a program needs is the file name and handle number.

Not all programmers agree that these features are advantages. Some programmers object to having to give up the control provided by FCBs; others insist that by not providing random-access record structures, the system becomes less powerful. These programmers are mollified by the fact that FCB functions are still available (their attitude may well change if FCBs eventually disappear).

Which group is right? Neither. For simple programming, nothing beats the handle functions for ease of use. Despite the objections of some programmers, programs seldom need to do their own file bookkeeping. Random file access still is available, but you must approach it differently.

A handle is simply a pointer into an internal DOS table that maintains all relevant information about an open file. Programmers do not have to maintain a detailed accounting of information, as they do when using the FCB functions; rather, the handle functions relinquish all bookkeeping functions to DOS. For most programming applications, this feature significantly eases the programmer's burden. Because you don't have to manipulate or worry about special file control blocks, your programs, conceptually, are simpler, easier to debug, and easier to keep compatible with future DOS releases.

Basic Handle File Handling

The basic technique for using handles to handle files is much simpler than that for using the corresponding FCB functions. Because the system handles the basic details, you simply identify the file you want and let DOS do the rest. In the handle file-handling method, you follow these steps:

1. Create an ASCIIZ file-name string.

2. OPEN (Int 21h, Function 3Dh) or CREATE (Int 21h, Function 3Ch) the file.

3. Set the file pointer into the file (Int 21h, Function 42h).

4. Complete the required operations.

5. Close the file.

An ASCIIZ string is simply an ASCII text string that ends in a NUL character (ASCII 0). See Chapter 4 for a discussion of ASCIIZ strings in various languages.

When To Use Handle Functions

In certain instances, which arise because of advanced functions provided by DOS V2 and later versions, you *must* use file handles rather than FCBs. For example, use file handles:

- ❑ Whenever you use path names
- ❑ Whenever I/O redirection and piping are important
- ❑ To support file sharing and locking
- ❑ To support networked environments
- ❑ To use enhanced error reporting
- ❑ For easy access to arbitrary locations in the file

I recommend that you use file handle functions whenever and wherever you can. (But be sure to use FCBs to create volume labels.) By using file handles for all your programs, you instantly gain portability for future environments in which FCBs will not exist. More important, you simplify your programming task.

Ordinarily, when you work with a high-level language such as C or BASIC, you won't want to come down to the level of detail covered in this chapter. High-level languages, after all, offer significant file-manipulation operations. But you will want to use compatible functions—handles. The latest C, BASIC, and Pascal releases all use handle functions for their file-access routines.

Directory Searching: A Practical Example

To illustrate the use of the DOS directory functions, let's develop a simple application that will tell us where a file resides in the hierarchical directory system. All we have to know is the file's name. The program described in the remainder of this chapter was developed to find a file (given its name) anywhere in the file system.

The program, called find.c, searches through the file structure. (C's recursive nature allows descent through the file system without making the program overly complicated.) This program illustrates how file handle functions can be used to access information quickly and naturally.

The basic technique for this simple program is

*For each argument on the command line,
search the file system for all files that have that name*

The program is implemented as follows:

```
/* Program: Find.c */

#include <stdio.h>

main(argc,argv)

/*
     find.c

     This search program locates file names within the directory
     structure of a hard disk. It illustrates the use of the DOS
     directory functions from a high-level language.

     Use the link switch

          /STACK:30000

     with Microsoft C.

*/
int   argc;
char *argv[];

{
     int   i;

     for(i=1; i<argc; i++)
          depth_search("", argv[i]);
}
```

Using file-search procedures that match the requirements of the file name, the search routine (depth_search) checks for files in each directory in the file system.

The basic algorithm follows:

Check the current directory for any files that match the desired file name.

Locate every subdirectory in the current directory and search all of them.

Whenever you enter this recursive routine, a new disk transfer area (DTA) is created. Whenever the function returns, the previous DTA is again made current. You don't have to work with only one DTA: you can have as many as you want, depending on what you need to solve your problem. In this case, the problem was best solved by the program in listing 9.1.

Listing 9.1

```
#include <stdio.h>

/* FIRST or NEXT search flags */
#define   FIRST    Ø
#define   NEXT     1

/* File attribute for search */
#define   FILE     Ø
#define   DIR      16

depth_search(dir,name)

/*
    Search for the name given. This recursive routine calls
    itself whenever it locates a new directory to search.

    Readers not familiar with searching should refer to a book
    about algorithms and/or data structures.
*/

char *dir,
     *name;

{
    char filename[256];   /* File name to search for   */
    char dirname[256];    /* Directory name to search */
    char dta[43];         /* Disk Transfer Area        */
    int  i;               /* Loop control variable     */
    int  flag;            /* Search type flag          */

    sprintf(filename,"%s\\%s",dir,name);
    /* Set the DTA to the local DTA buffer */
    set_dta(dta);

    /*
        Search for the file-name pattern in
        the current directory.
    */
```

Listing 9.1 continues

Listing 9.1 *continued*

```
flag = FIRST;
while(search(filename,flag,FILE)){
    printf("DEPTH:FOUND: %s\\%s\n",dir,dta +30);
    flag = NEXT;
}

/*
    Search for subdirectories in the current directory.
    NOTE: Directories are assumed to have file names
    without extensions and to have the correct attribute.
    When asked to search for a directory, the search
    routine returns all files (normal and directory).

*/
sprintf(filename,"%s\\*.",dir);
flag = FIRST;
while(search(filename,flag,DIR)){
    flag = NEXT;

    /* Specifically exclude "." and ".." from searching */

    if(!streql(".",dta +30) && !streql("..",dta +30)){
        sprintf(dirname,"%s\\%s",dir,dta +30);
        depth_search(dirname,name);
    }

    /* return to local DTA buffer for next directory */

    set_dta(dta);
}
}
```

This routine controls the search through the directory structure but uses the DOS *find file* function (4Eh) to locate files according to the specified search criteria. Whenever a file is found, DOS updates the DTA with information about that file. This information, which is derived from the file's directory entry, is used in depth_search() to print the file name (or to access the directory).

Search(), the routine that interfaces with the DOS functions, is shown in listing 9.2.

Notice in the search() routine that the same registers are set for each function call, whether you are looking for the first occurrence of the file or for any successive occurrences. The only difference is the setting in AH (4Eh for find first, 4Fh for find next). Although all the set information is required only

---

Listing 9.2

```
#include  <stdio.h>
#include  <dos.h>

#define   FALSE    Ø
#define   TRUE ! FALSE

search(fname,flag,type)

    /* Search for the file name given. */

char *fname;
int  flag;
int  type;

{

    union REGS regs;

    /*

        The first search results when the flag is set to Ø,
        which causes DOS Function 4Eh to be executed.
        Subsequent searches, which use DOS Function 4Fh,
        result when the flag is set to 1.

    */
    regs.h.ah = Øx4e  + flag;
    regs.x.cx = type;

    /*

        NOTE: The function requires DS:DX to point to the
        desired file name. We assume here that all variables
        are within the same segment so that DS points to all
        data. This assumption works for small programs but will
        not work when DS is manipulated to define multiple data
        areas.

    */
    regs.x.dx = (int)fname;
    intdos(&regs,&regs);
    if(regs.x.cflag==1)
        return(FALSE);
    return(TRUE);
}
```

---

for the find-first function (4Eh), it does not deter the operation of the find-next function (4Fh). For more detailed information about these functions, refer to the DOS Reference Section at the end of this book.

Whenever a search goes to another level in the hierarchical system, you must retain the DTA from the previous level(s) in order to continue searching. The following routine, set_dta(), lets you designate a buffer area as the current DTA:

```
#include <stdio.h>
#include <dos.h>

set_dta(ptr)

/*
     Sets the Disk Transfer Address (DTA) to the buffer pointed
     to by ptr. The function assumes that DS is already pointing
     to the data area. It is valid for most programs, except
     those with multiple data areas.

*/
char *ptr;

{
     union REGS regs;

     regs.h.ah = 26;
     regs.x.dx = (int)ptr;
     intdos(&regs,&regs);
}
```

The remaining routine, streql(), illustrates the convenience of programming with C functions. In this routine, strcmp() (the standard C library function used for comparing two strings) returns a 0 if the strings are the same. But sometimes, especially in the early development stages of building a program, you will find it convenient to create functions that serve as mnemonic reminders of what you *really* want them to do. For example, streql() returns either TRUE or FALSE, depending on whether the two strings are equal. By using the streql() function, we clarify our logic a little and can concentrate more on the problems that need to be solved. You can squeeze a little speed out of the routine by defining a streql() macro such as the following:

```
    #define streql(x,y)        (strcmp(x,y)==0)
```

By using the macro, you eliminate the overhead of a function call. Why not do it then? You can—depending on your intentions. By defining streql() as a function, you can include it in a library and the linker will make sure it's there when you need it. If you define it as a macro, you must define the macro in the program or in an include file to make it available. One way is simpler for development, one eliminates some overhead.

For most programs, the choice of which form to use depends on the programmer. Some programmers favor functions, others favor macros. The only critical factor during program development is clarity. You want to make everything as clear as possible in order to minimize development problems.

The code listing for the streql() routine follows:

```
#include <stdio.h>

streql(str1,str2)

/*
    Returns TRUE if the two strings are equal; FALSE otherwise.
    This routine is a convenience routine--I prefer thinking in
    terms of the equality of two strings to thinking of the
    comparison function as being equal to zero.
*/
char *str1,
     *str2;

{
    return(strcmp(str1,str2)==0);
}
```

Now that all the pieces of find.c have been described in detail, let's take the program for a test drive. The following test run searches for all occurrences of the file autoexec.*:

```
C>find autoexec.*
DEPTH:FOUND:  \AUTOEXEC.BAT
DEPTH:FOUND:  \AUTOEXEC.DV
DEPTH:FOUND:  \AUTOEXEC.BAK
DEPTH:FOUND:  \AUTOEXEC.WIN
DEPTH:FOUND:  \BIN\LOTUS\INSTALL\AUTOEXEC.BAT
DEPTH:FOUND:  \SYS\AUTOEXEC.DV
DEPTH:FOUND:  \SYS\AUTOEXEC.OLD
DEPTH:FOUND:  \SYS\AUTOEXEC.BAT
```

Summary

In this chapter, you have learned that file access is handled through one of two methods: File Control Blocks (FCBs) or file handles. FCBs are the older form of file access, compatible all the way back to DOS V1. Disk volume labels can be written only with FCB's, but every other kind of file access can be done with handle functions.

Handle functions can work within and with the hierarchical directory structure introduced at DOS V2. They also make programming much simpler because they let the operating system do the bookkeeping for a file.

Whenever you can, use the handle functions for compatibility with later releases of DOS and for maximum simplicity in programming.

Building, as always, on what you have learned, you are ready to move on to the next chapter, which deals with program execution.

Part IV

Memory Management and Miscellaneous Topics

CHAPTER 10

Program and Memory Management

To "get the job done," programmers have developed several dodges and devices for getting more into a program than could be contained in memory. Program chaining, overlays, and other techniques have long been staples of the programmer's art. The first system I worked on, for example, was an IBM 7040 with only 32K of memory; some programs simply could not be done without overlays (see the brief explanation of overlays at the end of this section).

Specialized techniques can turn into debugging nightmares that make programs highly nonportable to other systems. Because of the increased memory and processor speed of large systems, computer programmers have developed techniques for handling programs from within other programs. Command shells, such as COMMAND.COM, use these techniques to execute programs on demand.

On a DOS system, you can control the execution of a program from within another program by using the same functions used by COMMAND.COM. (This is similar to facilities provided on UNIX systems.) This is a relatively clean method of handling program functions. Major modules of the system can exist as stand-alone programs. Each such program can be thoroughly tested and debugged as an independent entity. UNIX programmers have found this technique to be extremely effective for program development.

271

This chapter begins by describing how memory works, how you can get more memory when you need it, and how to let DOS keep the memory you do not need. When you work in a high-level language, the compiler manages this process. In assembly language, however, you should be explicit about what you want to do with memory. The chapter also takes a closer look at expanded memory and examines what can be done with it.

The discussion then moves to program execution—how one process, the *parent*, executes another process, the *child*, and then regains control. A simple example is presented to show how this works.

Finally, a preliminary examination is made of a special kind of program, the TSR (Terminate and Stay Resident). TSRs are different in many ways from "normal" programs (such applications as wordprocessors, spreadsheets, and others). The most obvious difference is that, after they stop, TSRs stay in memory and are not overwritten. A TSR can get control from another program in several ways, the most important of which involves connecting to an interrupt (see Chapter 11, "Interrupt Handlers"). This chapter lays the groundwork for procedures to follow after you understand interrupts.

Let's go on, then, to memory management.

Program Overlays

A program overlay is a section of code or data which is not kept permanently in memory. The program may exist as several binary images, each of which handles some specific functions. The master segment handles overall coordination and usually has functions needed by all overlays.

In a typical program with overlays, the main menu and common functions are in the primary overlay, which is kept in memory at all times. Whenever the program needs a submenu, its overlay is loaded into an overlay area in memory that holds the overlay code. The main module then transfers control to the overlay, and the submenu and its functions are operable.

When the user is done with the submenu and returns to the program's main menu, control is transferred back to the primary overlay. Because the submenu's overlay in memory is no longer needed, the memory space can be used by another overlay (the submenu's program code is "overlaid" by the new code).

How Memory Works

The basic PC or compatible has an address space that holds as much as 1M of memory. (Remember that a megabyte is 1,024K.) As pointed out in Chapter 3, "The Dynamics of DOS," only 640K of this memory is available for program use. The remaining 384K is assigned to the ROM BIOS, display adapters, and cartridges.

The lower 640K of memory is not for user programs only, however. In this space, 1,024 bytes of interrupt vectors are reserved by the processor. Only interrupt vectors go in these locations which, as hardware engineers like to say, are *hard-wired* into the processor (see Chapter 11). Next come BIOS and DOS tables, the DOS kernel, system drivers, and finally the resident portion of the command processor. All of this memory comes from the "user" area of memory.

Calculating how much memory you lose is difficult because it depends on which system you use and which drivers you have loaded. The first user programs generally loaded (in the memory map) are TSRs such as Borland's SideKick. (Figure 10.1 is a graphic representation of memory use with TSRs loaded.) You must subtract their memory use from the available space. If you add a window package similar to DESQview, only about 350K of memory may remain from a starting point of 640K—and all without really starting a program to *do* something!

The space that remains after start-up (usually about 500K to 550K with SideKick loaded) is free and available for use. This space is called the Transient Program Area (TPA), a name used also for the equivalent area on CP/M systems. The name is appropriate because user programs are transient in this area—they come and go as users working on the system need them.

The machine's 640K limit on memory for a working area seemed virtually infinite when PCs were introduced. At that time, a PC with 64K of memory was considered standard; people who had 128K and the rich few who had machines with 256K were envied, although not much software was capable of using the extra memory. As needs grew, the 640K limit became more than an interesting sidelight—it became a major system limitation. Applied to computer memory, Murphy's law, "No matter how much you have, you will need more," became more than a joke.

Although some people (especially those committed to the Macintosh™ and its 68000 processor) have suggested that IBM made a major mistake in using the Intel microprocessor set, the machine has been a success despite its

Fig. 10.1. Memory use with TSRs loaded.

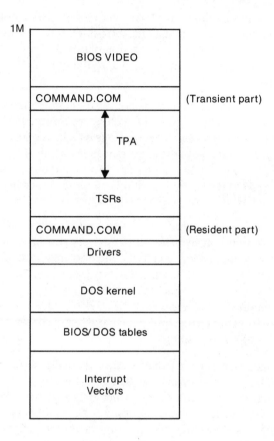

limitations. This is not an argument for or against any particular memory architecture; the important consideration here is what you have to live with *now*.

After the introduction of the 80286 chip, as much as 16M of memory became possible with the PC system. ("Hallelujah," some said. "Now we have a serious system," said others.) But DOS cannot utilize that memory in regular operation. The memory over the 1M limit is known as *extended memory* and is available on the 80286 processor and later models. DOS cannot use it, however; to access memory, the 80286 chip must operate in *protected* mode.

Protected Mode

The protected-mode feature on the 80286 and 80386 processors gives access to special processor functions that control multitasking operations. *Real* mode provides essentially the same environment as that of the 8088/8086 processors with access to only 1M of memory. When the processor is shifted to *protected* mode (generally done inside an operating system), the system can control the operation of multiple programs in memory and shift from one task to another.

This chapter does not describe the features of protected mode in great detail because DOS does not use that mode. To learn more about protected mode, consult any of the many books about 80286/80386 assembly language programming.

DOS runs everything in the processor's real mode; memory above 1M, therefore, is not accessible to programs that work through the normal DOS functions. Even when a system has the extra memory, you cannot use it effectively.

Although programs such as DESQview can tuck some of their operating code into RAM disk drivers that use extended memory like a disk, the memory is not accessible to most programs. (Programs must shift the processor to protected mode before they access the memory, and back to real mode when complete.) Even RAM disks are not necessarily fast when they operate in extended memory because the processor shifts from real mode to protected mode and back again to get to the data—a process that can be relatively slow. On an 80286 processor, going to the hard disk may be faster.

DOS provides two functions that help programs determine how much memory is available (Int 15h, Function 88h) and move data blocks to and from extended memory (Int 15h, Function 87h). But using these routines causes a serious problem because there is no management for the extended memory space. One program can easily write over data that another program (or a RAM disk driver) is keeping in the extended memory space; nothing senses the problem or reports the error.

Expanded memory, first introduced as a joint effort by Lotus ® and Intel at the 1985 spring COMDEX show (version 3.0), provides a way to allow PC access of as much as 8M of memory without requiring a special shift in processor mode. Expanded memory gives the processor access to extra memory through 16K *pages*, which can be mapped into an unused area of between

640K and 1M of memory. Four 16K pages are mapped into a 64K *page frame* at a location determined by users of the system when the board is installed. (See Chapter 3 for a more extensive discussion of expanded memory.)

The Expanded Memory Manager (EMM) causes expanded memory to act like a file with a handle. When your program asks for space in expanded memory, the expanded memory manager sets aside the space and returns a unique "handle" that can be used to get access to the space.

When you want to get to any 16K page from expanded memory, you use Int 67h to call the EMM and tell it to bring the page into the page frame. Then you can address the memory directly from your program. Figure 10.2 shows what happens.

Fig. 10.2. *Expanded memory access.*

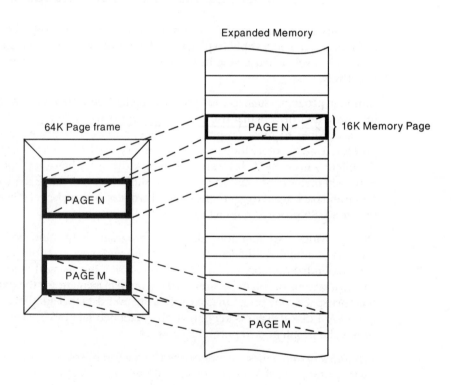

You install EMM.SYS (the Expanded Memory Manager driver) by adding the following line to your CONFIG.SYS file:

```
DRIVER=EMM.SYS
```

The Expanded Memory Manager driver works only partially like a true driver. (*True* drivers are described in Chapter 12, "Device Drivers"; for now, accept that it does not work normally.) Instead of accessing EMM.SYS like a file, as you would any other driver, you access its functions through Int 67h. See the DOS Reference Section for a detailed listing of the functions available through Int 67h.

The functions available through EMM.SYS include

- the status of expanded memory
- the allocation of pages in expanded memory
- the deallocation of pages in expanded memory
- diagnostics
- multitasking support
- the mapping of physical pages in expanded memory to logical pages assigned to programs

This paged-memory technique has been used in computers for a long time. There is no reason why your programs cannot take advantage of expanded memory when it is available.

Shortly after expanded memory was introduced, Microsoft announced its support for version 3.2 of the standard, which included facilities useful for multitasking operating systems. Version 3.2 became known as the LIM (Lotus-Intel-Microsoft) standard. Ashton-Tate ®, AST Research, and Quadram noticed a limitation in the standard: you could map only a 16K page into an unused area of memory. Why not, therefore, map a large area of memory from the TPA? These circumstances led to the development of Enhanced Expanded Memory (EEMS).

With EEMS memory, you can swap one whole program to the expanded memory area and substitute another program. This capability means that a PC can become multitasking in a real sense. LIM 4.0, introduced in 1988, includes EEMS as well as the old LIM 3.2 standard in its specification. All the companies that have been involved in expanded memory technology have announced support for this new standard. As this book is being written, LIM 4.0 has not yet hit the market except as a standard.

As long as we use the basic PC machines, we have to learn to live with the 640K area of space assigned to us. Newer machines lift these 640K restrictions.

Memory Management

Memory management under DOS concerns the free area in the TPA. To maintain compatibility between programs and future releases of the operating system, DOS calls should be used for all memory allocation and deallocation requests.

Although we currently can perform all kinds of tricks in memory, tricky programs will cease to work as we move toward multitasking. By learning now to work within the limitations of DOS, you should be able to write more portable programs in the future. Unfortunately, some of these tricks (such as direct access to the video-display memory) are the staples of DOS programming. Without them, the system is not responsive enough to give users the kind of "feel" necessary for a professional program. Although these tricks make the programs that use them less portable, some loss of portability is sometimes necessary to make good programs.

There are no tricks, however, in dealing with memory allocation. Even a tiny error causes the system to lock up. Let's look next at how DOS controls memory in the TPA.

The TPA is organized into a structure called the *memory arena*. DOS maintains a chained list of memory blocks called arena entries, each with its own special control block called an arena header. Three DOS functions (Int 21h, Functions 48h, 49h, and 4Ah) request or release memory. The DOS Reference Section describes each function in detail.

The arena chain (see fig. 10.3) connects each memory block into a list of memory blocks. Whenever two free memory blocks come in contact, they are combined into a single, larger block with only one arena header in the chain.

When a request is made for memory, DOS searches through the arena chain to locate a block big enough to fill the request. To assign the blocks, DOS employs a *First-Fit* strategy, in which it uses the first block big enough to meet the requirements. If the block contains more memory than is needed, it is split in two and the excess memory is put back in the list as a separate memory block.

DOS uses this First-Fit strategy because it is the most efficient one in general use. Beginning with DOS V3, you can change the allocation strategy to either of the following alternative methods:

❏ *Best Fit*: In this strategy, the whole memory is searched and the memory block that most closely matches the request fills it.

❏ *Last Fit*: The *last* block on the chain (the block with the *highest* memory address) that fits the allocation request is used.

Fig. 10.3. *Memory-allocation chain.*

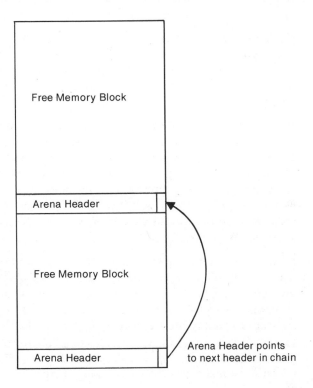

The memory allocation strategy does not need to be changed because the most efficient method is already in use.

Whenever DOS gets an allocation request, it checks the arena list to see whether any problems exist there. If you write over arena headers and otherwise destroy the list, your program is aborted and you see this message:

```
Memory Allocation Error
```

Shrinking Program Memory

When a COM program starts, it is assigned the first block in memory that is large enough to hold the program. Because DOS is inherently a single-user system that runs only one program at a time, memory has been collected into one large block that represents all the TPA. Instead of splitting the block, allocating a portion for the program, and returning the excess for other use, the operating system always assigns the whole block to a COM program. In this way, COM programs actually are assigned all memory.

EXE programs also are assigned all memory. (In this case, you can override the assignment if you want.) The EXE program's header has two parameters: MINALLOC and MAXALLOC. MINALLOC is the minimum memory allocation that the specific program needs in order to run. If a block with at least the minimum amount of memory needed is available, the program is run.

But DOS always tries to assign a block with as much memory as possible—up to MAXALLOC. The Microsoft linker always sets MAXALLOC to 1M. Whenever you link an EXE program, you guarantee that it has all available memory. Although you can change this by telling the linker the maximum number of paragraphs to request in MAXALLOC by including the /C:n switch (*n* is the number of paragraphs to set MAXALLOC for) or by using the EXEMOD program to change the MAXALLOC parameter directly, nobody does. Doing so is seldom necessary.

If you write programs in C, note that both Turbo C and Microsoft C automatically release excess memory when they start. Turbo Pascal, however, does not do so. In Turbo Pascal (versions 3 and 4) all available memory is used, with the highest area being managed as a heap. The only way to limit the amount of memory used by a program written in Turbo Pascal is to set a maximum size for the heap during compilation. Because of the way its memory is allocated with the stack and the heap above the program, no effective method exists for determining where a Pascal program will end.

BASIC also poses problems for programmers because there is no effective way to determine where the program ends in memory, nor is there a way to start a program except by accessing the EXEC function. A special MEMSET function lets the program set its upper memory limit, but this function is intended to allow a BASIC program to load assembly-language support routines rather than to provide for execution of other programs. CHAIN and RUN (BASIC statements for executing other BASIC programs) replace the existing program in memory with a new program instead of maintaining the present program's status.

Among high-level languages, only C is truly suitable for dynamic memory-allocation work. C provides good functions for memory allocation and deallocation; you never have to access the DOS functions for this purpose.

Only programs written in assembly language must explicitly return memory to the memory pool on start-up. Listing 10.1 shows how this is done.

Listing 10.1

```
        mov     sp,offset stack     ;Move stack to safe area
        mov     ah,4Ah              ;Setblock
        mov     bx,280h             ;Retain 10K of space
        int     21h
        jc      alloc_error         ;Allocation error

                [MORE PROGRAM CODE]

        dw      64 dup (?)
stack   equ     $
```

Getting More Memory

If a program needs more memory, it can call for additional memory using the Modify Memory Allocation function (Int 21h, Function 4Ah). If the memory is available, the carry flag is clear and register AX has the segment address of the base of the memory. If no memory is available, the carry flag is set, AX has an error flag (7 = memory control blocks destroyed, 8 = insufficient memory), and register BX has the size of the largest available block.

C provides useful functions for calling for additional memory, as it does for deallocating memory. Pascal's capability for calling for additional memory is minimal or nonexistent unless you use special compiler switches. BASIC provides no way to change allocation of memory to the BASIC program and no way to determine where to go in memory to restrict memory use.

Sometimes, tricky programming can be used in an attempt to free up memory. But Turbo BASIC, for example, while running in the interactive programming environment, stores a symbol table in high memory. This table would be overwritten by another program if you tried to use the memory to load programs.

Again, only in assembly language do we need to access the DOS allocation function directly. In C, the library allocation routines access the DOS functions for us. Listing 10.2 provides a way to get memory and determine how much memory is left if the first attempt is denied.

Several allocation and deallocation functions are available to programs written in C without access to the DOS calls for memory allocation. Using these available functions makes sense because they significantly simplify the operation and keep it under control of the language system. Turbo Pascal owns all available memory in the heap and, as needed, provides for allocation

Listing 10.2

```
getmem:
              mov      ah,48h          ;Allocate memory
              mov      bx,bufsize      ;16K memory
              int      21h
              jc       nomem           ;Can't allocate
              mov      bufseg,ax       ;Save pointer
              jmp      pgm             ;Continue program
nomem:
              cmp      ax,8
              jnz      quit            ;Major alloc error
              mov      bufsize,bx      ;Save buffer size
              mov      ah,48h          ;Allocate memory
              int      21h
              jc       quit            ;Still cannot allocate
pgm:

              [MAIN PART OF PROGRAM]

done:
              mov      ah,49h          ;Deallocate memory
              mov      es,bufseg       ;Point to buffer segment
              int      21h

bufsize  dw        400h
bufseg   dw        0
```

and deallocation of this space to the program. Pascal allocation and deallocation routines do not get or return space from the arena. BASIC requests and
returns nothing.

BASIC and Pascal programmers can limit the memory artificially with compiler switches and then use the DOS function calls to request and free
additional memory. But this exercise leads to confusion and poor memory
handling. Programs that must have dynamic memory handling should be
written in C or assembly language.

Expanded Memory

Sooner or later (when you run out of memory on your PC and have added all
the chips needed to take your system to the 640K limit), you probably will
buy an expanded memory board. Expanded memory allows quick, effective
access to huge amounts of data storage (EMS) or regions for multitasking
(EEMS).

Determining Expanded Memory's Availability

To determine whether expanded memory has been installed, use one of the following methods:

❏ Attempt to open the file EMMXXXX0 (the device driver's guaranteed name). If the open succeeds, either the driver is there or a file with the same name exists. To see whether the driver is there, use the IOCTL function to make a "get output status" request. The driver returns FFh; a file returns 00h. Close the file so that the handle can be reused.

❏ Inspect the address at the Int 67h vector location. This address is the interrupt entry point for the driver. If EMM.SYS is present, then the segment address given is the base of the driver; 10 bytes past that location, the file name appears where it is defined in the header. Although this process is faster than opening a file (open and close overhead is significant), the method relies on the program to access memory outside its normal memory range.

Listings 10.3 and 10.4 give two separate routines in C to check for the presence of the EMS driver.

Listing 10.3

```
#include <dos.h>

emmtest()

/***********************************************************
     Function: emmtest()
     Purpose:  Tests for the presence of expanded memory by
               attempting to open the file EMMXXXXØ (the name of
               the EMM driver). This routine does not run the
               IOCTL test to be sure that this is a driver.
               Returns TRUE if the driver is present; FALSE
               otherwise.
 **********************************************************/

{
        union REGS regs;
        struct SREGS sregs;
        short int result;
        long handle;
```

Listing 10.3 continues

Listing 10.3 continued

```
regs.h.ah = Øx3d;              /* Open file */
regs.h.al = Ø;                 /* Read mode only */
regs.x.dx = (int)"EMMXXXXØ";   /* File name */
sregs.ds = _DS;                /* Set the ds register */
intdosx(&regs,&regs,&sregs);

handle = regs.x.ax;            /* File handle */
/* If opened OK, then close the file */
if(result = (regs.x.cflag == Ø)){
        regs.h.ah = Øx3e;
        regs.x.bx = handle;
        intdos(&regs,&regs);
}
return(result);
}
```

Listing 10.3, which uses the opening-the-file method to determine whether the EMM is installed, doesn't bother to check the IOCTL call to see whether the open returned a file or a driver. In most cases this is not a problem. But to be safe you should add to the function a check of the IOCTL call.

Note that compiling this function with Turbo C yields a warning in the if( ) statement that sets result. This warning can be ignored safely because the desired effect is to set the result's value at TRUE or FALSE, depending on the result of the test. The compiler complains but handles it.

Listing 10.4 turned out to be a real problem for some C programmers who were unaccustomed to dealing with far pointers. When you work on a PC, you must realize the difference between pointers that point within a segment (near pointers); pointers that can point anywhere in memory, given the segment and offset address (far pointers); and pointers that can point anywhere in memory as though memory were not segmented (huge pointers). Whenever pointer arguments are used, you must be precise and always match them; otherwise, unexpected results prevent your program from running.

A more serious error stems from the way some books describe expanded memory. This error occurs because many expanded-memory discussions mistakenly explain that the pointer at Int 67h points to the beginning of the driver, and that 10 bytes from the memory location given in the Int 67h vector is the name EMMXXXX0. A moment's reflection tells you that this statement cannot be true because the interrupt vector points to the location at which control is transferred when the interrupt is called. Because an executable statement is at this location, the location cannot be the beginning of the driver (see Chapter 12, "Device Drivers").

Listing 10.4

```
#include <dos.h>

emmchk()

/*********************************************************
     Function:  emmchk()
     Purpose:   Checks for the presence of expanded memory by
                looking at an offset of 10 from the interrupt
                vector given in Int 67h.
*********************************************************/

{
        union REGS regs;
        struct SREGS sregs;
        char far *emptr, far *nameptr;
        long    testval;

        nameptr = "EMMXXXX0";

        regs.h.ah = 0x35;        /* Get interrupt vector */
        regs.h.al = 0x67;        /* Get it for the EMM */
        intdosx(&regs,&regs,&sregs);

        /* Make a FAR pointer to access the driver */
        emptr = MK_FP(sregs.es,0);

        /* Return TRUE if they are the same for eight characters */
        return(farcmp(emptr+10,nameptr,8));
}

#define         FALSE    0
#define         TRUE     !FALSE

farcmp(str1,str2,n)

char    far *str1,
        far *str2;
int     n;

{
        while(*str2 && n>0){
                if(*str1 != *str2)
                        return(FALSE);
                n--;
                str1++; str2++;
        }
        return(TRUE);
}
```

What actually happens is that the segment address stored with the Int 67h vector does point to the beginning of the driver. The driver memory is always allocated on paragraph boundaries (only multiples of paragraphs can be allocated); the segment address of the driver base is *normalized*—a fancy way of saying that the segment address is adjusted until the offset is zero.

With the segment address in the ES register, you can add 10 bytes to that location and find the driver name as expected. Listing 10.5 is a small program that tests for the presence of expanded memory by both methods and shows you what each one returns.

Listing 10.5

```
#include <stdio.h>

main()

/***********************************************************
      Function:    main()
      Purpose:     Drives demonstration of the functions emmchk()
                   and emmtest(), which test for the presence of
                   expanded memory.
      ***********************************************************/

{
        if(emmchk())
                printf("MEM: Expanded memory is present\n");
        else
                printf("MEM: Expanded memory is NOT present\n");
        if(emmtest())
                printf("OPEN: Expanded memory is present\n");
        else
                printf("OPEN: Expanded memory is NOT present\n");
}
```

Using Expanded Memory

When you know that expanded memory is available, you can use the expanded memory functions tied to Int 67h to get and use memory. (The EMS Reference Section describes the expanded memory functions.) Listings 10.6 and 10.7 show a simple example of the memory functions tied to Int 67.

The program in listing 10.6 demonstrates basic operation of expanded memory. The program does the following:

❏ tests to see whether expanded memory is there

❏ tests to see whether the expanded memory manager is working properly

❑ attempts to allocate 10 pages of expanded memory

❑ maps the pages one at a time into the page frame and writes a test string into each page

❑ maps the pages back into the page frame and then reads out and prints the test string

These are the most basic operations on expanded memory. They allow you to use the memory area in a wide variety of programs. You can use this type of technique to put a spreadsheet or database in expanded memory: to do so, you define an array of values in the page frame and fill them via their pointers. Remember to use far or huge pointers to access the page, because the area certainly will be out of the current segment.

Listing 10.6

```c
#include <stdio.h>

long emmalloc();

main()

/********************************************************
     Function:  main()
     Purpose:   Drives demonstration of the expanded memory-
                access functions.
********************************************************/

{
     long   emmhandle;
     char   teststr[80];
     int    i;

     /* Is there any expanded memory at all??? */
     if(!emmtest()){
          printf("Expanded memory is NOT present\n");
          printf("   cannot run this program\n");
          exit(0);
     }

     /* Is the Expanded Memory Manager functional?? */
     if(!emmok()){
          printf("Expanded memory manager NOT available\n");
          printf("   cannot run this program\n");
          exit(0);
     }
```

Listing 10.6 continues

Listing 10.6 continued

```
/* Get 10 pages of expanded memory for the demo */
if((emmhandle = emmalloc(10)) < 0){
        printf("There are not enough pages available\n");
        printf("   cannot run this program\n");
        exit(0);
}

/* Write the test string into each of the 10 pages. */
for(i=0; i<10; i++){
        sprintf(teststr,"%2d: Terry was here\n",i);
        emmmap(emmhandle,i,0);
        emmmove(0,teststr,strlen(teststr)+1);
}

/* Now read them back in and recover the test string. */
for(i=0; i<10; i++){
        emmmap(emmhandle,i,0);
        emmget(0,teststr,strlen(teststr)+1);
        printf("READING FROM BLOCK %d: %s\n",i,teststr);
}

/* Finally, release the expanded memory. */
emmclose(emmhandle);
}
```

Listing 10.7 is a small library of the expanded memory functions used in listing 10.6. In combination, these functions cover the expanded memory operations, although you might want to expand them and add error checking.

The functions included in the library are

emmtest	Tests for the presence in memory of the expanded memory driver
emmok	Tests the functionality of the expanded memory driver and determines the base address of the page frame
emmalloc	Requests a designated number of pages from the expanded memory manager
emmmap	Maps an expanded memory page into the page frame
emmmove	Moves data into a designated page in the page frame
emmget	Gets data from a designated page in the page frame

emmclose   Returns control of the expanded memory handle to
the expanded memory manager

Simple applications of expanded memory can start with these basic functions
and then grow as error checking and new features are added.

Listing 10.7

```
#include <dos.h>

#define        FALSE    Ø
#define        TRUE     !FALSE

#define        EMM      Øx67

char far *emmbase;

emmtest()

/***********************************************************
     Function:  emmtest()
     Purpose:   Tests for the presence of expanded memory by
                attempting to open the file EMMXXXXØ (the name of
                the EMM driver). This routine does not perform
                the IOCTL test to be sure that this is a driver.
                Returns TRUE if the driver is present; FALSE
                otherwise.
***********************************************************/

{
        union REGS regs;
        struct SREGS sregs;
        short int result;
        long handle;

        regs.h.ah = Øx3d;                  /* Open file */
        regs.h.al = Ø;                     /* Read mode only */
        regs.x.dx = (int)"EMMXXXXØ";       /* File name */
        sregs.ds = _DS;                    /* Set the ds register */
        intdosx(&regs,&regs,&sregs);

        handle = regs.x.ax;                /* File handle */
        if(result = (regs.x.cflag == Ø)){
                regs.h.ah = Øx3e;
                regs.x.bx = handle;
                intdos(&regs,&regs);
        }
        return(result);
```

Listing 10.7 continues

Listing 10.7 continued

```
}

emmok()

/********************************************************
     Function:  emmok()
     Purpose:   Checks to see whether the expanded memory manager
                responds correctly. If it does, it locates the
                base of the page frame. Returns FALSE if an error
                occurs in either operation; TRUE if everything is
                successful.
********************************************************/

{
        union REGS regs;

        regs.h.ah = Øx4Ø;                    /* Get manager status */
        int86(EMM,&regs,&regs);
        if(regs.h.ah != Ø)
                return(FALSE);

        regs.h.ah = Øx41;                    /* Get page frame segment */
        int86(EMM,&regs,&regs);
        if(regs.h.ah != Ø)
                return(FALSE);

        emmbase = MK_FP(regs.x.bx,Ø);
        return(TRUE);
}

long emmalloc(n)

/********************************************************
     Function:  emmalloc()
     Purpose:   Requests n pages of expanded memory and returns
                the file handle assigned to the pages or -1 if
                there is an error.

     Note: This routine should check to see whether the
                number of pages requested is available before
                making the call.
********************************************************/

int     n;

{
        union REGS regs;
```

Listing 10.7 continues

Listing 10.7 continued

```
        regs.h.ah = Øx43;           /* Get handle and allocate memory */
        regs.x.bx = n;
        int86(EMM,&regs,&regs);
        if(regs.h.ah != Ø)
                return(-1);
        return(regs.x.dx);
}

emmmap(handle,phys,page)

/********************************************************
    Function:   emmmap()
    Purpose:    This function maps a physical "page" from
                expanded memory into the page frame in the 16K
                window "frame."
********************************************************/

long    handle;
int     phys;
int     page;

{
        union REGS regs;

        regs.h.ah = Øx44;           /* Map memory */
        regs.h.al = page;
        regs.x.bx = phys;
        regs.x.dx = handle;
        int86(EMM,&regs,&regs);
        return(regs.h.ah == Ø);
}

emmmove(page,str,n)

/********************************************************
    Function:   emmmove()
    Purpose:    Moves n bytes from the local pointer "str" to the
                page specified in "frame."
********************************************************/

int     page;
char    *str;
int     n;

{
        char far *ptr;
```

Listing 10.7 continues

Listing 10.7 continued

```
        ptr = emmbase + page*16384;
        while(n-- > Ø)
                *ptr++ = *str++;
}

emmget(page,str,n)

/********************************************************
    Function:  emmget()
    Purpose:   Moves n bytes from the page "page" into the
               string "str."
********************************************************/

int     page;
char    *str;
int     n;

{
        char far *ptr;

        ptr = emmbase + page*16384;
        while(n-- > Ø)
                *str++ = *ptr++;
}

emmclose(handle)

/********************************************************
    Function:  emmclose()
    Purpose:   Releases the handle and returns control of the
               pages to the expanded memory manager.
********************************************************/

long    handle;

{
        union REGS regs;

        regs.h.ah = Øx45;               /* Release handle */
        regs.x.dx = handle;
        int86(EMM,&regs,&regs);
        return(regs.h.ah == Ø);
}
```

Program Execution

One of DOS's most useful features is its capability to run a program, the child, from within another program, the parent, without losing the original or parent program's current state. On a UNIX system, the function can spin off parallel processes. DOS is similar, but the parent process sleeps (stops functioning) while the new one runs.

Some of the EXEC function's basic features let programs perform the following tasks:

- ❏ spin off a child in the system's free memory
- ❏ wait for the completion of the child's operations
- ❏ receive from the child a return code that can be used for
  indicating normal completion, error terminations, or status codes

The DOS designers created the EXEC function as a stepping stone to a more powerful multitasking system in the future. That system probably will be OS/2; a significant DOS enhancement toward multitasking seems unlikely.

To use the EXEC function, enough memory must be available to run the new program. (See the earlier discussion to learn how to release memory.)

The EXEC Function

When enough program memory is available, you can execute another program with the EXEC function. When you call the EXEC function (Int 21h, Function 4Bh), the registers must be set up like this:

Register	Purpose
AL =0	Load and execute program
DS:DX	Pointer to full path name
ES:BX	Pointer to parameter block

AL can be set to 03h to tell the EXEC function to load into memory an overlay that the parent process already owns. Because overlays are not a factor at this point, you can concentrate on executing programs.

The DS:DX register pair points to the path name of the executable file. The path name can be one of the following:

- ❏ the file name of the program to execute, including the extension .EXE or .COM. (In this case, the program must be in the present directory.)

❑ a relative path name to the file, starting with a dot (.) and giving the directories in the path from the current working directory to the program

❑ a full path name to the file, starting at the root directory (\) and going to the file

Suppose, for example, that you want to execute the program DEMO.EXE in the \UTIL directory. If you are already in the \UTIL directory, you can refer to the program as

    DEMO.EXE

If you are in the \APPL directory, you can refer to the program by its relative path name:

    .\..\UTIL\DEMO.EXE

In this case, you can simplify the path name by starting with the "dot-dot" directory:

    ..\UTIL\DEMO.EXE

Finally, from any location, you can always refer to the program as

    \UTIL\DEMO.EXE

A path name must include everything needed to find the file; it can contain no wild-card characters. The file name must be spelled out in full and include the .EXE or .COM extension. Batch files (.BAT extension) cannot be executed with the EXEC function.

Features you are accustomed to using, such as wild cards in file names or path searches for the file, are functions of COMMAND.COM, not of the EXEC function. COMMAND.COM looks for files by searching the path environment variable. It also executes batch files using internal batch-file execution procedures. None of this can be done with the EXEC function. The same principle applies to COMMAND.COM internal commands. Commands such as DIR that are internal to COMMAND.COM cannot be executed separately.

The ES:BX register pair points to a parameter block that contains four additional addresses:

1. Environment block (two bytes, segment address)

2. Command tail (four bytes, offset then segment)

3. File control block 1 (four bytes, offset then segment)

4. File control block 2 (four bytes, offset then segment)

The environment block is the collection of program environment variables of the form VARIABLE =VALUE set by DOS or added by your SET instructions. For example, the variable TMP could be set equal to \TMP, a temporary directory area, so that some programs that create temporary files will create them there. The AUTOEXEC.BAT file would have the following line:

SET TMP =C:\TMP

All such variables together are what you point at with the environment block. For most circumstances, you simply want to retain the environment in which your present program works. Setting the environment block to zero causes EXEC to pass the parent program's environment to the child.

The command-tail pointer locates the portion of the command line that follows the command itself. For example, if you type the command

/BIN/COMMAND /C DIR

the command tail is /C DIR.

The command tail is stored as a count byte that gives the command-tail length, the command tail itself, and a carriage return (Function 0Dh). This command tail, fully laid out for use, would look like this:

```
1   2 3 4 5 6 7 8
Ø6h / C   D I R C/R
```

The last two parameters are initial settings for the File Control Blocks (FCB) included in the Program Segment Prefix (PSP). Unless you use FCB functions to maintain compatibility with DOS V1, you can safely let them point almost anywhere because you will ignore them. If you do intend to use FCBs, then they should be set up as described in Chapter 9.

The program in listing 10.8 executes the program \COMMAND.COM with the command tail /C DIR. There are some special features to note here:

❑ The stack pointer has not been saved explicitly, even though this function destroys it. intdos restores it automatically.

❑ The segment registers had to be retrieved in order to properly set all the pointers.

The program begins by getting the segment registers. This is the proper method in Microsoft C; in Turbo C, the segment registers are available as variables. See the emmtest() routine in the expanded memory program (listing 10.7) earlier in the chapter for an example of setting the DS register from the Turbo C-DS variable.

Listing 10.8

```c
#include <stdio.h>
#include <dos.h>

main()

/*******************************************************
    Function:  main()
    Purpose:   Demonstrates the use of the EXEC function to
               execute a program.
*******************************************************/

{
        union REGS regs;
        struct SREGS segs;
        struct {
                int     envblk;    /* Environment block */
                int     ocmd;      /* Command tail */
                int     scmd;
                int     ofcb;      /* FCB #1 */
                int     sfcb;
                int     ofcb2;     /* FCB #2 */
                int     sfcb2;
        } pblock;
        char    buffer[256];
        char    name[128];

        segread(&segs);
        strcpy(name,"\\command.com");
        printf("Executing program %s\n",name);

        /* Set up the Command Tail */
        buffer[Ø] = 6;                                  /* Number of characters */
        strcpy         (buffer+1,"/c dir\Ø15"); /* Command tail */
        pblock.ocmd = (int)buffer;
        pblock.scmd = segs.ds;

        /* Use parent's environment */
        pblock.envblk = Ø;

        /* Set up FCBs #1 and #2 */
        pblock.ofcb = (int)buffer;
        pblock.sfcb = segs.ds;
        pblock.ofcb2 = (int)buffer;
        pblock.sfcb2 = segs.ds;
```

Listing 10.8 continues

Listing 10.8 continued

```
/*
        Execute the designated program using the
        EXEC function 4Bh.
*/
regs.h.ah = 0x4b;
regs.h.al = 0;
regs.x.dx = (int)name;
segs.es = segs.ds;
regs.x.bx = (int)&pblock;
intdosx(&regs,&regs,&segs);

/*
        If the carry flag is set, then an error code is
        in the ax register.
*/
if(regs.x.cflag==1)
        printf("Error Code = %d\n",regs.x.ax);
}
```

After the program knows the segment register values, it sets up each parameter for the EXEC function call, command tail, environment (the default), and FCBs. Then it executes the function and checks whether any error codes are returned.

C's perfectly good exec() function for running children is preferred in all but the most unusual cases. As mentioned earlier, neither BASIC nor Turbo Pascal has equivalent facilities.

Program Exits

One of DOS EXEC's powerful features is its capability to have a program pass back a final status to the program that spawned it. By using Int 21h, Function 4Ch (the preferred exit function), a program can pass back an exit status that can be used for further decision making. UNIX systems use this capability all the time to manage the execution of systems of programs.

One recent example from my experience included a program that sequenced a series of other programs through a succession of operations. Depending on how certain programs ended, the main program could provide branches to alternative processing. In this case, the complicated process included interfacing with an IBM mainframe and making intelligent decisions about a database. If the IBM mainframe data transfer did not take place, the "add records to database" step was skipped and the database was processed for use.

The return code from a program is available inside a batch file as the variable ERRORLEVEL, which can be used to branch the logic in the file. If you are executing the program from another program, then the parent can get the return code from the child by calling Int 21h, Function 4Dh after the EXEC function returns. Register AH has one of the following exit types:

Exit code	Meaning
00	Normal termination
01	Terminated by a Ctrl-C command
02	Critical device error
03	TSR return (Int 21h, Function 31h)

Register AL has the return code from the child process.

Memory-Resident Programming

The TSR utility is a hot item for programming PCs. Borland's introduction of SideKick caused a major upheaval in the PC software market. So many TSR utilities are available now that if you used them all, there would not be room for executable programs. We always seem to want more TSRs than we can possibly accommodate.

Most people do not realize that what they consider to be a TSR is only one of two types of TSRs that can be set up and used. The TSR utility (like SideKick and others) was not the TSR function's intended purpose. TSRs originally were seen as extensions of the operating system.

The two types of TSRs are

- ☐ *Active TSRs:* These pop-up utilities such as SideKick and others are the most common type of TSRs. They usually are operated by responding to a specified keystroke called the hot key. When these utilities are activated, they take over the computer and perform their function before they return control to the program that originally controlled the machine.

- ☐ *Inactive TSRs:* These TSRs respond when a calling program calls a designated interrupt. When called, they perform a defined function, similar to a subroutine, and then return control to the calling program.

Active TSRs give users the impression of multitasking on a PC. TSRs do not actually multitask, but you get the definite impression that more than one operation is happening simultaneously. To give this illusion of operation, active TSRs are complex. As you know, DOS is not reentrant (you cannot break out of the middle of an internal DOS routine and restart it from somewhere else). If DOS is processing something (a disk access, for example) when a TSR activates to write something to the disk, you can cause serious problems and possibly mess up your disk.

Active TSRs have to watch what both DOS and users do. You will see some of these tricks in Chapter 11's discussion of TSRs as interrupt service routines.

Inactive TSRs work in a benign environment. An inactive TSR starts nothing until it is called by a program. Because DOS is a single-tasking environment, only one operation can be in progress at a time and we know that no DOS operation can be in progress when the TSR is called. Therefore, we are safe using DOS calls from an inactive TSR.

The TSR concept has undergone some major changes since DOS was introduced. The original TSR function (Int 27h) has been superseded by Int 21h, Function 31h. This function is more convenient to use because it allows a return code to be passed and lets the TSR use more than 64K of memory. Both of these factors justify using the preferred TSR call: Int 21h, Function 31h.

When a TSR runs, it sets up its memory tables and prepares for execution by connecting to a DOS interrupt. When everything is ready, the program determines how much memory it needs to keep; then it sets AH to 31h, AL to the return code, and DX to the number of paragraphs (16-byte blocks) to allocate to the TSR. When the program exits, the amount of memory available for executing programs is reduced by the amount assigned to the TSR, and the exit code passes back to the parent.

Sounds simple, doesn't it? It can be—for extremely simple TSRs. But if you are writing the next SideKick utility you will find that much more is involved than simply executing the TSR.

First, you must have a way to trigger the TSR's action. You can attach the TSR to the timer interrupt and activate the TSR's operation every specified number of seconds. More often, you attach the TSR to the keyboard service interrupt and look for a certain keystroke. With a proliferation of TSRs, collisions will occur because most keystrokes are used somewhere.

No matter how you attach a TSR to a system, the TSR must recognize the possible presence of other TSRs in the system. In order to allow other operations to occur on the trigger, a TSR must call the interrupt service routine that originally handled the interrupt before the start of the TSR. Furthermore, to prevent overlap with other functions, you should be able to change the keystrokes that trigger the TSR.

When you deal with DOS functions, TSRs and interrupt service routines (ISRs) are in the same danger. The MS-DOS system was always intended to be a single-user, single-task system and so is not reentrant (you cannot break out of an internal DOS function and restart it from another location). Because an active TSR or ISR responds to events that may not be synchronized to the operation of DOS functions, it is possible for a TSR or ISR to get control of the computer while an internal DOS function is in progress. Several undocumented DOS functions help us to determine when using DOS functions is safe and when it's not. These undocumented functions are discussed in Chapter 11.

Writing a successful TSR can be a major project, well worth a book of its own. A sophisticated TSR that includes many subfunctions, windows, and other features can take a team of sophisticated programmers a long time to implement. We'll build a simple TSR in Chapter 11 after you have learned enough about interrupts to make them work for you.

Summary

This chapter has covered memory management, expanded memory, and program execution. You have learned that TPA (Transient Program Area) memory is allocated by DOS to fill requests from programs that need memory. When programs start, they normally get all of available memory to work in and should release any memory that they will not use.

Assembly language programmers must explicitly release memory; C programmers have it done by the start-up code for their programs, and BASIC and Pascal programmers cannot release memory except at compile time.

Expanded memory gives us access to additional memory by paging a large amount of memory into the addressable 1M of PC memory. We can use this memory in 16K pages to store and retrieve data. To do so, we use the Int 67h function calls, which are detailed in the EMS Reference Section at the end of this book.

When we have enough memory available, DOS lets us run programs from within other programs (just as COMMAND.COM does). We can use this memory to tie together individual programs into a software system. TSRs (Terminate and Stay Resident programs) allow us to create programs that can coexist in memory while other programs are operating. With the techniques discussed in the next chapter, "Interrupt Handlers," we can create TSRs that can be invoked from the keyboard to give us the impression for multitasking.

CHAPTER 11

Interrupt Handlers

In this chapter, we look deep into the DOS system to discuss something that has a reputation for obscurity unlike anything else in computer programming—interrupt handlers. Interrupt handlers are programs that respond to the activation of an interrupt.

You may find that interrupt handling is really not so bad. At some levels, in fact, it is easily managed. But there are still a few "black holes" that you can drop into and never escape. The information in this chapter can keep you from getting lost.

Interrupts have been around for years. Part of their unsavory reputation was gained when they were first introduced as a major part of system design. On early computer systems, interrupts were often a major headache because programmers had no experience working with them and took unjustified shortcuts.

Interrupts have been the domain of systems programmers and hardware engineers for so long that many programmers were afraid to touch them. Luckily, a PC is a relatively benign place to work with interrupts. The problems you may have are managed simply if you write your interrupt handlers according to some general guidelines. As you gain experience, you will be able to control interrupts without thinking about it. Then, you will have arrived.

This chapter starts with a description of interrupts. There is a discussion of interrupts generated by internal and external hardware as well as those generated in software. As the discussion proceeds, you should begin to develop a feel for how interrupts can serve you. Some practical examples round out the interrupt handling discussion.

After you learn about interrupts, the chapter returns to the discussion that was started in the last chapter—the discussion of Terminate and Stay Resident (TSR) utilities. Nearly every TSR attaches itself in some way to an interrupt and responds to it as an Interrupt Service Routine (ISR). This chapter describes what makes a good TSR and discusses instances when using one does not make sense.

Let's start at the most basic level by trying to find out what an interrupt is.

What Is an Interrupt?

An interrupt is a signal to the processor that an event needing special attention has happened. It is used to catch the processor's attention for something important. If you didn't have interrupts, you would have to *poll* each device periodically and check whether it had something for you. Polling tends to waste a processor's time with a lot of useless checking.

If you have 60 devices on a polled system and checking a device takes 1 second, then each device is checked 1 time per minute. If you need a faster response to a condition, polling is just not suitable. An interrupt may occur, for example, when a disk drive signals that it has a sector of information ready to transfer to main memory. If the processor ignores the interrupt or waits before getting to it, the block is lost, so the processor is forced to stop what it is doing and immediately pick up the interrupt.

Interrupts like the one in the preceding example are caused by external events. They can be caused also by internal events such as a divide-by-zero error in a calculation or a program's specific request to execute a software interrupt.

Whenever your computer senses an interrupt condition, it saves whatever it is doing and transfers control to an interrupt handler, which is expected to service the condition and then return. Some processors provide only restricted interrupt identification and depend on the interrupt handler to identify the interrupt and take appropriate action. This type of handler wastes time identifying what has happened. Interrupts are handled more efficiently on the 8086 family by using interrupt vectors to speed you on your way for a specific interrupt.

Programming interrupt handlers has been a somewhat arcane art, known to only an enlightened few, especially on some older computer systems. Interrupt handling on some systems involved issues of precise timing and a knowledge of the intricacies of processor and computer design that went far beyond what typical programmers ever encountered. On systems in which interrupts can occur, multilevel interrupt errors are the bane of all programmers' existence because the path to an error may be random at best and nearly impossible to find. Errors that occur only once in a great while can be particularly difficult to find.

Interrupts on PCs, however, are relatively well behaved both because PCs are single-user and single-process systems and because the interrupt structure is much more sophisticated. You still have to be careful, but you can use this standard interrupt structure to handle the following situations:

1. Save anything that the processor did not save automatically when the interrupt occurred.

2. Block any interrupts that might interfere with the handler's operation.

3. Enable interrupts that can occur safely during the handler's operation.

4. Handle the interrupt.

5. Restore the processor registers saved in Step 1.

6. Reenable interrupts.

7. Return to normal processing.

This prescription does not guarantee good interrupt handling but it does guide you through this nest of vipers with your eyes open.

You already have encountered one situation, serial I/O, that cannot be handled effectively unless you tie an interrupt handler to the serial port. Microsoft BASIC provides an internal interrupt handler for communications that allows you to do serial I/O. In C, Pascal, or assembly language, you have to write your own handler.

The Ctrl-Break/Ctrl-C handler is another useful interrupt handler. For many programs, Ctrl-Break leaves the program in a bad state—with files not updated and so forth. To close down the program in an orderly manner, a Ctrl-Break handler lets your program control the exit.

How Interrupts Work

When an interrupt occurs, the processor can be in any state. A processor is designed so that it always completes any step in progress before it responds to an interrupt. When the processor sees an interrupt, it responds by pushing the flag register (the program status word), the instruction pointer (IP), and the code segment register (CS) on the stack and disabling interrupts.

After this critical machine-state information is saved, the processor looks to the system bus for an 8-bit number, the *interrupt vector*. Interrupt vectors are pointers to the programs that handle specific functions. The number, supplied by the interrupting device, directs the processor to check the *interrupt vector table* for the address of the program that processes the interrupt. The Intel 8086 processor family defines the first 1024 bytes of memory as the interrupt vector table. The program that processes the interrupt is the interrupt handler.

The processor simply multiplies the interrupt vector by 4 to get an offset address and then looks in segment 0000h to find the vector. This vector address is loaded into CS:IP, and the processor resumes operation from the new location pointed to by CS:IP.

After the processor is in the interrupt handler, the handler controls the processor. Most handlers first reenable interrupts so that higher-priority interrupts can be serviced. They also save any other registers that they use and then carry out their own operations as quickly as possible. For some devices a special acknowledgment signal must be passed so that the device knows it has been serviced. The handler must provide this where necessary.

Interrupt handlers generally must be written to be as tight and as fast as possible. Most of them are written in assembly language to eliminate all possible overhead and to ensure that the routine runs as quickly as possible. On large, powerful computers, handlers usually are written in a language like C to make them as simple as possible. On PCs, you can write handlers in C (there are C examples in this chapter) but time-critical interrupts should be handled with as little overhead as possible.

Interrupts triggered through the 8259A Programmable Interrupt Controller (PIC) must send an end-of-interrupt signal to the PIC when the processing is finished. All interrupts must restore the machine state by first restoring any registers saved and then executing an interrupt return (IRET) instruction that restores the flag register, CS, and IP to the values that existed before the interrupt occurred.

The Intel 8086 Family Interrupts

Interrupts on the 8086 microprocessor family come in three classes:

- ❏ Internal hardware
- ❏ External hardware
- ❏ Software

This section describes all three of these types of interrupts.

Internal Hardware Interrupts

Internal hardware interrupts are wired into a processor to handle special cases, such as a divide-by-zero error or other conditions in which a processor has recognized an error. These conditions are listed in table 11.1. ´

***Table 11.1.** Internal Hardware Interrupts*

Interrupt Level	Vector Offset Address	Meaning
8086 Processor Hardware Interrupts		
00h	00h	Divide by zero
01h	04h	Single step
02h	08h	Nonmaskable interrupt
03h	0Ch	Break point
04h	10h	Overflow
80286 Processor Hardware Interrupts		
05h	14h	Bound range exceeded
06h	18h	Invalid opcode
07h	1Ch	Processor extension not available
08h	20h	Double exception
09h	24h	Segment overrun
0Ah	28h	Invalid task-state segment
0Bh	2Ch	Segment not present
0Ch	30h	Stack segment overrun
0Dh	34h	General protection fault

We do not program directly with any of these interrupts. In the PC design, IBM reassigned some of these interrupts to deal with other conditions. A conflict remains between what is programmed in the 8086 family chips and what IBM has assigned the interrupt vectors for. This is not a good situation, but we have to deal with it. Table 11.2 lists the IBM-assigned interrupt vectors. Compare tables 11.1 and 11.2 to see the conflicts.

Table 11.2. Interrupt Vectors

Vector	Action
00h	Divide by zero
01h	Single step
02h	Nonmaskable interrupt
03h	Break point
04h	Overflow
05h	Print screen
06h	Unused
07h	Unused
08h	Hardware IRQ0 (timer tick)
09h	Keyboard input interrupt
0Ah	Reserved
0Bh	Asynchronous port controller 1 (COM2)
0Ch	Asynchronous port controller 0 (COM1)
0Dh	Fixed disk controller
0Eh	Floppy disk controller
0Fh	Printer controller
10h	Video driver
11h	Equipment-configuration check
12h	Memory-size check
13h	Floppy disk/fixed disk (PC/XT)
14h	Comm port driver
15h	Cassette/network service
16h	Keyboard driver
17h	Printer driver
18h	ROM BASIC
19h	Restart system
1Ah	Set/read real time clock
1Bh	Ctrl-Break handler
1Ch	Timer tick (user defined)
1Dh	Video parameter table
1Eh	Disk parameter table
1Fh	Graphics character table (characters 80–FFh)

Table 11.2 continues

Table 11.2 *continued*

Vector	Action
20h	Program terminate
21h	DOS function dispatcher
22h	Terminate vector
23h	Ctrl-C vector
24h	Critical-error vector
25h	Absolute disk read
26h	Absolute disk write
27h	Terminate and Stay Resident
28h	DOS OK interrupt
2Fh	Printer spooler
40h	Floppy disk driver (PC/XT)
41h	Fixed disk parameter table
43h	Graphics character table

External Hardware Interrupts

External hardware can be tied to the processor to allow the device to signal an interrupt. Most early microcomputer systems that used interrupts were built this way. Two connections are available: the nonmaskable interrupt (NMI) and the maskable interrupt (INTR). As the names imply, you can turn off the INTR but not the NMI.

NMI interrupts are used for problems in which you do not want the interrupt turned off for any reason. On some systems, a physical reset switch wired to an NMI interrupt lets operators get the processor's attention—no matter what.

INTR interrupts are wired through the 8259A PIC to take advantage of the chip's capability to prioritize and control interrupts under software control. Processor instructions can directly enable or disable interrupts, and instructions to the PIC can selectively enable and disable interrupts.

The interrupts, however, are set at the hardware level. In some cases, manufacturers set the interrupt levels, and nothing can change them. Some devices provide switches or jumpers that can reset the interrupt level within a limited range of values.

Software Interrupts

Software interrupts are caused by a program issuing the software interrupt instruction to make the processor act as though it received a hardware interrupt. This method is convenient for accessing DOS and BIOS services independent of any one program. The services can be linked to specific interrupts and changed at will without affecting application programs that call them.

Interrupt Vectors

The interrupt vector table is stored in the bottom 1,024 bytes of system memory with 4 bytes per interrupt, for a total of 256 distinct interrupt vectors. Each 4-byte entry is composed of the segment number and offset of the interrupt handler for that function or, in some cases, the address of a table of values—such as the graphic-character table pointed to by Int 1Fh.

Getting and Setting Interrupt Vectors

All the cautions about interrupt vectors should warn you that anything affecting the interrupt vectors can have damaging side effects. Imagine that you are two bytes into changing an interrupt vector four bytes long and you are interrupted by another process that needs the vector you are changing; the CPU jumps to an incomplete vector address and can end up virtually anywhere in memory. This situation most often results in "hanging" your computer.

How realistic is this scenario? DOS is a single-task system, in which only one operation can happen at a time. But another interrupt service routine, responding to a hardware interrupt, simply takes control and leaves your program halfway through it. Many a TSR takes control of interrupts when it (the TSR) is activated and then returns the interrupts to their original settings when the TSR is finished. This situation *can* happen.

More important is the upward-compatibility issue. Modifying an interrupt vector directly is not compatible with future DOS upgrades (including OS/2, if you want to view it as an upgrade). Although direct modification might work now, it is guaranteed not to work on a multitasking system. DOS, however, provides a safe way to change the interrupt vectors by using Int 21h, Functions 25h (set interrupt vector) and 35h (get interrupt vector).

To set an interrupt vector, follow these steps:

1. Use Function 35h to get the current vector value and store it for later use in restoring the interrupt and chaining to any routine already using the interrupt.

2. Use Function 25h to set the new vector.

This process is simple in assembly language (see listing 11.1).

Listing 11.1

```
;------------ Get the Ctrl-C Vector   ----------

        mov     ah,35h          ;Get vector
        mov     al,23h          ;Ctrl-C
        int     21h
        mov     oldseg,es       ;Store old vector
        mov     oldoff,bx


;------------ Set the Ctrl-C Vector   ----------

        mov     ah,25h              ;Set vector
        mov     al,23h              ;Ctrl-C
        mov     dx, seg c_hand
        mov     ds,dx
        mov     dx, offset c_hand
        int     21h
```

Turbo C provides two functions, getvect and setvect, that do the same thing as DOS Functions 35h and 25h without actually calling the DOS functions. Microsoft C Compiler version 5.0 adds the new functions _dos_getvect and _dos_setvect that perform the same actions. In Turbo Pascal 4.0, functions GetIntVec and SetIntVec perform the same actions.

You do not need to go down to the DOS level to set the interrupts. The available high-level language services help set them cleanly and eliminate concern over encountering a problem. These high-level language routines are more convenient ways of performing the Int 21h, Function 25h and 35h services.

When Should You Write an Interrupt Handler?

Creating an interrupt handler of your own makes sense in the following situations:

☐ *When you have to trap an interrupt to keep your program from failing in unusual cases.* When you write commercial programs, you should never let users "bomb out" of your program on a divide-by-zero error or on some other error. Your program should handle the error. Furthermore, if your program performs any "fancy" operations, you should trap Ctrl-C and Ctrl-Break events and handle them instead of letting the system cut you off.

☐ *When you have to link into an interrupt chain.* Here are two examples: writing a TSR that executes on certain keystrokes, or writing a special timing routine that you want to do from within a program.

☐ *When you have to control the serial port.* As I have mentioned, DOS doesn't provide adequate service for the serial ports. If you want to write a real terminal program, it must have an interrupt-driven, serial-port servicing routine.

In cases other than the ones just described, you should attempt to make your code as high-level as possible. If you can code the interrupt handler in a high-level language, by all means do so, unless the interrupt handler simply does not run fast enough in your program. Debugging is much easier in a high-level language than in assembly language. You can always recode the handler if it is not fast enough.

Wherever possible, take advantage of the high-level language facilities for interrupt handling. Turbo C provides the ctrlbrk() function for setting a Ctrl-C interrupt handler from a high-level code module. Microsoft C provides the UNIX-compatible signal() function for handling signal traps. Turbo BASIC and QuickBASIC each provide ON KEY/TIMER/etc.-type handlers for handling events. Turbo Pascal can handle interrupts that have in-line assembly code or the new Interrupt directive defined in Turbo Pascal 4.0. Choose the highest level that can do the job.

When you write an interrupt handler, you must be careful not to use DOS-type functions unless special care is taken. DOS is not reentrant: if it is interrupted while it is doing something, you could easily cause the system to lock up by calling DOS functions again.

One way not to invoke DOS functions is to have the interrupt handler do some setup processing (copy data to a memory buffer, for example). It can set a flag that can be recognized by the program currently using the system to do some additional processing, which might involve DOS calls. More to the point, DOS has some hidden ways to find out when DOS calls are safe. Hackers who spend their time trying to find out how other people perform computer techniques learned about and published the ways to learn what DOS does.

First, an undocumented Int 21h function (Function 34h) returns a pointer in the ES:BX registers. This pointer points to a DOS busy flag, called the *InDOS flag*. The flag is a single byte buried in the operating-system kernel. Whenever an Int 21h function starts, the flag is incremented by one. When the function ends, the flag is decremented by one. Whenever the flag is zero, no DOS functions are executing.

TSRs check for this flag whenever their hot key is pressed. If the flag is nonzero, then the TSR sets a hot-key flag in the TSR. TSRs that do this tie into the clock interrupt and check the status of InDOS 18.2 times per second until the flag clears. When InDOS is clear and the hot-key flag is set, the TSR starts its operations.

That is good, but leaves you hanging when the command processor is waiting for you to type a command line. Because the command processor uses DOS functions for command-line input, the InDOS flag is set while DOS waits for characters. Clearly, DOS is in a safe position and can be interrupted for other operations provided that you do not use the DOS functions to do any console I/O. To allow console I/O to occur, DOS has another undocumented interrupt, 28h, which is called repeatedly by the console input routines while they are waiting. This is the DOS Idle (or DOSOK) interrupt.

The DOS Idle interrupt normally does an IRET, which returns control to the console input routine. If a TSR is tied to the interrupt and notices that the hot-key flag is on, the body of the TSR can be executed immediately.

When you work with interrupts, be sure to follow a simple rule: *Always* assume that other programs may be involved. For example, you should never set interrupt vectors directly. Int 21h, Function 25h is provided for this purpose and prevents any mix-ups between programs setting the vectors. Unless you write something such as a Ctrl-C handler, you should preserve the original handler vector and branch to it when you complete your processing. You also can install another handler, which needs to be activated. If you don't observe this simple rule, you can get into trouble.

When your program ends, it should clear any interrupts it has set (the system automatically handles Ctrl-C). If you write a terminal program, for example, you should restore the interrupts before you leave the program, thus preventing an interrupt from branching to where the handler used to be. If your program is setting up a resident handler, then you should use the TSR exit rather than the normal exit so that the handler will be allocated the memory it needs and not be overwritten.

Writing a Ctrl-C Handler

A simple Ctrl-C handler serves as an example of interrupt handling. This handler is presented in several stages to show you several methods for handling the interrupt problem.

In the first example, handler.c, I have used the ctrlbrk() function in Turbo C to create a handler totally in C (see listing 11.2). Handler.c allows you to interrupt the process in progress and determine whether to leave. Because the ctrlbrk() function handles aborts, you return the appropriate code to the routine depending on the answer to the question.

This method of writing the routine is particularly convenient because it is high level, works the first time, and involves no arcane programming. Furthermore, Turbo C indicates that this routine may use longjmp and other functions to interact directly with the program at a high level.

Listing 11.2

```
#include <stdio.h>

#define    CR    Øx ØD
#define    LF    Øx ØA

int    handler();

main()

{
    int    c;
    int    i;

    if(getcbrk()==Ø)
        printf("BREAK checking is OFF\n");
    else
        printf("BREAK checking is ON\n");
```

Listing 11.2 continues

Listing 11.2 continued

```
ctrlbrk(handler);
for(i=0; i<100; i++){
    printf("%4.4d:TESTING CTRL BREAK\n",i);
}
printf("CHARACTER INPUT\n");
while((c=getche())!=0)
    if(c==CR || c==LF)
        putchar(LF);

}

handler()

{

    int   c;

    printf("\nCTRL BREAK HANDLER\n");
    printf("Do you want to quit? ");
    while((c = getch())!='y' && c!='Y' && c!='n' && c!='N');
    printf("\n");
    return(((c=='Y'||c=='y')?0:1));
}
```

Handler.c does two things to allow you to test the Ctrl-C handling:

1. It runs to the screen 100 lines that you can break into with Ctrl-C or Ctrl-Break.

2. It accepts characters from the keyboard so that you can try the Ctrl-C/Ctrl-Break during keyboard input.

You also can code directly in assembly language a function that works much the same as ctrlbrk, although the assembly-language function is greatly simplified. You must work in assembly language because you have to complete your handler with a return from interrupt (IRET) instead of the normal function return. The handler could be in-line code, but producing something that can be assembled is more instructive.

A good assembly-language programmer can produce an interrupt handler directly, but you may be unsure about how to put one together. To build this assembly-language routine, start with an empty C routine and compile it to assembly-language source code (the –S switch on either the Microsoft or Turbo C compiler):

Function: set_brk.c

set_brk()

```
{
}
```

brk()

```
{
    handler();
}
```

You compile the code like this:

```
C>CC -S set_brk.c;
```

to get the assembly language source code in listing 11.3 (Microsoft C).

Listing 11.3

Function: set_brk.asm

```
            name       set_brk

_text       segment    byte public 'code'
dgroup      group      _data,_bss
            assume     cs:_text,ds:dgroup,ss:dgroup
_text       ends

_data       segment    word public 'data'
_d@         label      byte
_data       ends

_bss        segment    word public 'bss'
_b@         label      byte
_bss        ends

_text       segment    byte public 'code'
_set_brk    proc       near
            ret
_set_brk    endp
```

Listing 11.3 continues

Listing 11.3 continued

```
_brk            proc        near
                call        near ptr _handler
                ret
_brk            endp
_text           ends

_data           segment     word public 'data'
_s@             label       byte
_data           ends

_text           segment     byte public 'code'
                extrn       _handler:near
                public      _brk
                public      _set_brk
_text           ends
                end
```

This NULL C program produces a kind of fill-in-the-blank routine with which you can build an interrupt handler. Some assembly language "hot shots" may laugh at this type of approach, but professional programmers have been using this method for years to learn how a compiler generates code or to provide a way for recoding a function in assembly language to save processing time.

Building an Assembly-Language Routine

Serious assembly-language programmers may cringe at the thought, but you can prepare an assembly-language routine by first writing it in a high-level language such as C and then compiling with an option that produces assembly-language source code. In the example from listing 11.3, development time has been reduced significantly because the skeleton of the routine was produced from the compiler.

This technique is good to remember if you have to produce an assembly-language program or if you want to optimize a program already in a high-level language. Converting the program to assembly code and editing the resulting file gives you a working program in a minimum amount of time.

To create the working interrupt handler in listing 11.4, follow these steps:

1. Let the _set_brk( ) function set up the interrupt handler, using Int 21h, Function 37.

2. Save all registers in the _brk function prior to calling the C function, and then restore them when it returns.

3. Change the RET to IRET.

In Turbo Pascal 4.0 you can declare a procedure with the interrupt directive to be an interrupt handler. The compiler automatically takes care of the registers and the IRET instruction.

Listing 11.4

Function: set_brk.asm

```
          name      set_brk

_text     segment   byte public 'code'
dgroup    group     _data,_bss
          assume    cs:_text,ds:dgroup,ss:dgroup
_text     ends

_data     segment   word public 'data'
_d@       label     byte
_data     ends

_bss      segment   word public 'bss'
_b@       label     byte
_bss      ends

_text     segment   byte public 'code'
_set_brk  proc      near
          push      bp              ;Save the registers
          push      ds
          push      di
          push      si

          mov       dx,cs
          mov       ds,dx
          mov       dx,offset _brk
          mov       ah,37           ;Set interrupt vector
          mov       al,23h          ;Ctrl-C handler
          int       21h

          pop       si              ;Retrieve the registers
          pop       di
          pop       ds
          pop       bp
          ret
_set_brk  endp
```

Listing 11.4 continues

Listing 11.4 continued

```
_brk      proc     near
          push     ax           ;Save the registers
          push     bx
          push     cx
          push     dx
          push     di
          push     si
          push     bp
          call     near ptr _handler
          pop      bp              ;Retrieve the registers
          pop      si
          pop      di
          pop      dx
          pop      cx
          pop      bx
          pop      ax
          iret
          _brk      endp
          _text     ends

_data     segment  word public 'data'
_s@       label    byte
_data     ends

_text     segment  byte public 'code'
          extrn    _handler:near
          public   _brk
          public   _set_brk
_text     ends
          end
```

Notice that no effort has been made to clean up the code beyond what was provided by the compiler. Some of the chaff could have been cleaned out (hot-shot assembly-language programmers will do so), but it isn't necessary. The only requirement is that the code works. It does.

Finally, the revision is added to the handler.c program (see listing 11.5).

Listing 11.5

```
Program: Handler2.c

#include <stdio.h>

#define      CR    ØxØD
#define      LF    ØxØA
```

Listing 11.5 continues

Listing 11.5 continued

```
main()

{
    int    c;
    int    i;

    if(getcbrk()==Ø)
        printf("BREAK checking is OFF\n");
    else
        printf("BREAK checking is ON\n");

    SET_BRK();
    for(i=Ø; i<1ØØ; i++){
        printf("%4.4d:TESTING CTRL BREAK\n",i);
    }
        printf("CHARACTER INPUT\n");
        while((c=getche())!=Ø)
            if(c==CR || c==LF)
                putchar(LF);
}

HANDLER()

{
    int    c;

    printf("\nCTRL BREAK HANDLER\n");
    printf("Do you want to quit? ");
    while((c = getch())!='y' && c!='Y' && c!='n' && c!='N');
    printf("\n");
    if(c=='Y'||c=='y')
        exit(Ø);
    return(Ø);
}
```

Compiling the program and linking it to the assembly-language routine yields a working Ctrl-C handler.

Now that you have learned something about interrupts and about how TSRs are activated, let's see how TSRs work.

Revisiting TSRs

TSRs originally were intended to be a convenient way to add ISRs to DOS by allowing programs to initialize themselves and link into the system-interrupt structure. Service routines that sort, search, and perform other utility functions were envisioned as normal uses for this function—and with good reason.

When DOS first entered the market, operating systems such as CP/M and TRSDOS had no TSR facility. But programmers had discovered how to build utilities and stash them in memory for other programs to use. Several popular packages with sorting utilities, display-handling utilities, and programmers' tools were available then; it seems likely that the designers of MS-DOS were aware of them and wanted to make building such utilities an easier process.

As users gained experience with DOS they learned that they could tie an interrupt service routine into the keyboard interrupt and see what was happening. Early copies of the PC's *Technical Reference Manual* included a ROM BIOS listing, so it was easy to see how things worked and what the effect would be of linking into the keyboard interrupt. On PCs, no effect would be visible to users; but for the TSR, it was another story.

When the TSR was linked to the keyboard interrupt, it no longer was a *passive* TSR. It became *active* because it could decide on its own when to do something; an active TSR took on an existence of its own.

A passive TSR would sit quietly in memory and respond only when a program passed a specific request for service. This type of TSR is easy to write because it needs no special coding tricks. When the TSR is called, you know that DOS is not active because the application program that invoked the interrupt had to have control of the machine. In this situation, anything the machine could do was legal. But that stopped with active TSRs.

An active TSR could interrupt the machine at any time. Knowing what the machine was executing when the TSR got control was impossible. Because DOS and PCs were designed as single-user, single-task systems, no provision had ever been made for the possibility that someone might run more than one program at the same time. BIOS and DOS, therefore, store large amounts of information in global tables. Intermediate results of data entry and calculations all use the same buffers. When you interrupt the system, the implication is that control *might* be inside DOS at the time of the interrupt. If you then call DOS again, you lose what DOS is doing and probably crash the system.

Early TSRs continually caused system crashes. They interfered not only with DOS but also with each other. Some were as tenacious as bulldogs in taking control of the machine. Hard-won experience has led to the following unofficial rules for writing TSRs:

❑ Never call DOS functions unless you have no other way to get what you want. (File system access is the major reason for having to call DOS.)

❑ If you have to do file I/O, you can do the following:

1. Use something other than DOS console I/O functions (Int 21h, Functions 01h–0Ch). Better ways of getting to the console are available.

2. Monitor the InDOS flag. When this flag is nonzero, DOS is executing an Int 21h function. Don't run your process when this flag is nonzero. (See the discussion of Int 21h, Function 34h in the DOS Reference Section for information about how to access this flag.)

3. Monitor Int 28h. This interrupt tells you that even though DOS is doing Int 21h functions, it is in a busy wait for console I/O. If you do your own console I/O below DOS, you can safely execute anything else. (See Int 28h in the DOS Reference Section for more information.)

❑ Provide a check function that lets your TSR indicate whether it is already installed. Linking to an unused interrupt vector lets the TSR check for the presence of an earlier copy in memory.

❑ Put a signature inside the executable code to tell whether the TSR is present.

❑ Always assume that other TSRs are present. Chain any interrupts used by your TSR by passing control to the interrupt vector your TSR found when it started.

❑ Use your own stack rather than the one controlled by the interrupted program. You have no way of knowing what might be on that stack, nor do you know the *size* of the stack or the amount of space that is left before you crash into something.

Interrupts Essential to TSRs

Some of the many interrupts are documented and some are not. Interrupts are important to anyone who writes a TSR. The DOS Reference Section gives as much detail as we know about each of them. This section introduces you to the interrupts so that you can see the kinds of assistance they can provide.

The Keyboard Interrupt

The keyboard interrupt (Int 09h) is the way an active TSR takes control. By monitoring what happens at the keyboard, the TSR can tell when the hot key is pressed and activated. Here is the basic method:

```
Int 09h activates on keystroke

Handler activates and reads keystroke
if(hot key has been found){
    throw away the keystroke
    check DOS
    if(in DOS){
        set a hot key flag
        return from the interrupt
    } else {
        activate the TSR
        when the TSR is done, return
            from the interrupt
    }
} else {
    chain to the next handler on Int 09h
}
```

What's this about "check DOS"? Remember that DOS is not reentrant. If you call DOS for anything, you might crash the system. To check DOS, use Int 21h, Function 34h, described in the next section.

The InDOS Flag, the DOSOK Interrupt, and the Timer Interrupt

Calling Int 21h, Function 34h returns a pointer to the InDOS flag (DOS busy flag). If this flag is nonzero, then DOS was interrupted while executing a function. If your TSR did interrupt DOS, the function will usually return in a fraction of a second. The preceding pseudocode for Int 09h shows where you would check the InDOS flag. After you set the hot-key flag, you must have a way to pick it up. For this purpose, you have the DOSOK interrupt and the timer interrupt.

When you start up, you initialize Int 28h, the DOSOK interrupt, like this:

```
Int 28h activates
check hot key flag
if(hot key flag is set){
    turn hot key flag off
    activate the TSR
```

Fragment continues

Fragment *continued*

```
    }
    call the next Int 28h service routine
    return from the interrupt
```

Int 28h (the DOSOK interrupt) activates when DOS is waiting for console input in Int 21h, Functions 01–0Ch. If you see this interrupt, you know that you can safely use other DOS functions. If DOS is not waiting for input, you use the timer interrupt.

The timer interrupt ticks 18.2 times per second. You can attach to this interrupt the following service routine that checks the hot-key flag:

```
    Timer Interrupt activates
    call next timer interrupt service
    check hot key flag
    if(hot key flag is set){
        turn hot key flag off
        activate the TSR
    }
    return from the interrupt
```

After you get control, you have other problems. Your TSR wants to work as simply as possible, but you do not know the state of the machine you are interrupting. How deep is the stack? How much space below the stack pointer is free for growth? More important, you do not want the TSR to be grabbed by a system error.

To make your TSR as robust as possible, you want to have it take control of the critical-error interrupt (Int 24h) and the Ctrl-Break interrupt (Int 23h). The TSR can also insert itself into the interrupt chain of the BIOS disk driver (Int 13h) and any other routines that might cause problems. Then, if a problem occurs, the TSR can correct it and you can shift to an internal stack and execute your functions.

Some programmers advocate *context switching*, where the DOS pointer to the active process's PSP is changed to point to the TSR's PSP. You use Int 21h, Function 51h to get the segment address of the interrupted program, save that address, and then use Int 21h, Function 50h to tell DOS that the TSR's Program Segment Prefix (PSP) is the current active process.

Context switching is a useful technique if you do complicated file I/O or otherwise want to have total control.

When the TSR finishes with its main business, it must "clean itself up," restore the interrupts, and reset the stack to normal. Then it can return to the interrupted program.

To demonstrate basic TSR operation, I have put some of the concepts to work in a simple clock program (clock.c) that sets itself up and then waits for a clock tick to activate (see listing 11.6).

Listing 11.6

```
/*
    Program: Clock.c
    Purpose: TSR Clock Demonstration
*/

#include <stdio.h>
#include <dos.h>

/*   Define needed constants */
#define       BOOL       int
#define       FALSE      Ø
#define       TRUE       !FALSE

/*   Define program size for the system */
#define       PGMSIZE    3ØØØ

/*   Define Base Address for Video Displays */
#define       MONOBASE   ØxbØØØ
#define       COLORBASE  Øxb8ØØ

/*   Define interrupt vectors for BIOS and DOS needed by program */
#define       GOTOXY     ØxØ2
#define       GETXY      ØxØ3
#define       TELETYPE   ØxØe
#define       VIDEO      Øx1Ø
#define       CLOCK      Øx1a
#define       TIMER      Øx1c
#define       DOS        Øx21
#define       TSR        Øx31
#define       TEST       Øx66

void interrupt (*orig_clock)();    /* original clock vector */
void interrupt clock();            /* declare clock() */
void interrupt test();             /* declare test() */

BOOL inclock = FALSE;              /* clock processing flag */
BOOL extra = FALSE;               /* extra tick flag */
int count = Ø;                    /* clock tick counter */
char buf[2Ø];                     /* time buffer */
char far *clkptr;                 /* pointer to screen location */
```

Listing 11.6 continues

Listing 11.6 continued

```
int   sp;                       /* stack pointer */
int   ss;                       /* stack segment */

int   hr, min, sec;             /* Current time */

main(argc,argv)

/*
      Main part of the clock routine. Does the following:

            1. Using vector 66h, checks whether the clock is
               already installed
            2. Saves the original clock vector
            3. Sets up the new clock vector
            4. Gets the initial system time
            5. Exits, using the TSR exit
*/

int   argc;
char *argv[];

{
      union REGS regs;
      int   mode;

/*    Initialize clock output buffer with a string for printing */
strcpy(buf,"  TEST  ");

/*
      Check for the presence of the clock TSR at Int 66h (normally
      unused and reserved for use by the user). If vector is
      zero, then assume not installed. If nonzero, report an error
      unless argv[1] is '¬u' which triggers a clock update.
      If found to be zero, set it to point to a local handler.
*/
orig_clock = getvect(TEST);

if(streql(argv[1],"¬u") && orig_clock!=Ø){
      printf("UPDATING THE CLOCK\n");
      int86(TEST,&regs,&regs);
      exit(Ø);
}
if(orig_clock != Ø){
      printf("ALREADY INSTALLED ... EXITING\n");
      exit(Ø);
```

Listing 11.6 continues

Listing 11.6 continued

```
}
setvect(TEST,test);

/*   Set up the clock interrupt handler */

orig_clock = getvect(TIMER);
setvect(TIMER,clock);

/*
     Read the initial value of the clock at start-up.
     Then set the clock pointer to the screen address.
*/
readclock(&hr,&min,&sec);
mode = getmode();
printf("DISPLAY MODE IS %d\n",mode);
if(mode==7)
     clkptr = MK_FP(MONOBASE,120);
else
     clkptr = MK_FP(COLORBASE,120);

/*   TSR exit to save the memory for the program */
tsrexit();
}

void interrupt clock()

/*
     Clock interrupt handler ... called by the timer interrupt
     18.2 times per second. Every 5th second we have to add one
     more tick before advancing so that we keep average time
     correct over periods longer than 5 seconds.
*/

{
union REGS regs;

/*   Call the original interrupt 1st */
(*orig_clock)();

/*
     Advance the tick counter. Every 5th second, add one tick
     to keep the time correct.
*/
count++;
if(sec%5==0 && count%18==0 && !extra){
     extra=TRUE;
     count--;
```

Listing 11.6 continues

Listing 11.6 continued

```
} else {
    extra=FALSE;
}

/*
    Every 18th tick (this will be 19th in 5th second)
    advance the displayed clock by 1 second
*/
if(count%18 == Ø){

/*
    Use internal stack, interrupts off until set.
    NOTE: The internal stack starts at the end of
    the area saved by the TSR exit and grows to low
    memory.
*/
    disable();
    sp = _SP;
    ss = _SS;
    _SS = _CS;
    _SP = PGMSIZE;
    enable();

/*  Advance seconds and correct hrs, mins, & secs */
    sec++;
    if(sec>=6Ø){
        sec=Ø; min++;
    }
    if(min>=6Ø){
        min=Ø;hr++;
    }
    if(hr>=24) hr = Ø;

/*  Display the clock on the screen if not already doing it */
    if(!inclock){
        inclock = TRUE;
        sprintf(buf+6,"%Ø2.2d:%Ø2.2d:%Ø2.2d ",hr,min,sec);
        displayclk(buf);
        inclock = FALSE;
    }

/*  Return stack to normal with interrupts off */
    disable();
    _SP = sp;
    _SS = ss;
    enable();
```

Listing 11.6 continues

Listing 11.6 continued

```
    }
}

tsrexit()

/*   Exit from the program, using the DOS TSR exit function */

{
    union REGS regs;

    regs.h.ah = TSR;
    regs.h.al = Ø;
    regs.x.dx = PGMSIZE;
    int86(DOS,&regs,&regs);
}

displayclk(str)

/*   Display the string at the clkptr position on the screen */

char       *str;

{
    char far       *ptr;

    ptr = clkptr;
    while(*str){
        *ptr++ = *str++;
        ptr++;
    }
}

readclock(hr,min,sec)

/*
    Read the BIOS clock and extract hours, minutes, and seconds
    from the clock. Store these in the arguments for use.
*/

int  *hr, *min, *sec;

{
    union REGS regs;
    unsigned long  clock;
    unsigned long  remain;
    unsigned long  x1, x2;
```

Listing 11.6 continues

Listing 11.6 *continued*

```
      regs.h.ah = Ø;
      int86(CLOCK,&regs,&regs);
      x1 = regs.x.cx*65536; x2 = regs.x.dx;
      clock = x1 + x2;
      *hr = clock/65543;
      remain = clock % 65543;
      *min = remain / 1Ø92;
      remain = remain % 1Ø92;
      *sec = remain / 18.21;
}

void interrupt test()

/*
      Test interrupt vector which will be checked on start-up.
      Also used to trigger a reread of the clock from an external
      program or with the '-u' argument for this one.
*/

{
      register int ds;

      disable();
      sp = _SP;
      ss = _SS;
      _SS = _CS;
      _SP = PGMSIZE;
      ds = _DS;
      _DS = _CS;
      readclock(&hr,&min,&sec);
      _DS = ds;
      _SP = sp;
      _SS = ss;
      enable();
}

streql(str1,str2)

/*   Returns TRUE if the strings are equal, FALSE otherwise */

char *str1, *str2;

{
      return(strcmp(str1,str2)==Ø);
}
```

Listing 11.6 *continues*

Listing 11.6 *continued*

```
getmode()

/*    Returns the video display mode of the system */

{
    union REGS regs;

    regs.h.ah = Øx0f;
    int86(VIDEO,&regs,&regs);
    return(regs.h.al);
}
```

Let's go over the program to see how it works.

You'll notice that part of the setup involves putting the word TEST at the beginning of the clock output buffer so that it will be displayed when the clock is updated. (This is just a convenience for the demonstration program.)

Standard Turbo C functions are used to access the interrupt vector table (instead of making the calls directly). But first we have to see whether the TSR is already installed. I've chosen a simple way to do this: I have used Int 66h as a marker because it is unused by most TSRs and its value normally is zero. If Int 66h is nonzero, the program assumes that the TSR has set it. If the value is zero, then you know that it has not been set.

Int 66h is used also to force the clock program to reset its current time from the system. Rather than write a new program to do that, simply start the TSR with a ' ¬u' flag. If the first argument is ' ¬u', reset the clock and leave.

The Turbo C function getvect() is used to get the value of the vector. Next, the program checks for the ' ¬u' flag if the Int 66h vector has been set. If it finds the ' ¬u' flag and if the vector is nonzero, an Int 66h is issued to reset the clock and exit.

If there is no ' ¬u' flag, the program checks whether the vector is nonzero. If it is, the program assumes that the clock program has already started. If another TSR that uses Int 66h is active, you will not be able to start the clock program (because of the Int 66h vector).

If after all your checks you find that the vector is zero, then you set the vector to point to the test() interrupt function (which forces the TSR to read the BIOS clock) and proceed to set up the clock function.

To set up the clock function, you first get the original clock vector, save it for future use, and then reset the vector to point to the clock() interrupt function. Then you read the initial clock time from the BIOS clock function, get the current display mode to identify a monochrome versus a color monitor, and establish a pointer (clkptr) to point to the screen location at which you will write the clock. To eliminate the use of BIOS or DOS functions while the TSR is operating, you put the clock directly to the screen display buffer. (*This will work only in text modes; programs that shift the display to graphics modes will show garbage from the clock.*)

After everything is set up, the TSR exit is called and the program is resident. The clock interrupt handler, clock( ), is the heart of the TSR. Let's go over it step by step to see how it operates.

First, we call the original clock timer so that it does whatever is required on each clock tick. Then we can proceed. The count variable keeps track of timer ticks (which occur at a rate of 18.2 per second). The clock advances one second every 18 ticks. Every five seconds, one extra tick is allowed in order to bring the average over five-second periods to 18.2 ticks per second. After advancing the count, check whether you are at a five-second interval. If you are, then you decrease the count by one to force a wait of one extra tick (giving you 19 ticks on this second). The extra flag tells you that you are doing the extra tick and prevents you from decrementing the count whenever you come back at the fifth second.

With the period between seconds covered, you now check for every 18th tick. When you find it, you reset the stack to your internal stack and then advance the timer by one second (sec++). Then, to keep the clock running correctly, you check for 60 seconds, 60 minutes, and 24 hours. After everything else is done, you display the clock.

If you are not already in the clock display section (inclock is set to FALSE), then you enter that portion of the program, set inclock to TRUE, and set up and display the clock. Finally, you reset the stack to its status when the clock( ) function was called.

The clock display is simple. You write directly to the screen memory, advancing the screen buffer pointer by 2 to get past the attribute byte for each byte of the clock that you write to the screen. The rest of the clock program is made up of some simple, self-explanatory functions.

The program is compiled with the Turbo C compiler, using the MAKE utility provided with Version 1.5 of the software. The makefile that compiles the program correctly is shown in listing 11.7.

The MAKE utility recompiles the program only when necessary. Such a utility, although of minimal use here, is especially useful on large projects.

Listing 11.7

```
clock.exe:     clock.obj
     tlink /x lib\cØt clock, clock,, lib\emu lib\maths lib\cs

clock.obj:     clock.c
     tcc -c -mt -f clock.c
```

The important thing about the compilation is that the program is compiled with the TINY memory model (the same as a COM program, so that Code, Data, and Stack segments are all the same). Consult your *Turbo C User Manual* for details on how to use the compiler switches.

If you are using Microsoft C, you can modify the program to handle segment registers within the limits of the Microsoft system and establish similar compilation switches for control of the program compilation.

Summary

This chapter has shown you how to work with interrupts. By using utilities provided as part of DOS Int 21h, you can change an interrupt vector to point to a function that you design. In C, you have written a sample handler with an assembly language front end to handle the interfacing. Turbo Pascal 4.0 provides a specific way for you to create interrupt handlers as Pascal functions.

Terminate and Stay Resident utilities can be written to trigger on interrupts (the keyboard and clock interrupts, for example). These utilities can be extremely dangerous to programs, however, because DOS was never intended to handle multitasking operations. DOS is a purely nonreentrant system and can fail when a TSR calls functions that were in progress when the TSR got control of the computer.

You have learned several ways to minimize problems with TSRs. You know not to call DOS functions unless absolutely necessary, and to use BIOS or direct calls for keyboard and screen I/O. You know about monitoring the InDOS flag to see when performing DOS functions is safe, and about monitoring Int 28h to determine when the system is waiting for keyboard input. You have learned to provide a check function that lets the TSR check to see whether it is already loaded and to always assume that another TSR is present. And you know that using an internal stack is a good way to prevent problems in stack operations.

CHAPTER 12

Device Drivers

In the early days of computing, programmers wrote all types of programs directly at the hardware level. Each program had to deal directly with the intricacies of card readers, printers, tape drives, and other equipment connected to computers. Programmers, therefore, had to master all kinds of arcane information about handling each type of error, processing correct input and output, and so on.

As computers developed, programmers saw that their time for this sort of repetitive work was at a premium. Handlers for external devices gradually became standard items that programmers added to their programs. Before long, these handlers were collected into a primitive operating system in which *all* programs could use the same set of device handlers, or *drivers*.

In the earliest operating systems the different *device drivers* were coded as integral parts of the system and interacted in intricate ways with the rest of the system. As a result of attempts to make device drivers more independent, systems programmers are able to install device drivers as needed during start-up.

Although most significant operating systems have some such flexibility, DOS provides the most flexibility for *users* to install drivers. Many microcomputer operating systems required tedious patching to accomplish what can be done with a prewritten driver and the system configuration file.

For most people who work with DOS, their only contact with drivers is to load them from distribution disks and make the required entry in the CONFIG.SYS file. (These entries are described later in this chapter.) Users follow written instructions that tell them, line for line, how to make the changes. In some systems, you do not have even this much contact because an installation program makes the changes for you.

333

Most programmers eventually begin to feel rather confident about their skills and decide to write a device driver. Experienced assembly language programmers find this a relatively easy task— they just have to follow a formula. You do not need source code for DOS, nor do you have to spend hours decoding DOS to determine how it works. (More power to you if you can, but it is not necessary.) If you follow the formula correctly, your driver will work correctly. Many programmers fail because they don't stick to the rigid outline of what a driver has to do and how it has to be laid out. In this chapter I hope to show you how to write good device drivers.

For maximum speed and coding convenience, device drivers usually are written in assembly language on PCs. Although parts of a device driver can be written in a language such as C, problems would occur in getting the correct structure and in minimizing overhead. Because of a device driver's rigid structure, modules compiled in C can provide only functional services to the driver. If you use C to build functions for a driver, you must start with an assembly language section that gets initial control and then calls C routines as needed. You *cannot* call C library functions because many of them refer to DOS functions. (A driver is not allowed to call DOS services. You will read more about this subject in this chapter's "Driver Initialization" section.)

Here are three good reasons for using assembly language to code the entire driver:

❏ Because a device driver is at the heart of all access to a device, it must be coded as tightly as possible to save execution time and memory space.

❏ The driver layout is rigidly defined; only assembly language gives you the required layout control.

❏ You must manipulate specified CPU registers at specific times. This is hard to do from C.

Coding device drivers in C is common in the UNIX world, but the interface requirements are different. An assembly language front end that you do not see links together and controls the operating system. Coding a driver in C can be fun, if you want to try it.

Before you learn how to build a device driver, you should understand how a device driver is laid out and how it works. Implementation will flow naturally from what you learn.

As you learn about drivers, you will build a driver shell into which you can drop additional code to make real drivers for real devices. You will start by learning about types of drivers and how they work.

Driver Types

The two basic types of device drivers—character devices and block devices—are fundamentally different. You should understand how they differ before you continue.

Character Device Drivers

Character devices are byte-oriented devices such as printer ports or serial ports. All communication with the device occurs on a character-by-character basis.

I/O from a character device occurs in one of two basic modes: cooked and raw. In *cooked* mode, DOS requests one character at a time from the driver and buffers the input internally. "Special" keystrokes such as Ctrl-C and the carriage return are processed by DOS. In *raw* mode, DOS does not buffer the data nor does it look for and respond to Ctrl-C or the carriage return. Rather, requests for input of a fixed number of characters are passed directly to the driver; the return is made up of the characters read by the driver.

Character devices are given names (CON, AUX, LPT, and so on) that can be up to eight characters long (like file names). The eight-character limitation arises because the driver's name held in the device header is only eight characters. (The header is discussed in the "Device Header" section later in this chapter.)

Block Device Drivers

Block devices process blocks of data such as those on tapes and disks. Each access to a block device *always* transfers data in the appropriate block sizes. With block devices, there is no equivalent to the character-device drivers' cooked and raw modes.

Block devices are assigned drive letters and become one or more of the system's logical drives (A:, B:, C:, and so on). A single block-device driver can handle more than one hardware unit or map one hardware unit into multiple logical devices. Each logical device is structured with a base-file system that includes a FAT (file allocation table) and root directory (for additional information about these structures, see Chapters 2 and 8).

How Device Drivers Work

When an application program calls DOS Int 21h, device drivers get involved in almost every case (except for system functions like extended error processing). Consider an example in which you try to write to a file on the disk.

Whether you explicitly code the file-writing operation as a call to DOS or use a library function, the application program sets up the registers and makes a call to Int 21h (DOS service routines) to handle the disk I/O. When the service routine gets control, it in turn sets up and makes a call to Int 26h (absolute disk write). Int 26h sets up a request header (a command buffer for the driver) in a reserved area of memory and calls the strategy routine for the device driver that handles the disk. The strategy routine simply saves the address of the request header and returns control to the interrupt handler.

Next, DOS calls the interrupt portion of the driver. (Its name, like that of the strategy routine, does not reflect its function.) The interrupt portion of the driver reads the request header and determines what is requested. The interrupt portion then transfers control to the appropriate internal routine and executes the disk write by calling the BIOS disk write function, Int 13h. When the disk write is completed, control returns through the chain to the application program, and status codes are adjusted to reflect what each calling routine expects.

Figure 12.1 shows the sequence of events. Each step of the operation involves a transfer of control to successively lower-level routines until the actual disk write occurs.

These steps take place for only one operation of the disk; there may be many such calls to the driver. If you use high-level language resources in the file call, you may need additional access to the disk to read the FAT, allocate space, and update parameters on the disk. Drivers can be extremely busy.

Although this example of a disk write is complicated, you can handle it with a call to the BIOS. You do not have to worry about the "down and dirty" interfacing details (the hardware operation itself). On each PC and compatible, the BIOS is supposed to make all devices look like a set of standard devices. But what if you add a custom piece of equipment? Figure 12.2 shows what happens. The driver has to manipulate the new hardware directly. There will be no BIOS to handle the interfacing details.

When you add a board that adds a new capability to the system, you must add a new device driver. When you add a CD-ROM drive, a mouse, a local area network, or a music synthesizer, you add hardware that the PC system

Fig. 12.1. *Calling for a disk write.*

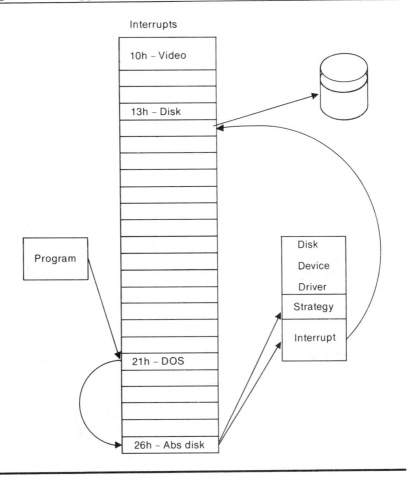

Interrupts

10h – Video

13h – Disk

Program

Disk
Device
Driver
Strategy
Interrupt

21h – DOS

26h – Abs disk

software was never designed to handle. MS-DOS has no software to handle a mouse device. The driver that comes with the mouse has to work directly with the hardware. This is where the complexity begins. In order to interface this hardware to the system, you need a driver.

The example of disk access through the driver (refer to fig. 12.1) hid one important fact: the BIOS already has taken care of the hardware details. All the timing details, bit manipulations, and so on are handled by the BIOS. For a custom add-on, your driver must handle the hardware details directly.

When you add a piece of hardware to the system and write the driver for it, *you* must complete all of the interfacing details. If you add an analog-digital

Fig. 12.2. *A custom device driver.*

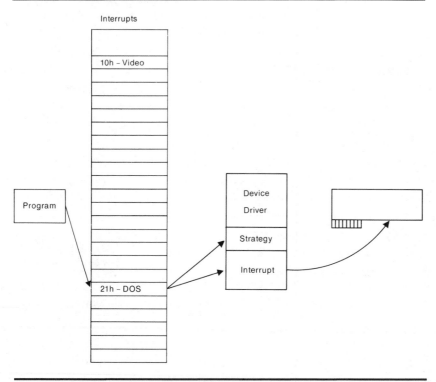

converter so that you can read some instrumentation, you must service the chips on the hardware level. If you have to observe timing restrictions or deal with other problems, *you* must know about them.

Demonstration of a working interface to a special board is beyond the scope of this book. To perform a successful interface, you must have an intimate knowledge of the hardware you want to run. Nothing less is acceptable. This book tries to give you a framework in which to make your driver work, whether you are writing a driver for a new piece of hardware to be added to a system or for some existing hardware.

Device Driver Structure

A device driver is made up of three parts: the device header, the strategy routine, and the interrupt routine. In DOS V2, the driver had to be a memory image (or a COM program) with no origin (ORG Ø, or no statement at all). And it had to be coded as a FAR procedure. The EXE2BIN program converts the assembled driver to an image file and the system loads the image during the boot operation. By convention, drivers usually have the extension .SYS (or sometimes .BIN). The file extension is changed to .SYS to prevent someone from accidentally executing the driver as a program.

In DOS V3.0 and later versions, drivers can be object files in EXE format. The operating system will load them correctly. But to maintain backward compatibility with DOS V2, most people who write drivers work with the COM format. (DOS V1 had no provision for loadable drivers.) The examples in this chapter are COM-type drivers.

The following section examines the structure of the driver. We will look first at the device header—the first important part of a working driver.

Device Header

The device header is an 18-byte area divided into five fields (see fig. 12.3).

Fig. 12.3. *The device header.*

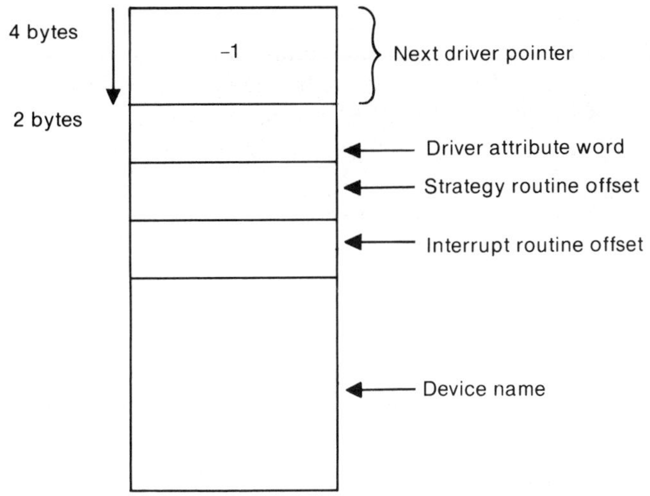

Here are the five fields:

❏ *Next driver pointer*: four bytes are initialized to –1 (FFFFFFFFh). DOS uses this field to load a pointer to the next driver in the list of drivers. The last driver in the list is marked with –1.

❏ *Driver attribute word*: two bytes that specify the driver characteristics (see table 12.1).

❏ *Strategy routine offset*: a two-byte offset to the strategy routine within the driver

❏ *Interrupt routine offset*: a two-byte offset to the interrupt routine within the driver

❏ *Device name*: an eight-character, left-justified, blank-filled device name. If the name is the same as that of an existing device, the new driver replaces the existing device. If the device is a block device, the first byte in this field is the number of logical devices associated with the driver; the other bytes are ignored.

Table 12.1. *Driver Attribute Word*

Bits FEDCBA98 76543210	Meaning
....1	Standard input
....∅	Not standard input
....1.	Standard output
....∅.	Not standard output
....1..	NUL device
....∅..	Not NUL device
....1...	Clock device
....∅...	Not clock device
....1....	Special
.....∅∅∅ ∅∅∅.....	Reserved (set to zero)
....∅...	OPEN/CLOSE/Removable media supported
....1...	OPEN/CLOSE/Removable media not supported
...∅....	Reserved (set to zero)
..1.....	IBM block format
..∅.....	Other block format
.1......	IOCTL supported
.∅......	IOCTL not supported
1.......	Character device
∅.......	Block device

As DOS initializes itself, it establishes a chain of the standard device drivers; the next driver pointer in each driver gives the address of the next driver in the chain (see fig. 12.4). The last driver in the chain has a pointer of –1 to indicate the end of the chain.

Fig. 12.4. *The driver chain.*

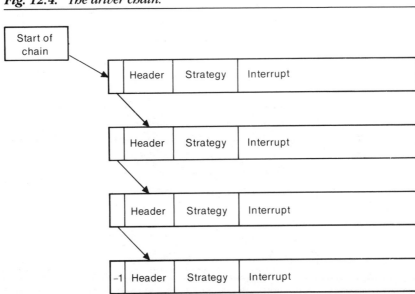

When DOS finally reads the CONFIG.SYS file, a driver chain already has been set up. New drivers are added at the head of the chain.

DOS looks for a driver by searching through the chain of drivers for a driver name that matches the name called for. Starting at the beginning of the driver list, DOS checks the name of the first driver to see whether it matches the requested name. If not, the Next Driver Pointer is consulted to find the next driver in the list and DOS then checks there. DOS checks each driver in the chain until it finds either the requested driver or the end of the list (marked by a –1 in the Next Driver Pointer field).

A new driver is always added to the beginning of the chain (see fig. 12.5). Then, when DOS searches for a driver, it will check the new driver first. If you add a driver with the same name as an existing driver (say, for example, that you add a new driver with the name PRN—the same name as that of the printer driver), the new driver will "replace" the existing one because a search always results in the new driver being used, never the old one.

Fig. 12.5. *Adding a new driver to the driver chain.*

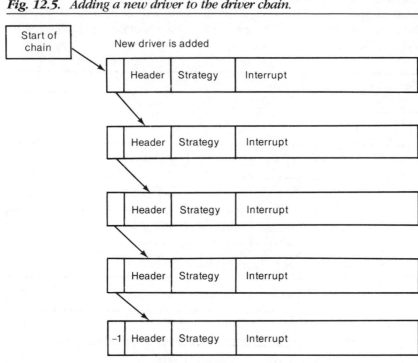

The ANSI.SYS driver works this way when it is included in the CONFIG.SYS file. It has the same name as the console driver (CON); when it is added to the driver chain, it will be found first whenever a console operation occurs. All console operations then work through the ANSI.SYS driver instead of the normal DOS console driver.

To illustrate how you set up and work with a driver, let's create a practical example (or at least a *working* shell for a real driver). Listing 12.1 is the header for a real driver called drvr.asm. Later in this chapter this driver is assembled into one that does not actually do anything. The assembled driver is a shell to which more code for actual applications can be added.

The first part of the driver is made up of instructions to the assembler. First, for convenience during the program, define several constants such as CR (carriage return), LF (line feed), MAXCMD (the maximum command number: 16 for DOS V3.0 and V3.1, 12 for V2.X), and so on. These definitions simplify your programming as you continue.

Listing 12.1

```
;    Header and assembler directives for drvr.asm

CR         EQU   ØDh             ;Carriage return
LF         EQU   ØAh             ;Line feed
MAXCMD     EQU   16              ;DOS V3.Ø, 12 DOS V2.Ø
ERROR      EQU   8ØØØh           ;Set error bit
BUSY       EQU   Ø2ØØh           ;Set busy bit
DONE       EQU   Ø1ØØh           ;Set done bit
UNKNOWN    EQU   8ØØ3h           ;Set unknown status
;
cseg segment    public 'code'   ;Start the code segment
     org        Ø               ;Zero origin
     assume     cs:cseg,ds:cseg,es:cseg
;
;========================================================
;    Device header for the driver
;    Next driver pointer is -1 (end of list)
;    Attribute is character device, does not
;      respond to IOCTL calls
;    Name of the driver is DRVR
;
drvr       proc       far          ;FAR procedure
           dd         -1           ;Next driver pointer
           dw         8ØØØh        ;Attribute
           dw         strategy     ;Pointer to strategy
           dw         interrupt    ;Pointer to interrupt
           db         'DRVR    '   ;Device name
;
```

As was mentioned earlier in this chapter, listing 12.1 has been defined as a *code* segment with a 0 origin (ORG Ø). All of the segment registers are set the same as the code segment so that you can assemble the driver as a binary image (COM format) file.

The first part of the driver that affects memory starts with the label drvr, where you declare that this is a FAR procedure. This is necessary because all drivers will be called by DOS with a FAR subroutine call. A FAR subroutine call is one that can go across segment boundaries—it pushes the return address (both segment and offset) on the stack as part of the call. By declaring this to be a FAR procedure, you ensure that the assembler will use a FAR return (which gets both segment and offset off the stack) to return control to DOS.

The first field in the header (a double word, or eight bytes) initially is declared to be –1. DOS sets this word to the address of the next driver in the chain. You then set the attribute word to 8000h to indicate that this character driver has no special capabilities (refer to table 12.1). This step is followed by the pointers (offsets only) to the driver's strategy and interrupt procedures, and then by this driver's eight-character name.

The header is critical to proper driver operation. When DOS needs to refer to the driver, it checks the attribute word to see what the driver can do and then uses the strategy and interrupt pointers to locate the routines. If the header isn't right, the driver fails before it starts. Because the header is all bookkeeping and the assembler does the bookkeeping for you, let's move on to the strategy routine.

Strategy Routine

A strategy routine has little to do with what usually is considered "strategy"— it does not try to devise the best way to drive the device or anything of that sort. You can write the strategy routing in as little as five lines; its purpose is to "remember" where in memory the operating system has assigned the location of the device's *request header* (RH). The RH serves the following two functions:

❏ It is a data area for DOS's internal operations.

❏ It is a communication area in which DOS tells the driver what to do and the driver responds with the result of the operation.

When a driver is asked to output data, the data address comes via the RH. The driver responds by performing its output task and then setting a flag or status byte in the request header to indicate completion.

When a driver is about to be called by DOS, the request header is built in a reserved area of memory and its address passed to the strategy routine in ES:BX. Although each call to the driver can have a new address, in practice the address generally is the same. The strategy routine saves this value for future use by the driver's interrupt routine.

Request headers vary in length but always have a fixed 13-byte header (sometimes called the "static portion" of the request header). The structure of the request header is shown in table 12.2.

Most of the fields in the request header are self explanatory. The status word (bytes 03–04h), however, needs clarification.

The status word passes the completion status of a request back to DOS in the format shown in table 12.3.

Table 12.2. Request Header Leading Bytes

Byte Offset	Field Length	Meaning
00h	Byte	Length of the request header
01h	Byte	Unit Code: the device number for block devices
02h	Byte	Command Code: the number of the most recent command sent to the driver
03h	Word	Status: status code set by the driver after each call. If bit 15 is set, then an error code occurs in the low-order eight bits. A status code of 0 means successful completion.
05h	Eight bytes	Reserved for use by DOS
0Dh	Variable	Data required by the driver

Table 12.3. Request Header Status Word

Bits FEDCBA98	76543210	Meaning
1.......	00000001	Write-protect violation error
1.......	00000010	Unknown unit error
1.......	00000011	Drive not ready error
1.......	00000100	CRC error
1.......	00000101	Bad drive request structure length error
1.......	00000110	Seek error
1.......	00000111	Unknown media error
1.......	00001000	Sector not found error
1.......	00001001	Printer out of paper error
1.......	00001010	Write fault
1.......	00001011	Read fault
1.......	00001100	General failure
.......1	....	Done
......1.	....	Busy
.00000..	....	Reserved
0.......	....	No error

The error bit in the status word is set to indicate that an error occurred in the operation of the driver. The error code is returned in the lower eight bits of the status word. When the error bit is not set, the error code should be set to zero to indicate satisfactory completion of the operation.

The busy bit is set to indicate that the device was busy when called. The done bit is set when the driver has completed the operation. The driver sets the bits to indicate the status of whatever operation is requested. All functions should set the done bit to indicate completion.

The strategy routine for the sample driver (drvr.asm) looks like listing 12.2.

Listing 12.2

```
;       Strategy Routine
;       Saves the pointer to the REQUEST HEADER (RH)
;       from the ES:BX registers to rh_seg and rh_off
;
rh_seg     dw    ?           ;RH segment address
rh_off     dw    ?           ;RH offset address
strategy:
           mov   cs:rh_seg,es
           mov   cs:rh_off,bx
           ret
;===========================================================
```

Listing 12.2 allocates space in which to store the segment and the offset of the request header. The whole strategy routine consists of saving the request header pointer (the segment address in the ES register and the offset address in the BX register). Why doesn't it do more? A more pointed question might be "Why have two entry points?" Why not pass the pointer to the interrupt routine in ES:BX and be done with it?

The answer involves the operating system's compatibility and internal mechanisms. The DOS designers designed the driver structure to be compatible with future extensions to a multitasking structure. When the operating system runs multiple tasks, more than one request may be sent to a specific driver before a single request can be handled. In other words, the requests may have to be queued.

If you make requests for disk-sector reads, for example, multiple requests may arrive before the first request can be satisfied, especially if the requested sector is far from the present location on the disk. You also can add intelligence to the strategy routine and let it try to optimize access to a disk device by sequencing multiple requests to minimize head movement. None of this is applicable to DOS.

Because DOS is a single-user, single-task system, the potential capability for multiple processes accessing any driver does not exist. But the structure is in place to allow an extension in that direction, should such an extension ever be deemed necessary.

After the request header's address is stored safely, you can return to DOS and await the call to the interrupt routine: it occurs immediately in a single-task system.

Interrupt Routine

The major portion of the driver, called the interrupt routine, does all the work. It is poorly named because it does not act like an interrupt and it ends with RET rather than IRET.

The interrupt routine contains code for as many as 20 functions required by the DOS system (13 on DOS V2, 17 on DOS V3, and 20 on DOS V3.2). Whenever the device driver is called, it gets the address of the request header and looks at the byte at offset 02h of the header to find the command code that indicates which function the driver will perform.

Most drivers create a table with pointers to the driver's functions. The command code is used as an index into the table to locate the desired function. Listing 12.3 shows the dispatch table for the sample driver.

Listing 12.3

```
;       Interrupt Section
;       Processes all driver requests
;
;-----------------------------------------------------------
;       Command Code Dispatch Table
;
d_tbl:
        dw      s_init          ;Initialization
        dw      s_mchk          ;Media check
        dw      s_bpb           ;BIOS parameter block
        dw      s_ird           ;IOCTL read
        dw      s_read          ;Read
        dw      s_nrd           ;Nondestructive read
        dw      s_inst          ;Current input status
        dw      s_infl          ;Flush input buffer
        dw      s_write         ;Write
        dw      s_vwrite        ;Write with verify
```

Listing 12.3 continues

Listing 12.3 *continued*

```
        dw    s_ostat        ;Current output status
        dw    s_oflush       ;Flush output buffers
        dw    s_iwrt         ;IOCTL write
        dw    s_open         ;Open
        dw    s_close        ;Close
        dw    s_media        ;Removable media
        dw    s_busy         ;Output until busy
;===========================================================
```

The table is particularly easy to lay out because the assembler keeps track of the functions and automatically inserts the correct offset addresses in the table. This driver (as written) does not support the special functions introduced in DOS V3.2 (Generic IOCTL and Get/Set Logical Device). This is not a problem, because the Get/Set Logical Device functions are for block drivers only (remember that this is a character device) and most programs do not use the calls that depend on these functions.

The body of the interrupt routine determines the nature of the request to be served. It branches from the dispatch table to the appropriate function. Listing 12.4 shows the rest of the body of the interrupt routine.

Listing 12.4

```
;
;-----------------------------------------------------------
;       Interrupt Handler
;
interrupt:
        cld                  ;Save machine state
        push es              ;Save all registers
        push ds
        push ax
        push bx
        push cx
        push dx
        push si
        push di
        push bp
;
;       Retrieve the rh pointer
;
        mov   dx,cs:rh_seg
        mov   es,dx
        mov   bx,cs:rh_off
```

Listing 12.4 continues

Listing 12.4 *continued*

```
;
        mov  al,es:[bx]+2    ;Command code
        xor  ah,ah
        cmp  ax,MAXCMD       ;Legal command?
        jle  ok              ;Jump if OK
        mov  ax,UNKNOWN      ;Unknown command
        jmp  finish
;
;    Execute driver function
;    All driver functions are responsible for
;       returning in AX the status
;
ok:
        shl  ax,1            ;Multiply by 2
        mov  bx,ax
        jmp  word ptr [bx + d_tbl]
;
;    End of the driver
;    Set completion status
;       and restore the registers
;
finish:
;
;    Retrieve the rh pointer
;
        mov  dx,cs:rh_seg
        mov  es,dx
        mov  bx,cs:rh_off
;
        or   ax,DONE         ;Set the DONE bit
        mov  es:[bx]+3,ax
;
        pop  bp              ;Restore the registers
        pop  di
        pop  si
        pop  dx
        pop  cx
        pop  bx
        pop  ax
        pop  ds
        pop  es
        ret                  ;Back to DOS
;===========================================================
```

The interrupt routine starts by saving the present machine state on the stack. Then it gets the pointer to the request header from the location at which the strategy routine stored it. The interrupt routine determines what it is supposed to do by looking at offset 02h in the request header. The routine then checks to make sure that the command is legal: if it is, the routine branches to the location at which it handles the function. An illegal command (one that is larger than the maximum command number) results in the driver returning an error flag set to indicate that the command was unknown.

When the command number is determined to be less than MAXCMD (the number of commands the driver supports), the driver multiplies the command number by two (by means of a left shift, which is the same as multiplying by two) to obtain the offset of the command code within the dispatch table. The shift is necessary because two bytes are stored for each table entry in the dispatch table. Then the offset is added to the dispatch table's base address and the driver jumps to the designated routine.

When the function finishes, the driver retrieves the pointer to the request header and sets the done bit in the status word to reflect the operation's completion. The registers saved at the beginning of the driver are restored and control is returned to the DOS kernel.

Before we look at each separate driver function, let's look at the sample driver's remaining code. As in any driver, only some functions need to be implemented. In cases in which a function is not needed, the driver can simply return a status code and do nothing. Some people advocate returning a zero code that indicates successful operation; others suggest returning an error code 3 (Command Unknown). If you write your own driver to use with your own software, you can make your own choice. But if you write a driver to replace an existing one, the new return codes should be consistent with those returned by the existing driver.

Listing 12.5 gives the remainder of drvr.asm.

Listing 12.5

```
;
;------------------------------------------------------------
;    Driver Commands
;
;    First the unused commands: we dispose of these
;        in an error exit
;
s_mchk:                         ;Media Check
s_bpb:                          ;BIOS parameter block
```

Listing 12.5 continues

Listing 12.5 continued

```
s_ird:                          ;IOCTL read
s_read:                         ;Read
s_nrd:                          ;Nondestructive read
s_inst:                         ;Current input status
s_infl:                         ;Flush input buffers
s_vwrite:                       ;Current output status
s_ostat:                        ;Current output status
s_oflush:                       ;Flush output buffers
s_iwrt:                         ;IOCTL write
s_open:                         ;Open
s_close:                        ;Close
s_media:                        ;Removable media
s_busy:                         ;Output until busy
        Xor  ax,ax             ;No error
        jmp  finish
;
;------------------------------------------------------------
;    Initialization
;
ident:
        db   CR,LF
        db   'Sample Device Driver - Version '
        db   'Ø.Ø'
        xdb  CR,LF,LF,'$'
;
s_init:
        mov  ah,9              ;Print string
        mov  dx, offset ident
        int  21h
;
;    Retrieve the rh pointer
;
        mov  dx,cs:rh_seg
        mov  es,dx
        mov  bx,cs:rh_off
;
        lea  ax,end_driver    ;Get end of driver address
        mov  es:[bx]+14,ax
        mov  es:[bx]+16,cs
;
        xor  ax,ax            ;Zero the ax register
        jmp  finish
;
;------------------------------------------------------------
;        Write data
;
```

Listing 12.5 continues

Listing 12.5 *continued*

```
s_write:
        xor   ax,ax          ;Zero ax register
        jmp   finish
;
;=========================================================
;     End of Driver
;
end_driver:
drvr endp
cseg ends
        end
;=========================================================
```

When you write a driver you can ignore all the functions that you do not need to do something with. In drvr.asm, for example, only the initialization function and the write function will do anything. All the remaining functions are handled with a single section that returns a code which tells DOS that the requested function was unknown. A driver that needs only read and write could provide only those functions.

The only function that *must* be included in all drivers is the initialization function: it must put the address of the end of the driver into the request header at offset 0Eh for use by the operating system's initialization code.

To ignore the functions, you simply return a code that says you do not know what DOS is requesting. Then you jump to the part of the interrupt routine that closes out the operation and sets the done bit (bit 8) in the request header's status word (offset 03h).

Initialization is next. You print a string to the screen (so that you know the driver is there) and then determine the address of the end of the driver. (The label end_driver is the end of this routine.) This address must be stored in the request header so that DOS knows where to load the next driver. Because drivers are loaded from low to high memory, the next driver will be loaded after the ending address of the current driver (see fig. 12.6).

Finally, the write routine sets to zero the AX register (the function return status for the driver) to indicate no errors in the operation of the driver. This type of simple function setup is typical of most drivers. Most drivers require only a few of the functions to do anything. As you will learn when we go over the functions individually, some of them make sense for only one type of driver. For example, the BIOS Parameter Block function is meaningless for a driver that deals with the keyboard.

Fig. 12.6. *Next driver loaded after ending address of current driver.*

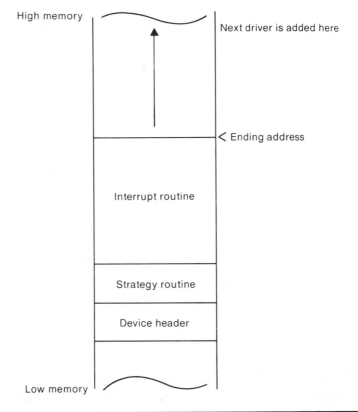

Table 12.4 lists the device-driver functions and indicates which are applicable to a specific version of DOS. We will examine each function in detail to see how it works.

Table 12.4. Device Driver Functions

Function	Meaning	DOS Version(s)
00h	Driver initialization	2, 3
01h	Media check	2, 3
02h	Build BIOS parameter block	2, 3
03h	I/O control read	2, 3

Table 12.4 continues

Table 12.4 *continued*

Function	Meaning	DOS Version(s)
04h	Read	2, 3
05h	Nondestructive read	2, 3
06h	Input status	2, 3
07h	Flush input buffers	2, 3
08h	Write	2, 3
09h	Write with verify	2, 3
0Ah	Output status	2, 3
0Bh	Flush output buffers	2, 3
0Ch	I/O control write	2, 3
0Dh	Open	3
0Eh	Device close	3
0Fh	Removable media	3
10h	Output until busy	3
11h	Generic IOCTL	3.2
17h	Get logical device	3.2
18h	Set logical device	3.2

Driver Initialization

The initialization function is the one function that *must* be present in all drivers. It performs any needed setup for the driver. One task of the initialization function is essential to DOS: it must set the address of the end of the driver into byte offset 0Eh of the request header. If your driver were driving a hard disk system, the initialization section would have to check for the presence and proper operation of the disk, initialize the disk parameters, and so forth. For a serial port, it should initialize the port and establish the default settings.

The driver's initialization section is the only section that can call DOS functions legally. No other part of the driver is allowed to call DOS. (Remember that DOS is not reentrant. While you are inside the driver, you *are* DOS!) Only Functions 01h-0Ch (Limited Console I/O) and 30h (Get DOS Version) are available for use. Because other parts of DOS have not been initialized when driver initialization occurs, calls to disk drives (and so on) fail and lock up the system.

The initialization process must update the request header by adding the following information:

Byte Offset	Contents
03h	Return status
0Dh	Number of units (for block devices)
0Eh	Address of first free memory above driver
12h	BIOS parameter block pointer (block devices)

Figure 12.7 shows the request header as it enters the initialization function; figure 12.8 shows the request header coming out of the function.

Fig. 12.7. Request header on entry to initialization function.

Request header

Offset		Contents
00h	00	Length
01h	01	Unit number
02h	02	Command code
03h	03	Return status
04h	04	
05h	05	
06h	06	
07h	07	
08h	08	Reserved for DOS
09h	09	
0Ah	10	
0Bh	11	
0Ch	12	
0Dh	13	
l0Eh	14	
0Fh	15	
10h	16	
11h	17	
12h	18	Offset of CONFIG.SYS
13h	19	
14h	20	Segment of CONFIG.SYS
15h	21	
16h	22	First unit #
17h	23	
18h	24	
19h	25	
1Ah	26	
1Bh	27	
1Ch	28	
1Dh	29	
1Eh	30	
1Fh	31	

Fig. 12.8.   Request header on return from initialization.

Request header
Offset   Contents

Offset		Contents
00h	00	Length
01h	01	Unit number
02h	02	Command code
03h	03	
04h	04	Return status
05h	05	
06h	06	
07h	07	
08h	08	Reserved for DOS
09h	09	
0Ah	10	
0Bh	11	
0Ch	12	
0Dh	13	# units
0Eh	14	Offset of free memory
0Fh	15	
10h	16	Segment of free memory
11h	17	
12h	18	Offset of BPB
13h	19	
14h	20	Segment of BPB
15h	21	
16h	22	
17h	23	
18h	24	
19h	25	
1Ah	26	
1Bh	27	
1Ch	28	
1Dh	29	
1Eh	30	
1Fh	31	

Because the initialization code is called only once, many programmers save memory by setting the address of the first free memory to the start of the initialization code. Big drivers with large initialization sections can gain a great deal of space this way. But the example is not that sophisticated. I simply used a defined address at the end of the code segment to define the end of the driver.

Media Check

DOS gives the media-check function the following information in the request header:

Byte	
Offset	*Contents*
01h	Unit code
02h	Command code (1 for media check)
0Dh	Media descriptor byte

The media-check function is supposed to check whether the disk medium on a block device has been changed since the last access. For a character device, the routine should always return DONE (the request header status word is set to 0100h; the done bit, bit 8, is set; all other bits are zero). This means "complete" (see listing 12.1 for a definition). For a fixed block device (such as a hard disk) the routine should always indicate that the medium has not changed by placing a *1* at byte offset 0Eh in the request header. But how can you tell whether a removable disk has been changed?

Many programmers have wrestled with this problem. But because the DOS world has never had standards for insisting on volume labels and so on, no one has been able to come up with a truly reliable answer. Here are some ideas that have been tried:

❏ Go back so fast for another disk access that the disk could not have been removed. So far, no one has figured out how fast is fast enough (as soon as someone does, the Olympics will have a new event—opening disk drive doors).

❏ If the drive door has been opened, you could assume that the medium has been changed. (But what if the door opened accidentally and was simply reclosed?)

❏ If the volume ID has not changed since the last disk access, you could assume that the medium is the same. (How many disks do you have with the same volume ID?)

Clearly, there are no foolproof ways to determine that the disk has not been changed. On the Macintosh ®, disks cannot be changed except through the operating system itself. There is no way (other than by a series of manipulations with a paper clip) to remove the disk without the operating system being involved. Because the PC is not this restrictive, the DOS programmer is left holding the proverbial "bag." We can never really be sure whether the disk we write to is the one intended. Regardless of whether we know which disk we are writing to, DOS will act on whatever this function returns.

DOS's reaction depends on the return code placed in byte offset 0Eh of the request header. If the value is a 1, DOS assumes that the device has not been changed and proceeds to write without rereading the FAT table from the disk.

A code of –1 tells DOS that the disk *has* been changed and forces DOS to dump any write buffers and then reread the FAT and directory from the device. When DOS dumps its buffers, the information in them is simply thrown away.

A code of 0 means "maybe" (the driver cannot tell whether the media has been changed). In this case, DOS assumes that everything is OK and flushes out any buffers directly to the disk. If the buffers are empty, DOS rereads the FAT and the directory to be sure that the buffers are empty. Generally, this is the safest response. If there is any doubt, DOS will at least try to save the information (if the disk *has* been changed, this may result in disk sectors being overwritten).

Beginning with DOS V3, this function also returns a pointer to the last volume-ID read from the disk. Figure 12.9 shows the request header on entry to the media-check function; figure 12.10 shows the request header on return.

Fig. 12.9.   Request header on entry to media-check function.

Request header

Offset		Contents
00h	00	Length
01h	01	Unit number
02h	02	Command code
03h	03	
04h	04	Return status
05h	05	
06h	06	
07h	07	
08h	08	Reserved for DOS
09h	09	
0Ah	10	
0Bh	11	
0Ch	12	
0Dh	13	Media ID
0Eh	14	
l0Fh	15	
10h	16	
11h	17	
12h	18	
13h	19	
14h	20	
15h	21	
16h	22	
17h	23	
18h	24	
19h	25	
1Ah	26	
1Bh	27	
1Ch	28	
1Dh	29	
1Eh	30	
1Fh	31	

Fig. 12.10. *Request header on return from media-check function.*

Request header
Offset   Contents

Offset	Number	Contents
00h	00	Length
01h	01	Unit number
02h	02	Command code
03h	03	
04h	04	Return status
05h	05	
06h	06	
07h	07	
08h	08	Reserved for DOS
09h	09	
0Ah	10	
0Bh	11	
0Ch	12	
0Dh	13	
0Eh	14	Media change code
0Fh	15	Offset of volume label
10h	16	
11h	17	Segment of volume label
12h	18	
13h	19	
14h	20	
15h	21	
16h	22	
17h	23	
18h	24	
19h	25	
1Ah	26	
1Bh	27	
1Ch	28	
1Dh	29	
1Eh	30	
1Fh	31	

} DOS V3 & later

The safe course of action for a disk driver is to always return NOT CHANGED (a value of 1 at byte offset 0Eh in the request header) for a hard disk and DON'T KNOW (a value of 0 at byte offset 0Eh in the request header) for a floppy disk.

Build BIOS Parameter Block (BPB)

For block devices only, these functions build a BIOS Parameter Block and return a pointer to it at offset 12h in the request header. Character devices should just return DONE. In DOS V3 and later systems, this routine should also read and store the device volume ID for later use by the media-check function, which must return a pointer to the volume label in DOS V3 and later (refer to fig. 12.10).

On entry to the build BPB function, the request header contains the following information:

Byte Offset	Meaning
01h	Unit code
02h	Command code (2)
0Dh	Media descriptor byte
0Eh	Buffer address

A one-sector buffer is passed to this routine. If the non-IBM format bit in the device attribute word is zero, the buffer contains the first sector of the FAT and should not be changed. If the bit is set, the buffer can be used as a scratch area in which to build the BPB.

Whenever the media check detects a disk change or "thinks" that the disk may have been changed, DOS calls the BPB routine to rebuild its BPB from the disk. The BPB's layout is shown in table 12.5.

Table 12.5. *BIOS Parameter Block (BPB) Layout*

Byte Offset	Field Length	Meaning
00h	Word	Number of bytes per sector
02h	Byte	Number of sectors per cluster
03h	Word	Number of reserved sectors that start at sector 0
05h	Byte	Number of FATs
06h	Word	Maximum number of root-directory entries
08h	Word	Total number of sectors
0Ah	Byte	Media descriptor
0Bh	Word	Number of sectors per FAT
0Dh	Word	Number of sectors per track (DOS V3)
0Fh	Word	Number of heads (DOS V3)
11h	Double word	Number of hidden sectors (DOS V3)
15h	Double word	Total sectors if word at 08h is zero (DOS V3)
19h	Seven bytes	Reserved

The request header on entry to the function is shown in figure 12.11; figure 12.12 shows it on return.

Fig. 12.11. *Request header on entry to build BPB function.*

Request header

Offset		Contents
00h	00	Length
01h	01	Unit number
02h	02	Command code
03h	03	
04h	04	Return status
05h	05	
06h	06	
07h	07	
08h	08	Reserved for DOS
09h	09	
0Ah	10	
0Bh	11	
0Ch	12	
0Dh	13	Media ID
0Eh	14	Offset of FAT buffer
0Fh	15	
10h	16	Segment of FAT buffer
11h	17	
12h	18	
13h	19	
14h	20	
15h	21	
16h	22	
17h	23	
18h	24	
19h	25	
1Ah	26	
1Bh	27	
1Ch	28	
1Dh	29	
1Eh	30	
1Fh	31	

Fig. 12.12.   Request header on return from build BPB function.

Request header
Offset   Contents

Offset	#	Contents
00h	00	Length
01h	01	Unit number
02h	02	Command code
03h	03	
04h	04	Return status
05h	05	
06h	06	
07h	07	
08h	08	Reserved for DOS
09h	09	
0Ah	10	
0Bh	11	
0Ch	12	
0Dh	13	
0Eh	14	
l0Fh	15	
10h	16	
11h	17	
12h	18	Offset of BPB
13h	19	
14h	20	Segment of BPB
15h	21	
16h	22	
17h	23	
18h	24	
19h	25	
1Ah	26	
1Bh	27	
1Ch	28	
1Dh	29	
1Eh	30	
1Fh	31	

I/O Control (IOCTL) Read

This function allows a program to access the device directly by means of the IOCTL call. This function is called *only* when the IOCTL bit is set in the attribute word of the device header. The request header includes the following information:

Byte Offset	Meaning
01h	Unit code
02h	Command code (3)
0Dh	Media descriptor byte
0Eh	Transfer address
12h	Byte/sector count
14h	Starting sector number (block devices)

The routine should return the status word at offset 03h and the actual number of bytes or sectors transferred at offset 12h. DOS does no error checking on the call.

All IOCTL calls (read, write, and the generic call added in DOS V3.2) communicate with the *driver,* not with the device. Programs use these calls to tell the driver what to do or how to configure itself. With a serial driver, for example, you might use an IOCTL write to set the baud rate, word length, stop bits, and parity; you could use an IOCTL read to determine the current settings. The problem is that IOCTL calls are extremely specific to the driver.

An IOCTL command has no structure. The command (in any form in which the application puts it) is stored at the transfer address. If a program wants to configure a serial port, it might place the string

```
WORD=8,BAUD=1200,STOP=1,PARITY=N
```

at the transfer address to indicate eight bits, 1200 baud, one stop bit, and no parity (for a discussion of the meaning of these terms, see Chapter 7). But *there is no guarantee that the driver will understand the control string*.

If you were to try an IOCTL call to our sample driver (refer to listing 12.5), the driver would ignore any information passed and the IOCTL call would be unsuccessful. The IOCTL call would never reach the driver because the IOCTL-supported bit (bit 14 in the device attribute word in table 12.1) has not been set. Furthermore, even if the driver is reached, the unknown function error from the IOCTL read and write functions is returned. Our sample driver has not been written to respond to IOCTL calls.

In most books, information about IOCTL is vague. In most cases, the information is not defined. IOCTL information that is defined is included in the DOS Reference Section of this book.

Read

The read function reads data from the device and returns the data to a designated buffer. The function also returns a completion code and the number of bytes or sectors transferred. All of these *must* be passed, even if an error occurs. In DOS V3 (and later versions), the driver must also return a pointer to the volume ID if error 0Fh is returned.

On entry to the function, the request header contains the same information that is passed to the IOCTL read, write, and write-with-verify functions (the information detailed at the beginning of the preceding section). The read function communicates with the device by reading from it and making what it reads available to the program that called the device driver.

The read function is called to read both character and block devices. When a single character read is supposed to take place, the driver is given a byte count of 1. Parameters that have no meaning for the driver are simply ignored. (The same principle applies also in the IOCTL and write calls.)

Nondestructive Read

Nondestructive read is a "look-ahead" read for character devices only. This command is meaningless for block drivers; they should return DONE. On entry, the request header contains only the command code (05h) at position 02h (see fig. 12.13). The driver should read the next character but leave it in the input buffer to be used by the read function when it is called. The character should be returned in the request header at position 0Dh, as it is in figure 12.14.

Fig. 12.13.   *Request header on entry to nondestructive read function.*

Request header

Offset		Contents
00h	00	Length
01h	01	Unit number
02h	02	Command code
03h	03	
04h	04	Return status
05h	05	
06h	06	
07h	07	
08h	08	Reserved for DOS
09h	09	
0Ah	10	
0Bh	11	
0Ch	12	
0Dh	13	
0Eh	14	
0Fh	15	
10h	16	
11h	17	
12h	18	
13h	19	
14h	20	
15h	21	
16h	22	
17h	23	
18h	24	
19h	25	
1Ah	26	
1Bh	27	
1Ch	28	
1Dh	29	
1Eh	30	
1Fh	31	

Fig. 12.14. *Request header on return from nondestructive read function.*

Request header Offset		Contents
00h	00	Length
01h	01	Unit number
02h	02	Command code
03h	03	
04h	04	Return status
05h	05	
06h	06	
07h	07	
08h	08	Reserved for DOS
09h	09	
0Ah	10	
0Bh	11	
0Ch	12	
0Dh	13	Character
0Eh	14	
0Fh	15	
10h	16	
11h	17	
12h	18	
13h	19	
14h	20	
15h	21	
16h	22	
17h	23	
18h	24	
19h	25	
1Ah	26	
1Bh	27	
1Ch	28	
1Dh	29	
1Eh	30	
1Fh	31	

DOS uses the nondestructive-read function for a look-ahead read during keyboard operations. Through this function, DOS looks for Ctrl-C characters in the input stream from the keyboard.

Input Status

DOS uses the input status function to check whether characters are waiting in the input buffer on a character device. Block devices automatically return DONE for this routine. Character devices return their status at position 03h of the request header. This function, unlike a nondestructive read, does not read any characters; it simply returns the busy status of the device.

When this function is available, DOS uses it to check whether the device is busy before attempting to read. On entry, the request header contains only the command code (06h) at position 02h.

Flush Input Buffers

This command code (07h, at position 02h in the request header on entry to the function) tells the driver to dump any characters waiting to be input from the device. The function should return the return status code at position 03h in the request header. Block drivers should always return DONE.

Write

The write function (command code 08h at position 02h in the request header) takes characters out of the buffer passed with the request header and outputs them to the device. The function returns the return status (at position 03h), the number of bytes or sectors transferred (at position 12h), and (with DOS V3.0 and later versions) a pointer to the volume ID (at position 16h) if error code 0Fh is returned. The error status and number of bytes transferred *must* be returned.

The layout of the request header is identical to that of the read function (and the IOCTL and write-with-verify functions).

Write with Verify

This function (command code 09h at position 02h in the request header), which is identical to the write function, should also verify the completed write.

Output Status

This function (command code 0Ah at position 02h in the request header) returns the status of a character device. To determine whether a device is busy, DOS calls this function before outputting to the device. When data to be printed is passed to the printer driver, the driver sees this call. The return status word (bytes 03–04h in the request header) is used to return the device status. If the lower eight bits are zero, the device is ready. If the device is not ready, its status is coded from the standard code in table 12.3.

Flush Output Buffers

This function (command code 0Bh at position 02h in the segment header) dumps the contents of the output buffers. Like the flush-input function, it is for character devices only. Block devices should return DONE.

I/O Control Write

Like the I/O control read function, this function (command code 0Ch at position 02h in the request header) accesses the device directly. It is called only if the IOCTL bit is set in the device header's attribute word. Everything (except the command code) said about the IOCTL read function applies here, but in reverse—IOCTL write passes information *to* the driver, for example. As with the read function, the driver *and* the application must agree on what should be sent and its format.

Functions 0Dh through 14h are supported *only* on DOS V3 and later.

Open

If the OPEN/CLOSE/RM bit is set in the device attribute word, this function (command code 0Dh at position 02h in the request header) is called when an open is attempted on the device. For block devices, the call can be used to keep track of the number of open files on the device. Unfortunately, FCB function calls can leave this count hanging because files opened with the FCB may not be closed. When you deal with handles, DOS automatically closes the files when a process ends. With FCB functions, however, there is no call to FCB close unless the process closes it. On character devices, the situation is easier because we commonly use this call to pass special start-up strings (such as printer-initialization strings) to the device or to deny simultaneous access to more than one process.

On entry to the function, the request header contains the unit code (at position 01h) and the command code (0Dh, at position 02h). On return from the function, you pass the status word at position 03h.

Device Close

The CLOSE function (command code 0Eh at position 02h in the request header) can help keep track of whether the device is currently open to one or more processes. If the open function (command code 0Dh) increments an internal counter whenever it is called, then the close function can decrement the count and flush buffers when the count reaches zero. But the problems with FCB OPENS remain. Termination strings (such as final form feeds) can be sent to character devices. The entry parameters for this function are like those of the open functions: the unit code at position 01h and the command code (0Eh) at position 02h.

Removable Media

If the OPEN/CLOSE/RM bit is set in the device header, the removable media call (command code 0Fh at position 02h of the request header) is used in DOS V3 and later versions to determine whether the device has removable media. If not, DOS can optimize its strategy for dealing with the device by loading disk tables into memory for faster access. Character devices should simply return DONE. Status codes are selected from table 12.3 to return in the status word at position 03h of the request header.

Output until Busy

The output-until-busy function (command code 10h at position 02h in the request header) was provided primarily for print spooling. Some types of devices, most notably printers with large internal buffers or printer buffers, can accept characters at an extremely high rate—higher than the computer can feed them. The driver, if allowed to do so, could transfer continuously a large number of bytes to the device without the device becoming busy. That is the purpose of this function.

When called, this function transfers bytes to the device as fast as it can. It will transfer as many bytes as it can, either until the device becomes busy or until all the bytes it was given to transfer have been transferred. On entry to the function, the request header has the command code at position 02h, the transfer address (where the bytes to write to the device are located) at position 0Eh, and the byte count to be transferred at position 12h.

On return from the function, the request header must have the return status at position 03h and the number of bytes transferred at position 12h. If the number of bytes transferred is less than the number to be transferred, there is no error. Block devices should return DONE for this function.

Functions 11h through 13h are available only on DOS V3.2 and later.

Generic IOCTL

Like the IOCTL read and IOCTL write functions, the generic IOCTL function (command code 11h at position 02h in the request header) depends on the use of an agreed upon set of signals between the driver and the application program. Because there are no rules, this function usually works best for programmers who write their own drivers. Generic IOCTL supports some of the new IOCTL functions in DOS V3.3. (These functions are described in detail in the DOS Reference Section.)

Figure 12.15 shows the layout of the request header on entry to the function; the layout on return is shown in figure 12.16.

Fig. 12.15. *Request header on entry to the generic IOCTL.*

Request header

Offset		Contents
00h	00	Length
01h	01	Unit number
02h	02	Command code
03h	03	
04h	04	Return status
05h	05	
06h	06	
07h	07	
08h	08	Reserved for DOS
09h	09	
0Ah	10	
0Bh	11	
0Ch	12	
0Dh	13	Category (major) code
0Eh	14	Function (minor) code
0Fh	15	SI register
10h	16	
11h	17	DI register
12h	18	
13h	19	Offset of IOCTL
14h	20	data packet
15h	21	Segment of IOCTL
16h	22	data packet
17h	23	
18h	24	
19h	25	
1Ah	26	
1Bh	27	
1Ch	28	
1Dh	29	
1Eh	30	
1Fh	31	

Fig. 12.16. *Request header on return from the generic IOCTL.*

Request header
Offset   Contents

Offset	Byte	Contents
00h	00	Length
01h	01	Unit number
02h	02	Command code
03h	03	
04h	04	Return status
05h	05	
06h	06	
07h	07	
08h	08	Reserved for DOS
09h	09	
0Ah	10	
0Bh	11	
0Ch	12	
0Dh	13	
0Eh	14	
0Fh	15	
10h	16	
11h	17	
12h	18	
13h	19	
14h	20	
15h	21	
16h	22	
17h	23	
18h	24	
19h	25	
1Ah	26	
1Bh	27	
1Ch	28	
1Dh	29	
1Eh	30	
1Fh	31	

Get/Set Logical Device

These functions (command codes 12h and 13h at position 02h in the request header) support the operation of Int 21h, Function 44h (Subfunctions 0Eh and 0Fh). They determine which block-device name was last used to refer to a given device and they tell the driver which device name will be used next. For additional information about these functions, see the DOS Reference Section.

The get and set logical device functions are called with the unit number at position 01h of the request header and the command code at position 02h. On return, the last device unit code is returned at position 01h and the device status is returned at position 03h.

The Whole Driver

The sample driver (drvr.asm) is listed in full in listing 12.6. You can produce a working driver by typing in this listing and assembling it according to the directions in the following section. (Although this driver doesn't do much, it is a beginning.) But be careful: although this driver has been tested, you can mess up your system if you mistype something, if a smudge in your book hides an important step, or if a step does not complete properly (and you miss it). Whenever you test drivers, be sure to work on a floppy rather than on your main system. And be sure to follow the precautions listed in the following section.

Listing 12.6

```
;       Driver:    DRVR.ASM
;
;       globals
;
CR          EQU     ØDh             ;Carriage return
LF          EQU     ØAh             ;Line feed
MAXCMD      EQU     16              ;DOS 3.Ø, 12 DOS 2.Ø
ERROR       EQU     8ØØØh           ;Set error bit
BUSY        EQU     Ø2ØØh           ;Set busy bit
DONE        EQU     Ø1ØØh           ;Set completion bit
UNKNOWN     EQU     8ØØ3h           ;Set unknown status
;
cseg segment     public 'code'     ;Start the code segment
     org         Ø                 ;Zero origin
     assume      cs:cseg,ds:cseg,es:cseg
;
;=========================================================
;       Device header for the driver
;       Next driver pointer is -1 (end of list)
;       Attribute is character device, does not
;          respond to IOCTL calls
;       Name of the driver is DRVR
;
drvr        proc        far         ;FAR procedure
            dd          -1          ;Next driver pointer
            dw          8ØØØh       ;Attribute
            dw          strategy    ;Pointer to strategy
            dw          interrupt   ;Pointer to interrupt
            db          'DRVR    '  ;Device name
```

Listing 12.6 continues

Listing 12.6 continued

```
;
;========================================================
;     Strategy Routine
;     Saves the pointer to the REQUEST HEADER (RH)
;       from the ES:BX registers to rh_seg and rh_off
;
rh_seg    dw    ?              ;RH segment address
rh_off    dw    ?              ;RH offset address
strategy:
          mov   cs:rh_seg,es
          mov   cs:rh_off,bx
          ret
;
;========================================================
;     Interrupt Section
;     Processes all driver requests
;
;
;--------------------------------------------------------
;     Command Code Dispatch Table
;
d_tbl:
      dw    s_init        ;Initialization
      dw    s_mchk        ;Media check
      dw    s_bpb         ;BIOS parameter block
      dw    s_ird         ;IOCTL read
      dw    s_read        ;Read
      dw    s_nrd         ;Nondestructive read
      dw    s_inst        ;Current input status
      dw    s_infl        ;Flush input buffer
      dw    s_write       ;Write
      dw    s_vwrite      ;Write with verify
      dw    s_ostat       ;Current output status
      dw    s_oflush      ;Flush output buffers
      dw    s_iwrt        ;IOCTL write
      dw    s_open        ;Open
      dw    s_close       ;Close
      dw    s_media       ;Removable media
      dw    s_busy        ;Output until busy
;
;--------------------------------------------------------
;     Interrupt Handler
;
interrupt:
      cld                 ;Save machine state
      push es             ;Save all registers
```

Listing 12.6 continues

Listing 12.6 continued

```
        push ds
        push ax
        push bx
        push cx
        push dx
        push si
        push di
        push bp
;
;       Retrieve the rh pointer
;
        mov   dx,cs:rh_seg
        mov   es,dx
        mov   bx,cs:rh_off
;
        mov   al,es:[bx]+2       ;Command code
        xor   ah,ah
        cmp   ax,MAXCMD          ;Legal command?
        jle   ok                 ;Jump if OK
        mov   ax,UNKNOWN         ;Unknown command
        jmp   finish
;
;       Execute driver function
;       All driver functions are responsible for
;          returning in AX the status
;
ok:
        shl   ax,1              ;Multiply by 2
        mov   bx,ax
        jmp   word ptr [bx + d_tbl]
;
;       End of the driver
;       Set completion status
;          and restore the registers
;
finish:
;
;       Retrieve the rh pointer
;
        mov   dx,cs:rh_seg
        mov   es,dx
        mov   bx,cs:rh_off
;
        or    ax,DONE           ;Set the DONE bit
        mov   es:[bx]+3,ax
```

Listing 12.6 continues

Listing 12.6 *continued*

```
;
      pop   bp                ;Restore the registers
      pop   di
      pop   si
      pop   dx
      pop   cx
      pop   bx
      pop   ax
      pop   ds
      pop   es
      ret                     ;Back to DOS
;
;-----------------------------------------------------------
;     Driver Commands
;
;     First the unused commands: we dispose of these
;         in an error exit
;
s_mchk:                       ;Media Check
s_bpb:                        ;BIOS parameter block
s_ird:                        ;IOCTL read
s_read:                       ;Read
s_nrd:                        ;Nondestructive read
s_inst:                       ;Current input status
s_infl:                       ;Flush input buffers
s_vwrite:                     ;Current output status
s_ostat:                      ;Current output status
s_oflush:                     ;Flush output buffers
s_iwrt:                       ;IOCTL write
s_open:                       ;Open
s_close:                      ;Close
s_media:                      ;Removable media
s_busy:                       ;Output until busy
      xor   ax, ax      ;No error
      jmp   finish
;
;-----------------------------------------------------------
;     Initialization
;
ident:
      db    CR,LF
      db    'Sample Device Driver - Version '
      db    '0.0'
      db    CR,LF,LF,'$'
s_init:
```

Listing 12.6 *continues*

Listing 12.6 continued

```
        mov   ah,9                ;Print string
        mov   dx, offset ident
        int   21h
;
;       Retrieve the rh pointer
;
        mov   dx,cs:rh_seg
        mov   es,dx
        mov   bx,cs:rh_off
;
        lea   ax,end_driver      ;Get end of driver address
        mov   es:[bx]+14,ax
        mov   es:[bx]+16,cs
;
        xor   ax,ax              ;Zero the ax register
        jmp   finish
;
;-------------------------------------------------------
;       Write data
;
s_write:
        xor   ax,ax              ;Zero ax register
        jmp   finish
;
;=========================================================
;       End of Driver
;
end_driver:
drvr endp
cseg ends
        end
;=========================================================
```

Assembling the Driver

To assemble the driver, you need to run the macro assembler, the linker, and then the EXE2BIN program to create the driver as a binary image. These steps have been combined into a standard batch file that also copies the driver to drive A: (just in case you forget to do so). Listing 12.7 gives the MAKEDRVR.BAT file.

The batch file first sets the PATH variable to include the compiler and command directories; then it assembles the driver. If the driver assembles properly, it gets linked. If the link is successful, EXE2BIN is executed to

Listing 12.7

```
;===========================================================
rem  Listing 12.7
rem  Makedrvr.bat

echo off

rem  Assemble driver with Microsoft Macro Assembler
rem  and stage for testing on drive a:

path=c:\bin\cc;c:\util;c:\dos
masm %1;
if errorlevel 1 goto mfail

link %1;
if errorlevel 1 goto lfail

exe2bin %1 %1.sys
if errorlevel 1 goto efail

copy %1.sys a:
goto done

:mfail
echo *** Assembly Failed ***
goto done

:lfail
echo *** Link Failed ***
goto done

:efail
echo *** Conversion to .sys failed ***
goto done

:done
echo on
c:\batch\setpath
===========================================================
```

convert the driver to a memory-image format. When the program terminates, the driver is copied to drive A: and the path is set back to normal.

When they work on a driver, most programmers repeatedly reassemble. The batch file helps ease the tension that surrounds repeated failures with *nothing* visible and no clear way to get an output. If you write a driver, expect to lock up the system a few times before you get it right.

To use the batch file, you must give it the name of the driver's source file (without the extension). To execute the drvr.asm program, you type:

C:> *makedrvr drvr*

The batch file will see automatically that the output is a file (called DRVR.SYS) that can be added to the CONFIG.SYS file.

Installing the Driver

The operating system installs device drivers when it processes the CONFIG.SYS file during the system boot procedure. If DRVR.SYS (your driver) is stored in the root directory on drive A:, you can add it to the system by editing the CONFIG.SYS file to include the line:

DEVICE =A:DRVR.SYS

Debugging the Driver

If your driver works the first time you run it, you are better than most programmers. Even the best programmers must test and retest the driver until they "get it right." Sometimes the problem is not something the programmer did wrong; it may be something he or she did not understand (or know) about the device.

To debug a device driver, you need to do a great deal of intensive head-scratching. A minor error in address modes during initialization can lock up a DOS system if the pointers it is looking for are somewhere else in memory. A call to a driver can disappear down a black hole, never to return again. Applications programs can be given incorrect responses to a function call because the driver returned the wrong count.

Because printing from inside a driver is not easy, getting information on an error is a nightmare. Sometimes, when an error is time-critical, just putting in the debugging code causes the driver to work perfectly. One driver that I worked on for a UNIX system would not work unless a certain amount of undetermined time was eaten up in the middle of the driver. Although many systems programmers have worked on the function, the delay is still there. DOS can get you the same way.

To debug a driver, remember the following guidelines:

❏ *Never test a new driver on your hard disk.* Make a bootable floppy disk and copy the driver and the CONFIG.SYS file to the floppy for testing. If you test on the hard disk and the driver fails on initialization, you cannot boot the hard disk directly. You will have to boot to a floppy to change CONFIG.SYS on the hard disk.

❑ *If you have a system without a hard disk, do the testing there.* Even a simple problem can have damaging consequences at the driver level. (What if your driver scrambles your hard disk's FAT?)

❑ *Use BIOS calls to print the driver's status at critical points.* If you want to understand the output, be careful not to include so many debugging outputs that you cannot read them as they go by.

❑ *Anything that records the screen display as it goes by during testing, and that can be played back at slow speed, can help.* Small computers, the system printer, or even a videotape can help if they can be configured to record what is happening.

Making a Practical Driver

You can make the sample driver more concrete by adding some substance to it. We'll add a write function to make the driver capable of writing to the printer as it gets characters. If you want this driver to replace the default printer driver, you can change its name (to PRN) in the device header.

Everything in drvr.asm remains the same, but we expand the write function (see listing 12.8).

Listing 12.8

```
;     Get print parameters
;
      mov   cx,es:[bx]+12h      ;Number of bytes to print
      mov   di,es:[bx]+0eh      ;Offset of data buffer
      mov   ax,es:[bx]+10h      ;Segment address of data buffer
      mov   es,ax
;
      mov   dl,0               ;Printer 0
      mov   bx,0               ;Count 0 bytes printed
;
s_prt1:
      cmp   bx,cx              ;Printed all characters yet?
      je    s_done            ;All done
;
      mov   al,es:[di]         ;Get a character
      inc   di                ;Point to the next one
;
      mov   ah,2              ;Check printer status
```

Listing 12.8 continues

Listing 12.8 continued

```
        int   17h
        test  ah,80h           ;Busy?
        jne   s_prtch          ;Print it
        jmp   s_err            ;Busy device, exit
s_prtch:
        cmp   al,LF            ;Is the character a line feed?
        je    s_bxinc          ;Skip it
        mov   ah,Ø             ;Print character
        int   17h
        test  ah,Ø9h           ;I/O error?
        jne   s_err            ;Handle it
s_bxinc:
        inc   bx               ;Count one printed
        jmp   s_prt1
s_err:
        mov   ax,8ØØch         ;General Failure Error
        jmp   s_end
s_done:
        mov   ax,bx            ;Save count
        mov   bx,cs:rh_off     ;Get req.hdr
        mov   es:[bx]+12h,ax   ;Store byte count
        xor   ax,ax            ;Zero ax register
s_end:
        jmp   finish
;============================================================
```

The new code prints characters to the printer and ignores line-feed characters on their way out. This function is useful if you want to use one of the older printers that interprets carriage returns or line feeds as a "carriage-return-line-feed" pair.

The function is simple. It begins by locating the request header pointer to the data buffer (offset 0Eh and 10h) and the number of bytes to transfer (offset 12h). Then it checks the printer status and, if the printer is busy, returns an error. If the printer is not busy, it prints the character. In this simplistic routine, any error that prevents you from writing the characters to the device causes the function to set an error code in the AX register (the device return status).

You could expand the entire function to do more sophisticated error-processing—such as recognizing which errors are which and returning appropriate codes—but the basic function is sound.

Using the Device Driver

In order to test the device driver, you have to use it. There are several simple ways to use it from a program or directly from the command-line prompt.

Our sample driver is named DRVR (refer to listing 12.6). Like all other devices, this driver is activated when called by name. If you wanted to redirect something to the printer with the normal driver (PRN), you could type:

C>*type autoexec.bat>prn:*

This would direct a copy of the AUTOEXEC.BAT file out to the printer. To use the driver, you can type:

C>*type autoexec.bat>drvr:*

When you attempt to write to drvr, DOS checks the driver chain to locate the name DRVR and then uses the driver to print the data.

You also can access the driver from a program by opening the device as you would a file. You could use a handle function call to open the device (see listing 12.9).

Listing 12.9

```
union REGS regs;

regs.h.ah = Øx3d;         /* Open-file function */
regs.h.al = Øx01;         /* Write access */
regs.x.dx = (int)"drvr";
intdos(&regs,&regs);      /* Call DOS function int */
handle = regs.x.ax;       /* Save the file handle */
```

Either way you choose to access the driver, you can test its operation according to its design. In the case of drvr, you want to be able to test whether it prints characters to the printer and whether it eliminates line feeds from the character stream.

Summary

This chapter has dealt with what most programmers find the hardest part of programming in DOS: creating device drivers. You have learned that you can create device drivers by following a standard "mold" for a driver.

All drivers are built in three primary sections:

❑ The device header
❑ The strategy routine
❑ The interrupt routine

Each has its own structure. The device header contains the name of the driver and the pointer to the next driver in the chain of system drivers. The strategy routine provides only for remembering where the system request header will be stored for communication between the driver and the operating-system kernel.

Most of the driver is contained in the individual functions (as many as 20 of them) that make up the interrupt routine. Any given driver may implement only a few of these functions and ignore the rest, returning a suitable completion code if such a request is made to the driver.

CHAPTER 13

Miscellaneous Functions

This chapter focuses on three basic types of functions: DOS information functions, date and time functions, and extended error processing. The first two types are simple and don't require extensive treatment. The third type of function is an extremely powerful extension to DOS's error-processing capabilities. However, because this type of function tends to be extremely program dependent, this chapter does not include a practical example of its usefulness.

DOS Version Information

A function was added in DOS V2.0 to let you retrieve the DOS version number. This function can be essential to knowing what functionality to use in running a system. Fortunately, because DOS versions earlier than V2.0 (in other words, V1.x) reliably return a zero, any return value of less than 2 indicates a DOS V1.x system. You can't tell V1.0 from V1.1, but at least you know that the major functionality change point hasn't been reached.

If detecting the DOS version doesn't seem important, remember that many people have never upgraded from DOS V1.0 or V1.1. For example, while writing this book I met a couple who had stopped at a Seattle computer store to buy extra hardware so that they could expand their two disk *original* IBM PC to a hard disk system. They were still running DOS V1.1 and had to be told that it wouldn't run the equipment they were buying. They walked out of the store with their hardware and DOS V3.2.

383

In order to maintain perfect compatibility across the various versions of DOS, you would have to restrict your programming to only those functions that were available in DOS V1—a laudable but silly goal. Most programming these days requires *at least* DOS V2.0; with earlier versions, features such as directories cannot even be used.

I recommend that you use the DOS version number in one of two ways:

1. Check for the proper DOS level and tell the user if it isn't high enough to support the program.

2. Check for the DOS level and compensate as necessary.

The second approach will create considerable overhead, unless you are limiting DOS-specific code to overlays (with a separate overlay for each DOS version) or doing an installation that will patch in the correct code version for the DOS in use.

The lines of code following this paragraph check for minimum functionality (at least DOS V2). The function returns two numbers: AL is the major version number (02h is DOS V2, 03h is DOS V3) and AH is the minor version number (10 is .10, 20 is .20, and so forth). Save registers BX and CX if you will need them after the call—the interrupt will destroy them.

Int 21h, Function 30h: Get DOS Version Number

```
mov     ah,48      ; DOS Version
int     21h
cmp     al,2       ; Check for greater than or equal to V2
jl      wrong      ; Wrong version
```

You can create (and use as a library function) a C subroutine that gives you the DOS version number. For example, if you simply want to check for a minimum version of DOS, you can use the subroutine chkver() in listing 13.1.

Listing 13.1

```
/* C version of chkver()  */

#include <stdio.h>

main()
```

Listing 13.1 continues

Listing 13.1 *continued*

```
/*
      This program checks for minimum V3, using the chkver()
      subroutine. If the version isn't at least 3, then the
      program will report failure. You can extract the subroutine
      and use it as part of a library.

*/

{
    int  ver;

    if((ver = chkver()) < 3){
        printf("ERROR - Version MUST be at least 3.Ø\n");
        printf("        Yours is only version %d\n",ver);
        exit(Ø);
    }
    printf("Thanks ... you have version %d of DOS\n",ver);
}

/**************************************************
      SUBROUTINE:    chkver()
      FUNCTION:      returns the major version number of the DOS
      ARGUMENTS:     none
      RETURNS:       integer version number
      COMMENTS:
**************************************************/

#include <dos.h>

chkver()

/*
      Subroutine uses Int 21h, Function 3Øh to determine the version of DOS.

      Function 3Øh returns Ø if earlier than V2.Ø, returns version
      number otherwise.

*/

{
    union REGS regs;

    regs.h.ah = Øx3Ø;
    intdos(&regs,&regs);
    if(regs.h.al == Ø) regs.h.al = 1;

    return(regs.h.al);
}
```

Because of the way this program is written, you can pull out the subroutine chkver(), place it in a subroutine library, and use it with other C programs. At the beginning of the program, be sure to add the statement

```
#include <stdio.h>
```

so that standard I/O functions are declared for the subroutine.

The subroutine itself simply calls Function 30h. Although the function returns both the major and minor numbers of the version (in registers AL and AH, respectively), only the major number is important.

Listing 13.2 is a BASIC version of the same program.

Listing 13.2

```
'BASIC version of chkver()

$include "REGNAMES.INC"

def fnchkver
'determine the DOS version from Int 21h, Function 30h
    reg %ax, &h3000
    call interrupt &h21

    if reg(%ax) and &h00ff = 0 then reg %ax,&h0001
    fnchkver = reg(%ax) and &h00ff
end def

'MAIN PROGRAM
'
'Use the check version function to print the
'system's version number

    if fnchkver <3 then
        print "OOPS - You have an operating system version"
        print "Earlier than 3.0, You need to upgrade."
    else
        print "Operating System version 3 or above"
    end if
end
```

If you want to print the DOS version number, you can use the getversion() subroutine shown in listing 13.3.

Listing 13.3

```
/* C version of getversion() */

#include  <stdio.h>

char *getversion();

main()

/*
    This program determines, from the return to Int 21h,
    Function 30h, which version of the operating system is
    installed. The program uses subroutine getversion(), which
    can be extracted, placed in a separate library file, and
    used with other programs.

 */

{
    printf("DOS Version %s\n",getversion());
}

/****************************************************
    SUBROUTINE:    getversion()
    FUNCTION:      returns a string with the
                   version number of the DOS
    ARGUMENTS:     none
    RETURNS:       pointer to a character buffer
    COMMENTS:
****************************************************/

#include  <dos.h>

char *getversion()

/*
    Subroutine uses Int 21h, Function 30h to determine the version of DOS.

    Function 30h returns 0 if earlier than V2.0, returns version
    number otherwise.

*/

{
    static char buffer[5];
    union REGS regs;
```

Listing 13.3 continues

Listing 13.3 *continued*

```
regs.h.ah = Øx3Ø;
intdos(&regs,&regs);
if(regs.h.al == Ø) regs.h.al = 1;
sprintf(buffer,"%d.%d",regs.h.al,regs.h.ah);

return(buffer);
}
```

The getversion( ) subroutine, which uses the DOS version's major and minor numbers, is more complex than the chkver( ) subroutine. To make the version numbers accessible for printing, you create a static character buffer into which the version string is written in the proper format. Be careful, because the static buffer is only five characters (the last of which *must* be a NULL character). A five-character buffer will work until versions of DOS have three-digit minor numbers or two-digit major numbers; if version numbers get too high, you will have to make the buffer larger.

Because you return a pointer to the static character buffer, your main routine can simply print the return value and—voilà—you have the DOS version. You can include this subroutine getversion( ) in a library and use it, as needed, for other programs.

Listing 13.4 is a BASIC version of the subroutine. The BASIC function is substantially the same as the C routine but (because of the way BASIC works) seems quite different.

Listing 13.4

```
'BASIC Version of getversion()

$include "REGNAMES.INC"

def fngetver
'determine the DOS version from Int 21h, Function 3Øh
'     vn = version number
'     rn = revision number

      reg %ax, &h3ØØØ
      call interrupt &h21

      if reg(%ax) and &hØØff = Ø then reg %ax,&hØØØ1
      vn = (reg(%ax) and &hØØff)
```

Listing 13.4 continues

Listing 13.4 continued

```
        rn = (reg(%ax) and &hffØØ)/256
        fngetver = vn + rn/1ØØ
end def

'MAIN PROGRAM
'
'Use the get version function to print the
'system's version number
'NOTE:    It's necessary to use PRINT USING to get the
'    proper number of decimal places

        cls
        print using "Version Number: #.##" ;fngetver


end
```

Equipment Information

You may want to know what equipment is included on your system as well as what the DOS version number is. BIOS Int 11h returns a code in register AX that indicates the equipment installed on the computer. Table 13.1 shows how the information is coded.

Table 13.1. BIOS Int 11h Return Code

Bit(s)	Meaning
0	Set if disk drives installed (bits 6–7 significant)
1	Set if math coprocessor installed (AT only)
2–3	Memory configuration (not meaningful for AT) 0 = 16K system board RAM 1 = 32K system board RAM 2 = 48K system board RAM 3 = 64K system board RAM
4–5	Initial video mode 1 = 40 × 25, text, color 2 = 80 × 25, text, color 3 = 80 × 25, text, mono

Table 13.1 continues

Table 13.1 *continued*

Bit(s)	Meaning
4–7	Number of disk drives minus 1 Valid only if bit 0 is 1
8	Not used
9–11	Number of RS232 ports
12	Set if game adapter installed (PC only)
13	Set if internal modem installed (AT only)
14–15	Number of printers attached

To determine the equipment in a computer, you simply invoke Int 11h and then interpret the return code. The C program in listing 13.5 uses the interrupt in a subroutine.

Listing 13.5

```
#include  <stdio.h>

#define   BOOL      int
#define   FALSE     Ø
#define   TRUE      !FALSE

main()

/*
     This program prints the equipment list for a computer; to do
     so, it uses function equipment().
*/

{
     int   eqpt;

     eqpt = equipment(TRUE);
     printf("Equipment Value is %x\n",eqpt);
}
```

Listing 13.5 continues

Listing 13.5 *continued*

```
/*********************************************************
        SUBROUTINE:    equipment()
        FUNCTION:      get the machine equipment list
        ARGUMENTS:     print flag
        RETURNS:       equipment word
        COMMENTS:      If the print flag is TRUE (non zero) the
                       routine will print the equipment list.
*********************************************************/
#include  <dos.h>

#define   EQUIPMENT Øx11

equipment(print)

/*

    Returns the equipment code from Int 11h. Optionally, will
    print the equipment list if the 'print' flag is TRUE

*/

BOOL print;

{
    union REGS regs;
    int  eqpt;

    int86(EQUIPMENT,&regs,&regs);
    if(print){
        eqpt = regs.x.ax;
        if(eqpt & Øx01)
            printf("Floppy Drives are attached\n");
        if(eqpt>>1 & Øx01)
            printf("Math Coprocessor installed (AT only)\n");
        switch(eqpt>>4 & Øx03){
            case 1:
                printf("Initial video mode 4ØX25 color\n");
                break;
            case 2:
                printf("Initial video mode 8ØX25 color\n");
                break;
            case 3:
                printf("Initial video mode 8ØX25 mono\n");
                break;
```

Listing 13.5 continues

Listing 13.5 *continued*

```
        }
    if(eqpt>>6 & 0x01)
        printf("Number of disk drives is %d\n",
            (eqpt>>6 & 0x03) + 1);
    printf("Number of RS-232 ports is %d\n",
        eqpt>>9 & 0x07);
    if(eqpt>>12 & 0x01)
        printf("Game adapter installed\n");
    if(eqpt>>13 & 0x01)
        printf("Internal modem installed (AT only)\n");
    printf("Number of printers is %d\n",
        eqpt>>14);
    }
    return(regs.x.ax);
}
```

The function equipment() can be pulled from this program and added to a function library of useful routines.

Notice the use of the definition EQUIPMENT in the interrupt call. By defining constants such as EQUIPMENT (0x11), you can simplify program maintenance and make your code much more readable.

Listing 13.6 shows the equipment program written in BASIC.

Listing 13.6

```
'BASIC Version of eqpt.bas

$include "REGNAMES.INC"

def fngeteqpt

    call interrupt &h11
    fngeteqpt = reg(%ax)

end def

'MAIN PROGRAM
'
'Get the installed equipment with the function
'geteqpt and interpret it with the subroutine
'printeqpt
```

Listing 13.6 *continues*

Listing 13.6 continued

```
        cls
        print "System Equipment Installed"
        eq% = fngeteqpt
        print "   Equipment code = ";HEx$(eq%)
        call printeqpt(eq%)
end

sub printeqpt(n%)
'
'This procedure prints the installed equipment list
'given the equipment code number

        if n% and &h01 then print "FLOPPY DRIVES ATTACHED"
        if n% and &h02 then print "MATH COPROCESSOR INSTALLED"
        if n% and &h1000 then print "GAME ADAPTER INSTALLED"
        vm = (n% and &h30)/16
        select case vm
            case 1
                print "40X25 text, color"
            case 2
                print "80X25 text, color"
            case 3
                print "80X25 text, mono"
        end select
        dd = (n% and &hC0)/64 + 1
        print "Number of disk drives: ";dd
        rs = (n% and &hE00)/512
        print "Number of RS-232 ports: ";rs
        pr = (n% and &hC000)/16384
        print "Number of printer ports: "'

end sub
```

Date and Time Functions

During system start-up, the date and time are initialized to their default values. If your system does not have an internal hardware clock, the default date is 1/1/80, and the default time is 00:00:00.00 (midnight). If your computer has an internal clock, the date and time are set from the values in the internal clock. From this point, the time is kept in the BIOS data area and the date is kept in COMMAND.COM. If you do not have an internal clock, the system date and time are reset with the DOS commands DATE and TIME.

The best way to access the time and date is to use the DOS functions provided for that purpose. In DOS V1.1 and later versions, the system date function gets the day, month, year, and day of the week as follows:

Int 21h, Function 2Ah: Get System Date

```
mov        ah,2ah       ; Get Date
int        21h
mov        dow,al       ; Day of Week
mov        mo,dh        ; Month
mov        dy,dl        ; Day
mov        yr,cx        ; Year
```

The returned values are in the following ranges:

Day	1–31
Month	1–12
Year	1980–2099
Day of Week	0–6 (0 =Sunday, 1 =Monday, etc.)

These ranges are used when you set the system date with DOS Int 21h, Function 2Bh. DOS returns AL =0 if the date is set successfully, FFh if the date is not valid.

You can also set the system date under program control through the use of the following DOS function:

Int 21h, Function 2Bh: Set System Date

```
mov        ah,2bh       ; Set date
mov        cx,yr        ; Year
mov        dh,mo        ; Month
mov        dl,dy        ; Day
int        21h
or         al,al        ; Test for invalid
jnz        error        ; Jump on error
```

In addition to the functions provided for getting and setting the system date, DOS includes functions for getting and setting the system time. When it gets the system time, DOS returns values within the following ranges:

Hours	0–23
Minutes	0–59
Seconds	0–59
Hundredths of seconds	0–99

Because of the relatively slow speed of some computer systems, the real-time clock may not have an accurate resolution of 100ths of seconds. On these systems, the DL value should not be used for accurate or critical timing.

You get the system time by executing the following DOS interrupt and function:

Int 21h, Function 2Ch: Get System Time

```
mov      ah,2ch      ; Get Time
int      21h
mov      hr,ch       ; Hours
mov      mn,cl       ; Minutes
mov      sc,dh       ; Seconds
mov      hn,dl       ; Hundredths of seconds
```

The range restrictions for setting the time are the same as those for getting the time. To set the time, use DOS Int 21h, Function 2Dh. The system will return AL =0 if the time is set successfully, AL =FFh if the time set is not valid.

Int 21h, Function 2Dh: Set System Time

```
mov      ah,2dh      ; Set Time
mov      ch,hr       ; Hour
mov      cl,mn       ; Minutes
mov      dx,Ø        ; Seconds = Ø
int      21h
or       al,al       ; Error?
jnz      error
```

Listing 13.7 includes a set of C functions for getting the time and date. The subroutines cdate( ) and ctime( ) can be pulled out of the listing and added to your library of functions. Each will return a string pointer to a static buffer inside the function, with the date or time formatted appropriately in this buffer.

Listing 13.7

```
/* Date/Time functions */

#include <stdio.h>

char *cdate(), *ctime();

main()

/*
    Retrieves and displays the system date and time. The
    subroutines can be extracted and placed in a function library.

*/
```

Listing 13.7 continues

Listing 13.7 continued

```
{
    printf("Date: %s Time: %s\n",cdate(), ctime());
}

/*******************************************************
    SUBROUTINE:     cdate()
    FUNCTION:       returns date string in form MM/DD/YY
    ARGUMENTS:      none
    RETURNS:        pointer to static string buffer
    COMMENTS:
********************************************************/

#include  <dos.h>

char *cdate()

/*
    Retrieve the system date and return a pointer to a string in
    the form MM/DD/YY.
*/

{
    static char buffer[9];
    union REGS regs;

    regs.h.ah = 0x2a;
    intdos(&regs,&regs);

    sprintf(buffer,"%02.2d/%02.2d/%02.2d",
        regs.h.dh, regs.h.dl, regs.x.cx-1900);
    return(buffer);
}

/*******************************************************
    SUBROUTINE:     ctime()
    FUNCTION:       returns time string in form HH:MM:SS
    ARGUMENTS:      none
    RETURNS:        pointer to static string buffer
    COMMENTS:
********************************************************/

char *ctime()
```

Listing 13.7 continues

Listing 13.7 continued

```
/*
    Returns a pointer to the time in the form HH:MM:SS
*/

{

    static char    buffer[9];
    union REGS regs;

    regs.h.ah = 0x2c;
    intdos(&regs,&regs);


    sprintf(buffer,"%02.2d:%02.2d:%02.2d",
        regs.h.ch, regs.h.cl, regs.h.dh);
    return(buffer);


}
```

Each function is put together to hold the string representation of the date or time until you can use the string. Such static variables are permanently allocated and can take up a great deal of memory that will be used only infrequently. Be careful not to use too many of them.

Listing 13.8, the Pascal program clock.pas, is another example of the use of the date and time functions. This program displays an on-screen clock until you press the escape key (Esc).

Listing 13.8

```
{ clock.pas - Screen Clock }

Program Clock;

{ Turbo Pascal 4.0. For 3.0, omit next code line }
{ and declare the Registers record type.         }

uses crt, Dos;

const    cr:  char = ^M;

var hour,min,sec,month,day,year : byte;
    ch : char;

Procedure get_time( var hr,mi,se : byte );
```

Listing 13.8 continues

Listing 13.8 continued

```
var
    I: Integer;
    Regs: Registers;

begin { get_time }
    With Regs Do
        begin
            AH:=$2C;
            Flags:=0;
            MsDos(Regs);    {execute software interrupt}
            hr:=CH;
            mi:=CL;
            se:=DH;
        end; { With Regs }
end; { end get_time }


Procedure get_date( var mo, da, yr : byte);

var
    I: Integer;
    Regs: Registers;

begin { get_date }
    With Regs Do
        begin
            AH:=$2A;
            Flags:=0;
            MsDos(Dos.Registers(Regs));    {execute software interrupt}
            yr:=(CX mod 100);
            da:=DL;
            mo:=DH;
        end; { With Regs }
end; { end get_date }

procedure print_time( hr,mi,se,mo,dy,yr : byte);

begin { procedure print_time }
    write(mo:2,'/',dy:2,'/',yr:2);
    write(' ',hr:2,':',mi:2,':',se:2);
    write(cr);
end; { end print_time }
```

Listing 13.8 continues

Listing 13.8 *continued*

```
begin { Main Routine }
    repeat
        get_time(hour,min,sec);
        get_date(month,day,year);
        print_time(hour,min,sec,month,day,year);
        delay(10);
    until keypressed;
    { flush the input buffer }
    while keypressed do ch := readkey;
    { for version 3.0, replace preceding line with }
    {     while keypressed do read(kbd,ch); }
end. { end Main Routine }
```

Clock.pas is a simplistic program. The main part of the program occurs at the end, between the begin-end pair marked as Main Routine. This main routine sets up a continuous loop (repeat-until) that gets the date and time and prints them every 10 seconds until a keyboard key is pressed. (Whenever a key is pressed, keypressed is set to TRUE so that Turbo Pascal can recognize it.)

After the clock loop ends, the program clears any keystrokes in the input buffer simply by reading characters as long as keypressed remains TRUE. Then the program terminates.

Extended Error Processing

A DOS function, introduced with DOS V3, lets you determine *extended error information*. Extended error information provides detailed information about an error that has just occurred (after a DOS service call) and suggests action to remedy the error. Although this function is most useful at the assembly language level, you also can get suggested recovery actions by using the routine from a high-level language.

If you are working in assembly language, you should save any essential registers before you call Function 59h because this special function destroys most of your register setups while it is processing. (If you are working in a high-level language, you do not need to save the registers.)

The following DOS function saves the registers and then gets the extended error information:

Int 21h, Function 59h: Get Extended Error Information

```
push        ax          ; Save registers before call
push        bx
push        cx
```

Fragment continues

Fragment *continued*

push	dx
push	si
push	di
push	bp
push	ds
push	es
mov	ah,89 ; Extended error info
mov	bx,Ø
int	21h

The routine returns the following codes:

AX = Extended error code
BH = Error class
BL = Recommended action
CH = Error locus

The meaning of these codes is detailed in tables 13.2, 13.3, 13.4, and 13.5. The codes are self explanatory; how you respond to them depends on the program and the nature of the call that generated the problem.

Table 13.2. *Extended Error Codes Returned in AX*

Code	Meaning
1	Invalid function
2	File not found
3	Path not found
4	No handles available
5	Access denied
6	Invalid handle
7	Memory control blocks destroyed
8	Insufficient memory
9	Invalid memory block address
10	Invalid environment
11	Invalid format
12	Invalid access code
13	Invalid data
14	Reserved
15	Invalid drive
16	Attempt to remove current directory
17	Not the same device
18	No more files
19	Disk write-protected
20	Unknown unit

Table 13.2 continues

Table 13.2 *continued*

Code	Meaning
21	Drive not ready
22	Unknown command
23	CRC error
24	Bad request structure length
25	Seek error
26	Unknown media type
27	Sector not found
28	Out of paper
29	Write fault
30	Read fault
31	General failure
32	Sharing violation
33	Lock violation
34	Invalid disk change
35	FCB unavailable
36	Sharing buffer overflow
37–49	Reserved
50	Network request not supported
51	Remote computer not listening
52	Duplicate name on network
53	Network name not found
54	Network busy
55	Network device no longer exists
56	Net BIOS command limit exceeded
57	Network adapter error
58	Incorrect network response
59	Unexpected network error
60	Incompatible remote adapter
61	Print queue full
62	Not enough space for print file
63	Print file deleted
64	Network name deleted
65	Access denied
66	Network device type incorrect
67	Network name not found
68	Network name limit exceeded
69	Net BIOS session limit exceeded

Table 13.2 continues

Table 13.2 *continued*

Code	Meaning
70	Temporarily paused
71	Network request not accepted
72	Print or disk redirection is paused
73–79	Reserved
80	File already exists
81	Reserved
82	Cannot make directory entry
83	Fail on INT 24
84	Too many redirections
85	Duplicate redirection
86	Invalid password
87	Invalid parameter
88	Network data fault

Table 13.2 lists the error codes with the primary error indication—in other words, the "what happened?" This type of error indication is familiar to programmers accustomed to working with operating system calls. Informational messages (maybe we should call them "semi-informational") give us something to tell the user but are not of much help to us unless only one thing could possibly be wrong. If there is more than one possible cause for an error, the informational message is only marginally helpful. In most cases, if you can expect the error, you should have programmed around it in the first place.

The error class codes in table 13.3 go one step beyond the error codes themselves. Error class codes classify the error, based on internal knowledge of the operating system.

Table 13.3. *Error Class Codes Returned in BH*

Class	Meaning
1	Out of resource
2	Temporary situation
3	Authorization
4	Internal
5	Hardware failure
6	System failure
7	Application program error
8	Not found

Table 13.3 continues

Table 13.3 *continued*

Class	Meaning
9	Bad format
10	Locked
11	Media
12	Already exists
13	Unknown

With most systems, an operating system error can arise from so many causes that the program must be extremely sophisticated in its error handling if it is to shield the user from problems. All experienced programmers have thought "it must be an operating system bug" as they've butted heads against a seemingly intractable problem. DOS will try to tell you if there seems to be such an error—but do you trust DOS to admit its own mistakes? If, when you're running a program intended for commercial use, you do get an indication of an error that cannot be corrected by the software, you can help minimize your own support problems if you make sure that the program clearly tells the user the source of the error. If you can point out a hardware failure, your customer service group will thank you for every call they *didn't* have to take.

Most experienced programmers have wondered what to do if certain errors occur. The recommended action codes shown in table 13.4 are meant to help but are not a total solution. By suggesting possible actions to the programmer, the designers of DOS have applied their knowledge of the system to your problems. You can take reasonable action based on the action codes.

Table 13.4. *Recommended Action Codes Returned in BL*

Action Code	Meaning
1	Retry. If not cleared in reasonable number of attempts, prompt user to Abort or Ignore
2	Delay then retry. If not cleared in reasonable number of attempts, prompt user to Abort or Ignore
3	Get corrected information from user (Bad filename or disk drive)
4	Abort application with cleanup

Table 13.4 continues

Table 13.4 *continued*

Action Code	Meaning
5	Abort application without cleanup (cleanup may increase problems)
6	Ignore error
7	Prompt user to correct error and then retry
	Errors that involve the user are especially prone to difficulties in error correction, particularly if the user doesn't understand your error message and prompts (Abort or Ignore error, for example). Suggested actions do not eliminate the programmer's responsibility for making the program as user-friendly as possible.

Action codes should be used as the basis for error recovery when an error condition is recognized. In most situations, only one or two of the recommended actions will make sense—you can ignore the others. But be careful—provide a graceful way to exit a program if an error (that cannot be fixed by software) occurs. If the user has to reboot the system to get out of an error-correction loop, the error has not been corrected. Always include an override to allow frustrated users to get out.

The error locus codes shown in table 13.5 expand information about an error and attempt to tell you something about the origin of the error—in other words, which device caused the error.

Table 13.5. *Error Locus Codes Returned in CH*

Locus Code	Meaning
1	Unknown
2	Block device (disk or disk emulator)
3	Network
4	Serial device
5	Memory related

On a single-user system, error locus code information is marginally useful because, in most cases, the original error code has told you what caused the error. This type of error information becomes useful in situations that deal with the possibilities inherent in redirection and device independence.

For example, if you write a program that works with the standard input and output devices, a user can redirect the output to a disk drive, a network, or the RS-232 port without the program being aware of the change. The error locus code can give you the key to interpreting and correcting the error.

Summary

This chapter has discussed a group of special functions that do not fit neatly into a single category: the DOS version functions, BIOS equipment function, DOS date and time functions, and the DOS error-handling function. All of these standard functions are valuable additions to a personal function library. You have learned how to build a few sample routines (in C, BASIC, and Pascal) for each of these functions.

The DOS error-handling function provides extensive information about DOS errors as well as suggestions for correcting problems. Although a generalized function that performs all types of error handling can be written, it would waste space on problems that won't occur. Here's a general rule: if you can foresee a problem, you should prevent it from happening. Other error handling should focus as much as possible on ways to help users.

Part V
Reference

BIOS Functions
DOS Functions
Mouse Functions
EMS Functions

BIOS Function Reference

The BIOS (Basic Input/Output System) functions are the fundamental level of any PC or compatible computer. BIOS functions embody the basic operations needed for successful use of the computer's hardware resources. These functions are used by DOS to carry out its own operations. Most programming on PCs or compatibles is done above the BIOS level. Programmers who need special functions call BIOS functions directly when no other method will work. In some cases, even the BIOS does not provide the services needed and programmers will go below it to the hardware itself.

The BIOS in a PC or compatible is largely contained in ROM (thus, the term ROM BIOS) as part of the hardware system. Ordinarily, the BIOS is provided by the manufacturer of a system, according to Microsoft's specifications for MS-DOS. Extensions of the ROM BIOS for EGA monitors or other devices can be added easily to the system. These extensions serve as one of the foundations of the PC environment's extendable nature. Some parts of the BIOS are loaded from disk when the system boots (a hidden system file, typically called either IBMBIO.SYS or IO.SYS). See Chapter 3 for a detailed description of how DOS is booted.

The ROM release date is located in the eight bytes starting at F000h:FFF5h. Some important BIOS release dates include:

Date	Machine Type
04/24/81	PC
10/19/81	Revised PC with bug fixes
08/16/82	PC XT
10/27/82	PC to XT upgrade
11/08/82	Portable PC
06/01/83	PCjr
01/10/84	Personal Computer AT
09/13/85	Convertible PC
04/21/86	PC XT 286
09/02/86	PS/2 line

These dates, which cover only the IBM ROM BIOS, are meaningful only if you are working with an IBM PC. Systems that do not have the true IBM ROM are likely to have different dates. The table does not cover *all* releases of the BIOS ROM. From time to time, notes in magazines or on bulletin boards (mostly reporting bugs) refer to other dates for ROM, but, to my knowledge, there is no comprehensive list of dates.

A model-identification byte (located at F000h:FFFEh) can be used to differentiate between models (see table BIOS.1). The PS/2 family continues to support this model-identification byte. For non-IBM machines, however, this byte is not uniform and cannot be relied on.

Table BIOS.1. Model Identification Bytes

Byte	System
9Ah	COMPAQ Plus
FFh	IBM PC
FEh	PC XT, Portable PC
FDh	PC*jr*
FCh	Personal Computer AT, PS/2 Models 50 and 60
FBh	PC XT (after 1/10/86)
FAh	PS/2 Model 30
F9h	Convertible PC
F8h	PS/2 Model 80

For additional information on the BIOS release dates and model identification, refer to the description of Int 15, Function C0h, later in this section.

On the PS/2, no BIOS stands between OS/2 and the hardware. All OS/2 hardware interfacing is done through device drivers. (See Chapter 12 for a discussion of device drivers.) MS-DOS continues to use the BIOS.

Device drivers are direct interfaces that are linked into the operating system to control access to hardware. In a multitasking operating system such as UNIX or OS/2, these drivers are capable of handling multiple requests from processes (programs) and of keeping everything in order. Access through drivers is essential in a multitasking environment such as OS/2 because any program with direct access to the hardware or to an all-encompassing BIOS could destroy what other programs are trying to do.

BIOS remains on the system for two reasons: to bootstrap the operating system and to support the Compatibility Box for running DOS programs. The Compatibility Box provided under OS/2 allows programs originally written for the PC to run as though they were running on a PC instead of a PS/2. Such programs will run successfully, although multitasking and other PS/2 features are not accessible to them.

A BIOS originally written to support DOS V3 would have trouble running under OS/2 because the BIOS will not run in protected mode. Some processor instructions are not allowed in protected mode, and programs are prevented from accessing portions of memory assigned to other programs. Protected mode makes multitasking operations possible, because you can write a program without worrying about its effect on other programs. The IBM PS/2 includes an advanced BIOS (ABIOS) that can work with a device driver in real and protected modes, support multitasking, and address up to 16M of memory.

On the PS/2, BIOS calls are supported for programs running in the Compatibility Box. Even Borland's Sidekick® (which uses undocumented system calls) will run on the PS/2, although the official position of Microsoft and IBM is to support only *documented* DOS calls. Under OS/2, however, DOS programs that must run in the background will be suspended. The OS/2 developers made the worst-case assumption that DOS programs are not compatible with multitasking because they directly access memory (writing directly to the screen, for example).

Readers moving into the OS/2 environment will find that this section indicates (wherever possible) the PS/2 aspects of interrupt processing in the BIOS. Keep in mind that IBM is *not* publishing the BIOS listing for the PS/2 as they did for the original PC. Instead, they are publishing only the entry points, which are almost entirely compatible with the old PC BIOS. Programs built on a BIOS foundation will continue to work with the PS/2. Programs whose timing depends on the speed of the BIOS will work much faster on the PS/2 family than they do on a PC.

The major changes in the PS/2 BIOS are shown in table BIOS.2.

Table BIOS.2. *Personal System/2 Differences*

Interrupt	Meaning
0Bh	Reserved, no longer communications
0Ch	Reserved, no longer communications
0Dh	Reserved
0Fh	Reserved
15h	System services (Cassette I/O)
40h	Diskette BIOS revector
41h	Fixed disk parameters
46h	Fixed disk parameters
4Ah	User alarm
71h–74h	Reserved
76h–77h	Reserved
F1h–FFh	User program interrupts

Except for communications programs that customarily take control of interrupts 0Bh and 0Ch, these changes should have no effect on most programs.

The BIOS Listings

The BIOS listings in this section are arranged in ascending numerical order by interrupt and function, from 00h through 1Fh and 70h. Interrupts or functions that are considered reserved are not detailed here unless they were detailed for earlier versions of BIOS and are marked as reserved in recent BIOS releases. The following information is included for each interrupt:

❏ **Purpose:** The interrupt's purpose

❏ **Interrupt:** The interrupt number

❏ **Function:** The function number, when applicable

❏ **Description:** A short description of the interrupt

❏ **Calling Registers:** The setup of the registers before the call to the interrupt

❏ **Return Registers:** The setup of the registers when the interrupt returns

❏ **Comments:** Explanatory comments and suggestions about the interrupt and its use

This section is intended as a reference to BIOS functions and their use. Because all BIOS function calls have the same form, this section does not include examples of how individual BIOS calls are used.

The information in this section was compiled from the widest available range of sources. Every effort was made to ensure the technical accuracy and timeliness of this information; if you find discrepancies, Que Corporation would be interested in your comments.

BIOS Function Quick Reference

BIOS Function Quick Reference continues

BIOS Function Quick Reference *continues*

Purpose: Divide-by-Zero Interrupt (Hardware Error)

Interrupt: 00h

Description: Called by the CPU if an attempt is made to divide by a zero value

Calling Registers: None

Return Registers: Nothing

Comments: The divide-by-zero interrupt is called when the processor is asked to perform the illegal operation "Divide by Zero." Because the mathematical result of dividing by zero is infinite (a number for which there is no representation on a computer), the operation is always treated as an error on any computer. The interrupt handler automatically takes care of the error.

At start-up, the BIOS sets this interrupt to point to an IRET instruction. But DOS resets the interrupt to point to a handler that generates the message Divide by Zero and then aborts the program that caused the error. This is handled at the DOS level because a corresponding handler does not exist at the BIOS level. A divide-by-zero error can leave the operating system unstable, resulting in other errors. If a divide-by-zero error occurs, the best course is to restart the system manually or to create a better handler (like the one for DOS Int 24h).

If you are writing a program in which user input may cause this type of error, you should trap the interrupt and handle it in a routine of your own. It's good programming practice to write your programs so that they screen the user input and never allow this error trap to occur. Sometimes, however, your program can generate the divide by zero in ways you hadn't thought of.

A divide-by-zero error can occur unexpectedly during operation of a program in which a stack problem results in attempts by the processor to execute Int 00h. Occasionally, a divide-by-zero error occurs when particularly intricate stack manipulation takes place during the process of debugging a program.

Purpose: Single Step Interrupt

Interrupt: 01h

Description: Called by the CPU if the trap flag is set

Calling Registers: None

Return Registers: Nothing

Comments: Whenever the trap flag (TF) is set, Int 01h will be called after each instruction has been executed. The debugger uses this interrupt to handle program single stepping. (Other types of programs should not call this interrupt.)

If you are writing a debugger, you need to take special care with the STI (Set Interrupt Flag) instruction to prevent trapping your own interrupt handler. When you enter your handler, interrupts are off and the trap flag is set. If you reenable interrupts before you turn off the trap flag, your interrupt handler will be single stepped. You will have to reboot in order to regain control.

Purpose: Non-Maskable Interrupt (NMI)

Interrupt: 02h

Description: Called by the CPU on memory parity error

Calling Registers: None

Return Registers: Nothing

Comments: From the programmer's standpoint, the Non-Maskable Interrupt (NMI) is one of the least useful interrupts because it represents a major system failure in progress. When an NMI occurs, you probably will not have time to recover. The NMI cannot be blocked or turned off—it simply must be accepted.

On the PC family of computers (including the PS/2 Model 30), this interrupt reports parity errors. When a memory parity error occurs on the system board, ROM BIOS displays PARITY CHECK 1 and then locks up the machine. PARITY CHECK 2 indicates an I/O channel parity error. A display of ????? indicates an intermittent-read problem with memory.

This interrupt is used also for parity checks on the rest of the PS/2 family but the error messages are numeric codes taken from the following table:

Code	Meaning
110	System-board memory failure
111	I/O channel-check activated
112	Watchdog timeout
113	Direct memory access bus timeout

A fault in I/O channel memory causes error 111. The Watchdog timeout is used to detect a missed IRQ0 (system timer) interrupt. When such an interrupt occurs with the Watchdog timeout enabled, NMI error 112 is generated. On systems driven by direct memory access (DMA), error 113 is generated if a DMA device is given control of the system bus for more than 7.8 microseconds.

Although you could trap the interrupt in order to shut down the system in an orderly manner, the interrupt handler may not be in good memory because this interrupt arises from a memory parity error. More important, if you attempt to flush disk buffers or to update your files, you may damage an otherwise good file.

Purpose: Breakpoint Interrupt

Interrupt: 03h

Description: Used by debuggers to trap program break points

Calling Registers: None

Return Registers: Nothing

Comments: Debugging programs put a vector that points to their breakpoint-handling routines at this interrupt. Debuggers place an Int 03h at the desired breakpoint and allow the program to run. When the program reaches the breakpoint, the interrupt handler returns control to the debugger.

Interrupts 03h and 01h are the primary hardware tools available for debugging assembly language programs.

Purpose: Arithmetic Overflow Interrupt

Interrupt: 04h

Description: Called by the CPU when an arithmetic operation overflows

Calling Registers: None

Return Registers: Nothing

Comments: When arithmetic operations generate results larger than the data type allows, you can call this interrupt by executing the INTO (Interrupt on Overflow) instruction. To enable the instruction, the Overflow Bit (bit 11) in the flag register must be set before the arithmetic instruction (such as MUL or IMUL) is executed. Because arithmetic overflow is not much of a problem for most programs, no action is taken. The default for the interrupt is to point to an IRET instruction and return immediately from the interrupt. No special handler is used to deal with overflow because the Intel micro-processor instruction set includes the JO and JNO (Jump if Overflow and Jump if Not Overflow) instructions, which ordinarily are used for handling overflow.

Purpose: Print Screen

Interrupt: 05h

Description: Prints the text screen to the printer

Calling Registers: None

Return Registers: Nothing

Comments: To trigger this function, which prints the current screen display to the printer, you press the PrtSc key (usually Shift-PrtSc). Function 05h transfers to a routine that sends to the printer the ASCII contents of the video screen buffer. Notice that I said *ASCII contents*—if you are working with a graphics screen, this interrupt will cause printing to occur, but what is printed will be unpredictable.

You can use this function under software control if you want to provide a way to print the screen display. Printing the screen display can be particularly useful in database programs, for example—you can print the contents of the screen instead of having to print records.

In some cases, you may need to replace the interrupt vector with a special handler that deals with special screen conditions or performs a completely different function. The standard function saves the cursor position and then prints the screen to printer 1 on the system. It runs with interrupts enabled so that any interrupt (except another print screen) can take control of the system.

This function, which modifies no registers, maintains a status byte at memory location 0050h:0000h. If this status byte is 1, printing is in progress. If the value is 0 a successful print operation has occurred, whereas FFh indicates that the last print operation was unsuccessful.

The PS/2 provides the same function, including the status byte.

Purpose: System Timer

Interrupt: 08h

Description: Called by the system clock approximately 18.2 times per second

Calling Registers: None

Return Registers: Nothing

Comments: Int 08h, which is called 18.2 times per second to advance the time-of-day counter, calls Int 1Ch (Timer Tick). This interrupt is tied directly to channel 0 of the system timer chip. People who write TSRs like Sidekick, for example, find Int 08h particularly useful for time-related triggering (as with a clock or alarm). Most TSRs should connect to Int 1Ch rather than to Int 08h.

Handlers for this interrupt need to execute as quickly as possible. Interrupt processing should be a small part of the normal use of the processor system. And because the timer is attached as IRQ0 (highest priority hardware interrupt), servicing this interrupt will take precedence over all other interrupts on the system. If this interrupt is poorly handled, it could lead to problems servicing other important interrupts such as disk servicing.

Address 0040:006Ch is a time-of-day indicator, counting the number of ticks since power up. Position 0040:0070h increases when the count reaches 24 hours.

This interrupt provides also for automatic motor-off function for disks, by decrementing location 0040:0040h. When location 0040:0040h reaches zero, the motor-running flag in the motor status at 0040:003Fh is reset to turn off the disk motor.

Purpose: Keyboard Interrupt

Interrupt: 09h

Description: The primary keystroke interrupt, called whenever a keyboard key is pressed or released

Calling Registers: None

Return Registers: Nothing

Comments: Whenever a key is pressed or released, the keyboard sends a signal that triggers this interrupt. The handler for this interrupt reads the key information from the keyboard port (port 60h), processes that information into character and scan code information, which it then puts into the 32-byte input character queue (stored at 0040:001Eh). The two codes are placed at the location pointed to by 0040:001Ch (keyboard buffer tail pointer) and the pointer is incremented by 2. If the buffer is already full, the pointer is recycled to the beginning of the buffer. Instead of accessing the keyboard directly, the BIOS console-input routines access this input queue, thereby allowing programmers some type-ahead and considerable flexibility in keyboard handling.

If you are using a PC XT with a BIOS release date after 1/10/86, or if you are using a Personal Computer AT, a PC XT 286, PC Convertible, or PS/2 system, this interrupt also issues an Int 15h, Function 91h (interrupt complete) with AL set to 02h after the keystroke has been processed. (See Int 15h, Function 91h for more information.)

TSRs (terminate-and-stay-resident utilities) that provide immediate response to keypresses frequently intercept and act upon this interrupt. Because the keyboard routines have to do a great deal of processing, intercepting keyboard requests from the normal BIOS keyboard routines is preferable to intercepting operations at this interrupt. If immediate responsiveness is essential, Int 09h is the best one to use.

Special keystrokes are interpreted by the handler as follows:

Keystroke	Handling
Ctrl	0040:0017h and 0040:0018h (keyboard control bytes) are updated and 0040:0096h (keyboard mode flags) are updated
Alt	Same as Ctrl
Shift	Same as Ctrl
Ctrl-Alt-Del	0040:0072h (reset flag) is set to 1234h, and system control is transferred to the POST (Power-On Self Test) routines. POST bypasses the normal start-up memory tests when this flag is set.
Pause	Causes the handler to loop until it gets a valid character
Print Screen	Issues Int 05h to call the print screen routine
Ctrl-Break	Issues Int 1Bh to call the Control-Break processor
System Request	PC XT BIOS (dates after 1/10/86), Personal Computer AT, PC XT 286, PC Convertibles, and PS/2 systems issue an Int 15h, Function 85h (SysReq key pressed).

Purpose: COM1 and COM3 interrupt service (PC, PC XT)
COM2 and COM4 interrupt service (Personal Computer AT)
Reserved (PS/2)

Interrupt: 0Bh

Description: Called when the serial port hardware issues an interrupt

Calling Registers: None

Return Registers: Nothing

Comments: Telecommunications programs generally intercept this interrupt vector. All other methods of accessing the serial port (BIOS or DOS functions) are not fast enough to handle speeds greater than 1,200 bps. (See Chapters 7 and 11 for a more detailed discussion.) By tying a custom interrupt handler here, the programmer can handle speeds up to the capacity of the machine (about 19.2K bits per second) if the interrupt handler is programmed carefully.

Int 0Ch handles the COM ports not handled by this interrupt.

Unfortunately, this interrupt is listed as Reserved on the PS/2. Communications programs that rely on this interrupt for speed will have to be rewritten on the PS/2.

Purpose: COM2 and COM4 interrupt service (PC, PC XT)
COM1 and COM3 interrupt service (Personal Computer AT)
Reserved (PS/2)

Interrupt: 0Ch

Description: Called when the serial port hardware issues an interrupt

Calling Registers: None

Return Registers: Nothing

Comments: Telecommunications programs generally intercept this interrupt vector. All other methods of accessing the serial port (BIOS or DOS functions) are not fast enough to handle speeds greater than 1,200 bps. (See Chapters 7 and 11 for a more detailed discussion.) By tying a custom interrupt handler here, the programmer can handle speeds up to the capacity of the machine (about 19.2K bits per second) if the interrupt handler is programmed carefully.

Int 0Bh handles the COM ports not handled by this handler.

Unfortunately, this interrupt is marked as Reserved on the PS/2. Communications programs that rely on this interrupt for speed will have to be rewritten on the PS/2.

Purpose: Hard Disk Management Interrupt (Disk Controller) (PC XT)
LPT2 Control (Personal Computer AT)
Reserved (PS/2)

Interrupt: 0Dh

Description: Called by the designated hardware controllers

Calling Registers: None

Return Registers: Nothing

Comments: This interrupt handler was added only in later versions of the ROM BIOS. It represents a function that is available only beginning with the PC XT.

On the Personal Computer AT, Int 0Dh is used for LPT2 handling. (See Int 0Fh for a discussion of printer services.)

On the PS/2, Int 0Dh is Reserved; its functions are redistributed elsewhere. Because few (if any) programs make direct use of this interrupt, this change will not affect most programmers.

Purpose: Floppy Disk Management

Interrupt: 0Eh

Description: Called by the floppy disk controller (hardware)

Calling Registers: None

Return Registers: Nothing

Comments: Int 0Eh is used by the floppy disk controller to detect disk transfer completions. Typically, because the operations available through this interrupt are attainable through other BIOS functions, this interrupt can be ignored. Most programmers do not use this interrupt.

Purpose: Printer Management (LPT1)
Reserved (PS/2)

Interrupt: 0Fh

Description: Internal printer-control interrupt

Calling Registers: None

Return Registers: Nothing

Comments: On the PC, Int 0Fh is used by the printer controller to detect printer errors and print completion. Generally, you can ignore this interrupt. Programmers typically do not use it.

On the PS/2, Int 0Fh is marked as Reserved; its functions are allocated elsewhere.

Purpose: Set Video Mode

Interrupt: 10h

Function: 00h

Description: Sets the display mode used by the video adapter

Calling Registers: AH = 00h
                          AL = Display mode (see table BIOS.3)

Return Registers: Nothing

Comments: This function sets the video mode, clears the screen, and selects the video adapter (if more than one is present). To prevent the screen-clear on EGA, MCGA, and VGA systems, set bit 7 of AL to 1.

Table BIOS.3. *Video Display Modes*

Video Mode	Mode Type	Display Adapter	Pixel Resolution	Box Size	Characters	Colors
00h	Text	CGA	320 × 200	8 × 8	40 × 25	16 (gray)
		EGA(2)	320 × 350	8 × 14	40 × 25	16 (gray)
		MCGA	320 × 400	8 × 16	40 × 25	16
		VGA(1)	360 × 400	9 × 16	40 × 25	16
01h	Text	CGA	320 × 200	8 × 8	40 × 25	16
		EGA(2)	320 × 350	8 × 14	40 × 25	16
		MCGA	320 × 400	8 × 16	40 × 25	16
		VGA(1)	360 × 400	9 × 16	40 × 25	16
02h	Text	CGA	640 × 200	8 × 8	80 × 25	16 (gray)
		EGA(2)	640 × 350	8 × 14	80 × 25	16 (gray)
		MCGA	640 × 400	8 × 16	80 × 25	16
		VGA(1)	720 × 400	9 × 16	80 × 25	16
03h	Text	CGA	640 × 200	8 × 8	80 × 25	16
		EGA(2)	640 × 350	8 × 14	80 × 25	16
		MCGA	640 × 400	8 × 16	80 × 25	16
		VGA(1)	720 × 400	9 × 16	80 × 25	16
04h	Graph	CGA/EGA/ MCGA/VGA	320 × 200	8 × 8	40 × 25	4
05h	Graph	CGA/EGA	320 × 200	8 × 8	40 × 25	4 (gray)
		MCGA/VGA	320 × 200	8 × 8	40 × 25	4
06h	Graph	CGA/EGA/ MCGA/VGA	640 × 200	8 × 8	80 × 25	2
07h	Text	MDA/EGA	720 × 350	9 × 14	80 × 25	Mono
		VGA(1)	720 × 400	9 × 16	80 × 25	Mono
08h	Graph	PC*jr*	160 × 200	8 × 8	20 × 25	16
09h	Graph	PC*jr*	320 × 200	8 × 8	40 × 25	16
0Ah	Graph	PC*jr*	640 × 200	8 × 8	80 × 25	4
0Bh		----- R E S E R V E D -----				
0Ch		----- R E S E R V E D -----				
0Dh	Graph	EGA/VGA	320 × 200	8 × 8	40 × 25	16
0Eh	Graph	EGA/VGA	640 × 200	8 × 8	80 × 25	16
0Fh	Graph	EGA/VGA	640 × 350	8 × 14	80 × 25	Mono
10h	Graph	EGA/VGA	640 × 350	8 × 14	80 × 25	16
11h	Graph	MCGA/VGA	640 × 480	8 × 16	80 × 30	2
12h	Graph	VGA	640 × 480	8 × 16	80 × 30	16
13h	Graph	MCGA/VGA	320 × 200	8 × 8	40 × 25	256

Notes: (1) Enhanced VGA mode; otherwise, the VGA can emulate either the CGA or the EGA characteristics for this mode.

(2) EGA mode when connected to an enhanced color display; otherwise, emulates the CGA characteristics for this mode.

Purpose: Set Cursor Type

Interrupt: 10h

Function: 01h

Description: Used to set height of video cursor

Calling Registers: AH = 01h
                         CH = Starting (top) scan line for cursor in
                               bits 0–4
                         CL = Ending (bottom) scan line for cursor in
                               bits 0–4

Return Registers: Nothing

Comments: This function sets the type of the text-mode cursor by specifying the cursor's starting and ending scan lines. The video-display system displays a blinking cursor by turning scan lines on and off. A character cell has eight scan lines in the CGA and 14 in the EGA. To specify the cursor size, the scan lines are numbered from the top, beginning with 0.

Cursor size in text mode is controlled by specifying the "start" and "end" scan line numbers of the character box, starting with line 0. The starting scan line is specified in CH; the ending scan line, in CL. On a CGA-equipped machine, for example, if you want to produce a two-line cursor that occupies the lower two lines of the character cell, you would set CX to 0607h.

Many programmers do not realize that the cursor will wrap around inside the character cell. If CH is less than CL, a normal one-piece cursor is displayed. By setting CH greater than CL, you can create a two-piece cursor. To disable the cursor, set CH =20h.

There is only one cursor type for all video pages. When a program uses different cursors on different video pages, it has to do the bookkeeping itself and explicitly change the cursor when changing screen pages.

For monochrome video modes, the default starting cursor scan line is 0Bh and the ending scan line is 0Ch. For color video modes, the default starting scan line is 06h and the ending scan line is 07h.

Purpose: Set Cursor Position

Interrupt: 10h

Function: 02h

Description: Used to specify cursor coordinates for video display

Calling Registers: AH = 02h
BH = Page number (0 for graphics modes)
DH = Row
DL = Column

Return Registers: Nothing

Comments: This function is used to position the cursor at a specific location on the text screen. Positions are defined relative to the upper left corner (position 0,0) when the screen is in text mode. The lower left corner is (79,24) in 80 × 25 text mode, (39,24) in 40 × 25 modes. Depending on the video mode, valid ranges for DL and DH are

80-column Text Mode	*40-column Text Mode*
DL = 0 to 79	DL = 0 to 39
DH = 0 to 24	DH = 0 to 24

You can turn off the cursor by placing it off the screen (position 0,25 is usually good).

You can position the cursor on any page to allow a program to do extensive work on a page that is not displayed on the screen. Then, when the completed screen is ready, you can present it almost instantaneously to the user. Table BIOS.4 shows the valid page numbers for different display types. You can display only those pages for which a specific video adapter has adequate memory. For example, the MDA has only one display page; depending on their mode, other display adapters can have as many as seven display pages.

Table BIOS.4. *Valid Page Numbers*

Page Numbers	Modes	Adapters
0–7	00–01h	CGA, EGA, MCGA, VGA
0–3	02–03h	CGA
0–7	02–03h	EGA, MCGA, VGA
0	07h	MDA
0–7	07h	EGA, VGA

If you are working in graphics modes, you should set the page number to 0. Use Function 05h to set the currently displayed page.

Purpose: Read Cursor Position and Configuration

Interrupt: 10h

Function: 03h

Description: Returns the cursor coordinates and type

Calling Registers: AH = 03h
                          BH = Page number

Return Registers: BH = Video page number
                          CH = Starting line for cursor
                          CL = Ending line for cursor
                          DH = Row
                          DL = Column

Comments: This function gets the current cursor position and returns the same values that were used to position the cursor with Function 02h. In 80 × 25 mode, (0,0) is the upper left corner and (79,24) is the lower right corner; in 40 × 25 mode, (39,24) is the lower left corner.

This function also returns the starting and ending rows for the cursor (see Function 01h for information on setting these values). You can use this function to determine the exact cursor type before you change it (so that you can restore it after your program has completed its work). If your program has to coexist in a mixed program environment, restoring the cursor type to what it was when your program started is good programming practice.

Purpose: Read Light Pen Position

Interrupt: 10h

Function: 04h

Description: Returns to coordinates of the light pen

Calling Registers: AH = 04h

Return Registers: AH = 0 Light pen not down/not triggered
1 Light pen down/triggered
BX = Pixel column (0–319 or 0–639,
depending on mode)
CH = Pixel row (0–199)
CX = Pixel row (0–nnn, depending on mode)
DH = Character row (0–24)
DL = Character column (0–79 or 0–39,
depending on mode)

Comments: This function reads the light pen's status and position. Although the mouse is more widely used than the light pen on the PC system, some applications use the light pen (and others could use it). Before using the light pen, you must check to see whether it has been triggered (AH = 1). If the light pen has been triggered, its location is given in the other registers; if it has not been triggered, the information contained in the other return registers has no meaning and should be ignored.

The light pen returns a vertical position accurate to only two scan lines. Horizontal accuracy of the light pen is no better than two pixels (320 pixels per scan line) or four pixels (640 pixels per scan line). Because of this, the light pen is not suitable for high-resolution graphics control. On most monochrome monitors, use of the light pen is not effective because of the display phosphors' long image-retention time.

The vertical resolution of some video modes is greater than 200 pixels. In such modes, the pixel row will be returned in CX, rather than in CH. Be sure to check the video mode to ascertain which register (CH or CX) will contain the value you should use.

PS/2 systems (MCGA or VGA) do not support the light pen (AH will always return 00h).

Purpose: Select Active Display Page

Interrupt: 10h

Function: 05h

Description: Used to display the video display page being viewed

Calling Registers: AH = 05h
AL = Page number selected (see table BIOS.5)

Return Registers: Nothing

Comments: This function, which selects the active (displayed) video page, works with the CGA, MCGA, EGA, or VGA adapters. It cannot be used with monochrome adapters, which have only one display page of memory. Table BIOS.5 shows the valid page numbers.

Table BIOS.5. Valid Page Numbers

Page Numbers	Modes	Adapters
0–7	00h, 01h	CGA, EGA, MCGA, VGA
0–3	02h, 03h	CGA
0–7	02h, 03h	EGA, MCGA, VGA
0–7	07h, 0Dh	EGA, VGA
0–3	0Eh	EGA, VGA
0–1	0Fh, 10h	EGA, VGA

This function is particularly useful for building spectacular text-screen displays. By building a screen in a nondisplayed page and then calling this function to display it, you can create an instantaneous screen change that gives your program an impressive, snappy look. Most of the important output functions can write to any page.

Purpose: Scroll Window Up

Interrupt: 10h

Function: 06h

Description: Used to scroll the text screen up by a specified number of lines within a defined area of the screen

Calling Registers: AH = 06h
 AL = Number of lines to scroll
  = 0 ⇒ entire window is blanked
 BH = Attribute used for blanked area
 CH = Row, upper left corner
 CL = Column, upper left corner
 DH = Row, lower right corner
 DL = Column, lower right corner

Return Registers: Nothing

Comments: This function (which is the opposite of Int 10h, Function 07h) initializes a window to blank with a specified attribute, or scrolls the window up a specified number of lines. The scroll function moves all lines in the window up one line, adds a blank line (with the designated attribute) at the bottom of the window, and eliminates the line that previously was at the top of the window. (If the new line is to be filled with text, your program must do the work.)

You can use this window-oriented function to define rectangular areas to clear (or scroll) on the screen and to set attribute values for the cleared line or lines within a window.

To clear the window, set AL either to 0 or to a value greater than the number of lines in the window. The BIOS listing in an *IBM Technical Reference Manual* shows this function implemented as a "clear a line, decrement the counter" function until the counter reaches zero. Given this algorithm, a "clear window" performed by setting AL to 0 will take longer than if you set AL to 25 (or some other value greater than the height of the rectangle being cleared). Unless your application is extremely screen-intensive, the time differential introduced by setting AL to 0 will not be noticeable. In any event, a simpler, faster way to clear the entire screen is to set the screen mode (Function 00h).

Purpose: Scroll Window Down

Interrupt: 10h

Function: 07h

Description: Used to scroll the text screen down by a specified number of lines within a defined area of the screen

Calling Registers: AH = 07h
AL = Number of lines to scroll
= 0 ⇒ entire window is blanked
BH = Attribute used for blanked area
CH = Row, upper left corner
CL = Column, upper left corner
DH = Row, lower right corner
DL = Column, lower right corner

Return Registers: Nothing

Comments: This function initializes a window to blank with a specified attribute, or scrolls the window down a specified number of lines. Use this function (which is the opposite of Int 10h, Function 06h) to scroll down the screen. The scroll function moves all lines in the window down one line, adds a blank line (with the designated attribute) at the top of the window, and eliminates the line that previously was at the bottom. (If the new line is to be filled with text, your program must do the work.)

You can use this window-oriented function to define rectangular areas to clear (or scroll) on the screen and to set attribute values for the cleared line or lines within the window.

To clear the window, set AL either to 0 or to a value greater than the number of lines in the window. The BIOS listing in an *IBM Technical Reference Manual* shows this function implemented as a "clear a line, decrement the counter" function until the counter reaches zero. Given this algorithm, a "clear window" performed by setting AL to 0 will take longer than if you set AL to 25 (or some other value greater than the height of the rectangle being cleared). Unless your application is extremely screen-intensive, the time differential introduced by setting AL to 0 will not be noticeable. In any event, a simpler, faster way to clear the entire screen is to set the screen mode (Function 00h).

Purpose: Read Character and Attribute

Interrupt: 10h

Function: 08h

Description: Returns the ASCII character and attribute at the current cursor position

Calling Registers: AH = 08h
BH = Display page

Return Registers: AH = Attribute byte
AL = ASCII character

Comments: This function reads the character and attribute bytes (for a specified display page) at the cursor's current position. Because you can get this information directly from the screen, you do not have to store information about the screen in your program, nor do you need tricky techniques to pass the screen display from one program to the next. The screen is in the screen memory.

TSR spelling and thesaurus utilities use this function to read the screen, so that they can determine which word to check. But if you are writing this type of utility, be careful. Because some programs access screen memory directly, without updating the screen cursor, the cursor mentioned in the descriptions of Functions 01h through 03h may *not* indicate the word you want.

Purpose: Write Character and Attribute

Interrupt: 10h

Function: 09h

Description: Stores at the cursor position a specific number of ASCII characters with a defined attribute

Calling Registers: AH = 09h
AL = ASCII character
BH = Display page
BL = Attribute byte of character in AL
CX = Number of characters to write

Return Registers: Nothing

Comments: This function writes ASCII-character and attribute bytes to the display at the cursor's current position on a specified display page. Use it to write many characters quickly to the screen (characters and attribute must all be the same).

In text mode, the function will write as many as 65,536 characters to the screen. As the function writes characters, it wraps lines—continuing from the end of one line to the beginning of the next without stopping. In graphics mode, the function goes only to the end of the line it was on at the start. As all the characters appear on the screen, the cursor position does not change.

An interesting way to use this function is to clear an area on-screen for text entry just before you call the input character function. You can set this area with a different color attribute to make it stand out. Because this function can clear an area much larger than the screen, the area can be as large as needed for data entry. Because the cursor does not move, you do not need to reposition it before you enter data.

In graphics modes, use the video attribute byte in BL to determine the color of the character written. But if bit 7 is set, the value in BL is XORed with the background color when the character is displayed (which can be extremely useful). You can erase a character from the screen by writing it to the display in graphics mode and then rewriting it with bit 7 on.

In graphics modes, the characters for ASCII codes 80–FFh come from a bit-map table whose address is stored in the interrupt vector 1Fh. By resetting this pointer to a table of your own, you can create your own table of characters. (See Function 1Fh for a discussion of the bit-map character table.) The characters for ASCII codes 00–7Fh are generated from a ROM character table that cannot be reset.

Purpose: Write Character at Cursor

Interrupt: 10h

Function: 0Ah

Description: Stores a specific number of ASCII characters at the cursor position without changing the attribute

Calling Registers: AH = 0Ah
AL = ASCII character
BH = Display page number
BL = Color of character in AL (in graphics modes only)
CX = Number of characters/attribute words to write

Return Registers: Nothing

Comments: This function (which is identical to Function 09h, except that you cannot set the attribute byte for the character in text mode) writes a number of characters at the cursor's current position on a specified display page. The attribute at the position each character is written remains unchanged.

Use this function when you want to write many characters quickly to the screen. In text mode, the function will write as many as 65,536 characters to the screen. As the function writes characters, it wraps lines (continuing from the end of one line to the beginning of the next without stopping). In graphics modes, the function will go only to the end of the line on which it started. The cursor position remains unchanged throughout the operation.

In graphics modes, BL is used to determine the color of the character written. If bit 7 is set, however, the value in BL is XORed with the background color when the character is displayed. This feature can be extremely useful for erasing a character from the screen—you simply write a character to the display in graphics mode and then rewrite it with bit 7 on.

In graphics modes, the characters for ASCII codes 80–FFh come from a bit-map table whose address is stored in the interrupt vector 1Fh. By resetting this pointer to a table of your own, you can create your own table of characters. (See Function 1Fh for a discussion of the bit-map character table.) The characters for ASCII codes 00–7Fh are generated from a ROM character table that cannot be reset.

Purpose: Set Color Palette

Interrupt: 10h

Function: 0Bh

Description: Selects colors for the graphics display

Calling Registers: AH = 0Bh
  BH = Color palette ID being set
   = 0 – BL has background and border color
   = 1 – BL has palette color
  BL = Color value to be used for that color ID

Return Registers: Nothing

Comments: This function, which selects or sets the contents of the color palette, works only for medium-resolution graphics displays such as mode 4. The function has no direct effect on memory. Rather, by interpreting the codes and changing the colors, this function affects the way that the 6845 CRT controller interprets the video memory. By using this function to rapidly change the palette, you can produce a flashing display.

In text mode, this function is used to set the screen's border color.

Table BIOS.6 lists the valid color palettes the function can set.

Table BIOS.6. Color Palettes

Palette	Pixel	Color
0	0	Same as background
	1	Green
	2	Red
	3	Brown
1	0	Same as background
	1	Cyan
	2	Magenta
	3	White

Purpose: Write Graphics Pixel

Interrupt: 10h

Function: 0Ch

Description: Writes a single pixel to the screen at the current cursor position

Calling Registers: AH = 0Ch
AL = Color value
BH = Page number
CX = Pixel column number
DX = Pixel row number

Return Registers: Nothing

Comments: This function, which writes a single pixel to the screen at a specified graphics coordinate, is the most basic graphics plotting service. Complex graphics-handling functions are built up by collections of operations that set the value of screen pixels.

In medium-resolution modes, the exact effect of the function depends on the palette in use. High-resolution CGA (mode 6) can show only black and white colors for pixels; mode 4 or 5 allows the pixels to be set from a four-color palette. With this function, if bit 7 of AL is set to 1, the new color is XORed with the current pixel; you can erase that pixel by writing it a second time.

The limits on the screen position that this function can address are 0–199 or 0–349 in the vertical and 0–319 or 0–639 in the horizontal, depending on the graphics mode. Refer to table BIOS.3 for details on screen limits by mode. Table BIOS.7 gives the valid page numbers (BH register) used by this function.

Table BIOS.7. Valid Page Numbers

Page Numbers	Modes	Adapters
0–7	0Dh	EGA, VGA
0–3	0Eh	EGA, VGA
0–1	0Fh, 10h	EGA, VGA

Purpose: Read Graphics Pixel

Interrupt: 10h

Function: 0Dh

Description: Returns the color of the pixel at a specific screen coordinate

Calling Registers: AH = 0Dh
BH = Page number
CX = Pixel column number
DX = Pixel row number

Return Registers: AL = Color value

Comments: This function, which gets the value of the pixel at the specified graphics coordinates, is often used in video games and advanced graphics applications. In video games, it is useful for collision detection. When they move a graphic object on the screen, advanced graphics programs can use this function to detect boundaries.

The limits for addressing are 0–199 or 0–349 in the vertical and 0–319 or 0–639 in the horizontal, depending on the video mode. Refer to table BIOS.3 for details on the addressing limits of the various video modes. Refer to table BIOS.7 for the valid page numbers that can be set in BH.

Purpose: Write Text in Teletype Mode

Interrupt: 10h

Function: 0Eh

Description: Outputs ASCII values with limited character processing

Calling Registers: AH = 0Eh
                                 AL = ASCII character
                                 BH = Display page (alpha modes)
                                 BL = Foreground color (graphics modes)

Return Registers: Nothing

Comments: This function writes text to the screen as if the screen were an old fashioned teletype machine. The function interprets the character codes for bell (ASCII 07h), backspace (ASCII 08h), carriage return (ASCII 0Dh), and line feed (ASCII 0Ah) in order to ring the console bell, backspace the cursor, move the cursor to the beginning of the line, or move to the next line. After the write, the cursor is moved to the next character position.

Despite its somewhat archaic designation (which may make you think of the old Teletypewriter machines), this function is useful. DOS uses it in the console driver to put operating system text and messages on the screen.

Like other important display functions, this one works on either displayed or nondisplayed pages. The significant difference between this and other display functions is that Function 0Eh automatically handles the normal control functions of bell, backspace, line feed, and carriage return, as well as line-wrap and scrolling. Although it does not allow you to change the video attributes of what you write, this is the best function for simple output.

Even if you are working on a nondisplayed page, the bell character will sound the system bell to call attention to any background operations. Unfortunately, this function does not expand Tab characters to spaces.

In order for this function to work on PC BIOS ROMs dated 4/24/81 and 10/19/81, the BH register *must* point to the currently displayed page.

Purpose: Get Current Display Mode

Interrupt: 10h

Function: 0Fh

Description: Returns the video display mode, screen width, and active page

Calling Registers: AH = 0Fh

Return Registers: AH = Number of columns on the screen
AL = Display mode (refer to table BIOS.3)
BH = Active display page

Comments: This function, which gets the video controller's display mode, including the number of character columns and the current display page, is most useful during program initialization. You use it to determine the present setting of the display system so that when your program is finished, it can return the display system to its original display mode.

Knowing the current display mode is especially important if you are writing TSR (Terminate-and-Stay-Resident) utilities that will "pop-up" on the screen during another application. Your utility may be working with a character screen, but the program that had control when your utility started may have been using a mode that is not what you need to use. Early TSRs failed to handle the screen display properly—in many cases, the resulting display looked as though a bomb had exploded inside the computer.

Although you can use Function 0Fh to determine the width of the screen, I recommend that you set the mode you want instead of trying to work out what is already there.

Purpose: Set Palette Registers

Interrupt: 10h

Function: 10h

Description: Controls operations on the color-palette registers within EGA/VGA video controllers

Calling Registers: AH = 10h

AL = 00h, Set palette register
BH = Color value
BL = Palette register to set

AL = 01h, Set border color register
BH = Color value

AL = 02h, Set all registers and border
ES:DX = Pointer to 17-byte color list

AL = 03h, Toggle blink/intensity
    (EGA only)
BL = Blink/intensity bit
    00h = Enable intensity
    01h = Enable blinking

AL = 07h, Read palette register (PS/2 only)
BL = Palette register to read (0-15)

AL = 08h, Read overscan register (PS/2 only)

AL = 09h, Read palette registers and border
    (PS/2 only)
ES:DX = Pointer to 17-byte table for values

AL = 10h, Set individual color register
BX = Color register to set
CH = Green value to set
CL = Blue value to set
DH = Red value to set

AL = 12h, Set block of color registers
BX = First color register to set
CX = Number of color registers to set
ES:DX = Pointer to color values

AL = 13h, Select color page
BL = 00h, Select paging mode
BH = Paging mode
    00h = 4 register blocks of 64 registers
    01h = 16 register blocks of 16 registers

AL = 13h, Select color page
BL = 01h, Select page
BH = Page number
    00–03h for 64 register blocks
    00–0Fh for 16 register blocks

AL = 15h, Read color register (PS/2 only)
BX = Color register to read

AL = 17h, Read block of color registers
BX = First color register to read
CX = Number of color registers to read
ES:DX = Pointer to buffer to hold color
        register values

AL = 1Ah, Read color page state

AL = 1Bh, Sum color values to gray shades
BX = First color register to sum
CX = Number of color registers to sum

Return Registers: Subfunctions 07h–08h
  BH = Value read
 Subfunction 09h
  ES:DX = Pointer to 17-byte table
 Subfunction 15h
  CH = Green value read
  CL = Blue value read
  DH = Red value read
 Subfunction 17h
  ES:DX = Pointer to color table
 Subfunction 1Ah
  BL = Current paging mode
  CX = Current page

Comments: On the PC*jr*, MCGA, EGA, and VGA display systems, this function controls the correspondence of colors to pixel values. Although listed as reserved in the IBM Personal Computer AT BIOS, this function is an extension to the BIOS, applicable to EGA/VGA display systems.

A detailed explanation of this function is beyond the scope of this book. If you are interested in programming display systems directly, refer to the bibliography for further guidance.

Some subfunctions (as designated by the contents of AL when calling this function) are not available on the PS/2 Model 30 system. This includes subfunctions 01h, 02h, 07h, 08h, 09h, 13h, and 1Ah.

Purpose: Character Generator

Interrupt: 10h

Function: 11h

Description: Supports the graphics character-generator functions, allowing a program to set up its own character-generator tables

Calling Registers:
AL = 00h, User alpha load
BH = Number of bytes per character
BL = Block to load
CX = Count to store
DX = Character offset into table
ES:BP = Pointer to user table

AL = 01h, ROM monochrome set
BL = Block to load

AL = 02h, ROM 8 ×8 double dot
BL = Block to load

AL = 03h, Set block specifier
BL = Character-generator block selection

AL = 10h, User alpha load
BH = Number of bytes per character
BL = Block to load
CX = Count to store
DX = Character offset into table
ES:BP = Pointer to user table

AL = 11h, ROM monochrome set
BL = Block to load

AL = 12h, ROM 8 ×8 double dot
BL = Block to load

AL = 20h, Set user graphics characters
pointer at 1Fh
ES:BP = Pointer to user table

AL = 21h, Set user graphics characters
pointer at 43h
BL = Row specifier
CX = Bytes per character
ES:BP = Pointer to user table

AL = 22h, ROM 8 ×14 set
BL = Row specifier

AL = 23h, ROM 8 ×8 double dot
BL = Row specifier

AL = 30h, System information
BH = Font pointer

Return Registers: Varies by subfunction

Comments: Although listed as reserved in the IBM Personal Computer AT BIOS, this function is an extension to the BIOS, applicable to EGA/VGA display systems.

A detailed explanation of this function is beyond the scope of this book. If you are interested in programming display systems directly, refer to the bibliography for further guidance.

Some subfunctions (as designated by the contents of AL when calling this function) are not available on the PS/2 Model 30 system. This includes subfunctions 01h, 10h, 11h, 12h, and 22h.

Purpose: Write String

Interrupt: 10h

Function: 13h

Description: Writes an ASCII string to the display

Calling Registers: AH = 13h
AL = Write mode (see table BIOS.8)
BH = Video page
BL = Attribute (write modes 0 and 1)
CX = Length of string
DH = Row at which to write string
DL = Column at which to write string
ES:BP = Pointer to string

Return Registers: Nothing

Table BIOS.8. Write String Modes

Mode	Comments
0	Attribute in BL. String is characters only. Cursor not updated.
1	Attribute in BL. String is characters only. Cursor updated.
2	String alternates characters and attributes. Cursor not updated.
3	String alternates characters and attributes. Cursor updated.

Comments: This function, *which is available only on PC XTs with BIOS dates of 1/10/86 or later, on the Personal Computer AT, and on machines in the PS/2 family,* writes a string of characters to the currently active display.

Use this function to designate a string (with embedded or global attributes for the characters) and then write it to the screen. Because it relies on other BIOS functions to actually write the string, this function is not particularly fast.

Because this function uses the Teletype interrupt (Int 10h, Function 0Eh) for output, it responds to the backspace (ASCII 08h), bell (ASCII 07h), line feed (ASCII 0Ah), and carriage return (ASCII 0Dh) characters by moving the cursor back one space, ringing the console bell, moving down one line, or moving the cursor to the beginning of the current line, respectively. It also performs line wrap and scrolling.

Purpose: Get Equipment Status

Interrupt: 11h

Description: Returns a rudimentary list of equipment attached to the computer

Calling Registers: None

Return Registers: AX = Equipment status word (see table BIOS.9)

Table BIOS.9. Equipment Status Word

Bits	Meaning
0	Disk drive installed = 1
1	Math coprocessor installed = 1
2-3	System board RAM
	00 = 16K
	01 = 32K
	10 = 48K
	11 = 64K
2	Pointing device installed = 1 (PS/2 line only)
3	Not used (PS/2 line only)
4-5	Initial video mode
	01 = 40 × 25 color
	10 = 80 × 25 color
	11 = 80 × 25 mono
6-7	Number of disk drives (if bit 0 = 1)
	00 = 1 drive attached
	01 = 2 drives attached
	10 = 3 drives attached
	11 = 4 drives attached
8	Not used
9-11	Number of serial cards attached
12	Game adapter installed = 1
12	Not used (PS/2 line only)
13	Not used
13	Internal modem installed = 1 (PS/2 line only)
14-15	Number of printers attached

Comments: During the booting process, the hardware status byte is set to indicate what equipment is attached to the computer. For example, bits 6 and 7 represent the number of floppy disk drives attached to the system. This status byte does not change after you boot the system.

This function is particularly useful to programmers who must adapt their programs to existing equipment. By checking for serial ports, disk drives, printers, and other equipment, your program can simplify the user's interaction with the program. Programs that have to ask for the characteristics of the system rely on the user to understand the PC well enough to answer the questions. The fewer questions your program has to ask, the easier it is to use.

As you can see from table BIOS.9, the meaning of the different bits varies according to computer type. To determine which type of machine you are using, check the computer's signature byte at address FFFF:FFFE.

Purpose: Get Memory Size

Interrupt: 12h

Description: Returns the number of contiguous 1K memory blocks available

Calling Registers: None

Return Registers: AX = Number of 1K memory blocks

Comments: This interrupt returns the number of *contiguous* 1K memory blocks found during start-up memory checks of the system. Contrary to what has been written about this interrupt, it has nothing to do with the switches on the motherboard of a standard PC or compatible.

Because the memory is determined from the power-on self test (POST), an incorrect number may be returned if defective memory causes the memory test to fail. (Should this happen, the interrupt will return the number of blocks found before the error.) The POST assumes that all installed memory is functional and that memory in the range of 0 to 640K is contiguous.

The method used to determine available memory depends on the system, but generally consists of an attempt to read and write to a memory block. As soon as the write/read cycle fails, the end of memory is assumed to have been reached.

When there is more than 640K of memory, Int 15h, Function 88h must be called to determine extended memory size.

On PS/2 systems, this interrupt returns a maximum amount of memory of up to 640K, minus the amount of memory set aside for the extended BIOS data area (EBDA). The EBDA may be as little as 1K. (See Int 15h, Function C1h for more information.)

Purpose: Reset Floppy Disk System

Interrupt: 13h

Function: 00h

Description: Resets the controller for the floppy disk drive

Calling Registers: AH = 00h
DL = Drive number (0 based)
bit 7 = 0 for a diskette
1 for fixed disk

Return Registers: Carry flag clear if successful
Carry flag set if error
AH = Return code (see table BIOS.10)

Comments: This function resets the floppy disk controller in preparation for floppy disk I/O. (A reset of the floppy disk system is essential for handling critical disk-access errors.) This function recalibrates the disk by forcing the drive to pull the heads to track 0 and to start the next I/O operation from track 0.

Invoking this operation does not cause the disk system to react immediately. Rather, a reset flag is set in the floppy disk controller (FDC) to recalibrate the drives the next time they are used. The recalibration causes the grinding sound one sometimes hears after a disk error.

When the drive number in DL has the high bit set, the diskette system will be reset, after which the hard disk (fixed disk) will be reset. The error return will refer to the hard disk reset. The diskette status can be found in the BIOS data area, at 0040:0041h.

This function is best used when an error has been returned in an attempt to use the diskette system. When a problem occurs, the reset function should be called and the function tried again. Depending on the program, you may want to do several retries. If you get consistent failure, you should notify the user and terminate the retry cycle.

Purpose: Get Floppy Disk System Status

Interrupt: 13h

Function: 01h

Description: Returns floppy disk status byte

Calling Registers: AH = 01h

Return Registers: AH = Status byte (see table BIOS.10)

Table BIOS.10. Disk Controller Status Bits

Bit 76543210	Meaning
. . . . 1	Illegal command to driver
. . . . . . 1 .	Address mark not located (bad sector)
. 11	Write-protected disk
. . . . . 1 . .	Requested sector not found
. . . . . 11 .	Diskette change line active
. . . . 1 . . .	DMA overrun
. . . . 1 . . 1	DMA attempt across 64K boundary
. . . . 11 . .	Invalid media
. . . 1	CRC error on disk read
. . 1	Controller error
. 1	Seek failure
1	Disk time out (failure to respond, drive not ready)

Comments: The status of the controller is set after each disk operation. With this function, your program can get the status of the disk as of the most recent disk operation. For example, you can use this function to detect a write-protected disk in the drive by examining bit 1.

Purpose: Read Floppy Disk

Interrupt: 13h

Function: 02h

Description: Retrieves a specific number of disk sectors

Calling Registers: AH = 02h
AL = Number of sectors to transfer (1–9)
ES:BX = Pointer to user's disk buffer
CH = Track number (0–39)
CL = Sector number (1–9)
DH = Head number (0–1)
DL = Drive number (0–3)

Return Registers: Carry flag clear if successful
AH = 0
AL = Number of sectors transferred

Carry flag set if error
AH = Status byte (refer to table BIOS.10)

Comments: This function transfers one or more sectors from the floppy disk into memory. Reading the floppy disk is such a standard operation that the lack of any error checking beyond the disk drive number is surprising. All input parameters should be checked carefully before you issue a call for service, because passing an invalid value can lead to unpredictable results.

Note: When you use this function, a peculiarity of the system is that the error code AH =9 (DMA Boundary Error) can occur when the DMA operation crosses a memory offset address that ends in three zeros. This type of memory boundary must correspond to a sector boundary in the disk read.

Purpose: Write Disk Sectors

Interrupt: 13h

Function: 03h

Description: Writes a specified area of memory to a designated number of disk sectors

Calling Registers: AH = 03h
AL = Number of sectors to transfer (1–9)
ES:BX = Pointer to user's disk buffer
CH = Track number (0–39)
CL = Sector number (1–9)
DH = Head number (0–1)
DL = Drive number (0–3)

Return Registers: Carry flag clear if successful
AH = 0
AL = Number of sectors transferred

Carry flag set if error
AH = Status byte (refer to table BIOS.10)

Comments: This function writes one or more sectors from memory to the floppy disk. Except for the disk drive number, none of the values passed to this function are checked for validity. Checking for validity is the programmer's responsibility. Reading the disk is such a standard operation that this lack of error checking is surprising. You should check all input parameters carefully before you issue a call for service, because passing an invalid value may lead to unpredictable results.

IBM documentation indicates that the number of sectors stored in AL is not required when you use this function on the PC XT 286. Leaving AL set will not matter in this case, because the passed values are not checked for validity.

Note: When you use this function, a peculiarity of the system is that the error code AH =9 (DMA Boundary Error) can occur when the DMA operation crosses a memory offset address that ends in three zeros. This type of memory boundary must correspond to a sector boundary in the disk write.

Purpose: Verify Disk Sectors

Interrupt: 13h

Function: 04h

Description: Checks accuracy of the CRC values of a specified number of disk sectors

Calling Registers: AH = 04h
AL = Number of sectors to verify (1–9)
CH = Track number (0–39)
CL = Sector number (1–9)
DH = Head number (0–1)
DL = Drive number (0–3)

Return Registers: Carry flag clear if successful
AH = 0

Carry flag set if error
AH = Status byte (refer to table BIOS.10)

Comments: Use this function to verify the address fields of the specified disk sectors. No data is transferred to or from the disk during this operation. Disk verification, which takes place on the disk, does not (as some people believe) involve verification of the data on the disk against the data in memory. This function does not read or write a disk; rather, it causes the system to read the data in the designated sector or sectors and to check its computed CRC (Cyclic Redundancy Check) against data stored on the disk.

When a sector is written to disk, the CRC is computed and stored on the disk as part of the sector header information. Because the verify operation checks this value, it is highly probable that the data in the disk sector is good.

As with most of the other disk functions, the disk drive number is the only input data that is checked for errors. Errors in input will cause unpredictable results.

This function can be used to check the disk drive for the presence of a readable disk. If the drive does not contain a properly formatted disk, the function will return an error.

Purpose: Format Disk Track

Interrupt: 13h

Function: 05h

Description: Formats a single disk track

Calling Registers: AH = 05h
ES:BX = Pointer to track address field list
CH = Track number
DH = Head number
DL = Drive number

Return Registers: AH = Return code (refer to table BIOS.10)

Comments: This function formats a disk track by initializing the disk address fields and data sectors. (See Chapter 8 for more information.) Be sure to use this function with great care, it can cause loss of all or part of any disk storage on your machine. Test it on a stripped-down system (floppy disk only) until you are absolutely certain of its correctness.

Formatting a disk track is only one part of formatting a disk. To format a disk, you must format each track correctly but, if the disk is to be used with DOS, you must also write the basic DOS disk structure to the disk (including the boot sector, initial FAT tables, and the disk's root directory).

The disk formatting operation is controlled by the track address field list (pointed to by ES:BX). The table is laid out as a series of 4-byte entries: one for each sector on the track. Each 4-byte entry is laid out like this:

Byte Offset	Meaning
00h	Track number
01h	Head number
02h	Sector number
03h	Size code

Table BIOS.11 shows allowable size codes; the entries are laid out in the order in which the sectors will appear on disk. This order need not be sequential. The sectors can be *interleaved* to improve disk access performance (see Chapter 8).

Table BIOS.11. *Track Address Field Size Code*

Size Code	Bytes per Sector
0	128
1	256
2	512
3	1024

Purpose: Return Disk Drive Parameters

Interrupt: 13h

Function: 08h

Description: Returns information about a specified disk drive

Calling Registers: AH = 08h
DL = Drive number (0 based)
   bit 7 = 0 for a diskette
        1 for fixed disk

Return Registers: Carry Flag clear if successful
CH = Number of tracks per side
CL = Number of sectors per track
DH = Number of sides
DL = Number of consecutive drives attached
ES:DI = Pointer to 11-byte diskette parameter
      table
BL = Valid drive-type value from CMOS
   01h = 5.25", 360K, 40 track
   02h = 5.25", 1.2M, 80 track
   03h = 3.5", 720K, 80 track
   04h = 3.6", 1.44M, 80 track

Carry Flag set if error
AH = Error status (refer to table BIOS.10)

Comments: *This function is available only on the Personal Computer AT (BIOS dated after 1/10/84) and the PS/2.* Use it to obtain the physical parameters of the disk.

Setting bit 7 of the DL register on calling the function refers to hard disks.

This function allows you to check the characteristics of the disk in the designated drive. On return, the table pointed to by ES:DI has the format shown in table BIOS.12.

Table BIOS.12. *Disk Media Characteristic Table*

Offset	Meaning
00h	First specify byte
01h	Second specify byte
02h	Number of timer ticks to wait before turning off drive motor
03h	Number of bytes per sector
	00h = 128
	01h = 256
	02h = 512
	03h = 1024
04h	Sectors per track
05h	Gap length
06h	Data length
07h	Gap length for format
08h	Fill byte for format
09h	Head settle time in milliseconds
0Ah	Motor startup time in 1/8ths seconds

Purpose: Initialize Fixed Disk Table

Interrupt: 13h

Function: 09h

Description: Sets (to their default values) the values in the specified fixed disk table

Calling Registers: AH = 09h
DL = Fixed disk drive number

Return Registers: Carry flag clear if successful
AH = 0

Carry flag set if error
AH = Status byte (refer to table BIOS.10)

Comments: Use this function, *which is available only on the Personal Computer AT and PS/2 line and works only on fixed (hard) disks,* to set the hard disk drive's physical parameters. The drive numbers used are not the standard BIOS drive numbers; rather, they are taken from a special series of numbers for fixed disks only (80h corresponds to the first disk, 81h to the second, and so on). Using an out-of-range disk drive number will lead to unpredictable results.

Initialization information for the drive is taken from the fixed disk parameter tables. Interrupt vector 41h points to the table for disk 1; vector 46h points to the table for disk 2. If a reference is made for any other disk, the function returns an "invalid command" status byte in AH.

Purpose: Read Long Sector
Reserved (PS/2)

Interrupt: 13h

Function: 0Ah

Description: Reads a specified number of "long" sectors from a hard disk

Calling Registers: AH = 0Ah
AL = Number of sectors
ES:BX = Pointer to data buffer
CH = Track
CL = Sector
DH = Head number
DL = Fixed disk drive number

Return Registers: Carry flag clear if successful
AH = 0

Carry flag set if error
AH = Status byte (refer to table BIOS.10)

Comments: This function, *which is available only on the Personal Computer AT and works only on fixed (hard) disks,* reads long sectors from the hard disk into memory. Long sectors are standard sectors that contain four bytes of error-correcting code in addition to regular data. This function, like the other read/write functions, is susceptible to the DMA boundary error (AH =9) that can occur when a DMA crosses a memory offset that ends in three zeros. Because there is no error checking of parameters with this function, errors in parameter values can lead to unexpected results.

The drive numbers used are not the standard BIOS drive numbers; rather, they are taken from a special series of numbers for fixed disks only (80h corresponds to the first disk, 81h to the second, and so on). Using an out-of-range disk drive number will lead to unpredictable results.

Table BIOS.13 gives the valid ranges for all of the parameters that can be passed to the function. *Note especially that the track number (CH and CL registers) is a 10-bit number stored with the high-order bits in bits 6 and 7 of register CL and the eight low-order bits in register CH.* The sector address (register CL) is a 6-bit number stored in bits 0–5 (the bits not used by the track number).

Table BIOS.13. *Valid Parameter Ranges*

Register	Parameter	Valid range
AL	# sectors	1–121
CH/CL	Track	0–1023
CL	Sector	1–17
DH	Head	0–15
DL	Drive	80h, 81h, etc.

Figure BIOS.1 shows how the bits in CH and CL are interpreted by this function.

Fig. BIOS.1. *Bits in CH and CL, as interpreted by Int 13h, Function 0Ah.*

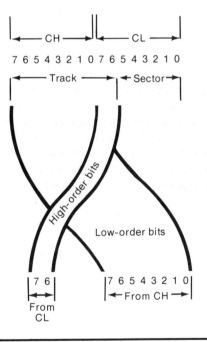

Purpose: Write Long Sector
Reserved (PS/2)

Interrupt: 13h

Function: 0Bh

Description: Writes a specified number of "long" sectors to the
hard disk

Calling Registers: AH = 0Bh
AL = Number of sectors
ES:BX = Pointer to data buffer
CH = Track
CL = Sector
DH = Head number
DL = Fixed disk drive number

Return Registers: Carry flag clear if successful
AH = 0

Carry flag set if error
AH = Status byte (refer to table BIOS.10)

Comments: *This function is available only on the Personal Computer AT
and works only on fixed (hard) disks.* Long sectors are standard sectors that
contain four bytes of error-correcting code in addition to regular data. This
function, like the other read/write functions, is susceptible to the DMA
boundary error (AH =9) which can occur when a DMA crosses a memory
offset that ends in three zeros. Because there is no error checking of
parameters, errors in parameter values can lead to unexpected results.

The drive numbers used are not the standard BIOS drive numbers; rather,
they are taken from a special series of numbers for fixed disks only (80h
corresponds to the first disk, 81h to the second, and so on). Using an out-of-
range disk drive number will lead to unpredictable results.

Purpose: Seek Cylinder

Interrupt: 13h

Function: 0Ch

Description: Moves read/write head to specified cylinder

Calling Registers: AH = 0Ch
                         CH = Low-order track
                         CL = High-order track
                         DH = Head number
                         DL = Fixed disk drive number

Return Registers: Carry flag clear if successful
                       AH = 0

                       Carry flag set if error
                       AH = Status byte (refer to table BIOS.10)

Comments: This function, *which is available only on the Personal Computer AT and works only on fixed (hard) disks,* moves the read/write heads to a specified cylinder. The drive numbers used are not the standard BIOS drive numbers; rather, they are taken from a special series of numbers for fixed disks only (80h corresponds to the first disk, 81h to the second, and so on). Using an out-of-range disk drive number will lead to unpredictable results. Unpredictable results can occur also from invalid parameter settings when the function is called.

Purpose: Alternate Disk Reset

Interrupt: 13h

Function: 0Dh

Description: Resets hard disk controller

Calling Registers: AH = 0Dh
                          DL = Fixed disk drive number

Return Registers: Carry flag clear if successful
                       AH = 0

                       Carry flag set if error
                       AH = Status byte (refer to table BIOS.10)

Comments: *This function is available only on the Personal Computer AT and works only on fixed (hard) disks.* The drive numbers used are not the standard BIOS drive numbers; rather, they are taken from a special series of numbers for fixed disks only (80h corresponds to the first disk, 81h to the second, and so on). Using an out-of-range disk drive number will lead to unpredictable results.

This function is identical to Int 13h, Function 00h. Both are used as critical-error handlers to force recalibration (by causing the disk heads to be repositioned to track zero before the next I/O operation is started). At present, this handler is coded to go to the same routine address as Int 13h, Function 00h. (This function is included for the future, when a single routine will no longer be sufficient for both floppy and hard disk recalibrations.)

Purpose: Return DASD (Direct Access Storage Device) Type

Interrupt: 13h

Function: 15h

Description: Gets driver's DASD type and number of sectors

Calling Registers: AH = 15h
   DL = Drive number

Return Registers: Carry flag clear if successful
   AH = DASD type of drive
   CX = Number of fixed disk sectors (high word)
   DX = Number of fixed disk sectors (low word)

   Carry flag set if error
   AH = Status byte (refer to table BIOS.10)

Comments: This function, *which is available only on the PC XT (BIOS dated 1/10/86 or later), PC XT 286, Personal Computer AT, or PS/2 line*, can use either the standard series of BIOS drive numbers (0 = drive A:, 1 = drive B:, etc.) or the fixed disk numbers (80h = first drive, 81h = second drive, etc.).

This function is used to determine whether Function 16h can be used to test the drive to see whether the floppy disk in the drive has been changed since the last access. Table BIOS.14 lists the function's valid return codes, which indicate whether you can tell anything about the status of the disk in the drive.

Table BIOS.14. DASD Types

Code	DASD Type
0	Drive requested is not available
1	Drive present, cannot detect disk change
2	Drive present, can detect disk change
3	Fixed disk

The value returned in CX:DX will be valid only if the DASD type returned in AH is 3.

Purpose: Read Disk Change Line Status

Interrupt: 13h

Function: 16h

Description: Determines whether disk in a specific drive has been changed

Calling Registers: AH = 16h
DL = Drive number

Return Registers: Carry flag clear and AH = 0 Disk not changed

Carry flag set
AH = 6 Disk changed
AH = 0 Error

Comments: Use this function, *which is available only on the PC XT (BIOS dated 1/10/86 or later), PC XT 286, Personal Computer AT, or PS/2 line*, to determine whether the disk in a drive has been changed or removed. This function can use either the standard series of BIOS drive numbers (0 = drive A:, 1 = drive B:, etc.) or the fixed-disk-only numbers (80h = first drive, 81h = second drive, etc.).

Note, in this function, the unfortunate use of the carry flag, which is confusing and inconsistent with its use in the interrupt's other functions. In this one instance, the presence of the carry flag does *not* indicate that an error has occurred. Rather, it indicates one of two possible conditions: that an error has occurred or that the disk has been removed. All of the other disk-access functions use the carry flag to indicate that an error has occurred.

Purpose: Set DASD Type for Disk Format

Interrupt: 13h

Function: 17h

Description: Specifies the Direct Access Storage Device (DASD) type for use by BIOS disk-formatting functions

Calling Registers: AH = 17h
AL = DASD format type (see table BIOS.15)
DL = Drive number (0 based)

Return Registers: Nothing

Comments: This function, *which is available only on the PC XT (BIOS dated 1/10/86 or later), PC XT 286, Personal Computer AT, or PS/2 line*, must be called before you format a disk. Its purpose is to tell the format function the DASD format type for formatting operations.

Table BIOS.15 lists the valid disk types that can be formatted on the Personal Computer AT system.

Table BIOS.15. DASD Format Types

Type	Meaning
1	Formatting 320/360K disk in 320/360K drive
2	Formatting 320/360K disk in 1.2M drive
3	Formatting 1.2M disk in 1.2M drive

The diskette status is kept in the BIOS data area at 004:0041.

Purpose: Set Media Type for Format

Interrupt: 13h

Function: 18h

Description: Specifies the type of media for BIOS to use in disk-formatting functions

Calling Registers: AH = 18h
                        CH = Number of tracks (0 based)
                        CL = Sectors per track
                        DL = Drive number (0 based)
                            bit 7 = 0 for a diskette
                                    1 for fixed disk

Return Registers: Carry flag clear if successful
                        ES:DI = Pointer to 11-byte parameter table
                              (refer to table BIOS.12)

                        Carry flag set if error
                        AH = Return code

Comments: This function, *which is available only on the Personal Computer AT (BIOS dated after 11/15/86), PC XT (BIOS dated after 1/10/86), PC XT Model 286, and the PS/2 line,* is intended to be used before Int 13h, Function 05h is used to format a disk track. This function specifies to BIOS the type of media it can expect to find in the disk drive.

Before using this function, you should note the use of the CH and CL registers to specify the track and sector information. The track can be a 10-bit value; as such, it requires the two high-order bits of CL. (Refer to fig. BIOS.1, which shows how this information is stored in the two registers.)

Purpose: Initialize Communications Port

Interrupt: 14h

Function: 00h

Description: Sets serial port parameters

Calling Registers: AH = 00h
AL = Initialization parameter
DX = Port number (0 =COM1, 1 =COM2)
(2 =COM3, 3 =COM4 on Personal
Computer AT)

Return Registers: AH = Port status
AL = Modem status

Comments: Use this function to initialize the communications port specified in DX. You can use the function to initialize COM ports 1 and 2 (DX = 0-1); on Personal Computer AT systems, COM ports 1–4 are allowed.

In AL, you specify how the communications port should be initialized. Use the parameters shown in table BIOS.16 to specify the baud rate, parity, word length, and stop bits.

Table BIOS.16. *Serial Port Initialization Parameters*

7,6,5 *Baud Rate*	4,3 *Parity*	2 *Stop Bits*	1,0 *Word Length*
000 = 110 baud	X0 =none	0 =1 bit	10 =7 bits
001 = 150 baud	01 =odd	1 =2 bits	11 =8 bits
010 = 300 baud	10 =none		
011 = 600 baud	11 =even		
100 =1200 baud			
101 =2400 baud			
110 =4800 baud			
111 =9600 baud			

The interrupt returns the status of the port (see table BIOS.17) and the modem (see table BIOS.18). The BIOS adds bit 7 of the port status bits (time out) to indicate excessive time spent waiting for a response. Otherwise, the status is what you would get directly from the hardware.

Table BIOS.17. *Port Status Bits*

Bit 76543210	Meaning
. . . . 1	Data ready
. . . . . . 1 .	Overrun error
. . . . . 1 . .	Parity error
. . . . 1 . . .	Framing error
. . . 1	Break detected
. . 1	Transmit holding register (THR) empty
. 1	Transmit shift register (TSR) empty
1	Time out

Table BIOS.18. *Modem Status Bits*

Bit 76543210	Meaning
. . . . 1	Change in Clear to Send (CTS) status
. . . . . . 1 .	Change in Data Set Ready (DSR) status
. . . . . 1 . .	Trailing edge ring indicator
. . . . 1 . . .	Change in receive line signal
. . . 1	Clear to Send (CTS)
. . 1	Data Set Ready (DSR)
. 1	Ring Indicator (RI)
1	Receive line signal detected

No matter how you want to use a communications port, initializing the port with this function gives you direct control over important parameters without involving many chip-dependent details. Even programmers who access the serial chips directly through their I/O port addresses will find this function a convenient way to control parameters with minimum complexity.

Purpose: Write Character to Communications Port

Interrupt: 14h

Function: 01h

Description: Outputs character to serial port

Calling Registers: AH = 01h
AL = Character to write
DX = Communications port (0 =COM1, 1 =COM2)
(2 =COM3, 3 =COM4 on Personal
Computer AT)

Return Registers: AH bit 7 = 0 (Function successful)
AH bit 7 = 1 (Function failed)
Bits 0–6 show cause of failure (refer to
table BIOS.17)

Comments: This function writes a character to and returns the status of the specified communications port. Ordinarily, writing a character to a serial port is not a time-critical task. It can be done whenever the character is ready. This function can write to serial ports 1 and 2 (COM1 and COM2). Before you call this function, be sure to use Int 14h, Function 00h to initialize the port. (On the Personal Computer AT, you can access ports COM1 to COM4.)

Communications programs that depend on this function can seldom exceed 1200 baud operation. In most cases, a rate of 1200 baud can transfer only a few characters at a time. This function is useless in most commercial applications because direct access to the I/O ports is needed to achieve the speed necessary for continued operation. Programs that do not depend on human interaction can work acceptably using this function. In control and monitoring applications, feeding characters to a serial device with this function is often practical and useful if the speed required is slow enough.

Table BIOS.17 shows the meaning of bits 0–6 in the AH register on return from the function (if the function failed).

Purpose: Read Character from Communications Port

Interrupt: 14h

Function: 02h

Description: Inputs character from serial port

Calling Registers: AH = 02h
                    DX = Communications port number (0 =COM1,
                              1 =COM2)
                              (2 =COM3, 3 =COM4 on Personal
                              Computer AT)

Return Registers: AH bit 7 = 0 (Function successful)
                    AL = Character
                    AH bit 7 = 1 (Function failed)
                          Bits 0–6 show cause of failure

Comments: This function reads a character from the specified communications port, returns the port's status, and can read from serial ports 1 and 2 (COM1 and COM2). (On the Personal Computer AT, you can access ports COM1 to COM4.) Before calling this function, be sure to initialize the port.

In any communications application, receiving characters is an extremely time-critical operation. When characters are coming in at uncontrolled intervals from an external device, the computer must be ready to respond to them immediately. Although output is controlled by the computer (but intimately tied to input in a communications program), input must respond to the external system. If the computer is not ready to respond before a new character arrives, that character will be lost.

Communications programs that depend on this function can seldom exceed 1200 baud operation. In most cases, a rate of 1200 baud can transfer only a few characters at a time. This function is useless in most commercial applications, because direct access to the I/O ports is needed to achieve the speed necessary for continued operation. Programs that do not depend on human interaction can work acceptably using this function. Reading a serial device with this function is often practical and useful in control and monitoring applications with relatively slow speeds.

Table BIOS.17 shows the meaning of bits 0–6 in the AH register on return from the function (if the function failed).

Purpose: Request Communications Port Status

Interrupt: 14h

Function: 03h

Description: Returns status information about a serial port

Calling Registers: AH = 03h
DX = Communications port number (0 =COM1, 1 =COM2)
(2 =COM3, 3 =COM4 on Personal Computer AT)

Return Registers: AH = Port status (refer to table BIOS.17)
AL = Modem status (refer to table BIOS.18)

Comments: This function, which returns the current status of the specified communications port, requests the status without doing any I/O or affecting the serial port in any other way. The function can access communications ports 1 and 2 (DX = 0–1). (On the Personal Computer AT, this function can access ports COM1–COM4.)

Tables BIOS.17 and BIOS.18 show the meaning of the status bits in the AH and AL registers on return from the call. Table BIOS.17 specifies the bits for the serial port, whereas table BIOS.18 gives the bits for the modem connected to the serial port.

Purpose: Extended Initialization (PS/2 only)

Interrupt: 14h

Function: 04h

Description: Initializes serial port parameters

Calling Registers: AH = 04h
AL = Break setting
BH = Parity
BL = Stop bits
CH = Data length
CL = Transmission rate (bps)
DX = Communications port number (0 =COM1,
1 =COM2, 2 =COM3, 3 =COM4)

Return Registers: AH = Port status (refer to table BIOS.17)
AL = Modem status (refer to table BIOS.18)

Comments: Function 04h provides (in a simpler fashion than that used by Function 00h) for RS-232 port initialization directly at the BIOS level on PS/2 machines. Table BIOS.19 shows the possible register settings for this function.

Table BIOS.19. *Possible Register Settings*

Register	Meaning	Settings	Meaning
AL	Break	00h	No break
		01h	Break
BH	Parity	00h	No parity
		01h	Odd parity
		02h	Even parity
		03h	Stick parity odd
		04h	Stick parity even
BL	Stop Bits	00h	One stop bit
		01h	Two stop bits (1 1/2 if data length setting in CH is 00h)
CH	Data Length	00h	5-bit word length
		01h	6-bit word length
		02h	7-bit word length
		03h	8-bit word length

Table BIOS.19 *continues*

Table BIOS.19 *continued*

Register	Meaning	Settings	Meaning
CL	BPS Rate	00h	110 baud
		01h	150 baud
		02h	300 baud
		03h	600 baud
		04h	1200 baud
		05h	2400 baud
		06h	4800 baud
		07h	9600 baud
		08h	19200 baud

On return from the function, the AH and AL registers reflect the current status of the port. Tables BIOS.17 and BIOS.18 give the meaning of each bit in the registers.

Purpose: Extended Communications Port Control (PS/2 only)

Interrupt: 14h

Function: 05h

Description: Allows extended control of the modem control register

Calling Registers: AH = 05h

AL = Read or write modem control register
(00h = read, 01h = write)

BL = Modem control register (if AL = 01h, see table BIOS.20)

DX = Communications port number (0 =COM1, 1 =COM2, 2 =COM3, 3 =COM4)

Return Registers: AH = Port status (refer to table BIOS.17)

AL = Modem status (refer to table BIOS.18)

BL = Modem control register (see table BIOS.20)

Comments: This function allows you to read or write the modem control register associated with the desired RS-232 port. This gives you direct access from the BIOS level to the port's modem-control lines. On read, you get the status of these lines; on write, you set the status. The bits in the BL register are defined in table BIOS.20.

Table BIOS.20. Modem Control Register Bits

Bit 76543210	Meaning
. . . . 1	Data Terminal Ready (DTR)
. . . . . . 1 .	Request to Send (RTS)
. . . . . 1 . .	Out1
. . . . 1 . . .	Out2
. . . 1	Loopback test
111	Reserved

When called, this function also returns the current status of the serial port and modem in registers AH and AL. Tables BIOS.17 and BIOS.18 give the meaning of each bit on return from the call.

Purpose: Turn On Cassette Motor

Interrupt: 15h

Function: 00h

Description: Turns on the motor of the cassette tape machine

Calling Registers: AH = 00h

Return Registers: Carry flag set if error
                                    AH = Return code (see table BIOS.21)

Comments: Because *this function works only on older PC models,* using it on PC XT, Personal Computer AT, or PS/2 systems will result in the carry flag being set and the return of AH =86h (see table BIOS.21).

Table BIOS.21. *Cassette Services Return Codes*

Code	Meaning
00h	Invalid command
01h	CRC error
02h	Data transitions lost
03h	No data located on tape
04h	Data not found (PC*jr* only)
86h	No cassette port available

Some owners of older systems with cassette relays have rewired the relays for other control functions. Such a step should be taken carefully, with a full understanding of the equipment's loading and other electrical requirements.

Purpose: Turn Off Cassette Motor

Interrupt: 15h

Function: 01h

Description: Turns off the motor of the cassette tape machine

Calling Registers: AH = 01h

Return Registers: Carry flag set if error
                        AH = Return code (refer to table BIOS.21)

Comments: Because *this function works only on older PC models,* using it on a PC XT, Personal Computer AT, or PS/2 system will result in the carry flag being set and the return of AH =86h (refer to table BIOS.21).

Some owners of older systems with cassette relays have rewired the relays for other control functions. Such a step should be taken carefully, with a full understanding of the equipment's loading and other electrical requirements.

Purpose: Read Data Blocks from Cassette Drive

Interrupt: 15h

Function: 02h

Description: Reads a specified number of bytes from the cassette

Calling Registers:　AH = 02h
　　　　　　　　　　　ES:BX = Pointer to data buffer
　　　　　　　　　　　CX = Number of bytes to read

Return Registers:　Carry flag clear if successful
　　　　　　　　　　　DX = Number of bytes read
　　　　　　　　　　　ES:BX = Pointer to byte following last byte
　　　　　　　　　　　　　　　read

　　　　　　　　　　　Carry flag set if error
　　　　　　　　　　　AH = Return code (refer to table BIOS.21)

Comments: Because *this function works only on older PC models,* using it on a PC XT, Personal Computer AT, or PS/2 system will result in the carry flag being set and the return of AH =86h (refer to table BIOS.21).

If you are using a cassette on a system with a cassette port, this function will transfer data from the cassette in 256-byte blocks but will deliver to the buffer only the number of bytes called for.

Some owners of older systems with cassette relays have rewired the relays for other control functions. Such a step should be taken carefully, with a full understanding of the equipment's loading and other electrical requirements.

Purpose: Write Data Blocks to Cassette Drive

Interrupt: 15h

Function: 03h

Description: Writes a specified number of bytes to the cassette

Calling Registers: AH = 03h
ES:BX = Pointer to data buffer
CX = Number of bytes to write

Return Registers: Carry flag clear if successful
ES:BX = Pointer to byte following last byte
written

Carry flag set if error
AH = Return code (refer to table BIOS.21)

Comments: Because *this function works only on older PC models,* using it on a PC XT, Personal Computer AT, or PS/2 system will result in the carry flag being set and the return of AH =86h (refer to table BIOS.21).

All transfers to the tape occur in 256-byte blocks, but only the number of bytes specified in the CX register will be transferred from the data buffer. Errors during the transfer indicate command, not transfer, errors. If you are writing an application that will use a cassette, the program should provide a way to verify the tape write before destroying the data in memory.

Some owners of older systems with cassette relays have rewired the relays for other control functions. Such a step should be taken carefully, with a full understanding of the equipment's loading and other electrical requirements.

Purpose: Format Unit Periodic Interrupt

Interrupt: 15h

Function: 0Fh

Description: Called by formatting routines at end of formatting each cylinder

Calling Registers: AH = 0Fh
AL = Phase code
        00h Reserved
        01h Surface analysis
        02h Formatting

Return Registers: Carry flag set, end of formatting or scanning
Carry flag clear, continue formatting/scanning

Comments: This function, *which is available only on PS/2 machines,* is used by programmers who want to gain control after formatting or scanning each disk cylinder. At that time, the format routine will call this interrupt.

If this function is invoked from any machine other than a PS/2, the carry flag will be set and AH will contain 80h (PC and PC*jr*) or 86h (all others) on return.

Purpose: Power-On Self-Test Error Log
(PS/2 line only, except Model 30)

Interrupt: 15h

Function: 21h

Description: Updates or reads POST error log

Calling Registers: AH = 21h
AL = 00h Read POST error log
01h Write error code to POST error log
BX = POST error code if AL =01h
BH = Device code
BL = Device error

Return Registers: If *reading* POST error log (AL = 0)
Carry flag clear if successful
AH = 00h
BX = Number of POST error codes stored
ES:DI = Pointer to POST error log

Carry flag set if error
AH = 80h (PC*jr* and PC)
AH = 86h (all others)

If *writing* error code to POST error log (AL = 1)
Carry flag clear if successful
AH = 00h

Carry flag set if error
AH = 01h POST error log full
AH = 80h (PC*jr* and PC)
AH = 86h (all others)

Comments: This function is used by the POST primarily to write information to the internal error log, or by diagnostic routines to gain information about the error codes detected during the POST. The values returned depend on whether you are posting or reading. The use of the POST error log is beyond the scope of this book.

This function works on all PS/2 machines except the Model 30. If this function is invoked from any machine other than a PS/2, the carry flag with be set and AH will contain 80h (PC and PC*jr*) or 86h (all others, including PS/2 Model 30) on return.

Purpose: Keyboard Intercept

Interrupt: 15h

Function: 4Fh

Description: Called by keyboard routines during I/O processing

Calling Registers: AH = 4Fh
Carry flag set, AL = Keyboard scan code

Return Registers: PC, PC*jr:*
Carry flag set, AH =80h

PC XT BIOS 11/08/82,
Personal Computer AT BIOS 1/10/84:
Carry flag set, AH =86h

All Others:
Carry flag set (New scan code in AL)
Carry flag clear (Original scan code in AL)

Comments: *This function is available only on the Personal Computer AT (BIOS dated after 1/10/84), PC XT (BIOS dated after 11/8/82), PC XT Model 286, and PS/2 series computers.* It is called by Int 09h and normally returns the scan code in the AL register with the carry flag set. The purpose of the routine is to translate scan codes for the keyboard interrupt. By providing a function to replace this one, a programmer can change scan codes to do character translations (such as one might do with an alternate keyboard layout).

If the function returns with the carry flag clear, Int 09h will ignore the character. In addition to doing character translations, a replacement function can use this to cause the system to ignore certain keystrokes.

Purpose: Device Open

Interrupt: 15h

Function: 80h

Description: Opens a device for a specific process

Calling Registers: AH = 80h
BX = Device ID
CX = Process ID

Return Registers: Carry flag set if error
AH = 80h (PC, PC*jr*)
AH = 86h (PC XT with BIOS 11/8/82)

Comments: *This function is available only on the Personal Computer AT, PC XT (BIOS dated after 11/8/82), PC XT Model 286, and PS/2 series computers.* It is intended for use in rudimentary multitasking operations, and is beyond the scope of this book.

Purpose: Device Close

Interrupt: 15h

Function: 81h

Description: Closes a device associated with a specific process

Calling Registers: AH = 81h
BX = Device ID
CX = Process ID

Return Registers: Carry flag set if error
AH = 80h (PC, PC*jr*)
AH = 86h (PC XT with BIOS 11/8/82)

Comments: *This function is available only on the Personal Computer AT, PC XT (BIOS dated after 11/8/82), PC XT Model 286, and PS/2 series computers.* It is intended for use in rudimentary multitasking operations, and is beyond the scope of this book.

Purpose: Program Termination

Interrupt: 15h

Function: 82h

Description: Used to terminate a process

Calling Registers: AH = 82h
                          BX = Device ID

Return Registers: Carry flag set if error
                        AH = 80h (PC, PC*jr*)
                        AH = 86h (PC XT with BIOS 11/8/82)

Comments: *This function is available only on the Personal Computer AT, PC XT (BIOS dated after 11/8/82), PC XT Model 286, and PS/2 series computers.* It is intended for use in rudimentary multitasking operations, and is beyond the scope of this book.

Purpose: Event Wait

Interrupt: 15h

Function: 83h

Description: Waits for process event to occur

Calling Registers: AH = 83h
AL = 00h, Set interval
CX:DX = Microseconds until posting
ES:BX = Pointer to byte with high-order bit
set as soon as possible after end of
interval
AL = 01h, Cancel set interval (PS/2 only)

Return Registers: Carry flag clear if successful

Carry flag set if error
AH = 80h (PC)
AH = 86h (PC XT, Personal Computer AT—BIOS
dated 1/10/84)

Comments: This function, *which is available only on the Personal Computer AT (BIOS dated after 1/10/84) and PS/2 series computers,* does not work with the PS/2 Model 30. The function is intended for use in rudimentary multitasking operations, and is beyond the scope of this book.

Purpose: Joystick Support

Interrupt: 15h

Function: 84h

Description: Returns status and coordinates of joystick

Calling Registers: AH = 84h
          DX = 00h Read switch settings
                  01h Read joystick position

Return Registers: PC, PC*jr:*
          Carry flag set, AH = 80h

          PC XT BIOS 11/08/82:
          Carry flag set, AH = 86h

          All others:
          DX = 00h
                  AL = Switch settings (bits 4–7)
                  Carry flag set if error
          DX = 01h
                  AX = A(X) value
                  BX = A(Y) value
                  CX = B(X) value
                  DX = B(Y) value

Comments: This function is used to control the operations of the joystick on all IBM computers (including the PS/2 line) *except* the PC, PC*jr*, and early PC XT (BIOS dated 11/08/82). On these computers, the function will return with the carry flag set, which indicates an error. AH will contain the error code: either 80h or 86h (for the PC XT).

The value in DX is used to indicate the type of information you want from the joystick. If DX is 0, this function will return the switch settings in the four most-significant bits of AL. If DX is 1, the position of the joystick is returned in the four general-purpose registers: AX, BX, CX, and DX. If no joystick is attached to the computer, the carry flag will be set on return.

Purpose: System Request Key Pressed

Interrupt: 15h

Function: 85h

Description: Called whenever SysRq (system request) key is
pressed

Calling Registers: AH = 85h

Return Registers: PC, PC*jr:*
Carry flag set, AH = 80h

PX XT BIOS 11/08/82:
Carry flag set, AH = 86h

All Others:
AL = 00h, Key pressed
01h, Key released

Comments: BIOS calls this function whenever the System Request key (Alt-
Print Screen) is pressed or released. *Only the more recent versions of BIOS
support this function,* which is accessible only from keyboards with a System
Request key.

If a computer's BIOS does not support this function, the carry flag will be set
and AH will contain either 80h or 86h (early PC XT) on return.

Ordinarily, the System Request key returns with the flags and registers set.
This is of no value, but your program can intercept this function to make
effective use of the key. To program the System Request key, you simply
revector Int 15h and save the old address. Then your routine should check the
contents of AH. If AH does not contain 85h, you should pass control to the
original Int 15h handler. If AH does contain 85h, the System Request key was
either pressed or released. AL reflects the key's state: if it is 00h, the key was
just pressed; if it is 01h, the key was just released.

Purpose: Wait

Interrupt: 15h

Function: 86h

Description: Pauses a certain amount of time before returning

Calling Registers: AH = 86h
                        CX,DX   Time before return in microseconds
                                (accurate to within 976 microseconds)

Return Registers: PC, PC*jr:*
                        Carry flag set, AH = 80h

                        PC XT:
                        Carry flag set, AH = 86h

                        All Others:
                        Carry flag set (Wait in progress)
                        Carry flag clear (Successful wait)

Comments: This function, *which works only on the Personal Computer AT and PS/2 line,* is designed to be used (within operating system software) for setting up system waits. It is not intended for use by applications programs.

Purpose: Move Block

Interrupt: 15h

Function: 87h

Description: Transfers a specified block of memory on 80286/80386 machines

Calling Registers: AH = 87h
CX = Word count of storage to be moved
ES:SI = Pointer to global descriptor table

Return Registers: PC, PC*jr:*
Carry flag set, AH = 80h

PC XT, PS/2 Model 30:
Carry flag set, AH = 86h

All Others:
Carry flag clear, Zero flag set
AH = 00h   Operation successful

Carry flag set, Zero flag clear
Operation failed
AH = 01h   RAM parity error
02h   Other exception occurred
03h   Gate address line 20h failed

Comments: With this function, IBM computers based on 80286 or 80386 microprocessors can transfer blocks of data to and from extended memory. (There must be more than 1M of memory.) The computer switches from the processor's real mode to protected mode. No interrupts are allowed during this type of transfer (interrupts may be missed if the move is a large one).

The global descriptor table pointed to by ES:SI is laid out as shown in table BIOS.22.

Table BIOS.22. *The Global Descriptor Table*

Offset	Description
00h	Dummy (Set to zero)
08h	GDT data segment location (Set to zero)
10h	Source GDT (Points to a GDT for the source memory block)
18h	Target GDT. Points to a GDT for the target memory block.
20h	Pointer to BIOS code segment, initialized to zero. BIOS will use this area to create the protected-mode code segment.
28h	Pointer to BIOS stack segment, initialized to zero. BIOS will use this area to create the protected mode stack segment.

Source/Target GDT Layout

Offset	Description
00h	Segment limit
02h	24-bit segment physical address
05h	Data access rights (set to 93h)
06h	Reserved word (must be zero)

Because the word count loaded into CX has a limit of 8000h, this routine can be used only to transfer as much as 64K of memory.

Purpose: Extended Memory Size Determination

Interrupt: 15h

Function: 88h

Description: Returns number of contiguous 1K memory blocks available in extended memory

Calling Registers: AH = 88h

Return Registers: PC, PC*jr:*
　　　　　Carry flag set, AH = 80h

　　　　PC XT, PS/2 Model 30:
　　　　　Carry flag set, AH = 86h

　　　　All Others:
　　　　　AX = Contiguous 1K blocks of memory beginning at 100000h

Comments: Returns the amount of memory determined available by POST checks above address 100000h. Notice that this function is available only for machines using either the 80286 or 80386 microprocessor.

Purpose: Switch Processor to Protected Mode

Interrupt: 15h

Function: 89h

Description: Switches the processor to protected mode so that it
can access extended memory and take advantage of
protected mode instructions

Calling Registers: AH = 89h
BL = IRQ0 interrupt vector offset
BH = IRQ8 interrupt vector offset
ES:SI = Pointer to Global Descriptor Table (GDT)
CX = Offset into protected mode CS to jump to

Return Registers: Carry flag clear if successful
Carry flag set if error

Comments: For a programmer with access to a system with extended
memory, the capability of switching the processor to protected mode is
potentially very interesting. Although protected mode gives you access to
additional memory and instructions, the price you pay is incompatibility with
many existing systems. Only machines with a 286 or 386 processor have this
capability (and they do not necessarily have the extra memory). Furthermore, DOS itself does not use protected mode. Subtle bugs may crop up
unless you write all of your own handling for this situation.

To use this function, you must first set up the Global Descriptor Table (GDT)
for the call. (Refer to table BIOS.22 for the GDT layout.)

While Function 89h is in use, the normal BIOS functions are not available to
the user. Programs running within protected mode must create their own
I/O commands. Furthermore, the standard interrupt vectors must be moved
in order to accommodate the 80286 interrupt definitions that overlay some
of the interrupt vectors assigned for real-mode use of the system. Interrupt
handlers for the hardware interrupts must also be defined.

Interrupt handling is a major part of any shift to protected mode using this
function. A more detailed discussion of 80286/80386 interrupt is beyond the
scope of this book. For details about the operation of protected mode
interrupts and the design of handlers for them, you should consult a good
reference on the 80286 and 80386 processor.

Purpose: Device Busy

Interrupt: 15h

Function: 90h

Description: Used by BIOS to indicate a "waiting state"

Calling Registers: AH = 90h
AL = Device type code
ES:BX = Pointer to network control block if
waiting for a network

Return Registers: PC, PC*jr:*
Carry flag set, AH = 80h

PC XT BIOS (11/08/82):
Carry flag set, AH = 86h

All Others:
Carry flag set (Minimum wait satisfied)
Carry flag clear (Wait not satisfied)

Comments: Use this function to tell the operating system that a program is about to wait for a device. This function is designed for developing multitasking software; it is not meant for use by applications programmers. Whenever BIOS is about to enter a "busy loop," (when it must wait for a device), it calls this function. Table BIOS.23 lists the type codes passed to the routine in AL.

Table BIOS.23. Type Codes Passed in AL

AL	Type Code
00h	Disk timeout
01h	Diskette timeout
02h	Keyboard (no timeout)
03h	Pointing device (timeout)
80h	Network (no timeout)
FCh	Fixed disk reset (PS/2 only)
FDh	Diskette drive motor start (timeout)
FEh	Printer (timeout)

This function (called at the beginning of an interrupt) is the opposite of Int 15h, Function 91h (called when the interrupt is complete). If you want to do other things while the computer is busy, you can hook into the Int 15h vector, which passes all functions (except 90h and 91h) to the original handler. After you save the machine's status, you are free to do another task.

Purpose: Interrupt Complete

Interrupt: 15h

Function: 91h

Description: Used by BIOS to indicate end of a "waiting state"

Calling Registers: AH = 91h

Return Registers: PC, PC*jr*:
                Carry flag set, AH = 80h

             PC XT BIOS (11/08/82):
                Carry flag set, AH = 86h

           All Others:
                AL = Type code

Comments: BIOS uses this function to report that the device interrupt is complete, according to the type code given in table BIOS.24. This function is not meant to be called by applications programmers; it is intended to be used internally by the operating system, or to develop multitasking systems. Device interrupts use Int 91h to indicate to the operating system that they are complete (see the comments for Int 09h).

Table BIOS.24. *Type Codes on Return from Function 91h*

AL	Type Code
00h	Disk timeout
01h	Diskette timeout
02h	Keyboard (no timeout)
03h	Pointing device (timeout)
80h	Network (no timeout)
FCh	Fixed disk reset (PS/2 only)
FDh	Diskette drive motor start (timeout)
FEh	Printer (timeout)

This function, which is called when an interrupt is complete, is the opposite of Int 15h, Function 90h (called when the interrupt begins).

Purpose: Return System-Configuration Parameters

Interrupt: 15h

Function: C0h

Description: Returns pointer to system-descriptor information

Calling Registers: AH = C0h

Return Registers: PC, PC*jr:*
Carry flag set, AH = 80h

PC XT BIOS (11/08/82),
Personal Computer AT BIOS (1/10/84):
Carry flag set, AH = 86h

All Others:
ES:BX = Pointer to system descriptor table in
ROM

Comments: The ROM system descriptor table contains useful information about the system. Table BIOS.25 shows the meaning of the entries.

Table BIOS.25. *System Descriptor Table*

Offset	Meaning
00h	Byte count of data that follows (minimum 8)
02h	Model byte
03h	Submodel byte
04h	BIOS revision level (00 = 1st release)
05h	Feature information (see table BIOS.26 for meaning)
06–09h	Reserved

The feature information byte is interpreted as shown in table BIOS.26.

The model byte contained at offset 02h of the system descriptor table should be the same as the system ID byte (stored at FFFF:FFFE). The submodel byte (offset 03h) can be used for additional system identification. From the information shown in table BIOS.27, you can determine what type of IBM computer is being used. (The BIOS date is provided to indicate differences between table entries for the same type of computer.)

Table BIOS.26. *The Feature Information Byte*

Bit 76543210	Meaning
. x	Reserved
. . . . . .Ø.	PC bus I/O channel
. . . . . .1.	Micro channel architecture
. . . . .1..	Extended BIOS data area (EBDA) allocated
. . . .1...	Wait for external event is supported
. . .1....	Keyboard intercept called by Int 09h
. .1.....	Real-time clock present
.1......	Second interrupt chip present
1.......	DMA channel 3 used by hard disk BIOS

Table BIOS.27. *System Model Identifications*

Computer Type	Model Byte (offset 02h)	Submodel (offset 03h)	BIOS Revision (offset 04h)	BIOS Date
PC	FFh			
PC XT	FEh			
PC XT	FBh	00h	01h	1/10/86
PC XT	FBh	00h	02h	5/09/86
PCjr	FDh			
AT	FCh			
AT	FCh	00h	01h	6/10/85
AT, COMPAQ 286	FCh	01h	00h	11/15/85
PC XT 286	FCh	02h	00h	
PC Convertible	F9h	00h	00h	
PS/2 Model 30	FAh	00h	00h	
PS/2 Model 50	FCh	04h	00h	
PS/2 Model 60	FCh	05h	00h	
PS/2 Model 80	F8h	00h	00h	

Purpose: Return Extended BIOS Data-Area Segment Address

Interrupt: 15h

Function: C1h

Description: Returns EBDA segment

Calling Registers: AH = C1h

Return Registers: PC, PC*jr:*
          Carry flag set, AH = 80h

     PC XT, Personal Computer AT:
          Carry flag set, AH = 86h

     PS/2:
          Carry flag set (Unsuccessful)
          Carry flag clear (Successful)
          ES = Extended BIOS data-area segment address

Comments: This function is used to determine the segment address of the extended BIOS data area (EBDA). Notice that (so far) this area is used only by the PS/2 line. You can determine whether it is supported on your system through Int 15h, Function C0h (refer to bit 2 of the feature information byte).

The EBDA is used internally by BIOS on the Personal System/2 line. It is allocated by the POST routines and resides at the top of the user memory area (usually as the last 1K of the 640K main memory area). POST adjusts the amount of free memory to allow for the EBDA. To determine the amount of free memory available, refer to Int 12h.

Purpose: Pointing Device BIOS Interface

Interrupt: 15h

Function: C2h

Description: Interface function for auxiliary printing devices

Calling Registers: AH = C2h
   AL = 00   Enable/Disable pointing device
        BH = 00 (Enable)
            01 (Disable)
   AL = 01   Reset pointing device
   AL = 02   Set sample rate
   AL = 03   Set resolution
   AL = 04   Read device type
   AL = 05   Pointing device interface
        initialization
   AL = 06   Extended commands
   AL = 07   Pointing device far call
        initialization

Return Registers: PC, PC*jr*:
        Carry flag set, AH = 80h

   PC XT, Personal Computer AT:
        Carry flag set, AH = 86h

   PS/2:
      Carry flag clear if successful
        Other registers vary by subfunction (see
        comments)
      Carry flag set if error
      AH = 01h Invalid function call
           02h Invalid input
           03h Interface error
           04h Resend
           05h No far call installed

Comments: This function, *which works only on the PS/2 line,* is designed to interface pointing devices (such as a mouse, digitizer, or puck) to DOS. Because most mouse software currently is interfaced through an Int 33h device driver, information about the mouse is covered under that interrupt.

Although detailed use of this function is beyond the scope of this book, I will touch quickly upon the parameters for each subfunction. Before you issue a subfunction, you should tell BIOS about the interrupt handler for the pointing device (set AL to 7 and ES:BX to the interrupt handler's far address). Next, enable the pointing device by setting AL and BL to 0 and calling this function.

After you have enabled the pointing device, you can reset it by setting AL to 1 and calling the function. On successful completion, BH will be set to the device ID of the pointing device, and the device's parameters will be reset.

Note that a similar subfunction (AL=5) is used to initialize the pointer device's interface. This subfunction is invoked with BH set to a number in the range of 1–8, which represents the number of bytes to be used for the data package size.

To allow for setting the pointing device's sampling rate, set AL to 2. A code that indicates the desired sampling rate is loaded into BH as follows:

Code	Sample Rate
00h	10 reports/second
01h	20 reports/second
02h	40 reports/second
03h	60 reports/second
04h	80 reports/second
05h	100 reports/second
06h	200 reports/second

To set the resolution of the pointing device, set AL to 3 and BH to the desired resolution (0 = 1 count per millimeter (cpm), 1 = 2 cpm, 2 = 4 cpm, and 3 = 8 cpm).

By setting AL to 4, you cause the device ID (returned in BH) to be read. This return value is the same as that returned when you reset the device (see AL = 5).

Purpose: Enable/Disable Watchdog Timeout

Interrupt: 15h

Function: C3h

Description: Provides control for PS/2 watchdog timer

Calling Registers: AH = C3h
                            AL = 00h Disable watchdog timeout
                                 01h Enable watchdog timeout
                            BX = Watchdog timer count (1–255)

Return Registers: PC, PC*jr*:
                     Carry flag set, AH = 80h

                     PC XT, Personal Computer AT, PS/2 Model 30:
                     Carry flag set, AH = 86h

                     PS/2:
                     Carry flag clear if successful
                     Carry flag set if error

Comments: This function is used to enable or disable the watchdog timer available with the PS/2 line of computers that use 80286 or 80386 microprocessors. On non-PS/2 computers, this function returns with the carry flag set and an error code in AH.

The watchdog timer uses timer channel 3, and is tied to the IRQ 0 line. When IRQ 0 is active for more than one cycle of the channel 0 timer (main system timer), the watchdog timer count is decremented. When the watchdog timer count reaches 0, a non-maskable interrupt (NMI) is generated. The main purpose of this function (and the watchdog timer) is to help in the detection of and recovery from errors.

Purpose: Programmable Option Select

Interrupt: 15h

Function: C4h

Description: Provides access to PS/2 system programmable
registers on option boards

Calling Registers: AH = C4h
AL = 00h Return base POS adapter register
address
01h Enable slot for setup
02h Adapter enable

Return Registers: PC, PC*jr:*
Carry flag set, AH = 80h

PC XT, Personal Computer AT, PS/2 Model 30:
Carry flag set, AH = 86h

PS/2:
Carry flag clear if successful
DL = Base POS adapter register address
(function 0)
BL = Slot number (function 1)

Carry flag set if error

Comments: The Programmable Option Select (POS), which is available on
PS/2 models that use the 80286 and 80386 microprocessors, eliminates the
need for system-board and adapter switches. The function of the switches is
replaced by programmable registers accessible through this function.

On non-PS/2 systems, this function returns an error. The carry flag is set and
AH contains an error code.

This function is intended primarily for use by system-configuration software,
not by applications programs. Should you decide to use it, be aware that
*improper use of the POS can cause loss of system integrity and may damage
some adapter boards.* The process for Personal System/2 system configuration and setup is beyond the scope of this book.

Purpose: Read Keyboard Character

Interrupt: 16h

Function: 00h

Description: Returns an ASCII value and scan code from the
keyboard buffer

Calling Registers: AH = 00h

Return Registers: AH = Keyboard scan code
AL = ASCII character code

Comments: This function, which reads a single character from the key-board buffer and returns the character and its scan code, is the one you most likely will use when you write a TSR that needs a "hot key" to trigger its operation (unless immediate response is needed, for which Int 09h should be used). By watching requests to this interrupt, you can trap and respond directly to occurrences of the hot key. The keyboard buffer is usually located at 0040:001A.

This function waits until a key is pressed and then returns the keyboard scan code and the ASCII code of the keystroke. If a key has no defined ASCII code, a value of 0 is returned for the ASCII code. (The arrow keys and function keys are examples of keys with no defined ASCII code.)

Although the Ctrl, Alt, and Shift keys return no code for themselves, they modify other keystrokes to produce unique codes. (See Int 16h, Function 02h for a way to tell the status of these keys.)

The special keystrokes Ctrl-Alt-Del (press and hold the Ctrl, Alt, and Del keys simultaneously) and PrtSc (press and hold the Shift key and the PrtSc key simultaneously) are not returned. BIOS recognizes these special keystrokes and immediately passes control to other interrupt-servicing routines.

This function allows you to enter any character by holding down the Alt key while you type its corresponding ASCII code on the keypad. For example, if you hold down the Alt key while you type *156,* the scan code 156 will be returned. If you type a number greater than 256, the returned code will be the number *modulo 256* (the number entered is divided by 256; the code will be the remainder).

Purpose: Read Keyboard Status

Interrupt: 16h

Function: 01h

Description: Checks for availability of a keystroke, returning the ASCII code and scan code if available

Calling Registers: AH = 01h

Return Registers: Zero flag clear (Key waiting)
            AH = Scan code
            AL = ASCII character
            Zero flag set (No key waiting)

Comments: Unlike Function 00h of Int 16h, this function does a quick check of the keyboard and then returns immediately. If a keystroke is ready, the function clears the zero flag and returns the keystroke's ASCII code and the keyboard scan code. If there is no keystroke to be processed, the function sets the zero flag. If the key has no defined ASCII code, a value of 0 is returned for the ASCII code. (The arrow keys and function keys are examples of keys with no defined ASCII code.)

Although the Ctrl, Alt, and Shift keys return no code for themselves, they modify other keystrokes to produce unique codes. (See Function 02h for a way to tell the status of these keys.) The special Ctrl-Alt-Del and PrtSc keystrokes are not returned, but cause other interrupts to occur immediately.

You can enter any ASCII code by holding down the Alt key while typing its corresponding three-digit code number. For example, holding down the Alt key while typing 156 will return the scan code 156. If you type a number greater than 256, the returned code will be the number *modulo 256* (the number entered is divided by 256; the code will be the remainder).

Int 16, Function 01h does not end with an IRET instruction, as other interrupt handlers do; rather, it uses a RET instruction with an option that allows the function to flush bytes from the stack. By returning in this way, the function can use the zero flag for a return flag. I don't know why the programmer chose to do this, but it works.

Purpose: Return Keyboard Flags

Interrupt: 16h

Function: 02h

Description: Returns a status byte indicating condition of
various Shift keys

Calling Registers: AH = 02h

Return Registers: AL = ROM BIOS keyboard flags byte

Comments: This function returns the status of keyboard toggles and Shift keys from the BIOS status register kept in memory location 0000:0417h.

Unusual key combinations make good triggers for special actions. In older programs, the Escape key (Esc) was often used for getting out of an application. But Esc is not a safe choice for irrevocable actions. The key is too easily pressed. To prevent accidental triggering, you would have to add an Are you sure? question if your program found the Esc key. You can provide a more positive initiator by triggering on a key sequence that is unlikely to occur accidentally (Ctrl-Left Shift-Right Shift, for example). Just be careful not to use key sequences that require double-jointed hands or other unusual characteristics!

Table BIOS.28 shows the meaning of the bits in the AL register on return from the function.

Table BIOS.28. *BIOS Keyboard Status Flags*

Bit 76543210	Meaning
. . . . 1	Right Shift key is depressed
. . . . . . 1 .	Left Shift key is depressed
. . . . . 1 . .	Ctrl key is depressed
. . . . 1 . . .	Alt key is depressed
. . . 1	Scroll Lock is enabled
. . 1	Num Lock is enabled
. 1	Caps Lock is enabled
1	Insert key has been toggled

Purpose: Write to Keyboard Buffer

Interrupt: 16h

Function: 05h

Description: Writes to an enhanced keyboard's buffer

Calling Registers: AH = 05h
CH = Scan code
CL = Character

Return Registers: AL = 1 if buffer is full

Comments: *This function works only on Personal Computer ATs and PS/2s with enhanced keyboards.* To determine whether a system has an enhanced keyboard, follow these steps:

1. Use Function 05h to write FFFFh to the keyboard's buffer.

2. Use Function 10h to read from the keyboard.

If you do not get FFFFh back within 16 tries (the size of the keyboard buffer) then you do not have an enhanced keyboard.

Purpose: Get Keystroke

Interrupt: 16h

Function: 10h

Description: Gets a keystroke from an enhanced keyboard

Calling Registers: AH = 10h

Return Registers: AH = Scan code
AL = Character

Comments: This function, *which works only on Personal Computer ATs and PS/2s with enhanced keyboards,* adds to keyboard processing a recognition of similarly named keys. For example, the keyboard has two Alt keys (Left and Right); this function adds recognition of the Left versus the Right Alt key. (For a table of additional available key identifications, see Int 15h, Function 12h.) The discussion of Int 16h, Function 05h tells you how to determine whether an enhanced keyboard is present.

Purpose: Check Keyboard

Interrupt: 16h

Function: 11h

Description: Checks an enhanced keyboard for a keystroke

Calling Registers: AH = 11h

Return Registers: Zero flag clear if keystroke is available
AH = Scan code
AL = Character

Zero flag set if no keystroke is available

Comments: *This function works only on Personal Computer ATs and PS/2s with enhanced keyboards.* Like other keyboard input routines, this function returns the character and scan code if a character is available and returns the zero flag set if no character is available. This function can be used to implement input routines that poll the keyboard regularly but do other work while waiting for input.

Purpose: Get Keyboard Status Flags

Interrupt: 16h

Function: 12h

Description: Returns status of enhanced keyboard Shift keys

Calling Registers: AH = 12h

Return Registers: AL = Status flag 1
AH = Status flag 2

Comments: This function, *which works only on Personal Computer ATs and PS/2s with enhanced keyboards,* is similar in purpose and operation to Int 16h, Function 02h, except that extended information is returned. The meaning of the status flags returned by this function is shown in tables BIOS.29 and BIOS.30. Notice that the information provided in table BIOS.29 (returned in AL) is the same as that returned in AL by Int 16h, Function 02h (refer to table BIOS.28).

Table BIOS.29. BIOS Keyboard Status Flag 1

Bit 76543210	*Meaning*
. 1	Right Shift key is depressed
. . . . . .1.	Left Shift key is depressed
. . . . .1. .	Either Ctrl key is depressed
. . . .1. . .	Either Alt key is depressed
. . .1. . . .	Scroll Lock is enabled
. .1.	Num Lock is enabled
.1.	Caps Lock is enabled
1.	Insert key has been toggled

Table BIOS.30. *BIOS Keyboard Status Flag 2*

Bit 76543210	Meaning
.......1	Right Ctrl key is depressed
......1.	Left Alt key is depressed
.....1..	Right Ctrl key is depressed
....1...	Right Alt key is depressed
...1....	Scroll Lock is depressed
..1.....	Num Lock key is depressed
.1......	Caps Lock key is depressed
1.......	SysReq Key is depressed

Purpose: Write Character to Printer

Interrupt: 17h

Function: 00h

Description: Outputs character to a parallel printer port

Calling Registers: AH = 00h
AL = Character
DX = Printer number (0–2)

Return Registers: AH = Printer status (see table BIOS.31)

Comments: This function writes the specified character to the printer port and returns the printer's current status, as shown in table BIOS.31.

Table BIOS.31. *Print Status Bits*

Bit 76543210	Meaning
. 1	Timeout
. . . . .xx.	Unused
. . . .1. . .	I/O error
. . .1. . . .	Printer selected
. .1.	Out of paper
.1.	Acknowledged
1.	Printer *not* busy

Purpose: Initialize Printer Port

Interrupt: 17h

Function: 01h

Description: Sends reset sequence to parallel printer port

Calling Registers: AH = 01h
DX = Printer number (0–2)

Return Registers: AH = Printer status (refer to table BIOS.31)

Comments: This function initializes the parallel printer port and returns the port's status (refer to table BIOS.31). The function outputs the character sequence 08h 0Ch to the printer port. EPSON and IBM printers respond to this sequence by performing a reset. Other printers, however, may not respond correctly and, if they are not EPSON- or IBM-compatible, may even exhibit undesirable effects from the code sequence.

Purpose: Request Printer Port Status

Interrupt: 17h

Function: 02h

Description: Returns status of a parallel printer port

Calling Registers: AH = 02h
DX = Printer number (0–2)

Return Registers: AH = Printer status (refer to table BIOS.31)

Comments: This function returns the current status of the specified parallel printer port (refer to table BIOS.31).

Note that if you are using a Personal Computer AT, a PC XT 286, or a Personal System/2 machine, and BIOS determines that the printer is busy (see bit 7 of table BIOS.31), BIOS will execute an Int 15h, Function 90h. (See the description of that function for additional information.)

Purpose: Execute ROM BASIC

Interrupt: 18h

Description: Starts up BASIC from ROM

Calling Registers: None

Return Registers: Nothing

Comments: On IBM systems, the ROM BASIC interpreter is still included in all BIOS ROM sets. During the boot process, if a floppy disk is not found and no hard disk is present, this interrupt is triggered to execute the ROM BASIC (a cassette BASIC interpreter). This interrupt is rarely used directly. User-written software should not trigger this interrupt.

But ROM BASIC is still necessary, because the BASICA interpreter on IBM distribution disks uses ROM BASIC for many of its routines. Because ROM BASIC is not present on compatibles, you cannot start IBM BASIC on a compatible.

On the new PS/2 systems, ROM BASIC is still included in the BIOS.

Purpose: System Warm Boot

Interrupt: 19h

Description: Initiates boot sequence

Calling Registers: None

Return Registers: Nothing

Comments: This function, which is similar to Ctrl-Alt-Del, performs a warm boot of the computer without losing the present status of memory. (Ctrl-Alt-Del performs a warm boot and also resets the machine state and the memory allocations.)

Contrary to some references, neither of these methods is the same as a power-off restart, which causes the entire system to be reset and power-on checks (including memory checks) to be performed.

When this interrupt is executed, it loads track 0, sector 1 (the boot code) from the disk at memory address 0000:7C00. The DL register is set to the drive number from which the boot is taking place, and then the boot code at that address (0000:7C00) is executed. If there is a hardware error (BIOS cannot locate a boot sector that can be loaded), an Int 18h is executed.

Purpose: Get Clock Counter

Interrupt: 1Ah

Function: 00h

Description: Returns the value of the system clock counter

Calling Registers: AH = 00h

Return Registers: AL = Midnight flag
CX = High-order word clock count
DX = Low-order word clock count

Comments: This interrupt retrieves the system clock counter, which ticks 18.2065 times per second, starting with zero (at midnight).

Midnight is determined as the number of ticks in a complete day of 86,400 seconds (1,573,040 ticks of the clock, for a total elapsed time of 86,399.9121 seconds). The AL register is set to 1 when midnight passes.

You reset AL to zero by executing this function. But be careful—other date routines may need the midnight-passage information.

Purpose: Set Clock Counter

Interrupt: 1Ah

Function: 01h

Description: Sets the value of the system clock counter

Calling Registers: AH = 01h
CX = High-order word clock count
DX = Low-order word clock count

Return Registers: Nothing

Comments: This interrupt retrieves the system clock counter, which ticks 18.2065 times per second, starting with zero (at midnight). To set the clock to a particular time, you compute the number of ticks (since midnight) that you want to represent. This number becomes the new setting for the clock.

To determine the number of ticks, you compute the number of seconds since midnight for the desired time setting and multiply that number by 18.2065 (the number of ticks per second). But be careful—the BIOS does not protect you from illegal values. If you specify a value outside a normal day's range (24 hours, or 1800Bh ticks), the BIOS will accept it.

Purpose: Read Real-Time Clock

Interrupt: 1Ah

Function: 02h

Description: Returns the time maintained by the real-time clock

Calling Registers: AH = 02h

Return Registers: Carry flag clear if successful

CH = Hours (BCD)
CL = Minutes (BCD)
DH = Seconds (BCD)
DL = Daylight savings time flag

Carry flag set if error

Comments: This function, *which is available only on the PC XT 286, Personal Computer AT, or PS/2 line,* returns the clock values in BCD (Binary Coded Decimal). If the Personal Computer AT BIOS is dated before 6/10/85, the value in DL, which indicates the presence of the daylight savings time option, is not returned.

BCD means that each 4-bit nibble is interpreted as a single decimal digit and that hexadecimal digits A through F are ignored. Table BIOS.32 shows the decimal values that correspond to the range of hex values in a 4-bit nibble representing BCD digits.

To use table BIOS.32, determine which digits correspond to a byte that has been coded BCD; then look at each nibble of the byte. For example, a byte value of 34h represents a decimal value of 34 in BCD. The byte A3h is undefined in BCD coding because the first nibble (A) is outside the range of allowed BCD representations.

If the carry flag is set, the clock is not functioning and the return values should be ignored.

Table BIOS.32. *BCD Correspondence Table*

Hex Value	Decimal Value
0	0
1	1
2	2
3	3
4	4
5	5
6	6
7	7
8	8
9	9
A	Undefined
B	Undefined
C	Undefined
D	Undefined
E	Undefined
F	Undefined

Purpose: Set Real-Time Clock

Interrupt: 1Ah

Function: 03h

Description: Sets the time maintained by the real-time clock

Calling Registers: AH = 03h
CH = Hours (BCD)
CL = Minutes (BCD)
DH = Seconds (BCD)
DL = Daylight saving time

Return Registers: Nothing

Comments: *This function is available only on the PC XT 286, Personal Computer AT, or PS/2 line.* Clock values should be set in BCD (Binary Coded Decimal). Each 4-bit nibble is interpreted as a single decimal digit; hexadecimal digits A through F are ignored. Table BIOS.32 shows the decimal values that correspond to the full range of hex values in a 4-bit nibble representing a BCD digit.

Register DL is coded to indicate whether the clock is keeping standard time (DL = 0) or daylight saving time (DL = 1).

Purpose: Read Date from Real-Time Clock

Interrupt: 1Ah

Function: 04h

Description: Returns the date maintained by the real-time clock

Calling Registers: AH = 04h

Return Registers: Carry flag clear if successful
$\qquad$ CH = Century (BCD)
$\qquad$ CL = Year (BCD)
$\qquad$ DH = Month (BCD)
$\qquad$ DL = Day (BCD)

$\qquad$ Carry flag set if error

Comments: This function, *which is available only on the PC XT 286, Personal Computer AT, and PS/2 line,* returns the clock values in BCD (Binary Coded Decimal). Each 4-bit nibble is interpreted as a single decimal digit; hexadecimal digits A through F are ignored. Table BIOS.32 shows the decimal values that correspond to the full range of hex values in a 4-bit nibble representing a BCD digit.

If the carry flag is set, the clock is not functioning. Return values should be ignored.

Purpose: Set Date of Real-Time Clock

Interrupt: 1Ah

Function: 05h

Description: Sets the date maintained by the real-time clock

Calling Registers:
AH = 05h
CH = Century (BCD) (19 or 20)
CL = Year (BCD)
DH = Month (BCD)
DL = Day (BCD)

Return Registers: Nothing

Comments: *This function is available only on the PC XT 286, Personal Computer AT, or PS/2 line.* Clock values should be set in BCD (Binary Coded Decimal). Each 4-bit nibble is interpreted as a single decimal digit; hexadecimal digits A through F are ignored. Table BIOS.32 shows the decimal values that correspond to the full range of hex values in a 4-bit nibble representing a BCD digit.

The values provided to the BIOS must be correct because no range checking is done on them. Incorrect values will cause unpredictable settings of the clock.

Purpose: Set System Alarm

Interrupt: 1Ah

Function: 06h

Description: Sets the system alarm timer to generate an interrupt
at a future time

Calling Registers: AH = 06h
                      CH = Hours (BCD)
                      CL = Minutes (BCD)
                      DH = Seconds (BCD)

Return Registers: Carry flag clear if successful
                      Carry flag set if error

Comments: *This function is available only on the PC XT 286, Personal Computer AT, or PS/2 line.* The alarm settings must be in BCD (Binary Coded Decimal). Each 4-bit nibble is interpreted as a single decimal digit; hexadecimal digits A through F are ignored. Table BIOS.32 shows the decimal values that correspond to the full range of hex values in a 4-bit nibble representing a BCD digit.

The alarm setting is an offset time from the present time. When the time runs out, the system will trigger Int 04h (arithmetic overflow). The program that sets the alarm must check the validity of the values provided, because BIOS does no checking. Before you reset an alarm, you must disable it with function 07h and set up an interrupt handler to deal with the alarm.

On return, a set carry flag indicates that an error has occurred. Either the alarm has been set previously without being disabled, or the clock is not functioning.

Purpose: Disable Real-Time Clock Alarm

Interrupt: 1Ah

Function: 07h

Description: Turns off the system alarm timer

Calling Registers: AH = 07h

Return Registers: Nothing

Comments: This function, *which is available only on the PC XT, Personal Computer AT, or PS/2 line,* disables the real-time alarm clock. If you have already set the alarm, this function must be called before you can reset it.

Purpose: Ctrl-Break Address

Interrupt: 1Bh

Description: Address of the Ctrl-Break interrupt handler

Calling Registers: None

Return Registers: Nothing

Comments: Interrupt vector 1Bh contains the address of the Ctrl-Break interrupt handler. Control is transferred to this address when a program is terminated by a Ctrl-Break key sequence. When the ROM BIOS finds the Ctrl-Break character during keyboard input, BIOS calls the handler immediately. This takes place during the character scan of the keyboard at the BIOS level and so is not guaranteed to be "safe" with respect to DOS. (See Chapter 11 for a discussion of "safe" interrupt handling.)

During initialization, the ROM BIOS sets this vector to point to an IRET instruction. DOS resets the vector to point to the Ctrl-C handler, thereby making the actions of both handlers identical. The Ctrl-C interrupt (Int 23h) is a DOS-level program break that is executed by DOS when DOS is in a "safe" position. Ctrl-Break, occurring as it does at the ROM BIOS level, cannot determine whether DOS is in a safe condition.

The simplest Ctrl-Break (or Ctrl-C) handler for a program points the interrupt to another IRET instruction so that the Ctrl-Break (or Ctrl-C) character is ignored. Then the program can process these characters as they arrive in the input stream.

Purpose: Timer Tick Interrupt

Interrupt: 1Ch

Description: Interrupt called by the system timer interrupts on each clock tick

Calling Registers: None

Return Registers: Nothing

Comments: Vector 1Ch, the timer tick interrupt called by Int 08h (System Metronome), is initialized to point to an IRET instruction. A TSR that needs to be triggered at each clock tick can reset the vector for this interrupt to point to a custom interrupt handler.

Purpose: Video-Initialization Parameter Table

Interrupt: 1Dh

Description: Pointer to a parameter table used for video controller initialization

Calling Registers: None

Return Registers: Nothing

Comments: Int 1Dh (which is not a true interrupt) points to a table of initialization parameters for the video controller. Because Int 1Dh is *not* executable code, this interrupt should not be called by a program. The results of an attempt to execute code at this interrupt will be unpredictable—most likely a system lockup.

Purpose: Disk-Initialization Parameter Table

Interrupt: 1Eh

Description: Pointer to a diskette base table used for disk controller initialization

Calling Registers: None

Return Registers: Nothing

Comments: Int 1Eh (which is not a true interrupt) points to the diskette base table, a table of initialization parameters for the disk controller. Because Int 1Eh is *not* executable code, this interrupt should not be called by a program. The results of an attempt to execute code at this interrupt will be unpredictable—most likely a system lockup.

Although this table can be modified to optimize disk accesses and tune a system, *any modification should be done with extreme care because the procedure can destroy anything and everything you have stored on disk.*

Purpose: Graphics Display Character Bit-Map Table

Interrupt: 1Fh

Description: Pointer to bit-map table used for video character generation

Calling Registers: None

Return Registers: Nothing

Comments: Int 1Fh (which is not a true interrupt) points to a table of character bit maps for the graphics mode representations of ASCII characters 128 to 255. Because Int 1Fh is *not* executable code, this interrupt should not be called by a program. The results of an attempt to execute code at this interrupt will be unpredictable—most likely a system lockup.

The bit-map table contains 128 characters (a total area of 1K) and is simply constructed. Each entry is eight bytes long and represents one 8-by-8 character. Each byte corresponds to one scan line in the character.

The following sample character represents an uppercase *I*—the coding includes a blank scan line at the top and bottom, one scan line each for the top and bottom bars, and four scan lines for the central vertical bar:

```
  1 2 3 4 5 6 7 8
1 Ø Ø Ø Ø Ø Ø Ø Ø
2 Ø 1 1 1 1 1 1 Ø
3 Ø Ø Ø 1 1 Ø Ø Ø
4 Ø Ø Ø 1 1 Ø Ø Ø
5 Ø Ø Ø 1 1 Ø Ø Ø
6 Ø Ø Ø 1 1 Ø Ø Ø
7 Ø 1 1 1 1 1 1 Ø
8 Ø Ø Ø Ø Ø Ø Ø Ø
```

Byte String: 00h, 7Eh, 14h, 14h, 14h, 14h, 7Eh, 00h

By resetting the pointer, you can create your own characters for use in CGA graphics modes.

Purpose: Real-Time Clock Interrupt

Interrupt: 70h

Description: Called 1,024 times per second to control periodic
and alarm functions

Calling Registers: None

Return Registers: Nothing

Comments: *This function applies only to PC AT, PC XT 286, and PS/2
product lines. (The periodic function is not included on the PS/2 Model 30.)*

The real-time clock interrupt is called nearly 1,024 times per second.
Whenever the interrupt is called, a double-word counter is decremented by
976 microseconds (1/1024 of a second). The initial value of this counter is
set by calls to Int 15h, Function 83h (Event Wait) or Function 86h (Wait) as
part of the call. When the counter reaches a value less than or equal to zero,
bit 7 of the designated wait flag is set. For Function 83h, the wait flag is
specified by the ES:BX register pointer. For Function 86h, the flag is at BIOS
data area location 0040:00A0h (Wait active flag).

If the real-time clock is activated as an alarm function by a call to Int 1Ah,
Function 06h, then when the time runs out, Int 4Ah is called by Int 70h to
activate the alarm handler. (The alarm handler must be set up prior to issuing
the call to Int 1Ah.)

DOS Reference

This section of *DOS Programmer's Reference* covers the services offered by DOS. These services are interrupts in the range of 20–2Fh and include many functions that are important for proper program execution. Separate reference sections cover the use of Int 33h for mouse functions and Int 67h for expanded memory management.

Before getting into the specifics of the DOS services, a few items must be covered so that you can have a solid understanding of how the services are used.

How DOS Services Are Invoked

DOS services are invoked in much the same fashion as the BIOS services—through the use of software interrupts. How interrupts are directly executed depends on the programming language you are using and, in many cases, on the dialect or implementation of that language. Examples throughout this book are in different languages, such as assembler, BASIC, C, and Pascal.

If the DOS interrupt is used for many different functions, the desired function number is loaded in the AH register before the interrupt is called. This may be further modified if the same function number is used for several different subfunctions. In this case, the subfunction number is loaded into the AL register before the interrupt is called.

In addition to the interrupt, function, and subfunction numbers, each DOS service generally requires specific parameters to be provided for proper operation. These parameters usually are provided through the use of CPU registers. Their use varies depending upon the needs of the DOS service and even upon the version of DOS in use.

To recap—in order to use DOS services successfully, several general steps must be followed. These are

1. Load the necessary registers with the proper parameters for the DOS service.

2. If the DOS interrupt is used for multiple functions, load AH with the proper function number.

3. If the DOS function is used for multiple subfunctions, load AL with the proper subfunction number.

4. Invoke the DOS interrupt.

5. Examine any returned values for validity and use.

If these steps are followed, then the successful use of virtually all DOS services can be ensured.

Reentrancy

DOS services were designed for a single-user, single-task computer system. There is much talk in the computer world these days about the importance of multitasking and multiuser systems. A response to this has been the development of OS/2, which provides for multitasking. Although this book does not cover OS/2 (or any other operating system besides DOS), it is important to realize that DOS does have design limitations.

Because DOS was designed as a single-user, single-task system, DOS services are not reentrant. This means that DOS services cannot be called from within other DOS services without running the risk of really mucking things up. The internal variables and stack used by DOS can become corrupted if the same DOS services are invoked from within each other. For example, if you have developed an interrupt-driven, whiz-bang system and have installed it as a Terminate and Stay Resident (TSR) utility, it is possible that while one interrupt is being handled by your software, another interrupt of the same nature could occur. What do you do? Well, if DOS were reentrant, you could merrily process away, handling each interrupt as it occurred. Because DOS is not reentrant, this is not possible. Figure DOS.1 illustrates the possible consequences of such an action.

Fig. DOS 1. *The effects of nonreentrancy in DOS.*

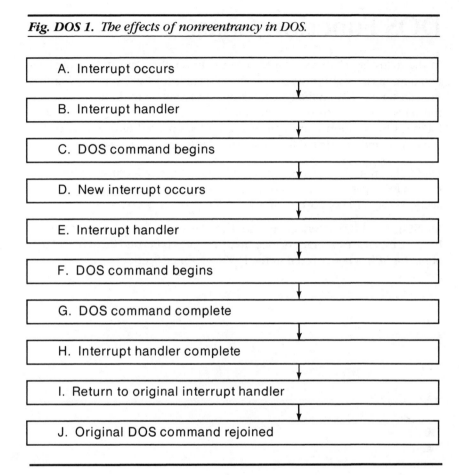

Notice that at Step D, while a DOS command was already in progress, a new interrupt was sensed that started the handler process all over again. The handling of that interrupt was completed with the execution of step I, and control was returned to the original point in the first iteration of the DOS command (step J). At this point, however, all the DOS variables and stack positions previously in use during step C have been changed or destroyed by steps F and G. The result is unpredictable and may have dire consequences on your program.

DOS Function Chart

In the following chart (see table DOS.1), all numbers are in hexadecimal notation. In the register-usage columns, *C* stands for Calling (meaning that the register is used in calling the function), and *R* stands for Return (meaning the register is used to return information). Those interrupts or functions followed by an asterisk are considered undocumented functions (see the section on undocumented functions later in this reference section).

Int 33h for mouse functions is covered in the Mouse Reference Section, and Int 67h for expanded memory management is covered in the EMS Reference Section. They are not covered in the DOS Reference Section.

Int 5Ch, NETBIOS interface, is listed in the chart for your information. Because extensive coverage of local area networks is beyond the scope of this book, Int 5Ch is not covered in the DOS Reference Section.

Table DOS.1. DOS Function Chart

Int	Func (AH)	Subfunc (AL)	Purpose	AX	BX	CX	DX	SI	DI	DS	ES	BP
20			Terminate program	C								
21		00	Terminate program	CR								
		01	Keyboard input with Echo	C								
		02	Display output	CR			C					
		03	Auxiliary input	C								
		04	Auxiliary output	C			C					
		05	Printer output	C			C					
		06	Direct console I/O	CR			C					
		07	Direct STDIN input	CR								
		08	STDIN input	CR								
		09	Display string	C			C			C		
		0A	Buffered STDIN input	C			C			C		
		0B	Check STDIN status	CR								
		0C	Clear buffer and input	CR			C			C		
		0D	Reset disk	C								
		0E	Select disk	CR			C					
		0F	Open file (FCB)	CR			C			C		
		10	Close file (FCB)	CR			C			C		
		11	Search for first entry (FCB)	CR			C			C		
		12	Search for next entry (FCB)	CR			C			C		
		13	Delete file (FCB)	CR			C			C		
		14	Read sequential file (FCB)	CR			C			C		
		15	Write sequential file (FCB)	CR			C			C		
		16	Create file (FCB)	CR			C			C		
		17	Rename file (FCB)	CR			C			C		
		18	Reserved									
		19	Get default drive	CR								
		1A	Set DTA address	C			C			C		
		1B	Get allocation table information	CR	R	R	R			C		
		1C	Get allocation table information for specific drive	CR	R	R	CR			R		
		1D	Reserved									

Table DOS.1. continues

Table DOS.1 continued

Int	Func (AH)	Subfunc (AL)	Purpose	Register Usage								
				AX	BX	CX	DX	SI	DI	DS	ES	BP
	1E		Reserved									
	1F*		Get default disk parameter block	CR			R			R		
	20		Reserved									
	21		Random file read (FCB)	CR			C			C		
	22		Random file write (FCB)	CR			C			C		
	23		Get file size (FCB)	CR			C			C		
	24		Set random record field (FCB)	C			C			C		
	25		Set interrupt vector	C			C			C		
	26		Create PSP	C			C					
	27		Random block read (FCB)	CR		CR	C			C		
	28		Random block write (FCB)	CR		CR	C			C		
	29		Parse file name	CR			CR	CR	CR	CR	CR	
	2A		Get system date	CR		R	R					
	2B		Set system date	CR		C	C					
	2C		Get system time	C		R	R					
	2D		Set system time	CR		C	C					
	2E		Set verify flag	C								
	2F		Get DTA address	C	R						R	
	30		Get DOS version number	CR	R	R						
	31		Terminate and stay resident	C			C					
	32*		Get drive parameter block	CR	R		C			R		
	33		Get/set Ctrl-Break flag	C			CR					
	34*		Return address of InDOS flag	C	R					R		
	35		Get interrupt vector	C	R					R		
	36		Get free disk space	CR	R	R	CR					
	37*		Get/set switchchar	CR			R					
	38		Get/set country information	CR	CR		CR			CR		
	39		Create subdirectory	CR			C			C		
	3A		Remove subdirectory	CR			C			C		
	3B		Set directory	CR			C			C		
	3C		Create/truncate file (handle)	CR		C	C			C		
	3D		Open file (handle)	CR			C			C		
	3E		Close file (handle)	CR	C							
	3F		Read file or device (handle)	CR	C	C	C			C		

Int	Func (AH)	Subfunc (AL)	Purpose	AX	BX	CX	DX	SI	DI	DS	ES	BP
	40		Write to file or device (handle)	CR	C	C	C			C		
	41		Delete file	CR	C	C	C			C		
	42		Move file pointer	CR	C	C	CR					
	43		Get/set file attributes	CR	C	CR	C			C		
	44	00	Get device information	CR	C		R					
		01	Set device information	CR	C		C					
		02	Character device read	CR	C	C	C			C		
		03	Character device write	CR	C	C	C			C		
		04	Block driver read	CR	C	C	C			C		
		05	Block driver write	CR	C	C	C			C		
		06	Get input status	CR	C							
		07	Get output status	CR	C							
		08	Block device removable?	CR	C							
		09	Block device local or remote?	CR	C		R					
		0A	Handle local or remote?	CR	C		R					
		0B	Set sharing retry count	CR		C	C					
	45		Duplicate handle	CR	C	C						
	46		Force duplicate handle	CR	C	C						
	47		Get current directory	CR	C		C	CR		CR		
	48		Allocate memory	CR	CR							
	49		Release memory	CR							C	
	4A		Modify Memory Allocation	CR	CR						C	
	4B	00	Execute program (EXEC)	CR	C	C	C			C	C	C
		03	Load overlay	CR	C		C			C	C	C
	4C		Terminate with return code	C								
	4D		Get return code	CR								
	4E		Search for first match	CR		C	C			C		
	4F		Search for next match	CR								
	50*		Set PSP segment	C	C							
	51*		Get PSP segment	C	R							
	52*		Get disk list	C	R					C	R	
	53*		Translate BPB	C				C		C	C	C
	54		Get verify flag	CR								
	55*		Create PSP	C			C			C	C	C

Table DOS.1 continues

Table DOS.1 continued

Int	Func (AH)	Subfunc (AL)	Purpose	Register Usage AX	BX	CX	DX	SI	DI	DS	ES	BP
	56		Rename file	CR			C		C	C	C	
	57	00	Get file date and time	CR	C	R	R		C	C	C	
		01	Set file date and time	CR	C	C	C					
	58*	00	Get allocation strategy	CR	C	C						
		01	Set allocation strategy	CR								
	59		Get extended error information	CR	CR	R						
	5A		Create temporary file	CR		C	CR		C	CR		
	5B		Create file	CR		C	C			C		
	5C		Set file access	CR	C	C	C	C				
	5D*	06	Get critical error flag address	C				R		R		
	5E	00	Get machine name	CR	C	R	CR			CR		
		02	Set printer setup	CR	C	C		C		C		
		03	Get printer setup	CR	CR	R			CR	CR	CR	
	5F	02	Get redirection list entry	CR	C	CR		CR	CR	CR	CR	
		03	Redirect device	CR		C		C	C	C	C	
		04	Cancel redirection	CR				C	C	C		
	60		Reserved									
	61		Reserved									
	62		Get PSP address	C	R							
	63	00	Get system lead byte table	C				R		R		
		01	Set interim console flag	C			C					
		02	Get interim console flag	C			R					
	64		Reserved									
	65		Get extended country information	CR	C	C	C		CR		CR	
	66	01	Get global code page	CR	R		R					
		02	Set global code page	CR	C		C					
	67		Set handle count	CR	C							
	68		Flush buffer	CR	C							
22			Terminate address									
23			Ctrl-C interrupt vector									
24			Critical error vector									
25			Absolute disk read	CR	C	C	C			C		
26			Absolute disk write	CR	C	C	C			C		
27			Terminate and stay resident	CR	C	C	C					

Register Usage

Int	Func (AH)	Subfunc (AL)	Purpose	AX	BX	CX	DX	SI	DI	DS	ES	BP
28*			Keyboard busy loop									
29*			Fast putchar									
2F	01	00	Print installation check	CR								
		01	Print submit file	CR			C			C		
		02	Print remove file	CR			C			C		
		03	Print remove all files	CR								
		04	Print hold queue/get status	CR			R	R		R		
		05	Print restart queue	CR								
	B7	00	APPEND installation check	CR								
		01*	APPEND									
33			Microsoft mouse									
5C			NETBIOS interface									
67	40		Get EMM status	CR								
	41		Get page frame segment	CR	R		R					
	42		Get number of pages	CR	R		R					
	43		Get handle/allocate memory	CR	C		C					
	44		Map memory	CR	C		C					
	45		Release handle and memory	CR								
	46		Get EMM version	CR								
	47		Save mapping context	CR			C					
	48		Restore mapping context	CR			C					
	49		Reserved									
	4A		Reserved									
	4B		Get number of EMM handle	CR	R							
	4C		Get pages owned by handle	CR	R		C					
	4D		Get pages for all handles	CR	R							
	4E	00	Get page mapping registers	CR					C		C	
		01	Set page mapping registers	CR				C		C		
		02	Get/set page mapping registers	CR				C	CR	C	CR	
		03	Get size of page mapping array	CR					CR		CR	

Note: Undocumented (reserved) functions are marked with an asterisk (*).

Reserved Functions

The following list of functions are those that are considered reserved by IBM and Microsoft and for which no other information could be determined (see table DOS.2). These functions, which are invoked through Int 21h, are not included in the DOS service reference listings later in this section.

Table DOS.2. *Reserved Functions*

Int	Function
21h	18h
	1Dh
	1Eh
	20h
	60h
	61h

Undocumented Functions

The following is a list of functions that are undocumented by IBM or Microsoft, but whose meaning and use have been documented by programmers over time (see table DOS.3). Many times the function's meaning and use

Table DOS.3. *Undocumented Interrupts and Functions*

Int	Function	Purpose
21h	1Fh	Get default disk parameter block
	32h	Get drive parameter block
	34h	Return address of InDOS flag
	37h	Get/set switchchar
	50h	Set PSP segment
	51h	Get PSP segment
	52h	Get disk list
	53h	Translate BPB
	55h	Create PSP
	58h	Get/set allocation strategy
	5Dh	Get critical-error flag address
28h		Keyboard busy loop
29h		Fast putchar
2Eh		Execute command

have been accrued by tedious trial-and-error and poring over code listings. The functions are presented here and later in the DOS service reference listings for your information. Keep in mind, however, that because they are officially undocumented, IBM, Microsoft, or other DOS vendors may change them at any time without notice. You should test out their operation on your system and verify that the same results are returned for your particular applications.

How DOS Services Are Presented

In this section, a standard format is used to present each DOS service. All services are organized in ascending numeric order by interrupt and function number. The presentation format includes the following information for each function: purpose, beginning, DOS version availability, interrupt number, function number, subfunction (if any), description, calling registers, return registers, and comments. Let's take a quick look at each of these items.

Purpose

This is simply a quick statement of the meaning of the DOS service. It is designed to give a quick overview of what the service is designed to accomplish. In most instances, the purpose is garnered from technical publications of IBM and Microsoft, the creators of DOS. In a few instances, however, their listed purposes are unclear, ambiguous, or imprecise. In these cases, the stated purposes have been semantically modified for greater clarity.

Beginning DOS Version

This is a designation of the DOS version number in which the service became available. This is of vital importance, because you do not want to try to invoke DOS services that are not supported by the operating system in use.

For instance, if your program uses a function that is supported only by DOS V3.0 or later, you may have unpredictable results if the function is used with DOS V2.1. To compensate for this, your program must check which version of DOS is in use and gracefully inform the user that the software cannot run on a system using DOS prior to V3.0. Chapter 13, "Miscellaneous Functions," covers the DOS services that are used to accomplish this. These services are also covered later in this section in reference format.

Interrupt Number

This is the interrupt number used to invoke the service. DOS interrupts covered in this section include those shown in table DOS.4.

Table DOS.4. *DOS Interrupts*

Interrupt	Purpose
20h	Program termination
21h	Multipurpose DOS interrupt
22h	Terminate address
23h	Ctrl-C interrupt vector
24h	Critical-error vector
25h	Absolute disk read
26h	Absolute disk write
27h	Terminate and stay resident
28h	Keyboard busy loop
29h	Fast putchar
2Ah	Network interface
2Eh	Execute command
2Fh	Multiplex interface
33h	Mouse interface
5Ch	NETBIOS interface
67h	LIM-EMS interface

Function Number

The function number, a designator loaded into the AH register, is used by the DOS interrupt to determine which service is desired. Although it is true that the function number is optional depending upon the interrupt being invoked, in reality it is almost a necessity. For instance, Int 21h has a possible 105 functions available as of this writing, all of which are covered in this section.

Subfunction Number

Like the function number, the subfunction is an optional designator that further defines the desired DOS service. Only a few DOS functions are divided into subfunctions, and these subfunctions are covered in this reference section as well. If the DOS function being selected requires the specification of a subfunction, the subfunction number is loaded into the AL register before the DOS interrupt is invoked. If no subfunctions are supported by the function, then the use of AL may not be defined, or it may be used to pass other parameters to the DOS service.

Description

This is a quick, one- or two-sentence indication of what this DOS service can do. It is similar to "Purpose" but is expanded to provide a brief explanation of the scope of the service.

Calling Registers

This is a list of the CPU register settings needed by the DOS service in order to function properly. Usually, these are referred to as parameters although they may include pointers to required parameter tables. This portion of the function listing is meant as a quick checklist of register settings required for the service.

Return Registers

Like the "Calling Registers" portion of the DOS function listing, this is a quick checklist of the values returned in registers by the DOS service. It gives a good, and often comprehensive, listing of what is provided by the particular DOS service.

Comments

This is the body of each DOS service listing. It is used to provide a narrative explanation of what the function does, how it is used, possible uses, and any quirks that should be noted. If the DOS function requires the use of parameter tables, either they are described in this section, or information that helps you determine the table content is provided.

DOS Services

Purpose: Terminate Program

Applicable DOS Systems: 1

Interrupt: 20h

Description: Terminates a program's operation and returns control to the process that spawned the program, normally COMMAND.COM prefix

Return Registers: None

Comments: Old DOS hands will recognize this function because it was the standard way to terminate programs on DOS V1. It performs the same basic operations as those provided by Function 00. With the introduction of DOS Functions 4Ch and 31h, this is no longer the recommended way to terminate a program unless it must maintain compatibility with DOS V1 systems. The newer functions allow exit codes to be returned to higher-level programs or batch files.

In addition to terminating the program and freeing the memory space occupied by the program, this interrupt does the following:

1. Restores the termination-handler vector from the Program Segment Prefix (offset 0Ah)

2. Restores the Ctrl-C vector from the Program Segment Prefix (offset 0Eh)

3. Restores the critical-error handler vector from the Program Segment Prefix (offset 12h)

4. Flushes the file buffers to disk

Item 3 is not done by versions of DOS prior to V2.0. After these four items are completed, system control is transferred to the termination-handler address as restored in Item 1.

Although this process sounds complete, if you are using File Control Block (FCB) file-handling functions it isn't complete enough. With FCB functions, the files are not closed by use of this command. Even though the information in the buffers is written to the disk (they have been flushed), the directory information is not updated to reflect changes to the file. Only the close-file function for FCBs (Function 10h) will properly close the file, update the directory, and free the buffer space for use by other programs. As a result, and as a practice of good programming style, it is a good idea to explicitly close any open files before using this program-termination function.

EXE programs calling this function must take extra care because the CS register must point to the segment the Program Segment Prefix (PSP) is in. With COM programs, you are guaranteed that this is the case, but there is no such guarantee with EXE programs. In most cases, this is not a problem, and a call without explicitly setting the CS register will work.

Upon completion of the program-termination function, system control is returned to the parent program that invoked the recently terminated child with the EXEC function (DOS Function 4Bh). Normally, this parent is COMMAND.COM, but it could be any other program. If returning to DOS, control is passed to the resident portion of COMMAND.COM where a memory test is done to determine if the transient section needs to be reloaded. If this checksum test fails, the transient portion is reloaded. Finally, if a batch file is in progress, the next line of the batch file is retrieved and executed.

Purpose: Terminate Program

DOS Version Availability: 1

Interrupt: 21h

Function: 00h

Description: Used to terminate the program and return control to the process that spawned the program

Calling Registers: AH = 00h
                                    CS = PSP segment address

Return Registers: None

Comments: This function is operationally identical to Int 20h. Refer to the comments section of the Int 20h description for more information.

Purpose: Keyboard Input with Echo

DOS Version Availability: 1

Interrupt: 21h

Function: 01h

Description: Reads a character from the keyboard (STDIN beginning with DOS V2) and echoes the character to the video display (STDOUT beginning with DOS V2)

Calling Registers: AH = 01h

Return Registers: AL = 8-bit data

Comments: This is the simplest method of keyboard input that programmers are likely to use. The function simply waits for a character to be input from the keyboard, echoes the character to the video display, and returns it to the program.

With DOS V1, it was this simple: the function retrieved characters only from the keyboard and displayed them only on the video display. Starting with DOS V2, however, the process was complicated somewhat with the introduction of redirection. Now a character is retrieved from the standard input device (STDIN) and displayed on the standard output device (STDOUT). Normally, STDIN is the keyboard and STDOUT is the video display, but these may be redirected by the user.

If no character is available at STDIN, this function will wait until one is available. If STDIN has been redirected to a device other than the keyboard, this may cause problems if the input is variable or sporadic. If working with the keyboard, however, this method of operation is reasonable and usually desirable.

When a character is available and has been displayed, its ASCII value is returned. If the character is an extended ASCII character, a zero will be returned, and another call to this function will be required to return the scan code of the key pressed. The extended ASCII codes are detailed in Appendix A.

When STDIN and STDOUT are redirected, problems may occur when using this function:

❏ If input is coming from a file, a zero byte that does not correspond to an extended keyboard code may be returned.

❏ The function cannot detect the end of a file.

These considerations may cause significant problems when STDIN has been redirected so that input is retrieved from a file. Because of this, you may want to use a different DOS input function: 06h, 07h, 08h, or 3Fh (when using handle 0, STDIN).

When you use this function, Ctrl-C or Ctrl-Break causes Int 23h to be invoked prior to returning from the function.

Purpose: Display Output

DOS Version Availability: 1

Interrupt: 21h

Function: 02h

Description: Outputs a character to the video display (STDOUT beginning with DOS V2.0)

Calling Registers: AH = 02h
                         DL = 8-bit character data

Return Registers: None

Comments: Like most of the other low-numbered I/O functions accessed through Int 21h, this function's use depends on the version of DOS being used. If operating under DOS V1, this function directs output to the video display only. Beginning with DOS V2, output is directed to the standard output device (STDOUT), which defaults to the video display.

The system will properly handle a backspace character as a nondestructive backspace on the screen. Ctrl-C and Ctrl-Break are also handled (through Int 23) if found during the operation.

If output is redirected by the user, there can be problems with using this function. If output is sent to a file, a disk error can cause your system to "hang" because there is no intrinsic method for this function to sense or handle disk errors. Notice that there are no return values for this function, and thus no way to indicate an error while attempting to output a character. Because of this consideration, you may wish to use a different DOS output function, such as Function 40h, using the predefined handle 01 (STDOUT).

Purpose: Auxiliary Input

DOS Version Availability: 1

Interrupt: 21h

Function: 03h

Description: Reads a character from the first serial port (STDAUX beginning with DOS V2)

Calling Registers: AH = 03h

Return Registers: AL = 8-bit input data from STDAUX

Comments: Unlike the keyboard, a serial device is unbuffered, which means that it handles characters one at a time as they are available. If characters become available faster than they can be handled by your software, they are lost. This function retrieves a character from the serial port. If no character is available, the function will wait until one is available before returning.

Beginning with DOS V2, this function retrieves characters from the standard auxiliary device (STDAUX), which defaults to COM1:. Under PC DOS, COM1: has a default initialization of 2400 bps, 8 data bits, no parity, and 1 stop bit. The DOS MODE command may be used to redirect STDAUX, and the data format settings can be changed either with BIOS functions (see Chapter 7, "Serial Devices," and the BIOS reference), or directly at a hardware level. This latter method is beyond the scope of this book.

Unfortunately, there is no access to information about the status of the serial port through this DOS function. You cannot tell whether a character is waiting or has been lost, nor can you set the parameters for the port. This is a major flaw in a system with serial devices. To do anything serious with serial ports, you must go at least to the BIOS level and generally to the hardware level with custom interrupt-handling software to run the port.

Ctrl-C and Ctrl-Break processing is enabled during this function. If either Ctrl-C or Ctrl-Break is detected, Int 23h is executed immediately.

In addition to this function, you can also use Function 3Fh with the predefined handle 03 (STDAUX) to read information from the serial port.

Purpose: Auxiliary Output

DOS Version Availability: 1

Interrupt: 21h

Function: 04h

Description: Outputs a character to the first serial port
(STDAUX beginning with DOS V2)

Calling Registers: AH = 04h
DL = 8-bit data to output to STDAUX

Return Registers: None

Comments: This function is used to send a character out the serial port. Beginning with DOS V2, output is directed to the standard auxiliary device (STDAUX), which defaults to the first serial port. PC DOS initializes COM1: as the default STDAUX at 2400 bps, 8 data bits, no parity, and 1 stop bit. Although other versions of DOS may differ in the default data format, all should default to COM1: as the standard auxiliary device.

If the STDAUX device is not free when output is attempted, this function waits until it is. Thus, "hanging" the computer is relatively easy if this function is invoked while STDAUX is not available. A more useful function would return status information about the status of the serial port. At present, this function is of limited value to the serious programmer. To do anything serious with serial ports, you must go at least to the BIOS level and generally to the hardware level with custom interrupt handling software to run the port.

Fortunately, Ctrl-C and Ctrl-Break processing is enabled during this call. Upon detection of either a Ctrl-C or Ctrl-Break, Int 23h is invoked. By intercepting the Ctrl-Break handler, it may be possible to recover from a "hung" computer which is waiting for a serial port that will never be available. This, however, is unwieldy and cumbersome. It is better (and more user friendly) to program other methods of controlling the serial port.

As with other DOS device control functions, you can send a character out STDAUX by using DOS Function 40h with the predefined handle 03.

Purpose: Printer Output

DOS Version Availability: 1

Interrupt: 21h

Function: 05h

Description: Outputs a character to the printer (STDPRN beginning with DOS V2)

Calling Registers: AH = 05h
DL = 8-bit data to print to STDPRN

Return Registers: None

Comments: This function waits until the printer is ready and then sends a byte. Because no printer status information is returned, the computer could "hang" while waiting for a printer that is not attached to the system or not ready. It is possible to achieve more satisfactory results with the BIOS printer functions (Int 17h) or through DOS Function 40h using the predefined handle 04.

Ctrl-C and Ctrl-Break are detected during this function and will cause the execution of Int 23h.

Purpose: Direct Console I/O

DOS Version Availability: 1

Interrupt: 21h

Function: 06h

Description: Reads and writes the console without processing by
DOS

Calling Registers: AH = 06h
DL = Function requested
00h through 0FEh—character to output
0FFh—input character request

Return Registers: If outputting a character, nothing is returned.

If inputting a character:
Zero flag set (ZF = 1) if no character is
available
Zero flag cleared (ZF = 0) if character is
available
AL = 8-bit data

Comments: This function is unique in that it inputs or outputs characters
depending on the setting of the DL register. Because FFh in the DL register
says "input," this function clearly cannot be used to output an FFh character
—not a major limitation but, in some cases, significant.

If not being able to output all possible ASCII codes is a drawback for your
application, you can accomplish the same type of input and output by using
DOS Functions 3Fh and 40h with predefined handles 01 (STDIN) and 02
(STDOUT).

This function is sometimes referred to as the *raw* I/O function: it reads
characters without echo and ignores Ctrl-C and Ctrl-Break characters, passing them to the program instead of branching to an interrupt handler.
Because they have to interpret all keystrokes, editing, word-processing, and
other programs that need complete keyboard control generally use this
function. (The opposite of raw I/O is *cooked* I/O; these terms come from the
UNIX terminal-handler world where they have specific meanings. See Chapter 12, "Device Drivers," for a discussion of raw and cooked I/O as it relates to
character-oriented device drivers.)

As with Function 01h, the codes returned from the keyboard are ASCII codes,
except when there is no corresponding ASCII code for the key pressed. If this
function returns a zero in AL, calling the function again will return the scan
code corresponding to the key pressed. See Appendix A for extended ASCII
code information.

Purpose: Direct STDIN Input

DOS Version Availability: 1

Interrupt: 21h

Function: 07h

Description: Reads a character from the standard input device
(STDIN) without Ctrl-C intercepting

Calling Registers: AH = 07h

Return Registers: AL = 8-bit input data

Comments: This function handles input similarly to Function 01h, except that the character is not echoed to the video display, and no Ctrl-C or Ctrl-Break handling is supported. On DOS V1 systems, a character is read only from the keyboard. If no character is ready, it waits for one to become available. On DOS V2 and higher, the function reads from the standard input device (STDIN) and thus supports redirection.

When a character is available, its ASCII value is returned. If the character is an extended ASCII character, a zero is returned and another call to this function is required to return the scan code of the key pressed. The extended ASCII codes are detailed in Appendix A.

This function does not echo characters to the display screen, allowing the program to control this function as desired. As with the direct I/O (Function 06h), this function ignores Ctrl-C and Ctrl-Break characters. If Ctrl-C or Ctrl-Break intervention is required, use Function 08h.

Purpose: STDIN Input

DOS Version Availability: 1

Interrupt: 21h

Function: 08h

Description: Reads a character from the standard input device (STDIN)

Calling Registers: AH = 08h

Return Registers: AL = 8-bit input data

Comments: This function handles input like other DOS input functions. It is most similar to Function 07h, except that Ctrl-C and Ctrl-Break interception is supported.

On DOS V1 systems, a character is read only from the keyboard. If no character is ready, one is waited for. On DOS V2 and higher, the function reads from the standard input device (STDIN) and thus supports redirection.

When a character is available, its ASCII value is returned. If the character is an extended ASCII character, a zero is returned and another call to this function is required to return the scan code of the key pressed. The extended ASCII codes are detailed in Appendix A.

This function does not echo characters to the display screen, allowing the program to control this function as desired. If either Ctrl-C or Ctrl-Break are detected, an Int 23h is executed.

Purpose: Display String

DOS Version Availability: 1

Interrupt: 21h

Function: 09h

Description: Outputs a string of characters to the standard
output device (STDOUT)

Calling Registers: AH = 09h
 DS:DX = Pointer to string terminated by a
 dollar sign ($, ASCII code 24h)

Return Registers: None

Comments: Displaying strings of characters on the screen is such a normal operation that it would seem strange if a function were not provided for this purpose. Function 09h allows string output operations by outputting a contiguous series of characters in the same way that Function 02h displays single characters. All characters beginning at the specified address are output until a dollar sign ($, ASCII code 24h) is encountered.

The strings handled by this function are unlike strings handled by any high-level language; they must be terminated by a dollar sign. C functions terminate strings with a NUL character, and Pascal and BASIC strings have a length byte (or word). Because of the choice of string terminator, which is a carryover from CP/M days, you cannot output a dollar sign with this function. This severely limits the usefulness of this function in application programs. Better results generally are achieved by using one of the other DOS output functions to write an efficient string-output routine matched to your high-level language requirements.

Purpose: Buffered STDIN Input

DOS Version Availability: 1

Interrupt: 21h

Function: 0Ah

Description: Reads characters from the standard input device
(STDIN) and places them in a user-specified buffer

Calling Registers: AH = 0Ah
DS:DX = Pointer to input buffer
BYTE 1 = Number of bytes the buffer
can hold
BYTE 2 = Number of bytes read
BYTE 3–? = Returned characters

Return Registers: None

Comments: Buffered STDIN input is a useful, commonly used function that gives you the full power of the normal input functions for keyboard handling. Input is taken from STDIN, which defaults to the keyboard, and is placed in a user-defined buffer area. The keyboard input buffer, which must be specified from the calling program, is set up as follows:

Byte Offset	Contents
0	Maximum number of bytes to read
1	Number of bytes read
2–?	Actual bytes from the keyboard

To use this function, simply store the number of bytes allowed for input in the first byte of the buffer pointed to by DS:DX. Because the buffer size must allow space for a terminating carriage return (ASCII 0Dh), the minimum buffer size is necessarily 1. In use, this would not allow for any actual keyboard input, because the 1 byte set aside for the buffer would be used by the terminating carriage return—not very useful. The realistic minimum buffer size is 2 bytes (1 byte of input plus the carriage return). The maximum buffer size is 255, which is logical because the buffer length specifier is only a single byte.

The function reads in characters from the keyboard and places them in the buffer, beginning with the third byte of the buffer. Each ASCII character requires one byte of buffer space with the exception of extended ASCII characters, which require two spaces—a NUL (ASCII 0) followed by the key's scan code. When the actual number of characters read reaches one less than the size of the buffer, new characters are ignored, and the bell rings with each keystroke. When the Enter key is finally pressed, the number of bytes retrieved and stored is placed in the second byte of the buffer, and control is returned to the calling program.

The input itself allows type ahead, and all keyboard editing commands are active. Ctrl-C and Ctrl-Break functions are active as well, resulting in the execution of Int 23h.

Notice that the size of the string is determined by the value returned in the length byte. This length does not include the terminating carriage return. Because this function stores extended ASCII values, and the first byte of such is set to zero, any strings input in this fashion cannot be used accurately by a high-level language such as C. Because C uses the NUL to mark the end of a string, part of an input string can be lost. Rather, some sort of preprocessing must be done to ensure that the input string is acceptable and complete.

Purpose: Check STDIN Status

DOS Version Availability: 1

Interrupt: 21h

Function: 0Bh

Description: Checks whether a character is available from the standard input device (STDIN)

Calling Registers: AH = 0Bh

Return Registers: AL = 00h, character not available from STDIN
FFh, character available from STDIN

Comments: This function checks whether a character is available from STDIN. Because STDIN normally is set to the keyboard, this function ordinarily is used to determine whether a keystroke is waiting in the keyboard buffer.

When called, this function returns immediately with a status in register AL indicating whether a character is waiting to be read. If a character is available, AL will contain FFh. Notice that the actual character is not returned by this function, which merely provides an indication of availability. This function continues to return the same status on successive calls until one of the DOS input functions (01h, 06h, 07h, 08h, or 0Ah) is used to read the character.

If, during the execution of this function, a Ctrl-C or Ctrl-Break is detected, an Int 23 is invoked.

Purpose: Clear Buffer and Input

DOS Version Availability: 1

Interrupt: 21h

Function: 0Ch

Description: Clears the standard input device (STDIN) buffer and then executes the designated input function call

Calling Registers: AH = 0Ch
                          AL = Function number to perform
                                01h, wait for keyboard input
                                06h, direct console I/O
                                      DL = FFh direct console input
                                      DL<> FFh char to write to STDOUT
                                07h, direct console input without echo
                                08h, console input without echo
                                0Ah, buffered keyboard input
                                      DS:DX = Pointer to input buffer

Return Registers: Return defined by function:
                         01h, wait for keyboard input
                               AL = Character from STDIN
                         06h, direct console I/O
                               ZF = 1, no character available from
                                     STDIN
                               ZF = 0, AL = Character from STDIN
                         07h, direct console input without echo
                               AL = Character from STDIN
                         08h, console input without echo
                               AL = Character from STDIN
                         0Ah, buffered keyboard input

Comments: This function is provided to allow the programmer to prevent type-ahead mistakes, which often arise during program operation. It prevents a user from accidentally typing past critical program input points. A good example might be a program that will format a disk. You want to ask the user whether he or she really wants to format the disk, because starting the operation destroys the disk. Using this function, you can prevent problems caused by accidental type-ahead.

This is an alternative entry point for earlier DOS input functions: 01h, 06h, 07h, 08h, and 0Ah. The only actual operation performed by this function is to clear the input buffer; then control is passed to the DOS input function requested in AL. Return values and programming considerations of each of the available DOS input functions apply when using this function.

Purpose: Reset Disk

DOS Version Availability: 1

Interrupt: 21h

Function: 0Dh

Description: Flushes all disk-buffer contents (if modified) to the appropriate disk files

Calling Registers: AH = 0Dh

Return Registers: None

Comments: This function writes the contents of the disk buffers to their corresponding disk files (flushes the disk buffers). It does not update the disk directory and should not be used in place of a file-close operation. No other disk operations are affected, nor are any other disk parameters reset.

On a 3Com® network, this function forces a new copy of the network volume File Allocation Table (FAT) to be loaded into memory when all files are closed.

Purpose: Select Disk

DOS Version Availability: 1

Interrupt: 21h

Function: 0Eh

Description: Changes the default disk drive

Calling Registers: AH = 0Eh
DL = Drive number (A: = 0 through Z: = 25)

Return Registers: AL = Last drive number (A: = 1 through Z: = 26)

Comments: In addition to selecting the default drive, this function can be used to determine the number of logical drives associated with the system. Logical drives are the number of block-oriented devices installed on the system—ram disks, hard disks, disk emulators, and so forth.

This function always returns a minimum value of 2, indicating the presence of two logical drives (DOS always views a single, physical, floppy disk drive as two logical drives, A: and B:). If you need to determine the number of physical floppy disk drives attached to the system, use BIOS Function 11h.

Beginning with DOS V3, this function returns a minimum last drive value equal to the number of logical drives or the LASTDRIVE value from the CONFIG.SYS file, whichever is greater. If there are only three logical drives and CONFIG.SYS does not specify a LASTDRIVE value, then a minimum last drive value of 5 is returned. This is the default value for LASTDRIVE.

The maximum number of drive designators has varied from one DOS version to another as shown in the following table:

DOS version	Available designators
1	16 (00–0Fh)
2	63 (00–3Fh)
3	26 (00–19h)

To maintain compatibility with all versions of DOS, applications should limit themselves to a maximum of 16 drives (the maximum number allowed for DOS V1).

Notice a peculiarity of this function: the value returned in AL is one-based and represents the number of disk drives attached to the system, but the value used to call the function is zero-based and represents the desired default disk drive. Thus, if you want to set the default drive to the last logical drive, you must complete the following steps:

1. Determine the current default drive (use Function 19h).

2. Call this function with AL set to the current default drive retrieved from Step 1.

3. Decrement the value returned from Step 2 (make it zero-based).

4. Call this function with the derived value from Step 3.

Purpose: Open File (FCB)

DOS Version Availability: 1

Interrupt: 21h

Function: 0Fh

Description: Searches the current directory for the named file. If the named file is found, it is opened, and the File Control Block (FCB) is filled in.

Calling Registers: AH = 0Fh
DS:DX = Pointer to unopened FCB

Return Registers: AL = 00h, file opened successfully
FFh, file not opened

Comments: This function is used to open an existing disk file that uses an FCB. This function will not create a file; that operation is left to Function 16h. Chapter 9, "Directories and Files," deals with files and explains FCBs in more detail. The open function is called after filling in the drive, file name, and extension fields of the FCB.

You should note that the proper drive designations are 0 for the default drive, 1 for A:, 2 for B:, etc. If the function is called with the drive field set for the default drive (0), the field value is automatically changed to the correct drive number so that subsequent calls to the file will not be messed up if the default drive is changed. In addition, the function sets the FCB block field to zero; the record size to 80h (128-character record length); and the file size, date, and time from the requested file's directory entry. If your file operations require the use of a different block number or record size, these values should be changed after this function is completed but before any other FCB file operations.

For applications operating in a network environment, it is important to note that this function automatically opens a file in compatibility mode. If a different mode is required, the handle operations should be used. If a file was created in a different mode and is subsequently opened in compatibility mode (as with this function), a DOS critical error is generated, and Int 24h is executed.

As with other FCB file operations, an error is indicated by the status code returned in the AL register. If AL is 0, no error was detected; if AL is FFh, there was an error during the operation.

Purpose: Close File (FCB)

DOS Version Availability: 1

Interrupt: 21h

Function: 10h

Description: Closes a previously opened file that uses a File
Control Block (FCB)

Calling Registers: AH = 10h
DS:DX = Pointer to opened FCB

Return Registers: AL = 00h, file closed successfully
FFh, file not closed

Comments: This function is used to close a previously opened disk file that uses an FCB. The close function is essential to proper operation in FCB files because there is no other way to force DOS to update the file's directory entry. Without properly closing a file, data may be lost. Chapter 9, "Directories and Files," deals with files and explains FCBs in more detail.

To use the function, you must provide information in the FCB's file-name, extension, and drive-designator fields. If you are working with a previously opened file, all this information should already be in place.

A feature of the close command is that the system checks for the position of the file within the directory. If it is not the same, the system is supposed to assume that the disk has changed, and AL will have an FFh character on return. It has been documented that this function does not work as advertised on DOS V2. It will, in fact, overwrite the File Allocation Table (FAT) and directory, thereby damaging the new disk.

As with other FCB file operations, an error is indicated by the status code returned in the AL register. If AL is 0, no error was detected; if it is FFh, there was an error during the operation.

Purpose: Search for First Entry (FCB)

DOS Version Availability: 1

Interrupt: 21h

Function: 11h

Description: Searches for first matching entry in current directory

Calling Registers: AH = 11h
DS:DX = Pointer to unopened FCB

Return Registers: AL = 00h, match was found
FFh, no match was found

Comments: This function is used to search for the first occurrence of a specified directory entry that uses a File Control Block (FCB). Chapter 9 explains FCBs in detail. This function is powerful and makes it easy to look for files in a consistent way without damaging the directory structure.

To use this function, you must provide the file name, extension, and drive designators in the appropriate FCB fields. Beginning with DOS V2.1, the question mark (?) is supported as a wild-card character in file-name specifications. Asterisks (*) are allowed as wild cards only under DOS V3.

To search for a file with a specific attribute, you must use an extended FCB (see Chapter 9). Valid attributes are derived from the various attribute bit settings and include the following:

Value	*File types matched*
00h	Normal
02h	Normal and hidden
04h	Normal and system
06h	Normal, hidden, and system
08h	Volume labels
10h	Directories

When the function completes successfully, the Disk Transfer Area (DTA) holds an unopened FCB for the file that was found. If the search is called with an extended FCB, the DTA has an extended FCB; otherwise it has a normal FCB. For more information on the DTA, refer to Chapter 9 and Function 1Ah.

As with other FCB file operations, an error is indicated by the status code returned in the AL register. If AL is 0, no error was detected; if AL is FFh, there was an error during the operation.

If you are using wild-card characters to search for files, and no error was returned from this function, you can continue the search for the next matching file by using Function 12h.

Purpose: Search for Next Entry (FCB)

DOS Version Availability: 1

Interrupt: 21h

Function: 12h

Description: Searches for the next matching entry in the current directory

Calling Registers: AH = 12h
DS:DX = Pointer to FCB returned by either Function 11h or 12h

Return Registers: AL = 00h, match was found
FFh, no match was found

Comments: This function, which continues a search begun with Function 11h, can be called as many times as necessary to locate a given file specification within a directory but will search only for the next matching entry, not the first entry. See Function 11h for further information.

Clearly, this function is of value only if the directory entry being searched uses wild-card characters. The File Control Block (FCB) pointed to by DS:DX should be the same FCB pointed to when Function 11h was called. Again, see the Function 11h comments for more information.

When this function completes successfully, the Disk Transfer Area (DTA) holds an unopened FCB for the file that was found. If the search was originally initiated with an extended FCB, the DTA will have an extended FCB; otherwise, it will have a normal FCB. For more information on the DTA, refer to Chapter 9, "Directories and Files," and Function 1Ah.

As with other FCB file operations, an error is indicated by the status code returned in the AL register. If AL is 0, no error was detected; if AL is FFh, there was an error during the operation.

If you are using wild-card characters to search for files, and no error was returned from this function, you can continue the search for the next matching file by using this function again.

Purpose: Delete File (FCB)

DOS Version Availability: 1

Interrupt: 21h

Function: 13h

Description: Deletes all allowable directory entries that match
the file specifications provided

Calling Registers: AH = 13h
DS:DX = Pointer to an unopened FCB

Return Registers: AL = 00h, file was deleted
FFh, file was not deleted

Comments: This function is used to delete files that use a File Control Block
(FCB). Chapter 9, "Directories and Files," deals with files and explains FCBs
in more detail. Only normal files can be deleted. Read-only files, system files,
hidden files, volume labels, or directories cannot be deleted with this
function.

To use this function, you must provide the file name, extension, and drive
designators in the appropriate FCB fields. Beginning with DOS V2.1, the
question mark (?) is supported as a wild-card character in file-name specifications. Asterisks (*) are allowed as wild cards only if you are running under
DOS V3.

Files deleted with this function are not cleared from the disk. The directory
entry is modified to indicate that the file has been deleted and that the
directory entry is available for use; the data clusters previously used by the file
are made available to other files. The data that was contained within the file is
left untouched and may be recovered with special file-recovery programs,
such as the Norton Utilities™.

As with other FCB file operations, an error is indicated by the status code
returned in the AL register. If AL is 0, no error was detected; if AL is FFh, there
was an error during the operation. Possible causes for error include trying to
delete an illegal file or not finding the specified file name.

Do not try to delete an open file. This can cause problems later when you try
to close the file or during program termination when DOS attempts to flush
the disk buffer to the deleted file. Files must be closed before you delete them.

In a network environment, you must have create-access rights in order to
delete files.

Purpose: Read Sequential File (FCB)

DOS Version Availability: 1

Interrupt: 21h

Function: 14h

Description: Beginning at the file pointer's current location, reads the next block of data and updates the file pointer

Calling Registers: AH = 14h
DS:DX = Pointer to an opened FCB

Return Registers: AL = 00h, read was successful
01h, no read, already at EOF
02h, read canceled, DTA boundary error
03h, partial read, now at EOF

Comments: This function facilitates the sequential reading of information from a disk file using a File Control Block (FCB). You can read information only from a file that has been previously opened (Function 0Fh). Chapter 9, "Directories and Files," deals with files and explains FCBs in more detail.

To use this function, you should ensure that DS:DX points to an FCB created after a file was opened successfully. Sequential reads are controlled by the parameters set in the FCB. The length of the read is given in the record-size field. The location is given by the current block number and the current record number. Before issuing this function, you can change the values of these FCB fields to values appropriate for your application.

When the read is completed, the information read from the disk is placed in the Disk Transfer Area (DTA), and the record address in the FCB is automatically incremented. For more information on the DTA, refer to Chapter 9 and Function 1Ah.

Because the information read from the disk is placed in the DTA, be sure that the DTA is large enough to receive the information. Otherwise, information from the disk could overwrite other data.

As with other FCB file operations, an error is indicated by the status code returned in the AL register. If AL is 0, no error was detected; any other value denotes an error during the operation. If the amount of data read by this function results in crossing a memory segment boundary in the DTA (a memory address ending in 000), a failure is indicated with AL = 2. Partial records (AL = 3) are read and padded with zero characters to the end.

In a network environment, you must have read-access rights in order to use this function.

Purpose: Write Sequential File (FCB)

DOS Version Availability: 1

Interrupt: 21h

Function: 15h

Description: Writes the record to the current block and record
locations from the File Control Block (FCB)

Calling Registers: AH = 15h
DS:DX = Pointer to an opened FCB

Return Registers: AL = 00h, write was successful
01h, no write attempted, disk full or
read-only file
02h, write canceled, DTA boundary error

Comments: This function facilitates the sequential writing of data to a disk
file using an FCB. You can write data only to a previously opened (Function
0Fh) or created (Function 16h) file. Chapter 9, "Directories and Files," deals
with files and explains FCBs in more detail.

To use this function, you should ensure that DS:DX points to an FCB created
after a file was opened or created successfully. The parameters set in the FCB
control sequential writes. The length of the write is given in the record-size
field. The location is given by the current block number and the current
record number. Before issuing this function, you can change the values of
these FCB fields to values appropriate for your application.

Because information written to disk comes from the Disk Transfer Area
(DTA), take care that the record size being written is the amount of data you
want. Otherwise, other data (garbage) could be written inadvertently to the
disk file. For more information on the DTA, refer to Chapter 9 and Function
1Ah.

If the amount of data being written does not fill the entire DOS disk buffer
(internal to DOS), the data simply is added to that already in the disk buffer
pending a need to write it to the disk. When this function is completed
successfully, the record address in the FCB is updated automatically.

As with other FCB file operations, an error is indicated by the status code
returned in the AL register. If AL is 0, no error was detected; any other value
denotes an error during the operation. If the disk is full or you try to write to a
read-only file, AL is equal to 1. If a memory-segment boundary in the DTA (a
memory address ending in 000) is crossed during a write operation, the
function will fail and return AL = 2.

In a network environment, you must have write-access rights in order to use
this function.

Purpose: Create File (FCB)

DOS Version Availability: 1

Interrupt: 21h

Function: 16h

Description: Creates a disk file based on the information
provided in the File Control Block (FCB)

Calling Registers: AH = 16h
DS:DX = Pointer to an unopened FCB

Return Registers: AL = 00h, file was created
FFh, file was not created

Comments: This function serves as a complement to opening a file (Function 0Fh). It creates the specified file and leaves it open for subsequent use with an FCB. Chapter 9, "Directories and Files," deals with files and explains FCBs in more detail.

Why not use this function all the time? Because file creation also truncates files that already exist—without warning! First, the function searches the current directory for the specified file. If the file is found, it is truncated and the FCB is updated; the file is open as if it were newly created. If the file doesn't exist, it is created, and the FCB is set for access to the new file.

To use this function, the FCB's drive, file-name, and extension fields must be provided. When you use an extended FCB, you also can assign an attribute to create a hidden file or a volume label. For information on file attributes, refer to Chapter 9.

As with other FCB file operations, an error is indicated by the status code returned in the AL register. If AL is 0, no error was detected; if AL is FFh, there was an error during the operation.

In a network environment, you must have create-access rights in order to use this function.

Purpose: Rename File (FCB)

DOS Version Availability: 1

Interrupt: 21h

Function: 17h

Description: Renames an existing file

Calling Registers: AH = 17h
DS:DX = Pointer to a modified FCB

Return Registers: AL = 00h, file was renamed
FFh, file was not renamed

Comments: This function allows you to change the name of existing disk files using a modified File Control Block (FCB). Only normal files can be renamed; thus read-only files, system files, hidden files, volume labels, or directories cannot be renamed with this function.

This function uses a modified FCB with the following format:

Offset	Meaning
00h	Drive designation
01h	Original file name
09h	Original file extension
11h	New file name
19h	New file extension

Notice that basically only three pieces of information are required: a drive designator (all renaming must occur on the same drive), and the old and new file names. Beginning with DOS V2.1, the question mark (?) is supported as a wild-card character in file-name specifications. Only under DOS V3 are asterisks (*) allowed as wild cards. Putting wild cards in the original file name causes the function to try to rename each file that matches the pattern. Putting wild cards in the new file name causes those character positions to remain unchanged in the new file.

Because file names in any given directory must be unique, this function will stop and return an error if it is ever asked to rename a file to a name that already exists. Through effective use of wild-card matching, you can build a sophisticated, multifile renamer. For example, suppose that you have a series of files named ABC01.DAT, ABC02.DAT, ABC03.DAT, etc., and that you want to rename them with the extension .OLD. If you choose the original file name ABC??.DAT and the new file name *.OLD, the rename process will proceed smoothly.

As with other FCB file operations, an error is indicated by the status code returned in the AL register. If AL is 0, no error was detected; if AL is FFh, there was an error during the operation.

In a network environment, you must have create-access rights in order to use this function.

Purpose: Get Default Drive

DOS Version Availability: 1

Interrupt: 21h

Function: 19h

Description: Returns the number of the current default drive

Calling Registers: AH = 19h

Return Registers: AL = Current drive number (A: = 0– Z: = 25)

Comments: This function is used to determine which disk drive DOS is using as the default drive. A number, representing the default drive, is returned in the AL register. The number is zero-based, with 0 for drive A:, 1 for drive B:, etc. This is a little different from other functions where a 0 may be used to specify the default drive. This function is related to Function 0Eh, which is used to set the default drive.

Purpose: Set DTA Address

DOS Version Availability: 1

Interrupt: 21h

Function: 1Ah

Description: Establishes an address that DOS will use as the beginning of the Disk Transfer Area (DTA)

Calling Registers: AH = 1Ah
DS:DX = Pointer to a new DTA

Return Registers: None

Comments: This function is used to specify a DTA to be used by DOS for disk operations. The DTA is used by many of the DOS functions, most notably the File Control Block (FCB) file functions. The handle functions used for file searching (Functions 4Eh and 4Fh) and Int 25 and Int 26 also use the DTA. When a program is started, a default DTA of 128 bytes is set aside at offset 80h in the Program Segment Prefix (PSP). The converse of this function is Function 2Fh, which is used to get the current DTA address.

The programmer is responsible for seeing that the DTA used for disk operations is adequate for the tasks undertaken. Because DOS keeps track only of the DTA's beginning address, the system has no way of knowing whether it has reached the end of the DTA during disk operations. The upshot is that program data or code can easily be overwritten by information transferred from the disk if the amount of data being transferred is more than the DTA can hold.

Purpose: Get Allocation Table Information

DOS Version Availability: 1

Interrupt: 21h

Function: 1Bh

Description: Gets basic information about disk allocation for the
disk in the default drive

Calling Registers: AH = 1Bh

Return Registers: AL = Sectors per cluster
CX = Bytes per physical sector
DX = Clusters per disk
DS:BX = Pointer to media descriptor byte

Comments: This function returns the information basic to a knowledge of
the capacity of the disk in the default drive. The information itself is seldom
used as much as the combination of CX*AL*DX, which gives the disk's total
capacity (in bytes). Function 1Ch returns identical information for a disk in a
specific drive, and Function 36h is used to determine the amount of free
space on a disk.

Beginning with DOS V2, DS:BX points to the media descriptor byte, contained within the File Allocation Table (FAT), but on DOS V1 it actually
points to the FAT in memory. The media descriptor (or FAT ID) byte can be
used to identify the media's formatting from the following table:

Value	Meaning
F0h	Not identifiable
F8h	Fixed disk
F9h	Double sided, 15 sectors per track (1.2M)
F9h	Double sided, 9 sectors per track (720K)
FCh	Single sided, 9 sectors per track
FDh	Double sided, 9 sectors per track (360K)
FEh	Single sided, 8 sectors per track
FFh	Double sided, 8 sectors per track

Notice that an FAT ID byte of F9h lets you know only that the disk was
formatted in a high-capacity disk drive. You must examine the other information returned by this function to determine the disk's actual capacity.
Furthermore, FAT IDs are not supported uniformly by all versions of DOS. The
standard as given is from the PC DOS technical manual and may not apply to a
particular manufacturer's version of DOS.

Purpose: Get Allocation Table Information for Specific Drive

DOS Version Availability: 2

Interrupt: 21h

Function: 1Ch

Description: Gets the basic information about disk allocation for the disk in a specified drive

Calling Registers: AH = 1Ch
DL = Drive number
Current drive = 0
(A: = 1 through Z: = 26)

Return Registers: AL = Sectors per cluster
CX = Bytes per physical sector
DX = Clusters per disk
DS:BX = Pointer to media descriptor byte

Comments: This function returns the information basic to a knowledge of the capacity of the disk in a specific drive. The information itself is seldom used as much as the combination of CX*AL*DX, which gives the disk's total capacity (in bytes). Function 1Bh returns identical information for a disk in the default drive, and Function 36h is used to determine the amount of free space on a disk.

Beginning with DOS V2, DS:BX points to the media descriptor byte contained within the File Allocation Table (FAT), but on DOS V1 DS:BX actually points to the FAT in memory. The media descriptor (or FAT ID) byte can be used to identify the media's format from the following table:

Value	Meaning
F0h	Not identifiable
F8h	Fixed disk
F9h	Double sided, 15 sectors per track (1.2M)
F9h	Double sided, 9 sectors per track (720K)
FCh	Single sided, 9 sectors per track
FDh	Double sided, 9 sectors per track (360K)
FEh	Single sided, 8 sectors per track
FFh	Double sided, 8 sectors per track

Notice that an FAT ID byte of F9h lets you know only that the disk was formatted in a high-capacity disk drive. You must examine the other information returned by this function to determine the disk's actual capacity. Furthermore, FAT IDs are not uniformly supported by all versions of DOS. The standard as given is from the PC DOS technical manual and may not apply to a particular manufacturer's implementation of DOS.

Purpose: Get Default Disk Parameter Block

DOS Version Availability: 2

Interrupt: 21h

Function: 1Fh

Description: Returns the address of the disk parameter block for the default drive

Calling Registers: AH = 1Fh

Return Registers: AL = 00h, no error
FFh, error
DS:BX = Address of drive parameter block

Comments: Microsoft and IBM officially specify this function as reserved. The description given here is derived from nonofficial technical information and thus is not to be construed as the function's official or permanent use. Its use, as documented here, may be changed in future versions of DOS. In fact, if your version of DOS is from a third-party vendor, this function may be used for an entirely different purpose. The information presented here is intended as a guide, and you should explore the function at your own leisure and risk.

Use this function to return the address of the disk parameter block used by DOS to determine specific structural information about the disk in the default drive. It returns, in DS:BX, the address shown in table DOS.5.

The purpose of each item in the table should be self-explanatory. One exception is the byte at offset 05h. Available information does not indicate the exact purpose of this piece of data, but it appears to be a code for the cluster size. Also, notice that the fields beginning at offsets 1Ch and 1Eh are for DOS V2 only. The purpose of these fields is unknown for DOS V1 and V3.

Because this function returns a value in the DS register, you should save the value of DS before you call the function.

Table DOS.5. *Drive Parameter Block*

Offset Byte	Field Length	Meaning
00h	Byte	Drive number (0 = A:, 1 = B:, etc.)
01h	Byte	Device driver unit number
02h	Word	Bytes per sector
04h	Byte	Sectors per cluster (zero based)
05h	Byte	Shift factor
06h	Word	Number of reserved boot sectors
08h	Byte	Number of FAT copies
09h	Word	Number of root directory entries
0Bh	Word	First data sector number
0Dh	Word	Highest cluster number plus 1
0Fh	Byte	Sectors per FAT
10h	Word	Root directory starting sector number
12h	Double word	Drive's device driver address
16h	Byte	Media descriptor byte
17h	Byte	Disk parameter block validity byte (0FFh indicates need to rebuild)
18h	Double word	Address of next device parameter block
1Ch	Word	Starting cluster number for current directory (DOS V2 only)
1Eh	64 bytes	ASCIIZ of current directory path (DOS V2 only)

Purpose: Random File Read (FCB)

DOS Version Availability: 1

Interrupt: 21h

Function: 21h

Description: Reads a specified record from a disk file, placing the information in the Disk Transfer Area (DTA)

Calling Registers: AH = 21h
DS:DX = Pointer to open FCB

Return Registers: AL = 00h, read was successful
01h, no read, EOF encountered
02h, read canceled, DTA boundary error
03h, partial record read, EOF encountered

Comments: This function facilitates the reading of random (nonsequential) information from a disk file with a File Control Block (FCB). Chapter 9, "Directories and Files," deals with files and explains FCBs in more detail. You can read information only from a file that has been previously opened (Function 0Fh).

To use this function, be sure that DS:DX points to an FCB created after a file was opened successfully. Random reads are controlled by parameters set in the FCB. The record to read is specified in the FCB by setting the random-record field, and the amount of data is controlled by the record-size field. Before issuing this function, you can change the values of these FCB fields to values appropriate for your application. DOS uses these two values to calculate the actual file position at which reading is begun.

When this function is completed, the information read from the disk is in the DTA. For more information on the DTA, refer to Chapter 9, "Directories and Files," and Function 1Ah. The FCB current position field is not updated by this function as it is with sequential functions. Unless the random record field is changed, subsequent accesses of the file return the same data.

Because information read from the disk is placed in the DTA, take care that the DTA is large enough to receive the data. Otherwise, information from the disk may overwrite other data.

As with other FCB file operations, an error is indicated by the status code returned in the AL register. If AL is 0, no error was detected; any other value denotes an error during the operation. If the amount of data read by this function results in crossing a memory segment boundary in the DTA (a memory address ending in 000), the function fails and returns AL = 2. Partial records (AL = 3) are read and padded with zero characters to the end.

In a network environment, you must have read-access rights in order to use this function.

Purpose: Random File Write (FCB)

DOS Version Availability: 1

Interrupt: 21h

Function: 22h

Description: Writes a specified record to a disk file, transferring the information from the Disk Transfer Area (DTA)

Calling Registers: AH = 22h
DS:DX = Pointer to open FCB

Return Registers: AL = 00h, write was successful
01h, no write attempted, disk full or read-only file
02h, write canceled, DTA boundary error

Comments: This function facilitates the writing of random (nonsequential) information to a disk file that uses a File Control Block (FCB). You can write information only to a previously opened (Function 0Fh) or created (Function 16h) file. Chapter 9, "Directories and Files," deals with files and explains FCBs in more detail.

To use this function, make sure that DS:DX points to an FCB created after a file is opened or created successfully. Parameters set in the FCB control random writes. The record to write is specified in the FCB by setting the random-record field; the amount of data is controlled by the record-size field. Before issuing this function, you can change the values of these FCB fields to values appropriate for your application. DOS uses these values to calculate the file position at which writing begins.

Because the information written to disk comes from the DTA, you must be careful that the record size being written is the amount of data you want. Otherwise, other data (garbage) could inadvertently be written to the disk file. For more information on the DTA, refer to Chapter 9 and Function 1Ah.

If the data being written does not fill the entire DOS disk buffer (internal to DOS), it is added to the data already in the disk buffer, pending a need to write it to the disk.

Unlike sequential functions, this function does not update the FCB current position field. Subsequent random writing to the file will transfer information to the same file record unless the random-record field is changed.

As with other FCB file operations, an error is indicated by the status code returned in the AL register. If AL is 0, no error was detected; any other value denotes an error during the operation. If the disk was full or if you attempted to write to a read-only file, AL is equal to 1. If, during a write operation, a memory segment boundary in the DTA (a memory address ending in 000) is crossed, the function fails and returns AL = 2.

In a network environment, you must have write-access rights in order to use this function.

Purpose: Get File Size (FCB)

DOS Version Availability: 1

Interrupt: 21h

Function: 23h

Description: Searches a directory for a matching file name; if the file is found, fills in the size information in the designated File Control Block (FCB)

Calling Registers: AH = 23h
DS:DX = Pointer to unopened FCB

Return Registers: AL = 00h, matching file found
FFh, no matching file found

Comments: This function is used to determine the number of records in a specified file through the use of an FCB. Chapter 9, "Directories and Files," deals with files and explains FCBs in more detail. The file should be unopened when using this function.

This function can be used after filling in the drive, file-name, extension, and record-size fields of the FCB. The supplied file name must be complete and unique; wild-card characters are not allowed. To find the size of the file in bytes, simply set the record-size field to 1.

If a file is located that matches the specified file name, the random-record field of the FCB pointed to by DS:DX is updated to indicate the number of records in the file. This number is determined by dividing the file size (in bytes) by the record size, resulting in the number of records. If there is any remainder from the division, the number of records is rounded up. If you forget to set the record-size field before calling this function, or for files in which the file-size portion of the directory entry may be incorrect or rounded to reflect a full sector, the information returned by this function may be of questionable value.

As with other FCB file operations, an error is indicated by the status code returned in the AL register. If AL is 0, no error was detected; if AL is FFh, an error occurred during the operation (generally, this means that the specified file was not found).

Purpose: Set Random Record Field (FCB)

DOS Version Availability: 1

Interrupt: 21h

Function: 24h

Description: When switching from sequential to random file I/O, used to set the File Control Block (FCB) random-record field based upon the current file position

Calling Registers: AH = 24h
DS:DX = Pointer to open FCB

Return Registers: None

Comments: This function modifies an open FCB to prepare it for random access functions. This function can be used after filling in the record-size, record-number, and block-number fields of the FCB. The function modifies the random-record field based on these field values. Chapter 9, "Directories and Files," deals with files and explains FCBs in more detail.

Purpose: Set Interrupt Vector

DOS Version Availability: 1

Interrupt: 21h

Function: 25h

Description: Safely modifies an interrupt vector to point to a specified interrupt handler

Calling Registers: AH = 25h
AL = Interrupt number
DS:DX = Pointer to interrupt handler

Return Registers: None

Comments: This function makes quick work of what can otherwise be a delicate operation—changing interrupt vectors. Because interrupt vectors are maintained in a table in low memory (see Chapter 11, "Interrupt Handlers"), they could easily be changed directly. This can be dangerous, however, if an interrupt occurs during the process—particularly while only a portion of the address has been transferred to the table.

Rather than write your own code to safely manage setting interrupts, DOS has provided this function, which guarantees to safely update the interrupt vector table to an address you supply. This is the only approved method of altering interrupt vectors.

Changing interrupt vectors can lead to some special problems. Interrupts 22h, 23h, and 24h are reset automatically to their original values when a program terminates in a normal manner (see Int 20h, Int 27h, and functions 00h, 31h, and 4Ch). If the program modifies any other interrupt vectors, these will remain at their changed values, even after the program terminates. This can cause problems; an interrupt condition that occurs after the program has terminated could cause a jump to a nonexistent interrupt handler.

In order to prevent such a situation, programs that change the interrupt vectors should first use Function 35h to get the original vector value and store it. The original vector value can be restored when the program ends. This has even greater implications for programs that change interrupt vectors. A program that changes vectors to interrupts other than 22h, 23h, or 24h must also be able to trap all the ways in which the program could be terminated abnormally. This means Ctrl-C/Ctrl-Break interrupt servicing, DOS critical-error servicing, and servicing for any other potential interrupt that might cause the program to terminate, such as dividing by zero.

If the program does not intercept any and all methods that might terminate it, hanging interrupt vectors could remain. If a program crashes without being able to reset the interrupt vectors, the only safe course is to reset the system before you do anything else.

Purpose: Create PSP

DOS Version Availability: 1

Interrupt: 21h

Function: 26h

Description: Copies the Program Segment Prefix (PSP) from the currently executing program to the specified segment address and then updates it for use by a new program.

Calling Registers: AH = 26h
DX = Segment address for new PSP

Return Registers: None

Comments: This function creates a PSP preparatory to running another program. A copy is made of the current program's PSP at the specified memory segment address. The PSP is covered in detail in Chapter 3, "The Dynamics of DOS."

In theory, you could copy a .COM file directly into the memory space after the new PSP and execute the program, but in actuality it would not be a good practice for the simple reason that this function is out of date. It has been superseded by the more sophisticated and much easier to use EXEC function (Function 4Bh). All Microsoft and IBM documentation recommends using the EXEC function in preference to Function 26h when spawning programs. EXEC better handles the details of program loading and execution and insulates the program from potential errors in operation. This function does not load or execute another program, it simply prepares a PSP for one. The function invoking the program must still load and execute the program.

If your program has changed the interrupt vectors for Int 22h, 23h, and 24h, the new vectors are copied into the newly created PSP. In addition, the memory allocation information is updated appropriately.

Purpose: Random Block Read (FCB)

DOS Version Availability: 1

Interrupt: 21h

Function: 27h

Description: Reads one or more consecutive random records from a disk file to the Disk Transfer Area (DTA)

Calling Registers: AH = 27h
CX = Number of records to read
DS:DX = Pointer to opened FCB

Return Registers: AL = 00h, all records read successfully
01h, no read, EOF encountered
02h, read canceled, DTA boundary error
03h, partial record read, EOF encountered
CX = Number of records read

Comments: This function facilitates the reading of a group of consecutive random records from a disk file using a File Control Block (FCB). You can read information only from a file that has been previously opened (Function 0Fh). Chapter 9, "Directories and Files," deals with files and explains FCBs in more detail.

To use this function, make sure that CX contains the number of records you want and that DS:DX points to an FCB created after a file was opened successfully. Parameters set in the FCB control random reads. The beginning record to read is specified in the FCB by setting the random-record field, and the size of each record is controlled by the record-size field. Before issuing this function, you can change the values of these FCB fields to values appropriate for your application. DOS uses these values to calculate the file position at which reading begins.

When this function is completed, the information read from the disk is in the DTA. (For more information on the DTA, refer to Chapter 9 and Function 1Ah.) When the function is successfully completed, the random record, current block, and current record fields of the FCB are updated.

Because the information read from the disk is placed in the DTA, you must be careful that the DTA is large enough to receive the total block of information. Otherwise, other data or program code could be overwritten with information from the disk.

As with other FCB file operations, an error is indicated by the status code returned in the AL register. If AL is 0, no error was detected; any other value denotes an error during the operation. If the amount of data being read by this function results in crossing a memory segment boundary in the DTA (a memory address ending in 000), the function will fail and return AL = 2. Partial records (AL = 3) are read and padded to the end with zero characters.

In a network environment, you must have read-access rights in order to use this function.

Purpose: Random Block Write (FCB)

DOS Version Availability: 1

Interrupt: 21h

Function: 28h

Description: Writes one or more consecutive random records to a disk file from the Disk Transfer Area (DTA)

Calling Registers: AH = 28h
CX = Number of records to write
DS:DX = Pointer to opened FCB

Return Registers: AL = 00h, all records successfully written
01h, no write attempted, disk full or read-only file
02h, write canceled, DTA boundary error
CX = Number of records written

Comments: This function facilitates the writing of a group of consecutive random records to a disk file using a File Control Block (FCB). You can write information only to a previously opened (Function 0Fh) or created (Function 16h) file. Chapter 9, "Directories and Files," deals with files and explains FCBs in more detail.

To use this function, make sure that CX contains the number of records to write and that DS:DX points to an FCB created after a file was successfully opened or created. Parameters set in the FCB control random writes. The beginning record to write is specified in the FCB by setting the random-record field, and the size of each record is controlled by the record-size field. Before issuing this function, you can change the values of these FCB fields to values appropriate for your application. DOS uses these values to calculate the file position at which reading begins.

Because the information written to disk comes from the DTA, you must be careful that the record size and number of records being written correspond to the amount of data you want. Otherwise, other data (garbage) could inadvertently be written to the disk file. For more information on the DTA, refer to Chapter 9 and Function 1Ah.

If the amount of data being written does not fill the entire DOS disk buffer (internal to DOS), the data is simply added to that already in the disk buffer pending a need to write it to the disk.

When the function has been completed successfully, the FCB's random-record, current-block, and current-record fields are updated.

As with other FCB file operations, an error is indicated by the status code returned in the AL register. If AL is 0, no error was detected; any other value denotes an error during the operation. If the disk was full or if you attempted to write to a read-only file, AL is equal to 1. During a write operation, if a memory segment boundary in the DTA (a memory address ending in 000) is crossed, the function fails and returns AL = 2.

In a network environment, you must have write-access rights in order to use this function.

Purpose: Parse File Name

DOS Version Availability: 1

Interrupt: 21h

Function: 29h

Description: Parses a file-name string into a File Control Block (FCB) for use. Separator characters in all versions are the period (.), the comma (,), the colon (:), the semicolon (;), the equal sign (=), the plus sign (+), Tab, and space. In DOS V1, the following additional characters serve as separators: the double quotation mark ("), the slash (/), the left bracket ([), and the right bracket (]).

Calling Registers: AH = 29h
AL = Parse control flag (see table DOS.6)
DS:SI = Pointer to text string
ES:DI = Pointer to FCB

Return Registers: AL = 00h, no wild cards encountered
01h, wild cards found
FFh, drive specifier invalid
DS:SI = Pointer to the first character after the parsed file name
ES:DI = Pointer to the updated, unopened FCB

Comments: Originally, the purpose of this function was to extract file names from command lines and place them in proper format for opening an FCB. To do so, you start with the pointer to the file-name string and a pointer to the FCB you plan to use. This FCB does not have to be in any sort of format—it can be a block of memory sufficient to hold an FCB.

The function returns a proper, unopened FCB for the desired file and a pointer to the first characters after the file name (clearly useful if you are parsing a command line within which the file name is one of several). Asterisk characters are converted automatically into one or more question-mark characters to the end of the file name or extension in this function.

Because this is an FCB function, it is not compatible with path names; therefore you cannot include directories in file names. This function can refer only to files in the current directory. The interpretation of the file name is controlled by a *parse flag* shown in table DOS.6.

Table DOS.6. *Parse Control Flag*

Bit 76543210	Meaning
. . . . Ø	Do not ignore leading separators.
. . . . 1	Ignore leading separators.
. . . . . . Ø .	Drive ID is modified whether specified or not. If not specified, drive ID defaults to 0.
. . . . . . 1 .	Drive ID is modified only if specified.
. . . . . Ø . .	File name is modified whether specified or not. If not specified, file name is set to BLANK.
. . . . . 1 . .	File name is modified only if specified.
. . . . Ø . . .	Extension field is modified. If string contains no extension, field is set to BLANK.
. . . . 1 . . .	Extension field in FCB is modified only if an extension is specified in the string.

When you work with FCB functions, this function is useful for setting up the FCB properly. This function results in a properly formatted FCB, ready to be opened. In order to use the FCB open or create functions, the pointer in ES: must be moved to DS:DX.

If there is no valid file name to parse, the function returns the pointer ES:DI so that ES:DI +1 points to a blank character.

Purpose: Get System Date

DOS Version Availability: 1

Interrupt: 21h

Function: 2Ah

Description: Gets the year, month, day, and day of the week from the system

Calling Registers: AH = 2Ah

Return Registers: CX = Year (1980-2099)
   DH = Month (1-12)
   DL = Day (1-31)
   AL = Day of week (0 = Sunday, 1 = Monday, etc.) DOS V1.1 or later

Comments: This function returns information about DOS's understanding of the current system date. This is simply a check of the DOS internal clock, not an access to a real-time clock/calendar if one is installed. As a general rule, if the system has an installed clock/calendar it is checked from the AUTOEXEC.BAT file when the system is started, or it is set manually by an operator.

Systems that run for days at a time can drift from accurate time in unexpected ways. System date or time may not be properly updated, or processes may interfere with or change the internal system time. This function might therefore return an incorrect date (but without access to a clock/calendar chip, you cannot check it).

The function uses the same register format as Function 2Bh (set system date) for ease of use.

Purpose: Set System Date

DOS Version Availability: 1

Interrupt: 21h

Function: 2Bh

Description: Sets the system date to the specified value without affecting the system time

Calling Registers: AH = 2Bh
CX = Year (1980–2099)
DH = Month (1–12)
DL = Day (1–31)

Return Registers: AL = 00h, date set successfully
FFh, date invalid, not set

Comments: This function uses the same register format as the get-date function. If you have a clock/calendar, you can access it to get the current date and update the system date using this function. Without a clock/calendar, you could prompt the user for input and then correct it in the operating system so that calls to the get-date function return the correct date.

The date set with this function is used to mark files during file operations.

If your computer system has a CMOS clock, this function causes its date to be set.

Purpose: Get System Time

DOS Version Availability: 1

Interrupt: 21h

Function: 2Ch

Description: Gets the system time in hours, minutes, seconds, and hundredths of seconds

Calling Registers: AH = 2Ch

Return Registers: CH = Hour (0–23)
CL = Minutes (0–59)
DH = Seconds (0–59)
DL = Hundredths of seconds (0–99)

Comments: Like getting the system date, getting the system time is a clearly useful function that we do not pay much attention to. You frequently need this information for reports or screen displays. However, you need to be aware of the following points:

1. This function does not retrieve time from a clock/calendar chip. It gets the DOS internal time, which is only as accurate as its setting.

2. On many systems, the system's real-time clock is not accurate enough to provide hundredths of a second resolution. In such a situation, the function could return a discontinuous time value for the hundredths of a second value.

Applications that use the time function for other than actual system time do not need to worry about the time setting. An application such as a timer that is started by setting the DOS time to zero and then checking elapsed time could be useful in some programs. If you write such a program, however, be aware that other programs expect to get the time of day from this clock. If you use it for elapsed time by setting it to zero and then leave it, the person using your program will be upset when other programs return the wrong system time.

The register format is the same as that used for Function 2Dh (set system time).

Purpose: Set System Time

DOS Version Availability: 1

Interrupt: 21h

Function: 2Dh

Description: Sets the system time to the specified hour, minute, second, and hundredth of a second without affecting the system date

Calling Registers: AH = 2Dh
CH = Hour (0–23)
CL = Minutes (0–59)
DH = Seconds (0–59)
DL = Hundredths of seconds (0–99)

Return Registers: AL = 00h, time set successfully
FFh, time invalid, not set

Comments: Setting the system time can be useful in a number of cases:

❏ Your program works with a clock/calendar and can set the date and time exactly from the chip.

❏ Your program queries the user for a time to set.

❏ You are using the clock as an elapsed time clock; you can reset it to zero and display or monitor it in terms of elapsed time instead of system time.

The register format, which is the same as that used for Function 2Ch (get time), allows you to get the time, ask about it, and then update only what has changed. In practical time setting, it is often best to set to an accuracy of no greater than plus or minus one second when working with a person. Trying to set hundredths of a second goes beyond what the typical user wants. Time setting to greater accuracy (for applications in astronomy, for example) requires special synchronizing techniques.

Programs working from a clock/calendar chip or from a time service, such as a WWV radio link, can set the time to hundredth-of-a-second accuracy. Some computers are unable to return this accuracy on a consistent basis because the real-time clock is not accurate enough.

If your computer system has a CMOS clock, this function will cause its time to be set.

Purpose: Set Verify Flag

DOS Version Availability: 1

Interrupt: 21h

Function: 2Eh

Description: Toggles the DOS read-after-write verify flag. Turning it on increases security when writing to disk and increases disk transfer time.

Calling Registers: AH = 2Eh
AL = 00h, turn off verify
01h, turn on verify
DH = 00h (DOS version earlier than 3.0)

Return Registers: None

Comments: How could you *not* want to verify your disk writes to make sure they are correct? It sounds like going against motherhood. But forcing a disk read-after-write verify of all data written to a disk increases by a factor of 2 the time needed to do the operation. On some non-IBM BIOS variants, the operation is not supported at all.

So why not do it? Time, obviously. When you do not need absolute assurance that every disk write is correct, leaving the verify flag off makes sense. Only for truly critical functions should you bother to set the flag, and then it should be turned off afterward.

Function 54h can be used to determine the current setting of the verify flag.

Purpose: Get DTA Address

DOS Version Availability: 2

Interrupt: 21h

Function: 2Fh

Description: Gets the current value of the Disk Transfer Area (DTA) pointer for File Control Block (FCB) file operations

Calling Registers: AH = 2Fh

Return Registers: ES:BX = Pointer to DTA

Comments: The default DTA is a 128-byte buffer at offset 80h in the Program Segment Prefix (PSP). Most programs do not need more than this for their operations. If you are working with larger record sizes or have special disk transfer requirements, however, setting up another DTA is useful.

Function 1Ah sets the DTA; this function (2Fh) tells you where it is. What this function does not tell you, however, (and the information is essential) is *how large the DTA is!* If you are not sure whether the DTA is big enough for what you are doing, you have no choice but to set it yourself to a block of memory big enough to handle the expected operations.

Purpose: Get DOS Version Number

DOS Version Availability: 2

Interrupt: 21h

Function: 30h

Description: Returns the DOS version number for reference so that an application can determine the capabilities of the software system. DOS versions earlier than 2.0 should return a version number of zero.

Calling Registers: AH = 30h

Return Registers: AL = Major version number (2, 3)
AH = Minor version number (2.1 = 10)
BX = 00h
CX = 00h

Comments: The DOS version number is important to programmers who deal directly with DOS; it allows them to customize a program to the system version installed. This function, which was added with DOS V2.0, gives you the major and minor version numbers for the DOS under which your program is expected to run. This is a good way to verify at the beginning of a program that the system can support the DOS calls you need. (Note: With both Microsoft C and Turbo C, these values are available as global variables.)

If your program works under a DOS earlier than V2.0, the function returns 0 for both major and minor version numbers. This immediately gives you such important information as no path names, no directories, and no hard disk support. If you are writing programs for DOS V2.0 and later find yourself on DOS 1.x versions, you should do the following:

1. Display an error message with Int 21h, Function 09h.

2. Exit the program with Int 21h, Function 00h.

If you intend to support DOS versions earlier than 2.0, use this information to restrict your use of DOS functions.

DOS V1.x restrictions are not the only ones of concern when you program. Programmers customarily use functions that extend their abilities, as those functions become available. DOS V3.3 adds some new functions that allow you to increase the number of open files and to flush file buffers to disk. By using these functions in a database program, you can make that database easier to write. But a user without DOS V3.3 would be left out (and would not be a prospective buyer) if you did not provide alternative ways of dealing with the problems for earlier versions of DOS.

Purpose: Terminate and Stay Resident

DOS Version Availability: 2

Interrupt: 21h

Function: 31h

Description: Terminates a process and returns control to the parent process. Everything else remains the same except that the process continues to occupy memory. The function is used by utilities that provide services via software interrupt.

Calling Registers: AH = 31h
AL = Return code
DX = Memory size to reserve (in paragraphs)

Return Registers: None

Comments: Terminate and Stay Resident (TSR) utilities are so common that you would be hard-pressed to find a system that does not use one or more of them. In addition to utilities like pop-up calculators, calendars, and notepads, TSRs can be used to provide common subroutine services for a series of programs. By building a library of functions activated by calls to a specific interrupt, you can provide standard utility routines for several programs without having to link the routines directly to the program. This reduces the size of such modules and speeds up loading them.

The purpose of the TSR function is to terminate (like Function 4Ch) the operation of a program but *not* to return the program's assigned memory to the pool of memory managed by DOS. This allows the program to remain active and to activate if it ties itself to an interrupt of some kind. For example, you could have a program activate and display a clock on the screen if it tied itself to the clock interrupt. Also, the handles could be activated if a key is pressed or if a program calls the interrupt function.

This function replaces the Int 27h TSR function originally provided with DOS V1. The original TSR function allowed only 64K of memory for the function and could not provide a return code. This function allows more than 64K of memory and allows control of the return code, which is available to the parent program through Function 4Dh. This allows batch files to control execution with the ERRORLEVEL parameter available inside the batch file.

The TSR function attempts to allocate the memory requested in the DX register out of the memory allocated when the program was started. It does not deal with memory that was assigned to the process via a call to Function 48h.

This function does not close any files that the program opened; files opened by the program remain open. However, handle functions are associated with the currently active process through an undefined area of the Program Segment Prefix (PSP). When the TSR function is not active, the open files it might refer to are those opened by the currently active process. This does not apply to File Control Block (FCB) functions, which are buffered through the process's own memory area. (See Chapter 9, "Directories and Files," for a discussion of FCB functions.)

Purpose: Get Drive Parameter Block

DOS Version Availability: 2

Interrupt: 21h

Function: 32h

Description: Retrieves the drive parameter block that defines the characteristics of the designated disk drive

Calling Registers: AH = 32h
DL = Drive number (0 = default, 1 = A:, etc.)

Return Registers: AL = FFh if drive number invalid
DS:BX = Address of drive parameter block

Comments: Microsoft and IBM officially specify this function as reserved. The description presented here is derived from nonofficial technical information and is not to be construed as the official or permanent use for the function. Its use, as documented here, may be changed in future versions of DOS. In fact, if your version of DOS is from a third-party vendor, this function may be used for an entirely different purpose. The information presented here is intended as a guide, and you should explore the function at your own leisure and risk.

This function is used to return the address of the disk parameter block used by DOS to determine specific structural information about the disk in the default drive. It is similar in purpose to Int 21h, Function 1Fh, except that this function allows the designation of a specific drive. When returned, DS:BX contains the address shown in table DOS.7.

The purpose of each table item is fairly self-explanatory. One exception is the byte at offset 05h. Available information does not indicate the exact purpose of this piece of data, but it appears to be a code for the cluster size. Also, notice that the fields beginning at offsets 1Ch and 1Eh are for DOS V2 only. The purpose of these fields is unknown for DOS V1 and V3.

Because this function returns a value in the DS register, it is a good idea to save the value of DS before you call the function.

Table DOS.7. *Drive Parameter Block Information*

Offset Byte	Field Length	Meaning
00h	Byte	Drive number (0 = A:, 1 = B:, etc.)
01h	Byte	Device driver unit number
02h	Word	Bytes per sector
04h	Byte	Sectors per cluster (zero based)
05h	Byte	Shift factor
06h	Word	Number of reserved boot sectors
08h	Byte	Number of FAT copies
09h	Word	Number of root-directory entries
0Bh	Word	First data-sector number
0Dh	Word	Highest cluster number plus one
0Fh	Byte	Sectors per FAT
10h	Word	Root directory starting sector number
12h	Double word	Drive's device driver address
16h	Byte	Media descriptor byte
17h	Byte	Disk parameter block validity byte (0FFh indicates need to rebuild)
18h	Double word	Address of next device parameter block
1Ch	Word	Starting cluster number for current directory (DOS V2 only)
1Eh	64 bytes	ASCIIZ of current directory path (DOS V2 only)

Purpose: Get/Set Ctrl-Break Flag

DOS Version Availability: 2

Interrupt: 21h

Function: 33h

Description: Either gets or sets the status of the Ctrl-Break/Ctrl-C check flag. With the flag set off, checking is done only during certain system I/O operations, effectively disabling Int 23h. This flag is a system global and affects all processes.

Calling Registers: AH = 33h
             AL = 00h, getting flag status
                   01h, setting flag status
             DL = 00h, Ctrl-Break checking off
                   01h, Ctrl-Break checking on

Return Registers: DL = 00h, Ctrl-Break checking off
                   01h, Ctrl-Break checking on

Comments: Except for a few I/O functions (see character I/O functions 01h–0Ch for the exceptions), there is no checking for Ctrl-Break/Ctrl-C characters during much of the Int 21h function handling. When this checking is turned on, the check is performed for *all* Int 21h functions.

When checking is enabled, if a Ctrl-Break or Ctrl-C is found, control is turned over to the handler for Int 23h. You can replace the Int 23h handler and deal with the Ctrl-Break or Ctrl-C in a function of your own rather than disabling it.

Be aware that the Ctrl-Break/Ctrl-C flag is a system global which affects all processes running on a DOS system. As a system global, some care must be taken with its handling because it is possible to affect processes other than the one activating or deactivating the function.

Purpose: Return Address of InDOS Flag

DOS Version Availability: 2

Interrupt: 21h

Function: 34h

Description: This is an internal DOS flag used to tell when DOS is processing an Int 21h function. When DOS enters such a function DOS increments the flag; when DOS leaves, it decrements the flag.

Calling Registers: AH = 34h

Return Registers: ES:BX = Pointer to InDOS flag

Comments: Microsoft and IBM officially specify this function as reserved. The description presented here is derived from nonofficial technical information and is not to be construed as the function's official or permanent use. Its use, as documented here, may be changed in future versions of DOS. In fact, if your version of DOS is from a third-party vendor, this function may be used for an entirely different purpose. The information presented here is intended as a guide, and you should explore the function at your own leisure and risk.

The InDOS flag is used by Terminate and Stay Resident (TSR) utilities to determine that at the time of invocation, DOS was inside the kernel processing an Int 21h function. When a TSR utility determines that DOS is currently in a function, it can do one of two things:

1. Go ahead with processing because no Int 21h function will be needed.

2. Refuse to process because Int 21h functions will be needed.

This need arises because the operating system kernel is not reentrant. This means that if an interrupt occurs while the operating system is already inside the kernel, the servicing routine cannot use Int 21h functions for processing because a call to a function might conflict with the previous call. In this case, you could easily crash the system, but not necessarily in any way that could be traced directly to the interrupt handler. At times, however, this flag is misleading.

When DOS waits for keyboard input, it idles in a loop, reading characters as they come in. As long as DOS is waiting at this point, it is safe to use the file handling and other functions. To let you know that you can safely use these functions, DOS polls the Int 28h (keyboard busy loop) during its character loop. A TSR can intercept Int 28h, which defaults to a pointer to an IRET, and check for things to do when it comes alive.

For example, if your TSR is started by pressing a "hot key" but finds that DOS is presently executing an Int 21h function because the InDOS flag is set, the TSR can set an internal flag that means, "I've been invoked, but I can't do anything." Whenever Int 28h is called, this flag could be checked. If the flag is set, the handler can branch immediately to the TSR part that performs the requested function.

A TSR should also intercept the clock interrupt and check the InDOS and TSR invocation flags during clock ticks. The purpose of this is to take care of the situation in which an Int 21h function (other than a character I/O function) was active when the TSR was first called. In this case, the clock interrupt sees the InDOS flag clear and the TSR invocation flag set, so that the requested function can be performed.

Purpose: Get Interrupt Vector

DOS Version Availability: 2

Interrupt: 21h

Function: 35h

Description: Gets the interrupt handler address for the specified interrupt. Although the address is readily available for a given interrupt, this is the preferred way to access the information for compatibility with multitasking environments.

Calling Registers: AH = 35h
                                AL = Interrupt number

Return Registers: ES:BX = Pointer to interrupt handler

Comments: This function is the only *approved* way to get the current setting of an interrupt vector. This function is guaranteed to work cleanly and return a reliable value for the vector. It is possible that another program, for example a Terminate and Stay Resident (TSR) utility, could change the interrupt vector after this function has returned the value. This is what happens when a single-user, single-tasking operating system is pushed beyond its limits.

When you set up a program that will work from an interrupt, you should use this function to determine the original setting of the interrupt so that you can restore it when you finish. You must be careful in doing this because you could come into conflict with TSRs or other interrupt handlers. If you remember an interrupt value, and a TSR starts and changes it, you might replace the interrupt vector in a way that would disable the TSR.

Purpose: Get Free Disk Space

DOS Version Availability: 2

Interrupt: 21h

Function: 36h

Description: Gets the amount of space available on a designated disk
drive along with other selected information about the drive

Calling Registers: AH = 36h
                          DL = Disk drive (0 = default, 1 = A, etc.)

Return Registers: AX = Sectors per cluster
                              FFFFh if the drive was invalid
                         BX = Number of available clusters
                         CX = Bytes per sector
                         DX = Clusters on the drive

Comments: This function, which is similar to Functions 1Bh and 1Ch,
returns basic information that can be used to determine the available space
on a disk.

You start by specifying the disk drive you want to check. You get back the
following raw information:

❑ the number of sectors per cluster
❑ the number of available clusters
❑ the number of bytes per sector
❑ the number of clusters on the drive

Using this information, the amount of space available is

(available clusters) × (sectors per cluster) × (bytes per sector)

This returns the number of bytes available on the drive. Divide by 1024 to get
the number of kilobytes, or divide by a record length to get the available space
in numbers of records for a database, and so on.

To get the total usable space on a disk, use:

(clusters on the drive) × (sectors per cluster) × (bytes per sector)

With this, you can write a function that prints something like this:

XXX bytes free out of YYY

Functions 1Bh and 1Ch return similar information.

Purpose: Get/Set Switchchar

DOS Version Availability: 2

Interrupt: 21h

Function: 37h

Description: Gets and allows you to reset the current switchchar

Calling Registers: AH = 37h

AL = Subfunction

    0, read switch character

    1, set switch character

    2, read device availability (DOS V2.x only)

    3, set device availability (DOS V2.x only)

Subfunction 3 only:

DL = 0 (/DEV/ precedes device names)

    >< 0 (/DEV/ does not need to precede device names)

Return Registers: AL = FFh, AL subfunction was not in the range 0–3

DL = Switch character (subfunctions 0 or 1)

    device availability flag (subfunctions 2–3)

Comments: Microsoft and IBM officially specify this function as reserved. The description presented here is derived from nonofficial technical information and is not to be construed as the function's official or permanent use. Its use, as documented here, may be changed in future versions of DOS. In fact, if your version of DOS is from a third-party vendor, this function may be used for an entirely different purpose. The information presented here is intended as a guide, and you should explore the function at your own leisure and risk.

The switchchar is the character used by DOS during parsing of strings to designated command switches. Normally, the switchchar is set to be the slash (/), but you can set it to some other character if your application requires it.

If you use this function, it is a good idea to determine the current switchchar (subfunction 0) and store it so that you can restore the original switchchar when your program is completed.

Purpose: Get/Set Country Information

DOS Version Availability: 2

Interrupt: 21h

Function: 38h

Description: Gets the current country information; with DOS V3.0 and later, allows the country information to be set as well.

Calling Registers: AH = 38h

Get Current Country Information
AL = 00, get current country information

With DOS V3.0 and later:
AL = 01, FEh specified country code <255
FFh country code is in BX register
BX = Country code if AL =FFh
DS:DX = Pointer to buffer for information

Set Current Country (DOS V3.0 and later)
AL = 01, FEh specified country code <255
FFh country code is in BX register
BX = Country code if AL =FFh
DX = FFFFh

Return Registers: Carry flag clear if successful
BX = Country code (DOS V3 only)
DS:DX = Pointer to returned country information

Carry flag set if error
AX = Error code
02h, invalid country (file not found)

Comments: Because DOS is an international disk operating system, programs sold for DOS may be expected to work in an international setting. This function tells your program what to use for many of the country-dependent parameters used for display of information. For example, date format typical of a certain country is encoded in bytes 0 and 1.

When the function gets the country-dependent information, it returns a pointer to a 32-byte buffer with the information. On DOS V3 and later, the function can be used also to set the country information for use by other programs.

The country code itself is usually the international telephone prefix code (DOS V3 and later). Some typical codes (for example, American Samoa —684, and Portugal—351) can be found at the front of almost any telephone book. The important point to notice here is that the numbers can be above 255. To accommodate this, the function provides for using the BX register to hold the country code when the AL register is set to FFh.

Table DOS.8 gives the format of the country information table, which is pointed to by DS:DX.

The case map call address listed at offset 12h in the table is the far address (segment:offset) of a format procedure that performs country-specific, lower- to uppercase mapping for character values above 7Fh. The mapping procedure should be called with the characters to be mapped in the AL register. The adjusted values are returned in the AL register.

Table DOS.8. *Country Information Buffer*

Bit Offset	Length	Meaning
DOS V2		
00h	Word	Date and time format
		0 = USA m d y, hh:mm:ss
		1 = Europe d m y, hh:mm:ss
		2 = Japan y m d, hh:mm:ss
02h	Byte	Currency symbol
03h	Byte	Zero
04h	Byte	Thousands separator
05h	Byte	Zero
06h	Byte	Decimal separator
07h	Byte	Zero
08h	18 bytes	Reserved
DOS V3		
00h	Word	Date format
		0 = USA m d y
		1 = Europe d m y
		2 = Japan y m d
02h	05h bytes	Currency symbol string (ASCIIZ)
07h	Byte	Thousands separator
08h	Byte	Zero

Table DOS.8 continues

Table DOS.8 *continued*

Bit Offset	Length	Meaning
09h	Byte	Decimal separator
0Ah	Byte	Zero
0Bh	Byte	Date separator
0Ch	Byte	Zero
0Dh	Byte	Time separator
0Eh	Byte	Zero
0Fh	Byte	Currency format
		00h = symbol leads currency, no space
		01h = symbol follows currency, no space
		02h = symbol leads currency, one space
		03h = symbol follows currency, one space
		04h = symbol replaces decimal separator
10h	Byte	Number of digits after decimal
11h	Byte	Time format
		Bit 0 = 0, 12-hour clock
		1, 24-hour clock
12h	Double word	Case map call address
16h	Byte	Data list separator
17h	Byte	Zero
18h	08h bytes	Reserved

Purpose: Create Subdirectory

DOS Version Availability: 2

Interrupt: 21h

Function: 39h

Description: Creates a subdirectory at the specified drive and path location

Calling Registers: AH = 39h
DS:DX = Pointer to ASCIIZ path specification

Return Registers: Carry flag clear if successful

Carry flag set if error
AX = Error code
03h, path not found
05h, access denied

Comments: DOS does not provide a way to manipulate directory entries other than through this function and the other directory functions (Functions 3Ah and 3Bh). This particular function allows you to create a new directory, which takes the path name of the directory and the drive designation if necessary.

This function will return an error and not create the requested directory if the directory already exists, if any element of the path name does not exist, or if the directory is from the root and the root is full.

In a network environment, you must have create-access rights in order to be allowed to create a subdirectory.

Purpose: Remove Subdirectory

DOS Version Availability: 2

Interrupt: 21h

Function: 3Ah

Description: Remove a subdirectory if it is empty

Calling Registers: AH = 3Ah
                          DS:DX = Pointer to ASCIIZ path specification

Return Registers: Carry flag clear if successful

Carry flag set if error
AX = Error code
03h, path not found
05h, access denied
06h, current directory
10h, current directory

Comments: This is one of only three functions provided to manipulate directory entries in other directories. It allows you to delete the specified directory but only if the directory exists and is empty and if the directory to be deleted is not the default directory.

In a network environment, you must have create-access rights in order to be allowed to delete a subdirectory.

Purpose: Set Directory

DOS Version Availability: 2

Interrupt: 21h

Function: 3Bh

Description: Sets the current or default directory to match the designated string

Calling Registers: AH = 3Bh
DS:DX = Pointer to ASCIIZ path string

Return Registers: Carry flag clear if successful

Carry flag set if error
AX = Error code
03h, path not found

Comments: This function allows you to place your program in a designated location within the directory system.

A useful technique for a program that works in a special directory is to use Function 47h to determine the current directory and save that information before using this function to set a new directory area. Then, when the program is finished, it can return to the original directory. Too few programs perform this simple step.

Purpose: Create/Truncate File

DOS Version Availability: 2

Interrupt: 21h

Function: 3Ch

Description: The designated file is created if it does not exist
or is truncated to zero length if it does.

Calling Registers: AH = 3Ch
CX = File attribute
DS:DX = Pointer to ASCIIZ file specification

Return Registers: Carry flag clear if successful
AX = File handle

Carry flag set if error
AX = Error code
03h, path not found
04h, no handles available
05h, access denied

Comments: The create/truncate file function is basic to file operations. It
does for handle-oriented functions what Function 16h does for File Control
Block (FCB) functions. It creates the named file if it doesn't exist or truncates
it to zero length if it does exist. The desired file is named by an ASCIIZ string,
which may contain drive and path specifiers. A 16-bit file handle is returned.
The file handle is used for further access to the file. The new file will have the
file attributes set in the CX register. The following table describes the file
types that are matched according to the different values.

Value	File types matched
00h	Normal
02h	Hidden
04h	System
06h	Hidden and system

When the truncate function is not wanted, you have two options, depending
on which DOS version is running:

1. With DOS V2, try to open the file with Function 3Dh. If the
function fails, call this function to create the file.

2. With DOS V3, try to create the file with Function 5Bh. If the
function fails, call Function 3Dh to open the file.

Either way, you need to think carefully about the use of this function. More than one programmer has called this function at the wrong time and destroyed important data.

This function will fail if any element of the path name does not exist, if the file is being created in the root directory and the root is full, or if a read-only file exists with the same name.

The file is created as a normal file with read/write permission returned. Function 43h can be used to change the file's attributes if desired. You cannot use this function to create either subdirectories or volume labels.

In a network environment, you must have create-access rights to be allowed to create/truncate a file.

Purpose: Open File

DOS Version Availability: 2

Interrupt: 21h

Function: 3Dh

Description: Opens the designated file and returns a file handle (16-bit number) used to reference the opened file

Calling Registers: AH = 3Dh
AL = Access mode (DOS V2)
Access and file-sharing mode (DOS V3)
DS:DX = Pointer to ASCIIZ file specification

Return Registers: Carry flag clear if successful
AX = File handle

Carry flag set if error
AX = Error code
01h, invalid function
02h, file not found
03h, path not found
04h, no handles available
05h, access denied
0Ch, invalid access code

Comments: To open a file, specify the file name as an ASCIIZ string. Normal, hidden, or system files are accessible to the function. Register AL tells the function what access you want to the file. Table DOS.9 shows how to set the AL register for DOS V2 and V3.

In DOS V3, in addition to requesting read/write access, you can request network access (file-sharing modes) and indicate whether the file is to be inherited by any children that this process may execute.

On return, the file is opened for access in the desired mode unless the file cannot be found or the desired access mode is not allowed (for example, accessing a read-only file with the access mode set to read/write). If the file-open function is successful, the read/write pointer will be at the beginning of the file.

In DOS V2, only bits 0–2 of the AL register are significant in this function. The remaining bits should be set to zero. In DOS V3 with the file-sharing software loaded, four bits of the AL register are devoted to permissions for other processes (bits 4–6, the sharing mode; and bit 7, the inherit bit). If a file

Table DOS.9. *Access and File-Sharing Modes*

Bits	Meaning
DOS V2	
76543210	
. 000	Read access
. 001	Write access
. 010	Read/write access
DOS V3	
76543210	
. 000	Read access
. 001	Write access
. 010	Read/write access
. . . .x. . .	Reserved
.000. . . .	Sharing mode—compatibility mode
.001. . . .	Sharing mode—read/write access denied
.010. . . .	Sharing mode—write access denied
.011. . . .	Sharing mode—read access denied
.100. . . .	Sharing mode—full access permitted
0.	Inherited by child processes
1.	Private to current process

handle is inherited by a child or duplicated by a process, these file-sharing modes are also inherited. On the dark side, a file-sharing error results in an Int 24h (critical error) with an error code 02h (drive not ready).

Compatibility mode (bits 3–7 set to zero) is the normal mode for most DOS software written before DOS V3, as well as for much of the software written afterwards. As long as the software is running on a single workstation, there is no conflict in file access. When networking software is introduced and file sharing becomes a reality, compatibility mode will no longer be suitable for file control.

To work with other programs in a network environment, programs will have to use sharing modes in the open call to provide for access within the limits of the programming task involved. Files opened using FCB functions are assumed to be in compatibility mode unless opened for read-only access, in which case they are assigned *deny write* sharing mode. Files opened by handle functions with read-only access also are considered to be in *deny write* sharing mode. All other compatibility access modes will deny all outside file access.

To use this function properly, the programmer must carefully think through the required access to the file and the implications of unrestricted write access to the file. The possible modes then are

- ❏ *Deny read/write:* Files opened in this mode cannot be opened again by another program (or the current program) either on the current machine or on another machine on the network. This type of access is necessary for control of database operations for critical updating.

- ❏ *Deny write:* Files opened in this mode can be opened only for reading by other programs.

- ❏ *Deny read:* Files opened in this mode cannot be opened for reading by other programs.

- ❏ *Deny none:* No access (read or write) is denied to other programs.

Multiple-program access to data files is a serious concern in a network environment. Databases can be corrupted by programs trying to update the same file record simultaneously. Methods of coordinating file access among different programs are beyond the scope of this book. You should consult books on networked databases or operating systems to learn about such coordination mechanisms.

Purpose: Close File

DOS Version Availability: 2

Interrupt: 21h

Function: 3Eh

Description: Closes a file previously opened with file handles

Calling Registers: AH = 3Eh
                          BX = File handle

Return Registers: Carry flag clear if successful

Carry flag set if error
AX = Error code
06h, invalid handle

Comments: This function is used to close a previously opened or created file using the DOS file-handling functions. The handle is returned to the system for use, and any updates to the file are performed. The file's date, as recorded in its directory entry, is updated if changes are made.

Good programming practice dictates that a program should always close any files it opens to force the operating system to update the file system properly. DOS automatically closes active file handles when a program terminates, but you should not rely on it, particularly if you want your programs to be portable.

Note: Be especially careful about closing file handle zero, which is the standard input device (normally, the keyboard). If you accidentally close file handle zero, you will lose communication through the keyboard.

Purpose: Read File or Device

DOS Version Availability: 2

Interrupt: 21h

Function: 3Fh

Description: Reads data from the file or device specified by the file-handle argument. This data is written to a designated memory location.

Calling Registers:　AH = 3Fh
　　　　　　　　　　　BX = File handle
　　　　　　　　　　　CX = Number of bytes
　　　　　　　　　　　DS:DX = Pointer to buffer area

Return Registers:　Carry flag clear if successful
　　　　　　　　　　　AX = Number of bytes read

　　　　　　　　　　　Carry flag set if error
　　　　　　　　　　　AX = Error code
　　　　　　　　　　　　　　05h, access denied
　　　　　　　　　　　　　　06h, invalid handle

Comments: A basic file read gets a designated number of bytes from the file to the buffer as specified. If a read completes successfully, but AX is less than CX, then a partial read occurred before the end of file (EOF) was detected. If the EOF has already been reached when this function is called, the carry flag will be set, but the AX register will be zero.

As with all the file-handle calls, devices can be treated exactly the same as files. We can use this function to read from character devices like the keyboard. Some special restrictions apply, however, when dealing with a character device. If a character device is in cooked mode (see Function 44h), the read is terminated by a carriage return (it reads a single line only).

In a network environment, you must have read-access rights in order to read a file or device.

Purpose: Write to a File or Device

DOS Version Availability: 2

Interrupt: 21h

Function: 40h

Description: Writes data to a file specified in the handle

Calling Registers: AH = 40h
BX = File handle
CX = Number of bytes to write
DS:DX = Pointer to buffer of data to write

Return Registers: Carry flag clear if successful
AX = Number of bytes written

Carry flag set if error
AX = Error code
05h, access denied
06h, invalid handle

Comments: Writing to a file using the file-handle function is as simple as specifying the file handle and the number of bytes and pointing to the data buffer. The function then writes that number of bytes to the current position in the file.

Register AX returns the number of bytes written or, if the function failed, an error code. Normally, the number of bytes returned in AX is the same as the number of bytes to write (CX register). If the write was successful and if AX is less than CX, a partial record was written. Partial-record writes could result if the disk is out of space; in this case, a check of available space with Function 36h, 1Bh, or 1Ch is a good test. An error code is returned if the file is marked as read-only.

In a network environment, you must have write-access rights in order to write to a file or device.

Purpose: Delete File

DOS Version Availability: 2

Interrupt: 21h

Function: 41h

Description: Deletes the specified file from the system. The actual file is not overwritten, but its directory entry is modified so that the space can be reused. Wild cards are not allowed in the file name.

Calling Registers: AH = 41h
DS:DX = Pointer to ASCIIZ file specification

Return Registers: Carry flag clear if successful
AX = Number of bytes written

Carry flag set if error
AX = Error code
02h, file not found
05h, access denied

Comments: This function deletes the file by marking the directory entry with an E5h in the first byte of the file name. This makes it possible to recover the "deleted" file if no other files are created or changed after the deletion. Nothing else is changed in the directory entry. The clusters allocated to the file are returned to the system for reuse.

Unlike the File Control Block (FCB) delete function (13h), wild cards are not allowed here. If you want to delete a group of files by matching a file name that uses wild cards, you must use the search functions (4Eh and 4Fh) to locate the files one by one. Because this function allows access to files in subdirectories, this restriction is easy to live with.

If the file exists but has the read-only attribute or if the file cannot be found, this function will fail.

In a network environment, you must have create-access rights in order to delete a file.

Purpose: Move File Pointer

DOS Version Availability: 2

Interrupt: 21h

Function: 42h

Description: Changes the current location in the file, the file pointer, to a position relative to the start of file, end of file, or the current position. The next read from the file will start at this location.

Calling Registers: AH = 42h
                           AL = Method code
                                   00h, offset from beginning of file
                                   01h, offset from current position
                                   02h, offset from end of file
                           BX = File handle
                           CX = Most significant part of offset
                           DX = Least significant part of offset

Return Registers: Carry flag clear if successful
                           DX:AX = New file-pointer location

                        Carry flag set if error
                           AX = Error code
                                   01h, invalid function (file sharing)
                                   06h, invalid handle

Comments: The file read/write pointer is adjusted by this function to a new position set from the beginning, end, or current position within the file. The offset can be specified as a 32-bit number (ranges up to 4,096M). You cannot practically use files of this size, however, because the operating system restricts you to a maximum 32M disk capacity for a single disk volume. When the file pointer is moved, this becomes the next point at which data will be written into the file.

A practical use of this function, other than setting the file position, is to determine the file size. You can get this by setting register AL to 2 (relative to end of file) and the CX and DX registers to 0 (offset from end of file). The location returned in the AX and DX registers represents the actual size of the file in bytes. Of course, this leaves the pointer at the end of the file. If this is not satisfactory, you must reset the position to the desired location before a read or write.

Another important use of the function is to implement an open-at-end-of-file or append function. You can use Function 3Dh to open the file and then use this function to reset immediately the read/write pointer to the end of file by the same method used to determine the file size ($AL = 2$, CX and $DX = 0$).

With this function, you can set the file pointer to a position before the beginning of the file or after the end of it. Setting the file pointer after the end of the file does not result in an error except when a read is attempted from this nonexistent location. A write to a location past the end of the file causes space to be allocated to the file and makes the file large enough to accommodate the write. Setting the file pointer before the beginning of the file results in an error when a read or write is attempted.

If this function is used on a network system with a file in deny-read or deny-none sharing mode, the file-pointer information is adjusted on the computer that has the file. If the file is in any other sharing mode, the file-pointer information is kept on the remote computer.

Purpose: Get/Set File Attributes

DOS Version Availability: 2

Interrupt: 21h

Function: 43h

Description: Gets or sets the attributes of a file. Only attributes read-only, hidden, system, or archive may be accessed.

Calling Registers: AH = 43h
AL = 00, get file attributes
    01, set file attributes
CX = New attribute when setting
DS:DX = Pointer to ASCIIZ file specification

Return Registers: Carry flag clear if successful
CX = Attribute if get

Carry flag set if error
AX = Error code
    01h, invalid function (file sharing)
    02h, file not found
    03h, path not found
    05h, access denied

Comments: The file attributes for a file can be set to the values shown in the following table:

Bit	Meaning
6543210	
......1	Read only
.....1.	Hidden
....1..	System
.1.....	Archive

You cannot set the subdirectory or volume label attributes with this function. To create a volume label, you must use the File Control Block (FCB) file-creation function and an extended FCB. Function 39h is the only function that allows you to create a directory.

In a network environment, you must have create-access rights in order to change any file-attribute bit except the archive bit. Changing the archive bit does not require any restrictive rights.

SYSTEM

Purpose: Device Driver Control (IOCTL)

DOS Version Availability: 2

Interrupt: 21h

Function: 44h

Description: Passes or retrieves control information to and from a device driver. The meaning of the information passed depends on which specific device driver is addressed.

Calling Registers: AH = 44h
AL = Device function code (see table DOS.10)
BX = Handle (function codes 00h, 01h, 02h, 03h, 06h, 07h, 0Ah)
BL = Drive code (0 = default, 1 = A:, etc.) (function codes 04h, 05h, 08h, 09h)
CX = Number of bytes to read or write
DS:DX = Pointer to buffer area (function codes 02h-05h)
DX = Device information (function code 01h...) (see table DOS.10)

Return Registers: Carry flag clear if successful
AX = Number of bytes transferred (function codes 02h–05h)
AL = Status (function codes 06h–07h)
00h = not ready
FFh = ready
AX = Value (function code 08h)
00h = removable
01h = fixed
DX = Device information (function code 00)

Carry flag set if error
AX = Error code
01h, invalid function (file sharing)
04h, no handles available
05h, access denied
06h, invalid handle
0Dh, invalid data
0Fh, invalid drive

Comments: The IOCTL function is one of the most comprehensive functions available under DOS. There are 16 separate subfunctions to this function. Table DOS.10 gives an overview of the subfunctions and the DOS version at which the subfunction was officially activated.

Table DOS.10. *Device Function Codes*

AL	Meaning	DOS version
00h	Get device information	2.0
01h	Set device information	2.0
02h	Character device read	2.0
03h	Character device write	2.0
04h	Block device read	2.0
05h	Block device write	2.0
06h	Get input status	2.0
07h	Get output status	2.0
08h	Block device changeable?	3.0
09h	Block device local or remote?	3.1
0Ah	Handle local or remote?	3.1
0Bh	Set sharing retry count	3.0
0Ch	Generic I/O control for handles	3.2
0Dh	Generic I/O control for block devices	3.2
0Eh	Get logical drive map	3.2
0Fh	Set logical drive map	3.2

The IOCTL function is a generalized device-driver interface program. Its purpose is not to transfer data but to communicate with a driver and tell it how to work.

Purpose: Get Device Information

DOS Version Availability: 2

Interrupt: 21h

Function: 44h

Subfunction: 00h

Description: Gets information about the device or file referred to by the handle

Calling Registers: AH = 44h
AL = 00h
BX = Handle

Return Registers: Carry flag clear if successful
DX = Device information (see table DOS.11)

Carry flag set if error
AX = Error code
01h, invalid function
05h, access denied
06h, invalid handle

Comments: The DX register returns coded information from the system about the character device or file referenced by the file handle in the BX register. Table DOS.11 shows the codes and their meaning. The handle must refer to an open file or character device.

Bit 5 for character devices is a particularly useful information bit. UNIX programmers are familiar with the terms *cooked mode* and *raw mode* when dealing with terminal devices. In DOS, cooked mode means that Ctrl-C, Ctrl-P, Ctrl-Q, Ctrl-S, and Ctrl-Z are processed. Cooked mode is the "full editing" entry mode. In raw mode, the operating system ignores the special meaning of these characters. They are passed directly to the application program. Special console input functions may still process Ctrl-C/Ctrl-Break unless Break checking is turned off.

The handle in the BX register must refer to an open file or device. If not, the function returns error code 06h (invalid handle).

Bits 8–15 of the DX register on return correspond to the same bits in the device driver's attribute word (see Chapter 12 for a more complete discussion of the attribute word and the driver header).

Table DOS.11. *Device Information Codes*

Bit	Meaning
Character Device	
FEDCBA98 76543210	
....1	Standard input device
....1.	Standard output device
....1..	NUL device
....1...	Clock device
....x....	Reserved
....0.....	Cooked mode
....1.....	Raw (binary) mode
.... .0......	End of file for input
.... 1.......	Character device
..xxxxxx	Reserved
.1......	Device can process control strings sent with subfunctions 02h and 03h. This bit can be read only. It must be set to zero initially.
x.......	Reserved
Block Device (Disk File)	
FEDCBA98 76543210	
....xxxxxx	Drive number (0 = A:, 1 = B:, etc.)
.... .0......	File has been written
.... 0.......	Disk file
xxxxxxxx	Reserved; must be set to zero when function is called

Purpose: Set Device Information

DOS Version Availability: 2

Interrupt: 21h

Function: 44h

Subfunction: 01h

Description: The complement of subfunction 00h for character devices only, this subfunction allows setting device information codes.

Calling Registers: AH = 44h
                          AL = 01h
                          BX = Handle
                          DX = Device data word

Return Registers: Carry flag clear if successful

                        Carry flag set if error
                          AX = Error code
                              01h, invalid function
                              05h, access denied
                              06h, invalid handle

Comments: Subfunction 01h allows you to set a limited portion of the device data word for character devices only. The only bit normally modified in this call is bit 5. (For an explanation of raw mode and cooked mode, see the discussion for subfunction 00h.)

If the DH register is not zero, the subfunction returns error code 01h (invalid function). This subfunction also requires that the handle refer to an open device. If the handle is a file, no information is updated. Table DOS.12 gives the interpretation of the Device Data Word (DX register).

Table DOS.12. *Device Data Word*

Bit	Meaning
FEDCBA98 76543210	
....1	Standard input device
....1.	Standard output device
....1..	NUL device
....1...	Clock device
....x....	Reserved
....∅.....	Cooked mode
....1.....	Raw (binary) mode
....∅......	End of file for input
.... 1.......	Character device
xxxxxxxx	Reserved

Purpose: Character Device Read

DOS Version Availability: 2

Interrupt: 21h

Function: 44h

Subfunction: 02h

Description: Gets control string information from the driver for use by the calling program

Calling Registers: AH = 44h
AL = 02h
BX = Handle
CX = Number of bytes to get
DS:DX = Pointer to data buffer

Return Registers: Carry flag clear if successful
AX = Number of bytes transferred

Carry flag set if error
AX = Error code
01h, invalid function
05h, access denied
06h, invalid handle

Comments: Arbitrary information about a driver can be passed through the calling program in a control string. This can be status information or whatever kind of information the driver is written to support. There are no standards for format or content of these messages.

This subfunction may initiate I/O to or from the device, but does not necessarily have to. How the driver responds to the request is up to the driver. Chapter 12, "Device Drivers," goes into more detail about control strings.

Bit 14 of Subfunction 00h indicates whether the driver can provide or respond to control strings.

Purpose: Character Device Write

DOS Version Availability: 2

Interrupt: 21h

Function: 44h

Subfunction: 03h

Description: Sends control-string information to the driver

Calling Registers: AH = 44h
AL = 03h
BX = Handle
CX = Number of bytes to send
DS:DX = Pointer to date buffer

Return Registers: Carry flag clear if successful
AX = Number of bytes transferred

Carry flag set if error
AX = Error code
01h, invalid function
05h, access denied
06h, invalid handle

Comments: Arbitrary information about a driver can be passed to the driver in a control string. This can be status information or whatever kind of information the driver is written to support. There are no standards for format or content of these messages.

This subfunction may initiate I/O to or from the device, but does not necessarily have to. How the driver responds to the request is up to the driver. Chapter 12, "Device Drivers," goes into more detail about control strings.

Bit 14 of Subfunction 00h indicates whether the driver can provide or respond to control strings.

This subfunction is often used to pass configuration information, such as baud rate or word length, to a driver.

Purpose: Block Driver Read

DOS Version Availability: 2

Interrupt: 21h

Function: 44h

Subfunction: 04h

Description: Gets control information from a block driver (disk type)

Calling Registers: AH = 44h
AL = 04h
BL = Drive number
CX = Number of bytes to get
DS:DX = Pointer to data buffer

Return Registers: Carry flag clear if successful
AX = Number of bytes transferred

Carry flag set if error
AX = Error code
01h, invalid function
05h, access denied
06h, invalid handle

Comments: Arbitrary information about a block driver can be passed from it in a control string. This can be status information or whatever kind of information the driver is written to support. There are no standards for format or content of these messages.

This subfunction may initiate I/O to or from the device, but does not necessarily have to. How the driver responds to the request is up to the driver. Chapter 12, "Device Drivers," goes into more detail about control strings.

Block device drivers are not required to support this subfunction. If the driver called does not support it, error code 01h, invalid function, is returned.

A frequent use of this subfunction involves readiness for operation of block devices. Devices such as CD ROM drives, tape drives, or other devices can be queried if the driver is written for it.

Purpose: Block Driver Write

DOS Version Availability: 2

Interrupt: 21h

Function: 44h

Subfunction: 05h

Description: Sends controlling information to a block device
(disk type)

Calling Registers: AH = 44h
AL = 05h
BL = Drive number
CX = Number of bytes to send
DS:DX = Pointer to data buffer

Return Registers: Carry flag clear if successful
AX = Number of bytes transferred

Carry flag set if error
AX = Error code
01h, invalid function
05h, access denied
06h, invalid handle

Comments: Arbitrary information about a block driver can be passed to it in a control string. This can include commands or whatever kind of information the driver is written to support. There are no standards for format or content of these messages.

This subfunction may initiate I/O to or from the device, but does not necessarily have to. How the driver responds to the request is up to the driver. Chapter 12, "Device Drivers," goes into more detail about control strings.

Block device drivers are not required to support this subfunction. If the driver called does not support it, error code 01h, invalid function, is returned.

Frequent uses of this subfunction include non-I/O device functions, such as tape rewind, disk eject, and so forth.

Purpose: Get Input Status

DOS Version Availability: 2

Interrupt: 21h

Function: 44h

Subfunction: 06h

Description: Returns status of the device or file for input
operations

Calling Registers: AH = 44h
AL = 06h
BX = Handle

Return Registers: Carry flag clear if successful
AL = Input status code (see table)

Carry flag set if error
AX = Error code
01h, invalid function
05h, access denied
06h, invalid handle

Comments: With this subfunction, you can tell whether a particular device
or file is ready for an input operation. You can test files for position at EOF
except when positioned by Function 42h, or you can test whether character
devices are ready to operate. The following table gives the input status code
(register AH) interpretation:

Code file	Device
00h at EOF	Not ready
FFh not at EOF	Ready

(*Special case:* A file will not return EOF if positioned at EOF by using
Int 21h, Function 42h.)

Purpose: Get Output Status

DOS Version Availability: 2

Interrupt: 21h

Function: 44h

Subfunction: 07h

Description: Returns status of the device or file for output
operations

Calling Registers: AH = 44h
AL = 07h
BX = Handle

Return Registers: Carry flag clear if successful
AL = Output status code (see table)

Carry flag set if error
AX = Error code
01h, invalid function
05h, access denied
06h, invalid handle

Comments: With this subfunction, you can tell whether a particular device
or file is ready for an output operation. As shown in the following table, files
always return *ready* for output; character devices do not.

Code	File	Device
00h	Ready	Not ready
FFh	Ready	Ready

Purpose: Block Device Removable?

DOS Version Availability: 3

Interrupt: 21h

Function: 44h

Subfunction: 08h

Description: Used to determine whether a block device is removable

Calling Registers: AH = 44h
AL = 08h
BL = Drive number

Return Registers: Carry flag clear if successful
AX = 00h, removable media
01h, nonremovable media

Carry flag set if error
AX = Error code
01h, invalid function
0Fh, invalid drive

Comments: Applications that need to locate data files or overlays on a particular device can determine with this subfunction whether the device is removable. If the desired file is not located on the device and the device is removable, the program should prompt the user to put in the correct disk to continue.

Some drivers do not support this function. In this case, the subfunction returns error code 01h.

Purpose: Block Device Local or Remote?

DOS Version Availability: 3.1

Interrupt: 21h

Function: 44h

Subfunction: 09h

Description: Determines whether the block device is local or remote

Calling Registers: AH = 44h
AL = 09h
BL = Drive number

Return Registers: Carry flag clear if successful
DX = Device attribute word
bit 12 = 1, drive is remote
0, drive is local

Carry flag set if error
AX = Error code
01h, invalid function
0Fh, invalid drive

Comments: If the network has not been started, this subfunction returns error code 01h, invalid function.

It is good programming practice to avoid this function. Programs should be written in such a way that they are not dependent on a particular device's location on a network.

Purpose: Handle Local or Remote?

DOS Version Availability: 3.1

Interrupt: 21h

Function: 44h

Subfunction: 0Ah

Description: Determines whether the handle is local or remote

Calling Registers: AH = 44h
AL = 0Ah
BX = Handle

Return Registers: Carry flag clear if successful
DX = Device attribute word
bit 15 = 1, handle is remote
0, handle is local

Carry flag set if error
AX = Error code
01h, invalid function
06h, invalid handle

Comments: If the network has not been started, this subfunction returns error code 01h, invalid function.

It is good programming practice to avoid this function. Programs should be written in such a way that they are not dependent on a particular device's location on a network.

Purpose: Set Sharing Retry Count

DOS Version Availability: 3.0

Interrupt: 21h

Function: 44h

Subfunction: 0Bh

Description: Changes the retry parameters for file sharing across a network

Calling Registers: AH = 44h
AL = 0Bh
CX = Pause between retries
DX = Number of retries

Return Registers: Carry flag clear if successful
Carry flag set if error
AX = Error code
01h, invalid function

Comments: When working with multiple PCs over a network, the retry parameters are associated with file-locking mechanisms. It is assumed that file locks are temporary and will be cleared after a short update. Such built-in mechanisms will retry automatically to establish access to a file if the file is locked when the first attempt is made.

The two parameters (retry count and pause between retries) are dependent on the system. Differences in CPU and clock speed have a significant effect on the actual length of the pause. The CX register controls the pause by giving the number of times a tight timing loop is executed. The timing loop repeats 65,536 times whenever it is called. Clearly, the retry count is the number of times the access will be attempted before failure is reported. Defaults are PAUSE =1 and RETRY =3.

These parameters can be used to tune the system to minimize file-sharing problems. If you expect long periods during which a desired file will be locked, you can extend the pause period when you make another attempt to access the file. If you change any of the defaults, however, restoring the defaults to prevent side effects on other programs is prudent.

Purpose: Generic I/O Control for Handles

DOS Version Availability: 3.2

Interrupt: 21h

Function: 44h

Subfunction: 0Ch

Description: In DOS V3.2, sets or gets the iteration count for a character-oriented device. In DOS V3.3, the function performs code-page switching.

Calling Registers: AH = 44h
AL = 0Ch
BX = Handle
CH = Category code (device type)
    DOS V3.2
        05h, printer
    DOS V3.3
        00h, unknown
        01h, COMx
        03h, CON
        05h, LPTx
CL = Minor function code
    DOS V3.2
        45h, set iteration count
        65h, get iteration count
    DOS V3.3
        4Ah, select
        4Ch, prepare start
        4Dh, prepare end
        6Ah, query select
        6Bh, query prepare list
DS:DX = Pointer to iteration count word (V3.2)
        Pointer to parameter block (V3.3)

Return Registers: Carry flag clear if successful

Carry flag set if error
AX = Error code
    01h, invalid function

Comments: The iteration count word specifies the number of times an operation will be attempted before giving up. With DOS V3.2, only category code 05h, printer, was allowed.

With DOS V3.3, this subfunction changed to handle code-page switching for devices. The minor functions include the following:

1. Prepare Start (4Ch) tells the driver to be ready for code-page font loading via subfunction 03h. A special start operation is a "refresh," which is generated by setting all code-page IDs to FFFFh.

2. Prepare End (4Dh) tells the driver that the code-page font loading is complete.

3. Select Code Page (4Ah) selects the code page to use.

4. Query Selected Code Page (6Ah) determines the status of the code page from the device.

5. Query Prepare List (6Bh) determines the list of code pages on the device.

Table DOS.13 defines the parameter block, pointed to by DS:DX.

Table DOS.13. *Parameter Block*

Bytes	Meaning
Minor Functions 4Ah, 4Dh, 6Ah	
0–1	Length of following data
2–3	Code-page ID
Minor Function 4Ch	
0–1	Flags
2–3	Length of parameter block (after this point)
4–5	Number of code pages
.	
.	Code-page designations
.	
Minor Function 6Ah	
0–1	Length of parameter block (after this point)
2–3	Number of hardware code pages
.	
.	Hardware code-page designations
.	
n–n +1	Number of prepared code pages
.	
.	Prepared code-page designations
.	

Purpose: Generic I/O Control for Block Devices

DOS Version Availability: 3.2

Interrupt: 21h

Function: 44h

Subfunction: 0Dh

Description: A collection of six input/output functions for handling special functions on block devices

Calling Registers: AH = 44h
AL = 0Dh
BL = Drive number
CH = Category code
08h, disk drive
CL = Minor function code
40h, set parameters for block device
41h, write track on logical drive
42h, format and verify track on logical drive
60h, get parameters for block device
61h, read track on logical device
62h, verify track on logical drive
DS:DX = Pointer to parameter block

Return Registers: Carry flag clear if successful

Carry flag set if error
AX = Error code
01h, invalid function
02h, invalid drive

Comments: This subfunction is provided to extend the capability to control block devices. A number of primitive operations can be controlled through this IOCTL call in device-independent fashion. Each minor function is examined individually.

Minor Function 40h (set device parameters) must be called before the other minor functions for a given device.

Minor Function 40h: Set Device Parameters

The parameter block for this minor function indicates the complete layout of the block device, including physical characteristics, media type, and so forth.

Parameter Block Layout

Byte offset	Meaning
00h	Special function codes
01h	Device type code
02–03h	Device attributes code
04–05h	Number of cylinders
06	Media type code
07–25h	Device BPB
26–?h	Track layout table

Special Function Codes

Bit 76543210	Meaning
.......∅	BPB entry is a new BPB
.......1	Use current BPB
......∅.	Use all fields in parameter block
......1.	Use only track layout field
.....∅..	Sectors in track may be different sizes
.....1..	Sectors in track are all the same size
∅∅∅∅∅...	Reserved

Device Type Codes

Code	Meaning
00h	320/360K 5 1/4-inch disk
01h	1.2M 5 1/4-inch disk
02h	720K 3 1/2-inch disk
03h	Single-density 8-inch disk
04h	Double-density 8-inch disk
05h	Fixed disk
06h	Tape drive
07h	Other block device

Device Attribute Codes

Bit 76543210	Meaning
.......∅	Removable storage
.......1	Nonremovable storage
......∅.	Device does not indicate change line status
......1.	Device does indicate change line status
xxxxxx..	Reserved

Media Type Code

Code	Meaning
00h	1.2M 5 1/4-inch disk
01h	320/360K 5 1/4-inch disk

BIOS Parameter Block (BPB) Layout

Offset Byte	Field Length	Meaning
00h	Word	Number of bytes per sector
02h	Byte	Number of sectors per cluster
03h	Word	Number of reserved sectors starting at sector 0
05h	Byte	Number of FATs
06h	Word	Maximum number of root directory entries
08h	Word	Total number of sectors
0Ah	Byte	Media descriptor
0Bh	Word	Number of sectors per FAT
0Dh	Word	Number of sectors per track
0Fh	Word	Number of heads
11h	Double word	Number of hidden sectors
15h	11 bytes	Reserved

Track Layout Table

Variable Length Table

Length	Meaning
Word	Number of sectors in track
Word	Number of first sector in track
Word	Size of first sector in track
.	
.	
Word	Number of last sector in track
Word	Size of last sector in track

Minor Function 41h: Write Track

The write-track function allows specification of all important parameters for a track (head, cylinder, sector, number of sectors, and location of data). For counting, the sector numbers and cylinder numbers start at zero.

Parameter Block

Offset	Meaning
00h	Special function = 0
01–02h	Number of disk head to use
03–04h	Number of disk cylinder to use
05–06h	First sector to use
07–08h	Number of sectors to transfer
09–0Ch	Pointer to data transfer buffer

Minor Function 42h: Format and Verify Track

This function formats and verifies a track on the disk. You need only to specify the disk head and cylinder to use; all the rest is handled by the driver.

Parameter Block

Offset	Meaning
00h	Special function = 0
01–02h	Number of disk head to use
03–04h	Number of disk cylinder to use

Parameter Block—Verify Format Status

Offset	Meaning
00h	Special function = 1
01–02h	Number of disk head to use
03–04h	Number of disk cylinder to use

Upon completion, if the special function field is checked for status, the following return values are possible:

0 = Supported by ROM BIOS, heads/cylinders allowed
1 = Not supported by ROM BIOS
2 = Supported by ROM BIOS, heads/cylinders not allowed
3 = Supported by ROM BIOS, ROM BIOS cannot determine if
supported (drive empty)

Minor Function 60h: Get Parameters

This function is the complement to minor Function 40h. This minor function uses the same parameter-block format as minor Function 40h to retrieve information about the device from the driver.

Minor Function 61h: Read Track

This function reads the track into the memory buffer provided in the parameter block. As with the write-track minor function, the location information is provided to the driver.

Parameter Block

Offset	Meaning
00h	Special function = 0
01–02h	Number of disk head to use
03–04h	Number of disk cylinder to use
05–06h	First sector to use
07–08h	Number of sectors to transfer
09–0Ch	Pointer to data transfer buffer

Minor Function 62h: Verify Track

This function performs the track-verify operation part of format/verify in minor Function 62h.

Parameter Block

Offset	Meaning
00h	Special function = 0
01–02h	Number of disk head to use
03–04h	Number of disk cylinder to use

Purpose: Get Logical Drive Map

DOS Version Availability: 3.2

Interrupt: 21h

Function: 44h

Subfunction: 0Eh

Description: Determines whether more than one logical drive name
is assigned to a device

Calling Registers: AH = 44h
AL = 0Eh
BL = Drive number

Return Registers: Carry flag clear if successful
AL = Drive number
0 = Only one logical drive assigned
1 = A:, 2 = B:, etc.

Carry flag set if error
AX = Error code
01h, invalid function
02h, invalid drive

Comments: The drive number returned by this call tells you the last drive
designation used to access the drive if more than one logical drive designation
applies to the device.

Purpose: Set Logical Drive Map

DOS Version Availability: 3.2

Interrupt: 21h

Function: 44h

Subfunction: 0Fh

Description: Sets the logical drive name that will be used to access this device next

Calling Registers: AH = 44h
AL = 0Fh
BL = Drive number

Return Registers: Carry flag clear if successful
AL = Drive number
0 = Only one logical drive assigned
1 = A:, 2 = B:, etc.

Carry flag set if error
AX = Error code
01h, invalid function
02h, invalid drive

Comments: When copying files between two disks, each of which corresponds to a different logical device but both of which must use the same physical device, you normally are prompted to change the disks when you do I/O to the device that is not presently in the drive. This function allows you to force the switch without getting the operating system prompt.

The function works by setting the next drive letter that would be issued to refer to this device. DOS then will not issue the **Insert Disk** prompt to the user. Subfunction 0Eh determines the name of the last logical drive used to access the device.

Purpose: Duplicate Handle

DOS Version Availability: 2

Interrupt: 21h

Function: 45h

Description: Provides a new handle for an already opened device
or file

Calling Registers: AH = 45h
BX = File handle

Return Registers: Carry flag clear if successful
AX = New handle

Carry flag set if error
AX = Error code
04h, no handles available
06h, invalid handle

Comments: Duplicating a file handle provides another handle for the same file. The file pointers move together. If you move the file pointer of one file, the file pointer for the other moves as well.

The most common use for this function is to force an update to a file's directory entry without having to incur the overhead of a file open and close. In DOS versions earlier than 3.3, this was the only way to force the update. DOS V3.3 introduced the new Function 68h to do the same thing more easily.

Purpose: Force Duplicate Handle

DOS Version Availability: 2

Interrupt: 21h

Function: 46h

Description: Makes two file handles refer to the same opened file at the same location. The file referred to by the second file handle will be closed first.

Calling Registers: AH = 46h
BX = First file handle
CX = Second file handle

Return Registers: Carry flag clear if successful

Carry flag set if error
AX = Error code
04h, no handles available
06h, invalid handle

Comments: The result of this function is similar to that of Function 45h; it causes two file handles to refer to the same file and move together. The most significant use of this function is to provide for device redirection. You can control the redirection process from inside another program and then return the device to normal with the following steps:

1. Use Function 45h to duplicate the handle to be redirected. Save the new handle for later restoration.

2. Use Function 46h for redirection by putting the "handle to be redirected" into CX and the "handle to be redirected to" in BX.

When you want to return conditions to normal, call Function 46h again with the redirected handle in CX and the duplicated handle returned by Function 45h in the BX register.

In the calling registers, if the handle in CX refers to an open file, the file will be closed first before the function starts.

Purpose: Get Current Directory

DOS Version Availability: 2

Interrupt: 21h

Function: 47h

Description: Returns an ASCIIZ string with the full path of the current directory, not including the drive and the leading backslash character (\ ). If the directory is the root directory, the string returned is NUL (first byte 0).

Calling Registers: AH = 47h
DL = Drive code (0 = default, 1 = A:, etc.)
DS:SI = Pointer to 64-byte scratch buffer

Return Registers: Carry flag clear if successful
DS:SI = Pointer to current directory path

Carry flag set if error
AX = Error code
0Fh, invalid drive

Comments: This function returns the path name of the current directory without the drive designator or the leading backslash (\ ). Because you set the drive code when you call the function, the absence of the drive designator and backslash is okay. (If you want to use the return from this function to build a file name, you will have to supply the drive and initial backslash for the file name.)

Many programs could benefit from using this function before changing the directory so that the user could be returned to the original directory when the program is complete. Programmers must be careful because an invalid drive code will cause the function to fail. To set the current directory, refer to Function 3Bh.

Purpose: Allocate Memory

DOS Version Availability: 2

Interrupt: 21h

Function: 48h

Description: Allocates a block of memory for use and returns a pointer to the beginning of the block

Calling Registers: AH = 48h
BX = Number of paragraphs needed

Return Registers: Carry flag clear if successful
AX = Initial segment of allocated block
BX = Size of largest available block if failed

Carry flag set if error
AX = Error code
07h, memory control blocks destroyed
08h, insufficient memory

Comments: The pointer is the segment address of the base of the block (the base address is AX:0000h). Because COM programs are always allocated all of memory, this function always fails when called from a COM program. (For more information, see Chapter 3, "The Dynamics of DOS," and Chapter 10, "Program and Memory Management.")

In multitasking environments, the "Top of Memory" seen by the process may not be the actual "Top of Memory." Programs such as DESQview and Windows give each program only as much space as the program is allowed in the program information files.

If the attempt to get space fails, the function returns the size of the largest available memory block. Another call requesting no more than this amount of space will be successful.

Purpose: Release Memory

DOS Version Availability: 2

Interrupt: 21h

Function: 49h

Description: Releases a block of memory to the pool managed by
DOS (makes the memory available for other programs)

Calling Registers: AH = 49h
ES = Segment of block to be released

Return Registers: Carry flag clear if successful

Carry flag set if error
AX = Error code
07h, memory control blocks destroyed
09h, invalid memory block address

Comments: This function assumes that the block of memory being freed
was acquired from Function 48h. If the block was not acquired from Function
48h, the function may simply fail (if you're lucky), or it may cause unpredictable errors in the program freeing the memory or in other programs residing
in memory. The problem arises because the system, in being told to free
memory, is expecting the address given to refer to a defined memory block as
part of the overall memory allocation scheme. Chapter 10, "Program and
Memory Management," goes into memory management in more detail.

Purpose: Modify Memory Allocation

DOS Version Availability: 2

Interrupt: 21h

Function: 4Ah

Description: Expands or shrinks a memory block previously allocated by Function 48h

Calling Registers: AH = 4Ah
BX = New requested block size in paragraphs
ES = Segment of block to be modified

Return Registers: Carry flag clear if successful

Carry flag set if error
AX = Error code
07h, memory control blocks destroyed
08h, insufficient memory
09h, invalid memory block address
BX = Maximum block size available (if AX = 08h)

Comments: Programs can use this function call to modify a memory block they received from a call to Function 48h or to modify their own memory allocation. Because COM programs are allocated all memory when they run, they must call this function if they expect to be able to EXEC other programs. EXE programs also need to call this function to free memory unless their MAXALLOC parameter in the EXE header has been modified to request less than all memory. Chapter 10, "Program and Memory Management," covers in more detail the subject of memory management for program execution.

This function is frequently referred to as SETBLOCK.

Purpose: Execute Program (EXEC)

DOS Version Availability: 2

Interrupt: 21h

Function: 4Bh

Description: Executes a program under control of another program

Calling Registers: AH = 4Bh
AL = 00, loading and executing a program
03, loading an overlay
ES:BX = Pointer to parameter block
DS:DX = Pointer to program specification

Return Registers: Carry flag clear if successful
All registers except CS and IP are destroyed, including the stack pointers. SS and SP should be stored locally before calling this function and restored after it returns.

Carry flag set if error
AX = Error code
01h, invalid function
02h, file not found
05h, access denied
08h, insufficient memory
0Ah, invalid environment
0Bh, invalid format

Comments: The EXEC function provides for executing programs and managing overlays in the system. The originating program (the parent process) regains control when the new program (the child process) has completed. The parent may receive an exit code from the child if the child uses a DOS termination function that transfers return codes.

This function can also load overlays. Overlays could consist of program segments or data. A major difference between program execution and overlay operation is that programs are allocated memory from whatever is free in the system. Overlays are loaded to memory already owned by the program invoking the overlay function. If needed, a program should release memory (a necessity for COM programs) before executing another program.

The primary control for the operation is the parameter block pointed to by the ES:BX registers. The format of the parameter block is given in table DOS.14.

Table DOS.14. *Parameter Block Layout*

Offset Byte	Field Length	Contents
EXEC Function (AL = 00h)		
00h	Word	Segment pointer to environment block
02h	Word	Offset of command tail
04h	Word	Segment of command tail
06h	Word	Offset of first FCB (offset 5Ch)
08h	Word	Segment of first FCB
0Ah	Word	Offset of second FCB (offset 6Ch)
0Ch	Word	Segment of second FCB
Overlay Function (AL = 03h)		
00h	Word	Segment pointer to load point for the overlay
002	Word	Relocation factor to be applied to the code image (.EXE files only)

The environment block is a series of ASCIIZ strings used to pass environment information to the program being executed. These strings are set at the command level by the SET function, or they can be created internally in the program. Usually, these strings include the COMSPEC variable (where to find the system command processor, COMMAND.COM), the PATH variable (where to look for executables), as well as other variables as specified on the system.

A typical environment block might look like this:

```
          1         2         3         4
1234567890123456789012345678901234567890
COMSPEC=C:\COMMAND.COM*PATH=C:\DOS**
```

The asterisks represent NUL or zero bytes. If the environment block pointer is zero, the child will inherit the same environment that the parent has. In DOS V3 and later, the final zero in the environment block is followed by a two-byte word with a character count followed by an ASCIIZ string with the drive and path name of the program file being executed.

The command tail is a single string that consists of whatever would have been typed on the command line after the command to be executed. The format is a single-byte length count, followed by the string of characters and terminated with a carriage return. The total length cannot exceed 128 bytes; it will be copied into the Program Segment Prefix (PSP) at offset 80h, giving the command tail only 128 bytes before it runs into the program. A typical command tail would look like this:

```
          1         2         3         4
123456789Ø123456789Ø123456789Ø123456789Ø
#\c CHAPTØ1.DOC@
```

The # is a single numeric byte with the value 14, and @ represents the single-byte carriage return.

A child process spawned in this way will inherit the parent process I/O files unless the parent explicitly specifies otherwise in the file-open call (Function 3Dh). Standard files remain open. If standard files were redirected for the parent, they will remain redirected for the child. The parent can redirect the files (see Function 46h).

When you call this function, precautions are in order. During any EXEC function, it must be assumed that all registers will be modified in the course of the function call because the purpose of the function is to run another program. When the EXEC function returns, only CS and IP can be assumed to be correct. Prior to the call, the parent program should store at least SS and SP (plus any other registers you want to retain). On return, SS and SP can be restored to their original values, but the restoration should take place with interrupts disabled so that the restoration cannot be stopped in the middle, a condition that would put the system in an unstable state.

The EXEC function cannot complete successfully unless there is sufficient memory to load the desired program. Assembly language programs should release needed memory with Function 4Ah prior to calling EXEC. When a C program starts, unneeded memory has already been released. For a more detailed discussion of memory allocation, see Chapter 10, "Program and Memory Management."

Purpose: Terminate with Return Code

DOS Version Availability: 2

Interrupt: 21h

Function: 4Ch

Description: Exits a program to its parent task. A return code is passed to the parent.

Calling Registers: AH = 4Ch
AL = Return code

Return Registers: None

Comments: On exit, DOS does the following:

❏ restores the termination handler vector from PSP:000Ah

❏ restores the Ctrl-Break handler vector from PSP:000Eh

❏ restores critical-error handler vector from PSP:0012h (DOS V3)

❏ flushes the file buffers (handle files)

❏ transfers to the termination-handler address

This is now the approved way to terminate a program. Programs that exist in DOS V2 and later should always use this function in preference to Int 20h or Int 21h, Function 00h. This function has two advantages over the earlier termination functions:

❏ It allows returning an exit code, which can be used as the ERRORLEVEL parameter in batch files or by the parent process through Function 4Dh to determine return information.

❏ It does not rely on any register settings for proper operation, such as the CS register pointing to the segment the PSP is in.

Because it automatically closes out file handles and updates the disk directory, this function protects against inadvertent errors in file handling. It will not, however, do anything for File Control Block (FCB) files.

Purpose: Get Return Code

DOS Version Availability: 2

Interrupt: 21h

Function: 4Dh

Description: Gets the return code from a successful EXEC function call. Returns both the system exit code and the child process's own exit code.

Calling Registers: AH = 4Dh

Return Registers: AH = System exit code
                00h = Normal termination
                01h = Termination by Ctrl-C
                02h = Termination by critical device
                     error
                03h = Termination by call to Function 49
           AL = Child exit code

Comments: When called, this function returns the exit code from a child process and from the system once (and only once). The system exit code tells you whether the program terminated normally. The child exit code tells you anything that the program wants to tell you. Its interpretation depends on the program you have run.

Purpose: Search for First Match

DOS Version Availability: 2

Interrupt: 21h

Function: 4Eh

Description: Given an ASCII string, which can include wild cards, this function will locate the first occurrence of a matching file name.

Calling Registers: AH = 4Eh
CX = Attribute to use in search
DS:DX = Pointer to ASCIIZ file specification

Return Registers: Carry flag clear if successful

Carry flag set if error
AX = Error code
02h, file not found
03h, invalid path
12h, no more files

Comments: This function, when given an ASCIIZ string that contains the full file name of a desired file (possibly including wild cards * and ?), fills information about the returned file into the Disk Transfer Area (DTA). The search is limited by the attribute provided to the function. Only those files that match the attributes specified will be found. The file attributes for the file can include the following values:

Value	File types matched
00h	Normal
02h	Normal and hidden
04h	Normal and system
06h	Normal, hidden, and system
08h	Volume labels
10h	Directories

Because the attribute is a byte, you can set CX by setting CL to the desired attribute and CH to zero. When the function returns, the DTA is set as shown here:

Offset Byte	Field Length	Contents
00h	21 bytes	Reserved for DOS use on subsequent searches

15h	Byte	Attribute of matched file
16h	Word	File time
18h	Word	File date
1Ah	Double word	File size
1Eh	13 bytes	File name and extension as ASCIIZ string. Blanks are stripped, and a period is placed in front of the extension

Time and date entries are interpreted like this:

Time Field Encoding

Bits	*Meaning*
FEDCBA98 76543210	
xxxxx...	Hours (0–23)
.....xxx xxx.....	Minutes (0–59)
....xxxxx	Two-second increments (0–29)

Date Field Encoding

FEDCBA98 76543210	
xxxxxxx.	Year – 1980
.......x xxx.....	Month (1–12)
....xxxxx	Day (1–31)

The DTA may be read to retrieve the information about the located file, which after all will have a different file name than the search string if it includes wild cards. However, the DTA should remain inviolate for use in further searches.

Purpose: Search for Next Match

DOS Version Availability: 2

Interrupt: 21h

Function: 4Fh

Description: After a successful call to Function 4Eh, this call continues to find files that match the specified criteria. The DTA must retain the information originally placed there by the call to Function 4Eh.

Calling Registers: AH = 4Fh

Return Registers: Carry flag clear if successful

Carry flag set if error
AX = Error code
12h, no more files

Comments: If wild cards are used in a first search (Function 4Eh), additional files that match the wild-card specification can be found by repeatedly calling this function. A failed search (carry flag set on return from the function) indicates that no additional file names match the pattern.

Searches with the "next match" function continue to use the same procedures used for the first match. The function updates the DTA to indicate the name of the file and other data regarding the file located by the search. The DTA must not be modified between calls to allow successive searches. The following table shows the layout of the data in the DTA on return from the function:

Offset Byte	Field Length	Contents
00h	21 bytes	Reserved for DOS use on subsequent searches
15h	Byte	Attribute of matched file
16h	Word	File time
18h	Word	File date
1Ah	Double word	File size
1Eh	13 bytes	File name and extension as ASCIIZ string. Blanks are stripped, and a period is placed in front of the extension.

Time and date entries are interpreted like this:

Time Field Encoding

Bits	Meaning
FEDCBA98 76543210	
xxxxx...	Hours (0–23)
.....xxx xxx.....	Minutes (0–59)
....xxxxx	Two-second increments (0–29)

Date Field Encoding

FEDCBA98 76543210	
xxxxxxx.	Year – 1980
.......x xxx.....	Month (1–12)
....xxxxx	Day (1–31)

The DTA may be read to retrieve the information about the located file, which after all will have a different file name than the search string if it includes wild cards. However, the DTA should remain inviolate for use in further searches.

Purpose: Set PSP Segment

DOS Version Availability: 2

Interrupt: 21h

Function: 50h

Description: Sets the address of the currently executing process's Program Segment Prefix (PSP)

Calling Registers: AH = 50h
BX = Segment address of the new PSP

Return Registers: None

Comments: Microsoft and IBM officially specify this function as reserved. The description presented here is derived from nonofficial technical information and is not to be construed as the function's official or permanent use. Its use, as documented here, may change in future versions of DOS. In fact, if your version of DOS is from a third-party vendor, this function may be used for an entirely different purpose. The information presented here is intended as a guide, and you should explore the function at your own leisure and risk.

Function 50h allows a Terminate and Stay Resident (TSR) program to implement *context switching* between the TSR process and the interrupted process on a DOS system. Context switching involves making the DOS system think that the TSR is the primary process rather than the interrupted process. To do this, you have to record the original PSP's address (Function 51h) and tell DOS that the TSR's PSP is the current one (Function 50h). When you are ready to return to the interrupted program, you return the PSPs to normal.

It has often been reported that this function is unreliable prior to DOS V3 and that, in particular, it does not work within an Int 28h handler (keyboard busy loop).

The PSP has come to be called the Process ID (PID) for the running process. This function is often known as SetPID.

Purpose: Get PSP Segment

DOS Version Availability: 2

Interrupt: 21h

Function: 51h

Description: Gets the address of the currently executing process's Program Segment Prefix (PSP)

Calling Registers: AH = 51h

Return Registers: BX = PSP of currently executing process

Comments: Microsoft and IBM officially specify this function as reserved. The description presented here is derived from nonofficial technical information and is not to be construed as the function's official or permanent use. Its use, as documented here, may change in future versions of DOS. In fact, if your version of DOS is from a third-party vendor, this function may be used for an entirely different purpose. The information presented here is intended as a guide, and you should explore the function at your own leisure and risk.

This function is used to determine the PSP of the process interrupted by a Terminate and Stay Resident (TSR) program. The TSR can save this address and then tell DOS that its own PSP is the executing one for the course of its processing. See Function 50h and Chapter 11, "Interrupt Handlers," for a more detailed discussion.

It has often been reported that this function is unreliable prior to DOS V3 and that, in particular, it does not work within an Int 28h handler (keyboard busy loop).

The PSP has come to be called the Process ID (PID) for the running process. This function is often known as GetPID.

Purpose: Get Disk List

DOS Version Availability: 2

Interrupt: 21h

Function: 52h

Description: The apparent function of this interrupt is to provide internal access to a master list of table pointers where DOS is storing information.

Calling Registers: AH = 52h

Return Registers: ES:BX = Pointer to DOS table as described below

Comments: Microsoft and IBM officially specify this function as reserved. The description presented here is derived from nonofficial technical information and is not to be construed as the official or permanent use for the function. Its use, as documented here, may change in future versions of DOS. In fact, if your version of DOS is from a third-party vendor, this function may be used for an entirely different purpose. The information presented here is intended as a guide, and you should explore the function at your own leisure and risk.

For internal purposes, DOS keeps track of pointers and tables that it needs to perform various functions. This function returns a pointer to an internal table that contains many of these pointers. There are many "holes" in the following description of the table—not because the unknown bytes have no purpose, but because their purpose is not known. What *is* known comes from dedicated DOS hackers who have been working out the details one piece at a time.

Notice that beginning with offset 10h, the construction of table DOS.15 varies, depending on whether DOS V2 or DOS V3 is in use.

Table DOS.15. *DOS Information Table*

Offset Byte	Field Length	Meaning
–02h	Word	Segment of first memory control block
00h	Double word	Pointer to first DOS disk block
04h	Double word	Possible pointer to first resident device driver
08h	Double word	Pointer to CLOCK$ device driver
0Ch	Double word	Pointer to CON: device driver
DOS V2.x		
10h	Byte	Number of logical drives
11h	Word	Maximum bytes per block of any block device
13h	Double word	Unknown
17h		Beginning of NUL device driver; first device in the device-driver chain.
DOS 3.x		
10h	Word	Maximum bytes per block on any block device
12h	Double word	Unknown
16h	Double word	Pointer to table of drive information (see following description)
1Ah	Double word	Unknown
1Eh	Word	Unknown
20h	Byte	Number of block devices
21h	Byte	Value of LASTDRIVE in CONFIG.SYS
22h	Byte	Beginning of NUL device driver; first device in the device-driver chain.

The following is what is known about the drive-information table pointed to by the pointer at offset 16h in table DOS.15 (DOS V3 only). The pointer is to the beginning of this table, and there is one table for each system drive, beginning with drive A:. The tables, each of which is 81 bytes long, follow one another in memory. There is one table for each drive on the system, the minimum being a default of five (A: through E:) or the value set in LASTDRIVE of the CONFIG.SYS file.

Offset Byte	Field Length	Meaning
00h	64 bytes	Current path for this drive as an ASCIIZ string (includes drive designator and root directory slash)
40h	Double word	Unknown
44h	Byte	Unknown
45h	Double word	Pointer to drive's DOS disk block
49h	8 bytes	Unknown

Purpose: Translate BPB to DPB

DOS Version Availability: 2

Interrupt: 21h

Function: 53h

Description: Translates a BIOS Parameter Block (BPB) into a DOS Parameter Block (DPB)

Calling Registers: AH = 53h
DS:SI = Pointer to BPB
ES:BP = Pointer to area for DPB

Return Registers: None

Comments: Microsoft and IBM officially specify this function as reserved. The description presented here is derived from nonofficial technical information and is not to be construed as the function's official or permanent use. Its use, as documented here, may change in future versions of DOS. In fact, if your version of DOS is from a third-party vendor, this function may be used for an entirely different purpose. The information presented here is intended as a guide, and you should explore the function at your own leisure and risk.

BIOS and DOS both keep their own information about the disks and drives attached to the system. This function allows you to change the BIOS Parameter Block (BPB) to a DOS Parameter Block (DPB). See also Int 21h, Functions 1Fh and 32h as well as Int 21h, Function 44h, subfunction 0Dh, minor function 40h. Table DOS.16 gives the layout of a BPB and a DPB. As you will notice, the information is primarily disk oriented, particularly in the BPB.

Table DOS.16. *BIOS and DOS Parameter Block Layout*

Offset Byte	Field Length	Meaning
BIOS Parameter Block Information		
00h	Word	Number of bytes per sector
02h	Byte	Number of sectors per cluster
03h	Word	Number of reserved sectors starting at sector 0
05h	Byte	Number of FATs
06h	Word	Maximum number of root-directory entries

Table DOS.16 continues

Table DOS.16 *continued*

Offset Byte	Field Length	Meaning
08h	Word	Total number of sectors
0Ah	Byte	Media descriptor
0Bh	Word	Number of sectors per FAT
0Dh	Word	Number of sectors per track
0Fh	Word	Number of heads
11h	Double word	Number of hidden sectors
15h	11 bytes	Reserved

DOS Parameter Block Information

Offset Byte	Field Length	Meaning
00h	Byte	Drive number (0 = A:, 1 = B:, etc.)
01h	Byte	Device driver unit number
02h	Word	Bytes per sector
04h	Byte	Sectors per cluster (zero based)
05h	Byte	Shift factor
06h	Word	Number of reserved boot sectors
08h	Byte	Number of FAT copies
09h	Word	Number of root-directory entries
0Bh	Word	First data-sector number
0Dh	Word	Highest cluster number plus 1
0Fh	Byte	Sectors per FAT
10h	Word	Root directory starting sector number
12h	Double word	Drive's device driver address
16h	Byte	Media descriptor byte

Table DOS.16 *continues*

Table DOS.16 *continued*

Offset Byte	Field Length	Meaning
17h	Byte	Disk parameter block validity byte (0FFh indicates need to rebuild)
18h	Double word	Address of next device parameter block
1Ch	Word	Starting cluster number for current directory (DOS V2 only)
1Eh	64 bytes	ASCIIZ of current directory path (DOS V2 only)

Purpose: Get Verify Flag

DOS Version Availability: 2

Interrupt: 21h

Function: 54h

Description: Gets the current value of the read-after-write (verify) flag

Calling Registers: AH = 54h

Return Registers: AL = 00h, verify off
01h, verify on

Comments: The verify flag controls whether the system will do a read-after-write verify of disk operations. The default for this flag is OFF (value 00).

Function 2Eh sets the verify flag. The effect of the setting is to slow down disk operations somewhat to allow the verify but increase the assurance that disk operations are successful.

Because network systems do not support the verify function, the return code is meaningless in these cases.

Purpose: Create PSP

DOS Version Availability: 2

Interrupt: 21h

Function: 55h

Description: Creates a Program Segment Prefix (PSP) at the designated segment-address location

Calling Registers: AH = 55h
                         DX = Segment at which to set up PSP

Return Registers: None

Comments: Microsoft and IBM officially specify this function as reserved. The description presented here is derived from nonofficial technical information and is not to be construed as the official or permanent use for the function. Its use, as documented here, may change in future versions of DOS. In fact, if your version of DOS is from a third-party vendor, this function may be used for an entirely different purpose. The information presented here is intended as a guide, and you should explore the function at your own leisure and risk.

This function is similar to Int 21h, Function 26h. The difference is that this function does not simply copy the PSP; it creates a separate and distinct "child" PSP in preparation for running another program. Like Int 21h, Function 26h, the usefulness of this function has been superseded by the EXEC function (Int 21h, Function 4Bh).

Purpose: Rename File

DOS Version Availability: 2

Interrupt: 21h

Function: 56h

Description: Renames a file or moves it to another directory on the same disk drive. The file name must be a specific file name, and no wild cards are allowed.

Calling Registers: AH = 56h
DS:DX = Pointer to ASCIIZ current file name
ES:DI = Pointer to ASCIIZ new file name

Return Registers: Carry flag clear if successful

Carry flag set if error
AX = Error code
02h, file not found
03h, path not found
05h, access denied
11h, not the same device

Comments: The present rename function is both more powerful and less powerful than the one provided for use with File Control Block (FCB) functions. This rename function allows you to use directory path names to locate files and can even move a file between directories. But because it does not allow wild cards, renaming groups of files is no longer a possibility.

For most normal work, the limitations are not significant. Renaming files in directories and moving them between directories is much more advantageous for general use. Multiple files can be handled by the calling program.

The function will not work if the path name does not exist or if a file of the desired name is already in the target directory. Nor will the function work across disk drives. If files being renamed are open, they should be closed first. Leaving a file open when renaming it can lead to unpredictable results.

In a network environment, you must have create-access rights in order to rename a file.

Purpose: Get/Set File Date and Time

DOS Version Availability: 2

Interrupt: 21h

Function: 57h

Description: Gets or sets the file's last modified date and time
in the directory entry

Calling Registers: AH = 57h
AL = 00h, get the date and time
         01h, set the date and time
BX = File handle
CX = Time if setting the date and time
DX = Date if setting the date and time

Return Registers: Carry flag clear if successful
CX = Time if getting date and time
DX = Date if getting date and time

Carry flag set if error
AX = Error code
         01h, invalid function (file sharing)
         06h, invalid handle

Comments: The date and time functions work on files opened with Functions 3Ch, 3Dh, 5Ah, or 5Bh (the handle open or create functions). The following table shows the layout of the bits and how they are interpreted for the date and time:

Time Field Encoding

Bits	*Meaning*
FEDCBA98 76543210	
xxxxx...	Hours (0–23)
.....xxx xxx.....	Minutes (0–59)
....xxxxx	Two-second increments (0–29)

Date Field Encoding

FEDCBA98 76543210	
xxxxxxx.	Year – 1980
.......x xxx.....	Month (1–12)
....xxxxx	Day (1–31)

Purpose: Get/Set Allocation Strategy

DOS Version Availability: 3

Interrupt: 21h

Function: 58h

Description: Gets or sets the code that tells which strategy to use for memory allocation

Calling Registers: AH = 58h
AL = 00h, get strategy code
　　 01h, set strategy code
BX = Strategy code if setting it
　　 00h, first fit (default)
　　 01h, best fit
　　 02h, last fit

Return Registers: Carry flag clear if successful
AX = Strategy code (if getting it)

Carry flag set if error
AX = Error code
　　 01h, invalid function (file sharing)

Comments: Microsoft and IBM officially specify this function as "used internally by DOS." The description presented here is derived from nonofficial technical information and is not to be construed as the function's official or permanent use. Its use, as documented here, may change in future versions of DOS. In fact, if your version of DOS is from a third-party vendor, this function may be used for an entirely different purpose. The information presented here is intended as a guide, and you should explore the function at your own leisure and risk.

This function deals with the strategy that DOS uses to allocate memory to processes when DOS is asked for memory. In general, this type of tuning parameter is meaningless for most programmers unless you have some reason to believe that one strategy will work better than another.

Possible strategies known to DOS include *first fit*, *best fit*, and *last fit*. The first-fit strategy searches for a memory block and returns the first one that is adequate to meet the allocation needs of the calling process. This search proceeds from low memory to high in search of the first block that is as large as or larger than the requested memory.

The best-fit strategy checks all available memory blocks to find the smallest block that will meet the allocation requested. Although this strategy results in the most efficient utilization of memory for the available processes, it also takes more processor time.

The last-fit strategy is the same as the first fit strategy except that the search proceeds from high to low memory rather than from low to high.

It should be noted that because the last-fit strategy (code 02) can actually be any value greater than or equal to 02, when getting the strategy, a number other than 02 may have been stored. A test for strategy should account for the potential that the number could be greater than 2.

Purpose: Get Extended Error Information

DOS Version Availability: 3

Interrupt: 21h

Function: 59h

Description: Gets extended error return information about a failed call to an Int 21h function, including recommended remedial action. This call destroys registers CL, DX, SI, DI, BP, DS, and ES.

Calling Registers: AH = 59h
BX = 00

Return Registers: AX = Extended error code
BH = Error class
BL = Recommended action
CH = Error locus

Comments: Extended error processing provides a significant extension to DOS error handling by making the DOS system a partner in diagnosing and solving run-time problems. This function adds a significant capability for analyzing and isolating an error that arises from a DOS call. It can be called after an error from any call to Int 21h or from Int 24h when an error status is returned. If there was no error, this function will return AX = 0000h. File Control Block (FCB) calls that return FFh can also be resolved with this function.

The information returned is classified in the accompanying tables. Register AX returns the Extended Error Code (see table DOS.17). These are general system errors already familiar as the error returned from many Int 21h functions. Register BH contains the Error Class, which provides further information about the error (see table DOS.18).

Table DOS.17. *Extended Error Codes Returned in AX*

Codes Decimal	Hex	Meaning
1	01	Invalid function
2	02	File not found
3	03	Path not found
4	04	No handles available
5	05	Access denied
6	06	Invalid handle
7	07	Memory control blocks destroyed

Table DOS.17 continues

Table DOS.17 *continued*

Codes Decimal	Hex	Meaning
8	08	Insufficient memory
9	09	Invalid memory block address
10	0A	Invalid environment
11	0B	Invalid format
12	0C	Invalid access code
13	0D	Invalid data
14	0E	Reserved
15	0F	Invalid drive
16	10	Attempt to remove current directory
17	11	Not the same device
18	12	No more files
19	13	Disk write-protected
20	14	Unknown unit
21	15	Drive not ready
22	16	Unknown command
23	17	CRC error
24	18	Bad request structure length
25	19	Seek error
26	1A	Unknown media type
27	1B	Sector not found
28	1C	Out of paper
29	1D	Write fault
30	1E	Read fault
31	1F	General failure
32	20	Sharing violation
33	21	Lock violation
34	22	Invalid disk change
35	23	FCB unavailable
36	24	Sharing buffer overflow
37–49	25–31	Reserved
50	32	Network request not supported
51	33	Remote computer not listening
52	34	Duplicate name on network
53	35	Network name not found
54	36	Network busy
55	37	Network device no longer exists
56	38	Net BIOS command limit exceeded

Table DOS.17 continues

Table DOS.17. *continued*

Codes Decimal	Hex	Meaning
57	39	Network adapter error
58	3A	Incorrect network response
59	3B	Unexpected network error
60	3C	Incompatible remote adapter
61	3D	Print queue full
62	3E	Not enough space for print file
63	3F	Print file deleted
64	40	Network name deleted
65	41	Access denied
66	42	Network device type incorrect
67	43	Network name not found
68	44	Network name limit exceeded
69	45	Net BIOS session limit exceeded
70	46	Temporarily paused
71	47	Network request not accepted
72	48	Print or disk redirection is paused
73–79	49–4F	Reserved
80	50	File already exists
81	51	Reserved
82	52	Cannot make directory entry
83	53	Fail on Int 24
84	54	Too many redirections
85	55	Duplicate redirection
86	56	Invalid password
87	57	Invalid parameter
88	58	Network data fault

Table DOS.18. *Error Class Codes Returned in BH*

Class Codes Decimal	Hex	Meaning
1	01	Out of resource
2	02	Temporary situation
3	03	Authorization
4	04	Internal
5	05	Hardware failure
6	06	System failure

Table DOS.18 *continues*

Table DOS.18 continued

Class Codes		
Decimal	*Hex*	*Meaning*
7	07	Application program error
8	08	Not found
9	09	Bad format
10	0A	Locked
11	0B	Media
12	0C	Already exists
13	0D	Unknown

The BL register returns the most interesting value, the recommended action to resolve the error (see table DOS.19). Finally, register CH returns the Error Locus, which helps identify the error's physical location (see table DOS.20). The only problem with all this information is that the wealth of it can be truly staggering. A generalized error handler would be out of the question. There are, however, some general steps to take depending on what type of error has occurred.

If a function indicates an error by setting the carry bit on return, its error handling should be written like this:

Table DOS.19. Recommended Action Codes Returned in BL

Action Code	Meaning
1	Retry. If not cleared in reasonable number of attempts, prompt user to Abort or Ignore.
2	Delay then retry. If not cleared in reasonable number of attempts, prompt user to Abort or Ignore.
3	Get corrected information from user (bad file name or disk drive).
4	Abort application with cleanup.
5	Abort application without cleanup (cleanup may increase problems).
6	Ignore error.
7	Prompt user to correct error and then retry.

1. Load the registers for the function.
2. Issue the Int 21h function call.
3. If the carry flag is clear, continue with normal operations.
4. If the carry flag is set, disregard the error code returned from the function and issue a call to Function 59h.
5. Use the suggested action in the BL register to determine the proper course of action.

Some functions indicate an error by returning a code in the AL register (AL = FFh). For these cases, the call should be written like this:

1. Load the registers for the function.
2. Issue the Int 21h function call.
3. If no error is reported in AL, continue with normal operations.
4. If an error is reported in AL, disregard the error code reported and issue a call to Function 59h.
5. Use the suggested action in the BL register to determine the proper course of action.

You must be careful using this function. On return, registers CL, DX, SI, DI, BP, DS, and ES are destroyed. You must also call the function *immediately* after an error has occurred. If another DOS function is executed before the call, the return will not correspond to the desired error.

Table DOS.20. *Error Locus Codes Returned in CH*

Locus Code	Meaning
1	Unknown
2	Block device (disk or disk emulator)
3	Network
4	Serial device
5	Memory related

Purpose: Create Temporary File

DOS Version Availability: 3

Interrupt: 21h

Function: 5Ah

Description: Creates a file with a guaranteed unique name in the specified directory. These types of files are generally used as temporary or working files and then deleted when the program is terminated.

Calling Registers: AH = 5Ah
CX = Attribute
DS:DX = Pointer to ASCIIZ path specification ending in a backslash (\ )

Return Registers: Carry flag clear if successful
AX = Handle
DS:DX = Pointer to ASCIIZ file specification with file name appended

Carry flag set if error
AX = Error code
03h, path not found
04h, no handles available
05h, access denied

Comments: Unique files always have uses as temporary files. By using the unique file creation call, you do not have to worry about the exact name created; you can leave that to the operating system.

To use the function, you provide a path name to the directory where you want the temporary file created. Use a full path name ending in a backslash character (for example, \TMP\ to put the file in the \TMP directory). You also can specify the attribute of the file you want created. The following table gives the valid attributes that can be set by this function. The function returns a unique file name according to its own internal rules.

Value	File types matched
00h	Normal
02h	Hidden
04h	System
06h	Hidden and system

The only ways to fail are if the path to the desired directory does not exist or if you are creating the file in the root directory and it is already full. You have to take some care though. Files created as temporary files have as much existence as files created to have continuing existence. Because such file are not deleted automatically when the program ends, your program should clean up after itself by deleting all such files.

In a network environment, you must have create-access rights in order to use this function.

Purpose: Create File

DOS Version Availability: 3

Interrupt: 21h

Function: 5Bh

Description: Creates a new file in the specified directory

Calling Registers: AH = 5Bh
CX = Attribute
DS:DX = Pointer to ASCIIZ file specification

Return Registers: Carry flag clear if successful
AX = Handle

Carry flag set if error
AX = Error code
03h, path not found
04h, no handles available
05h, access denied
50h, file already exists

Comments: This is the normal method of creating a file that you intend to use as more than just a temporary file. The function returns a file handle for access to the file. If the file cannot be created because the path does not exist or because you try to create it in the root directory and the root is full, the function will fail.

Unlike Function 3Ch, this function will fail if the file already exists. You can use this function to test for the existence of a designated file. If creation succeeds, the file did not exist.

The file is created as a normal file with read/write access. You can change the attributes with Function 43h. You cannot, however, create volume labels or subdirectories. The valid attributes are listed in the following table:

Value	File types matched
00h	Normal
02h	Hidden
04h	System
06h	Hidden and system

An interesting use for this file-creation function is to implement a semaphore mechanism across a PC network. If this function successfully creates a file, the program has the semaphore and can proceed into its critical code section. If it cannot create the file, you can retest the operation periodically.

When the program that created the file is finished with its critical section, it deletes the file and thereby releases the semaphore.

In a network environment, you must have create-access rights in order to use this function.

Purpose: Set File Access

DOS Version Availability: 3

Interrupt: 21h

Function: 5Ch

Description: Locks or unlocks a specified area of a file. This type of operation is used in multitasking or networking environments to prevent collisions in file updates.

Calling Registers: AH = 5Ch
AL = Function code
00h, locking
01h, unlocking
BX = File handle
CX = Most significant part of region offset
DX = Least significant part of region offset
SI = Most significant part of region length
DI = Least significant part of region length

Return Registers: Carry flag clear if successful
AX = Handle

Carry flag set if error
AX = Error code
01h, invalid function
06h, invalid handle
21h, lock violation

Comments: File locking is an essential operation in network environments for database- and other transaction-oriented functions. If more than one process is allowed to write to the same section of a file, the results of two such writes will be indeterminate. Record locking enforces an ordering on the operations so that one process must complete its write before another starts. It does not guarantee that the order of writes is sensible—it just makes sure that they do not interfere with each other.

Locks and unlocks are like BEGIN-END pairs in Pascal or braces ({}) in C; they must always be matched. For each file lock, there must be an exact duplicate file unlock in the same program. Failing to unlock a file results in a file whose state is indeterminate.

Programs that use file locking must take pains to trap all possible error exits from the program so that unlocks can be handled even in abnormal conditions. Programs that access files that are or can be locked should not attempt direct access to the file. The proper procedure for using the locking mechanism is not to rely on it to prevent collisions directly. Rather, an attempt should be made to lock the desired portion of the file and check the resulting error code for successful completion. If the lock can be created, file manipulation can proceed. If the lock cannot be created, the program should delay and try again.

The locking mechanism includes an automatic retry function. Using the IOCTL Function (44h), Subfunction 0Bh, you can change the number of retries and the retry interval.

File handles duplicated with Function 45h will inherit access to the locked regions. Programs spawned with the program EXEC Function (4Bh) do not inherit the file locks along with the files.

Purpose: Get Critical-Error Flag Address

DOS Version Availability: 2

Interrupt: 21h

Function: 5Dh

Description: This function returns a pointer to the location at which the system critical-error flag is stored.

Calling Registers: AH = 5Dh
AL = 06h

Return Registers: DS:SI = Pointer to critical-error flag

Comments: Microsoft and IBM officially specify this function as reserved. The description presented here is derived from nonofficial technical information and is not to be construed as the official or permanent use for the function. Its use, as documented here, may change in future versions of DOS. In fact, if your version of DOS is from a third-party vendor, this function may be used for an entirely different purpose. The information presented here is intended as a guide, and you should explore the function at your own leisure and risk.

This function returns a pointer to the error flag used by DOS to determine whether a critical error has occurred.

NETWORK

Purpose: Get Machine Name

DOS Version Availability: 3.1

Interrupt: 21h

Function: 5Eh

Description: Gets the network machine name; gets or sets the printer setup.

Calling Registers: AH = 5Eh

AL = Subfunction number
00h, get machine name
02h, set printer setup
03h, get printer setup

Subfunction 00, get machine name
DS:DX = Pointer to buffer to
receive machine name

Subfunction 02, set printer setup
BX = Redirection list index
CX = Length of setup string (maximum of
64 bytes)
DS:SI = Pointer to setup string

Subfunction 03, get printer setup
BX = Redirection list index
ES:DI = Pointer to buffer to receive
setup string

Return Registers: Subfunction 00, get machine name
Carry flag clear if successful
CH = 00, name not defined
CH > 00, name defined
CL = NETBIOS name number (CH>0)
DS:DX = Pointer to identifier (CH>0)

Carry flag set if error
AX = Error code
01h, invalid function

Subfunction 02, set printer setup
Carry flag clear if successful

Carry flag set if error
AX = Error code
01h, invalid function

Subfunction 03, get printer setup
Carry flag clear if successful
  CX = Length of printer setup string
  ES:DI = Pointer to printer setup string

Carry flag set if error
  AX = Error code
          01h, invalid function

Comments: The *machine name* is a 15-byte, ASCIIZ string used to identify the machine to a network. This function requires that the network be running. If the network is not running, the results of the function will be unpredictable. This function is applicable only to DOS V3.1 and later.

The printer setup is a string to be sent before any print job when accessing the network printer. This function allows setting or retrieving the string.

Purpose: Get Redirection List Entry

DOS Version Availability: 3.1

Interrupt: 21h

Function: 5Fh

Description: Gets or modifies the network redirection list entries

Calling Registers: AH = 5Fh
AL = Subfunction code
02 = Get redirection list entry
03 = Redirect device
04 = Cancel redirection

Subfunction 02, get redirection list entry
BX = Redirection list index
DS:SI = Pointer to 128-byte buffer for device name
ES:DI = Pointer to 128-byte buffer for network name

Subfunction 03, redirect device
BL = Device type
03 = Printer
04 = Disk drive
CX = Parameter to save for caller
DS:SI = Pointer to ASCIIZ local device name
ES:DI = Pointer to ASCIIZ network name followed by ASCIIZ password

Subfunction 04, cancel redirection
DS:SI = Pointer to ASCIIZ device name

Return Registers: Subfunction 02, get redirection list entry
Carry flag clear if successful
BH = Device status flag
Bit 0 = 0, device valid
1, device invalid
BL = Device type
03 = Printer
04 = Disk drive
CX = Stored parameter value
DX = Destroyed
BP = Destroyed
DS:SI = Pointer to ASCIIZ local device name
ES:DI = Pointer to ASCIIZ network name

Carry flag set if error
  AX = Error code
        01h, invalid function
        12h, no more files

Subfunction 03, redirect device
Carry flag clear if successful

Carry flag set if error
  AX = Error code
        01h, invalid function
        03h, path not found
        05h, access denied
        08h, insufficient memory

Subfunction 04, cancel redirection
Carry flag clear if successful

Carry flag set if error
  AX = Error code
        01h, invalid function

Comments: This function is used to get, set, or cancel network redirection for devices (printers or disk directories) on the network. It does this by modifying a list of local device names associated with network devices, files, or directories. The network must be running to support this function. Using this function, you can, for example, associate a disk-drive identifier with a network directory. You can also assign a remote printer device to be accessed with a local printer device name. The function supports remote passwords for remote disk access.

The file-sharing module must be loaded to use this function. All identifiers are passed as ASCIIZ strings and are thereby compatible with programming in C but not directly compatible with Pascal or BASIC. When you are getting a redirection entry, each call to subfunction 02 returns a single entry in the redirection table. The entries are ASCIIZ strings representing the local device name, to which DS:SI points, and the network name, to which ES:DI points.

As you make subsequent calls to subfunction 02, you can tell you have reached the end of the list when error code 12h (no more files) is returned. Calling this function destroys the contents of registers DX and BP, even though they are not used to return values.

Subfunction 03 (redirect device) allows you to specify a redirection to use. You can specify a printer or disk redirection (BL = device type) and indicate its local name (A:, B:, and so on for disk redirections; PRN:, LPT1:, and so on for printer redirection). When you redirect a printer, the output for the printer is buffered and sent to the network printer spooler for the desired device. Because this redirection occurs at the Int 17h level, you will trap all but hardware access to the printer itself.

Subfunction 04 (cancel redirection) uses only the local device name. The redirection is broken if that device has been reassigned. When the device name is a string starting with two backslashes, the connection between the local machine and the network directory is broken.

Despite the sophisticated redirection available, COM devices, STDOUT, and STDERR cannot be redirected.

Purpose: Get PSP Address

DOS Version Availability: 3

Interrupt: 21h

Function: 62h

Description: Gets the segment address of the Program Segment Prefix
(PSP) for the current program

Calling Registers: AH = 62h

Return Registers: BX = Segment address of PSP

Comments: The purpose of this function is to allow the program to retrieve
the address of its PSP at any time without having to explicitly save it in an
accessible area during program startup. Because most access to functions
should avoid direct access to the PSP, this function has only marginal utility.

Purpose: Get System Lead Byte Table

DOS Version Availability: 2.25 Only

Interrupt: 21h

Function: 63h

Description: Gets the address of the system lead byte table or controls the interim console flag

Calling Registers: AH = 63h
AL = Subfunction
  00h, getting address of the system lead byte table
  01h, setting or clearing interim console flag
  02h, getting value of interim console flag
DL = (if AL = 01)
  00h, setting interim console flag
  01h, clearing interim console flag

Return Registers: Subfunction 00
  DS:SI = Pointer to lead byte table

Subfunction 01
  None

Subfunction 02
  DL = Value of interim console flag

Comments: This function retrieves the address of the system lead byte table or allows control of the interim console flag. These data structures are associated with handling 2-byte-per-character display systems such as Kanji and Hangeul. This function applies to DOS V2.25 only; it is not available on DOS V3.

Purpose: Get Extended Country Information

DOS Version Availability: 3.3

Interrupt: 21h

Function: 65h

Description: Returns extended information for the specified country

Calling Registers: AH = 65h
AL = ID of information of interest (1, 2, 4, 5, or 6)
BX = Code page of interest (–1 = active CON device)
CX = Amount of data to return
DX = Country ID (default –1)
ES:DI = Pointer to buffer to return information to

Return Registers: Carry flag clear if successful
ES:DI = Pointer to returned information buffer

Carry flag set if error
AX = Error code
01h, invalid function
02h, file not found

Comments: Programmers working on international systems must have access to a wide range of country-specific information such as the currency symbol, date format, and so forth. Function 65h retrieves this information for your program, depending on the country you specify.

Table DOS.21 can be retrieved by country ID. The default (–1) represents the United States. The call retrieves only as much data as specified in CX. If the table contains additional data, that data will be truncated, and no error will be returned.

Table DOS.21. *Extended Country Information*

Offset Byte	Field Length	Meaning

Extended Country Information Buffer
Info ID: 01

Offset Byte	Field Length	Meaning
00h	Word	Info ID = 01
01h	Word	Size (38 or less)
03h	Word	Country ID
05h	Word	Code Page
07h	Word	Date and time format code 0 = USA m d y, hh:mm:ss 1 = Europe d m y, hh:mm:ss 2 = Japan y m d, hh:mm:ss
09h	5 bytes	Currency symbol string (ASCIIZ)
0Eh	Byte	Thousands separator
0Fh	Byte	Zero
10h	Byte	Decimal separator
11h	Byte	Zero
12h	Byte	Date separator
13h	Byte	Zero
14h	Byte	Time separator
15h	Byte	Zero
16h	Byte	Currency format 00h = Symbol leads currency, no space 01h = Symbol follows currency, no space 02h = Symbol leads currency, 1 space 03h = Symbol follows currency, 1 space 04h = Symbol replaces decimal separator
17h	Byte	Number of digits after decimal
18h	Byte	Time format Bit 0 = 0—12 hour clock 1—24 hour clock

Table DOS.21 *continues*

Table DOS.21 *continued*

Offset Byte	Field Length	Meaning
19h	Double word	Case map call address
1Dh	Word	Data list separator
1Eh	Byte	Zero
1Fh	10 bytes	Reserved

Extended Country Uppercase Table
Info ID: 02

00h	Byte	Info ID = 02
01h	Double word	Pointer to Uppercase Table. Uppercase Table is 130 bytes: 2-byte length + 128 uppercase values.

Extended Country File Name Uppercase Table
Info ID: 04

00h	Byte	Info ID = 04
01h	Double word	Pointer to File Name Uppercase Table. File Name Uppercase Table is 130 bytes: 2-byte length + 128 uppercase values.

Extended Country Collating Table
Info ID: 06

00h	Byte	Info ID = 06
01h	Double word	Pointer to Collating Table. Collating Table is 258 bytes: 2-byte length + 256 values in collating order.

Purpose: Get/Set Global Code Page

DOS Version Availability: 3.3

Interrupt: 21h

Function: 66h

Description: Gets or sets the code page for the current country

Calling Registers: AH = 66h
AL = Subfunction number
01h, get global code page
02h, set global code page
Subfunction 02, set global code page
BX = Active code page
DX = System code page

Return Registers: Carry flag clear if successful
Subfunction 01, get global code page
BX = Active code page
DX = System code page

Subfunction 02, set global code page
None

Carry flag set if error
AX = Error code
02h, File not found

Comments: This function moves the country data stored in COUNTRY.SYS into the resident country buffer area, the code page. Devices can be selected automatically for code page switching in the CONFIG.SYS file if the devices support it.

Purpose: Set Handle Count

DOS Version Availability: 3.3

Interrupt: 21h

Function: 67h

Description: Allows a process to modify dynamically the number of file handles (normally 20) allowed for a process

Calling Registers: AH = 67h
                          BX = Number of open handles to allow

Return Registers: Carry flag clear if successful

Carry flag set if error
AX = Error code

Comments: This function allows a program to control the number of file handles available for use while the program is running. This can be particularly important for complicated database programs, which often require a considerable amount of manipulation to handle the large number of files they need to keep open. Memory is allocated from memory freed by Function 74. If the amount of memory is less than the current number of files open, the memory will become effective when the current number of files drops below the limit.

The CONFIG.SYS entry FILES = can set up to 255 file handles in DOS V3.3. This function allows the number of file handles to rise to 64K entries. If the number specified is less than 20, the number defaults to 20.

Purpose: Flush Buffer

DOS Version Availability: 3

Interrupt: 21h

Function: 68h

Description: Flushes all buffered data for a file to the device

Calling Registers: AH = 68h
                         BX = File handle

Return Registers: Carry flag clear if successful

Carry flag set if error
AX = Error code

Comments: The standard way to flush buffers to disk has always been to close a file and then reopen it. A classic improvement on this was first to duplicate the file handle with Function 45h and then close the duplicate. This got the close without incurring the overhead of another open.

Function 68h eliminates the need to be tricky. If you want to flush the buffers, this function will do it faster and in a more secure fashion.

This function can be used instead of handle duplication or a close/open sequence to flush data buffers.

Purpose: Terminate Address

DOS Version Availability: 1

Interrupt: 22h

Description: This is not an interrupt at all but simply the address that control is transferred to when the currently executing program ends.

Calling Registers: Not Applicable

Return Registers: Not Applicable

Comments: When a program is loaded, the contents of this memory location are copied into the Program Segment Prefix (PSP) at offset byte 0Ah. When the program terminates, this value is restored from the same location. Because it is purely a storage area, it should never be executed directly.

Purpose: Ctrl-C Interrupt Vector

DOS Version Availability: 1

Interrupt: 23h

Description: This is not an interrupt. It is a vector that holds the address of the routine which receives control when a Ctrl-C or Ctrl-Break detection occurs.

Calling Registers: Not Applicable

Return Registers: Not Applicable

Comments: Whenever detection of a Ctrl-C or Ctrl-Break occurs during I/O operations or at other times when BREAK is on, the system branches to the address given in this vector. When a program is loaded, this vector is copied into its Program Segment Prefix (PSP) at byte 0Eh; the vector is restored by program termination.

Ctrl-C/Ctrl-Break handlers are two of the most commonly needed special handlers that programmers must write. Sophisticated programs cannot afford to relinquish control to a default handler. They must control any break operations to allow proper cleanup in the event of a problem. (Telecommunications programs written by inexperienced programmers are particularly subject to this type of error).

Because this is a vector storage location, you should never issue an Int 23h to activate the handler. The function will come into play soon enough as the system processes Ctrl-C and Ctrl-Break characters.

Ctrl-C/Ctrl-Break handlers have a number of options they can use for processing a break condition:

1. The handler can set a local flag, which can be polled by the main program for extensive action. Some limited action can be taken directly and then a *return from interrupt* (IRET) can be executed to return control to DOS. DOS restarts the interrupted function from the beginning and completes the call normally. This is useful for applications where every millisecond spent servicing the interrupt is important. High speed communications programs can be written this way.

2. The handler can take action on the condition that caused the interrupt and then do a *far return* (ret far) to return control to DOS. The carry flag should be set to indicate that the application must be aborted or cleared if the application is to be allowed to continue.

3. The handler can take whatever action it needs and then resume operation of the program directly without ever returning to DOS.

Any of the options are valid; the one you choose depends on what else you are doing. Option 1 should be chosen when it is necessary to minimize the time spent in a handler outside of normal processing. Option 2 is more generally useful as a processing procedure when an abort of the process is a possible option. Option 3 can be used to redirect operation and continue directly when it is not a good idea to return to the original operation in progress. It does no harm, but is not generally a wise idea except in special circumstances for which no other solution exists than a radical break from processing.

While in a Ctrl-C/Ctrl-Break handler, you can use any DOS function needed to process the condition.

Purpose: Critical-Error Vector

DOS Version Availability: 1

Interrupt: 24h

Description: This is not an interrupt. It is a vector that holds the address of the routine which receives control when a critical-error detection occurs. A critical error generally represents a hardware failure of some sort.

Calling Registers: Not Applicable

Return Registers: Not Applicable

Comments: When a program is loaded, the contents of this vector are read into the Program Segment Prefix (PSP) starting at byte 12h. When the program terminates, this vector is restored by the system termination handler. This interrupt should never be called directly.

When a critical-error handler is invoked, bit 7 of the AH register will be clear if the problem is due to a disk I/O error; otherwise bit 7 will be set. BP:SI will point to a device header control block where additional information about the error is stored. Registers SS, SP, DS, ES, BX, CX, and DX must be preserved by the critical-error handler.

DOS automatically retries three times before branching to the critical-error handler. When activated, the handler should perform necessary register saves and then attempt to handle the error. Only Functions 00–0Ch (Int 21h) can be invoked from inside a critical-error handler. Other calls destroy the DOS internal stack and should be avoided.

The register setup includes an error code in the lower byte of the DI register. These error codes are the same as those returned by the device drives in the request header (see table DOS.22).

This information can be used to help diagnose the problem. It is interesting to note that these error codes correspond directly to error codes 13h (19) through 1Fh (31) of the DOS extended error codes. For more on this, see Int 21h, Function 59h.

When the critical-error handler is ready to return, it should set an action code in the AL register according to the following table:

Code	Meaning
00h	Ignore error
01h	Retry operation
02h	Terminate program through Int 23h
03h	Version 3 only; fail system call in progress

Table DOS.22. Error Code (Lower Byte DI)

Code	Meaning
00h	Write-protect error
01h	Unknown unit
02h	Drive not ready
03h	Unknown command
04h	Data error (bad CRC)
05h	Bad request structure length
06h	Seek error
07h	Unknown media type
08h	Sector not found
09h	Printer out of paper
0Ah	Write fault
0Bh	Read fault
0Ch	General failure

With the action code set, the handler performs a return from interrupt (IRET), and the function is complete.

The handler can return directly to the user program, but if it does, it will be responsible for cleaning up the stack and removing all but the last three words from the stack prior to issuing an IRET. Control then returns to the statement directly after the I/O function that caused the error. This leaves DOS in an unstable condition until a call to an Int 21h function above 0Ch is performed.

Purpose: Absolute Disk Read

DOS Version Availability: 1

Interrupt: 25h

Description: Reads data from a specified disk sector to the designated memory area

Calling Registers: AL = Drive number (0 = A:, 1 = B:, etc.)
CX = Number of sectors to read
DX = Starting relative (logical) sector number
DS:BX = Pointer to DTA

Return Registers: Carry flag clear if successful

Carry flag set if error
AX = Error code

Comments: The absolute disk read reads a disk sector from the disk into memory by accessing the desired logical sector directly. This type of access must be handled with care because it bypasses the DOS directory structure.

Logical sectors are located starting with track 0, head 0. The first sector on this track is disk sector 0. Sectors then go to the next head, then the next track, and so on. Logical sectors correspond to the sequence of sector numbers stored magnetically on the disk itself and may not correspond to the physical sectors. By specifying interleaving factors, logical disk sectors can be physically separated on the disk. This is sometimes done to improve the efficiency of the disk.

If the carry flag is set when the function returns, then the AX register is interpreted as shown in the accompanying tables. AH and AL are interpreted as separate error codes (see table DOS.23.)

Because the absolute disk read can destroy any but the segment registers, care should be taken to preserve needed values prior to the call.

A special problem with this function makes it difficult to use directly from high-level languages. When the function returns, the CPU flags originally pushed on the stack by Int 25h are still there. To get rid of these extra numbers on the stack, you can do a POPF to take the number off the stack, or you can do an ADD SP,2 to increment the stack pointer past the number. Because high-level languages do not provide direct facilities for this kind of operation, this function has to be called from assembly language to prevent failure of the system. (It could be embedded assembly code, as in Turbo Pascal 3.)

Table DOS.23. *Interpretation of Error Codes*

Code	Meaning
AH Register Error Codes	
80h	Attachment failed to respond
40h	Seek operation failed
20h	Controller failed
10h	Data error (bad CRC)
08h	DMA failure
04h	Requested sector not found
03h	Write-protect fault
02h	Bad address mark
01h	Bad command
AL Register Error Codes	
00h	Write-protect error
01h	Unknown unit
02h	Drive not ready
03h	Unknown command
04h	Data error (bad CRC)
05h	Bad request structure length
06h	Seek error
07h	Unknown media type
08h	Sector not found
09h	Printer out of paper
0Ah	Write fault
0Bh	Read fault
0Ch	General failure

Purpose: Absolute Disk Write

DOS Version Availability: 1

Interrupt: 26h

Description: Writes data from the designated transfer area (DTS) to the disk sector(s) specified

Calling Registers: AL = Drive number (0 = A:, 1 = B:, etc.)
CX = Number of sectors to write
DX = Starting relative (logical) sector number
DS:BX = Pointer to DTA

Return Registers: Carry flag clear if successful

Carry flag set if error
AX = Error code

Comments: The absolute disk write writes a disk sector from memory by accessing the desired logical sector directly. This type of access must be handled with care because it bypasses the DOS directory structure.

Logical sectors are located starting with track 0, head 0. The first sector on this track is disk sector 0. Sectors then go to the next head, then the next track, and so on. Logical sectors correspond to the sequence of sector numbers stored magnetically on the disk itself and may not correspond to the physical sectors. By specifying interleaving factors, logical disk sectors can be physically separated on the disk. This is sometimes done to improve the disk's efficiency.

If the carry flag is set when the function returns, then the AX register is interpreted as shown in the accompanying tables. AH and AL are interpreted as separate error codes (see table DOS.24.)

A special problem with this function makes it difficult to use directly from high-level languages. When the function returns, the CPU flags originally pushed on the stack by Int 25h are still there. To get rid of these extra numbers on the stack, you can do a POPF to take the number off the stack, or you can do an ADD SP,2 to increment the stack pointer past the number. Because high-level languages do not provide direct facilities for this kind of operation, this function has to be called from assembly language to prevent failure of the system. (The assembly code could be embedded, as in Turbo Pascal 3.)

Table DOS.24. Interpretation of Error Codes

Code	Meaning

AH Register Error Codes

Code	Meaning
80h	Attachment failed to respond
40h	Seek operation failed
20h	Controller failed
10h	Data error (bad CRC)
08h	DMA failure
04h	Requested sector not found
03h	Write-protect fault
02h	Bad address mark
01h	Bad command

AL Register Error Codes

Code	Meaning
00h	Write-protect error
01h	Unknown unit
02h	Drive not ready
03h	Unknown command
04h	Data error (bad CRC)
05h	Bad request structure length
06h	Seek error
07h	Unknown media type
08h	Sector not found
09h	Printer out of paper
0Ah	Write fault
0Bh	Read fault
0Ch	General failure

Purpose: Terminate and Stay Resident

DOS Version Availability: 1

Interrupt: 27h

Description: Terminates the presently running program but preserves its memory area

Calling Registers: DX = Offset of last byte plus 1 (relative to PSP) of the program to remain resident
CS = Segment of the PSP

Return Registers: None

Comments: Terminate and Stay Resident (TSR) utilities are familiar to almost all of us working with PCs. Who doesn't have SideKick or some other utility that gives the feeling of multitasking operations without true multitasking? This interrupt was the original (DOS V1) TSR termination procedure, which would allow a program to set aside its memory after connecting itself to whatever interrupt it needed for processing.

On termination, the procedure restores Int 22h (terminate address), Int 23h (Ctrl-C interrupt vector), and Int 24h (critical-error vector) and then transfers control to the termination address. It allows the program to retain its memory area (DX register sizes the protected area) so that the TSR can remain active.

This termination is subject to some significant limitations. First, you must have the CS register set to the segment of the Program Segment Prefix (PSP) for the program. Generally, this is no problem, but you should make sure. Most significantly, only 64K bytes can be set aside for the TSR program. Under DOS V2 and V3, the preferred TSR termination is Int 21h, Function 31h, which allows any amount of memory and does not require that the CS register be set. Given the improvement in TSR termination handlers, Int 27h should be called only on DOS V1.x systems.

This interrupt does not close any files that may be open. If you want them closed, you must explicitly close them before using this interrupt.

Purpose: Keyboard Busy Loop

DOS Version Availability: 1

Interrupt: 28h

Description: Called regularly during the DOS console I/O polling loop to let a Terminate and Stay Resident (TSR) program know that it is okay to use file operations and other Int 21h functions above 0Ch

Calling Registers: Not Applicable

Return Registers: Not Applicable

Comments: Microsoft and IBM officially specify this function as reserved. The description presented here is derived from nonofficial technical information and is not to be construed as the official or permanent use for the function. Its use, as documented here, may change in future versions of DOS. In fact, if your version of DOS is from a third-party vendor, this function may be used for an entirely different purpose. The information presented here is intended as a guide, and you should explore the function at your own leisure and risk.

This interrupt is called by DOS while in its console input-polling loop. A TSR activated here knows that it is safe to do file system operations or other DOS functions above 0Ch. TSRs that need to allow other TSRs to execute should chain this interrupt to the next TSR in line.

Normally, this vector points at an IRET instruction.

Purpose: Fast Putchar

DOS Version Availability: 1

Interrupt: 29h

Description: DOS output routine interrupt

Calling Registers: Not Applicable

Return Registers: Not Applicable

Comments: Microsoft and IBM officially specify this function as reserved. The description presented here is derived from nonofficial technical information and is not to be construed as the official or permanent use for the function. Its use, as documented here, may change in future versions of DOS. In fact, if your version of DOS is from a third-party vendor, this function may be used for an entirely different purpose. The information presented here is intended as a guide, and you should explore the function at your own leisure and risk.

This interrupt is called by DOS output routines if the output is going to a device, and the device driver's attribute word has bit 3 set to 1.

This interrupt is intended for use with DOS device drivers, and it is not documented as being supported beyond DOS V2.0. It is *not* to be used in applications programs.

Purpose: Print Installation Check

DOS Version Availability: 3

Interrupt: 2Fh

Description: Handles access to the printer spooler

Calling Registers: AL = 00h, get installed status
01h, submit file to be printed
02h, remove file from print queue
03h, cancel all files in queue
04h, hold print jobs for status read
05h, end hold for status read
DS:DX = Pointer to packet address
(subfunction 01h)
Pointer to ASCIIZ file specification
(subfunction 02h)

Return Registers: Carry flag clear if successful
Subfunction 00h
AL = Status
00h, OK to install if not installed
01h, not OK to install if not installed
FFh, installed

Subfunction 04h
DX = Error count
DS:SI = Pointer to print queue

Carry flag set if error
AX = Error code

Comments: Print spooling has become a normal method of operation for many people who are too busy to stop what they're doing to wait for a printout. This function gives a program access to the printer spooler.

For subfunction 01, you provide a 5-byte packet with a priority level in the first byte and a pointer to an ASCIIZ file specification to be printed. The spooler takes over and automatically prints the file unless you intervene.

Subfunction 02 accepts wild cards (* and ?) in the file specification allowing multiple print file terminations from a single call to the function.

Subfunction 04 returns a pointer to a series of file-name entries, each 64 bytes long and containing an ASCIIZ string that is the file specification for one of the print files. The first in the list is the file presently being printed. The last entry has a NUL character in the first byte (zero length file-name string).

The error codes returned by the functions are shown in the following table:

Code	Meaning
01h	Function invalid
02h	File not found
03h	Path not found
04h	Too many open files
05h	Access denied
08h	Queue full
09h	Spooler busy
0Ch	Name too long
0Fh	Drive invalid

Purpose: APPEND Function

Interrupt: 2Fh

Function: B7h

Description: Network APPEND function

Calling Registers: AH = B7h
AL = 00h, Check for APPEND installation

Return Registers: AH <> 0 if APPEND installed

Comments: This function is used to determine whether APPEND has been installed. APPEND is installed at the DOS level through the APPEND command. The value returned in AH indicates whether it is installed. Because there has been little standardization in networking over the past several years, not all networks will respond correctly to this interrupt.

Interrupt 33h: Mouse Functions

The DOS mouse functions operate through an installed driver (MOUSE.SYS) which ties itself to Int 33h for access to the functions. The driver constantly updates the mouse cursor's position on the screen relative to the movement of the mouse itself. No action by the program is needed to maintain the driver's action.

At any time, a program can query the driver to find the current status of the mouse.

Purpose: Get Mouse Parameters

DOS Version Availability: 2

Interrupt: 33h

Function: 00h

Description: Determines whether a mouse is installed and returns the number of buttons on the mouse

Calling Registers: AX = 0000h

Return Registers: AX = 0000h, mouse not installed
FFFFh, mouse installed
BX = Number of buttons

Comments: Whenever a program in which you want to use the mouse starts, that program must call Function 0 to see whether a mouse is there. This function resets the mouse to the center of the screen, makes sure that the mouse is off, and sets the default mouse cursor and default movement ratios.

Purpose: Display Mouse Cursor

DOS Version Availability: 2

Interrupt: 33h

Function: 01h

Description: Causes the mouse cursor to appear on the display

Calling Registers: AX = 0001h

Return Registers: None

Comments: Turns on the mouse cursor, allowing display on the screen. This is not an absolute function; rather, it increments an internal mouse-cursor flag. Initially, this flag is set to a minus 1 (–1). Whenever the flag is zero, the mouse cursor will be displayed. Function 02h decrements the cursor flag, causing the cursor to disappear if the original value was zero.

Purpose: Turn Off Mouse Cursor

DOS Version Availability: 2

Interrupt: 33h

Function: 02h

Description: Turns off display of the mouse cursor

Calling Registers: AX = 0002h

Return Registers: None

Comments: This function turns off the display function but does not disable the driver. As noted in the comment for Function 01h, Function 02h decrements a cursor flag. If the value is not zero, the cursor is turned off.

Purpose: Get Mouse Position

DOS Version Availability: 2

Interrupt: 33h

Function: 03h

Description: Returns the current mouse position and button status

Calling Registers: AX = 0003h

Return Registers: BX = Button status
CX = X coordinate (horizontal)
DX = Y coordinate (vertical)

Comments: This function tells you where the mouse is located. No matter what mode the screen is in, Function 03h will return an x coordinate (row) of between 0 and 199 and a y coordinate (column) of between 0 and 639. Table M.1 shows the mouse cursor's position in terms of screen coordinates.

Table M.1. *Mouse Cursor's Position*

Screen Mode	Mouse Coordinates
00h, 01h	x = 16 ' column y = 8 ' row
02h, 03h	x = 8 ' column y = 8 ' row
04h, 05h	x = 2 ' screen X y = Screen Y
06h	x = Screen X y = Screen Y
07h	x = 8 ' screen column y = 8 ' screen row
0Eh-10h	x = Screen X y = Screen Y

The status of the mouse buttons is returned in BX; only the two low-order bits are significant. Table M.2 illustrates the meaning of the bits.

Table M.2. *Mouse Button Status Bits*

Bit 7654321Ø	*Meaning*
......Ø	Left button not depressed
......1	Left button depressed
.....Ø.	Right button not depressed
.....1.	Right button depressed
xxxxxx..	Undefined

Purpose: Set Mouse Position

DOS Version Availability: 2

Interrupt: 33h

Function: 04h

Description: Sets the mouse's position on the screen

Calling Registers: AX = 0004h
CX = New x coordinate (horizontal)
DX = New y coordinate (vertical)

Return Registers: None

Comments: You can use this function to place the mouse cursor anywhere on the screen. (The mouse driver will resume operating from that location.) This function is useful, for example, when you want to start the mouse at the first item on a menu that is brought up on the screen.

Purpose: Get Button-Press Information

DOS Version Availability: 2

Interrupt: 33h

Function: 05h

Description: Returns information about button presses on the
mouse

Calling Registers: AX = 0005h
BX = Button (0 =left, 1 =right)

Return Registers: AX = Button status
BX = Count of button presses
CX = Cursor's horizontal position at last
button press
DX = Cursor's vertical position at last
button press

Comments: Function 05h provides information about what has happened
to the specified cursor button since your last call to this function. You can tell
whether the button has been pressed, the number of times it was pressed, and
where the mouse was when the button was last pressed.

The button status is returned in register AX: 0 indicates that the button is
released (up); 1 indicates that the button is depressed.

Purpose: Get Button-Release Information

DOS Version Availability: 2

Interrupt: 33h

Function: 06h

Description: Returns information about a designated button's releases

Calling Registers: AX = 0006h
BX = Button (0 =left, 1 =right)

Return Registers: AX = Button status
BX = Count of button releases
CX = Cursor's horizontal position when last released
DX = Cursor's vertical position when last released

Comments: Function 06h returns information about the release of a mouse button. (Function 05h returns information about presses.) A button release (you let go of the button) is distinct from a press (you press down on the button) and can be identified if you use these two functions. Registers for this function contain information corresponding to the release operation.

Purpose: Set Mouse X Bounds

DOS Version Availability: 2

Interrupt: 33h

Function: 07h

Description: Sets the X limits of the mouse's travel on the screen

Calling Registers: AX = 0007h
                          CX = Minimum X bound
                          DX = Maximum X bound

Return Registers: None

Comments: When you want to limit the movement of the mouse cursor in the X direction (row), call Function 07h. This function is useful when you want to keep the mouse cursor within a defined area on-screen, as you might, for example, with a menu. Function 08h (Y Limits) also is useful for restricting the mouse cursor's movement.

Purpose: Set Mouse Y Bounds

DOS Version Availability: 2

Interrupt: 33h

Function: 08h

Description: Sets the Y limits of the mouse's travel on the screen

Calling Registers: AX = 0008h
CX = Minimum Y bound
DX = Maximum Y bound

Return Registers: None

Comments: When you want to limit the movement of the mouse cursor in the Y direction (column), call Function 08h. This function is useful when you want to keep the mouse cursor within a defined area on the screen, as you might, for example, with a menu. Function 07h (X Limits) also is useful for restricting the mouse cursor's movement.

Purpose: Set Graphics Cursor

DOS Version Availability: 2

Interrupt: 33h

Function: 09h

Description: Sets the cursor for use in graphics mode

Calling Registers: AX = 0009h
BX = Hot spot x position (–16 to 16)
CX = Hot spot y position (–16 to 16)
ES:DX = Pointer to screen and cursor masks

Return Registers: None

Comments: In graphics mode, the cursor is made up of a screen mask and a cursor mask. Function 09h specifies these masks *and* the hot spot (active area) within the cursor.

When the mouse cursor is generated in graphics mode, the screen mask is ANDed to the screen and the cursor mask is XORed. When two bytes are ANDed together, the resulting byte has a 1 bit wherever *both* of the two original bytes have a 1; all the other bits are set to zero. An XOR on two bytes results in a byte with a 1 bit wherever *only one* of the original bytes has a 1; all the other bits are set to zero.

As an example, if the screen mask is 9Ch and the byte is 3Bh, the result of ANDing them together is the following:

```
    AND              9Ch          10011100
                     3Bh          00111011
                                  --------
                                  00011000
```

If the cursor mask is 9Ch and the byte is 3Bh, the result of XORing them together is as follows:

```
    XOR              9Ch          10011100
                     3Bh          00111011
                                  --------
                                  10100111
```

The practical effect of these operations for graphics modes 1 through 6 is as follows for each bit:

Cursor Mask	Screen Mask 0	Screen Mask 1
0	0	1
1	No change	Inverted

For screen modes 7 and over, the effect is

Cursor Mask	Screen Mask 0	Screen Mask 1
0	Black	White
1	No change	No change

The masks stored at the location pointed to by ES:DX are bit-mapped blocks. Each byte of the bitmap corresponds to one row of the cursor (starting at the top row, screen mask first). Bytes 0 through 7 are the screen mask; bytes 8 through 15 are the cursor mask. Figure M.1 shows how the bytes correspond to cursor locations.

Fig. M.1. Bytes corresponding to cursor locations.

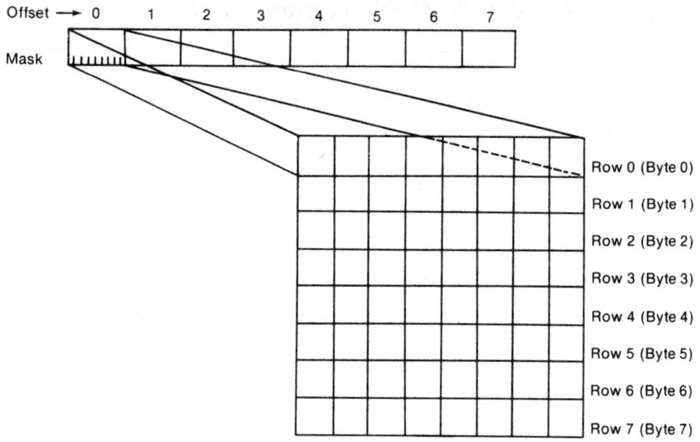

There are two bits per cursor pixel in graphics modes 4–6 and 14–16, even though the cursor size may differ.

Purpose: Set Text Cursor

DOS Version Availability: 2

Interrupt: 33h

Function: 0Ah

Description: Sets up the text mode cursor

Calling Registers: AX = 000Ah

BX = 0 to select attribute cursor
1 to select hardware cursor

CX = Start of screen mask or hardware cursor
scan line

DX = End of cursor mask or hardware cursor
scan line

Return Registers: None

Comments: In text mode, the cursor will be either an attribute cursor or a hardware cursor depending on how BX is set. With the attribute cursor, the CX and DX registers are screen and cursor masks, respectively. The screen mask preserves most of the original character's attributes. The cursor mask determines which attributes will be changed. The low byte of the screen mask should be FFh; the low byte of the cursor mask should be 00h.

The attribute and character bytes at the mouse cursor's location are ANDed with the screen mask and XORed with the cursor mask.

Purpose: Get Physical Movement

DOS Version Availability: 2

Interrupt: 33h

Function: 0Bh

Description: Determines the number of physical screen positions moved since the last call to this function

Calling Registers: AX = 000Bh

Return Registers: CX = Number of x positions moved (–32768 to 32768)

DX = Number of y positions moved (–32768 to 32768)

Comments: Function 0Bh will tell you the *relative* movement of the mouse cursor between calls. The internal software keeps track of the mouse cursor's location at all times and records its location at each call to this function.

The CX and DX registers return the relative movement (positive values correspond to right and down the screen). The numbers returned represent units equal to approximately .5 millimeters (.02 inches).

Purpose: Sets a User-Defined Input Mask

DOS Version Availability: 2

Interrupt: 33h

Function: 0Ch

Description: Allows the calling routine to set up a function that will be called by the device driver whenever a condition defined by the mask is found

Calling Registers: AX = 000Ch
                        CX = Call mask (see Comments)
                        DX = Address offset to function

Return Registers: None

Comments: This function creates a special handler for conditions recognized by the mouse device driver. A function can be written to respond to button presses or releases or to changes in the cursor's position.

Operation of the interrupt is controlled by a *call mask* that identifies which conditions will trigger the special handler. Wherever the call mask has a 1 bit, the function pointed to by the DX register will be executed when the condition occurs. A zero bit in the same position cancels the function. Table M.3 shows the assignment of bits in the call mask.

Table M.3. Call Mask Bits

Bit 76543210	Meaning
.......1	Cursor position changed
......1.	Left button pressed
.....1..	Left button released
....1...	Right button pressed
...1....	Right button released

When Function 0 is called, the entire call mask is reset to zero. Before a program that sets up a special handler for these conditions ends, the call mask should be reset by a call to Function 0Ch or to Function 00h.

Remember to restore the initial value of the call mask and subroutine addresses before you end your program.

Purpose: Set Light Pen Emulation

DOS Version Availability: 2

Interrupt: 33h

Function: 0Dh

Description: Turns on light pen emulation mode

Calling Registers: AX = 000Dh

Return Registers: None

Comments: In light pen emulation mode, the mouse position is the light pen position. Pressing both mouse buttons corresponds to pressing the light pen to the screen.

Purpose: Stop Light Pen Emulation

DOS Version Availability: 2

Interrupt: 33h

Function: 0Eh

Description: Turns off light pen emulation

Calling Registers: AX = 000Eh

Return Registers: None

Comments: This function is used to instruct the device driver to stop handling the mouse inputs as though they originated from a light pen. Function 0Eh causes the mouse to work in its normal manner, without driver translation.

Purpose: Set Physical Movement Ratio

DOS Version Availability: 2

Interrupt: 33h

Function: 0Fh

Description: Sets the ratio between physical movement of the cursor (1/200th of an inch) and coordinate changes

Calling Registers: AX = 000Fh

CX = # physical positions to indicate a change in 8 x coords (default 8)

DX = # physical positions to indicate a change in 8 y coords (default 16)

Return Registers: None

Comments: In both the CX and DX registers, the high bit must be zero. The minimum value for each ratio is 1.

Purpose: Conditional Off

DOS Version Availability: 2

Interrupt: 33h

Function: 10h

Description: Defines a screen area in which the cursor is erased

Calling Registers: AX = 0010h
CX = Upper X screen coordinate
DX = Upper Y screen coordinate
SI = Lower X screen coordinate
DI = Lower Y screen coordinate

Return Registers: None

Comments: Function 10h specifies an area on the screen where the cursor disappears. After using this function, be sure to call Function 01h again.

Purpose: Set Double Speed Threshold

DOS Version Availability: 2

Interrupt: 33h

Function: 13h

Description: Sets the threshold speed above which the cursor will move at twice the normal rate

Calling Registers: AX = 0013h
DX = Threshold speed

Return Registers: None

Comments: When the cursor moves across the screen at or above the threshold value (of physical positions per second), the cursor-movement factor is increased by a factor of 2.

Purpose: Swap User-Interrupt Vector

DOS Version Availability: 2

Interrupt: 33h

Function: 14h

Description: Sets the user-interrupt function and call mask

Calling Registers: AX = 0014h
CX = User-interrupt mask
ES:DX = Pointer to user-interrupt vector

Return Registers: CX = Old user-interrupt mask
ES:DX = Old user-interrupt vector

Comments: Like Function 0Ch, this function sets a user-defined handling function to respond to special events recognized by the mouse device driver. The call mask is the same one used in Function 0Ch (see table M.4).

Table M.4. Call Mask Bits

Bit 76543210	Meaning
. . . . 1	Cursor position changed
. . . . . . 1 .	Left button pressed
. . . . . 1 . .	Left button released
. . . . 1 . . .	Right button pressed
. . . 1	Right button released

With this function, unlike Function 0Ch, you specify the segment and offset vector to the handler routine and get the old values in return. Furthermore, when the handler is called, the CPU registers are set up with the information shown in table M.5.

Table M.5. *Register Setup when User Function Called*

Register	Contents
AX	Condition mask
BX	Button state
CX	Cursor's horizontal coordinate
DX	Cursor's vertical coordinate
DI	Horizontal counts
SI	Vertical counts

The DS register points to the mouse driver data segment when the user interrupt is called. If the user function needs to get its own data, the function will have to set DS to its own data segment.

Function 14h is enabled when the call-mask bit is set to 1; when it is set to 0, the function is disabled.

Remember to restore the initial value of the call mask and subroutine addresses before you end your program.

Purpose: Query Save-State Storage Size

DOS Version Availability: 2

Interrupt: 33h

Function: 15h

Description: Returns the size of the buffer for the current state
of the mouse device driver

Calling Registers: AX = 0015h

Return Registers: BX = Buffer size needed to hold current mouse
state

Comments: This function, which is used in preparation for Function 16h or
17h, determines the amount of memory needed to save the mouse's current
state before you use another program that also needs the mouse.

Purpose: Save Mouse Driver State

DOS Version Availability: 2

Interrupt: 33h

Function: 16h

Description: Copies the state of the mouse driver to the buffer pointed to by ES:DX

Calling Registers: AX = 0016h
ES:DX = Pointer to buffer to hold mouse state

Return Registers: None

Comments: This function copies the mouse's current state into the buffer pointed to by ES:DX. The buffer size needed is determined by a call to Function 15h.

Use this function whenever you want to suspend one program that is using the mouse and execute another such program. When the second program ends, you can restore the mouse's state to what it was before the second program started.

Purpose: Restore Mouse Driver State

DOS Version Availability: 2

Interrupt: 33h

Function: 17h

Description: Restores the mouse driver to its state when called
by Function 16h

Calling Registers: AX = 0017h
ES:DX = Pointer to buffer in which mouse
state is saved

Return Registers: None

Comments: When one program resumes after having executed another
program that used the mouse, this function allows you to restore the mouse's
state as it was immediately before the the second program was executed.

Purpose: Set Alternate Mouse User Handler

DOS Version Availability: 2

Interrupt: 33h

Function: 18h

Description: Allows setup of as many as three special-event handlers (similar to those defined in Function 0Ch)

Calling Registers: AX = 0018h
CX = Call mask (see "Comments")
DX = Address offset to function

Return Registers: None

Comments: This function creates a special handler for conditions recognized by the mouse device driver. A function can be written to respond to button presses or releases or to cursor position changes. As many as three such handlers can be defined by separate calls to Function 18h.

The operation of the interrupt is controlled by a *call mask* that identifies which conditions will trigger the special handler. Wherever the call mask has a 1 bit, the function pointed to by the DX register will be executed when the condition occurs. A zero bit in the same position cancels the function. Table M.6 shows the assignment of bits in the call mask.

Table M.6. Call Mask Bits

Bit 76543210	Meaning
. 1	Alt key pressed during event
. . . . . .1.	Ctrl key pressed during event
. . . . .1. .	Shift button pressed during event
. . . .1. . .	Right-button up event
. . .1. . . .	Right-button down event
. .1.	Left-button up event
.1.	Left-button down event
1.	Cursor moved

The entire call mask is reset to zero when Function 0 is called. Before it ends, a program that sets up a special handler for these conditions should reset the call mask by calling either Function 18h or Function 00h.

When the handler is called, the CPU registers are set up with the information shown in table M.7.

Table M.7. *Register Setup when User Function Called*

Register	Contents
AX	Condition mask
BX	Button state
CX	Cursor's horizontal coordinate
DX	Cursor's vertical coordinate
DI	Horizontal counts
SI	Vertical counts

Purpose: Get User Alternate Interrupt Vector

DOS Version Availability: 2

Interrupt: 33h

Function: 19h

Description: Returns a pointer to a function defined by a call to
Function 18h

Calling Registers: AX = 0019h
CX = Call mask

Return Registers: BX:DX = User interrupt vector
CX = Call mask (0 if no match was found)

Comments: This function searches the event handlers defined by Function
18h for one whose call mask matches the CX register.

Purpose: Set Mouse Sensitivity

DOS Version Availability: 2

Interrupt: 33h

Function: 1Ah

Description: Sets the mouse speed *and* double speed threshold values

Calling Registers: AX = 001Ah
BX = Horizontal coordinates per pixel
CX = Vertical coordinates per pixel
DX = Double speed threshold

Return Registers: None

Comments: This function combines Functions 0F and 13h into a single call. The values are not reset by a call to Function 00h. The maximum value for BX and CX is 100.

Purpose: Get Mouse Sensitivity

DOS Version Availability: 2

Interrupt: 33h

Function: 1Bh

Description: Returns the sensitivity values set by Function 1Ah

Calling Registers: AX = 001Bh

Return Registers: BX = Horizontal coordinates per pixel
CX = Vertical coordinates per pixel
DX = Double speed threshold

Comments: This function returns the sensitivity of the mouse, represented as the number of coordinates (horizontal and vertical) the mouse increments or decerements for each pixel of the screen.

Purpose: Set CRT Page Number

DOS Version Availability: 2

Interrupt: 33h

Function: 1Dh

Description: Sets the page on which the mouse cursor will be
displayed

Calling Registers: AX = 001Dh
BX = CRT page number

Return Registers: None

Comments: This function is used to set the screen page on which the mouse
cursor will be displayed.

Purpose: Get CRT Page Number

DOS Version Availability: 2

Interrupt: 33h

Function: 1Eh

Description: Gets the CRT page number on which the mouse cursor is displayed

Calling Registers: AX = 001Eh

Return Registers: BX = CRT page number

Comments: This function is used to determine the screen page on which the mouse cursor will be displayed.

Purpose: Disable Mouse Driver

DOS Version Availability: 2

Interrupt: 33h

Function: 1Fh

Description: Disables the mouse driver by restoring interrupt vectors used by the mouse driver

Calling Registers: AX = 001Fh

Return Registers: AX = 001Fh, successful
                                        FFFFh, unsuccessful
                          ES:BX = Previous vector for Int 33h

Comments: This function disables mouse operation by restoring the interrupt vectors for Int 10h and either Int 71h (8086 processor based systems) or Int 74h (80286 or 80386 based systems). Int 33h (the mouse function interrupt itself) is not affected directly by this call. But the original value of the Int 33h vector is returned in the ES:BX register pair. This value can be used to restore Int 33h to its original value, which will disable the handler completely.

Disabling any interrupt handler can be tricky. There is no way of knowing whether another handler has also attached itself to these interrupts after the mouse handler installed itself. The restored interrupt vectors will be the values from when the mouse driver was first installed. If another handler attached itself after that, calling this function will disable the the other handler also. This could lead to a system crash or worse.

Purpose: Enable Mouse Driver

DOS Version Availability: 2

Interrupt: 33h

Function: 20h

Description: Reinstalls the mouse driver for use

Calling Registers: AX = 0020h

Return Registers: None

Comments: Restores the interrupt vectors for Int 10h and 71h or 74h, which were removed by the call to Function 1Fh.

Purpose: Software Reset

DOS Version Availability: 2

Interrupt: 33h

Function: 21h

Description: Resets the mouse software (but not the mouse)

Calling Registers: AX = 0021h

Return Registers: AX = FFFFh, mouse driver installed
    0021h, mouse driver *not* installed
BX = 2 if mouse driver is installed

Comments: This function is identical to Function 00h except that it does not reset the mouse.

EMS Functions: Int 67h

Expanded memory (EMS memory, as explained in Chapter 2) allows up to eight megabytes of RAM to be accessed through a technique called *bank switching*.

In this technique, we define small sections of an extra memory area (the EMS memory) that can be switched into a processor's physical address area. Each section is called a *bank*. Bank switching has been used on computers for years as a way to extend access to high-speed temporary storage. With EMS memory, the 16K "banks" (referred to as "pages" in the EMS documentation) are switched to appear as normal memory within a defined "page frame." (See Chapters 2 and 10 for more detailed descriptions of the operation of EMS memory.)

A special driver is loaded to allow programs to access EMS memory. You access EMS memory as you would a file. After opening access to EMS memory with Int 67h, Function 43h, you tell the board (with Int 67h, Function 44h) which memory pages to make accessible. While a memory page is accessible, you can read from and write to the page. When you are finished, you use Int 67h, Function 45h to close the handle.

Version 3.0 of the EMS standard was developed jointly by Lotus, Intel, and Microsoft Corporations (hence LIM memory). Version 3.2 added support for such multitasking operating systems as Windows and DESQview. As I write this book, a new version (4.0) has been defined, but no products are yet available. Under the new version, you can run programs from and store information in expanded memory. This reference section was developed using information applicable to LIM version 3.2.

The only drawback to expanded memory is that programmers must keep track of where things are located within expanded memory. A great deal of effort has been gone into creating programming languages that hide the way memory works. You do not have to remember, for example, which memory block your variables are stored in. Even in assembly language, if you use labels to refer to the variables, an assembler keeps track of which one you are dealing with.

But with expanded memory, you, the programmer, must remember which expanded memory blocks are currently in the page frame and which expanded memory blocks data is stored in. You have to ask to have the correct block moved into the page frame when you want something that is not there. In other words, you are responsible for whether the right piece of memory is in use. Assembly language programmers who use multiple data segments have the same sorts of problems, but high-level language programmers do not.

Purpose: Get Manager Status

DOS Version Availability: 2

Interrupt: 67h

Function: 40h

Description: Tests whether expanded memory hardware (if installed) is functional

Calling Registers: AH = 40h

Return Registers: AH = 00h   OK
80h   Internal error in EMS software
81h   Malfunction in EMS hardware
84h   Requested function not defined

Comments: When you are sure that an expanded memory board is installed, this function will test to see whether it is functional. (Chapter 10 contains some techniques for determining whether a board is installed.)

Purpose: Get Page Frame Segment

DOS Version Availability: 2

Interrupt: 67h

Function: 41h

Description: Gets the segment address of the page frame used by the EMS

Calling Registers: AH = 41h

Return Registers: If successful
        AH = 00h
        BX = Segment of page frame

      If unsuccessful
        AH = 80h   Internal error in EMS software
            81h   Malfunction in EMS hardware
            84h   Undefined function

Comments: After you have determined that a board is installed and functional, you need to determine its location in memory. The board maps four 16K pages (a total of 64K) into an area of memory of between 640K and 1M. From the memory maps of up to 1M on the PC shown in Chapter 2, you can see that most of this space is taken up by video displays and ROMs, but that substantial amounts of free space are unused. When the physical board is installed, you usually select the address of the EMS window with switches on the board. You must be careful to select memory not being used for any other purposes.

The segment address returned is the base of the first 16K page. All other pages are offset from this location.

Purpose: Get Number of Pages

DOS Version Availability: 2

Interrupt: 67h

Function: 42h

Description: Gets the total number of pages of EMS memory in the system and the number of pages available

Calling Registers: AH = 42h

Return Registers: If successful
                       AH = 00h
                       BX = Number of unallocated pages
                       DX = Total number of pages in system

   If unsuccessful
                       AH = 80h   Internal error in EMS software
                            81h   Malfunction in EMS hardware
                            84h   Undefined function

Comments: Use this function to determine whether there is enough memory for your application (or to scale the application to the memory). With a single call, you can tell how much memory there is and how much of it is available. For instance, regardless of the number of pages returned in DX, if BX is equal to 0, all of expanded memory has been allocated and none is available for other uses.

Purpose: Get Handle and Allocate Memory

DOS Version Availability: 2

Interrupt: 67h

Function: 43h

Description: Opens an EMS handle for use and allocates a specified number of pages for the process

Calling Registers: AH = 43h
BX = Number of logical pages to allocate

Return Registers: If successful
AH = 00h
DX = Handle

If unsuccessful
AH	=	80h	Internal error in EMS software
		81h	Malfunction in EMS hardware
		84h	Undefined function
		85h	No more handles available
		87h	Allocation requested more pages than are physically available. No pages allocated.
		88h	Specified more logical pages than are currently available. No pages allocated.
		89h	Zero pages requested.

Comments: Use this function as a "File Open" for EMS memory. Although it does not perform the same functions as a regular File Open call, this function does provide a file-like interface to memory.

The handle returned in this call is used for all accesses to the board. This call associates the handle with a specified number of EMS memory pages that you can control with function 44h.

More than one EMS handle can be assigned to a single process during operation, but the process must close each handle properly by calling function 45h. Otherwise, the memory assigned to the handle will simply disappear and be unavailable for reuse until you restart the system.

Purpose: Map Memory

DOS Version Availability: 2

Interrupt: 67h

Function: 44h

Description: Maps one of the EMS pages assigned to the handle into one of the four physical pages in the calling process's page frame

Calling Registers: AH = 44h
AL = Physical page number (0–3)
BX = Logical page number
DX = Handle

Return Registers: If successful
AH = 00h

If unsuccessful
AH = 80h   Internal error in EMS software
81h   Malfunction in EMS hardware
83h   Invalid handle
84h   Undefined function
8Ah   Logical page not assigned to this handle
8Bh   Physical page number invalid

Comments: The logical pages are the EMS memory pages assigned to the handle by function call 43h. Logical pages are numbered from 0 to n–1, with *n* being the number of pages requested.

On the EMS board, the pages are not accessible to the program because they are outside the computer's physical address space. This function maps one logical page into the computer's physical address space so that memory instructions can be used to manipulate information in the page area. As many as four physical pages can be mapped from a single board (number 0–3).

Purpose: Release Handle and Memory

DOS Version Availability: 2

Interrupt: 67h

Function: 45h

Description: Closes the specified handle and returns the memory for use by other processes

Calling Registers: AH = 45h
DX = EMS handle

Return Registers: If successful
AH = 00h

If unsuccessful
AH = 80h   Internal error in EMS software
81h   Malfunction in EMS hardware
83h   Invalid handle
84h   Undefined function
86h   Error in save or restore of mapping context

Comments: The EMS memory equivalent of a file-close operation, this simple function is particularly important. Because the EMS memory manager functions as an add-on driver to the operating system, the operating system will not close an open EMS handle for you when your program ends. Before a program terminates, it must close the EMS handle. If it does not, the memory it has allocated remains allocated and cannot be used by any other program. The only way to free up the memory is to reboot the computer.

When the close function is executed, the memory that was assigned to the handle is returned to the pool of available EMS memory. If the function does not complete successfully, the memory has not been returned to the pool—you need to keep trying.

Most programs simply close files without checking whether the function was successful. Generally, this does not pose a problem for files (handle files, anyway) because DOS closes the file when the program terminates. But with EMS memory, you must check for the proper exit code and respond with a retry if the function was not successful.

Purpose: Get EMM Version

DOS Version Availability: 2

Interrupt: 67h

Function: 46h

Description: Returns the software version number

Calling Registers: AH = 46h

Return Registers: If successful

        AH = 00h

        AL = EMM version number

     If unsuccessful

        AH = 80h   Internal error in EMS software

           81h   Malfunction in EMS hardware

           84h   Undefined function

Comments: This function returns (in BCD) the version number of the EMM (Expanded Memory Management) software. The upper four bits of the AL register represent the major version number (the part to the left of the decimal point); the lower four bits represent the minor version number (the part to the right of the decimal).

Purpose: Save Mapping Context

DOS Version Availability: 2

Interrupt: 67h

Function: 47h

Description: Saves the current state of EMS hardware map

Calling Registers: AH = 47h
                         DX = Handle

Return Registers: If successful
                          AH = 00h

                      If unsuccessful
                          AH = 80h   Internal error in EMS software
                               81h   Malfunction in EMS hardware
                               83h   Invalid handle
                               84h   Undefined function
                               8Ch   Page-mapping hardware state save
                                        area full
                               8Dh   Save of mapping context failed
                                        because one already associated
                                        with the specified handle

Comments: If you are writing a resident program (TSR), an interrupt service routine, or a device driver that uses EMS memory, you must save the state of the mapping hardware before doing any EMS operations so that other programs don't interfere with your use of the memory. This function saves the state of the mapping hardware. Int 67h, Function 48h is used to restore the hardware map.

Purpose: Restore Mapping Context

DOS Version Availability: 2

Interrupt: 67h

Function: 48h

Description: Restores the EMS hardware map associated with the designated file handle

Calling Registers: AH = 48h
                          DX = Handle

Return Registers: If successful
                          AH = 00h

If unsuccessful
    AH = 80h   Internal error in EMS software
          81h   Malfunction in EMS hardware
          83h   Invalid handle
          84h   Undefined function
          8Eh   Restore failed, save area has no
                   context for the handle.

Comments: If you are writing a resident program (TSR), an interrupt service routine, or a device driver that uses EMS memory, you must restore the state of the mapping hardware upon completion of your program. Failure to do so may cause unpredictable results. While your software executes, for example, an applications program that uses EMS memory may be running and expecting the EMS mapping registers to be unchanged. This function restores the state of the mapping hardware. Int 67h, Function 47h is used to save the state of the hardware map.

Purpose: Reserved

DOS Version Availability: 2

Interrupt: 67h

Function: 49h

Description: This function is undefined in version 3.2 of the EMS standard.

Comments: In previous versions of LIM/EMS, this function was used to retrieve the page-mapping register I/O array from the EMS hardware. This function is now reserved. New software should not use it, but existing programs that use this function should still work correctly.

Purpose: Reserved

DOS Version Availability: 2

Interrupt: 67h

Function: 4Ah

Description: This function is undefined in version 3.2 of the EMS standard.

Comments: In previous versions of LIM/EMS, this function was used to retrieve the logical-to-physical page translation array from the EMS hardware. This function is now reserved. New software should not use it, but existing programs that use this function should still work correctly.

Purpose: Get Number of EMS Handles

DOS Version Availability: 2

Interrupt: 67h

Function: 4Bh

Description: Returns the number of active EMS handles

Calling Registers: AH = 4Bh

Return Registers: If successful
AH = 00h
BX = Number of active EMS handles

If unsuccessful
AH = 80h   Internal error in EMS software
81h   Malfunction in EMS hardware
83h   Invalid handle
84h   Undefined function

Comments: This function tells you how many handles are in active use at any given time. If BX =0, expanded memory is not being used. BX can range from 0 (not in use) to 255 (the maximum number of EMS handles).

Your program's interpretation of this number is less clear than it may seem. The number of active handles is not necessarily the same as the number of programs presently using expanded memory. Nothing restricts a program from using more than one EMS handle to access expanded memory. In fact, some programs use more than one handle to simplify bookkeeping for the data they are managing. Perhaps a more reasonable use of this function is to determine the number of handles still available, which is derived by subtracting the value in BX from 255. A program that knows how many EMS handles it needs to function properly can quickly determine whether it will be able to function with the number of handles remaining in EMS.

Purpose: Get Pages Owned by Handle

DOS Version Availability: 2

Interrupt: 67h

Function: 4Ch

Description: Determines the number of pages associated with a specific handle

Calling Registers: AH = 4Ch
DX = Handle

Return Registers: If successful
AH = 00h
BX = Number of logical pages

If unsuccessful
AH = 80h   Internal error in EMS software
81h   Malfunction in EMS hardware
83h   Invalid handle
84h   Undefined function

Comments: Any single handle can refer to from one to 512 pages of expanded memory. Because each page represents 16K of memory, a single handle can access from 16K to 8M. This function never returns 0 pages because at least one page must be assigned to a handle by the Expanded Memory Manager.

Purpose: Get Pages for All Handles

DOS Version Availability: 2

Interrupt: 67h

Function: 4Dh

Description: Returns the handles and the number of logical pages for all handles

Calling Registers: AH = 4Dh
ES:DI = Pointer to array to hold information

Return Registers: If successful
AH = 00h
BX = Number of active EMS handles

If unsuccessful
AH = 80h   Internal error in EMS software
81h   Malfunction in EMS hardware
84h   Undefined function

Comments: This function returns an array of values that indicate the current handles and the number of pages assigned to each of the handles. The EMS handle table is constructed of two-word entries, as follows:

Byte	Meaning
0–1	EMS handle
2–3	Number of pages

The formula for determining the amount of memory required for the table can be expressed as $4 \times BX$. Because there can be a maximum of 255 handles, 4×255 (or 1,020 bytes) is the maximum reasonable allocation for the table. BX will tell you the number of valid table entries. If BX is 0, the EMS manager is idle.

Be careful not to place the table (as specified by ES:DI) so that it will cause a segment wrap when the table is transferred to memory. This would result in an error.

Purpose: Get or Set Page Map

DOS Version Availability: 2

Interrupt: 67h

Function: 4Eh

Description: Gets or saves the EMS page-mapping registers from
a local array

Calling Registers: AH = 4Eh
AL = Subfunction

00h	Getting registers into array
01h	Setting registers from array
02h	Get and set operation
03h	Return size of page-mapping array

DS:SI = Pointer to array from which to set
information
ES:DI = Pointer to array to receive information

Return Registers: If successful
AH = 00h
AL = Bytes in page-mapping array (subfunction 3)

If unsuccessful

AH = 80h	Internal error in EMS software
81h	Malfunction in EMS hardware
84h	Undefined function
8Fh	Subfunction not defined

Comments: This function was added in version 3.2 of the EMM software to
support multitasking systems such as Windows or DESQview. Function 4Eh
gives the program direct access to the page-mapping information used
internally by the EMS board, information that is extremely hardware dependent. The array will hold information about the page-mapping registers and
additional control information.

Multitasking systems are the only programs that should use this type of
information—they can't work effectively without it. Single programs cannot
use this type of information.

Be careful not to place the table (as specified by ES:DI) so that it will cause a
segment wrap when the table is transferred to memory. This would result in
an error.

The ASCII Character Set

Hex	Dec	Screen	Ctrl	Key
00h	0		NUL	^@
01h	1	☺	SOH	^A
02h	2	●	STX	^B
03h	3	♥	ETX	^C
04h	4	♦	EOT	^D
05h	5	♣	ENQ	^E
06h	6	♠	ACK	^F
07h	7	•	BEL	^G
08h	8	◘	BS	^H
09h	9	○	HT	^I
0Ah	10	◙	LF	^J
0Bh	11	♂	VT	^K
0Ch	12	♀	FF	^L
0Dh	13	♪	CR	^M
0Eh	14	♫	SO	^N
0Fh	15	☼	SI	^O
10h	16	►	DLE	^P
11h	17	◄	DC1	^Q
12h	18	↕	DC2	^R
13h	19	‼	DC3	^S
14h	20	¶	DC4	^T
15h	21	§	NAK	^U
16h	22	▬	SYN	^V
17h	23	↨	ETB	^W
18h	24	↑	CAN	^X
19h	25	↓	EM	^Y

Hex	Dec	Screen	Ctrl	Key
1Ah	26	→	SUB	^Z
1Bh	27	←	ESC	^[
1Ch	28	∟	FS	^\
1Dh	29	↔	GS	^]
1Eh	30	▲	RS	^^
1Fh	31	▼	US	^_
20h	32			
21h	33	!		
22h	34	"		
23h	35	#		
24h	36	$		
25h	37	%		
26h	38	&		
27h	39	'		
28h	40	(		
29h	41	)		
2Ah	42	*		
2Bh	43	+		
2Ch	44	,		
2Dh	45	–		
2Eh	46	.		
2Fh	47	/		
30h	48	0		
31h	49	1		
32h	50	2		
33h	51	3		

Hex	Dec	Screen	Hex	Dec	Screen	Hex	Dec	Screen
34h	52	4	62h	98	b	90h	144	É
35h	53	5	63h	99	c	91h	145	æ
36h	54	6	64h	100	d	92h	146	Æ
37h	55	7	65h	101	e	93h	147	ô
38h	56	8	66h	102	f	94h	148	ö
39h	57	9	67h	103	g	95h	149	ò
3Ah	58	:	68h	104	h	96h	150	û
3Bh	59	;	69h	105	i	97h	151	ù
3Ch	60	<	6Ah	106	j	98h	152	ÿ
3Dh	61	=	6Bh	107	k	99h	153	Ö
3Eh	62	>	6Ch	108	l	9Ah	154	Ü
3Fh	63	?	6Dh	109	m	9Bh	155	¢
40h	64	@	6Eh	110	n	9Ch	156	£
41h	65	A	6Fh	111	o	9Dh	157	¥
42h	66	B	70h	112	p	9Eh	158	₧
43h	67	C	71h	113	q	9Fh	159	ƒ
44h	68	D	72h	114	r	A0h	160	á
45h	69	E	73h	115	s	A1h	161	í
46h	70	F	74h	116	t	A2h	162	ó
47h	71	G	75h	117	u	A3h	163	ú
48h	72	H	76h	118	v	A4h	164	ñ
49h	73	I	77h	119	w	A5h	165	Ñ
4Ah	74	J	78h	120	x	A6h	166	a
4Bh	75	K	79h	121	y	A7h	167	o
4Ch	76	L	7Ah	122	z	A8h	168	¿
4Dh	77	M	7Bh	123	{	A9h	169	⌐
4Eh	78	N	7Ch	124	|	AAh	170	¬
4Fh	79	O	7Dh	125	}	ABh	171	½
50h	80	P	7Eh	126	~	ACh	172	¼
51h	81	Q	7Fh	127	Δ	ADh	173	¡
52h	82	R	80h	128	Ç	AEh	174	«
53h	83	S	81h	129	ü	AFh	175	»
54h	84	T	82h	130	é	B0h	176	░
55h	85	U	83h	131	â	B1h	177	▒
56h	86	V	84h	132	ä	B2h	178	▓
57h	87	W	85h	133	à	B3h	179	│
58h	88	X	86h	134	å	B4h	180	┤
59h	89	Y	87h	135	ç	B5h	181	╡
5Ah	90	Z	88h	136	ê	B6h	182	╢
5Bh	91	[	89h	137	ë	B7h	183	╖
5Ch	92	\	8Ah	138	è	B8h	184	╕
5Dh	93	]	8Bh	139	ï	B9h	185	╣
5Eh	94	^	8Ch	140	î	BAh	186	║
5Fh	95	_	8Dh	141	ì	BBh	187	╗
60h	96	`	8Eh	142	Ä	BCh	188	╝
61h	97	a	8Fh	143	Å	BDh	189	╜

Hex	Dec	Screen		Hex	Dec	Screen		Hex	Dec	Screen
BEh	190	╛		D4h	212	╘		EAh	234	Ω
BFh	191	╗		D5h	213	╒		EBh	235	δ
C0h	192	╚		D6h	214	╓		ECh	236	∞
C1h	193	╩		D7h	215	╫		EDh	237	φ
C2h	194	╦		D8h	216	╪		EEh	238	∈
C3h	195	╠		D9h	217	╜		EFh	239	∩
C4h	196	─		DAh	218	╒		F0h	240	≡
C5h	197	╬		DBh	219	█		F1h	241	±
C6h	198	╞		DCh	220	▄		F2h	242	≥
C7h	199	╟		DDh	221	▌		F3h	243	≤
C8h	200	╚		DEh	222	▐		F4h	244	⌠
C9h	201	╔		DFh	223	▀		F5h	245	⌡
CAh	202	╩		E0h	224	α		F6h	246	÷
CBh	203	╦		E1h	225	β		F7h	247	≈
CCh	204	╠		E2h	226	Γ		F8h	248	°
CDh	205	═		E3h	227	π		F9h	249	•
CEh	206	╬		E4h	228	Σ		FAh	250	·
CFh	207	╧		E5h	229	σ		FBh	251	√
D0h	208	╨		E6h	230	μ		FCh	252	ⁿ
D1h	209	╤		E7h	231	τ		FDh	253	²
D2h	210	╥		E8h	232	Φ		FEh	254	■
D3h	211	╙		E9h	233	θ		FFh	255	

Selected Memory Locations

Note: This table of selected memory locations is provided to help you understand the way the system functions. Direct access to any of these memory locations makes a program extremely nonportable and should be avoided unless there is no other way to provide the features or response you want.

At best, knowing the locations of this information in memory can help you get information. Changing the information in the BIOS and DOS data areas can be extremely damaging, however (and a lot of fun if you don't mind crashing your system).

Addresses	*Description*
00000–00400	**Interrupt Vector Tables:**
00000	Int 00, Hardware divide by zero
00004	Int 01, Hardware single step trap
00008	Int 02, Non Maskable
0000C	Int 03, Debugger breakpoint set
00010	Int 04, Arithmetic overflow
00014	Int 05, BIOS print screen
00020	Int 08, IRQ0–Clock tick
00024	Int 09, IRQ1–Keyboard action
00028	Int 0A, IRQ2
0002C	Int 0B, IRQ3–COM2

00030	Int 0C, IRQ4–COM1
00034	Int 0D, IRQ5–PC/XT Hard Disk
	PC AT LPT2
00038	Int 0E, IRQ6–Diskette
0003C	Int 0F, IRQ7–LPT1
00040	Int 10, BIOS video services
00044	Int 11, BIOS equipment list services
00048	Int 12, BIOS memory size services
0004C	Int 13, BIOS disk/diskette services
00050	Int 14, BIOS communications services
00054	Int 15, BIOS cassette services
	PC AT: Extended services
00058	Int 16, BIOS keyboard services
0005C	Int 17, BIOS printer services
00060	Int 18, Activates ROM BASIC
00064	Int 19, Reboots system
00068	Int 1A, BIOS time-of-day services
0006C	Int 1B, Called by Ctrl-Break handler
00070	Int 1C, Called by Int 08 handler
00074	Int 1D, Video init. parameter table
00078	Int 1E, Disk parameter table
0007C	Int 1F, Hi graphics character table
00080	Int 20, DOS program terminate
00084	Int 21, DOS function services
00088	Int 22, Program terminate
0008C	Int 23, DOS Ctrl-Break interrupt
00090	Int 24, Critical-error handler
00094	Int 25, DOS absolute disk read
00098	Int 26, DOS absolute disk write
0009C	Int 27, DOS TSR
000A0	Int 28, DOS Idle interrupt
000A8	Int 2A, MS-Net access
000BC	Int 2F, DOS print spooler/multiplex Int
00100	Int 40, Diskette Int Vector if hard disk is installed
00104	Int 41, Fixed disk parameter table
00108	Int 42, EGA BIOS uses this to redirect the video interrupt
0010C	Int 43, EGA init. parameter table
00110	Int 44, EGA character table
00128	Int 4A, PC AT: Int 70 alarm
00168	Int 5A, Cluster
0016C	Int 5B, Used by cluster program

0019C	Int 67, Expanded memory manager services
001C0	Int 70, IRQ8–PC AT Real-time clock
001C4	Int 71, IRQ9–PC AT redirect to Int 0A
001D4	Int 75, IRQ13–PC AT math coprocessor
00400–00500	**ROM BIOS Data Area:**
00400	COM1 address
00402	COM2 address
00408	LPT1 address
0040A	LPT2 address
0040C	LPT3 address
00410	Equipment flag
00412	Initialization flag
00413	Memory size in K
00415	Amount of memory in I/O channel
00417	Keyboard status flags
00419	Alternate keypad entry storage
0041A	Keyboard type-ahead buffer
0043E	Diskette data
00449	Current display mode
0044A	Number of screen columns
0044C	Size in bytes of display memory page
0044E	Offset to current display page
00450	Cursor position for each page
00460	Current cursor mode
00462	Number of active video page
00463	Port address of active display card
00465	Hardware mode select register value
00466	Color palette setting
00467	Cassette data
0046C	Low word of time data
0046E	High word of time data
00470	Passed midnight since last read
00471	Break flag
00472	Reset flag
00474	Fixed disk data area
00478	PC*jr* printer and serial timeouts
00480	Start of keyboard data area
00482	End of keyboard data area
00484	EGA additional video parameters
004F0	User communication area
00500–00600	**DOS/BASIC Data Area**
00500	Print screen status flag

APPENDIX C

A Resource List

Hardware

Intel Corporation. *iAPX 286 Programmer's Reference Manual*. Intel Corp., Santa Clara, Calif., 1983.

International Business Machines Corporation. *Personal Computer Technical Reference*. IBM, Boca Raton, Fla., 1984.

——. *Mouse Technical Reference*. IBM, Boca Raton, Fla., 1987.

——. *Personal System/2 and Personal Computer BIOS Technical Reference*. IBM, Boca Raton, Fla., 1987.

Morse, Stephen P. *The 8086/8088 Primer*, 2nd Edition. Hayden Book Company, Rochelle Park, N.J., 1982.

Woram, John. *The PC Configuration Handbook*. Bantam Books, New York, N.Y., 1987.

MS-DOS and BIOS Programming

Angermeyer, John and Keven Jaeger. *MS-DOS Developer's Guide*. Howard W. Sams, Indianapolis, Ind., 1986.

Campbell, Joe. *C Programmer's Guide to Serial Communications*. Howard W. Sams and Company, Indianapolis, Ind., 1987.

Chesley, Harry R. and Mitchell Waite. *Supercharging C with Assembly Language*. Addision-Wesley, Reading, Mass., 1987.

Hyman, Michael. *Memory Resident Utilities, Interrupts, and Disk Management with MS and PC DOS*. MIS Press, Portland, Oreg., 1986.

International Business Machines Corporation. *Disk Operating System Technical Reference Version 3.3*. IBM, Boca Raton, Fla., 1987.

Jump, Dennis N. *Programmer's Guide to MS-DOS*. Brady Books, New York, N.Y., 1987.

Lai, Robert S. *Writing MS-DOS Device Drivers*. Addison-Wesley, Reading, Mass., 1987.

Porter, Kent. *Stretching Turbo Pascal*. Brady Books, New York, N.Y., 1987.

Wadlow, Thomas A. *Memory Resident Programming on the IBM PC*. Addison-Wesley, Reading, Mass., 1987.

Wilton, Richard. *Programmer's Guide to PC and PS/2 Video Systems*. Microsoft Press, Redmond, Wash., 1987.

Young, Michael J. *Performance Programming Under MS-DOS*. Sybex, San Francisco, Calif., 1987.

Programming Languages

Abel, Peter. *Assembler for the IBM PC and PC-XT*. Reston Publishing, Reston, Va., 1984.

Duntemann, Jeff. *Complete Turbo Pascal*. Scott, Foresman and Company, Glenview, Ill., 1986.

Harbison, Samuel P. and Guy L. Steele, Jr. *C: A Reference Manual*. Prentice Hall, Englewood Cliffs, N.J., 1987.

Holzner, Steve. *Advanced Assembly Language on the IBM PC*. Brady Books, New York, N.Y., 1987.

Lafore, Robert. *Microsoft C Programming for the IBM*. Howard W. Sams and Company, Indianapolis, Ind., 1987.

Scanlon, Leo. *IBM PC and XT Assembly Language*. Brady Books, Bowie, Md., 1983.

Wyatt, Allen. *Using Assembly Language*. Que Corporation, Carmel, Ind., 1987.

General Programming

Birrell, N.D. and M.A. Ould. *A Practical Handbook for Software Development*. Cambridge University Press, Cambridge, England, 1986.

Ledgard, Henry. *Software Engineering Concepts*. Addison-Wesley, Reading, Mass., 1987.

Liffick, Blaise W. *The Software Developer's Handbook*. Addison-Wesley, Reading, Mass., 1985.

Yourdon, Edward. *Techniques of Program Structure and Design*. Prentice Hall, Englewood Cliffs, N.J., 1975.

General DOS

DeVoney, Chris. *Using PC DOS*, 2nd Edition. Que Corporation, Indianapolis, Ind., 1987.

International Business Machines Corporation. *Disk Operating System Version 3.3*. IBM, Boca Raton, Fla., 1987.

Illustration Index

Tables

Index

input (Int, 21h Function 03h), 541, 556
output (Int, 21h Function 04h), 541, 556

B

BASIC programming language
   access of 8086 registers, 25, 155-156
   access of 8250 UART through I/O ports, 208
   ASCIIZ format for strings in, 85
   functions, 14-15
      INKEY$, 154-155
      INP, 208
      MEMSET, 280
      OUT, 208
   memory allocation, 80, 281-282
   overhead, 67
   ROM, 48
   statements
      CHAIN, 280
      RUN, 280
   use of DOS and BIOS functions, 65
batch file
   commands, 43-44
   EXEC function cannot execute, 294
   terminate program (Int 20h) and, 551
baud rate, 178
binary coded decimal (BCD), 523-528
BIOS (Basic Input/Output System)
   access from programs, 83-87
   actions for key presses, 31
   baud rate for early versions of, 182
   boot record loaded by, 220
   bootable partition determined by, 219
   communications port initialization settings, 187-188
   display mode tracking, 127
   first software level in virtual machine, 40-41
   functions
      platform for DOS provided by, 8
      undocumented, 1
   as DOS module, 7
   high-level language calls to, 87-116
   integration of "computer system," 13
   interface from programs, 83-116
   interrupts, 41
   location, 7, 273
   parameter block (BPB). *See* BIOS Parameter Block
      (BPB)
   PS/2 entry points for, 411
   purpose, 41
   reference section, 409-536
   release date list, 409
   resident device drivers in, 49
   ROM, 40-41, 47-49, 150
   stored as first file on disk, 247
   SYSINIT to load, 41
BIOS interrupts, 412
   00h divide-by-zero, 413, 416
   01h single step, 413, 417

02h nonmaskable, 72, 413, 418
03h breakpoint, 413, 419
04h arithmetic overflow interrupt, 413, 420
05h print screen, 413, 421
06h and 07h reserved, 413
08h system timer, 413, 422
09h keyboard, 31, 150, 320, 413, 423-424
0Ah reserved, 413
0Bh communications, 413, 425
0Ch communications, 413, 426
0Dh hard disk controller, 413, 427
0Eh floppy disk management, 413, 428
0Fh printer management, 413, 429
10h video, 413
   00h set video mode, 413, 430-431
   01h set cursor type, 413, 432
   02h set cursor position, 413, 433
   03h read cursor position and configuration, 413,
      434
   04h read light pen position, 413, 435
   05h select active display page, 413, 436
   06h scroll window up, 413, 437
   07h scroll window down, 413, 438
   08h read character and attribute, 413, 439
   09h write character and attribute, 413, 440
   0Ah write character at cursor, 413, 441
   0Bh set color palette, 413, 442
   0Ch write graphics pixel, 413, 443
   0Dh read graphics pixel, 413, 444
   0Eh write text in teletype mode, 413, 445
   0Fh get current display mode, 413, 446
   10h set palette registers, 413, 447
   11h character generator, 413, 449-450
   13h write string, 413, 451
11h get equipment status, 389-390, 452-453
12h get memory size, 413, 454
13h diskette, 322, 336, 414
   00h reset floppy disk system, 241, 414, 455
   01h get floppy disk system status, 414, 456
   02h read floppy disk, 414, 457
   03h write disk sectors, 414, 458
   04h verify disk sectors, 414, 459
   05h format disk track, 237-238, 414, 460
   06h and 07h reserved, 414
   08h return disk-drive parameters, 414, 461-462
   09h initialize fixed disk table, 414, 463
   0Ah read long sector, 414, 464-465
   0Bh write long sector, 414, 466
   0Ch seek cylinder, 414, 467
   0Dh alternate disk reset, 414, 468
   0Eh-14h reserved, 414
   15h return direct access storage device (DASD)
      type, 414, 469
   16h read disk change line status, 414, 470
   17h set DASD type for disk format, 414, 471
   18h set media type for format, 414, 472
14h asynchronous communications function, 188,
   190, 414

C

T

More Computer Knowledge from Que

LOTUS SOFTWARE TITLES

1-2-3 QueCards	21.95
1-2-3 QuickStart	21.95
1-2-3 Quick Reference	6.95
1-2-3 for Business, 2nd Edition	22.95
1-2-3 Business Formula Handbook	19.95
1-2-3 Command Language	21.95
1-2-3 Macro Library, 2nd Edition	21.95
1-2-3 Tips, Tricks, and Traps, 2nd Edition	21.95
Using 1-2-3, Special Edition	24.95
Using 1-2-3 Workbook and Disk, 2nd Edition	29.95
Using Lotus HAL	19.95
Using Symphony, 2nd Edition	26.95

DATABASE TITLES

dBASE III Plus Applications Library	21.95
dBASE III Plus Handbook, 2nd Edition	22.95
dBASE III Plus Advanced Programming, 2nd Edition	22.95
dBASE III Plus Tips, Tricks, and Traps	21.95
dBASE IV Quick Reference	6.95
dBXL and Quicksilver Programming: Beyond dBASE	24.95
R:BASE Solutions: Applications and Resources	19.95
R:BASE System V Techniques and Applications	21.95
R:BASE User's Guide, 3rd Edition	19.95
Using Clipper	24.95
Using Reflex	19.95
Using Paradox, 2nd Edition	22.95
Using Q & A, 2nd Edition	21.95

MACINTOSH AND APPLE II TITLES

HyperCard QuickStart: A Graphics Approach	21.95
Using AppleWorks, 2nd Edition	21.95
Using dBASE Mac	19.95
Using Dollars and Sense	19.95
Using Excel	21.95
Using HyperCard: From Home to HyperTalk	24.95
Using Microsoft Word: Macintosh Version	21.95
Using Microsoft Works	19.95
Using WordPerfect: Macintosh Version	19.95

APPLICATIONS SOFTWARE TITLES

Smart Tips, Tricks, and Traps	23.95
Using DacEasy	21.95
Using Dollars and Sense: IBM Version, 2nd Edition	19.95
Using Enable, 2nd Edition	22.95
Using Excel: IBM Version	24.95
Using Managing Your Money	19.95
Using Quattro	21.95
Using Smart	22.95
Using SuperCalc4	21.95

WORD-PROCESSING AND DESKTOP PUBLISHING TITLES

Microsoft Word Techniques and Applications	19.95
Microsoft Word Tips, Tricks, and Traps	19.95
Using DisplayWrite 4	19.95
Using Microsoft Word, 2nd Edition	21.95
Using MultiMate Advantage, 2nd Edition	19.95
Using PageMaker on the IBM	24.95
Using Sprint	21.95
Using Ventura Publisher	24.95
Using WordPerfect, 3rd Edition	21.95
Using WordPerfect 5	24.95
Using WordPerfect Workbook and Disk	29.95
Using WordStar	18.95
WordPerfect Advanced Techniques	19.95
WordPerfect Macro Library	21.95
WordPerfect QueCards	21.95
WordPerfect Quick Reference	6.95
WordPerfect QuickStart	21.95
WordPerfect Tips, Tricks, and Traps, 2nd Edition	21.95

HARDWARE AND SYSTEMS TITLES

DOS Programmer's Reference	24.95
DOS QueCards	21.95
DOS Workbook and Disk	29.95
IBM PS/2 Handbook	21.95
Managing Your Hard Disk, 2nd Edition	22.95
MS-DOS Quick Reference	6.95
MS-DOS QuickStart	21.95
MS-DOS User's Guide, 3rd Edition	22.95
Networking IBM PCs, 2nd Edition	19.95
Programming with Windows	22.95
Understanding UNIX: A Conceptual Guide, 2nd Edition	21.95
Upgrading and Repairing PCs	24.95
Using Microsoft Windows	19.95
Using PC DOS, 2nd Edition	22.95

PROGRAMMING AND TECHNICAL TITLES

Advanced C: Techniques and Applications	21.95
C Programmer's Library	21.95
C Programming Guide, 3rd Edition	24.95
C Quick Reference	6.95
C Standard Library	21.95
Debugging C	19.95
QuickBASIC Quick Reference	6.95
Turbo Pascal for BASIC Programmers	18.95
Turbo Pascal Program Library	19.95
Turbo Pascal Tips, Tricks, and Traps	19.95
Using Assembly Language	24.95
Using QuickBASIC 4	19.95
Using Turbo Prolog	19.95

Que Order Line: **1-800-428-5331**

All prices subject to change without notice. Prices and charges are for domestic orders only.
Non-U.S. prices might be higher.

SELECT QUE BOOKS TO INCREASE
YOUR PERSONAL COMPUTER PRODUCTIVITY

Using PC DOS, 2nd Edition

by Chris DeVoney

The best-selling guide to PC DOS is now even better! DOS master Chris DeVoney has updated *Using PC DOS*—the Que classic that covers every aspect of the IBM operating system. Critically acclaimed, *Using PC DOS* is a combination of beginning tutorial and lasting reference, now covering PC DOS through version 3.3. This new 2nd Edition adds up-to-date information on IBM's PS/2 computers and shows how to work with 3 1/2-inch disks. Also featured is a comprehensive beginning tutorial and the popular Command Reference, an easy-to-use consolidation of essential DOS commands. No IBM microcomputer user should be without a copy of *Using PC DOS, 2nd Edition!*

C Programming Guide, 3rd Edition

by Jack Purdum, Ph.D.

A completely new edition of a Que classic. Rewritten to reflect C's ongoing development—including the new ANSI standard—this text contains many programming tips that let readers benefit from the author's practical programming experience. Also included are a complete keyword reference guide, a host of program examples, and a tear-out quick reference card. This is the perfect guide for beginning programmers in the C language.

Programming with Windows

by Tim Farrell

You can save up to three months of programming start-up time with Que's *Programming with Windows*. Written by a major Windows applications developer, this book includes basics that are not part of the Microsoft Windows Developer's kit. Programming with Windows includes an introduction to the Windows environment, techniques for applications design, and hints on how to debug your programs. Whether you are programming with Windows 2 or Windows 386, *Programming with Windows* is the ideal guide to both custom and general applications programming. Companion software is available.

Using Assembly Language

by Allen Wyatt

Let *Using Assembly Language* show you how to make the most of your programs with assembly language subroutines. This book will help you understand assembly language instructions, commands, and functions—how they are used and what effects they produce. You will learn to interface assembly language with high-level languages, develop and manage libraries of subroutines, successfully debug subroutines, and access BIOS and DOS services. Functioning both as a learning aid and a reference guide, *Using Assembly Language* demonstrates how to harness the speed, versatility, flexibility, and code compaction possible with assembly language.

ORDER FROM QUE TODAY

Mail to: Que Corporation • P.O. Box 90, Carmel, IN 46032

Item	Title	Price	Quantity	Extension
807	Using PC DOS, 2nd Edition	$22.95		
99	Programming with Windows	$22.95		
107	Using Assembly Language	$24.95		
850	C Programming Guide, 3rd Edition	$24.95		

Book Subtotal _____

Shipping & Handling ($2.50 per item) _____

Indiana Residents Add 5% Sales Tax _____

GRAND TOTAL _____

Method of Payment

☐ Check ☐ VISA ☐ MasterCard ☐ American Express

Card Number _____ Exp. Date _____

Cardholder's Name _____

Ship to _____

Address _____

City _____ State _____ ZIP _____

If you can't wait, call **1-800-428-5331** and order TODAY.

All prices subject to change without notice.

FOLD HERE

Place
Stamp
Here

_____
_____
_____
_____

Que Corporation
P.O. Box 90
Carmel, IN 46032

REGISTRATION CARD

Register your copy of *DOS Programmer's Reference* and receive information about Que's newest products. Complete this registration card and return it to Que Corporation, P.O. Box 90, Carmel, IN 46032.

Name _____ Phone _____

Company _____ Title _____

Address _____

City _____ State _____ ZIP _____

Please check the appropriate answers:

Where did you buy *DOS Programmer's Reference*?
- ☐ Bookstore (name: _____)
- ☐ Computer store (name: _____)
- ☐ Catalog (name: _____)
- ☐ Direct from Que _____
- ☐ Other: _____

How many computer books do you buy a year?
- ☐ 1 or less   ☐ 6-10
- ☐ 2-5   ☐ More than 10

How many Que books do you own?
- ☐ 1   ☐ 6-10
- ☐ 2-5   ☐ More than 10

How long have you been programming on PCs?
- ☐ Less than 6 months
- ☐ 6 months to 1 year
- ☐ 1-3 years
- ☐ More than 3 years

What influenced your purchase of *DOS Programmer's Reference*?
- ☐ Personal recommendation
- ☐ Advertisement   ☐ Que catalog
- ☐ In-store display   ☐ Que mailing
- ☐ Price   ☐ Que reputation
- ☐ Other: _____

How would you rate the overall content of *DOS Programmer's Reference*?
- ☐ Very good   ☐ Satisfactory
- ☐ Good   ☐ Poor

How would you rate the overall content of *DOS and BIOS Reference Sections*?
- ☐ Very good   ☐ Satisfactory
- ☐ Good   ☐ Poor

COMMENTS: _____

How would you rate *Part I: Introduction to DOS*?
- ☐ Very good   ☐ Satisfactory
- ☐ Good   ☐ Poor

How interested would you be in obtaining sample programs from this book on diskette?
- ☐ Very interested
- ☐ Somewhat interested
- ☐ Not at all interested

How much would you be willing to pay for a disk of sample programs from this book?
- ☐ Under $20   ☐ $30 to $40
- ☐ $20 to $30

What do you like *best* about *DOS Programmer's Reference*?

What do you like *least* about *DOS Programmer's Reference*?

How do you use *DOS Programmer's Reference*?

What other Que products do you own?

For what other programs would a Que book be helpful?

Please feel free to list any other comments you may have about *DOS Programmer's Reference*.

_____

_____

_____

_____

_____

FOLD HERE

_____

_____

_____

_____

Place
Stamp
Here

Que Corporation
P.O. Box 90
Carmel, IN 46032

Registration Card

Put Essential Information at Your Fingertips . . .

With the Que Quick Reference Series!

When you need a convenient reference to your favorite applications, choose the **Que Quick Reference Series**. Each Que **Quick Reference** is a low-priced, easy-to-use reference to common program commands and functions, and contains the high-quality information you expect from Que. Essential information in a compact format—the **Que Quick Reference Series**!

ORDER TODAY! CALL 1-800-428-5331, EXT. A105

- -

YES!

Please send me the following Que **Quick Reference** books:

Qty.	No.	Title	Price
____	865	*MS-DOS Quick Reference*	$6.95
____	862	*1-2-3 Quick Reference*	$6.95
____	866	*WordPerfect Quick Reference*	$6.95
____	868	*C Quick Reference*	$6.95
____	869	*QuickBASIC Quick Reference*	$6.95

Return this card to:
Que Corporation
11711 N. College Ave.
Carmel, IN 46032
For even faster service, call toll-free:
1-800-428-5331, ext. A105

Name _____

Title _____

Company _____

Address _____

City _____

State _____ ZIP _____

Home Phone _____

Work Phone _____

☐ MasterCard   ☐ VISA   ☐ American Express

Card Number _____

Signature _____

Please include 50¢ per item shipping and handling.
All prices subject to change without notice.
Prices and charges are for domestic orders only.
Non-U.S. prices might be higher.

- **MS-DOS**
- **1-2-3**
- **WordPerfect 5**
- **C**
- **QuickBASIC 4**

If you use any of these popular applications, you should be using the Que Quick Reference Series!

Whether you use a laptop or a desktop personal computer, the **Que Quick Reference Series** provides immediate access to information often buried in traditional texts. These portable references help you quickly determine the proper use for important commands and functions, without wading through pages and pages of inapplicable information. When you need essential information fast, turn to the quality information contained in the **Que Quick Reference Series**!

MS-DOS Quick Reference
Gain immediate control of MS-DOS 3.3 with this compact reference. Includes information on:
- DOS commands and error messages
- EDLIN commands
- Batch Files

Order #865, $6.95

1-2-3 Quick Reference
The instant 1-2-3 reference. Includes information on:
- Fundamental 1-2-3 commands
- Essential @functions
- Important macros

Order # 862, $6.95

WordPerfect Quick Reference
The easy-to-use reference for all users of new WordPerfect 5. Includes information on:
- Essential commands
- Common tasks and applications
- Uses of program function keys

Order #866, $6.95

C Quick Reference
The portable reference to programming with the forthcoming ANSI C standard. Includes information on:
- Essential commands and keywords
- Important concepts
- Proper programming protocol

Order #868, $6.95

QuickBASIC Quick Reference
The convenient reference to the functions and keywords available with the Quick-BASIC 4 compiler. Includes information on:
- Essential commands & keywords
- Important concepts
- Proper programming protocol

Order #869, $6.95

COMING SOON:
dBASE IV Quick Reference
Order #867, $6.95

ORDER TODAY! CALL 1-800-428-5331, EXT. A105

BUSINESS REPLY MAIL
FIRST CLASS PERMIT NO. 278   CARMEL, IN

Postage will be paid by the addressee

Que Corporation
11711 N. College Ave., Ste. 140
Carmel, IN 46032

NO POSTAGE
NECESSARY
IF MAILED
IN THE
UNITED STATES

If you use 1-2-3 or Symphony more than two hours a day, please accept a FREE evaluation copy of *Absolute Reference.*

FREE ISSUE OFFER! Just mail postage-paid order form today!

Introducing the only journal for serious spreadsheet users. It's *guaranteed* to save you time and dramatically increase your capability.

Most spreadsheet users tap only a fraction of the tremendous power lying dormant within 1-2-3 and Symphony. Unfortunately, the user's guidebooks—even Que's own—can only scratch the surface.

That's why if you work regularly with 1-2-3 or Symphony, you owe it to yourself to examine *Absolute Reference.*

Save more than one week's time in the coming year

First of all, *Absolute Reference* will save you time . . . and time is money. In fact, we guarantee that the techniques you gain in your monthly issues *will save you at least an hour a week* over the next year—that's 52

hours! Multiply 52 hours by a minimum of $25 per hour for your time—and you've increased your productivity *by $1,300.*

But that's the least of what *Absolute Reference* will do for you.

How *Absolute Reference* helps you become a spreadsheet master.

Every month, with a passion for practicality, *Absolute Reference* articles tell you how to increase your capability with 1-2-3 and Symphony. Neat new macros, new applications, shortcuts, more professional printouts, more logical layout, avoiding pitfalls, outspoken product reviews, and reader tips—you'll get concise reports like these in every monthly issue. (See next page for sample articles.)

Our 100% Moneyback Guarantee makes this offer risk free.

Use the subscription form below, but SEND NO MONEY. Examine your

first issue with no obligation. If for any reason you are not satisfied, simply write cancel on your invoice. Even after you've paid, if you're not delighted with *Absolute Reference*, we'll refund your entire subscription fee.

YES! Please send my FREE SAMPLE ISSUE with no obligation.

Please start my one-year, no-risk subscription and send my FREE SAMPLE ISSUE immediately. I'll receive 12 additional monthly issues at your discounted subscription rate of $59—a $25 savings off the normal $84 price. (Subscriptions payable in U.S. funds. Foreign orders add $20.) I NEED *NOT* SEND ANY MONEY NOW, and if I am *not satisfied* after evaluating my first issue for 30 days, I may write "CANCEL" on my invoice and owe nothing. I have signed below.

Signature Required_____

Name_____

Title_____

Company_____ **Phone (____)** _____

Address_____

City, State, Zip_____

☎ **For even faster service, call toll free: 1-800-227-7999, ext. 552. (In Indiana: 1-317-573-2540)**

Que Corporation
11711 N. College Avenue
Carmel, Indiana 46032-9903

Here's a tiny sample of the kinds of articles you'll read in every issue of *Absolute Reference:*

Discover the incredible power of macros—shortcuts for hundreds of applications and subroutines.
- A macro for formatting text
- Monitoring preset database conditions with a macro
- Three ways to design macro menus
- Building macros with string formulas
- Having fun with the marching macro
- Using the ROWs macro
- Generating a macro for tracking elapsed time

New applications and new solutions—every issue gives you novel ways to harness 1-2-3 and Symphony
- Creating customized menus for your spreadsheets
- How to use criteria to unlock your spreadsheet program's data management power
- Using spreadsheets to monitor investments
- Improving profits with more effective sales forecasts
- An easy way to calculate year-to-date performance
- Using /**D**ata **F**ill to streamline counting and range filling

Extend your uses—and your command—of spreadsheets
- Printing spreadsheets sideways can help sell your ideas
- How to add goal-seeking capabilities to your spreadsheet

- Hiding columns to create custom worksheet printouts
- Lay out your spreadsheet for optimum memory management
- Toward an "intelligent" spreadsheet
- A quick way to erase extraneous zeros

Techniques for avoiding pitfalls and repairing the damage when disaster occurs
- Preventing and trapping errors in your worksheet
- How to create an auditable spreadsheet
- Pinpointing specific errors in your spreadsheets
- Ways to avoid failing formulas
- Catching common debugging and data-entry errors
- Detecting data-entry errors
- Protecting worksheets from accidental (or deliberate) destruction
- Avoiding disaster with the /**S**ystem command

Objective product reviews—we accept *no advertising*, so you can trust our editors' outspoken opinions
- Metro Desktop Manager
- Freelance Plus
- Informix
- 4Word, InWord, Write-in
- Spreadsheet Analyst
- 101 macros for 1-2-3

Mail this card today!

BUSINESS REPLY MAIL
FIRST CLASS PERMIT NO. 278   INDIANAPOLIS, IN

Postage will be paid by the addressee

ABSOLUTE REFERENCE
THE JOURNAL FOR 1-2-3 AND SYMPHONY USERS

Que Corporation
11711 N. College Avenue
Carmel, Indiana 46032-9903

NO POSTAGE
NECESSARY
IF MAILED
IN THE
UNITED STATES